# PARADE
## *of* FAITH

## Other Books by Ruth A. Tucker

*From Jerusalem to Irian Jaya*

*Daughters of the Church* (with Walter Liefeld)

*Private Lives of Pastors' Wives*

*Guardians of the Great Commission*

*Christian Speakers Treasury*

*Another Gospel: Cults and New Religions*

*Stories of Faith*

*Women in the Maze*

*Multiple Choices*

*Family Album*

*Seasons of Motherhood*

*Not Ashamed: The Story of Jews for Jesus*

*Walking Away from Faith*

*God Talk*

*Left Behind in a Mega-Church World*

*Leadership Reconsidered*

# RUTH A. TUCKER

# PARADE
## _of_ FAITH

A Biographical History of the Christian Church

**ZONDERVAN®**

**ZONDERVAN**.com/
**AUTHORTRACKER**
_follow your favorite authors_

ZONDERVAN

*Parade of Faith*
Copyright © 2011 by Ruth A. Tucker

This title is also available as a Zondervan ebook. Visit www.zondervan.com/ebooks.

Requests for information should be addressed to:

Zondervan, *Grand Rapids, Michigan 49530*

Library of Congress Cataloging-in-Publication Data

Tucker, Ruth, 1945-
    Parade of faith : a biographical history of the Christian church / Ruth A. Tucker.
        p. cm.
        Includes index.
        ISBN 978-0-310-20638-5 (hardcover)
        1.  Church history. 2.  Christian biography. I. Title. II. Title: Biographical history of the Christian
    church.
    BR145.3.T83 2010
    270.092'2--dc22                                                                      2010053516

Maps by International Mapping. Copyright © 2011 by Zondervan. All rights reserved.

*Cover design: John Hamilton Design*
*Cover photography: SuperStock; The Bridgeman Art Library; Bettmann/Corbis;*
    *Billy Graham Evangelistic Association*
*Interior design: Sherri L. Hoffman*

*Printed in the United States of America*

11 12 13 14 15 /DCI/ 27 26 25 24 23 22 21 20 19 18 17 16 15 14 13 12 11 10 9 8 7 6 5 4 3 2 1

To the Students who were my Teachers
in my first
Church History Class
at
Moffat Bible College
Kijabe, Kenya
1985

---

*Paul Manyara Gichoya*

*Sammy Munywoki Ivali*

*Paul Mwangi Kamunge*

*John Mbugua Kariuki*

*Kennedy Kipkemoi Kiplelum*

*Timothy Musyoka Kituo*

*William Kipruto Kotut*

*Gabriel Kitheka Mbuvi*

*Johnstone Kioko Musa*

*Betrice Muthoki Musau*

*Reuben Karare Ng'ang'a*

*Benson Raphael Omungu*

*Joseph Kimaru Setaney*

*Samuel Katuma Nzoka Wambua*

*George Muiruri Wanjema*

*Emily Wambui Waweru*

# Contents

# Preface

One of the most memorable church history courses I ever taught was at Fuller Theological Seminary some two decades ago. In the front row was Rik Stevenson, the only African American in the class. The first to arrive and the last to walk out the door at the end of the session, he peppered me with questions. He was determined to make church history his own—so much so that before the short course ended, he traveled to Philadelphia to research the ministry of Charles Tindley, a nineteenth-century black megachurch minister.

Our acquaintance blossomed into friendship, and now, after nearly two decades, we are both settled in Grand Rapids, Michigan. A local minister and professor, Rik often stops by to talk church history. His current field of research is the black church in Canada. But Rik sees all of church history as belonging to African Americans. Whether Thomas Aquinas or John Bunyan or Mary Slessor, he identifies with his spiritual forbearers and makes them his own. I do the same. I do not demand that the history of Christianity be a woman's history in order to make it my own.

Today the Christian church is growing most rapidly in the Southern Hemisphere and is more multicultural and gender inclusive than ever before. Diversity, however, has not been a hallmark of Christian history. The Jewish leadership of the New Testament church was soon replaced by what might be termed *ethnic Mediterranean* leadership. Later, as the faith shifted northward, ethnic Europeans come to the fore, the vast majority of leaders in every generation being male. Nevertheless, women and people of color have found their way into the pages of contemporary church history texts, as they rightly should.

But simply adding color and gender to the historical mix fails to appreciate the chasm separating people of color—and women—from white, male-oriented academia. Fact-based rather than story-based history has reigned for centuries in Europe and America, and such history often leaves others, including *postmoderns* of every stripe, behind by its very formulation. Indeed, the *story* was the vehicle for transmitting history in the Old and New Testaments and in the generations since. But it lost its way as it moved into the modern world. Today story is making a comeback—thanks in part to feminine and multicultural influences.

This book is dedicated to my first class of church history students at Moffat Bible College in Kenya. How well I recall Kotut and Kennedy and Gabriel and Timothy, ethnic Kilenjins and Kambas, studious scholars in the middle of Kikuyu country. I remember that class as though it were yesterday. Sixteen students, sitting at their desks wondering what a rookie white lady teacher might have to offer them. The truth is, they offered me a lot more than I offered them. I had been warned by missionaries before I arrived that Africans are used to learning by rote in elementary school and that this practice often continues into college. *Don't expect them to jump into class discussion*, they said. I panicked. If I don't get feedback, I fade away. I vowed things would be different. I would force them to challenge me. And challenge me they did.

I had an advantage over the other American teachers — my gender. Challenging a white American male professor back in those days was intimidating for some. But a woman who was baiting them with her sometimes outrageous comments and questions — that was different. I got them stirred up by the end of the first day of that three-week session. We interacted and argued, clucked in despair and howled with laughter. The colorful characters in our Christian heritage, it turns out, were just like Africans — at least they behaved like Africans. They worshiped and grieved and bickered and celebrated just like Africans do.

I discovered this truth most profoundly when my students were performing their end-of-course drama that we turned into an exciting campus event. Polycarp and Perpetua and other persecuted Christians came to life — and death — as they were burned at the stake. In fact, we nearly lost Kituo, our Kenyan Polycarp, in the fire. A scream of horror rose up from the crowd as his choir robe (didn't all early martyrs wear choir robes?) was singed by the flames. The following year Martin Luther and Katie von Bora were the stars — as authentically African as that celebrated couple has ever been.

Church history belongs to Africans (and all Christians of the world) when they embrace it as their own. I, after all, claim church history for myself even though Polycarp and Augustine and dozens of others in this volume are much closer geographically — and perhaps psychologically and spiritually — to Africans than they have ever been to me. One need not be an African to identify with Perpetua or Augustine, nor Jewish to claim a connection with Jesus and Paul. We are one family across culture and time: one Lord, one faith, one baptism.

# Introduction

When Saint Bruno in his younger years was studying in Paris, the city was caught up in a sea of mourning. A renowned monastic scholar, much admired for his holy life, had died. But as the funeral cortege proceeded to the tomb, the dead scholar rose out of the coffin and cried out, "By God's righteous judgment, I am accursed." Utterly astounded, the officiating clerics delay the funeral until the following day. But the same shocking episode occurs again, and still again the day after. So terrified—and convicted of sin—is Bruno that he goes straightaway into the desert to meditate and soon thereafter, in 1084, he founds the Carthusians, a cloistered order of monks and nuns. On September 14, 1224, while praying on the mountain of Verna, Saint Francis receives the stigmata—the very wounds of the crucified Christ. On July 2, 1505, Martin Luther, having been struck down by lightning, promises Saint Anne that he will become a monk. Some two centuries later, American evangelist William Tennent awakens in the night realizing the toes on one foot are missing—snatched by the Devil.

The history of Christianity is a fascinating narrative, roiling with legends and lies, facts and figures, daring feats and disputations. Wild and well-nigh impenetrable, it snares the unsuspecting reader by its captivating content. Indeed, having once started down the rabbit trail of church history, it turns into an exhilarating hunt. That is why studying the subject is not only a serious enterprise but also entertaining—and addictive.

A metaphor for church history is a journey, a pilgrimage, or perhaps a parade—a parade that begins as the Messiah marches out of the pages of the Old Testament. The parade meanders through Palestine and reaches a pinnacle with the triumphal entry into Old Jerusalem, only to be followed by a charade: trial and execution. The parade will end one day in New Jerusalem when, from every tongue and tribe and nation, *the saints go marching in*. But in the millennia before that glorious new day, the parade of Christian history marches on with colorful fanfare, complete with clowns and garish floats and the steady beating of the bass drum.

How does a historian even begin to narrate this strange and sometimes shocking story to readers? For me it would be natural to offer the drama in the very chaotic jumble in which it presents itself. But I have found that my students desire structure and organization. So what I seek to offer here is the delightfully messy disarray of our Christian heritage in a free and easy style but with a highly organized structure. The book has 24 chapters in two parts of 12 chapters each. Eash chapter contains all the same components, including an opening page of personal remarks, a parade-of-history sidebar, and everyday-life section, a *What if* segment serving as wrap-up, and a bibliography for further reading.

There are countless ways to partition the history of Christianity as one formulates a textbook, the chronological always competing with the topical. In this volume, Part I covers the time beginning with the New Testament, continuing through the post-apostolic period and medieval Catholicism, ending with the Magisterial Reformation led by Luther, Zwingli, and Calvin.

Part II highlights a new movement within the church, proceeding with fits and starts, only to gain momentum as it triumphs in the twentieth century. The first and foundational chapter of Part II features the Anabaptists, who called for separation of church and state in opposition to the Magisterial Reformers and the Catholic Church of the previous centuries. The following chapters carry on with the institutionalized church as seen in the Catholic Counter-Reformation and the English Reformation, while picking up the trail of Puritans and Quakers and diverse communities of believers worldwide—a trail that ends at the turn of the twenty-first century.

This volume is not a reference work or an exhaustive history of Christianity, nor is the selection of individuals and topics free from subjectivity. It contains no comprehensive bibliography or notes, though each chapter ends with a short list of books for further reading. Quotes featured in sidebars from historians and other present-day writers are referenced by author and title. Quotes within the body of the text are taken from original sources, most of which can be found online at such sites as *Medieval Sourcebook*.

The book is not written primarily for those headed for doctoral studies in church history, though I would hope such individuals would find the book most useful. Rather, it is written as an introductory college and seminary text—especially for those studying for ministry or already involved in ministry. And if lay people and smart home-schoolers snatch the book off the shelves, I will feel supremely honored.

The subject matter is *people*. How could it be anything other? Ralph Waldo Emerson was correct in saying there is "properly no history, only biography." Yet history often gets a bum rap for being an endless stream of names and dates or, as Henry Ford suggested, *one damn fact after another*. The best way to learn history, then, is through stories. Narrative history puts flesh on the dry bones long buried as voices rise out of the graves and speak directly to us and identify with our concerns. But we dare not confuse what we hear in the stories with their actual words and meanings. On an everyday level communication easily breaks down as we speak across a dinner table, and even more so when words are spoken across time and culture.

The personal musings opening each chapter should not be mistaken for mere self-promotion. Christian history is a family history, one that becomes personalized as we put ourselves into the story. I hope that readers will find their own points of connection as they identify with individuals and events. The *What if* ending of each chapter should also stimulate students—in this case to identify their own counterfactuals. We easily imagine that historical events were inevitable—that Martin Luther, for example, could have done nothing other than separate from the Church of Rome. Not so. Contemplating the counterfactuals of history helps us better comprehend not only how consequential decisions can be but also how seemingly insignificant events can change the whole course of history.

The definitive counterfactual for the church historian is *What if Jesus had not lived and died and been resurrected from the grave?* What if? There is no answer apart from acknowledging how extraordinarily different the entire course of history would have been. And through that acknowledgment, we begin to comprehend the incredible significance of the salvation drama.

*Soli Deo Gloria.*

# Acknowledgments

I extend sincere appreciation to Zondervan's Executive Vice President and Editor-in-Chief, Dr. Stan Gundry, for his nearly three decades of judicious guidance, challenging and chiding me while at the same time expressing supreme confidence in my work. I also wish to thank Jim Ruark, who has expertly guided this volume through the editorial process. To Professor Lyle Bierma, outstanding church historian and theologian, I am most grateful for critiquing and for correcting mistakes in the manuscript in its early stages. To Robert Hosack, friend and Executive Editor at Baker Books, I am especially appreciative of his fine indexing and sharp eye for errors. To my husband, John Worst, I am deeply indebted for reading and re-reading and encouraging me every step of the way, making this book his own. For all errors and shortcomings that remain, I take full responsibility.

# PART I

# The Early Church through the Magisterial Reformation

# CHAPTER 1

# A Resurrection People

## *The New Testament Era*

*I first learned about New Testament characters from a flannelgraph propped on an easel. The colorful paper characters and props set against a nondescript green and blue landscape made the stories come alive. I later taught a beginner Sunday school class in the same way.*

*Life was simple back then, and so were the stories. No longer. As I've studied the Bible over the years, I have come to realize how complex it really is. I welcome controversial interpretations and unconventional insights. And I am not alone. The field of biblical studies is a dynamic and growing enterprise, capturing the attention of scholars from wide-ranging disciplines and from vastly different cultural backgrounds and theological perspectives.*

*This chapter on the New Testament era is foundational—the raison d'etre for the entire book. Without the first witnesses of Jesus, there would be no church history. But the chapter is also unique because of its source limitation: it is based solely on the biblical account without challenge to its historical accuracy.*

*I have often told my students that the freewheeling profession of historian is more suited to my temperament than that of biblical scholar. If newly discovered documents, for example, revealed that Martin Luther late in life had recanted his "Protestant" faith, I could accept the verdict and add the documentation to this text. But there is no such latitude with closed canon of Scripture. As a historical source book—and sacred text—the Bible stands alone. I do not challenge its accuracy, nor do I seek to resolve apparent contradictions or engage in* higher criticism *as I might with other sources. So it is with this disclaimer that I offer the first chapter—a chapter rooted in my faith commitment more than in my profession as a church historian.*

> The past remains integral to us all, individually and collectively.
> We must concede the ancients their place.... But their place is not simply back there....
> [I]t is assimilated in ourselves, and resurrected into an ever-changing present.
>
> DAVID LOWENTHAL

No history is more assimilated into ourselves and resurrected into an ever-changing present than biblical history. Christians have never granted the ancient biblical characters a place simply back there. We assume we know them and that they are us — the virtuous ones pleasantly participating in our potlucks and Bible studies, and the wicked ones in cults or terrorist camps. We cannot help but make them our contemporaries. But we must also let them be themselves in their own times as much as the fragmented documents of their lives allow them to be.

As the era of the Old Testament flowed into that of the New, there was far more blending of belief and practice than clear lines of demarcation. There was no sharp Judeo-Christian divide. Jesus' followers were Jews who were utterly unaware they were on the ground floor of the Christian faith. Ever conscious of their religious heritage, they were faithful to their traditions — as one can observe in the lives of Mary, the mother of Jesus, John the Baptist, Peter, and Paul.

The earliest record of the Christian church — the documents contained in the New Testament — makes frequent reference to the Hebrew Bible (or Old Testament). Dozens of names are mentioned without elaboration as though the reader knows them well. The gospels of Matthew and Luke both include foundational genealogies from the Jewish past. Noah and Abraham and Moses are referenced without introduction. Paul compares Jesus with Adam and brings Eve into the discussion. The writer of the book of Hebrews lists a Who's Who of biblical greats as a "cloud of witnesses" to inspire Christians for all times. The infant church was standing on the shoulders of giants as it found its way into the first century.

Following the destruction of the temple and the fall of Jerusalem in AD 70, only two Jewish-based groups would survive in significant numbers: the Pharisees portrayed in the Gospels (a movement later known as Rabbinic Judaism) and Christians. Their fraternal differences in Jesus' day would escalate into competing religions. Gnostic sects and separatists such as the Ebionites were fading away, though only to be resurrected in other manifestations in the following centuries. Only Christians, united by

---

## PARADE OF HISTORY

The infant Christian church meanders not only through Palestine and beyond but also through texts of the New Testament, though never in an entirely neat and orderly chronological fashion. Some events are humdrum; others, like the boisterous triumphal entry, pop right out of the pages. All of the twelve disciples were probably present — and many more. Luke records that prior to the parade two disciples were sent to fetch a colt, but as the parade was getting underway, "the whole crowd of disciples began joyfully to praise God in loud voices" — so much so that Pharisees told Jesus to shush them. Then come the Lord's unforgettable words: "If they keep quiet, the stones will cry out." No parade has ever matched that one.

## No Missions in the Old Testament

It might be asked whether one should not begin with the Old Testament in the search for an understanding of mission. This is a legitimate question. There is, for the Christian church and Christian theology, no New Testament divorced from the Old. However, on the issue of mission we run into difficulties here, particularly if we adhere to the traditional understanding of mission as the sending of preachers to distant places.... There is, in the Old Testament, no indication of the believers of the old covenant being sent by God to cross geographical, religious, and social frontiers in order to win others to faith in Yahweh.

David Bosch, *Transforming Mission*

apostolic teachings and the bonding of persecution, would see significant growth in succeeding generations.

But the evolution of Christianity as a religion distinct from Judaism was not an obvious development in the first century. Even Jesus was not the *Christian* he is easily thought to be. To all appearances, he was just another Jewish rabbi whose God-ordained message and mission might have been lost in the annals of history had it not been for one factor: Jesus commissioned his disciples to take the message far beyond the borders of Palestine. This missionary feature of the faith more than anything else, from a practical standpoint, separated the old from the new. When the doors flew open to *all the world* of Gentiles, differences arose, tempers flared, and lines were drawn. It was a painful process. Indeed, as doors flew open, others were slammed shut. The very heritage out of which Christianity was born would later become abhorrent. Discrimination would lead to persecution, and the Jewish culture passed down since the time of the patriarchs would be spurned.

Things might have turned out differently had early Christians taken seriously the words of Jesus to love one another—even one's enemies. But as time passed, the chasm between Christian and Jew widened. Early Christians did, however, take seriously Jesus' message to spread

the gospel, and that passion propelled the message throughout the Roman world and beyond.

Even before he issued the Great Commission, commanding his disciples to go out into all the world and preach the gospel, Jesus sent disciples out two by two. And during his post-resurrection appearances, he again commanded his followers to be witnesses "in Jerusalem, and in all Judea and Samaria, and to the ends of the

Planet Art

Virgin Mary

## Growing Up in Nazareth

A medium-sized Jewish town, Nazareth was home to Syrians as well as to Romans and Greeks. The city center, the hub of official activity, was the synagogue. Nearby, the marketplace offered a variety of shops where food and footwear and other necessities were bartered or bought. Stonemasons, tentmakers, and weavers plied their trade in adjacent family dwellings. Such houses, situated close together, consisted of one or two rooms with a low and narrow entrance. They featured flat roofs and dirt floors. Living quarters doubled as sleeping quarters with mats rolled onto the floor—or onto the roof if the nights were hot. Housework was a communal activity conducted outside in the courtyard by women and girls who cooked and baked over open fires. Water, carried in clay pots from a nearby well, served its many purposes for drinking, food preparation, bathing, and washing clothes. A communal neighborhood atmosphere with very little privacy was the normal way of life.

Diligently adhering to strict Sabbath codes, ancient Jews dispensed with work at sundown on Friday. Following prayer and lighting of candles, extended families joined together for a meal as preparation for their day of rest and worship. Typical fare would have included fish or fowl and vegetables, often cooked together in a pot. Eggs, olives, dates, and fruit of various kinds were staples, as was wine. As a day of rest, the Sabbath was a time marked by rules and regulations—as well as a merry time of laughter and sharing memories. Worship at the synagogue featured public reading of the Torah and, after that, two more ritual meals.

> ### NEW TESTAMENT SUNDAY-SCHOOL FIGURES
>
> A blur of romance clings to our notions of "publicans," "sinners," "the poor," "the people in the marketplace," "our neighbors," as though of course God should reveal himself, if at all, to these simple people, these Sunday school watercolor figures, who are so purely themselves in their tattered robes, who are single in themselves, while we now are various, complex, and full at heart.
>
> Annie Dillard, *Holy the Firm*

Passover was the foremost celebration on the religious calendar—a holy week commemorating the Jewish exodus from slavery in Egypt. Families left their homes and poured into the holy city of Jerusalem, now teaming with multitudes, little children running underfoot amid donkeys, dogs, and other domesticated animals. A much-anticipated holiday, it was a festive occasion to leave cares behind for a less-than-relaxing religious retreat.

Back home work was routine; children labored alongside parents unless they were enrolled in school. Girls, taught by their mothers at home, specialized in domestic pursuits; boys gathered at the synagogue to study under a rabbi. First taught at home to read and

## More than a One-Horse Town

Jesus' immediate environment was more culturally diverse and cosmopolitan than has generally been recognized. It is probable, and perhaps likely, that Jesus had enough competence in Greek to converse in that language during his itinerant ministry.... Although Nazareth was a village of some 1,600 to 2,000 in population and relied heavily on agriculture as its economic base, it is not accurate to think that Jesus grew up in cultural and geographical isolation. Nazareth was situated alongside of, and overlooking, one of the busiest trade routes in ancient Palestine, the Via Maris, which stretched all the way from Damascus to the Mediterranean. Capernaum, a town of 12,000 to 15,000, was yet more culturally diverse than Nazareth.

Michael James McClymond, *Familiar Stranger*

write, they began by age ten a more formal study of the Torah. The eager scholars among them might continue their studies for as many as eight years and then seek out a more distinguished rabbi for advanced learning. Most boys typically carried on in their father's line of work. Girls married young and had babies—unless they were barren, a condition that brought a woman much grief.

earth." (It is often said that this command of Jesus in Acts 1:8 was put in motion by Acts 8:1 when "a great persecution broke out against the church at Jerusalem, and all except the apostles were scattered throughout Judea and Samaria.") Later, Paul took up the missionary mantle, a calling that became almost an obsession. But others joined the cause as well—Barnabas and Silas and John Mark, most notably. What role the original disciples played is less certain. There is no doubt, however, about the central role of mission outreach in the early church. Whether fact or legend, tradition offers an inspiring account of the Twelve fanning out into the Mediterranean world, Thomas traveling as far as India.

Matthew, according to tradition, evangelized in Ethiopia; James the Less in Egypt; Bartholomew in Armenia; and Andrew, Philip, John, and others spread out to the north. They all went their separate ways, faithfully following the command of Jesus. These stories, however, may say more about the mission emphasis of a later day than any urgency the apostles may have felt. In fact, the biblical text suggests that the disciples did not rush out to conduct cross-cultural ministry. Luke reports in Acts 8 that following the stoning of Stephen, "a great persecution broke out against the church at Jerusalem" and that the believers were scattered—"all except the apostles." The twelve disciples seem to have had feet of clay and may have remained in Jerusalem for many years. But while there is reason to doubt the veracity of some of these traditional accounts, they do suggest that taking the gospel to far-flung foreign fields was a high priority for the early church.

If some of the disciples failed to fully embrace the Great Commission, they also fell short of Jesus' message to minister to the marginalized. Jesus was radical in his social outlook. His concern was for the poor, the prisoners, the persecuted, the prostitutes, and all others who were on the outside and the underside of society. But Jesus reached out to the rich and powerful as well. As a matter of course, he called out to a despised tax collector to join his band. Nor did he overlook the female half of society, including the socially ostracized Samaritan woman he met at a well. Women also played important roles in his ministry — strong and opinionated women like Mary and Martha. In fact, Jesus gathered around him an odd assortment of individuals — uneducated laborers and others who were less than reliable when they were most needed. Argumentative, competitive, churlish, they followed with mixed motives as much as with devotion.

Virgin Mary

Jesus' parables were enigmatic, surely not designed as a catechism. Crowds dogged his every move, five thousand to feed, miracle upon miracle. Time was short. Events were unfolding: triumphal entry, Last Supper, Gethsemane, crucifixion, resurrection. And then he was gone, leaving behind a motley crew of resurrection people.

## Mary: Mother and Disciple of Jesus

In recent years Mary has undergone a facelift — more than that, a complete physical and personality makeover — especially among Protestants. No longer is she the Renaissance artist's depiction of demure and perfect womanhood, a haloed, fine-featured Italian lady. Gone is her ever-meek-and-mild temperament. She is rather portrayed as a strong-willed, outspoken Jewish matron. Unlike the garden statuary in blue and white garb, she may have been stout, with a full face and dark complexion, a typical first-century peasant woman from Palestine.

The Christian era begins with the story of Mary, a young woman from Nazareth whose heritage lies deep in the Jewish drama of the

---

### A SERMON EXCERPT ON THE NATIVITY

Shame on you, wretched Bethlehem! The inn ought to have been burned with brimstone.... There are many of you in this congregation who think to yourselves: "If only I had been there! How quick I would have been to help the Baby!... You say that because you know how great Christ is, but if you had been there at that time you would have done no better than the people of Bethlehem.... Why don't you do it now! You have Christ in your neighbor. You ought to serve him, for what you do to your neighbor in need you do to the Lord Christ Himself.

Martin Luther, *Christmas Book*

## MUSLIM VERSION OF THE CHRISTMAS STORY

When she bore him, she isolated herself to a faraway place. The birth process came to her by the trunk of a palm tree. She said, "I wish I were dead before this happened, and completely forgotten." [The infant] called her from beneath her, saying, "Do not grieve. Your Lord has provided you with a stream...." She came to her family, carrying him. They said, "O Mary, you have committed something that is totally unexpected...." She pointed to him. They said, "How can we talk with an infant in the crib?" [The infant said] "I am a servant of GOD. He has given me the scripture, and has appointed me a prophet...."

Qur'an, Sura 19:22–30

Old Testament. The angel Gabriel tells her she has found favor with God, that she will conceive and bear a son by the Holy Spirit—and not just a son but the "Son of the Most High." Her fiancé, Joseph, "a righteous man," is not the father. When he becomes aware of the situation, he faces the dilemma of how to deal with very unfortunate circumstances. According to the law, betrothal is legally binding. The only way to sever the relationship is through divorce. Joseph plans to do this with as little public fanfare as possible, but an angel intervenes, telling him that Mary has conceived by the Holy Spirit and that he should take her as his wife. Mary, informed by the angel that her barren cousin Elizabeth is also pregnant, sets off for a three-month visit with the soon-to-be mother of John the Baptist. She returns to Nazareth before Jesus is born.

According to gospel accounts, Jesus was born during the reign of Herod the Great, thus sometime before 4 BCE. The birth narrative in Luke's gospel is one of the most familiar passages in the Bible. Leaving their hometown of Nazareth, Mary and Joseph travel to Bethlehem to pay taxes. Arriving late, they find no vacancy at the inn. But they are offered a stable, most likely a second room attached to a family dwelling where animals were sheltered—a room that would offer some privacy from the main family room for cooking, eating, and sleeping.

Although some scholars question whether Bethlehem was the location of the nativity, there is no other town so filled with history and prophecy. It is the setting for the story of Ruth and Boaz, but more than that, it is the site of David's birth and where Samuel anointed him king. This "city of David" is the *little town of Bethlehem* of Christmas-carol fame, a starlit silhouette indelibly etched on Christmas cards. No sooner was the baby born than angels announced the news to shepherds who spread the word. "But Mary treasured all these things and pondered them in her heart."

Very little is revealed of Mary following the birth of Jesus apart from a series of isolated events: Magi visit, bringing gifts. Mary and Joseph travel to Jerusalem to present Jesus at the temple. They return to Nazareth only to be warned by an angel that they must flee to Egypt to protect their boy from the wrath of King Herod. After a sojourn in Egypt, the family returns to Nazareth. There is no further reference to Mary until some years later when she is perhaps thirty. The setting is the Passover in Jerusalem. Jesus, at age twelve, has disappeared to listen to teachers in the temple court. When Mary and Joseph, already a day's journey out of Jerusalem, discover that he is not with the company of travelers, they turn back. When they find him in the temple interacting with elders

## ON THE ROAD WITH MARY

Mary [as many Bible teachers have claimed] may well have been retiring and home-loving, but with the possible exception of the angel's announcement of the coming conception, the scriptural record never shows us Mary at home. She is hurrying off to Elizabeth, then going to Bethlehem for the census, then to Jerusalem for purification rites, down to Egypt, back to Nazareth, then to Jerusalem again for the Passover, to Cana for the wedding, to Capernaum, to a city near the Sea of Galilee with her other sons to persuade Jesus to come home, and finally to Jerusalem again. It therefore requires an exercise of imagination to learn from her lessons "mostly related to home."

Dorothy Pape,
*In Search of God's Ideal Woman*

and rabbis, Mary appears agitated by his willfulness. He responds: "Didn't you know I had to be in my Father's house?"

Following that incident, the story of Mary—and of Jesus—disappears for nearly two decades. Indeed, the whole biblical drama shuts down until John the Baptist appears on the scene. From later references it is assumed that during this interim Mary is busy raising her family.

Throughout the biblical story Joseph plays a secondary role. Mary is always named first when the couple is referenced. Indeed, Joseph disappears from the record after Jesus' twelfth year, and perhaps Mary raised the children as a single parent. That Mary had other children has been rejected by Roman Catholics (who insist she ever remained a virgin), but the biblical account refers to brothers and sisters: "Isn't this the carpenter's son?" asked observers from Nazareth. "Isn't his mother's name Mary, and aren't his brothers James, Joseph, Simon and Judas? Aren't all his sisters with us?"

In her role as a mother, Mary appears to have been perplexed regarding her relationship with Jesus, in particular when Jesus is left behind at the temple and again years later at the wedding in Cana. When she asks Jesus to get more wine, his response is direct: "Woman, why do you involve me? . . . My time has not yet come." This may have been his very straightforward way of letting her know that she, as a

## JESUS AND WOMEN

Perhaps is it no wonder that women were first at the cradle and last at the cross. They had never known a man like this Man — there never had been such another. A prophet and teacher who never nagged at them, never flattered or coaxed or patronized; who never made arch jokes about them, never treated them either as "The women, God help us!" or "The ladies, God bless them!"; who rebuked without querulousness and praised without condescension; who took their questions and arguments seriously; who never mapped out their sphere for them, never urged them to be feminine or jeered at them for being female; who had no axe to grind and no uneasy male dignity to defend; who took them as he found them and was completely unselfconscious. There is no act, no sermon, no parable in the whole Gospel that borrows its pungency from female perversity; nobody could possibly guess from the words and deeds of Jesus that there was anything "funny" about women's nature.

Dorothy Sayers, *Are Women Human?*

disciple, is not relating to him properly, or it may have implied that his time of miraculous wonders has not yet been inaugurated.

Mary's relationship with Jesus is further clarified during his itinerant ministry in Galilee. While crowds throng him to hear his message and benefit by his healing powers, Mary and his brothers come "to take charge of him, for they said, 'He is out of his mind.'" When Jesus is informed that they are there, his response is blunt: "Who are my mother and my brothers?" he asks rhetorically. Pointing to his followers, he says: "Here are my mother and my brothers!" Typical of his teaching style, Jesus uses a mundane interruption to illustrate an eternal truth. He gives a similar response on another occasion when a woman in the crowd calls out "Blessed is the mother who gave you birth and nursed you." He simply responds, "Blessed rather are those who hear the word of God and obey it."

These incidents should not be interpreted as demeaning of Mary. She is more than mother; she becomes a prominent disciple. She grieves in anguish at the crucifixion, but her dedication to Jesus and his teachings goes far beyond the cross. As the book of Acts opens, she and her sons are among those who are gathered in the upper room, praying and waiting for the Holy Spirit in fulfillment of Jesus' promise. Her presence reinforces the credibility of the new faith.

John the Baptist

## John the Baptist: Desert Preacher

John the Baptist, when viewed alongside other New Testament characters, seems to be marching to a different drummer. Living apart in the desert near the Dead Sea, he is an ascetic whose lifestyle more closely resembles that of the Essenes, than that of the Pharisees, Sadducees, or Zealots, who were active in their own ways in pubic life. For that reason alone, his life merits study, especially since monastic asceticism would become such a prominent lifestyle for Christian ministry in the centuries following.

An Old Testament character showing up on the scene of first-century Palestine, John was born only months before Jesus. His birth story, like that of Jesus, is included in Scripture—an inclusion that portends his greatness. His parents, Zechariah and Elizabeth, a childless elderly couple living in the hill country of Palestine, were devout Jews. A descendent of Aaron, Zechariah was a priest privileged to travel to Jerusalem with other priests from his "division" for a once-in-a-lifetime opportunity to go alone inside the temple and burn incense to the Lord. While conducting this ceremony, an angel

## A Prophet Leaping Out of the Gospel Pages

John the Baptist cuts an imposing figure in the opening pages of the New Testament. Wearing coarse camel's hair and leather, eating locusts and wild honey, shouting at the top of his lungs in a wilderness place to the penitents and curious, John leaps out of the Gospel pages as the frightening first figure of a new age. He rants of the coming judgment when the unjust will be destroyed, he demands conversion, he washes those who've begun to change their lives, and he is ultimately beheaded by a ruler who would not repent.... John the Baptist inaugurates the good news of God's kingdom like a champagne bottle shattered against the hull of a new ship.

Catherine M. Murphy,
*John the Baptist: Prophet of Purity for a New Age*

startles him with a message that his persistent prayer for a child will be granted: Elizabeth will give birth to a son who "will be great in the sight of the Lord ... in the spirit and power of Elijah." When Zechariah expresses doubts, an angel identifying himself as Gabriel penalizes him by taking away his voice.

Zechariah returns home speechless, and nine months later becomes a first-time father. On the eighth day, when he and Elizabeth take the baby to be circumcised, it is assumed the infant will be named for his father. But instead Elizabeth insists, "No! He is to be called John." Those present argue that *John* is not a family name. They turn to Zechariah for confirmation. He writes the name *John*—and recovers his voice. Then he makes a prophecy in lyrical form: his son "will go on before the Lord to prepare the way for him, to give his people the knowledge of salvation."

John next appears in the biblical record as an adult and in the desert, where "the word of the Lord came to him." It is a call to preach, and he wastes no time. "He went into all the country around the Jordan, preaching a baptism of repentance for the forgiveness of sins." Dressed in camel's hair, he looks the part of a desert holy man. Neither polished nor professional, he is a ranting prophet who captures people's attention.

Some scholars believe that John was a Nazirite, as is implied in the angel's message to his father: "He is never to take wine or other fermented drink, and he will be filled with the Holy Spirit even from birth." But there is little evidence indicating that he held to the Nazirite vows. In fact, his very public prophetic outreach suggests otherwise. Nor was John a leader of an organized sect. Yet he was a compelling preacher. According to Jewish historian Josephus, Herod Antipas was threatened by John's popularity—"afraid that his great persuasive power over men might lead to an [up]rising, for they seemed ready to follow his counsel in everything."

The most noteworthy event in John's preaching career is his inauguration of Jesus' ministry. As he baptizes Jesus, a voice from heaven proclaims, "Behold, the Lamb of God who takes away the sins of the world." Jesus later declares that John is the greatest of anyone ever born to a woman. But then he almost seems to take it back by saying that John is the least in the kingdom of God. Perhaps he is differentiating his own message from that of John. But John does not appear to fully understand. He continues his baptizing ministry. Jesus goes to Galilee, and he and John preach different messages. John's is more politically focused. Herod, who had earlier been impressed by John's preaching, arrests him. He fears that John will incite a rebellion and is infuriated that John has attacked him by name for his unlawful marriage to Herodias, his sister-in-law.

During John's imprisonment Jesus' ministry continues to grow. John sends his disciples to question Jesus: "Are you he that comes, or should we look for another?" Jesus tells them: "Go and tell John what you see and hear." What they had seen were miracles—signs of the supernatural not associated with John's ministry.

Herodias is angered that John had railed against her relationship with Herod, but she bides her time. Then, on Herod's birthday, she arranges for Salome, her sexy daughter by her first marriage, to dance before the king. So charmed—and no doubt inebriated—is he that he promises her anything she wants. Consulting her mother, she makes her request: "Give me the head of John the Baptizer on a platter." Though he is "exceedingly sorry," Herod dispatches his henchmen to execute the prisoner and bring the bloody head on a platter.

Barely thirty years old, John is executed without even a mock trial. His disciples, no longer hunkering down outside his prison cell, are scattered. They could not have imagined how the horror of that murderous night would one day be gruesomely memorialized. Indeed, one of the most prized relics during medieval times was the head of John the Baptist, claimed to be in the possession of several of the great European churches.

## Peter: First of the Apostles

Is Peter the "rock" on which the Christian church is built, the founder and head of the Church of Rome during the last decades of his life? Or is he merely one of the Twelve whose larger-than-life personality grabs the attention of the gospel writers? The New Testament writings do not offer an open-and-shut case.

In the Gospels, Peter is listed first among the twelve disciples and the inner circle: Peter, James, and John. But following Jesus' death and resurrection, James, the brother of Jesus, is the head of the Jewish Jerusalem church, and Paul is sent to the Gentiles. In his letter to the Galatians, Paul credits three of the Jerusalem leaders for the commissioning: "James, Peter, and John ... gave me and Barnabas the right hands of fellowship" and "agreed that we should go to the Gentiles, and they to the Jews." Here he lists James first, though earlier in the same letter he states that after being in Arabia for three years, he had gone up to Jerusalem "to get acquainted with Peter," adding that "I saw none of the other apostles—only James, the Lord's brother."

Later, Paul writes his letter to the Romans, a detailed document on Christian doctrine, telling them of his desire to one day visit them in that great city. He makes no mention of Peter's founding the church, nor is Peter mentioned in his long list of greetings at the end. Either Peter is not the founder of that church or he is not in Rome at the time. Or perhaps Paul is purposely diminishing his role. We know from other New Testament writings that they had serious differences.

Simon Peter, son of Jonah and brother of Andrew, grew up in Bethsaida, a town on the Sea of Galilee. A married man (whose mother-in-law is later healed by Jesus), he had a boat and teamed up with Andrew in a fishing business in Capernaum. Andrew was a disciple of John the Baptist, but when John identified Jesus as the "Lamb of God," Andrew and another unnamed disciple followed Jesus. Andrew then sought out Peter and told him, "We have found the Messiah." He brought Peter to Jesus and Jesus named him Cephas (*petros* in Greek), meaning "rock."

The calling of the disciples is told in various versions. In one account Peter is fishing all night with James and John but catching nothing. Jesus tells them to put their nets down on the other side of the boat. They pull in a big haul and follow him. Considering Peter's impetuous personality, his early ministry appears to be one of fits and starts, requiring more than one calling. As time passes, Andrew fades into the background as Peter, with his type-A personality, assumes leadership of the disciples. Quick to speak, his interaction with Jesus on the Mount of Transfiguration is typical:

> Jesus took Peter, James and John with him and led them up a high mountain, where they were all alone. There he was transfigured.... And there appeared before them Elijah and Moses, who were talking with Jesus. Peter said to Jesus, "Rabbi, it is good for us to be here. Let us put up three shelters—one for you, one for Moses and one for Elijah." (He did not know what to say, they were so frightened.) Then a cloud appeared and enveloped them, and a voice came from the cloud: "This is my Son, whom I love. Listen to him!" Suddenly, when they looked around, they no longer saw anyone with them except Jesus (Mark 9:1–8).

Peter's impetuosity is also evident when he and the disciples are out at sea amid a storm. They see a "ghost" walking on the water toward them and are terrified. When Jesus identifies

Peter denying the Lord

himself, Peter throws out the challenge: *If it's really you, bid me to walk to you.* When Jesus does, Peter "walked on the water and came toward Jesus. But when he saw the wind, he was afraid and, beginning to sink, cried out." Jesus rescues him.

On another occasion Peter had answered Jesus' question about his identity by boldly pronouncing him to be the *Christ, Son of the Living God.* But when Jesus explained that he "must be killed and on the third day be raised to life," Peter rebuked him: "This shall never happen to you!" Jesus' response was searing: "Get behind me, Satan! You are a stumbling block to me; you do not have in mind the things of God, but the things of men." Again, when Jesus knelt to wash the disciples' feet at the Last Supper, Peter insisted that Jesus not wash his feet; Jesus, after all, is their leader. When Jesus responded, "Unless I wash you, you have no part with me," Peter insisted that Jesus wash his hands and head as well.

When Jesus warns the Twelve that one of them will deny him, Peter nudges John to ask him what he means. Later, when Peter asks the Lord where he is going, Jesus gives a less-than-precise answer, telling him he cannot come along. Peter counters: "Lord, why can't I follow you now? I will lay down my life for you." With that, Jesus predicts Peter's betrayal: "Before the rooster crows, you will disown me three times!" But before his denial Peter has one last opportunity for bravado. Following supper, they all go into the Garden of Gethsemane. As authorities come to arrest Jesus, Peter brandishes his sword and cuts off the ear of the high priest's bodyguard. Visibly annoyed, Jesus miraculously reattaches the ear.

As Jesus has predicted, Peter denies him before dawn. The setting is memorable. Peter is warming his hands over an open fire and talking, still unable to turn off his motor-mouth. His Galilean accent is recognized. A servant girl points to him as a follower of Jesus. When others ask his identity, he curses, insisting he does not even know Jesus. Three times he denies. Then the rooster crows. He remembers the words of Jesus and is remorseful; he does not disclose his identity and is neither pummeled by the bystanders nor arrested by authorities.

Testimonies in eyewitness accounts typically vary. One individual reports a particular aspect of the drama; another focuses on something else. So it was with the passion and resurrection narratives. Where is Peter at the cross? The apostle John reportedly is there, as are the women, including Mary the mother of Jesus and Mary Magdalene. But Peter is nowhere to be found. After the burial, women report that the tomb is empty. Peter outruns John to verify the story and walks right into the tomb.

Mystified by the disappearance of the body, Peter, like others, thinks he is seeing a ghost when Jesus appears in his resurrected form.

After forty days of post-resurrection appearances, Jesus is "taken up before their very eyes" into heaven. The disciples return to Jerusalem and Peter takes charge of finding a replacement for the turncoat Judas. His leadership, however, appears to be anything but authoritarian. When the others propose they cast lots, Peter goes along with the proposal, and "the lot fell to Matthias."

Peter's prominent public role soars with the hurricane winds and the tongues of fire at Pentecost. Peter's Pentecost sermon ranks high as a biblical pulpit-pounder. "These men [referring to the tongues-speakers]," he fumes, "are not drunk as you suppose." Thousands listen as he explains their conduct as a fulfillment of Joel's prophecy. Then his anger explodes. "Men of Israel, you, with the help of wicked men, put him to death by nailing him to the cross." But the bad news is followed with good: "God has made this Jesus, whom you crucified, both Lord and Christ."

Without so much as an altar call, some three thousand come forward, are baptized, and join the church. Is Peter fulfilling the words of Jesus, "Upon this rock I will build my church"? Following Pentecost, he is clearly the leader involved in all the major events, including the shocking double demise of Ananias and Sapphira (for lying to the Holy Spirit). But the

## PETER: MAGNIFIED AND MISREPRESENTED

No character of the Bible, we may say, no personage in all history, has been so much magnified, misrepresented and misused for doctrinal and hierarchical ends as the plain fisherman of Galilee who stands at the head of the apostolic college.... He was the strongest and the weakest of the Twelve.... He had all the excellences and all the defects of a sanguine temperament. He was kind-hearted, quick, ardent, hopeful, impulsive, changeable, and apt to run from one extreme to another. He received from Christ the highest praise and the severest censure.... With all his weakness he was a noble, generous soul, and of the greatest service to the church.

Philip Schaff, *History of the Christian Church*

situation quickly changes when persecution breaks out and the leaders of the infant church are scattered.

Acts 9 records Paul's conversion, and as his star rises, Peter's begins to fade. He continues to perform on center stage through chapter 12, healing Aeneas and Dorcas, but no longer as a towering leader. In fact, in chapter 10 he is presented in a lengthy and in some ways less-than-flattering account. The story features a Gentile seeker: "At Caesarea there was a man named Cornelius, a centurion in what was known as the Italian Regiment. He and all his family were devout and God-fearing; he gave generously to those in need and prayed to God regularly."

Prompted by an angel, Cornelius sends men to fetch Peter. He might have turned the visitors away but for a vision of unclean animals and the unambiguous message: "Do not call anything impure that God has made clean." Peter agrees to accompany the men and is welcomed into the home filled with "a large gathering of people." The first thing he says is not *Thanks so much for your invitation*. Rather, he says, "You are well aware that it is against our law for a Jew to associate with a Gentile or visit him. But

God has shown me that I should not call any man impure or unclean. So when I was sent for, I came without raising any objection." Here is Peter, years after Jesus commanded the disciples to "go and make disciples of all nations," still fussing about associating with Gentiles. Hardly a flattering picture.

To be fair to Peter, however, there was an identity crisis in the early church. Indeed, Jewish Christians in Jerusalem were agitated when they learned of Peter's being entertained by Gentiles — and not only that, baptizing them. When Peter recounted the entire story, including his own standard of strict separation that God had overruled, the debate was so heated that James called a council. Peter was vindicated and the "Judaizers" and "circumcision party" were on the losing side, though the wrangling was not over. In fact, several years later Paul rebuked Peter on this very issue:

> When Peter came to Antioch, I opposed him to his face, because he was clearly in the wrong. Before certain men came from James, he used to eat with the Gentiles. But when they arrived, he began to draw back and separate himself from the Gentiles because he was

## LEAVING PETER WITH THE PAPACY

Despite his prominence in the New Testament story, the apostle Peter has been whisked away from the center of Christian reflection. He has become one of the "Lost Boys," orphaned by turns in ecclesiastical history, the pen of the critics, and the popular consciousness of Christians. Protestants were separated from Peter by no less a figure than Martin Luther, who discovered the true Gospel in the writings of Paul.... In recounting the biblical narrative, Luther had his eye on Rome. The Reformation put Paul in Protestant hands, gladly leaving Peter with the papacy. "Good riddance to you, Peter, and your successors!" was the cry. While Roman Catholics inherit Peter and the Holy See, Protestants end up with Paul and the true Gospel.... Peter gets at best a few lines in our books, where he is portrayed as the confused theologian who serves as the perfect foil for our beloved Paul.

Gene L. Green, *Peter: Apostolic Foundation*

afraid of those who belonged to the circumcision group. The other Jews joined him in his hypocrisy, so that by their hypocrisy even Barnabas was led astray.

When I saw that they were not acting in line with the truth of the gospel, I said to Peter in front of them all, "You are a Jew, yet you live like a Gentile and not like a Jew. How is it, then, that you force Gentiles to follow Jewish customs?" (Gal. 2:11–14).

Peter's interaction with Paul is the last event of his life that Scripture records. According to tradition, he was martyred in Rome under the reign of Nero. After noting the strife and hardships Peter endured, Clement of Rome later reported that "he had at length suffered martyrdom [and] departed to the place of glory due to him."

## Paul: Apostle and Missionary

More than any other New Testament figure, Paul was responsible for the proliferation of the Christian faith. Indeed, it is difficult if not impossible to exaggerate his influence on the early church. He penned indispensable documents, personally evangelized vast regions of the Mediterranean world, and served as a larger-than-life role model. Born early in the first century some years after the birth of Jesus, he was reared in the Greco-Roman city of Tarsus, located on the Mediterranean Sea in what is present-day Turkey. He was a Roman citizen, perhaps inheriting the status from his father. But by his own account he was first and foremost a Jew, "circumcised on the eighth day, of the people of Israel, of the tribe of Benjamin,

The apostle Paul

a Hebrew of Hebrews; in regard to the law, a Pharisee."

Despite the cosmopolitan nature of Tarsus—described by Paul as "no mean city"—he was reared in an orthodox home affording him few occasions to enjoy the cultural offerings. As a young man he studied in Jerusalem under the distinguished teacher Gamaliel, a Pharisee. The other major schools of Jewish thought, the Sadducees and Essenes, held opposite positions on a number of issues, including determinism and free will—the Essenes asserting that God predetermines all that happens, the Sadducees insisting that individuals are in control of their own destiny and also downplaying the notion of a literal resurrection. The Pharisees, on the other hand, emphasized both divine sovereignty and human free will and believed in a literal resurrection. More notably, they were known for their zeal for the law. The fundamentalists of their day, the Pharisees shunned fellowship with other Jews and split into various factions. The two major divisions were the school of Hillel and the school of Shammai, the latter being the stricter of the two. According to one tradition, Gamaliel was associated with the school of Hillel; another tradition suggests he founded a distinct school of his own. That Paul closely followed his teaching is uncertain. He may have been an unidentified student who is described as having "impudence in matters of learning"—one who frequently challenges his teacher.

Paul is first introduced in Scripture as Saul, a zealous Jew seeking to destroy the new faith in its infancy. He spurns the wisdom of Gamaliel, who had recommended restraint. Instead, Paul demands the death penalty and lends his support to the stoning of a disciple named Stephen. "Breathing out murderous threats against the Lord's disciples," he seeks referrals from Damascus synagogues in order to smoke out any who "belonged to the Way" and haul them off to be interrogated in Jerusalem.

Did Paul ever encounter Jesus in person? Palestine is a small area. It is not rash to imagine that he was interested in this teacher who was drawing such large crowds. Indeed, he may not only have heard Jesus preach but may also have sought him out. Some have wondered if Saul might have been like the young man in the Garden of Gethsemane (Mark 14 KJV) the night before the crucifixion: "And there followed [Jesus] a certain young man, having a linen cloth cast about his naked body; and the [soldiers] laid hold on him: And he left the linen cloth, and fled from them naked." (There is a tradition that suggests this may have been Mark himself.)

But is it possible that Saul was stalking Jesus before his Damascus Road experience? He almost seems prepared for his conversion. The voice confirms what he knows too well: "It is hard for thee to kick against the pricks" (KJV). An ox goaded on by the master would sometimes kick against the spiked shaft—the prick—making the goading even more unpleasant. For Paul the prick was conscience; the more he persecuted Christians, the more miserable he became. Then he was stopped dead in his tracks. "Suddenly a light from heaven flashed around him." It is fitting that this man, destined to become the greatest of the apostles, should undergo a profound visionary confrontation. Here the risen Christ is audibly challenging him, calling him by his given name: "Saul, Saul, why do you persecute me?" When Paul questions the identity of the voice, he hears an astonishing answer: "I am Jesus whom you are persecuting."

In that moment all of his rabbinical arguments against Jesus are swept away. Indeed, so physically potent is the experience that for three days Paul loses both his sight and strength. He is counseled by Ananias and then baptized. After spending a brief time in Damascus, where he amazes his fellow Jews by preaching the resurrection of Christ in the synagogues, his activities are unclear. During at least part of the next three years he is in Arabia. Some have speculated that he might have spent time in the region of Mount Sinai, pondering the law of Moses in light of his new revelation. Others have assumed he was involved in ministry, perhaps so unsuccessful that it remained largely unrecorded.

After three years Paul returns to Jerusalem, and there he confers with James and Peter. He faces violent opposition from his fellow Jews, but he escapes to Caesarea and then continues on to Tarsus. For the next several years he ministers in the surrounding province, sometimes

---

## A CHANGING LANDSCAPE

The City breathes through [Paul's] language. Jesus' parables of sowers and weeds, sharecroppers, and mud-roofed cottages call forth smells of manure and earth, and the Aramaic of the Palestinian villages often echoes in the Greek. When Paul constructs a metaphor of olive trees or gardens, on the other hand, the Greek is fluent and evokes schoolroom more than farm; he seems more at home with the clichés of Greek rhetoric, drawn from gymnasium, stadium, or workshop.... In those early years, then, within a decade of the crucifixion of Jesus, the village culture of Palestine had been left behind, and the Greco-Roman city became the dominant environment of the Christian Movement.

Wayne A. Meeks,
*The First Urban Christians*

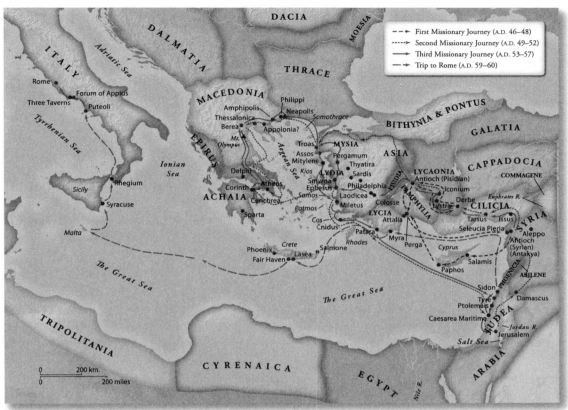

Paul's missionary journeys

facing severe persecution. On at least one occasion he is tortured with thirty-nine lashes. At the invitation of Barnabas he moves his base of ministry to Antioch, where his zeal to evangelize far exceeds that of the Jerusalem leaders. Preaching in the synagogues, he finds minimal receptivity with the exception of those born to mixed marriages and "proselytes of the gate" (Gentiles who worshiped the God of Israel by choice).

Thus turning to the Gentiles, Paul launches his ambitious missionary journeys, the first with Barnabas and Mark, traveling to Cyprus and then to the strategic cities in the province of Galatia in Asia Minor. The success of this itinerant ministry sets the stage for two more such trips. But there are delicate matters relating to practical theology and personal relationships that lie ahead. The most hotly disputed issue is circumcision. Must Gentile converts be circumcised? So explosive is the issue that Paul and Barnabas travel to Jerusalem seeking to settle the question once and for all. After an extended heated debate, James, head of the Jerusalem church, concedes that requiring Gentiles to be circumcised would only impede evangelism. The problem, however, is not so easily resolved. In the following years it continues to divide the early church.

Before embarking on the second missionary journey, Paul and Barnabas quarrel bitterly. Barnabas insists that John Mark accompany them as he had done on the first journey. Paul

## PAUL'S BUSY SCHEDULE

But get around he did. Corinth, Ephesus, Thessalonica, Galatia, Colossea, not to mention side trips to Jerusalem, Cyprus, Crete, Malta, Athens, Syracuse, Rome — there was hardly a whistle-stop in the Mediterranean world that he didn't make it to eventually, and sightseeing was the least of it. He planted churches the way Johnny Appleseed planted trees. And whenever he had ten minutes to spare he wrote letters. He bullied. He coaxed. He comforted. He cursed. He bared his soul. He reminisced. He complained. He theologized. He inspired. He exulted....

And where did it all start? On the road, as you might expect. He was still in charge of a Pharisee goon squad in those days and was hell-bent for Damascus to round up some trouble-making Christians and bring them to justice. And then it happened.

It was about noon when he was knocked flat by a blaze of light that made the sun look like a forty-watt bulb....

Frederick Buechner, *Peculiar Treasures*

adamantly refuses, convinced that John Mark is untrustworthy. He had deserted them the first time around, and Paul is furious that Barnabas simply wants to let bygones be bygones. Neither one backs down. Instead they go their separate ways, Barnabas and John Mark heading for Cyprus, and Paul and Silas for Syria.

On this second journey Paul visits many of the churches he had previously established, bringing good news: circumcision is not required. He then travels to Troas in western Asia Minor and on to present-day Greece to establish congregations in Philippi, Thessalonica, Athens, and Corinth. Along the way he invites Timothy, a young convert, to join them. Most puzzling is Paul's decision to induct Timothy into ministry through circumcision. What was he thinking? Was he merely attempting to placate Jewish Christians?

On his third and final missionary tour, Paul returns to the western shore of Asia Minor, where he spends more than two years establishing a church in Ephesus, working closely with Priscilla and Aquila. Here he witnesses some of his greatest successes while at the same time encountering grave threats, especially from the ardent devotees of the Greek goddess Artemis as well as fellow Jews. He speaks of fighting with "wild beasts" in Ephesus and of being "under great pressure, far beyond our ability to endure, so that we despaired even of life."

Paul's missionary outreach is seen by some biblical scholars as nothing short of spectacular. In a matter of a decade he establishes churches in four of the provinces of the Roman Empire. His success is due in part to his forceful personality, but he is surely not a lone ranger. His is a team ministry, and he repeatedly credits his associates, both male and female, for their indispensable partnership in the gospel. He has enemies, to be sure, and strong disagreements with co-workers, but never do we find him alone. Yet on a personal level he is alone. He is unmarried and free from domestic responsibilities. He is not, however, without family altogether. Seven of his relatives are mentioned in his letters: his sister and nephew help him when he is in prison, and other relatives are greeted in his letter to the Romans: Andronicus and Junia, Jason, Sosipater, and Lucius.

More than any other biblical figure, Paul candidly confesses his spiritual struggles—so much so that a therapist today might diagnose him with OCD (Obsessive Compulsive Disorder): "I am unspiritual, sold as a slave to sin. I do not understand what I do. For what I want to do I do not do, but what I hate I do.... I have the desire to do what is good, but I cannot carry it out. For what I do is not the good I want to do; no, the evil I do not want to do—this I keep on doing."

Straightforward and transparent, his personality is exposed in both word and action. He is argumentative and irritable, and he lashes out and complains as easily as he expresses affection and concern. His relatives, friends, and fellow workers number in the dozens. Unlike career clerics, Paul is bi-vocational, depending both on the goodwill of fellow Christians and on his own earning power. Working closely with Priscilla and Aquila in Ephesus, he spends his days as a craftsman and evangelist. He is a *skenopoios*, most likely a tent-maker, a smelly job of tanning hides and weaving goat hair into fabric (though the term could also refer to a trade in sandal making). And persecution is ever present.

Having received conflicting prophecies about their impending visit to Jerusalem, Paul and certain co-workers nevertheless make their way to that city. Though fully aware of the danger, he is "compelled by the Spirit." After reporting on his missionary travels, he responds to rumors that he is telling Jewish converts they need not circumcise their baby boys. To prove his faithfulness to Jewish law, Paul agrees to participate in a Nazirite temple ceremony. His visit to the temple draws the attention of out-of-town Jews who are aware of his teaching "against our people and our law." What follows is terrifying:

The whole city was aroused, and the people came running from all directions. Seizing Paul, they dragged him from the temple, and immediately the gates were shut. While they were trying to kill him, news reached the commander of the Roman troops that the whole city of Jerusalem was in an uproar. He at once took some officers and soldiers and ran down to the crowd. When the rioters saw the commander and his soldiers, they stopped beating Paul (Acts 21:30–32).

Arrested and about to be incarcerated, Paul requests an opportunity to speak to the people. The crowd listens attentively to his conversion testimony, but when he reports that he is commissioned by God to preach to the *Gentiles*, they again fly into a frenzy. Roman authorities seek to settle the matter in Jerusalem, but when they learn of a plot to kill him, they transfer him to Caesarea by the Sea for protection. He is charged with disturbing the peace and is kept in custody for the next two years. Somewhat of a celebrity, he gains the attention of local authorities interested in his message. Indeed, Luke devotes three chapters to Paul's interaction with people in high places, including two Roman governors, Felix and Festus, and the Jewish High Priest and Jewish King Agrippa. Women are also involved: Drusilla, wife of Felix, and Bernice, sister of Agrippa.

Paul "succeeded exactly where we fail. The first and most striking difference between his action and ours is that he founded 'Churches' whilst we found 'Missions.'"

Roland Allen

Roman authorities would have preferred to let religious leaders in Jerusalem handle the controversy, but Paul, a Roman citizen, appeals to Caesar. The voyage to Rome, like almost everything in Paul's life, is fraught with peril. One terrifying storm after another finally ends the journey in shipwreck on the island of Malta, although crew and prisoners survive. Three months later Paul boards another ship to Rome, where he is greeted by Christians awaiting his arrival. Now under house arrest, he lives in his own residence with a guard at the door. "For two whole years Paul stayed there in his own rented house and welcomed all who came to see him. Boldly and without hindrance he preached the kingdom of God and taught about the Lord Jesus Christ."

Luke's story in Acts ends with no details of Paul's appeal to the emperor. During his incarceration he writes what are known as the Prison Epistles: Colossians, Philemon, Ephesians, and Philippians. According to tradition, he was martyred during the intense persecution by Nero in the year 64. Another account dates his death on June 29 of 67, the same day that Peter was crucified upside down. Peter's death was for all to see; Paul, a Roman citizen, was beheaded outside the view of the crowds. He was marched through the walls of the city along the Ostian Way. The end came quickly with the slash of a sword.

New Testament figures—particularly Mary, John the Baptist, Peter, and Paul—are among the most familiar names in the annals of history. They are subjects of great works of art and literature and are studied by scholars and memorialized in sermons. Indeed, we easily imagine that we know a lot about them. In actuality, we have very few sources that illuminate their lives. They are forever obscured behind a vast veil f myth and legend that stretches across the centuries.

## What If ...

What if Jesus had not said to Peter, *Upon this rock I will build my church*? Papal authority is derived from the claim that Peter was the first pope. Would there be no long succession of popes, or would the papacy have developed in the Catholic Church based on other grounds? Would there be one, rather than three, branches of Christendom? Or might a *popeless* Catholic Church have led to many other branches?

What if Peter had not backed down when confronted by Paul's rebuke, and what if his stance on circumcision had carried the day? Would the relationship between Christians and Jews have been different in the early church and in the centuries that followed?

What if Paul had interpreted the flash of light on the road to Damascus as a hallucination spurred by a migraine headache? Might he have gone on persecuting Christians, while James or Barnabas or Peter took the title of chief of the apostles? Paul was not only a writer whose letters have profoundly influenced Christian belief, but he was the tireless missionary to the Gentiles. Would the Roman world have been evangelized without him?

## Further Reading

Bailey, Kenneth E. *Jesus Through Middle Eastern Eyes: Cultural Studies in the Gospels.* Downers Grove, Ill.: InterVarsity, 2008.

Brownrigg, Ronald. *Who's Who in the New Testament*, 2nd ed. New York: Taylor and Francis, 2002.

Bruce, F. F. *Paul: Apostle of the Heart Set Free.* Grand Rapids: Eerdmans, 1977.

Burke, Alexander J., Jr. *John the Baptist: Prophet and Disciple.* Cincinnati: St. Anthony Messenger Press, 2006.

Card, Michael, and Brennan Manning. *A Fragile Stone: The Emotional Life of Simon Peter.* Downers Grove, Ill.: InterVarsity, 2006.

Ferguson, Everett. *Backgrounds of Early Christianity*, 3rd ed. Grand Rapids: Eerdmans, 2003.

Flemming, Dean. *Contextualization in the New Testament: Pattern for Theology and Mission.* Downers Grove, Ill.: InterVarsity, 2005.

McClymond, Michael James. *Familiar Stranger: An Introduction to Jesus of Nazareth.* Grand Rapids: Eerdmans, 2004.

McKnight, Scot. *The Real Mary.* Brewster, Mass: Paraclete Press, 2007.

Metzger, Bruce M. *New Testament: Its Background, Growth and Content*, 3rd ed. Nashville: Abingdon, 2003.

Meeks, Wayne A. *The First Urban Christians: The Social World of the Apostle Paul*, 2nd ed. New Haven: Yale University Press, 2003.

Murphy, Catherine M. *John the Baptist: Prophet of Purity for a New Age.* Collegeville, Minn.: Liturgical Press, 2003.

Pelikan, Jaroslav. *Mary through the Centuries.* New Haven: Yale University Press, 1996.

Pollock, John. *The Apostle: A Life of Paul.* Wheaton, Ill. Victor, 1994.

Sanders, E. P. *Paul: A Very Short Introduction.* New York: Oxford University Press, 2001.

Walker, Scott. *Footsteps of the Fisherman: With St. Peter on the Path of Discipleship.* Minneapolis: Augsburg Fortress, 2003.

Wright, N. T. *Paul: In Fresh Perspective.* Minneapolis: Fortress Press, 2006.

# CHAPTER 2

# A Persecuted People

## *The Post-Apostolic Generations*

*What was she thinking, I ask myself. It is the beginning of the third century, and Perpetua is facing her executioners. Here is a young mother, leaving behind her infant son. Her aged father is pleading with her to consider his needs and spare her life. All she would have to do is put off her catechism class to a less dangerous time. But instead she willingly becomes a martyr remembered through the centuries for her sacrifice.*

*If I try to put myself in Perpetua's shoes, it is hard to imagine that I would have made the same choice. Leaving behind a motherless child was one of my biggest fears until my son reached adulthood. And I'm no doubt much too cowardly to face the executioner's sword. I probably would have looked for an easy way out.*

*This is not to say that I don't have great reverence for martyrs and those who have been persecuted. Polycarp, in his eighties, was dragged out of the hayloft where he was hiding, only to be burned at the stake. Today, from the Middle East to India and China and around the world, there are reports of churches and property destroyed and of Christians terrorized, assaulted, and killed.*

*Most North Americans have little comprehension of persecution. "Oh, yes they do," a student will quickly retort. What about the scholar who failed her dissertation defense at UCLA because of her evangelical beliefs? What about the Christian minister who was not permitted to pray at the Colorado governor's inauguration while a Native American spiritualist was? Such examples do not deserve the label of persecution, however. For the one struggling to complete a dissertation, the opposition may truly feel like persecution, but it dare not be ranked with the horror that accompanies a door kicked down in the night and a father hauled away to a dungeon never to be heard from again.*

*American Christians expect tax breaks for their Sunday offerings, and churches enjoy property tax exemptions. They take for granted religious programming on radio and television and freedom of religion on every soapbox and in every stadium. Anything that falls short of such freedom is easily labeled persecution. Not so, I tell my students. Before you use the term, put yourself in the place of Polycarp or Perpetua.*

> The historian has before him a jigsaw puzzle from which many pieces
> have disappeared. These gaps can be filled only by his imagination.
> GAETANO SALVEMINI, *HISTORIAN AND SCIENTIST*

Most of the pieces of the jigsaw puzzle of the early church have disappeared. But that is not the only problem the historian confronts. The giant puzzle of church history simply will not fit onto the tiny space of a textbook. Here and there are random shapes that faintly resemble an individual, others that form a flame shooting from the pyre, and another a partial page torn from a manuscript. The rest of our heritage of faith is pieced together by imagination, both ancient and modern.

If the writings that comprise the New Testament are authoritative for Christians, the collection of writings immediately following the apostolic age are the next most trustworthy, some scholars reason. But the writings of the ante-Nicene fathers (those writing prior to the Council of Nicaea) are a mixed bag. The early writers were working with an incomplete canon and were influenced by cultural trappings, as are Christians today. True, they were geographically and chronologically close to the apostles, but knowing an apostle or the disciple of an apostle does not translate into theological understanding. Such insights developed gradually—and imprecisely—in the third and fourth centuries

as apologists and clerics argued among themselves, each basing his claims on documentary evidence.

The Christians of this era made significant written contributions, but equally important were worship practices and lifestyle issues—and a willingness to die for the faith. The stories of sacrifice and self-denial are a testimony to the power of a transformed life. Such trials brought a sense of unity, but at the same time there were many differences in belief and practice, as is seen in the lives of Polycarp, Ignatius, Justin Martyr, Irenaeus, Perpetua, and Tertullian.

Religion flourished in the Roman Empire. Scholars and senators and soldiers and slaves all had religious opinions and customs. Syncretism was widespread, and the ancients were surely not strangers to stories of the supernatural. Indeed, there was a smorgasbord of pagan superstitions, beliefs, relics, and rituals from which to choose. Christianity competed in the marketplace of religion.

Unlike other religious beliefs, apart from Judaism, Christianity was rooted in history. Jesus was not another Roman god populating the heavens. He was a man of flesh and bone

## PARADE OF HISTORY

Before the New Testament era comes to a close, the parade of martyrs begins. Stephen leads as grand marshal. Paul proceeds to martyrdom, according to tradition, outside the gates of Rome along the Ostian Way. A generation later Ignatius makes the martyrs' march from Syria to Rome, met along the way by cheering Christians — Christians instructed not to interfere with his execution: "I beg you," he admonishes them, "do not do me an untimely kindness." On arrival in Rome, he is executed in the amphitheater. Polycarp follows on in the parade of persecution, put to death in Smyrna a generation later. Perpetua and Felicitas and others continue the procession to the slow beat of the funeral dirge.

## FIRST-CENTURY PAGAN WORSHIP OF MARS LENUS

While I am unable to bear the dire pangs of body
And spirit, wandering forever near the edges of death,
I, Tychicus, by Mars' divine love, am saved.
This little thanks-offering I dedicate in return for his great caring.

who walked the dusty roads of Judea. As such, the entry of Christianity into the Roman religious world made headlines, especially as it grew and was perceived to be a threat to the empire.

One of the direct historical links between the apostolic and the post-apostolic period comes with Clement of Rome, believed by some to be a companion of the apostle Paul and perhaps the Clement to whom Paul refers in his letter to the Philippians. Clement's words on church structure are often quoted in referencing bishops and deacons who ruled post-apostolic churches. But his writing also illustrates how quickly a doctrine can be twisted if left unchallenged.

Clement's defense of the resurrection of Christ, for example, illustrates early syncretism: "There is a certain bird which is called a phoenix," he wrote to the Corinthians. "This is the only one of its kind, and lives five hundred years." As death approaches, "it builds itself a

## POST-APOSTOLIC CHURCH GROWTH

Never in the history of the race has this record ever quite been equaled. Never in so short a time has any other religious faith, or, for that matter, any other set of ideas, religious political, or economic, without the aid of physical force or of social or cultural prestige, achieved so commanding a position in such as important culture.

Kenneth Scott Latourette,
*A History of the Expansion of Christianity*

nest of frankincense, and myrrh, and other spices, into which, when the time is fulfilled, it enters and dies. But as the flesh decays a certain kind of worm is produced, which, being nourished by the juices of the dead bird, brings forth feathers. Then, when it has acquired strength, it takes up that nest in which are the bones of its parent" and lives for another five-hundred year cycle. An interesting story, but hardly one that offers insight on the biblical concept of resurrection.

With each succeeding post-apostolic generation, theological issues and debates became more complex. Each question drew a variety of answers. Worship style became more varied as the faith passed from one generation to the next. Some things, like church infighting, stayed the same, however. Challenging Corinthian believers to reread "the epistle of the blessed Apostle Paul," Clement reminds them that in Paul's day "parties had been formed among you" though now the "sedition" is even worse.

With no formulated New Testament canon, faith communities often depended on sparse copies of one or two of Paul's letters. Yet, the church realized remarkable growth, though the estimated numbers vary widely and are much debated today. Some scholars argue that there were as many as a million Christians by the end of the first century; others insist there were fewer than ten thousand. Statistics aside, there were several factors that contributed to the increase in numbers in the early centuries, most notably through the tireless work of itinerant preachers. Eusebius of Caesarea writes of the dedication of the second-century traveling evangelists, no doubt with some exaggeration:

> At that time many Christians felt their souls inspired ... to sell their goods and to distribute them to the poor. Then, leaving their homes, they set out to fulfill the work of an evangelist, making it their ambition to preach the word of the faith to those who as yet had heard nothing of it, and to commit to them the book of the divine Gospels. They were content simply to lay the foundations of the faith among these foreign peoples: they then appointed other pastors and committed to them the responsibility for building up those whom they had merely brought to the faith.

Another avenue of evangelism was the teaching of apologists, defending the faith against Jewish and pagan adversaries. Often well-versed in philosophy, they captured the attention of the educated classes. Equally important was the informal everyday witness of believers. In his *Book of Martyrs*, John Foxe writes: "In that age every Christian was a missionary. The soldier tried to win recruits ... ; the prisoner sought to bring his jailer to Christ; the slave girl whispered the gospel in the ears of her mistress; the young wife begged her husband to be baptized." The testimony of critics is also telling. Celsius writes with sarcasm and scorn:

> Their aim is to convince only worthless and contemptible people, idiots, slaves, poor women, and children.... They would not dare to address an audience of intelligent men ... but if they see a group of young people or slaves or rough folk, there they push themselves in and seek to win the admiration of the crowd. It is the same in private houses. We see wool-carders, cobblers, washermen, people of the utmost ignorance and lack of education.

Then as now, good deeds of Christians were a key factor in evangelism. Indeed, Emperor Julian was distressed that Christians, more than pagans, were the ones who served others. Christianity, he said, "advanced through the loving service rendered to strangers, and through their care for the burial of the dead." It is scandalous, he continued, that the "godless Galileans care not only for their own poor but for ours as well; while those who belong to us look in vain for the help that we should render them."

The demonstration of faith in the face of persecution and martyrdom was another avenue of evangelism. Although early outbreaks of persecution were sporadic and localized, stories of courage were nevertheless a source of inspiration. In many instances pagans were deeply moved and converted by such testimonies. But

## DON'T BE STINGY WITH MONEY AND POSSESSIONS

Do not be one who holds his hand out to take, but shuts it when it comes to giving. If your labor has brought you earnings, pay a ransom for your sins. Do not hesitate to give and do not give with a bad grace, for you will discover who He is that pays you back a reward with a good grace. Do not turn your back on the needy, but share everything with your brother and call nothing your own. For if you have what is eternal in common, how much more should you have what is transient!

*The Didache* (Teaching of the Twelve), second century

*The Christian Martyrs' Last Prayer* by Jean-Léon Gérôme

there were serious setbacks as well. Some believers fell away from the faith. Pliny the Younger, governor of Bithynia (Asia Minor), wrote to Emperor Trajan in 112 regarding his interrogation of Christians: "So far this has been my procedure when people were charged before me with being Christians. I have asked the accused themselves if they were Christians; if they said 'Yes,' I asked them a second and third time, warning them of the penalty; if they persisted I ordered them to be led off to execution."

When threatened with death, many cursed Christ and sacrificed to images of the emperor and the gods. The majority facing martyrdom may indeed have denied the faith; Pliny reported that "the temples, which had been well-nigh abandoned, are beginning to be frequented again" and "fodder for the sacrificial animals, too, is beginning to find a sale again." He concluded on a positive note: "From all this it is easy to judge what a multitude of people can be reclaimed, if an opportunity is granted them to renounce Christianity." Eusebius reported a similar outcome in Alexandria during the crackdown by Emperor Decius in the middle of the third century. But he also emphasized the courageous accounts of martyrs:

They seized first an old man named Metras, and commanded him to utter impious words. But as he would not obey, they beat him with clubs, and tore his face and eyes with sharp sticks, and dragged him out of the city and stoned him. [When] Quinta ... turned away in detestation, they bound her feet and dragged her through the entire city over the stone-paved streets, and dashed her against the millstones, and at the same time scourged her; then, taking her to the same place, they stoned her to death.... Then they seized also that most admirable virgin, Apollonia, an old woman, and, smiting her on the jaws, broke out all her teeth. And they made a fire outside the city and threatened to burn her alive if she would not join with them in their impious cries. And she, supplicating a little, was released, when she leaped eagerly into the fire and was consumed.... Serapion [was thrown] headlong from an upper story.

The emperor's brutality knew no bounds. "Much terror was now threatening us," writes Eusebius, "so that, if it were possible, the very elect would stumble." And some did stumble. Some who came forward were "pale and trembled." Others approached the pagan altars and "boldly asserted that they had never before been Christians." Some held out and "after a few days imprisonment abjured"; and still others, "after enduring the torture for a time, at last renounced." Among those who stood firm in the face of martyrdom was the Bishop of Antioch.

## Ignatius: Bishop of Antioch

By the end of the first century most Christians knew Jesus only second hand. But there were surely some still around who had touched the hem of his garment or sat on his lap when he was blessing the little ones. According to legend, Ignatius (c. 35 – 108) is the little one whom Jesus blessed: "Sitting down, Jesus ... took a little child and had him stand among them. Taking him in his arms, he said to them, 'Whoever welcomes one of these little children in my name welcomes me; and whoever welcomes me does not welcome me but the one who sent me.'"

While distancing himself from Judaism, Ignatius sought to bring Christians under one *universal* or catholic, church. Already in Paul's day there had been factions, some following Apollos, some Peter, and some following him. Now, a generation later, the likelihood of a splintered church seems very real. In his letter to Smyrna, Ignatius writes: "Wherever the bishop appears, there let the people be; as wherever Jesus Christ is, there is the catholic Church. It is not lawful to baptize or give communion without the consent of the bishop. On the other hand, whatever has his approval is pleasing to God."

Ignatius

At the same time Ignatius is not opening the door for just anyone—bishop or not—to claim membership in the universal church. "Take note of those who hold unsound opinions on the grace of Jesus Christ," he warns. "They abstain from the Eucharist and from prayer because they do not confess that the Eucharist is the flesh of our Savior Jesus Christ, flesh which suffered for our sins and which that Father, in his goodness, raised up again."

As Bishop of Antioch in Syria, Ignatius boldly challenges Emperor Trajan, who has officially decreed worship of the pagan gods. Ignatius rails against the new decree—apparently ignoring the fact that Trajan is vacationing nearby in Antioch. In fact, Ignatius accuses the emperor of breaking his own rule. He mocks him, suggesting in a sermon, *If he doesn't have*

*to worship the gods, neither do we.* Trajan is not amused, and Ignatius is arrested. In the months that follow, he is a prisoner on the way to Rome, ever fearing that someone might secure his freedom. In his letter to the Romans, he pleads with Christians to rebuff such nonsense. "I am writing to all the Churches and I enjoin all, that I am dying willingly for God's sake, if only you do not prevent it. I beg you, do not do me an untimely kindness."

Besides writing letters filled with theological reflections, Ignatius keeps a journal of maltreatment by his captors. Whether literal or figurative, his accounts are graphic: "From Syria even to Rome I fight with wild beasts, by land and sea, by night and by day, being bound amidst ten leopards, even a company of soldiers, who only grow worse when they are kindly treated." It is a good story, and many along the way come out to meet him and listen to his message. The journey takes him through Smyrna, where he gives his benediction to the Christians served by his friend Bishop Polycarp. Soon after he arrives in Rome, he is executed in an amphitheater, getting what he wanted—a martyr's crown. His bones are carefully carried back to Antioch, precious relics for people who have lost their pastor. Today they can be found at St. Clement's Church in Rome.

## Polycarp: Bishop and Martyr of Smyrna

When the apostle John put in words the cinematic sound and spectacular visuals of his

## Early Christian Worship

Christian belief and worship practices soon became distinct from Jewish forms. As congregations grew, they moved from homes into larger public buildings—perhaps a warehouse or another structure with open space. The first church structure to be so identified is a third-century remodeled building in Syria. Early in the next century, under Emperor Constantine, churches and cathedrals became a common part of the landscape.

Christians begin worshiping on Sunday during apostolic times (Acts 20, 1 Cor. 16), but not until a generation later is the practice clearly enunciated by Ignatius. To distinguish

Fresco of female figure holding chalice in the Agape Feast. Catacomb of Saints Pietro e Marcellino (Saints Peter and Marcellinus), Via Labicana, Rome, Italy

Christianity from Judaism, he argues that believers must worship on the first day of the week. Those who have "newness of hope" should "no longer [be] observing Sabbaths but fashioning their lives after the Lord's day, on which our life also arose through Him and through His death."

Whatever day of the week, Christians often met in secret so as to avoid harassment from authorities. Pliny the Younger writes of Christian practices divulged during interrogation: "On an appointed day they had been accustomed to meet before daybreak, and to recite a hymn antiphonally to Christ, as to a god." After taking a ceremonial oath (*sacramentum*) "to abstain from theft, robbery, adultery, and breach of faith," they separated and later came together again for a meal, "but it was ordinary and harmless food" as opposed to the rumored cannibalism of communion. Justin's *First Apology*, written to the emperor in 155, offers a more detailed description of worship:

> On the day called Sunday there is a gathering together in the same place of all who live in a given city or rural district. The memoirs of the apostles or the writings of the prophets are read, as long as time permits.... When we cease from our prayer, bread is presented and wine and water. The president in the same manner sends up prayers and thanksgivings, according to his ability, and the people sing out their assent, saying the 'Amen.' ... Those who have means and are willing, each according to his own choice, gives what he wills, and what is collected is deposited with the president. He provides for the orphans and widows, those who are in need on account of sickness or some other cause, those who are in bonds, strangers who are sojourning, and in a word he becomes the protector of all who are in need.

## Liturgical Evangelism

Third-century liturgical evangelism consisted of . . . the rite of entrance; catechumenate; rite of election; purification and enlightenment; rites of initiation; and mystagogy. . . . Here is how it worked: A person who evidenced interest in the gospel was brought to the pastor and elders of the church. An inquiry into or a formal presentation of the gospel took place which emphasized not so much belief in this or that doctrine but the converting person's willingness to adopt the Christian lifestyle. . . . During the catechumenate, which could last up to three years . . . the converting person was able to demonstrate clearly a commitment to the ethical demands of the gospel, he or she entered the period of purification and enlightenment via the rite of election. . . . A final renunciation of the power of evil was made in baptism as the converting person stood in the waters. Finally, during the mystagogic period, the convert received teaching regarding the Christian life and the doing of good works. . . . This form of evangelism in the early church must be viewed in its cultural context, the paganism of the Roman Empire. The people of the Roman world were steeped in an amoral way of life: accustomed to belief in many gods, reliance on magic, and faith in the stars. Consequently, evangelism had to confront people both in the sphere of belief and the realm of lifestyle. . . .

Robert Webber, "Ethics and Evangelism" (*Christian Century*)

As was true in the apostolic church, there were growing factions as the faith spread, some revealing a much more ecstatic style of worship than others. One of these factions was Montanism. Of the Montanists, Tertullian (who later became one of them) writes, "They see visions; and, turning their face downward, they even hear manifest voices." Hippolytus, a preacher and scholar, condemned them: They are "captivated by [two] wretched women, called a certain Priscilla and Maximilla, whom they supposed prophetesses. And they assert that into these the Paraclete Spirit had [dwelt] and . . . they magnify these wretched women above the Apostles and every gift of Grace, so that some of them presume to assert that there is in them a something superior to Christ."

Raising their voices above the discord, however, were those calling church unity—a call that has echoed through the centuries to the present day.

revelation on the Island of Patmos, meaning and mystery became one. Even he could not have known how precise his prophetic words to the church in Smyrna would be: "Do not be afraid of what you are about to suffer. I tell you, the devil will put some of you in prison to test you, and you will suffer persecution for ten days. Be faithful, even to the point of death." Nor could he have imagined those words were prophetically pointed at his own dear disciple, Polycarp.

Polycarp (69–155) is most remembered for his martyrdom as an old man. An early church leader known as a kindly pastor and a defender of orthodox doctrine, he later served as Bishop of Smyrna. That the threat of persecution was very real is evident in his letter to the church at Philippi. Here he warns Christians of the dangers of materialism and instructs them in proper handling of funds that are too easily misappropriated. His concerns are everyday matters as well as theological issues. He vehemently rejects the claims of Marcion, who, while following the teachings of Paul, dismisses the remainder of Scripture, insisting that the God of the Old Testament is surely no God of Christians. So upset is Polycarp with Marcion's beliefs that he assails him to his face as "the first-born of Satan." But persecution is heavy on his heart. He reminds believers that "Christ endured for our sins even to face death," and exhorts them to "Pray for emperors, magistrates, rulers, and for those who persecute and hate you."

Polycarp

Unlike Ignatius, Polycarp has no hankering for a martyr's death. But he is considered a prime target. During an athletic festival in Smyrna in AD 155, Christians refusing to worship the emperor are threatened with execution. Officials particularly want the revered Polycarp, hoping he will deny the faith and disgrace the Christian community. Polycarp's friends provide a hiding place in a hayloft outside the city, but a boy reports his whereabouts to authorities. Soon the hunt is on, and the old man is discovered, shackled, and brought before authorities. But he is not ready to die. He has good years ahead of him for writing and counseling and caring for the sick and suffering. He might have simply offered incense to the emperor. Did not Jesus say, "Render onto Caesar what is Caesar's"? The imperial official begs him to cooperate: "What harm is there to say 'Lord Caesar,' and to offer incense?"

Polycarp was a beloved bishop. His congregations would have no doubt forgiven the old man any weakness displayed in such desperate circumstances. But burning incense meant far more in the pagan mind than merely showing respect. Moreover, the Proconsul now goes a step further. To spare his life Polycarp must curse Christ and take an oath to Caesar. He is now standing before a sea of people. He understands the consequences. He does not flinch. The crowd hushes to the sound of his voice. "For eighty-six years I have served Him," he reminds them. "He has never done me wrong. How can I blaspheme my King who saved me?"

He may have taken opportunity to make some last-ditch doctrinal points and to warn the

## MARCION

Born in Sinope near the Black Sea, Marcion (ca. 110–160) was a theologian whose widely circulated teachings were a serious threat to the second-century church. According to Justin, he was "teaching men to deny that God is the maker of all things in heaven and earth and that the Christ predicted by the prophets is His Son." Sometimes referred to as a Gnostic, his teachings, albeit dualistic, were quite different. He saw only an evil God in the Old Testament and a good God in parts of the New. Rejecting the whole Hebrew Bible and much of the New Testament, he sought to transform the faith by denying anything he perceived to be Jewish. His hero was Paul, the only one who truly understood the message of salvation.

crowd of their greed and indolence and tendency to wallow in self-pity. But the imperial official does not permit this to turn into a religious rally. He clarifies the punishment in graphic terms. There is no need to explain that he will not be read his rights or be offered a defense attorney. In fact, no trial at all. So it was with Jesus. Polycarp knows the passion story all too well. His own death will not be on a cross, but the pyre is bad enough.

The crowd is growing and becoming restless. It is obvious that this is overkill—the powerful Roman Empire waving its flares in the face of a frail old man. So the official explains again the torture he will endure, pleading with him to just get it over with: *Deny Christ, go home, and get on with whatever you do as a Bishop.* But Polycarp is not taking the bait. He has one last chance to address the crowd—though his words are aimed at the official: "The fire you threaten burns for a time and is soon extinguished; there is a fire you know nothing about—the fire of the judgment to come and of eternal punish-

---

### THE IMPORTANCE OF MARCION

The chief importance of Marcion in the second century lies in the reaction which he provoked among the leaders of the Apostolic Churches. Just as Marcion's canon stimulated the more precise defining of the NT canon by the Catholic Church, not to supersede but to supplement the canon of the OT, so, more generally, Marcion's teaching led the Catholic Church to define its faith more carefully, in terms calculated to exclude a Marcionite interpretation.

F. F. Bruce, *The Spreading Flame*

---

ment, the fire reserved for the ungodly. But why do you hesitate? Do what you want."

Realizing Polycarp will not back down, the official motions for rowdies to get involved—perhaps to shift responsibility away from himself. They grab slats of wood, pile up the pyre, and light the flames—though only after Polycarp has an opportunity to say a final prayer. He

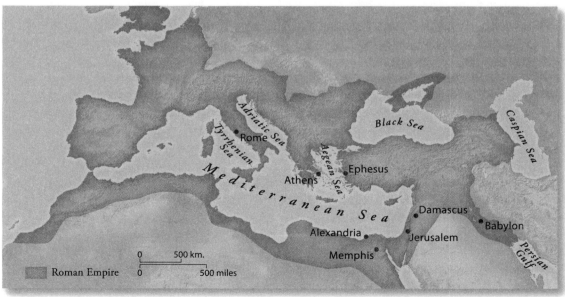

Roman Empire of the second century

dies an unspeakable death, believing that there will literally be hell to pay for anyone who turns away from God should he himself not remain faithful.

## Justin Martyr: Apologist for Pagans

Unlike many other noted Christians of the early centuries, Justin (100–165) was an adult convert to the faith. Reared in a prosperous pagan family in Samaria, he was well educated and he retained his property and his philosopher's gown after his conversion. Indeed, he was convinced that he had found the true philosophy—philosophy discovered only after studying the sterile gospel of the Stoics and Plato, who gave "wings for his soul" but ultimately left him unsatisfied.

Justin Martyr

Then, around the year 130, a chance meeting with an old man by the sea transforms Justin's life. The man points him not only to the prophets whose words had been fulfilled in Christ but also to Christians who had suffered and died for their faith. "A fire was suddenly kindled in my soul. I fell in love with the prophets and these men who had loved Christ," he writes. "I reflected on all their words and found that this philosophy alone was true and profitable. That is how and why I became a philosopher. And I wish that everyone felt the same way that I do."

So convinced is he that he becomes an evangelist to the educated intellectuals of the ancient world. His debating skills are widely recognized, as are his teachings and writings. He is a Christian apologist who retains his pagan philosophy insisting that the truth of pagan philosophy, particularly Platonism, serves as "a schoolmaster to bring us to Christ." Indeed, more than any other prominent Christian apologist of the early centuries, he unabashedly embraces philosophy, much to the chagrin of his critics. Greek philosophy, he believes, is drawn from the Old Testament; and Socrates and Heraclitus are men of true faith, as are Old Testament saints. For Justin, Christ, the Word (*Logos*), is absolute truth and all truth is thus the truth of Christ.

Justin defends the way of Christ on two fronts: Judaism and paganism. While residing in Ephesus, he debates a Jewish scholar whose arguments are found in Justin's treatise *The Dialogue with Trypho*. Here he asserts that the old covenant is replaced by the new, even as Gentiles are the new Israel. He later founds a school in Rome, where his focus is on pagan philosophy. In his *First Apology*, offered "on behalf of men of every nation who are unjustly hated and reviled," he argues that the Christian faith is not a dangerous religion to be feared. Addressing his treatise to the emperor, he insists Christians are the "best helpers and allies in securing good order, convinced as we are that no wicked man … can be hidden from God, and that everyone goes to eternal punishment or salvation in accordance with the character of his actions." Written in 155, the *Apology* is an attempt to justify the faith and show that paganism is an inferior imitation. More importantly, it elucidates the conduct and religious practices of Christians. Their worship is straightforward religious devotion. The emperor has nothing to fear.

## THE POST-APOSTOLIC PRO-LIFE MOVEMENT

Letter of Barnabas (AD 74): "You shall not slay the child by procuring abortion; nor ... destroy it after it is born."

Didache (AD 150): "You shall not murder.... You shall not use potions. You shall not procure [an] abortion, nor destroy a newborn child."

Mark Felix (AD 170): "There are some women among you who by drinking special potions extinguish the life of the future human in their very bowels, thus committing murder before they even give birth."

Athenagoras (AD 177): "What man of sound mind, therefore, will affirm, while such is our character, that we are murderers? ... We say that those women who use drugs to bring on abortion commit murder, and will have to give an account to God for the abortion."

Tertullian (AD 210): "In our case, a murder being once for all forbidden, we may not destroy even the fetus in the womb.... To hinder a birth is merely a speedier man-killing; nor does it matter whether you take away a life that is born, or destroy one that is coming to birth. That is a man which is going to be one; you have the fruit already in its seed."

Hippolytus (AD 228): "Women who were reputed to be believers began to take drugs to render themselves sterile, and to bind themselves tightly so as to expel what was being conceived, since they would not, on account of relatives and excess wealth, want to have a child by a slave or by any insignificant person. See, then, into what great impiety that lawless one has proceeded, by teaching adultery and murder at the same time!"

But holding high Greek philosophy and making the faith to appear reasonable and rational was not enough to satisfy the Roman authorities. In 165 Justin was arrested. Had he been tempted to buckle under the threat of death, he might have recalled the old man who, on the shore many years earlier, had pointed him to Christ, emphasizing the courage of those who were faithful unto death. Like them, he now refuses to forsake Christ and sacrifice to the gods. "No one who is rightly minded," he tells the prefect, "turns from true belief to false." According to tradition, Justin was martyred in Rome under Emperor Marcus Aurelius.

### Irenaeus: Exposing Gnostic Heresy

A leading theologian of the third century, Irenaeus (c. 138–202) is remembered as the Bishop of Lyons (modern France). Mission outreach, apologetics, and persecution are prominent themes in his writings. In fact, while he was away in 177, Bishop Pothinus was martyred, and Irenaeus returned to fill that very dangerous post. But the heavy hand of the Roman Empire was not the only enemy he faced. Among those calling themselves Christians were Gnostics. Iranaeus's writings, particularly *Against Heresies*, define parameters of the true faith against a counterfeit religion, citing as authoritative the Gospels, Acts, and the letters of Paul.

Born in Polycarp's hometown of Smyrna, Irenaeus was in his late teens when the great bishop was martyred, and he may have drawn inspiration for ministry from that most historic event. His testimony shows an important link to the apostolic church:

I remember the events of that time more clearly than those of recent years ... so that I am able to describe the very place in which the blessed Polycarp sat as he discoursed, and his goings out and his comings in, and the manner of his life, and his physical appearance, and his discourses to the people, and the accounts which he gave of his intercourse with John and with the others who had seen the Lord.

Serving as a presbyter in Lyons was the beginning of his official ministry. By the middle of the second century, the informal house church of earlier generations was gradually becoming more centralized and institutional. As church office holders gained prestige and power, conflict increased. Competing claims to truth and authority arose and the church was feeling the heat.

> "Even though Eve had Adam for a husband, she was still a virgin... By disobeying, Eve became the cause of death for herself and for the whole human race. In the same way Mary, though she had a husband, was still a virgin, and by obeying, she became the cause of salvation for herself and for the whole human race."
>
> Irenaeus

This is the situation that confronts Irenaeus in Lyons. As the bishop, he is in charge of the church in the entire region—one threatened more by internal strife than external persecution. The trendy *cult* of the day is Gnosticism, though it is anything but a single movement with one individual as prophet or messiah. Some Gnostics profess to be Christians, but Irenaeus insists they are no more than wolves in sheep's clothing. Indeed, this Gnostic "error," he argues, "is never set forth in its naked deformity" so as to be easily exposed. Rather, it is "craftily decked out in an attractive dress ... to make it appear to the inexperienced ... more true than truth itself." What appeared to be "more true"

was the higher esoteric *gnosis* (knowledge) that was necessary for salvation—a knowledge that many believed transformed the man Jesus into the higher form of *the Christ.*

The most disturbing aspect of Gnosticism is its fashionable appeal. Irenaeus sees right through it and is concerned about his flock, many of whom are flirting with this heresy. He knows that he has to take action, and he does just that with the power of the pen. Soon after he is appointed bishop, he writes a five-volume work, *Against Heresies.* Here he lays out the false beliefs and counters them with biblical references. He attacks the dualism of a transcendent good God of love in the Gospels and an evil god of the Old Testament—the one who created the sinful physical world. In doing this "they disregard the order and connection of the Scriptures and ... dismember and destroy the truth." There is only one God, Irenaeus thunders: "He is Father, He is God, He the founder, He the Maker, He the Creator.... He it is whom the law proclaims, whom the prophets preach, whom Christ reveals, whom the Apostles make known to us, and in whom the church believes."

Even as he emphasizes the God whom Christ reveals, Irenaeus holds high Jesus, both subject and author of Scripture. He is convinced that the writings of Moses and later prophets are Jesus' words. He counsels his readers: "Read with earnest care that Gospel which has been given to us by the apostles, and read with earnest care the prophets, and you will find that the whole conduct, and all the doctrine and all the sufferings of our Lord, were predicted through them." Virtually everything in the Hebrew Bible points to Christ. How then, he wonders, could so-called Christians be attracted to Gnosticism and its denigrating of the Old Testament?

But the Gnostics not only pit new against old and God against god, they also contrast

## RADICALLY DIFFERING KINDS OF CHRISTIANS

Contemporary Christianity, diverse and complex as we find it, actually may show more unanimity than the Christian churches of the first and second centuries. For nearly all Christians since that time ... have shared three basic premises. First ... the canon of the New Testament; second ... the apostolic creed; and third ... specific forms of church institution.... Before that time, as Irenaeus and others attest, numerous gospels circulated among various Christian groups.... Those who identified themselves as Christians entertained many — and radically differing — religious beliefs and practices.

Elaine Pagels, *The Gnostic Gospels*

light and darkness and spiritual and material. They claim that Christ and Jesus are two different entities — that Christ was spiritual and only *appeared* to inhabit a physical body — the body of Jesus the man. Likewise, they insist that Christ did not actually die on a cross. How could he if he were only a spiritual being? Irenaeus rails against those who claim that Jesus only appeared to be human and who claim that "Simon, a certain man of Cyrene, being compelled, bore the cross in his stead [and was] thought to be Jesus, was crucified, through ignorance and error, while Jesus himself received the form of Simon."

Such flimflam, in the mind of the bishop, is preposterous. Jesus Christ truly suffered on the cross. Martyrdom is too real to allow that central doctrine to be dismissed by the Gnostics. Christ knew that his followers would suffer persecution, Irenaeus argues, "and He did not speak of any other cross, but of the suffering which He should Himself undergo first, and His disciples afterward." Theological matters are personal, relating directly to the spiritual growth of the church. Studying the writings of the Gnostics, Irenaeus counters their claims first and foremost as an evangelist, seeking to win them back to the true faith.

In his battles with Gnostics, Irenaeus was determined to maintain the orthodoxy of the apostolic church. That could be accomplished, he reasoned, only by identifying a continuous chain going back to the apostles linked together in orthodoxy, past and future. Thus was born the doctrine of apostolic succession — that there is an uninterrupted line of succession of bishops that can be traced back to the twelve apostles (and claimed by Catholics in succeeding generations until today — to be found in the Roman Catholic Church alone).

Irenaeus was a peacemaker in the manner of his mentor, Polycarp, whom he cites when he seeks to bring about a resolution between Victor, the Bishop of Rome, and Eastern Christians who had refused to comply with the western date for Easter. When Victor excommunicates them, Irenaeus challenges him, pleading for moderation. He points to Victor's predecessors, who did not observe the eastern date for Easter, "nor did they permit those after them to do so. And yet, though not observing it, they were none the less at peace with those who came to them from the parishes in which it was observed." The same was true, Irenaeus points out, with Polycarp and Anicetus. "For neither could Anicetus persuade Polycarp ... nor Polycarp Anicetus.... But ... they communed together.... And they parted from each other in peace."

Irenaeus walks out of the pages of patristic history as though he were living today amid

## CLEMENT OF ALEXANDRIA: PHILOSOPHER AND VEGETARIAN

Converted from paganism, Clement (c. 150–215) was a convert of Pantaenus, who founded the great Christian intellectual center of the era, the Catechetical School at Alexandria. He succeeded Pantaenus in that post, serving more than two decades before passing the position on to his student, Origen. An apologist who engaged pagan philosophers on their own terms, Clement insisted that science and philosophy pave the way for evangelism. Critics found him too enamored with Gnosticism. "The man of understanding and discernment is, then, a Gnostic," he wrote. "And his business is not abstinence from what is evil ... or the doing of good out of fear ... [or] promised recompense ... but only the doing of good out of love, and for the sake of its own excellence is the Gnostic's choice." An early vegan, he argued: "It is good, then, neither to eat flesh.... For this is rather characteristic of a beast; and the fumes arising from them being dense, darken the soul.... For a voice will whisper to him, saying, 'Destroy not the work of God for the sake of food.'"

New Age and postmodern spiritualities. He is a peacemaker, but he does not suffer fools lightly.

### Perpetua and Felicitas: Faith Above Family

As the Christian faith spread through words and deeds of ordinary people, apologists, and traveling missionaries, the number of catechumens and converts increased. Every Christian was presumed to be a missionary. The consequence was frightening to Roman officials, who feared this "cult" might soon get out of hand. With zealous evangelism came persecution, often resulting in conflict and family breakdown—even as Jesus had warned: "Do not suppose that I have come to bring peace to the earth. I did not come to bring peace, but a sword. For I have come to turn a man against his father, a daughter against her mother.... a man's enemies will be the members of his own household." This struggle was painfully played out in the life of Perpetua. All she had to do was "perform the sacrifice" to the emperor and her life would have been spared.

The year is 202. Emperor Septimus Severus issues a decree against conversion to Judaism or Christianity. All new converts in North Africa will be executed unless they publicly perform a sacrifice to him. Perpetua, her servant girl Felicitas, and three men who had not yet completed catechism could make a sacrifice to honor the head of state. But they refuse. They know there is a price to pay for professing Christ, not the emperor, as Lord. Dying a martyr's death is considered a glorious entry into heaven, but dealing with family members is pure anguish. Perpetua's husband, who is not mentioned in the account, had perhaps died or abandoned her due to her newfound faith. The painful testimony below begins after she and Felicitas and the men are confined to prison:

A few days after, the report went abroad that we were to be tried. Also my father returned from the city spent with weariness; and he came up to me to cast down my faith saying: "Have pity, daughter, on my grey hairs; have pity on your father, if I am worthy to be called father by you; if with these hands I have brought you unto this flower of youth and I have preferred you before all your brothers; give me not over to the reproach of men. Look upon your brothers; look upon your mother and mother's sister; look upon your son, who will not endure to live after you. Give up your resolution; do not destroy us all together...."

This he said fatherly in his love, kissing my hands and groveling at my feet; and with tears he named me, not daughter, but lady.... And he went from me very sorrowful.

Soon after, when a report goes out that this indeed is the execution day, Perpetua's father returns, this time bringing her infant son. "Perform the Sacrifice; have mercy on the child," he pleads. Then he steps forward to forcibly prevent her from laying down her life. At this point an officer begins beating the old man. The execution having been delayed, Perpetua begs to breastfeed her baby one more time. Her father (and perhaps authorities) refuse, thinking such a denial might yet cause her to change her mind.

In the meantime, Felicitas, now eight months pregnant, fears that the execution of Christians in the arena (by wild animals) might be carried out without her, for Roman law prohibits a pregnant woman from being put to death. Here she has a perfect opportunity to escape punishment—at least for a time—but she pleads with God to bring on labor pains. "After their prayer her pains came upon her," writes an observer. "So she was delivered of a daughter, whom a sister reared up to be her own daughter."

On the day of execution, before they are led to the arena, the five prisoners are baptized. That Perpetua might have been spared due to her social class and gender is false hope for her aging father. She and Felicitas together enter the arena:

> But for the women the devil had made ready a most savage cow, prepared for this purpose against all custom; for even in this beast he would mock their sex. They were stripped.... The people shuddered, seeing one a tender girl, the other her breasts yet dropping from her late childbearing. So they were called back and clothed in loose robes. Perpetua was first thrown.... She stood up; and when she saw Felicity smitten down, she went up and gave her hand and raised her up....

The men had been brought into the arena first to be killed by wild animals—a bear, a leopard, and a boar. This spectacle was typically a real crowd-pleaser. But the gory torture of young women turns the frenzied spectators from cheering to jeering. They begin shouting, "Enough!" Perpetua is then taken to the gladiator to be beheaded. Whether due to hesitancy or to lack of skill, the first slash of his sword is not sufficiently severe. She cries out in pain, takes the gladiator's trembling hand, directs the sword to her neck, and it is over.

After this wave of persecution, there followed a half-century of relative peace. But such faith as seen in the arena that day was a testimony that sparked faith in others. Today Perpetua and Felicitas are commemorated as saints by Catholics, Anglicans, and Lutherans.

---

## PACIFISM IN THE EARLY CHURCH

The age of persecution down to the time of Constantine was the age of pacifism to the degree that during this period no Christian author to our knowledge approved of Christian participation in battle. The position of the Church was not absolutist, however. There were some Christians in the army and they were not on that account excluded from communion.

Roland Bainton, *Christian Attitudes Toward War and Peace*

---

**WHY A CHRISTIAN WOMAN SHOULD NOT MARRY A PAGAN**

Who would be willing to let his wife go through one street after another to other men's houses, and indeed to the poorer cottages, in order to visit the brethren? Who would like to see her being taken from his side by some duty of attending a nocturnal gathering? At Easter time who will quietly tolerate her absence all the night? Who will unsuspiciously let her go to the Lord's Supper, that feast upon which they heap such calumnies? Who will let her creep into jail to kiss the martyr's chains? Or bring water for the saints' feet? [The answer? Only a Christian man.]

Tertullian, *Letter to his wife*

---

## Tertullian: What Has Athens to Do with Jerusalem?

Like Justin Martyr, Quintus Septimius Florente Tertullianus (c. 160–235) was an early apologist converted as an adult. He is remembered as the first of the Latin Fathers—church fathers whose thinking was influenced more by Roman than by Greek sensibilities. An African born in Carthage, he was the son of a Roman military officer and became a prominent lawyer, well versed in imperial government policy. He wrote prolifically in both Greek and Latin and was biting in his satire, particularly in comparing Christians with pagans who ridiculed and persecuted believers:

> This is the reason, then, why Christians are counted public enemies: that they pay no vain, nor false, nor foolish honors to the emperor; that, as men believing in the true religion, they prefer to celebrate their festal days with a good conscience, instead of with the common wan-

---

**TERTULLIAN'S NEW TESTAMENT**

Four Gospels
Acts
Letters of Paul
1 John
Jude
Revelation

---

tonness. It is, forsooth, a notable homage to bring fires and couches out before the public, to have feasting from street to street, to turn the city into one great tavern, to make mud with wine, to run in troops to acts of violence, to deeds of shamelessness to lust allurements! What! Is public joy manifested by public disgrace? . . . We do not celebrate along with you the holidays of the Caesars in a manner forbidden alike by modesty, decency, and purity. . . . In this matter I am anxious to point out how faithful and true you are, lest [you] be found . . . worse than we wicked Christians!

Unlike Justin and other early apologists, Tertullian strongly denounced Greek philosophy as the promulgator of heresy:

> For philosophy is the material of the world's wisdom, the rash interpreter of the nature and dispensation of God. Indeed, heresies are themselves instigated by philosophy. . . . What indeed has Athens to do with Jerusalem? What has the Academy to do with the Church? What have heretics to do with Christians? Our instruction comes from the porch of Solomon, who had himself taught that the Lord should be sought in simplicity of heart. Away with all attempts to produce a Stoic, Platonic, and dialectic Christianity! We want no curious disputation after possessing

Christ Jesus, no inquisition after receiving the gospel! When we believe, we desire no further belief. For this is our first article of faith, that there is nothing which we ought to believe besides.

For this stance against secular learning, he is sometimes viewed as the ultimate anti-intellectual of the early church.

Tertullian

Tertullian, however, was a supremely influential theologian. He introduced the term *Trinity* into theological discourse as well as the concept of three persons and one substance, which would later become critical terminology as a test for orthodoxy. He was the first to distinguish biblical writings as *Old Testament* and *New Testament*. He argued that Christianity was the only *true* religion (*vera religio*), denouncing paganism and sectarian movements as superstitions while pronouncing doctrines that he did not hold as heretical. Yet at age fifty, with a quarter-century ahead of him, Tertullian joined a cult. The Montanists, named for the prophet founder Montanus, had all the earmarks of a superstitious sectarian movement that he had condemned.

Montanus, a late-second-century traveling preacher accompanied by two prophetesses, professed to be the Paraclete, the Holy Spirit in human form, complete with new revelations. *The Three*, as they were known, gained a following by promising direct words from God through their ecstatic utterances, believing their prophecies took precedence over those of the apostles. Why did Tertullian join the Montanists? For one thing, he was distressed by the institutionalization of the church — "the church of a lot of bishops." And he may have been attracted to them for their strict, tightly regulated lifestyle. After a time, however, he separated from the larger movement to form an even stricter

## CYPRIAN, BISHOP OF CARTHAGE

Like Tertullian, whom he revered, Cyprian (d. 258) hailed from North Africa. A wealthy pagan orator and legal expert, he was baptized as a middle-aged adult. Donating much of his wealth to charity, he was ordained a deacon, presbyter, and Bishop of Carthage — all in the space of a few years. He might have gone down in history as just another African bishop but for a reign of terror — the persecution of Christians under Emperor Decius in 250. He fled Carthage, claiming that God had directed him in a vision to do so. Many lay Christians as well as clerics caved in to authorities and sacrificed to the emperor. Despite his own weakness in the face of persecution, Cyprian had little sympathy for those who had "fallen away." Christians could be received back into the church only on their deathbed, and faith-denying clerics were stripped of their office. Salvation, he was convinced, comes only through the church: "No one can have God as Father who does not have the church as mother." He initially faced strong opposition, but later he won over many of the people through his own good deeds. Before he died, he faced one more controversy: Is baptism valid if officiated by a heretic? His answer was no, thus putting him at odds with the Bishop of Rome and the position of the Catholic Church in the centuries since then.

version of Montanists who became known as the Tertullianists.

Tertullian's perspective on women is most interesting. Although he is married and becomes part of a movement where two women wield charismatic authority second only to Montanus himself, in his mind, women are the "devil's gateway": "You destroyed so easily God's image (man)." In his earlier denigration of heretical groups, he had marshaled forth proof: "The very women of these heretics, how wanton they are! For they are bold enough to teach, to dispute, to enact exorcisms, to undertake cures — it may be even to baptize." Women, he argued, are daughters of Eve: "Every woman should be . . . walking about as Eve mourning and repentant, in order that by every garb of penitence she might the more fully expiate that which she derives from Eve — the ignominy, I mean, of the first sin, and the odium . . . of human perdition."

Yet Tertullian stands out in the early church in his profound reverence for Christian marriage. His words are appropriate for a wedding ceremony in the twenty-first century:

How beautiful, then, the marriage of two Christians, two who are one in hope, one in desire, one in the way of life they follow, one in the religion they practice. They are as brother and sister, both servants of the same Master. Nothing divides them, either in flesh or in spirit. They are, in very truth, two in one flesh; and where there is but one flesh there is also but one spirit. They pray together, they worship together, they fast together; instructing one another, encouraging one another, strengthening one another. Side by side they visit God's church and partake of God's Banquet; side by side they face difficulties and persecution, share their consolations. They have no secrets from one another; they never shun each other's company; they never bring sorrow to each other's hearts.

Like other prominent believers of this era, Tertullian left behind a mixed legacy. His words and actions were often contradictory and sometimes inflammatory. Yet, his reflection on persecution is one of the most oft-quoted lines from the post-Apostolic period: "The blood of the martyrs is the seed of the church."

## What if . . .

What if Polycarp had burned the incense and taken an oath to Caesar to avert his fiery death? How would the beloved bishop's denial of Christ have affected the course of Christianity? What if Perpetua and Felicitas had shrunk back in the arena and agreed to deny their faith?

What if Marcion's claims had won the day? Would Christianity have become a cult of Paul? Would the Sunday school assignment of memo-rizing the books of the Bible begin and end with a portion of Paul's epistles?

What if Irenaeus had not fought so tenaciously against the Gnostics? Would the Christian faith today be a form of New Age spirituality?

What if Tertullian's arguments had triumphed? Would philosophical concepts be less prevalent in early theological development? Was his question valid: What has Athens to do with Jerusalem?

## Further Reading

Aquilina, Mike. *The Fathers of the Church.* Huntington, Ind.: Our Sunday Visitor, 2006.

Brent, Allen. *Ignatius of Antioch: A Martyr Bishop and the Origin of Episcopacy.* New York: T&T Clark, 2007.

de Ste. Croix, Geoffrey. *Christian Persecution, Martyrdom, and Orthodoxy.* New York: Oxford University Press, 2006.

Dunn, Geoffrey D. *Tertullian.* New York: Routledge, 2004.

Frend, William H. C. *Martyrdom and Persecution in the Early Church.* Cambridge, UK: James Clark, 2008.

Grant, Robert M. *Irenaeus of Lyons.* New York: Routledge, 1996.

Jungers, Wallace S. *The Victory of the Early Christian Martyrs.* Bloomington, Ind.: First Books Library, 2002.

Litfin, Bryan M. *Getting to Know the Church Fathers: An Evangelical Introduction.* Grand Rapids: Brazos, 2007.

Osborn, Eric. *Tertullian, First Theologian of the West.* New York: Cambridge University Press, 2003.

Parvis, Sara. *Justin Martyr and His Worlds.* Minneapolis: Fortress Press, 2007.

Richardson, Cyril C. *Early Christian Fathers.* Louisville: Westminster John Knox Press, 2006.

Robeck, Cecil. *Prophecy in Carthage: Perpetua, Tertullian, and Cyprian.* Cleveland: Pilgrim Press, 1992.

Salisbury, Joyce. *Perpetua's Passion.* New York: Routledge, 1997.

# CHAPTER 3

# Creeds and Councils

## *Debating and Defining Doctrine*

*I sometimes wonder if I would have been a follower of Jesus had I been his contemporary and been aware of his teachings. I also wonder what position I would have taken in the swirl of the fourth-century Arian controversy—with no access to the Bible as we have it today. Most people take for granted the Christian doctrines they confess with no thought of how difficult it would be to devise a systematic theology if the only text available were the Bible—and worse yet, not even a complete canon of Scripture. This was the predicament facing Christians in the early centuries of the church's history.*

*Complicating matters were political factors and personality clashes. It is impossible to find a parallel situation today, but imagine a wide spectrum of American Christians trying to agree on a doctrinal statement. What if the President got involved and in the end the Supreme Court settled the matter? It sounds preposterous, but in some ways it would not be altogether different from what occurred at the Council of Nicaea in 325.*

*Today the situation is made more complex by established denominations and entrenched hierarchies unknown in ancient times. Such institutionalized religion, infused with money and power, is rarely open to change or compromise. With centuries of scholarship behind us, we stand on the shoulders of theological giants. But how would we ever agree—even on the broadest framework of a doctrinal formula? Would Mennonites and Quakers, for example, insist that pacifism be part of the formula? (They could argue after all that, like the deity of Christ, pacifism was almost universally affirmed by early Christians.) If so, would that derail the process before it could even get off the ground?*

*Add to the matter of pacifism a hundred or a thousand other competing issues, and we begin to realize the many differences to overcome in forming a consensus. So when we look back to the early church's deliberations, even though they were infused with back-alley maneuvering and political pressure, we ought to stand in awe. The Council of Nicaea—and councils that followed—set the parameters for Christian belief in the following centuries.*

The theologian may indulge the pleasing task of describing Religion as she descended from Heaven, arrayed in her native purity. A more melancholy duty is imposed on the historian. He must discover the inevitable mixture of error and corruption which she contracted in a long residence upon earth, among a weak and degenerate race of beings.

EDWARD GIBBON, *THE HISTORY OF THE DECLINE AND FALL OF THE ROMAN EMPIRE*

It is difficult to write about the ancient wrangling over theological propositions and opinions without taking sides. Religion, we are convinced, descended from heaven in the purity of our own particular perspective. Thus the ancients, whom we say are on our side, are on heaven's side. The historian truly does have the melancholy duty to shed light on the error and corruption inevitable among a weak and degenerate race of human beings, both ancient and modern.

Multivolume tomes expound the arguments and counter-arguments surrounding the third- and fourth-century theological debates and the related issues spinning off in succeeding generations. Even so, the story is incomplete—and virtually incomprehensible. Nevertheless, a basic understanding of Christianity's theological underpinnings is aided by a glimpse at the lives of some of the leading protagonists: Origen, Arius, Athanasius, and Emperor Constantine.

The earliest generations of Christians, beginning with the apostles, faced the task of clarifying the differences between the new faith and Judaism. While the Hebrew Bible was held in high esteem as Holy Scripture, practicing Jews were considered the enemy. "Judaizers" were so named because they regarded circumcision and other Jewish ceremonies and laws as necessary facets of religious life. By the fourth and fifth centuries, most church leaders severed all ties with Judaism and disciplined those who did not fall in line. This period also saw a corresponding rise in anti-Semitism—a hatred of Jews that has reared its ugly head across the entire span of Christian history.

As the faith spread into the Hellenistic world, the focus on Judaism receded and other issues came to the fore. Church leaders sought to define the faith against both Gnosticism and paganism, the former known for its esoteric secret knowledge and the latter for its vast pantheon of gods. Gnostic Christianity was typically considered more dangerous because it was viewed as counterfeit—pretending to be a higher form of the faith. Paganism was perceived to be outside the realm of the Christian faith. Yet it too influenced early Christianity. Leaders such as Tertullian wrote treatises against Gnosticism and adamantly insisted that Christian

---

### PARADE OF HISTORY

As the procession of the early church moves into the fourth century, the air is filled with fury as churchmen hold forth in debate over doctrinal differences, debates that culminate in a procession of bishops, lesser clerics, criminals, and prostitutes to the First Ecumenical Council of Nicaea. The arguments of Athanasius win the day, but within a decade he begins the first of several marches into exile. In the meantime, his nemesis, Arius, dies in a most ignoble way while, according to an adversary, he "paraded proudly through the midst of the city."

beliefs must not be influenced by pagan philosophy. But the urge to contextualize won the day, as it would in succeeding centuries. As full-time evangelists, apologists, and ordinary lay people brought new converts into the church, pagan terminology and rituals came with them.

It is erroneous to imagine the Christian church as a major force in the Mediterranean world during the centuries before Constantine. Despite growing numbers, it remained an outlawed religion. Christians—both educated and ignorant classes alike—were generally looked upon as a nuisance and were known primarily as the objects of persecution. Population figures vary widely, but some historians have estimated that by the year 250 they made up less than 2 percent of the empire of some fifty million people. Others have claimed that there may have been as many as a million Christians in Egypt alone by the end of the third century. Whatever the statistics, the church began to wield influence beyond its numbers, especially as it was becoming institutionalized.

By 250 there were some one hundred bishops scattered throughout Italy, the most prestigious of these the Bishop of Rome. According to church records, he was supported by nearly fifty priests, fourteen deacons and subdeacons, some forty acolytes, and fifty exorcists as well as doorkeepers and readers. In the shadow of this hierarchy were fifteen hundred needy people, primarily widows and children who were said to be "fed by the grace and kindness of the Lord," meaning from the church coffers. Rome was by no means the only thriving center of the faith during this time. Africa boasted more than one hub of the church, Carthage and Alexandria being the most prominent. Carthage was home to Tertullian, Cyprian, Augustine, and other North African churchmen, all Latin (as opposed to Greek) Christians.

During the third century Alexandria rapidly gained a reputation as an intellectual center of Christian scholarship and piety. Here Arius developed his theology. Before him came Clement, who, unlike Tertullian, was not afraid of pagan

## THE EMPEROR CALLS A COUNCIL

Then ... he convoked a general council, and invited the speedy attendance of bishops from all quarters, in letters expressive of the honorable estimation in which he held them. Nor was this merely the issuing of a bare command but the emperor's good will contributed much to its being carried into effect: for he allowed some the use of the public means of conveyance, while he afforded to others an ample supply of horses for their transport. The place, too, selected for the synod, the city Nicaea in Bithynia (named from "victory"), was appropriate to the occasion. As soon then as the imperial injunction was generally made known, all with the utmost willingness hastened thither, as though they would outstrip one another in a race; for they were impelled by the anticipation of a happy result to the conference, by the hope of enjoying present peace, and the desire of beholding something new and strange in the person of so admirable an emperor. Now when they were all assembled, it appeared evident that the proceeding was the work of God, inasmuch as men who had been most widely separated, not merely in sentiment but also personally, and by difference of country, place, and nation, were here brought together, and comprised within the walls of a single city, forming as it were a vast garland of priests, composed of a variety of the choicest flowers.

Eusebius of Caesarea, *The Life of the Blessed Emperor Constantine*

philosophy or Gnosticism. His student Origen specialized in allegorical interpretations of the biblical text and was in turn challenged by Antiochian scholars who had a much more literal bent.

In the early centuries after the apostle Paul made his massive footprint, no central figure can be credited for single-handedly furthering the cause of the faith. Evangelism was considered the work of every Christian, and anonymity was in many ways a positive attribute. An apostle Paul would have been an easy target, but tens of thousands of nameless evangelists were easily lost in the crowd.

If there is one figure who stands above all others during the early centuries of the church, it is Emperor Constantine. Official persecution in the Roman Empire ended with his reign. For that reason alone, he was a powerful force in the development of the Christian church. But his influence was perhaps even more striking as a theological arbiter. With the Edict of Milan in 313 (coming on the heels of the 311 Edict of Toleration), Christian worship was legalized, paving the way for future favored status. But Constantine's pivotal role in the church was his call for the Council of Nicaea in 325. Nor did he step aside when the Council convened. His oversight profoundly influenced the course of church history.

## Origen of Alexandria: Theologian and Allegorical Exegete

The blistering persecution set in motion by Emperor Septimus Severus in 202 that claimed the lives of Perpetua and her fellow catechumens tore apart the family of the young Origenes Adamatius (185–254). His story illustrates how devastating such state-sponsored terrorism was to families, often separated by dislocation, death, and desertions of the faith. But the very oppression that separated loved ones sometimes served to bring them closer together spiritually.

So it was with young Origen, who would become one of the leading systematic theologians of the early church. Born into a Christian home in Alexandria, he was the oldest of seven children. As a youth he memorized lengthy passages of the Bible and often perplexed his father, Leonides, with difficult theological questions. Leonides, a teacher of the Bible and Greek literature, was a Roman citizen. The happy home life was suddenly disrupted in 202, however, when Origen's father was imprisoned.

The sixteen-year-old boy might have been utterly distraught, but instead the ordeal served to strengthen his faith. Fearing his father might forsake his faith out of devotion to the family, he pleads: "Do not change your mind because of us." Indeed, he is so wrought up that he makes

### Finding Hidden Gems of Spiritual Truth

One major difference between Alexandrian and Antiochene theologies revolved around hermeneutics (biblical interpretation).... Clement and Origen both sought to dig down through the various layers of meaning in the Bible to discover its hidden gems of spiritual truth separated from the crude literal and historical narratives and images.

When Alexandrian Christian scholars — whether living in Alexandria or elsewhere — read the Prophets and Apostles, they tended to find hidden references to the Logos and heavenly, spiritual existence everywhere.

Roger E. Olson, *The Story of Christian Theology*

## Rival Cities and Schools

It is easy to imagine the Arian controversy arising in a remote period of time. But in some ways fourth-century cities were more modern than were cities in the intervening centuries. Scholars in Antioch and Alexandria would have been entirely out of place living in London among the teeming masses of the eighteenth-century Industrial Revolution.

A budding theologian residing in the ancient city of Antioch would have opportunities to stroll the colonnaded streets, walking by palaces and the public amphitheater. Though most likely living as an ascetic, he would have observed others enjoying the baths at its famed spa, drinking from the public fountains, attending the theater, and feasting in luxury at a Roman dining room adorned with colorful mosaics. Antioch was known as the "Athens" of the Near East—a cosmopolitan city of learning, literature, philosophy, religion, and the arts.

Located in southern Turkey, Antioch was the capital of Ancient Syria and the leading city of the Roman East. It was the trading hub on the crossroads of East and West and ranked with Rome, Carthage, and Constantinople as one of the four great cities of the Roman Empire. Its population grew to more than half a million by the fourth century.

A rival city, Alexandria boasted one of the seven wonders of the ancient world, its Pharos, or Lighthouse, as well as its second-to-none library established by Alexander the Great himself. Holding some 700,000 manuscripts—the whole corpus of knowledge accumulated by ancient philosophers, scientists, and poets—the library and museum are said to have been of unsurpassed beauty. The city was also a center of theological scholarship, providing

### THE CITY OF ALEXANDRIA

The first thing one noticed in entering Alexandria by the Gate of the Sun was the beauty of the city. A range of columns went from one end of it to the other. Advancing down them, I came in time to the place which bears the name of Alexander and there could see the other half of the town which was equally beautiful. For just as the colonnades stretched ahead of me, so did other colonnades now appear at right angles to them.

Achilles Tatius, AD 400

Illustration of the Pharos of Alexandria, lighthouse, one of the Seven Wonders of the ancient World, by Maerten van Heemskerck (1498-1574)

residence for some of the most recognized scholars of the day: Clement, Origin, and Arius, to name a few.

For early Christian scholars, the two cities were worlds apart in their theological perspectives. Antioch, where believers were first called Christians, was home of the Antiochene school, fostering a straightforward biblical hermeneutic that interprets the text essentially as it reads, without spiritual or allegorical renderings. In Alexandria, more influenced by Greek philosophy, allegorical interpretation flourished, particularly through the influential work of Origen.

plans to turn himself over to authorities in the hope of joining his father in prison. His mother, however, foils his plans. She hides his clothes, knowing full well that her son could not endure the embarrassment of public nudity. Shortly afterward, Leonides is beheaded and his property confiscated, leaving his widow and young children in dire straits.

Through the generosity of a benefactor, Origen is able to continue his studies for a year and then becomes a teacher in order to support his mother and siblings. Like his father, he teaches Greek literature and is particularly influenced by Plato. In the following years he serves as head of the catechetical school in Alexandria, a position left vacant when his predecessor fled persecution.

For Origen, theology is intricately tied to spiritual formation. He practices strict asceticism, denying himself normal pleasures in order to suffer with Christ. In fact, he takes the extreme measure of castrating himself to avert sexual desires, interpreting Matthew 19:12 literally: "There are those who have made themselves eunuchs for the sake of the kingdom of heaven." Such drastic action, he likewise reasons, would preclude scandal in his teaching of young women. With his asceticism comes humanitarian outreach, primarily aiding those suffering under persecution. Some of his students are sentenced to death, and his own life is always in danger. Gone is his youthful desire for martyrdom. He now hides in homes of both pagans and Christians in order to escape execution.

Under Origen's teaching and administration, the Alexandrian school grows. He sets aside time to learn Hebrew to facilitate his teaching of the Old Testament. His scholarship captures the attention of church leaders, and he is invited to preach and teach elsewhere, much to the chagrin of his bishop, Demetrius, who demands that he return home. How dare he tour as a celebrity speaker! "It has never been heard of and it never happens now," the bishop seethes, "that laymen preach homilies in the presence of bishops." But Origen's fame continues to soar. Still in his early thirties, he is invited to tutor the empress, mother of Emperor Alexander Severus. Eusebius tells us: "As Origen's renown spread everywhere and even came to her ears, she thought it very important to be favored with the sight of this man and to sample his understanding of divine matters which everyone was admiring."

That Origen is so widely recognized as a great teacher and preacher is a threat to the less-than-secure Bishop Demetrius. Then as now, there is turf to defend for fear of losing prestige and status. And Origen, for his part, is not easily muzzled. When he is traveling through the Mediterranean world, he spends time in Caesarea, where he is ordained by the bishop, who believes such acknowledgment of his ministerial gifts is appropriate. When Demetrius learns of this "breach of jurisdiction," he is livid. He accuses Origen of teaching heresy and exposes the secret of his youthful self-castration. In the ensuing conflict, Origen is banned from Alexandria and his ordination is rendered null and void.

Other bishops, however, ignore the retraction of his ordination, and he is invited to serve as a priest and teacher under their jurisdictions. He eventually makes his home in Caesarea, where he combines his work of teaching, preaching, and writing in wide-ranging fields of biblical studies, theology, philosophy, natural science, and ethics. His intention, however, is not to establish a liberal arts program. Rather, his focus is mission outreach—bringing pagans into the faith through his appealing educational offerings. During the later years of his life, Origen travels as a theological consultant, frequently called upon to judge the orthodoxy of a particular churchman or teacher whose beliefs are in question. With the help of a wealthy benefactor, he is able to devote his time to research and writing.

Origen's allegorical method of biblical interpretation places the spiritual meaning above the literal meaning of a given text. Yet to him the Bible is the very Word of God, divinely inspired—albeit filled with mysteries and double and triple meanings. How else, for example, could he view the creation account? Schooled in the sciences, he asks: "What man of intelligence will believe that the first and the second and the third day, and the evening and the morning, existed without the sun and moon and stars?" More than anything else, Origen's writings offer a window of understanding into early Christian scholarship and imagination. His major treatise *Against Celsus* serves as a powerful defense of the faith. *First Principles* shows him to be an ostensibly orthodox theologian.

During the persecution under Emperor Decius, Origen was arrested and imprisoned. Although nearing seventy, he was afforded no mercy. According to Eusebius, his torture was severe. Among other agonies, his legs were "pulled four paces apart in the torturer's stocks." Released from prison, he died soon afterward.

Unlike many of the leading Christians of the early church, Origen will never be given the title of saint. In the sixth century he was deemed a heretic for several of his controversial views,

## GREGORY THE WONDERWORKER

What Origen does with words and allegorical biblical interpretation, Gregory (213–270) does with missions and miracles. Both are at heart evangelists. A student who converted to Christianity from paganism under the teaching of Origen, Gregory, a Bishop in Asia Minor, is best known for what might be termed allegorical miracles. For example, when two brothers are fighting over the ownership of a lake, Gregory splits the lake in two parts and gives a big pond to each of the boys. In another instance he moves a mountain. "Gregory was a great and conspicuous lamp, illuminating the church of God," writes Basil, one of his biographers. "He possessed, from the co-operation of the Spirit, a formidable power against the demons, that he turned the course of rivers by giving them orders in the name of Christ; and that his predictions of the future made him the equal of other prophets."

including his belief in a Trinitarian hierarchy. But he held views even more abhorrent, what a critic called "the fabulous preexistence of souls" and "the monstrous restoration which follows from it." This restoration was a form of universalism in which God's love in the end prevails over his wrath.

## Arius: Challenging the Full Deity of Christ

The most significant and far-reaching matter of theological dispute in the fourth century was the Arian controversy, a showdown between those who held tenaciously to the trinitarian Godhead and the full deity of Christ and those who subordinated the Son to the Father — those who challenged the co-eternity and consubstantiality (of one being or substance) of the Son with the Father and regarded him as a created being. This conflict would be officially settled at the landmark Council of Nicaea, but the matter would live on for generations — indeed, to the present day.

Imagine Arius, a seminary student in Antioch with access to copies of ancient texts and having interaction with respected teachers like Lucian who guides his research. He is grappling with biblical issues, some very practical and related to daily living, others more theological in nature — though the discipline of theology is still an ill-defined area of scholarship. From "seminary" Arius moves on into ministry, first serving as a presbyter in Antioch and then in 313 moving to Alexandria to serve as a presbyter at St. Mark's. He quickly discovers that challenging church authority is not the way to climb the clerical career ladder of success. He is a presbyter, a position that provides him a pulpit, but his bishop is upset with his teachings, initially blaming his training at the rival school in Antioch.

Born in Libya and raised in Antioch, Arius (c. 250–336) is a fervent Christian and dedicated disciple of Jesus. Blessed with a brilliant mind and an engaging style, he has a reputation as a captivating preacher. He is described by an acquaintance as a tall, thin, serious ascetic, walking barefoot and unable to disguise his winsome personality. Above all, he is a superb salesman. He knows the popular mind and how to attract attention. He composes popular verses — little ditties — and puts them to music. One of his opponents complains that he can not go to the market without hearing such songs and becoming engaged in theological disputes with the butcher, the fruit vendor, and the bath attendant. Some point out that this young teacher has a disproportionate number of female supporters — women with loose morals, according to his bishop, Alexander.

The issues of the day are very complicated and culturally embedded. For example, how should Christians define themselves in relation to Jews and to the pagan culture and cults around them, especially in relation to Greek philosophy? The oneness of God is the clear teaching of the Jews, and the Christians accept the Hebrew canon as their own. That is a key consideration for Arius. The "cult of Jesus" dare not forget its roots in Abraham, Isaac, and Jacob. Nor dare it become just another pagan cult by fashioning a man into a God.

In 319 these issues come to a head with Bishop Alexander, a key church leader in Alexandria under whom Arius is a mere presbyter. Alexander, suspicious of Arius, preaches a sermon meant especially for all the presbyters on "the great mystery of the Trinity in Unity." Arius is frustrated. By merely couching the problem in mystery, he reasons, Alexander is refusing to face the issue head on. So Arius attacks his sermon, insisting that it fails to uphold a distinction among the persons in the Godhead. He is adamant that Christians avoid a polytheistic conception of God. He maintains that the concept of God must not be watered down—that God is God, absolutely transcendent.

Arius writes a letter to Alexander declaring that the faith he learned from his forefathers and even from Alexander himself must stand. That faith, he argues, is very simply summed up:

> "We acknowledge one God ... alone everlasting, alone without beginning ... alone sovereign ... God of the law and prophets and New Testament."

Arius is well aware that followers of Jesus easily speak of Jesus as God. They speak of Christ as the Lord, the Savior, but he insists that these titles refer to Jesus in relationship to his disciples. He challenges the questions: *How is Jesus Christ related to us? What does he mean for us?* Rather, he insists, the question is: *Who is Jesus Christ?* Is he fully God, co-eternal and consubstantive, or is he subordinate to the Father? This question must not be clouded in mystery.

Arius could not have known that the questions he raised would have profound implications. Indeed, he responded so specifically and so vigorously that he forced the church to devote its energies to clarifying the matter, and for that alone he made a major contribution to theology.

Arius draws much of his own argument from the prologue to the Gospel of John. There is a difference, he contends, between God the Father and the Word (the Son of God). He likewise points to the writings of Paul: "For us there is one God, the Father from whom are all things and for whom we exist, and one Lord, Jesus Christ, through whom are all things and through whom we exist" (1 Cor. 8:6).

He also claims to be supporting the long-held beliefs of church tradition. Justin, for example, had written two *Apologies* that were widely heralded in the early church. "The most true God, the Father of righteousness," Justin wrote, "and the Son, who came forth from him and taught us these things, and the army of the other good angels who follow him and are made like him, and the prophetic Spirit...."

Needless to say, Arius stirs up controversy. Alexander is irate. He suspends him from office. But Arius is not easily silenced. His theology is rational and appealing. He is a loyal and conservative Christian—fundamentalist, some would say—who is safeguarding the truth, especially that foundational truth the church must not abandon, namely, the monarchy or the sole rule of God. Saying that the Son is co-eternal with the Father, he insists, suggests polytheism, a claim that his Hebrew forefathers would have adamantly opposed. They looked for the messiah, but not a messiah who is the Son of God— God himself.

The tables are turned as Arius, accused of making Jesus lesser than God, is charged with a polytheistic construction. As the debate grows more intense, Alexander manages to have Arius condemned. But Arius has his own friends in high places. He flees to the palace of Eusebius, the bishop of Nicomedia (not to be confused with his contemporary, Bishop Eusebius of Caesarea, the "Father of Church History").

Like Arius, Eusebius has studied under Lucian and insists that Greek philosophical understanding of such terms as *substance* is alien to the Judeo-Christian experience and sacred Scripture. Yet their opponents are employing these words as though they come straight out of the Gospels. Eusebius admires Arius's youth and spunk and is pleased to have him saying things he dare not say himself. But the safe haven at the palace solves nothing. The quarrel only escalates. Everyone, it seems, is getting involved.

The First Council of Nicaea

Indeed, so contentious is the conflict that it is threatening the unity of the empire. Emperor Constantine tries to settle the dispute through letters, but failing to do so, he calls a council of the bishops of the church — the Council of Nicaea (AD 325).

Here Athanasius comes to the fore, challenging the rational arguments of Arius with solid biblical reasoning of his own. He insists that there is no place in Christian thought for any kind of an intermediate being between God and man, between Creator and creature. And he argues persuasively that true redemption is accomplished only through God the Son, not an intermediary. Athanasius wins the day at the Council of Nicaea: the Father and the Son are co-eternal and of one substance (*homoousios*). Arius is exiled from Alexandria. But the story is not over. Arius has a large and loyal following, support that seems to be growing with every passing year. The emperor is sympathetic and demands that he be restored to his former position. Athanasius is adamant. He knows all too well that the theological views of Arius have not changed. He wins a temporary victory, but his authoritarian spirit rubs many people the wrong way.

By 335 at the First Synod of Tyre, a decade after the Council of Nicaea, the tide is turning toward Arius, and now Athanasius is exiled to Gaul, a coup accomplished largely by Eusebius, thanks to his connections with Emperor Constantine. The bishops who support Athanasius are barred from the meeting. False accusations help seal the deal, including an accusation by a woman who claims that Athanasius tried to seduce her. Other witnesses claim that he threatened to keep shipments of grain from leaving Alexandria on their way to Constantinople.

So once again Arius is back. But before he can re-enter the church and celebrate communion, he dies very suddenly. An unfriendly source records the gory details:

> It was then Saturday, and ... going out of the imperial palace, attended by a crowd of Eusebian partisans like guards, [Arius] paraded proudly through the midst of the city, attracting the notice of all the people. As he approached the place called Constantine's Forum, where the column of porphyry

## ARIANS WORSHIPING CHRIST

The Arians found prayer to the Logos an unavoidable element of Christian worship.... The Arians also continued the practice of baptizing in the name not only of the Father, but also of the Son and of the Holy Spirit.... The Arian doctrine of Christ as creature collided with the tradition of describing him as God; but the Arian use of the titles Logos and Son of God, which together had come to summarize the central meaning of that tradition, made the collision between the two quite ambiguous. In fact, it is misleading to speak of "the two" as though Arianism and orthodoxy were such obvious alternatives throughout the controversy.

Jaroslav Pelikan, *The Christian Tradition*

is erected, a terror arising from the remorse of conscience seized Arius, and with the terror a violent relaxation of the bowels: he therefore enquired whether there was a convenient place near, and being directed to the back of Constantine's Forum, he hastened thither.

Soon after a faintness came over him, and together with the evacuations his bowels protruded, followed by a copious hemorrhage, and the descent of the smaller intestines: moreover portions of his spleen and liver were brought off in the effusion of blood, so that he almost immediately died. The scene of this catastrophe still is shown at Constantinople, as I have said, behind the shambles in the colonnade: and by persons going by pointing the finger at the place....

Whether this less-than-believable account of his death was God's supernatural judgment, as many Nicene Christians believed, or whether he was the victim of poisoning by his enemies, is a matter that has long been debated. Arius was gone but not soon forgotten. His legacy would be carried on by "heretics" throughout church history.

### Athanasius: Defending Orthodoxy

Like Arius, Athanasius was a man with many enemies. "Black Dwarf," they sneered. Short of stature and dark-skinned, Athanasius (c. 296–373) was born into a Christian family in Alexandria. Entering school at an early age, he was well educated in Greek literature, theology, and biblical studies. The church was a natural occupational choice—a career path offering prominence but not without pain. He was exiled five times—banished from Alexandria for a total of seventeen years out of his forty-five-year tenure as bishop. The life of Saint Athanasius, who is considered one of the greatest saints of Eastern Orthodoxy, is couched in legend, perhaps the most beloved story being that of his *baptism* into holy orders.

Hosting a gathering at his house by the sea, Bishop Alexander of Alexandria looks out across the sand one day and notices a group of boys playing in the water. But then, peering more closely, he realizes that they are not playing a game or engaging in horseplay as boys typically do. There is something strange about their activities—activities that appear to be all too church-like. So he sends an aide to "catch" the boys and bring them back for interrogation. The boys initially lie, but under pressure they break down and admit they are playing church. Little Athanasius, as the story goes, is pretending to be a bishop, following church order in quizzing his friends, and then administering the sacrament of baptism. So impressed is Alexander with this little boy bishop, that he takes him under his wing, and Athanasius dutifully follows in his footsteps.

According to Gregory of Nazianzus, Athanasius "was brought up, from the first, in religious habits and practices, after a brief study of literature and philosophy, so that he might not be utterly unskilled in such subjects." But the pious youth "could not brook being occupied in vanities." So he began "meditating on every book of the Old and New Testament, [and] with a depth such as none else has applied even to one of them, he grew rich in contemplation, rich in splendor of life."

After completing his formal studies, Athanasius is ordained a deacon and serves as Bishop Alexander's secretary, living in his home. Soon after the much older Arius makes known his theological views, the bishop issues an encyclical signed by Athanasius accusing Arius of heretical beliefs: "The Son is a creature and a work; neither is he like in essence to the Father; neither is he the true and natural Word of the Father; neither is he his true wisdom; but he is one of the things made and created and is called the Word and Wisdom by an abuse of terms." Alexander calls for a council in Alexandria, and more than one hundred bishops in the region attend. It is no surprise that Arius is declared anathema. Yet he continues preaching until he is forcibly driven out of the area.

Athanasius

Emperor Constantine has no patience for what he imagines are petty issues. He sends letters to both Alexander and Arius, insisting they settle the matter between them and their respective supporters. Having only recently consolidated his imperial power as sole emperor, he is determined to preserve unity in the empire. The church is a key to success. "Division in the church," he grumbles, "is worse than war."

With little hope of resolution, Constantine decides to call a council at Nicaea in the summer of 325, chosen in part for good weather forecasts and for its close proximity to his palatial mansion. Although some eighteen hundred bishops throughout the empire are invited, only a few hundred show up. This is the First Ecumenical Council—a meeting of the whole church as opposed to a church in one region. Here Arius is condemned as a heretic, and anyone preaching his ideas or even possessing his manuscripts may be convicted of a capital crime. The trinitarian concept of the Godhead is deemed orthodoxy—a concept as complicated as it is simple. *Homoousios*, the full deity of Christ the Son, is defined by that Greek word meaning "of one substance"—Christ is one substance with the Father.

Athanasius publishes *On the Incarnation* and is celebrating victory. But the compromise made at the Council of Nicaea quickly begins to fall apart. By 328 Constantine is having second thoughts, and he brings out of exile two

## BIBLE VERSES VERSUS GREEK WORDS AT THE COUNCIL OF NICAEA

The Arians and their sympathizers argued strongly for the use only of biblical wording. Alexander and his aide Athanasius recognized this as a ploy. The Arians had become adept at "Scripture twisting" so that any biblical terminology could be interpreted in their favor. The only way to bring closure to the debate and make clear once for all that Arian subordinationism was heretical was to use extrabiblical terminology that clearly spells out the unity of Father and Son as equal within the Godhead.

Roger E. Olson, *The Story of Christian Theology*

key Arian bishops. In that same year Alexander dies, and Athanasius, who only three years earlier has become a deacon, takes his place—all part of the political intrigue of the fourth century. But that promotion does not preclude banishment, nor does it signal growing support for the Nicene formula. The occasion of his first banishment brings together all the rumor and subterfuge the ancient world can muster. Both sides specialize in tall tales. Banishing a bishop for heresy is not nearly as interesting as intrigue involving murder and magic.

> *"Jesus whom I know as my Redeemer cannot be less than God."*
>
> Athanasius

One side hurls accusations; the other side fends them off and hurls their own. A particular case relates to Arian Bishop Arsenius. Was he really kidnapped? If so, was it a contrived plot by the Arian side to blame Athanasius for plotting to murder him through magic? Or was the whole thing cooked up by the Athanasian forces in an effort to discredit the Arians? The matter comes to a head at a Synod in Tyre in 335. Charges of prostitution are added to those of murder. In the end, the prostitute apparently picks someone other than Athanasius out of the line-up. But the soap opera does not end here.

Slander is piled upon slander, and the late-night pagan comedians have the last laugh.

In the end, Athanasius is banished to Gaul (present-day France and Germany) on charges that he conspired to withhold Egyptian wheat from the market in an apparent effort to starve the Arian East into submission. He returns home in 337 but is banished again in 339 by the new emperor, Constantius, who is allied with the Arians. Away for seven years, Athanasius spends most of his time in Rome and Milan.

Upon Athanasius's return home in 346 the citizens of Alexandria are so excited that a revival breaks out. "How many unmarried women who were before ready to enter upon marriage," exults Athanasius, "now remained virgins to Christ! How many young men, seeing the examples of others, embraced the monastic life!" The widows and orphans are now cared for—so much so "that you would have thought every family and every house a Church by reason of the goodness of its inmates and the prayers which were offered to God."

But a decade later Athanasius is again banished. During this time he writes, among other works, his own history of Arianism and several tracts against the heresy. His best-selling manuscript, however, is a biography, *Life of St. Antony*. He knows the desert monk, and he accepts his stories as truth, including incredible tales of Antony's tangling with Satan. Exiled twice more, Athanasius finally returns to Alexandria for the remaining seven years of his life. A year after his final exile he writes his yearly letter to the churches under his care, setting forth the definitive list of documents contained in the New Testament canon, listing all twenty-seven books as we know them today.

Several years after his death in 373, the Ecumenical Council of Constantinople reaffirmed the Nicene orthodoxy that he had put forward some fifty years earlier. More than any other fourth-century churchman, he is responsible for the orthodox position hammered out at Nicaea. Perdition awaited those who did not fall in line: "Which Faith except every one do keep whole and undefiled, without doubt he shall perish everlastingly."

From this point on in church history there is often a vast chasm between the Nicene Christians and the Arian Christians, though they both continue to claim insider status in the church until the Ecumenical Council of Constantinople in 381 that settles once and for all that Arians are heretics. Thus it is no surprise that throughout church history Athanasius has been given a good press. During the decades of controversy between the two councils, however, there is no certainty as to which side will pre-

The Eastern Mediterranean

vail. Indeed, the Arians outnumber those in the orthodox camp by large majorities. According to a report from Jerome, millions had been captured by the Arian heresy, including some eighty percent of the bishops. Athanasius receives letters expressing alarm at what is going on. "The heresy long ago disseminated by that enemy of

---

## Which Christ Will You Die For?

Athanasius stared down murderous intruders into his church. He stood before emperors who could have killed him as easily as exiled him. He risked the wrath of parents and other clergy by consciously training young people to give their all for Christ, including martyrdom.... What was clear to Athanasius was that propositions about Christ carried convictions that could send you to heaven or to hell.... I believe Athanasius would have abominated, with tears ... the so-called "reformists" and "the emerging church," "younger evangelicals," "postfundamentalists," "postfoundationalists," "postpropositionalists," and "postevangelicals." I think he would have said, "Our young people in Alexandria die for the truth of propositions about Christ. What do your young people die for?" And if the answer came back, "We die for Christ, not propositions about Christ," I think he would have said, "That's what Arius says. So which Christ will you die for?"

John Piper, *Contending for Our All*, 2006

truth, Arius, grew to a shameless height," writes a correspondent, "and like a bitter root it is bearing its pernicious fruit and already gaining the upper hand."

So uncertain is the future that Arianism is portrayed in end-times proportions. "Has the Lord completely abandoned His Church?" asks a dejected supporter of Athanasius. "Has the hour then come and is the fall beginning in this way so that now the man of sin is clearly revealed, the son of perdition, who ... is lifted up above all that is called God or that is worshiped?" Despite the sense of despair, there are many attempts to mend fences. During the decades between 340 and 360, councils are convened in Sardica, Sirminum, Rimini, and Selucia. Indeed, there are so many meetings that a pagan writer makes sport of the situation, claiming that "the highways were covered with galloping bishops." By another account, "bishop was contending against bishop, and the people were contending against one another, like swarms of gnats fighting in the air"—all part of the messy history of theology.

## Constantine: A Questionably Christian Emperor

Emperor Constantine (c. 272–327) was the first Christian emperor. Or was he? Whether he was a sincere believer or only used religion as a talisman or as a way to unite his empire has been debated for centuries. Growing up an army brat in Serbia, he saw little of his father, Flavius Constantius, an officer who worked his way up through the ranks. Constantine's mother, Helena, had grown up in a poor family living near the Black Sea. Working as an inn-keeper when she met his father, Helena was a "consort" rather than a wife and thus became an "unwed mother." The lack of a marriage certificate did not diminish her prospects for sainthood, however. In fact, in Eastern Orthodoxy she is commemorated with her son, Emperor Constantine, on May 21, the "Feast of the Holy Great Sov-

---

### CHURCH FATHERS VERSUS HERETICS

The study of early Christian doctrine has been transformed by a change in attitude toward heresy and the heresiarchs. Gone is the picture of the gradual flowering of a single, consistent vision of Christian truth, developing only in the sense of receiving an increasing precision of expression, something forced on the church by the need to combat perversions of that truth deliberately introduced by malevolent heretics. In its place has come a picture of the Christian church seeking to discover what the truth might be in the context of always-changing conditions and new problems. In that revised picture the roles of "father" and "heretic" are much less sharply contrasted. Pelagius and Nestorius are not seen as men of evil will; they are seen rather as Christians determined to defend some aspect of Christian truth that was genuinely at risk in the teaching of St. Augustine or of St. Cyril. Even if their overall presentation of the faith be judged less satisfactory than that of their ultimately canonized opponents, they were standing out for important Christian insights to which their orthodox Christian opponents did not do full justice.... Such an attitude does not involve denying the reality of the issues that divided them. It only involves saying that true insight was not the exclusive prerogative of one side.

Maurice F. Wiles, *Archetypal Heresy*

## THE SEVEN ECUMENICAL COUNCILS

325 First Council of Nicaea: convened by Constantine, established the Nicene Creed that affirmed the full deity of Christ

381 First Council of Constantinople: convened by Theodosius I, reaffirming the Council of Nicaea and its rejection of Arianism

432 Council of Ephesus: convened to renounce the teaching of Nestorius that Christ has two separate natures, human and divine; declared that Mary is *theotokos*, Mother of God

451 Council of Chalcedon: convened to reaffirm that Christ is at the same time "truly man and truly God" in one person

553 Second Council of Constantinople: convened by Justinian in a move to placate Monophysite Christians by condemning more Nestorian writings

680 Third Council of Constantinople: convened to refute the teaching that Christ had two natures but only one will and asserted that Christ had both a human and divine will

787 Second Council of Nicaea: convened by Constantine V to restore the veneration of icons in the Eastern church

ereigns Constantine and Helen, Equal to the Apostles."

When Constantine is twenty, his father, on orders of Emperor Diocletian, separates from Helena and marries Theodora. Helena then loses her status and lives in the shadows until her son rises to power after the death of his father more than a decade later. In 325 she is brought back to live a royal life at the center of power. Now she becomes a collector of relics, and through her travels she not only popularizes the practice of pilgrimage but also identifies the most significant holy sites. She reportedly points to the very spot where the cross was buried and later discovers the stump of the tree from which the cross was hewn and the very nails that pierced the hands and feet of Jesus. This queen of relics even identifies the bones of the three wise men from the East. Through

Emperor Constantine I with a model of the city

her influence great churches are built on hallowed ground that she identifies—in Bethlehem at the site of the nativity and in Jerusalem at the place of the ascension.

Helena's saintliness is attested by the historian Eusebius: "She became under [her son's] influence such a devout servant of God that one might believe her to have been from her very childhood a disciple of the Redeemer of mankind." The story of Constantine's vision of a cross in the noon-day sky also comes from Eusebius and is one of the most well-known conversion accounts in Christian literature—if it is indeed a conversion account.

The date is October 28, 312. The setting is the ancient stone Milvian Bridge that spans the Tiber River near the gate of Rome. Constantine is nervous. His troops are outnumbered by the army of Maxentius stationed behind the walls of Rome with enough provisions to withstand a long siege. The prospects of winning are not good for the pagan general. Then at noon he sees a cross above the sun with the words "Conquer by this."

Why Maxentius came out of town to do open battle with his adversary is a mystery to military experts. In the end, due to his poor strategy or to the intervention of God, the victory belongs to Constantine, paving the way for him to become the sole emperor of both East and West.

As a Christian emperor, Constantine gets high marks for the Edict of Milan in 313 that secures toleration of Christianity and ends the persecution that began with Nero. But while ending persecution from pagans he disregards the Christian pacifist tradition and inaugurates a long history of Christian fratricide. He sends troops to North Africa to attack the Donatists, a breakaway sect of Christian purists.

Constantine's sins also include murder—and not merely murder of his distant enemies. He arranges the murder even of his son and one of his wives. His Christian credentials are found wanting in other matters as well. Before he professed to follow the Christian God, he was partial to the sun god, a god who continued to be in good standing with him long after his cross-above-the-sun vision. His coins featured the sun god on one side and the name of Christ on the other. Thus *Sun*day, so-called by Constantine, was on his orders set aside as the day of worship.

Constantine's delayed baptism also throws a damper on any claim to his saintliness. Apparently fearing the sacrament would not take because of his wicked ways, he postpones it until he is on his deathbed in 337. Then he contacts

## THE FATHER OF CHURCH HISTORY

Historians cannot help thinking and writing subjectively, particularly if the subject matter is held dear. This was true of Eusebius of Caesarea (c. 263–339), the most noted church historian of the early centuries. But despite his pro-Christian and pro-Arian bias, his works are invaluable. He saved records that would otherwise have been lost. But his own biography (written by the bishop who succeeded him) did not survive the ravages of time, so his life is shrouded in obscurity. Most references to Eusebius in church history texts are to Bishop Eusebius of Caesarea as opposed to his contemporary, Bishop Eusebius of Nicomedia, who was so pro-Arian that Athanasius referred to the Arians as the Eusebians.

Eusebius of Caesarea was more concerned with Christian unity than with taking a strong stand on one side or the other. But the passion he passed down as a gift to later generations was his work as a historian. "I feel inadequate to do it justice as the first to venture on such an undertaking, a traveler on a lonely and untrodden path," he penned in the introduction to his multivolume *Ecclesiastical History.* "But I pray that God may guide me and the power of the Lord assist me, for I have not found even the footprints of any predecessors on this path, only traces in which some have left various accounts of the times in which they lived."

These prior record-keepers sustained him: "Calling as from a distant watchtower, they tell me how I must walk in guiding the course of this work to avoid error." He set the stage for good primary research, in part because there was so little opportunity for research in secondary sources: "I have gathered from the scattered memoirs of my predecessors whatever seems appropriate to this project, plucking, as it were, flowers from the literary fields of the ancient authors themselves."

## MURDERS AND RUMORS OF ILLICIT LOVE

As Constantine's wife, Fausta would have had good reason to oppose Crispus as Constantine's favorite, in favor of her own son.... Some historians conjecture that Fausta hatched a plot to inspire Constantine's suspicions against Crispus. All that is certain is that in 326 ... Constantine ordered the murder of his firstborn son and the obliteration of the name Crispus from imperial history.... If Fausta did falsely conspire against Crispus, and if, after the murder, Constantine learned [perhaps from Helena] that he had been misled by Fausta, that would account for what happened next. So would another, simpler explanation that some historians favor — namely, that Crispus and his stepmother Fausta were lovers. What we do know is in that same fateful year, shortly after murdering his son, Constantine murdered his wife.... Eusebius promoted only the happiest of images in all his accounts, and having designated Constantine as the new Moses, he makes no mention of the murders of his wife and son.

James Carroll, *Constantine's Sword*

Bishop Eusebius of Nicomedia to officiate. Setting aside his imperial purple garb, he dresses in white and rests on a white sofa to symbolize his new spiritual status. That Eusebius is an Arian is one final snub by the emperor to Athanasius and orthodoxy in the Western church. In an effort to rectify the matter, however, an apocryphal account was later circulated that falsely claims that Constantine was baptized in Rome by Pope Sylvester. The end for Constantine comes, according to Eusebius, at "about the time of the midday sun," reminiscent of the vision a quarter-century earlier — symbolism fitting an emperor.

Constantine's life illustrates the malevolence and messiness of this era — an era that set the stage for orthodox faith for the ensuing centuries. Saintly heroes were in short supply. Sin and shame had free reign, then as now.

---

## What if ....

What if Constantine had been killed in battle or by a zealous and jealous rival or wife? What if the church had remained a persecuted pilgrim faith? What if the Council of Nicaea had not been called together and become a pivotal turning point in the early church? How different the Christian faith would be today.

What if the Arians had carried the day at the Council of Nicaea and in the generations that followed? What if the church had split down the middle over Arianism with the Eastern church going one way and the Western another? Or, what if the Western church had split into two camps or gone the way of the Arians? The counterfactuals are infinite. Imagine church "orthodoxy" being the view of Arius. Would the Reformation have come early with the insistence that Athanasius was right? Would the sixteenth-century Reformation, fashioned as it was, have occurred at all?

What if Eusebius had found himself too busy with his ministry as bishop to pursue his avocation as a historian? How much poorer we would be today without his writings.

## Further Reading

Anatolios, Khaled. *Athanasius*. New York: Routledge, 2004.

Ayers, Lewis. *Nicaea and Its Legacy: An Approach to Fourth-Century Trinitarian Theology*. New York: Oxford University Press, 2006.

Carroll, James. *Constantine's Sword: The Church and the Jews*. New York: Houghton Mifflin, 2001.

Kousoulas, D. G. *The Life and Times of Constantine the Great: The First Christian Emperor*. New York: Routledge, 1997.

McGuckin, John Anthony. *The Westminster Handbook to Patristic Theology*. Louisville: Westminster John Knox Press, 2004.

MacMullen, Ramsay. *Voting about God in Early Church Councils*. New Haven: Yale University Press, 2006.

Olson, Roger E. *The Story of Christian Theology*. Downers Grove, Ill.: InterVarsity, 1999.

Rusch, William C. *The Trinitarian Controversy*. Minneapolis: Augsburg Fortress, 1980.

Trigg, Joseph W. *Origen*. New York: Routledge, 1998.

Wiles, Maurice F. *Archetypal Heresy: Arianism Through the Centuries*. New York: Oxford University Press, 2001.

Williams, Rowan. *Arius: Heresy and Tradition*. Grand Rapids: Eerdmans, 1987.

# CHAPTER 4

# Desert Fathers

*Early Monastic Life and Writings*

*Saints, as we all know, are regular people. Or are they? The Catholic Church does not canonize saints willy-nilly. To be deemed a saint, one must have reportedly lived a holy life and performed at least one miracle. Today, in an age of cynicism, miracles are more difficult to prove, but from biblical times to the Renaissance and beyond, their validity was typically taken for granted. Moreover, miracles were performed in the names of holy men and women long after they died.*

*Last year I was diagnosed with shingles, a painful neurological malady that is first manifested by a rash. In my case I knew something was wrong when I began feeling sharp pains above my ear, radiating down my neck. Two days later I spotted a rash on my chest. I immediately called my doctor and got a prescription that promised to relieve the pain and irritation. The medicine worked, though more than a year later my ear still itches.*

*Had I been living in medieval times, a physician would have had little or nothing to offer me. I would have prayed for healing, but not necessarily to God. I would more likely have prayed to St. Anthony, the saint called upon to cure infectious diseases—especially shingles (herpes zoster). Indeed, the affliction is still known in Italy and elsewhere as Anthony's Fire.*

*Credited with even greater responsibility is Laziosi Peregrine, the patron saint of people afflicted with cancer or AIDS. Saint Dymphna is called upon to cure insanity. But when all hope is gone—when other saints have failed—Saint Jude remains. One of the twelve disciples, Jude is the patron saint of "lost causes." The prayer is "Saint Jude, hope of the hopeless, pray for me."*

*Modern medicine and technology, we might imagine, thwart an impulse to depend on saints. But saints have come of age on the Internet. They thrive right alongside news alerts on medical breakthroughs.*

We are not certain that the best histories are not those in which a little
of the exaggeration of fictitious narrative is judiciously employed.
Something is lost in accuracy; but much is gained in effect.

THOMAS BABINGTON MACAULAY

It is naïve for a historian to assume that everything he or she publishes is objective truth. If we had to prove the veracity of every word we wrote, there would be little left but sterile facts and figures—and much of that might be fictitious. Exaggeration is an art form in some historical accounts, both ancient and modern. The more we dig, the more we realize that fictitious narrative is not found in fiction alone. So it is with the stories of Desert Fathers—and Mothers—and the early monasticism of the Mediterranean world.

There was no clear line of demarcation in the early church between theologians and contemplatives as there often is today. Athanasius, with his razor-sharp mind, for example, could just as easily write the fabled *Life of Antony* as a heavy theological tome. Mysticism, supernaturalism, and theological studies were easily blended in the writings of the early desert monks and their contemporaries such as Anthony of Egypt, Simon Stylites, Marcella and Paula, Jerome, Ambrose, Augustine, Monica, and Mary of Egypt.

Surely Athanasius was exaggerating when he said that the mass exodus of ascetic Christians from the population centers turned the Egyptian desert into a city. It was hardly that. But who knows, if someone were to have *hurled an egg* (to paraphrase H. L. Mencken) from a camel caravan, it just might have landed on a penitential praying hermit.

The desert has served as an alluring focal point, both allegorical and geographical, throughout Christian history. Moses and the children of Israel wandered for forty years in its rugged and unforgiving terrain. The prophet Isaiah was "the voice of one crying out in the wilderness." John the Baptist was a desert ascetic wearing camel's hair and acting crazy. Jesus ventured into the barren wilderness for forty days and nights, enduring torment and temptation. Paul went straight away into the Arabian desert after his conversion.

Among the first of the desert monks were Christians fleeing imperial persecution. There they hid in caves rather than facing prison or execution. But word spread that this was also a place to find God. There was beauty in the desert—the beauty of God's presence and of spiritual victories over Satan. "O Desert, bright with the flowers of Christ," sang Jerome, himself a desert monk. "O Solitude, whence come

## PARADE OF HISTORY

As the parade of the early church moves forward, we see a pilgrimage of ascetics moving into the desert. They hide in caves and mountain cliffs. Simon Stylites finds solace—and celebrity—on a pillar. Soon the desert is dotted with pillars, and processions of tourists arrive, seeking spiritual support from these saints of the sand. Among the ascetics is Mary of Egypt, converted from her sinful life at a parade in Jerusalem—a parade marking the holy day of the Exaltation of the Cross.

the stones of which the Apocalypse, the city of the Great King, is built! O Wilderness, gladdened with God's special presence! What keeps you in the world, my brother, you who are above the world? How long shall gloomy roofs oppress you? Oh, that I could behold the desert, lovelier to me than any city."

But the desert was callous, cold-hearted — surely no environment for sissies. Its punishing sun, frigid nights, and disdain for nourishment tested even the most muscular ascetics. Here the spirit was either broken or rejuvenated. Temptation thrived in the parched soil. Demons slithered like serpents among the rocks. That was its appeal. As incidents of persecution and martyrdom declined, the desert became a venue for suffering with Christ. There were no beds, no baths, and barely bread for shrunken stomachs. Indeed, the desolate landscape sucked the physical satisfactions of life out of its inhabitants as surely as did state persecution.

Those who ventured out regarded themselves athletes engaged in a perpetual contest with demons. Many of these cave-dwelling holy men and women lived solitary lives. Others lived in community. But there was no safety in numbers either from the elements or from enemy attacks. In 380 an unruly army of marauders from the north swept down on a remote Egyptian monastery, killing thirty-eight of its residents. A survivor has left behind a chilling account:

> For who, even if his heart were of stone, would not weep for the holy martyrs who had grown old in the garb of Christians, flung upon the ground in merciless suffering; each one of them struck down, one with his head cut off and another with his head split in two. What can I say about the number of merciless blows which struck the saints who were killed limb by limb and were flung upon the ground?

Nevertheless, the solitary ascetics kept on coming, though few of them having taken formal monastic vows. Tourists came as well, staying on as long as their desert vacations allowed. Not all the ascetics were pleased with this turn of events. Swarms of people and spirituality were not as easily meshed in the fourth-century monastic mindset as they are in the megachurch mentality today. Nor were government officials overjoyed. Where had all the soldiers gone — and the taxpayers?

Perhaps an anorexic holy man had little to offer a crumbling empire, but the insight and spiritual sayings of these Desert Fathers and Mothers have had a remarkably long shelf life. Twenty-first-century Christians continue to mine for treasure among the words and wisdom of these saints and sages of old.

## Anthony of Egypt: First of the Desert Monks

"If you want to be perfect, go and sell everything you have and give the money to the poor." These are the words that stopped the rich kid dead in his tracks. His parents had died, and now all their wealth belongs to him. The much-heralded city of Alexandria offers infinite opportunities for luxurious living. His whole life is ahead of him. He can travel in comfort and see the wonders of the world if he so desires. But he hears the call of God in that very pointed gospel passage. His only travel will be to the desert. His journey of the soul begins by giving his wealth to the poor and leaving his childhood home. His goal is to become a true lover of God — to give himself entirely to Christ, ever vigilant in resisting the devil. His motto: "The mind of the soul is strong when the pleasures of the body are weak." He nourishes himself on bread and water, fasting altogether

Anthony's life in panorama

In one instance when a would-be follower tells him that he has given all his wealth away but for a small amount for necessities, the response is vintage Anthony: "If you want to be a monk, go into the village, buy some meat, cover your naked body with it and come here like that." When the man returns, his body is bloody and torn by wild dogs and vultures. The moral of the story: "Those who renounce the world but want to keep something for themselves are torn in this way by the demons who make war on them."

every other day and denying himself sleep, preferring to pray through the night.

Anthony (251 – 356), whose life story is told by Athanasius, lives among the tombs, where he is assaulted by wild animals and demons. This is God's way of training him to fight and win spiritual battles like an athlete prevailing in the arena. After a time he leaves the tombs, seeking an even more secluded area, where he remains for twenty years, becoming a celebrity — a superstar among desert saints. Disciples seek him out, and their encounters with him inspire generations of ascetics.

Anthony's activities intersect with the lives of other well-known figures of the era. During the brutal persecution under Emperor Diocletian in 303, he travels to Rome to minister to the suffering. He is also enmeshed in the theological controversies of the day. Athanasius persuades him to come to Alexandria from his desert hideaway to speak out against Arius, whose views are catching fire. Though he is no theologian, Anthony epitomizes sainthood. His life of self-

## FIGHTING DEMONS

As he was watching in the night the devil sent wild beasts against him. And almost all the hyenas in that desert came forth from their dens and surrounded him; and he was in the midst, while each one threatened to bite. Seeing that it was a trick of the enemy he said to them all: 'If ye have received power against me I am ready to be devoured by you; but if ye were sent against me by demons, stay not, but depart, for I am a servant of Christ.' When Antony said this they fled, driven by that word as with a whip.

A few days after ... he saw a beast like a man to the thighs but having legs and feet like those of an ass. And Antony only signed himself and said, 'I am a servant of Christ. If thou art sent against me, behold I am here.' But the beast together with his evil spirits fled, so that, through his speed, he fell and died. And the death of the beast was the fall of the demons. For they strove in all manner of ways to lead Antony from the desert and were not able.

Athanasius, *Life of St. Antony*

## Asceticism and Sexuality

The suffering ascetic looked not only to Jesus as the ultimate ideal but also to the first man, Adam. In the garden, Adam communed with God in sinless perfection. His paradise may have been lush with fruit trees and other vegetation, but there was no sin of gluttony or lust—at least, not until the introduction of Eve. In order to reconstruct Adam's sinless state, ascetics went to the desert, living as far from women as possible. But they quickly discovered that lust erupted in solitude more often than amid company. To rid oneself of lustful thoughts, many reasoned, one must starve oneself. If hunger pangs became all-consuming, the sex drive would likely diminish.

The monastic worldview regarded chastity in terms of redemption or salvation. While ordinary lay people could inherit eternal life if they maintained their sacramental duties, ascetics could attain angelic—or Adamic—status here on earth. Celibacy without lust allowed the ascetic to sever attachments to worldly pleasures and arrive at a heavenly state— a oneness with God.

But celibacy was considered more than a mere human construct. It was a mark of the Trinity. Those who find ultimate godliness visualized the triune God in virginity. Sexual desire was a result of the fall and God's curse on humankind. Attaining true godliness demanded the eradication of all sexual desire. Jerome testified about how difficult that was for him:

> How often, when I was living in the desert, in the vast solitude which gives to hermits a savage dwelling-place, parched by a burning sun, how often did I fancy myself among the pleasures of Rome!... I had no companions but scorpions and wild beasts, I often found myself amid bevies of girls. My face was pale and my frame chilled with fasting; yet my mind was burning with desire, and the fires of lust kept bubbling up before me when my flesh was as good as dead. Helpless, I cast myself at the feet of Jesus.

Women as well as men sought oneness with God through asceticism. But women faced an additional burden, as was true of Macrina, sister of Gregory of Nyssa. A fourth-century holy woman known for her wisdom, she was hindered by her gender. In writing about his saintly sister, Gregory wonders "if indeed she should be styled woman, for I do not know whether it is fitting to designate her by her sex, who so surpassed her sex." Another "desert mother" confessed: "According to nature I am a woman, but not according to my thoughts." True godliness, then, was manly virginity, minus lust—a most difficult state to attain.

denial is the support Athanasius most desires. Saint Augustine will later be put to shame by reading Athanasius's story of Anthony.

After his trip to Alexandria, Anthony returns to the desert with two companions who care for him in his final years. Despite all the privations he endures he lives to age one hundred and five, according to Athanasius, having secured the promise that his body will be buried in an unmarked grave. His concerns are not for dogs or vultures. He does not want his bones and remnants of clothing fought over and revered as relics. For him spirituality is self-denial and sacrifice, not saint-worship.

Simon Stylites tempted by the devil

## Simon Stylites: Saint on the Pillar

Among all the so-called Desert Fathers, Simon Stylites (390–459) is often regarded as the most bizarre. His claim to fame was his perch on a pillar in a Syrian desert for nearly forty years. Today his celebrity has faded, but in his own day pilgrims came from great distances to hear him preach and offer counsel.

Simon grew up a shepherd boy profoundly influenced by his pious mother, Martha. By the age of thirteen he is fasting and denying himself the normal pleasures of life. At sixteen he enters a monastery but finds monastic life too comfortable. He leaves the community and begins a regimen of self-mutilation and starvation. Indeed, he is close to death before he is discovered and nursed back to life. As time passes, his ways become still more eccentric—even among the desert monks themselves. He escapes to a tiny hut, now not only starving himself but also

forcing himself to stand upright until he faints and falls to the ground.

After three years he moves to a narrow mountain crevasse, where he expects to be left alone. But pilgrims are on his trail, eager that his holiness rub off on them. He has no place to hide, until he comes up with an ingenious idea. With the help of sympathizers, he devises a pillar that grows in stages to rise, eventually, several stories high. His platform offers him no more floor space than a small bedroom. Now even more tourists arrive. Every afternoon he speaks to the crowds, though never encouraging them to follow him in his extreme asceticism. He maintains a wide-ranging correspondence and gains the respect of common people and emperors, including Theodosius and his wife, Eudocia. His support for the Council of Chalcedon is much sought after by Emperor Leo.

During his lifetime and after his death, living on pillars as "stylite" monks became the rage among the desert ascetics. Indeed, the desert was said to be dotted with pillars.

## Marcella and Women in Monasticism

Monasticism attracted more men than women. Women were rarely found in wilderness caves or atop desert pillars, but from the earliest centuries they did play important roles in houses of charity. In the early centuries, the houses were loosely formed without a monastic rule or formal vows. Marcella (c. 325–410) exemplifies this way of life that caught on among other women of the time.

Growing up in Rome, she was influenced by her pious mother, Albina, an educated woman of wealth and benevolence. Childhood memories centered around piety, and one in particular related to Athanasius, who lodged in her home during one of his many exiles. He may have taken special interest in her, thinking back to his own youthful practice of playing church. Athanasius interacted with his hosts on theological matters and recounted anecdotes of his own monastic life. His most spellbinding stories, however, were the miraculous tales of the desert monks. As a parting gift he left behind the first copy of his biography, *Life of St. Anthony.*

Marcella's wealth and beauty placed her at the center of fashionable Roman society. She married young, to a wealthy aristocrat, but less than a year later he died. Her time of mourning over, young men soon come calling again. However, convinced that God is directing her to a life of poverty and service, she shocks her social circle when she leaves behind her fashionable dresses for a coarse brown garment and abandons her usual extravagant hair styling and makeup. Appearing as a low-class woman, she starts a trend as other young women join her. They form a community known as the brown dress society, spending their time praying, singing, reading the Bible, and serving the needy. Her palatial home is now a refuge for weary pilgrims and for the poor.

Summoned by Bishop Damasus (who arranges lodging at Marcella's hospitality house), Jerome arrives in 382. It is an exhilarating time for this woman of letters, who has immersed herself in both Greek and Hebrew, to be entertaining one of the great minds of the age. He spends the next three years in what he calls her "domestic church," translating the Bible into Latin. She learns under his teaching even as she critiques his translation. He speaks

and writes of her Christian devotion and scholarship and commends her influence on Anastasius, bishop of Rome—particularly in his condemning Origen's doctrines, which Jerome declares a "glorious victory." Indeed, his admiration of Marcella is unbounded, not only for her intellectual acumen but also for her deference to men who might be threatened by her vast store of knowledge:

> All that I had gathered by long study and constant meditation, she drank in, learned and possessed, and after I left Rome, she answered any arguments that were put to her about scripture, including obscure and ambiguous inquiries from priests, saying that the answers came from me or another man, even when they were her own, claiming always to be a pupil even when she was teaching, so that she did not seem to injure the male sex because the apostle [Paul] did not permit women to teach.

Marcella, however, is also known for her efforts to restrain Jerome from quarrelling with his opponents—or at least helping him control his legendary temper. Eleven of his extant letters are addressed to her, and she is mentioned in many of his other writings. In one of his letters he responds to her query about the truth of Montanism. Someone is apparently attempting to convert her, and she is deeply interested in what she is hearing, though suspecting that the claim that they possess a more authentic spirituality might be false. Jerome writes a lengthy point-by-point refutation of the movement and then concludes:

> To expose the infidelity of the Montanists is to triumph over it. Nor is it necessary that in so short a letter as this I should overthrow the several absurdities which they bring forward. You are well acquainted with the Scriptures; and, as I take it, you have written, not because

you have been disturbed by their cavils, but only to learn my opinion about them.

It was at the home of Marcella that Jerome first met Paula, a devoted and scholarly woman who would become his long-time intellectual counterpart. When Jerome returns to the Holy Land, Paula later relocates there as well. They invite Marcella to join them, but she remains in Rome to oversee her growing house of virgins, where she is addressed as Mother. But hard times are ahead of her. She is in her late seventies in 410, when the Goths, led by Alaric, pillage the city. Soldiers storm the residence demanding she relinquish her hidden jewels and wealth, which long before had been sold to fund her charitable work. When she has nothing to give them, they strike her down. She is taken to a church set up as a sanctuary, but she dies the next day. Marcella was later canonized by the Roman Catholic Church; her feast day is January 31.

Jerome's sudden departure from Rome to Bethlehem and Paula's own departure soon afterward is shrouded in mystery. Paula, also a widow and relative of Marcella, was the mother of five children. In Palestine she established a monastery for women and her prestige grew — but not without lingering rumors whispered in Rome. Both she and Jerome promote celibacy; however, this practice does not preclude a very close friendship — so close that it would be associated with scandal. "Before I knew the house of saintly Paula," writes Jerome, after he has left Rome, "my praises were sung through the city." But that has quickly changed due to an "evil report." He laments that "the only fault found in me is my sex, and that only when Paula comes to Jerusalem."

> "She was in the front line in condemning the heretics."
>
> Jerome, speaking of Marcella

## Jerome: Monk, Scholar, and Bible Translator

"Make knowledge of the Scripture your love and you will not love the views of the flesh." These are the words of Jerome (c. 331 – 420), who is regarded by some as the greatest of all translators of the Bible. He was far more than a Bible translator, however. In addition to his Latin Vulgate version of the Bible, he wrote numerous biblical commentaries and was deeply involved in theological controversies of the day as well as with matters of asceticism and spiritual formation. His historical writing and vast correspondence offer a fascinating insight on an era when doctrinal disputation blends easily with the asceticism of the Desert Fathers.

Jerome is also the subject of a medieval legend that draws from pre-Christian stories. In one account Jerome removes a thorn from the paw of a lion, who returns the kindness by stay-

---

### THE STORY OF AN AGED ABBESS

In this city of Antinoe there are twelve convents of women; in one of them I met Amma Talis, an old woman who had spent eighty years in asceticism, as she and the neighbors told me. With her dwelt sixty young women who loved her so greatly that no key even was fixed on the outer wall of the monastery, as in other monasteries, but they were kept in by love of her. Such a height of impassivity did the old woman reach that when I entered and sat down she came and sat by me and put her hands on my shoulders in a transport of freedom.

Palladius, *Lausiac History*
(early 5th century)

ing on to guard the monastery and watch over the donkey. When the donkey goes missing, the lion is blamed, but Jerome stands by his pet, and the lion takes over the work of the donkey. When the donkey is eventually found, they all live happily ever after. In medieval art, Jerome is depicted with a grateful lion lying at his feet.

At age twenty Jerome journeys to Rome to be baptized. The details of his conversion are hazy, but according to one source he becomes involved with the homosexual community in Rome and experiences terrible remorse that draws him on Sundays to holy places—especially to the catacombs, where the martyrs are interred: "Often I would find myself entering those crypts, deep dug in the earth, with their walls on either side lined with the bodies of the dead, where everything was so dark."

Following his baptism, Jerome's educational pursuits and various ministries take him from one region to another until he eventually settles down at a monastery in Bethlehem, the setting for the legend of the lion. Jerome's celebrated wisdom and kindness is only one side of this often-volatile man, however. He is harsh in his criticism of other church leaders and pointedly condemns the corruption of the bearded clerics in Rome, of whom he sarcastically writes, "The only thought of such men is their clothes—are they pleasantly perfumed, do their shoes fit smoothly.... If there is any holiness in a beard, nobody is holier than a goat."

Having been forced out of Rome in his forties, he resents these enemies of the truth. But more controversies continue while he is residing in Bethlehem. One of his best-known correspondents is his younger contemporary, Augustine, who first writes to him challenging his translation of a phrase in Galatians. The letter takes nearly a decade to reach its destination in Bethlehem, after apparently being read

by many people along the way. And, as Jerome assumed, it may very well have been written for public consumption: "It is a sign of youthful arrogance to try to build up a reputation by assailing prominent figures." Nevertheless, the correspondence—both harsh and pleasant—continues for many years.

> *"Do not let your deeds belie your words, lest when you speak in church someone may say to himself, 'Why do you not practice what you preach?'"*
>
> Jerome

Jerome's writings span a wide range of subjects, including his perspective on marriage and monasticism. In comparing celibacy with marital bonds, he gives marriage a numerical value of thirty, rating widowhood and virginity sixty and one hundred, respectively. He insists, however, that he has high regard for marriage—but only for its potential to increase the number of virgins: "To prefer chastity is not to disparage matrimony.... Married ladies can be proud to come after nuns, for God Himself told them to be fruitful, multiply and replenish the earth.... A child born from marriage is virgin flesh.... I praise matrimony. But only because it produces virgins."

His concern for the education of children prompts him to write a lengthy letter to Paula's daughter-in-law about home-schooling her baby girl, also named Paula—a letter written for public dissemination.

Let your child of promise have a training from her parents worthy of her birth.... Let boys with their wanton frolics be kept far from Paula: let even her maids and attendants hold aloof from association with the worldly, lest they render their evil knowledge worse by

Jerome with Marcella and Paula

all take care not to make her lessons distasteful; a childish dislike often lasts longer than childhood.

Paula's wealth funded Jerome's library in Bethlehem, and from his cell came a steady stream of scholarly works. During his thirty-four years in that location he wrote commentaries and annotated bibliographies as well as treatises against heresies, particularly against the teachings of Pelagius and Origen. In fact, so blistering are his attacks on Pelagianism that some partisan thugs break into the monastery, set fire to the buildings, and assault the monks, killing one of them, although Jerome himself escapes. He dies some years later, poring over manuscripts to the very end.

## Ambrose: Orator and Bishop

The stories of the saints formed an important part of popular Christian literature in the early church and the centuries immediately following. Frequently, the accounts included tales of infant and childhood miracles—some that strain credulity. St. Nicholas, for example, stands upright only hours after he is born to announce he is beginning a schedule of fasting by nursing only once a day on Wednesdays and Fridays. Other infancy tales are more believable but no less decisive in indicating God's favor. Pointing to his future greatness, the infant Saint Ambrose endures a frightful encounter with bees:

> Ambrose . . . was sleeping in his cradle with his mouth open, in the courtyard of the governor's palace, when suddenly a swarm of bees came and so covered his face and mouth that they kept on going in and out of his mouth in continuous succession. . . . And presently the bees flew off and soared to such a height in the air that it was impossible for human eyes to

teaching it to her. Have a set of letters made for her, of boxwood or of ivory, and tell her their names. Let her play with them, making play a road to learning, and let her not only grasp the right order of the letters and remember their names in a simple song, but also frequently upset their order and mix the last letters with the middle ones, the middle with the first. Thus she will know them all by sight as well as by sound. When she begins with uncertain hand to use the pen, either let another hand be put over hers to guide her baby fingers, or else have the letters marked on the tablet so that her writing may follow their outlines and keep their limits without straying away. Offer her prizes for spelling, tempting her with such trifling gifts as please young children. Let her have companions too in her lessons, so that she may seek to rival them and be stimulated by any praise they win. You must not scold her if she is somewhat slow; praise is the best sharpener of wits. Let her be glad when she is first and sorry when she falls behind. Above

see them. It frightened his father. "If that little one lives," he said, "he will become something very big."

The patron saint of beekeepers, Ambrose (c. 338 — 397) was born into a Christian family in Gaul. He followed his father, a government official, into that profession and became a popular administrator in Milan.

In 374, when Ambrose is in his mid-thirties, his life is suddenly upended. The bishop of Milan dies in the midst of bitter Arian strife, and Ambrose is seen as a mediating figure. The Arians in Milan are opposing the one designated to succeed the bishop, and the election at the basilica is in turmoil. Ambrose, an interested bystander, suddenly hears a call from the crowd, "Ambrose for bishop!" Others join in, and before he fully realizes what is happening, he is elected the next bishop of Milan.

He has two strikes against him. He is neither trained in theology nor baptized. Without proper credentials, he takes the most logical course: he goes into hiding. But bringing peace to Milan is more than a local matter. When the emperor learns of the election, he praises the choice. This prompts the guard giving cover to Ambrose to reveal his whereabouts. Brought to the basilica against his will, Ambrose is baptized and installed as bishop of Milan.

Any optimism that the Arian controversy would diminish with Ambrose in high-church office is premature. He averts open combat with Arians until 386, when the Emperor Valentinian and his mother, Justina, insist that two churches in Milan be turned into Arian strongholds. Ambrose refuses. He meets the emperor's officials with powerful words: "If you demand my person, I am ready to submit: carry me to prison or to death, I will not resist; but I will never betray the church of Christ. I will not call

upon the people to succour me; I will die at the foot of the altar rather than desert it." He does not want strife. "The tumult of the people I will not encourage," he promises, "but God alone can appease it."

The emperor backs down and later calls on Ambrose to serve as an ambassador and mediator. Some years later, Ambrose confronts Emperor Theodosius I. When rioters murder the Roman governor, Theodosius sends in troops and slaughters some seven thousand people. Ambrose is outraged and is prepared to excommunicate him. He backs down only when the emperor admits his guilt and repents. After several months of penance, he is permitted the Eucharist.

Characteristic of his ability to compromise and make peace, Ambrose holds to a form of universalism. In the end, he believes, all will find God. "Our Savior has appointed two kinds of resurrection in the Apocalypse," he argues. " 'Blessed is he that hath part in the first resurrection,' for such come to grace without the judgment. As for those who do not come to the first, but are reserved unto the second resurrection, these shall be disciplined until their appointed times, between the first and the second resurrection."

Most students of church history remember Ambrose as the great preacher who inspired Augustine. Having heard of his rhetorical skills, Augustine seeks him out. In fact, it was Augustine who prompted Ambrose's famous line, *When in Rome do as the Romans do.* When Augustine wonders why the churches in Milan do not follow Rome in fasting on Saturday, Ambrose responds: "When I am at Rome, I fast on a Saturday; when I am at Milan, I do not. Follow the custom of the Church where you are."

Augustine makes other personal references to Ambrose, including one that reminds moderns that reading silently to oneself was not always a common practice: "When he read, his eyes scanned the page and his heart sought out the meaning, but his voice was silent and his tongue was still. Anyone could approach him freely and guests were not commonly announced, so that often, when we came to visit him, we found him reading like this in silence, for he never read aloud."

Augustine, insightful in sizing up emotions (as is evident in his *Confessions*), analyzed his mentor: "Ambrose himself I esteemed a happy man, as the world counted happiness, because great personages held him in honor. Only his celibacy appeared to me a painful burden."

## Augustine: Saint for all Seasons

Augustine of Hippo (354 – 430) is one of the giants of church history. In the fifteen-hundred-year span between the apostle Paul and Martin Luther, no one looms larger in the minds of most Protestants. With the possible exception of Thomas Aquinas and John Calvin, his influence as a theologian is unparalleled. He was deeply entrenched in the theological debates of his day—debates that still invoke his name today. And his memoir, *Confessions,* is given a place in literature as the first recorded memoir. Augustine was an African, and it is fitting that this man of such great stature is still read and debated today, when the African church, having come full circle, is again a center of vibrancy and scholarship.

Much of what we know about Augustine from a personal perspective comes from his *Confessions.* But memoirs are, among other things, unreliable truth. He writes his story, as is often the case, long after the events have occurred. And like all memoirists, he presents a portrait of himself that offers lessons from a

Augustine and his mother, Monica

particular perspective. The theme moves from sin to salvation.

As a sexually charged youth, Augustine finds himself in "the thorny branches of sex and temptation trapped . . . in a briar patch that grew over my head." The reader might be surprised to read of this great saint lusting after naked street women in Carthage, "where a caldron of unholy loves was seething and bubbling around me." And he places himself at the center: "I was looking for something to love, and . . . so I took joy with the body of my lover, and so polluted the spring of friendship with the slime of lust." But if he struggled with sexual temptations after his garden conversion, he does not divulge that to the reader.

Before converting—or returning—to the Christian faith of his mother in which he had been reared, Augustine sows his wild oats for several years as an adherent of Manichaeism, a dualistic religion that reveres Jesus as well as Buddha and other prophets. As in Gnostic cults, in Manichaeism the spiritual realm is manifested in conflict between light and darkness—between spirit and body. There is no good God who reigns supreme or has the wherewithal to save sinners. Individuals are essentially on their own, seeking knowledge to save themselves. Reflecting back on these years, Augustine writes:

> I still thought that it is not we who sin but some other nature that sins within us. It flattered my pride to think that I incurred no guilt and, when I did wrong, not to confess it.... The truth, of course, was that it was all my own self, and my own impiety had divided me against myself. My sin was all the more incurable because I did not think myself a sinner.

Manichaeism eventually proves to be intellectually unsatisfying for the teacher of rhetoric and budding scholar. He turns to skepticism for a time, and then his interest in philosophy brings him (in the form of Neo-Platonism) to the feet of Plato, whose reputation from the grave had grown with every succeeding century. Here is a philosophy of transcendence—a secular spirituality extolling truth, goodness, and beauty. This intellectual shift parallels a geographical move from Carthage to Rome, in part to escape his meddling mother. From Rome he moves to Milan, where his mother joins him and soon becomes enamored with Ambrose and influences her son to attend his sermons. All the while, Augustine is moving away from his Manichaeism and philosophical worldview toward orthodox Christianity. His "garden conversion" is the spiritual climax—and the most quoted scene—of his memoir. In his *Confessions* (a prayer to God), he writes:

> I cast myself down, I know not how, under a fig-tree, giving full vent to my tears; and the floods of mine eyes gushed out, an acceptable sacrifice to Thee.... I spake much unto Thee: "And Thou, O Lord, how long? How long, Lord, wilt thou be angry, for ever?" ...

## AUGUSTINE, AUTOBIOGRAPHY, FICTION, PSYCHOLOGY

Then we reach Augustine, who tells us everything — his jealousies in infancy, his thieving as a boy, his stormy relationship with his overbearing mother (the ever-certain Monica), his years of philandering, his breakdowns, his shameful love for an unnamed peasant woman, whom he finally sends away. His self-loathing is as modern as that of a character in Camus or Beckett — and as concrete: "I carried inside me a cut and bleeding soul, and how to get rid of it I just didn't know."

No one had ever talked this way before. If we page quickly through world literature from its beginnings to the advent of Augustine, we realize that with Augustine human consciousness takes a quantum leap forward — and becomes self-consciousness. Here for the first time is a man consistently observing himself not as Man but as this singular man — Augustine. From this point on, true autobiography becomes possible, and so does its near relative, subjective and autobiographical fiction. Fiction had always been there, in the form of storytelling. But now for the first time there glimmers the possibility of psychological fiction: the subjective story, the story of a soul. Though the cry of Augustine — the Man Who Cried "I" — will seldom be heard again in full force until the early modern period, he is the father not only of autobiography but of the modern novel. He is also a distinguished forebear of the modern science of psychology.

Thomas Cahill, *How the Irish Saved Civilization*

So was I speaking, and weeping in the most bitter contrition of my heart, when, lo!, I heard from a neighboring house a voice, as of a boy or girl, I know not, chanting, and often repeating, "Take up, read; take up, read." Instantly my countenance altered and I began to think most intently, whether children were wont in any kind of play to sing such words, nor could I remember ever to have heard the like.

Augustine takes this as a sign from God, remembering St. Anthony, who, when he heard the words of the gospel, gave away his wealth and followed the Lord. So he returns to his friend Alypius (who is with him in the garden) and reaches for a manuscript of Paul they had been reading. And there his eyes fall on these words: "Not in rioting and drunkenness, not in chambering and wantonness, not in strife and envying: but put ye on the Lord Jesus Christ, and make not provision for the flesh in concupiscence" (Rom. 13:13–14).

"No further would I read, nor did I need to," he writes, "for instantly at the end of this sentence, by a light of serenity infused into my heart, all darkness of doubt fled away." Biographers and historians have pointed out that this was a conversion to a celibate monastic life as much as a recommitment to the Christian faith of his heritage and that it had been some time in coming. Indeed, some historians have suggested that the garden story is little more than symbolic fiction that Augustine imagined when he wrote it down some ten years later.

Another aspect of this story that is frequently highlighted (and sometimes challenged) is the fatherly role played by Ambrose. Augustine's life was supposedly turned around by listening to the powerful sermons of Ambrose, who convinced Augustine by pointing to the Jewish scriptures that prophesied of Christ. In reality,

Augustine found Ambrose to be a first-rate orator; it was style, not content, that enthralled him. But when Augustine sought out the bishop of Milan, he found him unapproachable — consumed with other matters (administration and diplomacy). "He was unaware of my seethings at the pit of peril," Augustine recalled. "I could not inquire of him what I wished, crowded out as I was from his hearing and speaking by a swarm of those with worldly needs, to whose demands he gave his attention."

Still another key aspect of Augustine's life is his relationship with his mother, Monica, and her influence on his conversion. In his *Confessions* he portrays himself as a young man seeking to escape an overbearing, meddling mother, nagging him about his wayward lifestyle and erroneous beliefs. He sails from Africa to Rome without informing her. From Rome he moves on to become a professor of rhetoric in Milan.

> And, soon enough, Augustine's mother will arrive on the scene [in Milan], creating, as she always does, emotional tornadoes and hurricanes — a sort of one-woman African *Sturm und Drang*.
>
> Thomas Cahill

So why does Augustine come across as the adoring son when penning his *Confessions*? That he had come full circle in returning to the Christian faith of his childhood is a factor. Likewise, Monica has been dead for several years when he eulogizes her. His gratitude for her is offered in a prayer to God:

That faithful servant of yours, my mother, came to you in my behalf with more tears than most mothers shed at a child's funeral. Her faith in you had made plain to her that I was spiritually dead. And you heard her, Lord.... You heard her and sent her a dream.... In her dream she saw herself standing on a kind of measuring rule or wooden yardstick, wailing and overcome with grief. A radiant young man approached her in a happy and laughing mood and asked her the reasons for all this protracted weeping.... She replied that she was mourning the ruin of my soul. He then admonished her and, in a reassuring way, ordered her to look more carefully and she would see that I was standing next to her on the same measuring rule.... When Mother told me about her dream, I tried to disparage it, saying I interpreted it to mean she shouldn't give up hope, because one day she would be as I was. She, however, came back at me immediately, saying, "No, it was not told me 'Where he is, there you will be,' but rather, 'Where you are, there he will be.'"... Nearly nine years were to pass during which I sank deeper into the mire and false darkness.... And all the while this devout, gentle, modest widow ... was heartened by this hope.

His mother's dream comes true on Easter Sunday 387, when her favorite preacher Ambrose baptizes not only Augustine but also her grandson Adeodatus. Augustine leaves behind his teaching position to immerse himself in Scripture for the next few years. He then returns to Africa to live in his hometown of Tasgate as a monk with his books and his theological contemplations. But the locals have other ideas. They recognize his capabilities and elect him to be their priest. Then, in 395, only eight years after his baptism, he is elected bishop of Hippo. Unlike many bishops of the era, he seeks to retain a monastic way of life while preaching several times a week and writing more than a thousand treatises in addition to extensive correspondence. His letters are primarily biblical and theological in nature but rarely without a personal touch—sometimes scolding and caustic. In an introductory letter to Jerome in 394, he writes with graciousness and warmth:

> Never was the face of any one more familiar to another, than the peaceful, happy, and truly noble diligence of your studies in the Lord has become to me. For although I long greatly to be acquainted with you, I feel that already my knowledge of you is deficient in respect of nothing but a very small part of you—namely, your personal appearance; and even as to this, I cannot deny that since my most blessed brother Alypius ... has seen you, and has on his return been seen by me, it has been almost completely imprinted on my mind by his report of you; nay, I may say that before his return, when he saw you there, I was seeing you myself with his eyes.

At times, Augustine is seething with rage—particularly when he is dealing with Donatists. The Donatist sect arose in the aftermath of the Great Persecution of Emperor Diocletian in the early years of the fourth century, fifty years before Augustine was born. The issue that bound Donatists together more than any other was how one responds in the face of persecution. Imperial officials demanded that Christians hand over the Scriptures under penalty of death. Some handed over their precious manuscripts; others refused and paid the penalty. Still others voluntarily stepped forward, baiting the officials by brashly refusing to surrender the Scriptures they claim to have hidden. In the eyes of many, these martyrs were hero saints, while those who surrendered were *traditors*.

How then should a *traditor* be disciplined by the church? Is it enough for a priest to say "I'm sorry" and go back to work administering the sacraments? The Donatists regarded denial of the faith to be the ultimate crime against the church and against God. Such an individual was no longer even part of the church. Penance was not enough. Only rebaptism by a "pure" bishop could restore the one to the true church. What had begun as a serious matter of church discipline deteriorated quickly into a cult of martyrs and shrines and relics, with a violent streak that lead to intervention by Constantine and his successors. In the end, the Donatists were suppressed.

In defense of priests and bishops who had surrendered the Scriptures, Augustine argues that the sacrament is valid irrespective of the sinfulness of the priest who administers it. He is not the first to hold this position, but he develops what will become official Catholic doctrine. The grace of Christ, he argues, is operative in the sacrament; thus the worthiness of the priest is irrelevant. Conferring grace through the sacraments finds theological support with Augustine.

But differences with Donatists are not doctrinal only. In some cases they are personal and are based on hearsay as much as solid facts. In a letter to Eusebius in 396, Augustine begins by emphasizing that he is a man of peace and that he does not wish "that any one should against his will be coerced into the Catholic communion." Rather, the truth should "so commend itself as to make them embrace and follow it." Then he becomes very specific and emotional in reporting a story. Not only do the Donatists preach another gospel, but they also open their doors to the most vile individuals. Indeed, the facts of this case are so despicable that Augustine's fury is almost palpable:

"What could be more worthy of detestation than what has just happened?" he demands. "A young man is reproved by his bishop for frequently beating his mother like a madman, and

not restraining his impious hands from wounding her who bore him." Augustine does not explain why the mother is not taken to a safe haven, but he reports that the man continues to "beat with incredible ferocity" and threatens to kill her. What does the man do next? He "then passes over to the Donatists, and is rebaptized while filled with wicked rage, and is arrayed in white vestments while he is burning to shed his mother's blood. He is placed in a prominent and conspicuous position within the railing in the church; and ... exhibited as a regenerate man."

Augustine praises Eusebius "as a man of most mature judgment" and "wisdom" and then demands to know: "Can these things find favor in your eyes?" He reminds Eusebius in this open letter that there are two mothers involved in this case: "A [biological] mother is wounded by ... the ungrateful wretch; and when the Church, his spiritual mother, interferes, she too is wounded in those sacraments by which, to the same ungrateful son, she ministered life and nourishment." Augustine rails against anyone who could so violate the church. Indeed, it appears that his primary concern is for the second of these mothers, and it leaves the literary critic wondering if the first mother might be more metaphorical than real.

> "Thou hast made us for thyself, and our hearts are restless till they find their rest in Thee."
> Augustine, *Confessions*

Countering heresies is a major focus of Augustine's writing, and the Donatists rank high on his list. But whether censuring Manichaeism or philosophical rationalism or Donatism, he is above all defending his Mother Church. The one-time eclectic freethinker is now solidly in the camp of orthodox Christianity—the One True Church. That Donatists dare make the same claim is as repugnant as it is heretical. Although he has earlier insisted that no one should be coerced into professing the true faith, he later argues that civil authority has not only the right but also the obligation to force heretical sects such as the Donatists back into the church. Without such unity, both the church and civil government are vulnerable to barbarian attacks from the outside. Such reasoning is later cited in defense of the terrorist tactics of the Inquisition.

> The first condition of happiness is that it be permanent. To love what can be lost is to live in fear. Freedom of fear, therefore, can be found only in the immutable possession of an unchanging object, and the only object independent of flux is God.
>
> Augustine

Augustine's most bitter theological controversies involve Pelagius, a devout and stout British monk, also born in 354, who catches the attention of both clerics and laity with his alluring emphasis on free will. Augustine's emphasis on God's sovereignty and election and human sinfulness is thought by some to be too deterministic. Pelagius, on the other hand, teaches that individuals are responsible for their sins, even as they are for their good deeds. That humans inherit original sin from Adam he deems patently false; whether one sins or not is a matter of self-control and choice, free will rather than determinism. Augustine counters that our sinful nature propels us to sin and that no one has the innate capability to do good.

Augustine's philosophical background thwarts any temptation he might have to offer easy theological answers—at least for the big-

gest question: Who is God? He knows above all else that God is entangled with mystery. "Since it is God we are speaking of," he cautions, "you do not understand it. If you could understand it, it would not be God."

On more down-to-earth matters, he is less hesitant to play the *mystery* card. He is quick to point out the close connection between original sin and sex. In his correspondence with Julian of Eclanum, a spirited young married priest, he argues that original sin is passed from one generation to the next not only through seminal fluid but also through the very act of sex itself. Since the fall, he reasons, sexual intercourse is a sin because it is no longer rationally controlled as it was in the Garden of Eden. Julian baits him by insisting sex is good and that he and his wife enjoy the activity whenever they desire. Augustine is outraged by such iniquity. He lives in perilous times. Life is serious. There is no time for frivolous entertainment, surely not sexual intimacies. At least not in a manner that would bring pleasure.

## Mary of Egypt: Sex Addict and Saint

Augustine's *Confessions* is often regarded as the ultimate fourth-century tell-all tale. But his story pales in comparison to that of Mary of Egypt (344–421). Like many such confessions, hers may have been embellished with sleazy stories for the desired effect: a scoundrel saved from the garbage pails of sin. However, few Christians, contemporary or ancient, have a more spellbinding story of redemption than does Mary.

Her narrative was passed on to a desert pilgrim, Father Zosimas, though not written down until St. Sophronius, the Patriarch of Jerusalem put it in print some two centuries after her death. The story is best told in her own words as she relates it during a chance meeting in the desert with Zosimas. She is naked and seems to appear out of nowhere. After some introductory small talk and spiritual salutations, Zosimas asks Mary to reveal her circumstances, and she bares her soul:

> I am ashamed.... But as you have already seen my naked body I shall likewise lay bare before you my work, so that you may know with what shame and obscenity my soul is filled.... Already during the lifetime of my parents, when I was twelve years old, I renounced their love and went to Alexandria.... For about seventeen years ... I was like a fire of public debauchery.... Then one summer I saw a large crowd of Lybians and Egyptians running towards the sea. I asked

one of them ... "Will they take me with them if I wish to go?" [He said], "No one will hinder you if you have money to pay for the journey and for food." And I said to him, "To tell you truth, I have no money, neither have I food. But I ... have a body.... Seeing some young men standing on the shore, about ten or more of them, full of vigour and alert in their movements, I decided that they would do for my purpose.... I frequently forced those miserable youths even against their own will. There is no mentionable or unmentionable depravity of which I was not their teacher.... At last we arrived in Jerusalem. I spent the days before the festival in the town, living the same kind of life.... The holy day of the Exaltation of the Cross dawned while I was still flying about—hunting for youths. At daybreak I saw that everyone was hurrying to the church, so I ran with the rest. When the hour for the holy elevation approached, I was trying to make my way in with the crowd which was struggling to get through the church doors.... But when I trod on the doorstep which everyone passed, I was stopped by some force which prevented my entering....

At this point Mary is stricken with remorse, and soon after she confesses her sin before an "icon of the most holy Mother of God." After that she crosses the Jordan and retreats into the desert, living as a hermit for forty-seven years until she meets Zosimas and tells her story. After her story is over, they go their separate ways with the promise to meet each year so that she can take communion from him. On one such appointed meeting, he finds her dead. She is today celebrated as a saint in both the Catholic and the Eastern Orthodox Church.

For the desert fathers and mothers, self-denial was the ultimate sign of holiness. They were sincerely striving for a deeper spiritual

Mary of Egypt with Father Zosimas

path. There is no doubt they truly loved God. Yet in the eyes of twenty-first century Christians, they are surely a strange lot. But how will we appear seventeen centuries hence?

---

## What if ....

What if Simon Stylites had never climbed atop a pillar? What if Mary of Egypt had not become a Christian and changed her errant ways? Have the stories of their lives made an impact on the Christian faith?

What if Jerome had not translated the Bible into the Latin Vulgate? That volume served the church for many centuries, and it is difficult to imagine the medieval — or Reformation — church without it.

What if Ambrose, innocently standing in the midst of a mass of people in a Milan sports arena, had walked away — and kept on walking — when the crowd started screaming his name for bishop?

What if his hiding place not been discovered, and he would not have been in a position to sway Augustine to follow in his footsteps?

What if Augustine had gone the way of the Manicheans and put his persuasive powers to work for that cultic movement? What if he had not become such an influential theologian and if Pelagius had prevailed instead? It is difficult to imagine the Reformation playing out as it did without the profound influence of Augustine. Luther, an Augustinian monk, drew heavily from him, as did Calvin and Knox and countless Puritans and others in the generations that followed.

## Further Reading

Athanasius. *The Life of Antony and the Letter To Marcellinus.* Translated and edited by Robert C. Gregg. Mahwah, N.J.: Paulist Press, 1979.

Augustine. *Confessions.* New York: Oxford University, 1998.

Brakke, David. *Demons and the Making of the Monk: Spiritual Combat in Early Christianity.* Cambridge, Mass.: Harvard University Press, 2006.

Brown, Peter. *Society and the Holy in Late Antiquity.* Berkeley: University of California Press, 1982.

Chitty, Derwas. *The Desert: A City.* Crestwood, N.Y.: St. Vladimir's Seminary Press, 1997.

Clark, Gillian. *This Female Man of God: Women and Spiritual Power in the Patristic Age, AD 350–450.* New York: Routledge, 1995.

Dietz, Maribel. *Wandering Monks, Virgins, and Pilgrims: Ascetic Travel in the Mediterranean World, A.D. 300–800.* University Park, Pa.: Penn State University, 2005.

Dunn, Marilyn. *The Emergence of Monasticism: From the Desert Fathers to the Early Middle Ages.* Oxford: Blackwell, 2000.

Goehring, James E. *Ascetics, Society, and the Desert: Studies in Early Egyptian Monasticism.* Harrisburg, Pa.: Trinity Press International, 1999.

Green, Michael. *Evangelism in the Early Church,* rev. ed. Grand Rapids: Eerdmans, 2004.

Luckman, Harriet A., and Linda Kulzer, eds. *Purity of Heart in Early Ascetic and Monastic Literature.* Collegeville, Minn.: Liturgical Press, 1999.

Ramsey, Boniface. *Ambrose.* New York: Routledge, 1997.

Rebenich, Stefan. *Jerome.* New York: Routledge, 2002.

Wills, Garry. *Saint Augustine: A Life.* New York: Penguin, 2005.

# CHAPTER 5

# City of God in the "Dark Ages"

## Benedict to Gregory the Great

*The funniest book I have ever read is John Kennedy Toole's* A Confederacy of Dunces, *often labeled a cult classic. The main character, Ignatius Reilly, is a slob. He's not just grossly overweight and a sloppy dresser with serious intestinal and gas issues, but he's lazy and disrespectful and—though it's hard to believe—incredibly arrogant. His primary occupation is writing his book, each section beginning with "Dear Reader." But finally his mother pushes her freeloading son out to get a job. He works for a time in a pants factory and then pushes a hotdog-cart, a job that ends abruptly when his employer discovers he is eating all the profits.*

*What I find most amusing about the book is that Ignatius, himself a philosopher of sorts, looks to Boethius, the early medieval author of* The Consolation of Philosophy, *as his idol. I had memorized the name Boethius in order to pass a college philosophy test, but I had never given him further thought until I read this novel.*

*A late riser, Ignatius, lying in bed, "pulled his flannel nightshirt up and looked at his bloated stomach . . . contemplating the unfortunate turn that events had taken since the Reformation." He is worried about his bad fortune, fearing he will go the way of Boethius and be tortured and killed.*

*Later in the book the "large, elegant, limited edition" of* The Consolation of Philosophy *is used as a weapon by a crime suspect about to be arrested by an undercover policeman. Still later, the name Boethius serves as a pick-up line for Ignatius, who meets Miss O'Hara, a "Boethian" stripper, in a dirty, dingy nightclub. The last time we hear of the book, we learn that "somebody stole it off him in the toilet"—a key piece of evidence in a conspiracy against Ignatius.*

*Of all the medieval writers, Boethius is truly the most accessible today, and thanks to Ignatius Reilly,* The Consolation of Philosophy *has enjoyed a bit of a revival in recent years.*

History with its flickering lamp stumbles along the trail of the past,
trying to reconstruct its scenes, to revive its echoes,
and kindle with pale gleams the passion of former days.
WINSTON CHURCHILL

The rocky road between ancient and medieval times, peppered with potholes, affords no mile markers or signposts. The church stumbles along, its flickering lamp casting shadows along the trail of the past as it tries to reconstruct its scenes, revive its echoes, and kindle the passion it once possessed. The glories of the ancient days, however, can never be recovered — most notably "Christian" Rome. Like Humpty Dumpty, the city has had a great fall, and all the king's horses and all the king's men can never put Rome back together again.

Augustine stands spread-eagled, like a colossus, straddling both the fourth and the fifth centuries. His immensely influential *City of God* seeks to explain the great calamities that have come upon the world from his — and from God's — perspective. Other important figures arrive later on the scene to make their imprints not only on the church but in political, military, and economic affairs as well. This is a time when church and state are struggling through courtship conflicts, going their separate ways in anger, and then finding romance again. Most rulers after the era of Constantine had close

Christian connections. The on-again, off-again courtship of church and state is seen in the lives of the leading figures of the age, including Boethius, Pope Leo I, Benedict, Pope Gregory the Great, and Saint Patrick.

By the beginning of the fifth century the church was well established in Rome, a cultural center as well as the financial hub of the entire region. The statement "All roads lead to Rome" was not an exaggeration. In the century before the birth of Christ, manual laborers and slaves had constructed a vast network of concrete roads leading to and from the city. Churches and government buildings, constructed from stone and concrete, were made to last. They demonstrated the marvels of advanced engineering, as did the hundreds of miles of underground aqueducts providing water for agricultural and industrial enterprises as well as for private homes, public fountains, sewers, and the city's celebrated baths.

Situated on seven hills, Rome was home not only to the Coliseum, the Forum, the Pantheon, and other government edifices, but also to aristocrats living in palatial wooded estates as well

## PARADE OF HISTORY

The western church of the fifth century seems almost to retreat, as wave after wave of barbarian marauders march into Rome. But amid the desecration there are bright spots. Martin of Tours is parading his cavalry regiment through the countryside of France when his life is instantly transformed in an encounter with Christ in the form of a beggar. Patrick, taken as a slave to Ireland, escapes and returns to Britain only to courageously march back to Ireland as a missionary. Today no saint outranks him for sheer parade power, as cities around the world celebrate St. Patrick's Day.

as teeming masses of manual laborers packed into crowded inner-city ghettos. With a population of a million, Rome was the most economically diverse and cosmopolitan city of the age. What other location in the era of Emperor Constantine afforded the church so many resources for consolidation and expansion? Indeed, Constantine's ambitious program of basilica building was remarkable, and the name *Christian* carried prestige. The once rag-tag church on the run was now holding its head high.

But storm clouds had been brewing on the horizon — and not for the church only. Despite efforts to ratchet up homeland security, terrorists were penetrating the leaky borders. It would be simplistic to compare the centuries-old Roman Empire with a twentieth-century superpower, but there are some similarities; and the sack of Rome on August 24, 410, was similar in some respects to New York City's 9–11. As was the case in New York, Rome had been previously attacked, and more attacks should have been expected. But there was a sense of invincibility. Alaric, like Osama bin Laden, reigned over innumerable terrorist cells and was hiding a stash of weapons. But it was presumed that the empire, with its powerful military advantage,

---

## WHAT DOES A BARBARIAN USE FOR KINDLING?

From time to time, a tribe of barbarians roared into Rome and made a terrible mess. Since these stalwart fellows largely lacked written languages, they did not understand about libraries. What was the use of having huge rooms stacked full of crackly stuff rolled around a stick? These weird objects burned very easily, however, and the wisdom of the ages went to kindle campfires.

Rose Williams,
*The Lighter Side of the Dark Ages*

---

would prevail. "Mission accomplished" would be prematurely emblazoned on the banners flying over the capital.

As is true today, there was in Roman culture a disturbing penchant for casting blame, for trying to make sense of the catastrophic events from a sociological and theological and historical perspective. Pagans blamed Christians (who had enjoyed preferential status for most of a century) for what was wrong in the empire, including their lack of military service and their useless monastic escape to the desert.

---

## FALL OF ROME

The story of its ruin is simple and obvious; and, instead of inquiring why the Roman empire was destroyed, we should rather be surprised that it had subsisted so long.... As the happiness of a future life is the great object of religion, we may hear, without surprise or scandal, that the introduction, or at least the abuse, of Christianity had some influence on the decline and fall of the Roman empire. The clergy successfully preached the doctrines of patience and [weakness]; the active virtues of society were discouraged; and the last remains of the military spirit were buried in the cloister; a large portion of public and private wealth was consecrated to the [cloister]...; the church, and even the state, were distracted by religious factions, whose conflicts were sometimes bloody, and always implacable; the attention of the emperors was diverted from camps to synods....

Edward Gibbon, *The Decline and Fall of the Roman Empire*

Augustine shot back, arguing that Rome had long been a decadent city. In his philosophy of history, *The City of God,* he interpreted history in light of God's redemptive acts, pointing to the struggle between the heavenly city and the earthly city symbolized by Jerusalem and Babylon. Though a laborious tome, it served to guide both scholars and clerics for more than a millennium.

A generation earlier, when the Roman army was overwhelmed at Adrianople in 378, Ambrose of Milan drew his conclusion from an Old Testament prophet. The enemy, he speculated, was the very Gog of which Ezekiel had warned: "The end of the world is coming upon us," he wailed.

While Augustine argued that Christians should not be blamed for the fall of Rome — that pagans themselves were culpable — his two-city model did not encourage Christians to actively defend the worldly empire. Unlike Jerome, Augustine did not painfully lament the fall of Rome. Indeed, he saw Rome in all its materialistic glory and rebellion against God as the epitome of worldliness. The heavenly City of God, on the other hand, was centered on spiritual things. Nevertheless, Augustine's magnum opus not only served medieval monasticism well but also set the stage for the growing power of the Roman Catholic Church.

Speculation on the causes of the decline and fall of the Roman Empire were rife in the fifth century and following. One story widely circulated pointed a finger at the emperor himself. According to Procopius, the palace at Ravenna was occupied by nothing less than imperial fools. When informed by his chief of staff that Rome had perished, Emperor Honorius wailed in anguish, "Tis not an hour [has passed since] she was feeding from my hand," imagining that his pet chicken by that name had died. When the official explained to him that he had been referring to the metropolis of Rome, the emperor was relieved.

## ULFILAS AND MISSION OUTREACH

Some imagine that Alaric's military attacks on Rome came from irreligious barbarians. In actuality most of them were professing Christians whose conversion to the faith was prompted by the ministry of Ulfilas (c. 310–383). Born one hundred years before Alaric's sack of Rome, Ulfilas had been deeply concerned about the warlike ways of the Gothic peoples he had come to serve. Indeed, so concerned was he that when he translated the Bible into their language he omitted the books of Samuel and Chronicles because of their militaristic content. But any such lack of biblical support for their warring ways did not deter these Goths in battle.

Even if these barbarians were Christians, they were Arians and thus shunned by the Roman Church — worse in the minds of many than out-and-out pagans. Jerome, with strong anti-Arian bias, sarcastically describes them: "Those who had formerly used wagons for dwellings, now use a wagon for a church." What did they learn in their wagon churches? Here is the creed of Ulfilas:

I, Ulfila, bishop and confessor, have always so believed, and in this, the one true faith, I make the journey to my Lord; I believe in one God the Father, the only unbegotten and invisible, and in his only-begotten son, our Lord and God, the designer and maker of all creation, having none other like him (so that one alone among all beings is God the Father, who is also the God of our God); and in one Holy Spirit, the illuminating and sanctifying power....

## The Coming of Territorial Christianity

In earlier Christian history, in the Christianity of the old Roman Empire, conversion, sealed by baptism, marked a person's entrance into a new community. In the experience of northern and western Europe, Christian conversion led rather to a symbolic reordering of the community already existing.

This is the birthplace of territorial Christianity, the origin of the idea of the Christian nation. No Constantine, no Theodosius, could have envisaged the form of the territorial Christianity that developed in the north. The Roman Empire that they ruled had too much diversity, too many interest groups, too much inbuilt pluralism, to sustain anything of the kind. But the northern peoples, with no easy way of dividing sacred and profane custom, produced territorial Christianity by their need to have a single body of custom. A single people must follow a single code.

To this extent, territorial Christianity reflected the continuation of a principle inherent in the primal cultures of the north. But it also transcended these cultures.... In a sense the church continued the Roman Empire; if Rome had lost imperial political significance, it was still the set of the Empire of Christ.... In entering the Christian faith the peoples of the north and west entered a wider universe, recognized wider kinships, than they had done before: a single assembly of Christian princes and peoples, a single church, a single sacred language, a single tradition of learning.

Andrew F. Walls, *The Cross-Cultural Process in Christian History*

Alaric I is often identified as the one individual most responsible for the Fall of Rome. Born into a Gothic military family of Arian Christians, he rose to the rank of a Visigoth warrior king whose military expertise served the Roman Empire well until he, with good reasons, turned against his employer. His aim, however, was never to bring Rome to ruins. Far from it. He aspired to be the empire's leading general, and for that role he was willing to negotiate. But Honorius was more concerned about his own safety than that of Rome. Alaric and his hoards of backwoods soldiers and their women and children simply moved into the city. Rape and murder were uncommon, but fear was everywhere.

Alaric died soon after his army sacked Rome and before he realized his goal of occupying North Africa. The barbarian invaders who followed in his wake appeared to have no misgivings about rape and murder and pillage. Then, in 476, a German warrior chief forced Emperor Romulus Augustus to abdicate his throne, thus ending once and for all the Western Roman Empire that had spanned continents for some twelve hundred years. Fleeing the barbarian hordes, many of the urban dwellers escaped to North Africa or into the European countryside, leaving behind all the lavish wealth and conveniences of old Rome.

Despite the devastation in 410, Rome would remain an important center of church activities, though by the end of the fifth century the population had dropped to some fifty thousand. The bishop of Rome had for some time been recognized as the "first among equals" (the other "equals" being the bishops of Antioch, Alexandria, Constantinople, and Jerusalem). The recognition of the bishop of Rome as pope, however, would not be fully developed until the time of Leo I, who set forth not only the primacy of Rome but also the supreme power of the pope. He was an administrative genius who strongly defended Rome and is remembered

## The Backwoods of the "Dark Ages"

The term *Dark Ages,* long used to identify the early Middle Ages and no longer politically correct, is not without justification. Civilization seemed to go in reverse and retreat into the back woods. "What is there to please us in this world?" Pope Gregory lamented. "Everywhere we see sorrow and lamentation. The cities and towns are destroyed, the fields are laid waste and the land returns to solitude. No peasant is left to till the fields, there are few inhabitants left in the cities, and yet even these scanty remnants of humanity are still subject to ceaseless sufferings.... Some are led away captive, others are mutilated and still more slain before our eyes."

It is difficult to exaggerate the backward fall of civilization into the "Dark Ages." The high civilizations of classical Greece and Rome had virtually disappeared in many regions in the generations after the sack of Rome. Outside the Mediterranean world, Europe was populated with primitive bands of warring barbarians who had no established towns or written languages, not even stone architecture. Nor were there organized political or religious entities. Indeed, Europe was largely a cultural vacuum.

Enter the church. With military and missionary power combined, the Christian faith, beginning in the fifth century, would move north even as barbarians were pushing south. Once a Mediterranean religion, Christianity would spread throughout the whole of Europe. A vast army of missionary monks, initially commissioned by Gregory, brought their culture with them: education, agriculture, politics, and law, all under the umbrella of the Christian faith. Indeed, Pope Gregory I is sometimes identified as the Father of Western Culture.

The monks not only brought Latin culture, but they also helped restore the ruined countryside by tilling the soil and introducing new agricultural methods. Monasteries were

### LIFE IN THE VAST WESTERN BACKWOODS

The new Western world which emerged, the world of the first half of the Middle Ages, was to be a world where countrysides were vastly more important than towns — which indeed shrank to a vanishing point — and where life was a very primitive thing and a great contrast to life in the centuries-old urban civilization of the Hellenistic East where the Church was born and for four hundred years had its first developments. This world of peasants and country-bred, fighting warrior-lords and barbarian princes was an all but illiterate world, and the language they spoke was moving ever further and further away, not from the tongue of Cicero only, but from anything that resembled grammatical Latin.... Life in this vast Western backwoods — on this vast frontier — was hard and cruel, of course; filled with all the violent crime one cares to imagine.

Philip Hughes, *A Popular History of the Reformation*

farms and schools of learning all in one. It is incorrect, however, to imagine Christianity coming via Latin higher learning. Rather, it came largely through what has been described as Christian mythology or the cult of the saints—a cult dependent on relics and associated miracles. The faith was often introduced through power encounter, with monks countering shamans on their own terms.

for his diplomatic coup in meeting Attila the Hun outside the city walls in 452, successfully convincing the barbarian general not to sack the city.

## Leo I: First *Real* Pope

Born into an aristocratic family ten years before the sack of Rome, Leo (c. 400–461) was singled out by the emperor to serve as a diplomatic envoy in settling a dispute in Gaul. While he was away, the bishop of Rome died, and Leo was unanimously elected to fill the post. He moved quickly to secure power, insisting that popes were in a direct line of succession from the apostles and that anyone who rejected papal authority was not within the "body of Christ." He consolidated this authority by moving against heretics, particularly Pelagians and Manicheans.

Leo, in the judgment of many historians was the first *real* pope. The term *pope* (*papas* in Greek) did not always specify the head of the church. It was used for bishops and even more broadly as a term of respect for church officials. But beginning with Leo, the term began to be used almost exclusively for the bishop of Rome. Less than a century earlier, Damasus I (who authorized the Vulgate translation) sought to elevate his position as bishop of Rome to head of the church. But true papal supremacy was not clearly defined until the reign of Leo, coming to full bloom under Gregory I.

Leo's rule was theological as well as political. As was true in earlier centuries, so-called heretics often served to clarify doctrine. Such was the case when Leo received a letter in 448 from Eutyches, an abbot in a monastery near Constantinople. Eutyches writes of the influence of the Nestorian heresy (that separated Christ's two natures by insisting God could not be a baby in a manger). But then he himself comes under fire for allegedly subscribing to the same heresy and is excommunicated by Bishop Flavian. He asks Leo to reinstate him, and when Leo fails to act, he is absolved in a "robber council," an action that is perceived to be a threat to papal power and is promptly annulled by Leo—supported by Emperor Theodosius II (of the East).

In 449 Leo writes a letter to Bishop Flavian. This "Tome of Leo" becomes a key document as the church continues to define orthodoxy at the Council of Chalcedon in 451. Here Leo's definition of the two natures of Christ is deemed the orthodox position. He illustrates the problem by referencing the "scandal" relating to Eutyches. The abbot seeks to "dissolve Jesus" in his endeavor "to separate the human nature from him, and to make void by shameless inventions that mystery by which alone we have been saved." Leo charges Eutyches with "senseless blindness with regard to his Passion" in thinking "the Lord's crucifixion to be unreal."

Eutyches is anything but a rookie just out of seminary. He is seventy years old and the head of a monastery of some three hundred monks. He refuses to appear before Bishop Flavian, convinced that the deck is stacked against him. When he finally does appear and is questioned, he waffles on precisely what he is willing to confess. But the statement he makes leaves no doubt among the supporters of Leo that he is a heretic. "I confess that our Lord was of two natures before the union, but after the union I confess one nature."

Leo regards such a confession as blatant heresy, not only "absurd and perverse" but also "extremely foolish and extremely blasphemous." He seeks to clarify the incarnation and the two-fold nature of Christ with words that rise above dry dogma:

> Without detriment therefore to the properties of either nature and substance which then came together in one person, majesty took on humility, strength weakness, eternity mortality: and for the paying off of the debt belonging to our condition inviolable nature was united with possible nature, so that, as suited the needs of our case, one and the same Mediator between God and men, the Man Christ

Jesus, could both die with the one and not die with the other.

Heresy is not the only matter weighing Leo down. Only a few years after the landmark Council of Chalcedon, he is facing a desperate situation in Rome—those pesky barbarians again threatening to sack the city. Attila, nicknamed "the scourge of God," is making his way to Rome. One early account serves to establish Leo as "the Great" for the centuries that follow. According to the anonymous author, Attila "came into Italy, inflamed with fury, after he had laid waste with most savage frenzy Thrace and Illyricum, Macedonia and Moesia, Achaia and Greece, Pannonia and Germany. He was utterly cruel in inflicting torture, greedy in plundering, insolent in abuse." Leo, in his fifties, stands strong. Though he might have objected to the way he is portrayed, his saintliness is secure:

> The old man of harmless simplicity, venerable in his gray hair and his majestic garb, ready of his own will to give himself entirely for the defense of his flock, went forth to meet the tyrant ... and he spoke to the grim monarch, saying "The senate and the people of Rome, once conquerors of the world, now indeed vanquished, come before thee as suppliants. We pray for mercy and deliverance. O Attila, thou king of kings ... the people have felt thy scourge; now as suppliants they would feel thy mercy."
>
> As Leo said these things ... suddenly there were seen the apostles Peter and Paul, clad like bishops, standing by Leo, the one on

Pope Leo the Great meets Attalia

the right hand, the other on the left. They held swords stretched out over his head, and threatened Attila with death if he did not obey the pope's command. Wherefore Attila ... straightway promised a lasting peace and withdrew beyond the Danube.

That Leo served both as head of state and chief diplomat demonstrated the weakness of Imperial Rome since the events of 410. But his talking down Attila surely did not signal the end of the invasions of the city. Some years later, Vandal marauders moving northward from Africa pillaged the city despite Leo's pleas. For the next years, until his death in 461, he took charge of cleanup and restoration as well as ministering to those who had been taken captive to Africa.

## Benedict of Nursia: Father of Western Monasticism

Today in the Catholic Church the Feast of St. Benedict is celebrated on July 11, and Benedictine monasticism flourishes around the world. Born into a prosperous family in northern Italy, Benedict (480–550) grew up with his twin sister, Scholastica, who later founded a sister order of Benedictines and is also heralded as a saint.

As a young man, Benedict traveled to Rome seeking education and spiritual development, but all he finds is worldliness. Disgusted with the increasing wealth of the church, he soon leaves town, seeking solitude. Setting out for a remote mountainous region, he tells no one but a family servant who insists on joining him and caring for his needs. So the young man, not

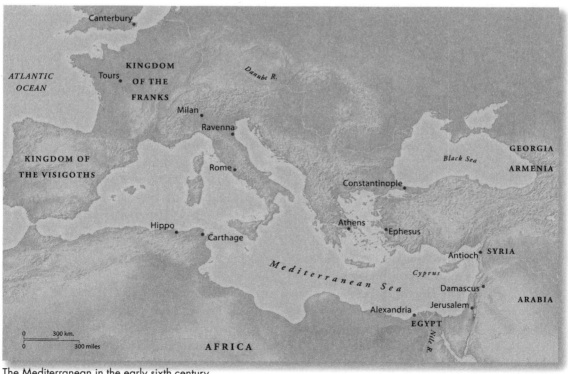

The Mediterranean in the early sixth century

yet twenty, trudges north with an old woman. While stopping in a village along the way, the old woman breaks a clay jar and then tells the locals that Benedict has miraculously restored it.

Not wanting to gain fame as a miracle-worker, he leaves the garrulous servant behind and sets out alone to live a life of solitude. On his way he meets Romanus, a resident monk in a small monastery who agrees to show him the way of a hermit. The monk supplies him with a warm hooded robe fashioned from animal skins and helps him find a cave overhanging a cliff. Each day for the next three years Romanus brings a portion of his own meal and lowers it by basket from above. Benedict is left entirely alone to his solitary thoughts.

Miracle stories are later associated with these three years of solitude. On the first Easter Sunday, for example, a priest preparing for his own celebratory feast hears a voice saying: "Thou art preparing thyself a savoury dish while my servant Benedict is afflicted with hunger." With these words, the priest is out the door in search of the hungry man. He finds him, and together they enjoy an Easter picnic. In other instances the voices and visions—including one of an alluring woman—are from Satan, as his biographer Pope Gregory recounts:

Benedict of Nursia

> On a certain day when he was alone the tempter presented himself. A small dark bird, commonly called a blackbird, began to fly around his face and came so near him that, if he had wished, he could have seized it with his hand. But on his making the sign of the cross, the bird flew away. Then followed a violent temptation of the flesh, such as he had never before experienced. The evil spirit brought before his imagination a woman whom he had formerly seen, and inflamed his heart with such vehement desire at the memory of her

that he had very great difficulty in repressing it. He was almost overcome and thought of leaving his solitude. Suddenly, however, with the help of divine grace, he found the strength he needed. Seeing near at hand a thick growth of briars and nettles, he stripped off his habit and cast himself into the midst of them and plunged and tossed about until his whole body was lacerated. Thus, through those bodily wounds, he cured the wounds of his soul.

Later, as Benedict ventures out of his cave, he is spotted by shepherds. News of the hermit sighting quickly spreads, and pilgrims make their way to the cave offering food and seeking counsel. Among those who climb the cliffs are a band of monks begging Benedict to become their abbot. He agrees, only to realize that his strict asceticism does not agree with their careless ways. In fact, so repugnant is his discipline that they poison his wine. But as he makes the sign of the cross over his glass, it miraculously breaks, spilling on the floor. Forgiving them, he asks: "Why have you plotted this wicked thing against me? Did I not tell you beforehand that my ways would not accord with yours? Go and find an abbot to your taste." With those words he leaves and returns to his cave.

Hearing of this fiasco—and miracle—more pilgrims arrive, many wishing to follow him in strict discipline. For Benedict this is an answered prayer. He realizes that solitude is not the way of discipleship. He is now prepared to organize a community. In the succeeding years he establishes monastic houses of twelve monks each. Along the way, he performs miracles. When a monk is clearing land along a lakeshore, the head of his axe flies off and lands deep in the water. When Benedict lowers the wooden handle into the water, "immediately from the bottom rose the iron head and fastened itself in the shaft."

But troubles are never far away. His success causes animosities with a local priest who, according to Gregory, sends him a gift of poisoned bread and induces lewd women to tempt his monks. Convinced that he must move on, Benedict abandons his twelve monastic houses and travels with a small group of disciples to an even more remote area that lies in ruins from the devastation of the marauding Goths, its inhabitants having reverted to paganism. Soon Benedict and his disciples are preaching the wrath of God and tearing down the pagan altars. In the ruins of the pagan temple they build the monastic compound of Monte Cassino. Again pilgrims arrive, pleading to join the brotherhood and the movement rapidly expands.

In the years that follow, the one-time cave-dweller amasses large tracts of land, villas, and churches, as wealthy benefactors donate their property. His popularity and reputation as a holy man of miracles swells. Travelers come from great distances just to be in his presence.

More significant than money and land and increasing numbers of disciples is Benedict's Rule. Having previously borrowed guidelines from other monastic leaders, he is determined to write a rule that mirrors his own principles. The Rule requires that followers relinquish their wills in submission to authority—that being "the strong armor of obedience, to fight under our Lord Christ." But overall, the rule is judicious in its way of monastic living. The first sentence of the document promises that "we shall ordain nothing severe and nothing burdensome."

The monk's daily life is a combination of solitude and community living. Times of prayer

## THE RULE OF BENEDICT IN NORTH DAKOTA

Few books have so strongly influenced Western history as the Rule of St. Benedict.... I met the Rule by happy accident, when I found myself staying in a small Benedictine convent during a North Dakota Council on the Arts residency at a Catholic school.... I felt it necessary to tell the sisters, however, that I wasn't much of a churchgoer, had a completely Protestant background, and knew next to nothing about them.... The sisters listened politely and then one of them said, with a wit I'm just learning to fathom, "Would you like to read our Rule?" .... What happened to me then has no doubt happened to many unsuspecting souls in the fifteen-hundred-plus years that Benedictines have existed. Quite simply, the Rule spoke to me.

Kathleen Norris, *The Cloister Walk*

and liturgy are balanced with manual labor, study, and communal activities. "Idleness is the enemy of the soul," Benedict warns in the Rule. "At set times, accordingly, the brethren should be occupied with manual work, and again, at set times, with spiritual reading." The monks fast until their noonday meal and even then are not allowed to eat meat. But austere asceticism is strongly discouraged. When a monk chained himself to a rock, Benedict sent word: "If thou art truly a servant of God, chain thyself not with a chain of iron but with a chain of Christ."

Despite the rule, internal conflicts continued. Indeed, Benedict's troubles were not over. The lands that had been reclaimed for Christianity were once again overrun by marauding hoards, this time the Lombards. The monastery was attacked and the monks were in danger. But the Rule of Benedict lived on, serving as the primary monastic guide for some five hundred years.

## Boethius: A Medieval Modern Man

In many ways, Anicius Manlius Severinus Boethius (c. 480–524) stands apart from all other great Christian thinkers and writers before the Renaissance. A Christian whose worldview surely influenced his writing, he did not write or translate Christian books per se as did those who came before and after him; his writings have a more *secular* feel. He was born into a centuries-old aristocratic family, a nursery for popes and emperors and other high officials. Like his father, he was a Roman consul, as were both of his own sons. But before he died when Boethius was seven, his father had also been a teacher in Alexandria. With his father's books, he was likely home-schooled in the classics in either Alexandria or Athens. Whatever the mode

of his education, it is clear from his writing that he enjoyed well-rounded classical learning.

With a government appointment, Boethius ventures into scholarly endeavors as a true renaissance man. He translates scholarly Greek works into Latin on topics ranging from philosophy and theology and astronomy to math and music. His dream is to translate all the works of Aristotle and Plato, but his life is cut short. Religious convictions and ethical principles prompt him to take a stand that he knows will enrage Theodoric of Italy, the very king who has granted him and his sons their government offices. The Arian controversy is still dragging on, and the king is allied with Arians. Boethius, true to his orthodox faith, is accused of plotting against Theodoric and supporting the Eastern emperor.

In 523 he is charged with treason, imprisoned, and brutally executed the following year. A contemporary observer offers a clipped account of what happened: "He was tortured for a very long time by a cord that was twisted round his forehead so that his eyes started from his head. Then at last amidst his torments he was killed with a club."

During the preceding year of imprisonment, Boethius wrote his masterpiece, *The Consolation of Philosophy*, the most widely read philosophy book of the Middle Ages, still very readable today. The book begins with a poem that reflects on the joys of his past pleasures and his present state of suffering:

> To pleasant songs my work was erstwhile given,
> and bright were all my labours then;
> but now in tears to sad refrains
> am I compelled to turn.

He laments his loss of companions, who had been "the pride of my earlier bright-lived days." And he laments his old age: "White hairs are scattered untimely on my head, and the skin hangs loosely from my worn-out limbs." But he is not just an old man facing hard times. He is in prison waiting execution:

> Fortune's fickle bounty,
> and while yet she smiled upon me,
> the hour of gloom
> had well-nigh overwhelmed my head. . . .
> Why, O my friends, did ye so often puff
>     me up,
> telling me that I was fortunate?
> For he that is fallen low
> did never firmly stand.

Here is Boethius, in his final days, receiving consolation from a visionary friend, Lady Philosophy: "While I was pondering thus in silence, and using my pen to set down so tearful a complaint, there appeared standing over my head a woman's form." Lady Philosophy is here to diagnose — and to cure — his disease. Indeed, she rebukes him for his poetic lines and reminds him that he had been "nourished upon the milk of my learning, brought up with my food until you had won your way to the power of a manly soul."

But now he is wallowing in self-pity, forgetting the "weapons as would keep you safe." With her opening words, the "dark night [was] dispelled, the shadows fled away, and my eyes received returning power as before." It is only now that Boethius is recognizing who this visionary woman is:

> So when I turned my eyes towards her and fixed my gaze upon her, I recognized my nurse, Philosophy, in whose chambers I had spent my life from earliest manhood. And I asked her, "Wherefore have you, mistress of all virtues, come down from heaven above to visit my lonely place of banishment? Is it that you, as well as I, may be harried, the victim of false charges?" "Should I," said she, "desert you, my nursling?"

Using the dialectical method, Lady Philosophy questions Boethius regarding the guidance and direction of the universe. Boethius answers that he does not know if God is actively involved, to which Lady Philosophy responds that his very answer allows her to diagnose his disease. He has forgotten who he is and what his place is in the universe. How, she wonders aloud, does he presume to know the beginning but not the end and purpose of all things. She reminds him that his attitude toward his misfortune is misguided — that happiness comes from within rather than from outward circumstances. No outside power — not even the king who has wrongly imprisoned him — has the power to destroy inner peace that comes from God. All that which is derived from wealth and power is fleeting and does not offer real happiness.

At the beginning of Book III, Boethius praises Lady Philosophy: "Greatest comforter of weary minds, how have you cheered me with your deep thoughts and sweet singing too! No more shall I doubt my power to meet the blows of Fortune."

In their conversations, the two deal with the age-old conundrum of evil — its source and how a good God can permit evil. Boethius also raises questions about predestination, free will, and chance. What does God know and determine, and what is left to free will and chance? Throughout the four books are prayers, particularly prayers for understanding:

> Grant then, O Father, that this mind of ours may rise to Thy throne of majesty; grant us to reach that fount of good. Grant that we may so find light that we may set on Thee unblinded eyes; cast Thou therefrom the heavy clouds of this material world. Shine forth upon us in Thine own true glory.

Despite his acclaim throughout the medieval period and beyond, Boethius has been largely lost to the modern-day student of church history. However, his words and his questions are as relevant today as they were nearly fifteen centuries ago. Of this great masterpiece, C. S. Lewis wrote: "Until about two hundred years ago it would, I think, have been hard to find an educated man in any European country who did not love it." The legacy of Boethius was most appropriately a gift bestowed on Christian scholars in the generations following his own. These "Dark Ages" caused many to wonder where, indeed, was the hand of God.

## Gregory the Great: Pope and Politician

Like Pope Leo and Boethius, Gregory (c. 540–604) descended from Roman nobility and was himself a propertied government administrator. But the church was in his blood. Three aunts were nuns, as was his widowed mother, Silvia; and all four of them were canonized as saints. His great-great-grandfather was Pope Felix III, uncle of Pope Agapitus.

Gregory was a young boy when Benedict died and had given no consideration to becoming a Benedictine monk. He would rather follow his father into government service. Although reared in moderate wealth, he knows nothing of a carefree and lavish lifestyle. Wave after wave of barbarian armies have brought ruin to

S·GREGORIVS·I·MAGNVS·ROMANVS

Pope Gregory I

the region. His dream is to escape, though not to the monastery. "Late and long," he recalled, "I put off the grace of conversion." But in his mid-thirties he leaves behind his government post, donates his property to charity, and sets out to establish Benedictine monasteries. Later he becomes a cloistered monk himself. In 579 he is appointed papal ambassador to Constantinople, where he becomes embroiled in a theological controversy.

Even as Pope Leo had confronted Eutyches, Gregory (at this time only a deacon) confronts Eutychius, the patriarch of the city. More than a century has passed, but the same issues still smolder. Eutychius argues against the bodily resurrection of believers, while Gregory insists that just as Christ's physical body was raised from the dead so also would the bodies of his followers be raised. Eutychius loses the battle. His treatise is condemned and burned. Gregory returns to Rome to serve as abbot of St. Andrew's monastery before he is elevated to the papacy in 590. For nearly a century the church has not demonstrated strong leadership in the West, but Gregory quickly consolidates his power. A self-described "servant of the servants of God," he defends his absolute authority over the church.

During his fourteen-year reign as pope, Gregory suffers ill health primarily due to strict asceticism combined with heavy responsibilities and long workdays. In addition to administrative duties (serving virtually as head of state during wartime), he oversees welfare for refugees

## MARTIN AND GREGORY OF TOURS

In medieval times and earlier, Tours was a popular destination. Five Roman roads and one river passed through it. For a serious pilgrim, Tours was on the itinerary. It was the religious metropolis of Gaul, and its shrines promised miracles. Believers came in droves. Both Martin and Gregory, separated by two centuries, were bishops of Tours. Gregory wrote the *Life of St. Martin,* featuring his supernatural wonders. But Martin had been a legend in his own time. Today more than three thousand churches are dedicated to him in France alone.

The story most often associated with Martin (c. 316–397) touches his life as a Hungarian cavalry officer. He is leading a regiment of troops through the countryside on a blustery winter day when he encounters a beggar. Instead of kicking him out of the way with his boot, which might have been a normal response, Martin stops, takes off his warm cape, and wraps it around the pitiful vagabond, thus easing his own conscience. What happens next changes his life. Glancing again at the man, he realizes that the beggar now clothed in his cape is actually Jesus. Transformed, Martin leaves the military, founds a monastery, and works miracles.

Gregory of Tours (c. 538–594) was born into a family with a long clerical lineage. Reportedly, thirteen of the eighteen previous bishops of Tours were related to him, including his great grandfather Gregory of Langres (in an era when bishops were fathers and grandfathers). An inspirational writer, Gregory endeavored to "fire others with that enthusiasm by which the saints deservedly climbed to heaven," while at the same time exposing heresy. But his most noted work was *Historia Francorum* (*History of the Franks*), a work that stood alone for centuries with little challenge, serving yet today as a key primary source.

*Gregory of Tours* by Jean Marcellin. Stone, before 1853

and others displaced by hostilities. But he is primarily a preacher who speaks with urgency, convinced that he is living in the end times. At the same time, he seeks to bring solemnity to public worship, establishing a training school for church musicians. The hauntingly beautiful Gregorian chants date to this period, as do standard liturgies of scripture readings and prayers for each Sunday of the year.

Pastoral care is also one of his passions. *Liber Regulae Pastoralis* (Book of Pastoral Rule) was written in response to questions on the topic.

The conduct of the minister is critical and should be "so far ... superior to the conduct of the people as the life of a shepherd is accustomed to exalt him above the flock." He must "consider how great a necessity is laid upon him to maintain uprightness." He uses the symbols wine and oil offered by the Good Samaritan to denote the balance between discipline and compassion: "Thus it is necessary that he who sees to the healing of wounds should apply in wine biting pain and in oil soothing tenderness, for wine cleanses ... and oil promotes the course of healing. In other words, gentleness is to be mingled with severity."

Gregory also plays a major role in theological matters, particularly in advancing the concept of purgatory, with its corresponding merit of the saints, particularly those who were miracle workers. His *Dialogues,* filled with miracle stories, ranks high as popular devotional literature for more than a thousand years. In some cases the miracle is less than spectacular. For example, Honoratus, a young man who has vowed to abstain from meat, is mocked by his parents until a servant who has gone to draw water from the well finds in the bucket a fish—and more than a mere minnow at that. "The fish was so great that it served Honoratus very well for all that day.... and afterward, in that place which is called Funda, he built an Abbey, wherein he was the father of almost two hundred monks."

> "We make Idols of our concepts, but Wisdom is born of wonder."
>
> Pope Gregory I

But according to Gregory, the greater miracles are associated with Honoratus's merit as a saint. After he dies, Libertinus, one of the monks at the abbey, is traveling abroad, and as "always, did he bear about him in his bosom one of [Honoratus's] stockings." Along the way he meets a woman "carrying the corpse of her dead son." She pleads with Libertinus to raise her son from the dead. After some hesitation, "the holy man ... fell upon his knees, lifted up his hands to heaven, drew the stocking out of his bosom, laid it upon the breast of the dead corpse; and behold, while he was at his prayers, the soul of the child returned into the body." The merit of Honoratus, Gregory insists, is effective in the working of this miracle.

Another story that Gregory reports in his *Dialogues* goes to the heart of his belief in purgatory. Justus, a monk at his monastery who has earlier stowed away money, dies repentant of this sin. However, Gregory, concerned for his soul, offers a month of Masses for him. On the thirtieth day, a visionary Justus appears to another monk, announcing that he has been freed from the flames of purgatory. These thirty Masses are believed to be so effective that the practice—known as "Gregorian Masses"—continues for centuries, particularly in Benedictine monasteries.

Merits and good works, according to Gregory, do not affect one's place in purgatory only. Indeed, they have a direct correspondence to one's place in heaven: "For if there were not inequality of rewards in ... heaven," Gregory argues, "then [why] were there ... many mansions ... in which divers orders and degrees of God's saints [will] be distinguished ... in ... their merits and ... good works."

Even as barbarians plunder Italy and neighboring regions, Gregory is setting the stage for medieval missionary outreach. Before he is elevated to the papacy, he spots blond boys on the slave auction block in the Roman forum. He asks where they are from and is told they are Angles. "Angles?" he declares. "Say rather they are angels! What a pity that God's grace does not dwell within those beautiful brows!" He buys the boys, brings them back to the monastery, and catechizes and baptizes them. He then makes plans to go to their homeland as a missionary but is occupied with other duties.

In the meantime Æthelbert, the third Scottish king of Kent, marries Bertha. She is a princess and a Christian; he is a pagan who (influenced by Bertha and the prospect of political gain) later becomes a Christian. Through Bertha's active involvement the church, with

## THE LAST OF THE LATIN FATHERS

Gregory the First, or the Great, the last of the Latin fathers [Ambrose, Augustine, and Jerome preceding him] and the first of the popes, connects the ancient with the medieval church, the Graeco-Roman with the Romano-Germanic type of Christianity. He is one of the best representatives of medieval Catholicism: monastic, ascetic, devout, and superstitious; hierarchical, haughty, and ambitious, yet humble before God; indifferent, if not hostile, to classical and secular culture, but friendly to sacred and ecclesiastical learning; just, humane, and liberal to ostentation; full of missionary zeal in the interest of Christianity and the Roman see, which to his mind were inseparably connected. He combined great executive ability with untiring industry, and amid all his official cares he never forgot the claims of personal piety. In genius he was surpassed by Leo I., Gregory VII., Innocent III.; but as a man and as a Christian, he ranks with the purest and most useful of the popes. Goodness is the highest kind of greatness, and the church has done right in according the title of the Great to him rather than to other popes of superior intellectual power.

Philip Schaff, *History of Christianity*

its own bishop, is reestablished in Canterbury (a centuries-old church that has been in ruins). Now in contact with Pope Gregory, she and her husband welcome the prospect of missionaries.

In 596 Gregory, as pope, commissions Augustine, the prior of St. Anthony in Rome, and forty monks to serve as missionaries in Britain. It is a dangerous mission, and before they arrive at the destination Augustine has second thoughts and turns back to Rome. But when word reaches Gregory, he orders them to turn around and carry on with their journey. On Christmas 597, soon after they arrive, Augustine baptizes ten thousand of Æthelbert's subjects. The mass baptism, remembered as the "Miracle of Canterbury," paves the way for the reestablishment of the church in that region. Gregory's concern for this mission venture is evident in his response to Augustine's inquiries, insights that have stood the test of time for Catholic missionaries:

> The heathen temples of these people need not be destroyed, only the idols which are to be found in them.... If the temples are well-built, it is a good idea to detach them from the service of the devil, and to adapt them for the worship

of the true God.... And since the people are accustomed, when they assemble for sacrifice, to kill many oxen in sacrifice to the devils, it seems reasonable to appoint a festival for the people by way of exchange. The people must learn to slay their cattle not in honor of the devil, but in honour of God and for their own food.... If we allow them these outward joys, they are more likely to find their way to the true inner joy.... It is doubtless impossible to cut off all abuses at once from rough hearts, just as a man who sets out to climb a high mountain does not advance by leaps and bounds, but goes upward step by step and pace by pace.

Gregory later promotes Augustine to the position of archbishop of Canterbury. Augustine dies in 604, just months after the death of Gregory. Their combined efforts leave the church in this region on a solid foundation.

### Saint Patrick: A Legendary Life

Long before Augustine journeyed to convert the Angles, Christianity had been carried to the region by Celtic monks. Growing out of their ministry is the work of an illustrious missionary to Ireland. Patrick (c. 389–461) is a much-celebrated saint though his actual identity is shrouded in legend. Indeed, historians have for centuries wondered if there were actually two individuals (Pelladius and Patrick) melded into one. The first of these individuals is thought to have died in 461, and the second in 493. History is not always an exact science, and the story of St. Patrick is too good to be set aside for want of solid data. So Patrick and his double become one, and we recognize that hagiography and biography are often blended.

Patrick was born in Britain into a Celtic Christian family of clerics—his father a deacon and his grandfather a priest, both married, as were most clerics at this time. Kidnapped by a band of Irish plunderers when still a youth, Patrick is sold into slavery. For six long years he herds swine and seeks God:

> The Lord opened the understanding of my unbelief, that, late as it was, I might remember my faults and turn to the Lord my God with all my heart; and He had regard to my low estate, and pitied my youth and ignorance, and kept guard over me even before I knew Him, and before I attained wisdom to distinguish good from evil; and He strengthened and comforted me as a father does his son.

During this time he is convinced that he hears the voice of God telling him that a ship is waiting to take him home. He escapes and journeys to a port where he works aboard ship for his passage home. Now a free man, he finds refuge in a monastery and then returns to his home. There, "in the depth of the night," God speaks in a vision:

> I saw a man named Victoricus, coming as if from Ireland, with innumerable letters; and he gave me one of these, and ... while I was reading out the beginning of the letter, I thought that at that very moment I heard the voice of those who were beside the wood of Focluth, near the western sea; and this is what they called out: "Please, holy boy, come and walk among us again." Their cry pierced to my very heart, and I could read no more; and so I awoke.

For Patrick the vision is God's call, but the clerics are not convinced. In spite of one delay after another, however, he finally arrives back in Ireland in 432, now past the age of forty. His mission field is isolated and hostile, beyond the borders of the empire. There are scattered Christian communities, but his encounters are primarily with pagans who have no desire

Mountain in County Antrim, where St. Patrick is reputed to have shepherded as a slave

## THE DUTIES OF A DOZEN MISSIONARY MONKS

Their method was to visit a country and, where it seemed suitable, found a missionary village. In the centre they built a simple wooden church, around which were clustered schoolrooms and huts for the Celtic monks, who were the builders, preachers, and teachers. Outside this circle, as required, dwellings were built for the students and their families, who gradually gathered around them. The whole was enclosed by a wall, but the colony often spread beyond the original enclosure. Groups of twelve monks would go out, each under the leadership of an abbot, to open up fresh fields for the Gospel. Those who remained taught in the school, and, as soon as they had sufficiently learned the language of the people among whom they were, translated and wrote out portions of Scripture, and also hymns.... When some converts were made, the missionaries chose from among them small groups of young men who had ability, trained them specially in some handicraft and in languages, and taught them the Bible and how to explain it to others, so that they might be able to work among their own people.... They avoided attacking the religions of the people, counting it more profitable to preach the truth to them than to expose their errors.

E. H. Broadbent, *The Pilgrim Church*

to turn away from their traditional ways of worship. They revere the sun and wind and fire and rocks, a worldview that finds magic and spirits everywhere in nature. The druid priests mount strong opposition, but Patrick eventually prevails. He trumps their magic with magic (or miracles) of his own, causing some historians to wonder if Patrick might have been the mightiest druid of them all.

In the years that follow, Patrick impresses political leaders and makes alliances that promote church growth. Within fifteen years much of Ireland is reportedly evangelized. His missionary story features perilous journeys, life-threatening opposition, kidnapping, and captivity. After some thirty years of ministry, he laments: "I fear to lose the labor which I began" lest God "would note me as guilty."

The evangelization of Ireland by Patrick and others was a venture conducted primarily by the Celtic church, as opposed to the Roman church. A noteworthy Celtic abbot-missionary was Columba, who was born into a prosperous Irish family in 521 and brought up in the Christian faith. As a young man Columba entered a monastery and in the decades that followed is credited with establishing churches and monasteries throughout Ireland, including ones at Derry, Durrow, and Kells. But his greatest work was in Britain. With twelve clerics to serve under him, he established his headquarters just off the coast of Scotland on Iona, a small bleak, barren, foggy island, battered year-round by pounding waves. Here he set forth a monastic life of prayer, fasting, meditation, Bible study, and manual labor—and, most importantly, training for evangelists who are then commissioned to preach, build churches, and establish more monasteries.

Although Gregory I is credited with initiating the conversion of Europe through missionary and military undertakings, the work of Patrick, Columba, and others is also an important piece of the puzzle. Indeed, this is an era when missionary ventures spurred by monastic expansion begin in earnest.

## What if . . . .

What if Alaric, the warrior king of the Visigoths, had made peace with Emperor Honorius and become a great Roman army general known for defending, rather than sacking, Rome? How might history be different today if the Roman Empire had lived on through the Middle Ages?

What if Leo had not proclaimed that anyone who rejected papal authority was not to be considered within the body of Christ? What if Gregory had not upheld that claim?

What if Boethius had never been imprisoned and seen a vision of Lady Philosophy? His *Consolation of Philosophy*, which had a profound influence on the medieval mind, might not have been written.

What if Patrick — or his double — had never caught a vision in the night and evangelized Ireland?

## Selected Bibliography

Boethius, Ancius. *The Consolation of Philosophy.* New York: Penguin, 1999.

Butcher, Carmen. *Man of Blessing: A Life of St. Benedict.* Cape Cod, Mass.: Paraclete, 2006.

Cahill, Thomas. *How the Irish Saved Civilization: The Untold Story of Ireland's Heroic Role from the Fall of Rome to the Rise of Medieval Europe.* New York: Doubleday, 1995.

Collins, Roger. *Early Medieval Europe: 300–1000,* 2nd ed. New York: Palgrave Macmillan, 1999.

Dawson, Christopher. *Religion and the Rise of Western Culture.* New York: Doubleday, 1950.

Freeman, Philip. *St. Patrick of Ireland: A Biography.* New York: Simon and Schuster, 2005.

Heather, Peter. *The Fall of the Roman Empire: A New History of Rome and the Barbarians.* New York: Oxford University, 2007.

Marenbon, John. *Boethius.* New York: Oxford University, 2003.

Markus, R. A. *Gregory the Great and His World.* New York: Cambridge University Press, 1997.

Ward-Perkins, Bryan. *The Fall of Rome and the End of Civilization.* New York: Oxford University Press, 2006.

Wells, Peter S. *Barbarians to Angels: The Dark Ages Reconsidered.* New York: W.W. Norton, 2008.

White, Caroline, ed. *The Rule of St. Benedict.* New York: Penguin, 2008.

# CHAPTER 6

# Byzantine Religion

*The Expansion of Eastern Orthodoxy*

*Years ago I spent an afternoon in the magnificent chapel of Princeton University, where hundreds of icons were on display. I found them interesting, but they seemed alien to my own evangelical heritage. I did not find them to be windows to God. The same was true as I visited and viewed the domed Orthodox cathedrals in Moscow. There was great beauty but nothing that inspired a direct connection with God.*

*Recently, after worshipping at our own church, my husband and I decided to visit an Orthodox Church. St. George Antiochian and St. John Chrysostom Russian are nearby in downtown Grand Rapids, but we decided to travel across town to the much larger St. Nicholas Antiochian Orthodox Church. In an introductory session, Deacon Justin pointed out that the various "brands" of Orthodoxy in America are unique. Orthodoxy elsewhere in the world is simply that, with no prefix. But when immigrants began flooding into the United States, they established churches in their own cultures and languages—thus Russian and Serbian and Greek Orthodox churches.*

*As we entered the sanctuary, I was expecting a large open room with no seating. This is true in the old countries, Justin told us, but most Orthodox churches here have made concessions to American sensibilities and provide pews. But no compromise had been made on incense, bells, ornate robes, and high-church liturgy. Icons with gold-leafed halos adorned the walls and ceiling: Mary with arms outstretched and baby Jesus in her heart was above the altar, and directly above us in the dome, Jesus was depicted, surrounded by great figures of the Old Testament.*

*The people in the pews seemed sincere and no less genuinely Christian than those in my own church. Yet there was a chasm separating us. That we were asked not to participate in the Eucharist was as much their loss as ours.*

> Even the most painstaking history is a bridge across an eternal mystery.
> BRUCE CATTON, *PREFACES TO HISTORY*

A twenty-first-century Protestant seeking to understand Eastern Orthodoxy may become bogged down in what seems like a most painstaking history. To do so the individual must bridge the chasm across an eternal mystery. Orthodox Christianity is indeed a religion of mystery. As we move through the history of Christianity, the direction is both geographical and ecclesiastical, and sometimes we pick up the story from an earlier era. The Christian faith began in Palestine, initially centered in Jerusalem and the eastern Mediterranean world. As Paul and others journeyed to Rome and beyond, the stage was set for the gradually differing forms of Greek and Latin Christianity.

Early Christian leaders are Greek speakers and writers, and there is no obvious division between East and West. By the fourth century, however, the so-called church fathers are often differentiated as the Greek or Latin Fathers. They are also categorized chronologically, those prior to the Council of Nicaea in 325 as the ante-Nicene Fathers, and those after as the post-Nicene Fathers.

Most of the individuals already discussed fit into either the East or the West. Included in the East (or Greek) are Irenaeus, Origen, and Athanasius. In the West (or Latin) are Tertullian, Ambrose, Jerome, Augustine of Hippo, and Gregory I. But the lines are often blurred. Jerome, for example, studied in Constantinople but spent most of his adult life in a monastery near Bethlehem. The differences between East and West only intensify as one century rolled into another. Those who are most identified with the Eastern church in the first millennium include ones held in high regard by the whole church as well as ones deemed heretics, and ones revered by Orthodox Christians alone. They include the Cappadocian Fathers (and Mothers), John Chrysostom, Nestorius, John of Damascus, Emperor Justinian, Cyril and Methodius, and Princess Olga and Vladimir.

By the time of Gregory the Great, subtle changes began creeping into the eastern and western branches of the church. One of these changes was language. Greek had been the common language spoken throughout the Roman Empire. Paul wrote his epistle to the Romans in Greek, and most church leaders in the next five or six centuries knew Greek (with the notable exception of Augustine of Hippo). By the sixth century that began to change. Although Gregory had served as the pope's representative in

## PARADE OF HISTORY

In the Eastern Church the procession of icons on the first Sunday of Lent marks Orthodoxy in its unique style of worship. But this is only one example of its colorful processions. The setting is eighth-century Athens, the night before Easter. John of Damascus, along with the king and queen and countless clerics are processing from church and ascending a platform that stands high above the multitudes. As the night wears on, the melancholy chant of the monks grows louder. Then the timekeeper announces the stroke of midnight. The drums roll. John raises the cross and joyfully proclaims: *Christos Anesti*, Christ is risen. The people, lighting torches, shout back the refrain and sing and dance and process around the platform until dawn. *Christos Anesti!*

## GREEK AS MOTHER, ROME AS DAUGHTER

The Greek Church reminds us of the time when the tongue, not of Rome, but of Greece, was the sacred language of Christendom. It was a striking remark of the Emperor Napoleon, that the introduction of Christianity itself was, in a certain sense, the triumph of Greece over Rome.... The name of *pope* is not Latin, but Greek, the common and now despised name of every pastor in the Eastern Church. *She is the mother,* and Rome the daughter. It is her privilege to claim a direct continuity of speech with the earliest times; to boast of reading the whole code of Scripture, Old as well as New, in the language in which it was read and spoken by the Apostles. The humblest peasant who reads his Septuagint or Greek Testament in his own mother-tongue on the hills of Bœotia may proudly feel that he has access to the original oracles of divine truth which pope and cardinal reach by a barbarous and imperfect translation; that he has a key of knowledge which in the West is only to be found in the hands of the learned classes.

Arthur Stanley, *Lectures on the History of the Eastern Church*

Constantinople in his younger years, he did not know Greek. His example no doubt influenced others, and Latin became the language of the church in the West. With this language barrier came increased theological and cultural barriers.

But language was only one factor. Long before 604 when Gregory died, East and West had been developing their own traditions while at the same time sharing a common history. One of the most significant issues separating the two sides was papal supremacy. Orthodoxy has defined itself as the church of the seven councils (First Council of Nicaea, Constantinople I, Ephesus, Chalcedon, Constantinople II, Constantinople III, Second Council of Nicaea), believing that councils, not the pope, hold final authority. Nevertheless, Christian leaders continued to be heralded in both East and West. The four western Fathers (Ambrose, Jerome, Augustine of Hippo, and Gregory I) are balanced by four eastern Fathers: Athanasius, Basil the Great, Gregory of Nazianzus, and John Chrysostom.

Today there are some 250 million Orthodox Christians worldwide, the largest being Russian, with upwards of 100 million, followed by Romanian, with some 15 million, with Greek, Serbian, and Bulgarian close behind. Of the more than two billion professing Christians in the world, more than half are Catholics, Protestants being the second-largest branch. Consequently, Orthodox Christians have often been sidelined by Western Christians. Indeed, as Catholics and Protestants have fought each other over the centuries, Orthodox Christians have simply carried on their traditions, seemingly paying little heed. In the minds of some scholars, however, they had seriously veered off course. The noted nineteenth-century church historian Adolf von Harnack wrote: "The Orthodox Church is in her entire structure alien to the gospel and represents a perversion of the Christian religion, its reduction to the level of pagan antiquity." In the early centuries, however, East and West were one. A *saint* like John Chrysostom belonged to the whole church.

### The Cappadocians: Molded by a Woman's Touch

The Cappadocian Fathers, as they later came to be known, were brothers Basil and Gregory and Gregory Nazianzen, all from Cappadocia,

## EVERYDAY LIFE

## Food, Fasts, and Feasts

One of the most popular genres of literature today is food and meal preparation. Every kind of recipe collection or cookbook or diet manual imaginable is either available or on the way to publication. Such was not the case in the ancient world, though Rome featured a second-century cookbook and ancient Greece offered a store of sources that serve the food historian well. But the Byzantine Empire provides only hints of its cuisine.

In the East, food regulations came down from on high. Meat and fish were prohibited on fast days, including every Wednesday and Friday. In fact, Orthodox fast days encompass more than half the days of a year, some stricter than others. And fasting does not involve food alone. On certain fast days married couples were to abstain from sex. But if one became weary of fast days, there were many feast days to celebrate.

Included in food restrictions were restraints on the sale of items. Rules forbad the setting up a food booth close to churches, particularly the grandest church of all, Saint Sophia in Constantinople, though such rules were often challenged. Merchants insisted that the aromas of spices lofting into the air was a means of honoring Mother Church and the saints.

> "And if you come to the holy city of famous Byzantion, I urge you again to eat a steak of peak-season tuna; for it is very good and soft."
>
> Archestratus, letter, c. 350 BC

A favorite Byzantine recipe was monokythron, cooked in one pot and calling for cabbage, fourteen eggs, three different kinds of cheese, five varieties of fish, olive oil, garlic, pepper, and wine. The dish would be the main course for a feast. But both upper and lower classes enjoyed a wide variety of staples, including eggs, cheese, apples, pears, oranges, lemons, figs, walnuts, almonds, olives (in brine), and olive oil. In fact, a visitor complained that Byzantine food was too saturated with olive oil.

A feast fit for a king might feature a goat stuffed with onions, leeks, garlic, and a wide range of savory spices. Situated along trade routes from the Orient, the Eastern Empire quickly became a major spice market. Sold alongside saffron, cinnamon, clovers, ginger, and black pepper were aromatics, some doubling for perfume and food flavoring. Musk, imported from Afghanistan, was a favorite. "It is a scent," sniffed Saint Jerome, "for lovers and hedonists."

Sauces were often copied from other regions, including the Roman Empire's famed garum, prepared by fermenting fish and then mixing the guts, gills, and blood. A commoner's delicacy that crossed class lines, it found its way to the table to flavor whatever food was being served. A stuffed goat would not be complete without garum.

Dessert was a delicacy. Favorites were the many varieties of pastries, some, including Greek baklava, incorporating almonds, walnuts, and chestnuts. Jam was a special delight, sometimes eaten by the spoonful. Treats for a poorer family included rice pudding with honey. A good meal was incomplete without wine, particularly spicy varieties. Coffee and buttermilk often accompanied dining as well.

Bread was the most important staple of the diet. In fact, so critical was bread for family meals, for feast days, and for the sacrament that bakers were exempt from the military draft or other forms of public service.

a region in central Turkey. Recognized for their monastic leadership, they were also astute theologians. The term *Cappadocians*, however, is more fitting than Cappadocian Fathers because it captures three generations of a family, both women and men. The grandmother of Basil and Gregory was Macrina the Elder, who fled persecution only to be left widowed and impoverished. Yet she ministered to those who were even more needy and was canonized as the patron saint of widows.

One of Macrina's sons was Basil (the elder), who married the wealthy Emmelia and together with her had nine children, five of whom were designated as saints. Macrina (the younger) (324–379), named for her grandmother, was the older sister who had a profound influence on her siblings as well as on her mother. Her brother Gregory presents a glowing account in his *Life of Macrina,* as follows:

Macrina the Younger

Orthodox Church in America, www.oca.org

Macrina's brother, the great Basil, returned after his long period of education, already a practiced rhetorician. He was puffed up beyond measure with the pride of oratory and looked down on the local dignitaries.... Nevertheless Macrina took him in hand, and with such speed did she draw him also toward the mark of philosophy that he forsook the glories of this world and despised fame gained by speaking, and deserted it for this busy life where one toils with one's hands. His renunciation of property was complete, lest anything should impede the life of virtue.... Now that all the distractions of the material life had been removed, Macrina persuaded her mother to give up her ordinary life and all showy style of living and the services of domestics to which she had been accustomed before, and bring her point of view down to that of the masses, and to share the life of the maids, treating all her slave girls and menials as if they were sisters and belonged to the same rank as herself.

Macrina had chosen a life of asceticism after her fiancé died, maintaining that lifestyle in the home while her siblings were growing up. She later joined with her brother Basil to form a convent in conjunction with his monastery. The most celebrated of the Cappadocians, he is recognized as Basil the Great (329–379), Father of Eastern Monasticism. Setting aside worldly aspirations and touring monasteries in Egypt, Basil returned to Cappadocia, where he established a monastery. His "Longer Rules" and "Shorter Rules" are still used today, and all monks in the Eastern church are Basilian monks. Basil viewed monastic life as one of service to those in need, setting the example by selling his family's estate for famine relief and calling on other wealthy landholders to do likewise. He worked in the kitchen and dispersed provisions alongside ordinary monks and laypeople. Food was distributed freely to any in need, regardless of ethnicity, pointing out to his critics that the digestive system of a Jew is no different from that of a Christian.

Basil had a flare for words and is remembered particularly for "The Six Days," his series of nine sermons on creation that display the beauty of God's natural wonders. In 370 he was named bishop of Caesarea, pitting him against Emperor Valens, an Arian. When he died in 379, the entire population of Caesarea—Christians, Jews, and pagans—is said to have followed his funeral cortege with weeping.

Basil's younger brother Gregory of Nyssa (335–394) did not enter the monastery and may have been married to Theosebia, a much-heralded deaconess in the church at Nyssa, where Gregory served as bishop. His writing set the stage for the Eastern church's focus on apophatic theology, which emphasizes that God is ultimately unknowable. While strongly defending the doctrine of the Trinity, he insisted that God is infinite and transcendent and thus beyond our understanding. The true way to God is through darkness—even as Moses found God in the luminous darkness. In *Life of Moses* he writes:

> Since Moses was alone, by having been stripped as it were of the people's fear, he boldly approached the very darkness itself and entered the invisible things where he was no longer seen by those watching. After he entered the inner sanctuary of the divine mystical doctrine, there, while not being seen, he was in company with the Invisible. He teaches, I think, by the things he did that the one who is going to associate intimately with God must go beyond all that is visible and ... believe that the divine is there where the understanding does not reach.

Gregory Nazianzen (c. 325—389), the third of the Cappadocian Fathers, was a close associate and friend of Basil and Gregory of Nyssa. His mother was instrumental in converting her husband, Gregory, who subsequently became bishop of Nazianzus. Young Gregory accused his father of tyranny and left home, only to later return and work with his father in the church. He was consecrated bishop of Sasima by Basil, but he protested that Basil was using him simply to promote his own standing in the church. Of his location, Gregory writes, it is an "utterly dreadful, pokey little hole; a paltry horse-stop on the main road ... devoid of water, vegetation, or the company of gentlemen.... This was my Church of Sasima!"

Gregory later gives away his wealth and enters a monastery. On his deathbed Basil, not a man to hold grudges, recommends his friend

## A CRITIQUE OF FOURTH-CENTURY LUXURY

We repose in splendor on high and sumptuous cushions, upon the most exquisite covers, which one is almost afraid to touch, and are vexed if we but hear the voice of a moaning pauper; our chamber must breathe the odor of flowers.... Slaves must stand ready ... some to hold cups both delicately and firmly with the tips of their fingers, others to fan fresh air upon the head. Our tables must bend under the load of dishes.... The poor man is content with water; but we fill our goblets with wine to drunkenness, nay, immeasurably beyond it. We refuse one wine, another we pronounce excellent when well flavored....

Gregory Nazianzen

Gregory to a post as the leading theologian in Constantinople with the hope that he will defeat Arianism. As such, Gregory's tenure in Constantinople is anything but peaceful. The city is deeply divided, but he begins drawing crowds with his powerful preaching. His "Five Theological Orations," defending the Trinity and the deity of Christ, are aimed at Arians.

Arian opponents storm his church in 379 during the Easter vigil, killing one bishop and wounding Gregory. Matters improve when Theodosius ascends the throne and vows to rid the East of Arians once and for all. Gregory is elected bishop of Constantinople to replace the Arian bishop dismissed by the emperor, but his problems are far from over. Accused of attaining his position illegally, he resigns: "Let me be as the Prophet Jonah! I was responsible for the storm.... Seize me and throw me." The emperor accepts his resignation, and Gregory returns to Cappadocia where his ministry began.

### John Chrysostom: Preacher *Par Excellence*

John Chrysostom (c. 347–407), like Gregory of Nazianzus, was a bishop of Constantinople and known for eloquence in preaching—hence, his name Chrysostom, meaning "golden mouth." So captivating are his words that his congregation is sometimes moved to tears. On other occasions they applaud and stomp their feet, a response he finds utterly out of place in a worship service. In fact, he is so disturbed that he devotes a sermon to proper worship conduct and the impropriety of boisterous clapping and stomping. So moved are the people that they give him rousing approval with their hands and feet.

Born in Antioch, John was raised by his widowed mother, Anthusa, who arranged for his education with Libanius, one of the most renowned teachers of rhetoric in the ancient world—and a pagan. On his deathbed, Libanius confided to a friend that John would naturally have been his successor "if the Christians had not taken him from us."

Initially living as a hermit, John denies himself sleep and stands most of the day and night reading and memorizing Scripture. After two years and in ill health, he returns to Antioch, where he is ordained a deacon and then a priest. In this capacity he develops his rhetorical skills. His sermons reveal a wide range of perspectives, from deep theological and spiritual insights to outright anti-Semitism and spiteful notions about women. He is bold in his attacks, on one occasion calling Empress Eudoxia the second Jezebel. He realizes he has preached himself "out of the pulpit and into exile"—though that would not happen for several years.

John Chrysostom

As to discipline: "Punish him, now with a stern look, now with incisive, now with reproachful, words" or "win him with gentleness and promises."

The home is to be ordered with husbands and wives fulfilling their assigned roles, though the husband, in Chrysostom's construct, is not *head* of the home.

> To woman is assigned the presidency of the household.... A woman is not able to hurl a spear or shoot an arrow, but she can grasp the distaff, weave at the loom.... She cannot express her opinion in a legislative assembly, but she can express it at home, and often she is more shrewd about household matters than her husband ... and frees him from all such household concerns ... about money.

With so much freedom for women, John might appear to be a fourth-century feminist, but he is not. He restricts women in church leadership because "the woman taught the man once, and made him guilty of disobedience, and wrought our ruin." But he is inconsistent. In reference to Junia, in Romans 16, he writes, "Think how great the devotion of this woman must have been, that she should be worthy to be called an apostle!" Yet again, he suggests that men would be better served by being taught by lower forms of animals than by women.

In the meantime he preaches thousands of sermons based on a literal rather than an allegorical interpretation of Scripture. His application is often pointed. "Do you wish to honor the body of Christ?" he demands of wealthy parishioners. "If so, do not imagine you are doing so when you show up at worship in your finest attire, bowing before an ornate altar, while you neglect the poor all around you." He also preaches on childrearing: "Higher than every painter, higher than every sculptor and than all artists do I regard the one who is skilled in the art of forming the souls of children." The key is to begin while "the soul is tender." Parents should not parade their boys around in "fine raiment and golden ornaments" and "long hair." Rather, funds should support a "strict tutor."

> *"I know my own soul, how feeble and puny it is: I know the magnitude of this ministry, and the great difficulty of the work; for more stormy billows vex the soul of the priest than the gales which disturb the sea."*
>
> John Chrysostom

Women, however, fare much better in John's sermonizing than do Jews. His harshest attacks against Jews come in 386 while serving as a presbyter in Antioch. Christians are freely participating in Jewish holidays and rituals, which John regards as "Judaizing." He preaches eight sermons timed to correspond with Rosh Hashanah and Yom Kippur. Here he rails that the synagogue is no better than a theater or brothel. And worse: "The Jews have degenerated to the level of dogs. They are drunkards and gluttons. They beat their servants. They are ignorant of God. Their festivals are worthless.... [They are] the Christ killers"—words used by Christians (and Nazis) to persecute Jews in later generations.

In many ways, John is an equal-opportunity slanderer. His attacks reach the inner sanctums of power where Empress Eudoxia reigns in extravagant luxury. When a silver statue is erected in her honor within sight of his cathedral, he explodes. "Again Herodias raves, again she is troubled; she dances again; and again desires to receive John's head in a charger." He is banished a second and final time and dies in exile.

## Nestorius and the Church That Bears His Name

Long before there was a split between Eastern Orthodoxy and the West, some "Nestorian" Christians in the East separated from the rest of the Christian church. Geographically, the movement stretched from the Mediterranean world to Iraq and Iran and India and all the way to China. Although it is referred to today as the Assyrian Church of the East, the name most often used in the West is Nestorian. This identification was inspired in part by John Stewart's *Nestorian Missionary Enterprise: The Story of a Church on Fire* (first published in 1928).

A patriarch of Constantinople, Nestorius (c. 386–451) was born in Asia Minor. Educated in rhetoric, he was a popular preacher and was

---

### A SAINT NAMED NICHOLAS

"Jolly Old St. Nicholas" is a song taken from a legend — and perhaps from a real saint, though there are no dated records referencing him as a fourth-century bishop in Myra (present-day Turkey). Born into a prosperous family, he inherits bags of gold that he throws to beautiful young girls to prevent them from becoming prostitutes. When his bags of gold are gone, he works miracles and keeps Arians out of the city. His legend grows over the generations, and today St. Nicholas — or Santa Claus — brings his bags of booty down the chimney.

---

sometimes compared to golden-mouthed John Chrysostom. Like John and the Cappadocians, he strikes out against Arianism and all heresies — until he is deemed a heretic himself. He refuses to acknowledge Mary as the "mother of God," insisting rather she is the mother of Christ but not the mother of God. *Heretic,* bellows Cyril of Alexandria. *How can she be mother of Christ in his humanity without being mother of Christ in his divinity without dividing Christ into two persons?*

So serious is the tension that Emperor Theodosius II calls a general council to settle the matter. Strife between Alexandria and Antioch (as represented by Cyril and Nestorius) is surely not new. When the Council of Ephesus convenes in 431, Cyril takes charge and opens the meetings before those from Antioch even arrive. In the end, Cyril, not surprisingly, wins the day. Nestorius is deposed; Mary is the mother of God. Christ is only one person. Within two years the church rids itself of seventeen bishops who had supported Nestorius, and a separate church is born. Persecution pushes the movement further east, and as it moves it picks up new adherents

## NESTORIANS: A CHURCH ON FIRE

These are the men who the arrogance of Rome has branded as heretics all down the centuries. Would to God that the churches and missions of to-day might be inoculated with the same brand of heresy if it but led to such a mighty work of grace as was wrought through these missionaries of the "Church of the East," the Nestorian Church of the sixth, seventh and subsequent centuries of the Christian era!

John Stewart, *Nestorian Missionary Enterprise*

and new beliefs—so much so that the Nestorians in later generations are often unaware of the issues that ignited the separation.

Long before the Council of Ephesus in 431, Christians had fled east beyond the borders of the empire to escape persecution. But hardly had the persecution in the West ceased than it began in the Persian Empire, particularly under Sapor II (339–379) and his fifth-century successors. The numbers of martyrs in the West pale in comparison to those in the East. Under Sapor II, the named martyrs were some sixteen thousand. The height of the slaughter came under Kirkuk, when ten bishops, hundreds of other clerics, and more than one hundred thousand lay Christians were reportedly martyred. Survivors were driven further east.

In India Nestorians claim ancient roots with the already-existing Thomas Christians—those who, according to tradition, were evangelized by the apostle Thomas. The Nestorians then spread out across Asia, arriving in China and Mongolia in the seventh century, spurred on by zeal to evangelize. Their monasteries are Bible institutes, and by the end of the eighth century the Persian Empire is reportedly filled with monastic missionary training centers that send out men and women with large portions of Scripture committed to memory.

By the thirteenth century there were nearly thirty metropolitan church seats and some two hundred bishops extending across Asia. Within

a century, however, Nestorians were in decline. Internal corruption combined with the destructive forces of Genghis Khan and Islam led to the dismantling of a once vibrant church.

### Emperor Justinian I and Empress Theodora

He stepped into office as the most powerful ruler in the world in an era of hard times, promising to turn the economy around, reform the tax code, revitalize education, make improvements on the infrastructure, and consolidate foreign policy. It did not hurt that he had a beautiful and brilliant wife at his side. Conscious of the failures of the previous administration, his program was ambitious and his promise was *change*. "We have decided now to grant to the world [what others failed to do] with the help of Almighty God." A modern American story? This was the year 527, and the state was the Roman Empire.

Emperor Justinian I exudes confidence. Intelligent, easy-going, and energetic, he is indeed a workaholic, often referred to as "the Emperor who never sleeps." But he faces almost insurmountable problems, including a bubonic plague that decimates nearly half the population. Born into a poor peasant family and orphaned early, Flavius Peterus Sabbatius (c. 483–565) was adopted and raised by his uncle, Justin, an army officer also of peasant stock. Justin quickly recognizes the boy's precocious ways, and young Flavius is given the best education Constantinople has to offer. In return he serves as an invaluable, albeit young, consultant to his illiterate uncle, who aspires to become emperor. With the young man's help and a cortege of advisors and troops, in addition to some hefty bribes, Justin ascends the throne in his late sixties and reigns for seven years.

Some historians cite evidence that Justinian was actually the power behind the throne, but it is unlikely that this powerful military officer would have handed over the reins of government to his son. Justinian more likely served only as his adopted father's most trusted advisor. He convinces his father to repeal a law in 525, allowing him to marry Theodora (c. 500–548), a low-class woman. Justin, considered by historians a mediocre emperor, names Justinian as co-emperor and dies shortly thereafter.

Justinian and Theodora are the talk of the town. He is the brilliant and engaging prince, and she, seventeen years his junior, is as beautiful and elegant as she is cunning and clever.

She was born in Cyprus, where her father was a circus animal trainer and her mother a dancer performing in the grand Hippodrome of Constantinople. When she was twelve her father died, and she and her sisters soon joined their mother in circus dancing and acting routines. According to one early source, "She was ... [a] comedienne who delights ... by letting herself be cuffed and slapped on the cheeks ... raising her skirts to reveal to the spectators ... feminine secrets."

As First Lady, she is no mere hostess. Nor is she a behind-the-scenes advisor. She makes her opinions known publicly, and her adoring husband, with self-image intact, appears not to be threatened. Her influence is seen in imperial decisions such as a ban on selling girls as prostitutes. Aware of this life of degradation, she establishes a home — the Convent of Repentance — for young women escaping prostitution.

But like all married couples, Justinian and Theodora have their differences. Religion divides them more than anything else. They

## THE COPTIC (MONOPHYSITE) CHURCH IN EGYPT

The origins of this church are claimed to date from the Holy Family's escape to Egypt and to have been carried on by the testimony of the Ethiopian eunuch as he passed through the region on his way south. But the actual founding of the church, according to tradition, came when Mark journeyed to Egypt as a missionary. Until the fifth century Copts were considered part of the church, but the Chalcedon Definition demanded that Christ, while being one person (*hypostasis*), has two natures, human and divine. The word *mono-physite* is derived from Greek terms meaning *one* and *nature*. Opposite of the Monophysite position was that of Nestorius, who insisted on a distinct separation of Christ's divine and human nature — so much so that Mary must not be regarded *Theotokos* (God-bearer or Mother of God) because she was mother *only* of the human Jesus. The Christians of Egypt insisted that their theology was in accord with that of Cyril, patriarch of Alexandria, a respected theologian who attacked Nestorius. Coptic beliefs are summed up on the Church of Alexandria official website:

> Copts believe that the Lord is perfect in His divinity, and He is perfect in His humanity, but His divinity and His humanity were united in one nature called "the nature of the incarnate word" — united in one "without mingling, without confusion, and without alteration." ... These two natures "did not separate for a moment or the twinkling of an eye."

are both Christians but he is Orthodox, she a Monophysite—a sector of Christianity refusing to accept the conclusions of the Council of Chalcedon. Denying the two natures of Christ, the adherents of this movement insist rather that Jesus is wholly divine, his humanity having been swallowed up in the divine, in the words of Eutyches, like a "drop of wine in the ocean." For the sake of his wife—and for the sake of maintaining a stable grain trade with Monophysite Egypt—Justinian seeks to downplay the differences. Like Constantine before him, more than anything he wants peace and prosperity in the empire.

This plan works well for him as it had for Constantine. Regarding church and state, he declares: "There are two great gifts which God, in his love for man, has granted from on high: the priesthood and the imperial dignity. The first serves divine things, while the latter directs and administers human affairs; both, however, proceed from the same origin and adorn the life of mankind."

Through much of his reign, Justinian is fighting internal and external enemies. At times he ruthlessly crushes rebellions to save his government and to hold his empire together.

Indeed, he pushes back boundaries, seeking to restore the empire to its past glory. But cost overruns and a devastating plague dash his dreams. Nevertheless, he moves forward on legal reforms and architectural wonders, including the magnificent Hagia Sophia in Constantinople, with its second-to-none mosaics and spectacular cathedral dome. Constructed in only five years, it becomes one of the wonders of the world.

Justinian survives the decades-long plague, as does Theodora. But she is brought down at age forty-eight by apparent cancer. Her husband lives on for another two decades. Having been childless, the couple has no direct heirs. But in the years that follow, the empire is ruled by Justin II (Justinian's nephew) and his wife Sophia (Theodora's niece).

## Muhammad and the Advance of Islam

The rise of Islam in the seventh century was actually aided by some Christian communities that initially joined forces with the followers of Muhammad to subdue non-Christian tribes in the region. But with their mutual enemies suppressed, the more powerful Muslims turned

---

### THE JUSTINIAN ADMINISTRATION

529 The Justinian Code, a codification of Roman law, is laid out in a series of volumes, *Corpus Juris Civilis*. The word *justice* comes from this Byzantine emperor, as do countless legal maxims based on the code such as, "The things which are common to all (and not capable of being owned) are: the air, running water, the sea and the seashores."

533 Convinced that the Second Coming of Christ is imminent, Justinian prepares by ordering military forces to recapture large regions of the Roman Empire.

542 The bubonic plague, known as the Great Plague of Justinian, ravages Europe for more than a half-century, killing an estimated half of the population.

552 The emperor is convinced that Europe is ripe for new business ventures, so he sends missionary monks to Ceylon (Sri Lanka) and China as undercover silk-worm-egg smugglers. They return with the worm, and the silk industry is born.

## CHRISTIANITY IN ASIA AND AFRICA

Much of what we today call the Islamic world was once Christian. The faith originated and took shape in Syria-Palestine and in Egypt, and these areas continued to have major Christian communities long after the Arab conquests. As late as the eleventh century, Asia was still home to at least a third of the world's Christians, and perhaps a tenth of all Christians still lived in Africa.

Philip Jenkins, *The Lost History of Christianity*

against the Christians. Some Christians converted to Islam to protect their property and livelihood. Others became part of the great migration east.

Muhammad (c. 570–632), founder and prophet of Islam, was born in Mecca. His visions that later became the basis for the *Qur'an* began in 610, and twelve years later, in 622, the *Hegira*—fleeing Mecca to Medina—marked the birth of the movement. In 630 Muhammad's forces prevailed in Mecca. Following his death in 632, Muslim armies moved west in a conquest that inaugurated Islamic rule in Jerusalem in 636, with Antioch and Damascus falling to Muslim rule soon after. They then moved on to North Africa, to the Christian centers of Alexandria and Carthage. The goal was conversion not killing, but those who resisted lost property and in some cases their lives. Within twenty years, large regions of the Persian and Byzantine empires were under Islamic control.

The speed at which the Islamic armies conquered is striking. In less than a hundred years the Prophet's warriors had overrun much of the region from Persia to Spain. In Eastern Europe, they were stopped before they conquered Vienna. In the West, the decisive turning point came with the Battle of Tours in 732, when Muslim forces were defeated by Charles Martel. The threat of Islam to Eastern Orthodoxy would continue for centuries, with no reso-

lution in the Crusades. Today Christianity has all but disappeared in a region once dotted with churches and led by some five hundred bishops.

### John of Damascus and the Iconoclastic Crisis

The most disruptive controversy in the Eastern Church related to icons—depictions of Christ, Mary, the apostles, and other saints that were considered to be windows to God. For some—called iconoclasts (or image-breakers)—icons signified the idol worship forbidden in the Ten Commandments. Icon supporters, however, insisted icons were means of grace as were the bread and wine of the Lord's Supper. In 692, after generations of bickering, the Council of Quinsextum (also called the Trullan Synod) issued a canon in their defense: "The human figure of Christ our God, the Lamb, who took on the sins of the world, [should] be set up even in the images.... Through this figure, we realize the height of the humiliation of God the Word and are led to remember His life in the flesh, His suffering and His saving death and the redemption ensuing from it for the world."

Various emperors had taken issue with icons, but it was not until the reign of Leo III in 726 that they were ordered destroyed and monks who were their most zealous defenders were severely persecuted. Icons, opponents insisted, prevented Muslims and Jews from converting to Christianity. Emperor Leo sought support from Pope Gregory II in Rome, while at the same time threatening to destroy the images in the churches in the West. The pope defended the use of icons, but after further threats from the emperor he confided that his only defense in the face of military might was to pray that a demon would so torture the emperor that he would repent of his evil ways.

In the meantime, the empire was in the midst of a bloody civil war. Monks were the target of angry mobs and state-sponsored persecution. Iconoclasts wreaked havoc on churches and shrines. Even dead saints were not spared, their bodies dug up and burned. Those who opposed the ban on icons fought back. In 730, Emperor Leo issued a stronger decree, ratcheting up the persecution and penalties against icon supporters. The divide between East and West deepened when a papal representative was imprisoned. In the years that followed, the bloody struggle continued, only to abate after Emperor Leo IV died and his wife Irene, a devoted icon-worshiper, succeeded him

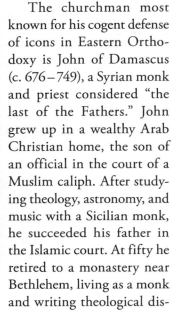

John of Damascus

as empress (regent for her nine-year-old son). Throughout her reign and her son's, the use of icons was restored, only to be prohibited again in 943 during the reign of Empress Theodora.

The churchman most known for his cogent defense of icons in Eastern Orthodoxy is John of Damascus (c. 676–749), a Syrian monk and priest considered "the last of the Fathers." John grew up in a wealthy Arab Christian home, the son of an official in the court of a Muslim caliph. After studying theology, astronomy, and music with a Sicilian monk, he succeeded his father in the Islamic court. At fifty he retired to a monastery near Bethlehem, living as a monk and writing theological discourses and hymns. Among his hymns still sung today are, "Come ye faithful, raise the strain" and "The day of resurrection! Earth, tell it out abroad!"

The theological work for which John is best known is *The Fountain of Wisdom*, which lays out the philosophical and theological underpinnings of the Eastern Church. His defense of icons comes at a time when icons are banned, but he is safely ensconced in the caliph's court,

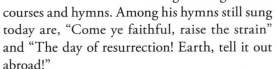

## A DEFENSE OF ICONS

Icons are not primarily historical but spiritual portrayals.... An icon is more like the Bible. A Bible is not "identical in essence" with the living Word, Jesus Christ, yet the Bible mediates the grace of Christ as we read it.... The ... church fathers like Athanasius, Basil, and John Chrysostom ... supported the use of icons.

Bradley Nassif, "Kissers and Smashers"

outside the emperor's reach. That he would find a safe haven among Muslims who denounce all images is curious. But this is where he writes his three *Apologetic Treatises against Those Decrying the Holy Images*. Written in a style easily understood by ordinary Christians, the work spurs protests and intense theological debate, most specifically at the Second Council of Nicaea in 787, called to resolve the icon controversy.

Amid the controversy, Emperor Leo allegedly forges a letter in John's handwriting, showing John to be double-crossing the Islamic regime to which he owes his office. John vigorously denies writing the letter, but to no avail. He not only loses his job, but his right hand—the hand that wrote the letter—is cut off at the wrist. However, there is a happy and fitting ending. His hand is restored in answer to a prayer before an icon of Mary. So moved is the caliph, according to John's tenth-century hagiographer, that he offers to reinstate John in his high court position. But John declines the offer and moves to the monastic fortress of Mar Saba, where he lays out his support for icons: "If we made an image of the invisible God, we would certainly be in error," he writes, "but we do nothing of the sort; for we are not in error if we make the image of the incarnate God, who appeared on earth in the flesh."

The logic of representing Christ and the saints because they appeared in human form is fiercely challenged by the iconoclasts, who continue to condemn icons. Indeed, they dredge up the previous debates on Christ's human and divine natures and insist that those who favor the use of icons are perpetuating the ideas of Nestorius, who divided the two natures of Christ. "If the image represents the humanity of Christ to the exclusion of His divinity," writes an opponent of icons, "it implies a Nestorian Christology and separates in Christ, God

---

### AN ANCIENT RESURRECTION HYMN

The day of resurrection! Earth, tell it out abroad;
The Passover of gladness, the Passover of God.
From death to life eternal, from earth unto the sky,
Our Christ hath brought us over, with hymns of victory. . . .
Now let the heavens be joyful! Let earth the song begin!
Let the round world keep triumph, and all that is therein!
Let all things seen and unseen their notes in gladness blend,
For Christ the Lord hath risen, our joy that hath no end.

John of Damascus

---

from man; if on the contrary, the iconographer pretends to represent Christ in the individual fullness of his divinity and his humanity, he assumes that the divinity itself can be circumscribed, which is absurd."

Icon defenders are not easily silenced: "If someone dares make an image of the immaterial and in corporal divinity," writes John, "we repudiate him." John argues that icons actually uphold a worship that is more faithful to the doctrine set forth at the Council of Chalcedon. Patristic theology, he insists, opens the way for the veneration of icons. The Tome of Leo is offered as evidence, particularly the oft-quoted passage on the two natures of Christ that sought to illuminate the mystery of the incarnation:

The Inconceivable is conceived in the womb of a Virgin, the Unmeasurable becomes three cubits high; the Unqualifiable acquires a quality; the Undefinable stands up, sits down and lies down: He who is everywhere is put

## The Controversial Little Word *Filioque*

The matter of icons is not the only theological issue that troubles the Eastern Church during this era, though in the case of the *filioque* the debate is not internal. The Nicene Creed adopted by the churches in both the East and the West states, "I believe . . . in the Holy Spirit, the Lord, the Giver of Life, *who proceeds from the Father. . . .*" But in the generations that follow, the Arian claim that the Son was lesser than the Father had taken root. In an effort to dampen such teachings, theologians begin adding the phrase *and the Son* (the *filioque*) — thus making the Son equal to the Father. The addition of the *filioque* becomes widespread throughout the West, where it not only receives a stamp of approval from Charlemagne but is also adopted in 794 at the Council of Frankfurt — though not deemed official orthodoxy by Rome until some two centuries later.

In 808 Pope Leo III writes to Charlemagne that he personally has no problem with the *filioque*, but that the Creed itself is sacrosanct. *Don't mess with the Creed* is his message. The Creed belongs to the *whole* church, and no one could simply change it. But future popes are not so protective, particularly amid growing East-West hostility. When the Council of Frankfurt confirms the *filioque*, the lines are drawn. How dare the West change the doctrine of the church? Such is no less than "moral fratricide" — a flagrant sin of church disunity. Moreover, the *filioque* is heresy — it entails upsetting the very balance of the Godhead.

into a crib; He who is above time gradually reaches the age of twelve; He who is formless appears with the shape of a man and the Incorporeal enters into a body . . . , therefore the same is describable and indescribable.

Despite John's best efforts, the iconoclasts prevail, and in 754 Emperor Constantine V (son of Leo III) calls a synod, the Iconoclast Council, proclaiming that "the only lawful representation of Christ is the Holy Eucharist" and that images of Christ and saints are to be "abhorred" as "blasphemous." The council also pronounces a curse against three defenders of icons, including John of Damascus. In fact, the synod declares: "The Trinity has destroyed these three."

With a new emperor—and Empress Irene— the balance of power tips in favor of icons. In 787 the Second Council of Nicaea restores icons as "holy images." But not until the tenth century, with Empress Theodora, would they be permanently secure in the Eastern Church.

## Cyril and Methodius: Missionary Monks

Caught between the East and the West, Cyril and his brother Methodius were missionary translators to the Slavs. Born in Thessalonica in 825 and 827 respectively, they were reared by an uncle who held a high government position in Constantinople. As a teenager Cyril studied theology, Hebrew, and Arabic. He later served as a theology professor in Constantinople and as a diplomat with Arab religious leaders at the Abbisid Caliphate. His assignment was theological in nature, and he focused on the doctrine of the Trinity, becoming one of the first to serve as a missionary to Muslims. Methodius joined a monastery after briefly serving as an official among the Slavs.

Together the brothers teamed up as ambassadors to the Khazars, a large nomadic tribe in a vast region that is today southern Russia. Over previous generations, the Khazars had successfully warded off a Muslim invasion and were being courted by the Byzantine Empire. The brothers were unsuccessful in their mission, and the Khazars, before being overrun by Genghis Khan, accepted Judaism as their faith.

Undeterred, in 860 the brothers, at the invitation of a Moravian prince, begin their life-long ministry of formulating an alphabet and translating the Bible into the Slavic language. Such tireless labors would seem on the surface to be commendable, but clerics, resentful of the "foreign missionaries," insist that Latin alone is the language of the Bible and report them to Pope Nicholas I. He demands an explanation, and the brothers dutifully report to Rome since their mission field is within the Western church's jurisdiction. But by the time they arrive in 869, Nicholas has died and Adrian II is on the papal throne. To his credit, the new pope not only commends their ministry but also consecrates Methodius as bishop and soon thereafter as archbishop. Cyril, apparently too ill to return, remains in Rome and joins a Greek monastery, where he dies.

Returning to Moravia with the pope's blessing does not lessen the opposition Methodius faces from clerics and ruling authorities. He is deposed and imprisoned. Three years later, after political reverses, he is released and resumes his position as archbishop. His health broken, he dies in 885, though not without completing his translation of the Bible into Slavic.

## Princess Olga, Vladimir, and Russian Orthodoxy

When Princess Olga converted to Christianity she laid the foundation for the Russian Orthodox Church. Born into a powerful family of Viking descent, Olga marries Prince Igor I of Kiev. In 954, due in part to his costly wars and political ineptness, Igor is assassinated and Olga begins her term as regent for her young son. After executing her husband's assassins, she sets about bringing fiscal, social, and religious reforms. In 955 she makes a public profession of faith, and two years later she journeys to Constantinople to be baptized and arrange for teachers to come to Russia. But any progress toward Orthodoxy is quickly undone when her son and his supporters assume power. He

---

### EASTERN EXASPERATION WITH ROME

My dearest brother, we do not deny to the Roman Church the primacy amongst the five sister patriarchates [Rome, Constantinople, Alexandria, Antioch, and Jerusalem], and we recognize her right to the most honorable seat at an ecumenical synod. But, she has separated herself from us by her own deeds, when through pride she assumed a monarchy which does not belong to her office.... How shall we accept decrees from her that have been issued without consulting us and even without our knowledge? If the Roman pontiff, seated on the lofty throne of his glory, wishes to thunder at us and, so to speak, hurl his mandates at us and our churches not by taking counsel with us but at his own arbitrary pleasure, what kind of brotherhood or even what kind of parenthood can this be? We would be the slaves not the sons of such of a church.... In such a case what could have been the use of the scriptures? The writings and the teachings of the Fathers would be useless. The authority of the Roman pontiff would nullify the value of all because he would be the only bishop, the sole teacher and master.

Niketas, Archbishop of Nikomedia, to Anselm, Bishop of Havelberg, 1136

Baptism of Saint Prince Vladimir, by Viktor Vasnetsov

renounces Christianity, and for a time, for political gain, he flirts with Islam.

Not until nearly twenty years after Olga's death in 988 did Orthodoxy become the official religion of Russia. Her illegitimate grandson, Vladimir (c. 958–1015), seems the most unlikely royal to bring this about. He is only ten when his grandmother dies and already on his way to becoming a ruthless and degenerate warrior. When his father dies, Vladimir prevails over his half-brothers in a bloody rivalry and eventually gains control of Kiev and other key strongholds. Like his father, he rejects his grandmother's religion, which is now taking root among many of his subjects. He is a pagan—

## THE "INCIDENT" OF 1054

Even as Orthodoxy was taking root in Russia, it was being strained to the breaking point with the Western Latin church. Theological perspectives as well as cultural and political rivalry had created tension for centuries, but one particular incident stands out as a turning point in hostilities. Bishop Kallistos Ware, in his classic *The Orthodox Church*, tells the story best:

> One summer afternoon in the year 1054, as a service was about to begin in the Church of the Holy Wisdom (Hagia Sophia) at Constantinople, Cardinal Humbert and two other legates of the Pope entered the building and made their way up to the sanctuary. They had not come to pray. They placed a Bull of Excommunication upon the altar and marched out once more. As he passed through the western door, the Cardinal shook the dust from his feet with the words: "Let God look and judge." A deacon ran out after him in great distress and begged him to take back the Bull. Humbert refused; and it was dropped in the street.

The pope's representatives had apparently waited for months to gain an audience with the Patriarch of the Eastern Church. Finally, on July 16, 1054, their patience had worn thin. The Bull of Excommunication, spurred by the apparent rebuff, dredged up old squabbles, including the *filioque*, married clergy, and various liturgical differences.

Within days, the Patriarch had dispatched his own bull of excommunication to Rome, pointing out the errors of the Latin Church. In the centuries that followed, there would be many efforts to bring about reconciliation — efforts that still continue today. There would also be terrible animosity, however, as in 1204, during the Fourth Crusade, when Constantinople was overrun and captured. But the Great Schism of 1054 has symbolically stood for the separation and split of the Church — an event of historic proportions. The most calamitous date for the Eastern Orthodox Church came in 1453 when the Eastern Empire fell with the capture of Constantinople by the Turks — and the great church of Holy Wisdom would become a mosque.

particularly in lifestyle, with several wives and numerous concubines.

Paganism, lacking cohesive unity, is not an ideal state religion, however. With nation-building in mind, Vladimir commissions envoys to investigate other religions: Judaism, Islam, Catholicism, and Orthodoxy. The first two are ruled out because of dietary laws and other factors. In the end, Catholicism does not rise to the high liturgical standard of Orthodoxy. The report of the commission on seeing the Hagia Sophia in Constantinople is memorable: "We no longer knew whether we were in heaven or on earth.... Such beauty, and we know not how to tell of it." With that endorsement, Vladimir picks Orthodoxy as the state religion, takes another wife (Anna, the sister of Basil II, the Byzantine emperor), dispatches troops for another war, and secures his place as a saint in the Orthodox tradition.

With its long history and millions of adherents, Eastern Orthodoxy remains today an enigma to many Christians in the West—particularly its apophatic theology and icons. With no pope or famous evangelists, it rarely makes news and often seems aloof and set apart from the other branches of Christianity.

## What If ...

What if the Eastern and Western churches had been able to work out their differences and had remained under one umbrella? How would the church look today? Would the Protestant Reformation have occurred? Would the churches in Asia, Africa, and Latin America be expanding in size as they are today?

What if the iconoclasts had won the day? How distinct would Eastern Orthodoxy be today?

What if Justinian and his adoptive father, with their peasant backgrounds, had not ascended the throne and made their marks on statecraft and judicial law? How might our laws and courts be different today?

What if Cyril and Methodius had stayed home instead of serving as missionaries to the Slavs, or if Vladimir had chosen Islam over Orthodoxy? How would the world be different today?

## Selected Bibliography

Bridge, Antony, *Theodora: Portrait in a Byzantine Landscape*. Chicago: Academy Chicago, 1993.

Daley, Brian. *Gregory of Nazianzus*. New York: Routledge, 2006.

Evans, James Allan. *The Empress Theodora: Partner of Justinian*. Austin: University of Texas, 2003.

Hall, Christopher A. *Reading Scripture With the Church Fathers*. Downers Grove, Ill.: InterVarsity, 1998.

Herrin, Judith. *Women in Purple: Rules of Medieval Byzantium*. Princeton, N.J.: Princeton University, 2004.

Kelly, J. N. D. *Golden Mouth: The Story of John Chrysostom.* Ithaca, N.Y.: Cornell University Press, 1998.

Rosen, William. *Justinian's Flea: Plague, Empire, and the Birth of Europe.* New York: Viking, 2007.

Smith, Richard Travers. *St. Basil the Great.* Whitefish, Mont.: Kessinger Publishing, 2007.

Stewart, John. *Nestorian Missionary Enterprise: The Story of a Church on Fire.* Piscataway, N.J.: Georgia Press, 2007.

Tradigo, Alfredo. *Icons and Saints of the Eastern Orthodox Church.* Los Angeles: Getty, 2006.

Ware, Timothy Kallistos. *The Orthodox Church.* New York: Penguin, 1993.

# CHAPTER 7

# The Reconstituted Roman Empire

## *Charlemagne and Papal Power*

*In the late 1970s when I was a new professor teaching my first courses in church history, one of the questions students sometimes asked as we moved into the Middle Ages was: "Do you think there were any real Christians then?" Though I should not have been surprised, I was nevertheless jolted by the query.*

*My response today is the same as then: of course there were! Moreover, there is no way for Protestants to trace their heritage back to the New Testament era or to the church fathers except by going through the Roman Catholic Church. We may rightly ask whether certain popes were truly Christian. But whatever the answer, they are our popes. The Western church did not disappear in the generations following the apostle Paul and then suddenly reappear as Martin Luther was nailing his Ninety-five Theses to the church door in Wittenberg. Nor is the matter solved by identifying "Protestant" stepping stones such as Waldo, Wycliffe, and Hus.*

*Mormons maintain that the gospel was lost at the end of the apostolic age and that it reappeared in the form of the "Restored Gospel" when Joseph Smith dug gold plates from the Hill Cumorah. That is Mormon history. It is not Christian history—even if we were to shrink the "lost" centuries down to ten or fewer.*

*I am a Catholic through the Middle Ages. My people (Lutheran by ancestry, Reformed by adoption) came straight out of the Roman Catholic Church. Martin Luther and John Calvin were both Catholics, as were the vast majority of first-generation Protestants.*

*As Protestants, we do our own heritage a disservice if we imagine that medieval Catholicism belongs to Catholics only. It is a heritage we share. With that perspective, it is natural for us to regard Catholics today as brothers and sisters whose ancestors, unlike ours, did not veer off the Roman Catholic road in the sixteenth century.*

Nil manet aeternum, nihil immutabile vere est,
Obscurat sacrum nox tenebrosa diem.
Nothing remains forever, nothing is truly unchangeable,
Shadowy night blots out the holy day.
ALCUIN (D. 804)

When we contemplate the Catholic Church, we have no difficulty affirming that nothing remains unchangeable or even remains forever. Of course the church has remained, but it is not the same church that existed in medieval times. A thousand years ago the Catholic Church was often as wild and unruly as the barbarians it sought to convert. Clerical sins ranged from adultery and embezzlement to rape and murder. And unlike the scandals of today, some of the clergy from popes on down seemed almost to glory in their crimes.

Any study of medieval popes reveals a close proximity to heads of state. This is a time when the church reigns supreme but never without interference or challenge. Here we see the full flowering of *Christendom*—a theocracy of sorts born in the reign of Emperor Constantine and reignited on Christmas Day 800, when Charlemagne was crowned Holy Roman Emperor. The papacy maintains close connections with "secular" government; at times the two are virtually one and the same. Missionary outreach, bolstered by the military, is considered a critical component of foreign policy.

But missions and monasteries also foster literacy and libraries and a spirited upsurge in scholarship. The medieval period that indulges violence and church corruption also promotes mathematics and metaphysics and manuscript copying. And there is a keen awareness that individuals and events are part of the record that will stand the test of time. History matters, and names are not to be forgotten. Among them are Boniface, Alcuin, Charlemagne, Anskar, Pope Joan, Pope Gregory VII (Hildebrand), Urban II, and Innocent III.

The Byzantine civilization centered in Constantinople blossoms as the Western Roman Empire is falling into decay. Many of the glories of Rome are transported east and adapted by the Byzantine culture. Roman law and statecraft is absorbed into Justinian's codes, and from the Hellenistic culture of Greece comes science, philosophy, poetry, and prose as well as music, art, and architecture. During the three centuries following Gregory the Great, civilization in the East is more advanced than in the West, where culture often seems to be regressing, spurred on by inequalities of feudalism. Territorial kings

## PARADE OF HISTORY

The pomp and pageantry of the Eastern church is matched by that of the Western church as a procession of popes moves through medieval times. The power of the empire competes with the power of the church in a parade of pickpockets, clerics, clowns, court jesters, and criminals of every kind. The most titillating story features a female pope who gives birth during the fanfare of a parade from St. Peter's to the Lateran. But the most shameful of parades of this era are the Crusades. Marching off to the Holy Land with a flourish, these frenzied swarms of civilian soldiers and besotted citizens mark the low point of the period.

rule over warrior lords of the manor. The lords contract not only knights as fighting men but also a host of others. All are vassals in a system that ranks every individual from top to bottom, peasant serfs being at the very bottom, trading arduous labor for security and use of the land. But the disparity between the landed nobles and the impoverished peasants cannot last. Nor are knights — or peasants — always reliable. There are uprisings of serfs and battles among kings and among nobles. Indeed, there is a continual rearranging of society, all in the shadow of Viking raids from the undefined borders to the north.

Built on a foundation of sand, the feudal hierarchy begins to crumble into anarchy, despite the widely quoted clerical claim of its being authorized by God:

> God himself has willed that among men, some must be lords and some serfs, in such a fashion that the lords venerate and love God, and that the serfs love and venerate their lord following the word of the Apostle; serfs obey your temporal lords with fear and trembling; lords treat your serfs according to justice and equity.

Popes in the generations following Gregory I are mostly Romans (or at least Italians) who view their reigns as political plums. Their independence, however, is curtailed by the still-powerful Byzantine emperor. But by the eighth century, the political power of the West is beginning to emerge, in fits and starts, from barbarian devastation. And by the time of Gregory II, whose sixteen-year reign begins in 715, the East is struggling on two fronts — the iconoclastic controversy from within and Muslim threats from without.

Another factor that offers the Western church a measure of independence is poor communication — the distance between Rome and Constantinople and the fact that the well-designed Roman roads are now in disrepair. What once was a northern land of barbarians is now being tamed in the name of the Roman Catholic Church. The Franks — from the time of Clovis — and the Germans are on their way to adopting a European Catholic mentality through the influence of Charles Martel and Boniface and later Charlemagne.

As the power of kings becomes more centralized, so also does the power of popes — power based in some instances on outright forgeries, the most notorious being the *Donatio Constantini* (Donation of Constantine), written around 750. Pope Hadrian I is the first to cite it as justification for Charlemagne to recognize the authority of the church. His letter, dated 778, references "blessed Sylvester, Roman Pontiff," who was given "the right to bestow authority" over vast realms by Emperor Constantine. Although this was long before Pope Leo III crowned him Emperor of the Romans, Charlemagne has a give-and-take relationship with the papacy, and the letter perhaps seemed to him as routine bartering. Such had been the case with his father and grandfather. His father, Pippin (the Short, whose grandson was Pippin the Hunchback), was crowned King of the Franks in 754 by Pope Stephen II; and his grandfather, Charles (the Hammer) Martel (the illegitimate son of Pippin the Middle), was also indebted to popes and bishops for his power.

Charles Martel was the warrior king who unified the Franks, preparing the way for his grandson, Charlemagne. A ruthless military general, he beat back the Saxons and later the Frisians. But his most celebrated claim to fame came in 732 at the Battle of Tours. His was a decisive victory over the Muslim invaders, though not the one-sided exaggeration portrayed by a chronicler:

## EVERYDAY LIFE

### Same Sex Love

When historians read letters and other documents from the medieval Mediterranean world, it is easy to view customs through the lens of their own culture. But such a perspective can be very misleading. Expressions of same-sex love and friendship, for example, are often presumed to be homosexual in nature. Homosexuality was not uncommon in ancient and medieval times, but what appears to a contemporary Western eye to be gay or lesbian love may have been nothing of the sort.

In early medieval times passionate pledges of "brotherly love" were the norm. In fact, there were sometimes signed contracts binding "blood-brothers" together, not as in a marriage contract but as a bond of loyalty to one another. Such bonds also exhibited physical expressions of love. For example, in the eleventh century Anselm wrote to two young men embarking on a monastic life: "My eyes eagerly long to see your face, most beloved; my arms stretch out to your embraces. My lips long for your kisses; whatever remains of my life desires your company." On another occasion, he wrote to a monk assigned to another monastery: "We cannot now

---

#### ALCUIN'S PASSIONATE POETRY AND LOVE

During the early Middle Ages ... "passionate friendship" ... was common and comprised the subject matter of much clerical writing....

A distinctly erotic element, for instance, is notable in the circle of clerical friends presided over by Alcuin at the court of Charlemagne. This group included some of the most brilliant scholars of the day ... but the erotic element subsisted principally between Alcuin and his pupils ... The prominence of love in Alcuin's writings, all of which are addressed to males, is striking. In one poem he writes, "You, sweet love, are the most welcome guest of all."

Another is addressed to someone older:

Love has pierced my heart with its flame ...,
And love always burns with fresh fire....
Let me therefore flee to you with my whole heart,
And do you flee to me from the vanishing world....

He wrote to a friend (a bishop and possibly the recipient of the poem quoted above),

I think of your love and friendship with such sweet memories, reverend bishop, that I long for that lovely time when I may be able to clutch the neck of your sweetness with the fingers of my desires. Alas, if only it were granted to me ... to be transported to you, how would I sink into your embraces ... how would I cover, with tightly pressed lips, not only your eyes, ears, and mouth but also your every finger and your toes, not once but many a time.

John Boswell, *Christianity, Social Tolerance, and Homosexuality*

be separated without tearing apart our joint soul and severing our heart." Such passion should not necessarily be equated with sexual desires. After all, Anselm later initiated the Council of London, which among other things, regulated against homosexual activity among clerics.

Later in the Middle Ages, the intense love that Hildegaard of Bingen expresses toward a younger nun, Richardis von Stade (who served her faithfully and then departed to another convent), is sometimes presumed to be a lesbian love. But the context suggests, rather a deep motherly love. Monastic culture often encouraged the writing of love letters to God and Jesus and the saints—and to fellow monks and nuns. The spiritual love they expressed to one another was often just that—a form of intense platonic affection. It would be naïve to assume, however, that homosexuality was not at times a factor.

The Muslims planned to go to Tours to destroy the Church of St. Martin, the city, and the whole country. Then came against them the glorious Prince Charles, at the head of his whole force.... By the grace of Our Lord, he wrought a great slaughter upon the enemies of Christian faith, so that—as history bears witness—he slew in that battle 300,000 men, likewise their king.... And what was the greatest marvel of all, he only lost in that battle 1500 men.

Charles commissioned Willibrord, bishop of Utrecht, to evangelize the Frisians and Boniface (Winfrid) to evangelize the Germanic tribes. He seemed to see no conflict in combining military might with missions.

## Boniface (Winfrid): Apostle to the Germans

The most celebrated medieval missionary was Winfrid Boniface (c. 672–754), an ordained priest and monk from Devonshire England. Willibald, who wrote *The Life of St. Boniface* in 768, presents his as a typical "saintly" childhood. After he was weaned and reared with his mother's "anxious care," Winfrid decided "to

enter the service of God and began to think deeply ... of the monastic life." He sought the counsel of clerics on how to overcome "the frailties of his nature." When his father learned of his desire to become a monk, he rebuked him "with violence" and paraded "before him all the inducements of pleasure and luxury." But he resisted, "filled with the spirit of God." Then his father, "struck down by a sudden and fatal sickness," at last gives the boy his blessing.

Hearing the stories of missionary monks, Winfrid recognizes his calling to cross the English channel and evangelize the "heathen" on the continent. After an unsuccessful ministry in Friesland, he returns home. But three years later, in 718, he sets out again, though first traveling to Rome, where he receives a papal commission. After facing more failures, he finally settles in the Rhineland, where he will serve for the remainder of his life. In 723 he again visits Rome, this time to be commissioned a missionary bishop by Pope Gregory II, who gives him the name Boniface.

His most celebrated confrontation with paganism is his attack on the thunder god at Geismar. A mighty oak tree stands as a sacred symbol, the very spirit of the god. Some in the

Boniface's martyrdom in 754

region are faithful Christians, but others offer sacrifices to trees and springs and conduct various divinations and incantations. Upon his arrival, Boniface strides into the middle of the crowd, grabs an axe, and begins chopping down the gigantic tree. "Suddenly, the oak's vast bulk, shaken by a mighty blast of wind from above crashed to the ground" forming a Cross, writes Willibald. Indeed, "the oak burst asunder into four parts, each part having a trunk of equal length. At the sight of this extraordinary spectacle the heathens who had been cursing ceased to revile and began, on the contrary, to believe and bless the Lord."

> "Can there be a more fitting pursuit in youth or a more valuable possession in old age than a knowledge of Holy Writ? In the midst of storms it will preserve you from the dangers of shipwreck and guide you to the shore of an enchanting paradise and the ever-lasting bliss of the angels."
>
> Boniface

Like other earlier missionaries, Boniface establishes monastic mission outposts, always with military support. Among these monasteries is the double (coed) monastery of Bischofsheim, where his cousin Lioba serves as the abbess, ruling over both nuns and monks in separate communities. The nuns—both English and native women—are cloistered, rarely going outside the convent walls. But regional officials, church leaders, and commoners come for counsel with the great abbess, "whose reputation for holiness and virtuous teaching," according to Boniface, "had penetrated across wide lands and fill the hearts of many with praise."

Lioba quickly realizes, however, that this is dangerous work. Boniface laments that local rulers "have shown their evil disposition and have sinned in a criminal way against the teaching of the gospels" by persisting "in the seduction of nuns." Nevertheless, she perseveres and goes on to establish more outposts. Soon there is "hardly a convent of nuns in that part which had not one of her disciples as abbess."

Meanwhile, Boniface is establishing a monastery at Fulda with the military support of Charles Martel. "Without the protection of the prince of the Franks," he writes, "I can neither rule the people or the church nor defend the priests and clerks, monks and nuns; nor can I prevent the practice of pagan rites and sacrilegious worship of idols without his mandate and the awe inspired by his name."

Boniface often clashes with Celtic and French Monks, whom he regards as disloyal to Rome. His greatest clash, however, occurs when he turns his work over to others and returns to pioneer missionary outreach. In 754 he journeys back to Friesland, where he and some fifty of his associates are ambushed and killed by local pagan forces. In 771, less than two decades following his death, Charlemagne ascends the throne, and during the nearly half-century of his reign, he combines missions and military might to extend the boundaries of the empire.

## Alcuin: Principal of the Palace School

Prior to the reign of Charlemagne, a fine scholar and educator lit a candle, and the "Dark Ages" began to fade into dawn. Alcuin (c. 735–804) stands out as the greatest educator of this era. He was in many ways Charlemagne's opposite.

A highly literate and literary monk, he seemed an unlikely associate of the often-vicious warrior king. But Charlemagne's choice of Alcuin to head his Palace School in France was a stroke of genius.

Anything but a one-man show, Alcuin assembled the greatest scholars of the age in the Palace School. Late in life, he summed up his accomplishments, saying he had "dispensed the honey of the scripture, intoxicated my students with the wine of ancient learning, fed them the apples of grammatical refinement, and adorned them with the knowledge of astronomy." He did far more than that, and his scholarly reach stretched across Europe and beyond. Among his achievements are not only the founding of libraries but also the production of books, wherein he introduces a smaller font than was previously used—a calligraphy (Carolingian Miniscule) that allows for many more words per page of parchment, thus significantly reducing the cost of manuscripts.

Born into a noble family from York in Northumbria (northeast England), the precocious Alcuin (nicknamed Albinus) is placed in the Cathedral School at York as a young child. He quickly sprints to the head of his class, and his renowned master Egbert gives him special tutoring and takes him on his travels to the

### MISSIONS AND MILITARY MIGHT

Since the times of Charlemagne's grandfather, the idea of reforming the Frankish Church was linked to that of evangelizing the Saxon and Frisian pagans of the north. The energy and cultural training required to restore discipline and propriety among the bishops and monks of Gaul were the same qualities required to undertake missionary work beyond the borders of Christendom. It is no surprise then that the most important churchman and the architect of the first reforms under Charles Martel and later under Carloman and Pepin was a missionary. Boniface enjoyed the friendship of the Frankish mayors of the palace, and they provided him with indispensable political and military backing for his apostolate in Germany.

Alessandro Barbero and Allan Cameron, *Charlemagne*

continent. When Egbert is elevated to the position of archbishop, he names Alcuin to succeed him. For the next fifteen years Alcuin maintains high academic standards while expanding the library, faculty, and enrollment. The best and brightest come to sit under his teaching.

His big break comes in the spring of 781 in Parma, Italy, when he meets Charlemagne (then King of the Franks) who convinces him to leave his position and head up the Palace School in the royal court in the town of Aachen (Aix-la-Chapelle). An admirer of Charlemagne, Alcuin accepts the challenge and sets the stage for what would become known as the Carolingian Renaissance. The Palace School is the academy of choice for sons of the royal families and nobility, including Charlemagne's son Pepin. With funds from his patron, Alcuin expands the library and attracts the best minds of Europe to this prestigious center of learning.

Alcuin is known primarily through his enormous capacity for correspondence, his letters copied and passed along for their wisdom and counsel. He challenges monks overseeing young scholars in Northumbria to "consider the splendour of your churches, the beauty of your buildings, your way of life according to the Rule." They should be appreciative of the architecture that surrounds them every day. Knowing the temptations of the scholars under their charge, he continues: "Let the boys be present with praises of the heavenly king and not be digging foxes out of holes or following the fleeting courses of hares.... He who does not learn when he is young does not teach when he is old."

Alcuin lives during difficult times. Learning is often interrupted by fierce invaders from the north who have no appreciation for high culture. When he learns that Vikings have ravaged his homeland, he is inconsolable. But his own emperor, Charlemagne, could be equally ruthless in crushing the opposition. He imposes the death penalty on Saxons who refuse to be baptized. It is no wonder, then, that revolt begins with the burning of churches and the slaughter of priests. Alcuin strongly objects to the bloodshed, writing to Charlemagne that "faith arises from the will, not from compulsion. You can persuade a man to believe, but you cannot force

## ALCUIN AND HIS PUZZLES

In addition to his expertise in theology, linguistics, and biblical studies, Alcuin was a master of liberal arts, fine arts, mathematics, and science. In fact, he is considered one of the fathers of mathematics. Mathematics and logic, he reasoned, could be best understood through story problems. With that in mind, he developed and passed along puzzles that were designed to sharpen the minds of young students. The best known of these brain teasers are the stories of the wolf, the goat, and the cabbage and the story of the three jealous husbands, each of whom would not let the others be alone with his wife. The stories are similar; in each case there must be a crossing of a river. The problem relates to how many times the boat must go across the river to accomplish its purpose. In the case of the wolf, the goat, and the cabbage, if left alone to their own devices, the wolf will eat the goat or the goat will eat the cabbage. So how does one mentally think the way out of this problem? At some point the oarsman must bring back something that has already been left on the other shore. The same is true of the jealous husbands and their wives. The only way people advance in life, Alcuin asserted, is to think their way out of problems.

## THE VENERABLE BEDE

A scholar of the Carolingian Renaissance, Bede (c. 672–735) was first and foremost a writer and teacher. In addition to his biblical commentaries, he wrote his celebrated masterpiece, *A History of the English Church and People.* The text is a remarkably objective treatment of the period, drawn "from ancient documents, from the traditions of our forebears, and from my own personal knowledge."

Born into a prosperous family in Northumbria, he entered a monastery at age seven and died in a monastery more than a half-century later. Monastery life, however, did not preclude his having a wife. In one of his commentaries he writes: "Prayers are hindered by the conjugal duty because as often as I perform what is due to my wife I am not able to pray." In another commentary, he confesses: "Formerly I possessed a wife in the lustful passion of desire and now I possess her in honourable sanctification and true love of Christ."

Bede is remembered not only as the father of English history but also for his passion for having the Bible translated into the language of his own people. To Archbishop Egbert, he wrote of the need for Scripture "to be known and constantly repeated in their own tongue by those that are unlearned, that is, by them who have knowledge only of their proper tongue" — this he wrote centuries prior to the Protestant Reformation. His own contribution to this cause was an Old English translation of the gospel of John, which was completed on his deathbed.

him. You may even be able to force him to be baptized, but this will not help to instill the faith within him." The Saxons, he insists, need "preachers, not predators." Neither is the imposition of tithes acceptable. "The tithes, they say, destroyed the faith of the Saxons."

In affairs of state, Alcuin is regarded as one of Charlemagne's chief advisors; but, missing his homeland, he returns to England in 790. Within a few short years, however, Charlemagne recalls him. He is needed to stand up against Felix, archbishop of Urgel, and the growing Adoptionist heresy—belief that Jesus was only an adopted son and became divine through sinless fidelity to God. The matter is settled, largely through Alcuin's arguments, at the Council of Frankfurt in 794. But Alcuin insists that heretics, like pagans, should not face the death penalty. Indeed, Felix, whose Adoptionist position is soundly rejected at the Council, is allowed to return to his home in Spain, where he continues for many years to preach his heresy.

In 796 Alcuin becomes the abbot of Saint Martin's abbey at Tours. Now in his sixties, he is determined to leave the life of court luxury and return to monastic living. In 800, four years before his death, he encourages Charlemagne to go to Rome to be crowned Holy Roman Emperor by the pope.

By this time, Theodulf of Orleans has stepped into the position Alcuin vacated when he departed to the abbey four years earlier. He carries on the educational and ecclesiastical reforms of the Carolingian Renaissance for more than a decade after the death of Alcuin. Accused of conspiracy in 817, he is exiled and dies in 821 from poisoning. Today Saint Theodulf might be forgotten but for his great Palm Sunday hymn, which is often sung while children process into the sanctuary waving palm branches:

> All glory, laud, and honor to thee,
>      Redeemer, king,
> To whom the lips of children made sweet
>      hosannas ring.

## Emperor Charlemagne: Education, Women, and War

Like military leaders before him, Charlemagne (742–814) was a ruthless warrior bent on expanding his vast domains. Yet by all accounts he was a religious man who promoted and funded monasteries. The oldest son of Pippin III and grandson of Charles Martel, Charlemagne grew up in a military family that controlled a large portion of what is today Switzerland and France. His mother, Bertha, a daughter of royalty, brought prestige and lands to the marriage. Little is known of his childhood but, according to his earliest biographer, his physical presence as an adult was unmistakable: "He was six feet four inches tall, and built to scale. He had beautiful white hair, animated eyes, a powerful nose … always stately and dignified." Disciplined in eating and drinking, his mealtime entertain-

Emperor Charlemagne

ment was not the usual fare of court jesters. Rather, an aide read aloud the best literature of the day. He was conversant in other languages, believing that "to have another language is to possess a second soul."

On his father's death in 668, when Charles is in his mid-twenties, he and his brother Carolman become co-heirs to the vast kingdom. When Carolman dies three years later, Charles becomes sole king of the Franks. His mother arranges a marriage with Desiderata, daughter of the king of the Lombards, for obvious political gain, but the marriage is annulled the following year. Charles reportedly puts her out—against his mother's wishes—and marries thirteen-year-old Hildegard, a duke's daughter. She bears him nine children, several of whom grow up to be their father's land-grabbing warriors.

With Desiderata out of the way, Charles declares war on her father and conquers the Lombards in northern Italy. From there he moves south and also pushes the borders of his kingdom into what is today Spain, Hungary, and Germany. Ruthless as a commander, he reportedly executes more than four thousand Saxon prisoners in a single day. Nor is he a gentleman on the home front. Hildegard competes with eight wives and concubines and many more children.

In addition to his campaigns of aggression, Charles holds back invading Muslims. But expansion is his forte, often through relatively peaceful means with little dismantling of local culture. Indeed, surrendering to his forces has positive effects. With a unified administration, local wars diminish, and commerce, farming, and education are vastly improved.

The turning point in Charlemagne's reign comes in 800. A year earlier Pope Leo III had appealed for protection. Having risen up through the ranks from the lower classes, Leo is scorned by Roman aristocrats and fears for his life. Charles uses the opportunity to boost his own standing. He comes to Saint Peter's Basilica on Christmas Day 800 to pray, and there the pope crowns him Holy Roman Emperor. Labeled "Charlemagne's Pope," Leo reigns until he dies in 816. Yet he stands his ground against the emperor on some matters, particularly when Charlemagne, motivated by expansionist aims, seeks to change the Nicene Creed by adding the *filioque* ("and the son"), a move considered heretical by the Eastern Church.

With wars yet to wage, Charlemagne reforms the realms already under his rule. Inaugurating the "Carolingian Renaissance," he courts scholars, most notably Alcuin, and encourages education across the empire. His court at Aachen becomes an impressive cultural and educational center. With Alcuin's expertise, he creates a university town, drawing talent from all social levels and fostering a wide range of academic disciplines. Music, art, architecture, roads, bridges, and thermal baths add to the city's prestige.

But to the end of his life, Charlemagne the warrior is sending troops into battle, sometimes leading the charge himself. In 811, when he is marching his men north to attack King Godefrid and his Norse army, he learns that the king has been murdered. The seventy-year-old Charlemagne turns back. It would be his last campaign. He dies in 814 with his son, Louis the Pious, succeeding him. His long reign of forty-seven years can be summed up in his own terms: "By the sword and the cross." Most of his subjects had known no other ruler. A monk penned lines that spoke for many:

> From the lands where the sun rises to western shores, People are crying and wailing ... the Franks, the Romans, all Christians, are stung with mourning and great worry ... the

young and old, glorious nobles, all lament the loss of their Caesar.... The world laments the death of Charles.... O Christ, you who govern the heavenly host, grant a peaceful place to Charles in your kingdom. Alas for miserable me.

Following the reign of Charlemagne, the papacy begins a lengthy period of decline. Thirty-five popes reign in the 170 years between 880 and 1050, averaging less than five years each. Indeed, between 896 and 904 there are nine popes—the same number that reigned in the whole of the twentieth century. The short tenure is not because they are old and sickly: some begin their reign as teenagers. Some are deposed, others murdered; some reign only a few weeks or months. Five popes are assassinated. Besides popes, there are antipopes, making a tidy chronology of succession well nigh impossible. The era is tainted by papal corruption of every kind. It thus might be natural to suppose that a feminine touch would bring some decorum to this male-only club.

## Pope Joan: Legend and Legacy

That a woman would sit in the papal throne is not so inconceivable in light of the fact that some popes in this era were unordained teenagers. Furthermore, women often held an honored place in the church, sometimes, like Lioba, overseeing large monastic complexes.

John Anglicus was reportedly an English scientist who relocated in Rome and gained a reputation for erudite scholarship. His status and renown paved the way for church office. Indeed, the scientist soon became a cardinal and, with the death of Pope Leo IV, was elevated to the papacy in 853. All goes well until one day, while in procession to the Lateran

## THE CADAVER SYNOD

In an era of papal sleaze some popes — most notably Stephen VII — almost seem to revel in their wickedness. The act for which Stephen is most remembered is his presiding over the "Cadaver Synod" in January of 897. Ordering the body of his predecessor, Formosus (891–896), unearthed, he demands that the "stinking corpse" be attired in papal robes, propped up in a chair, and put on trial. Formosus, who had reigned as pope for five years, was by all accounts able, intelligent, and saintly — at least by ninth-century standards. But Stephen, acting as judge, rails at the decayed corpse. Formosus, not surprisingly, loses his case and is duly punished. Three fingers from his right hand by which he had given the papal blessing are chopped off, and his papal garments are exchanged for the garments of a pauper. All his acts and decrees as pope are invalidated — as was his papacy itself. Stephen reigns only a matter of months before he is stripped of his papal crown, imprisoned, and strangled. In 897, long after his body was thrown in the Tiber (on the orders of Stephen) and retrieved by a devoted follower, Formosus is reinstated as a legitimate (albeit dead) pope and given a proper papal burial. A decade later, however, his body is once again unearthed on the orders of Pope Sergius III. This time he would be properly humiliated by being beheaded.

from St. Peter's Basilica, the carriage is forced to make a quick stop while the pope gives birth to a baby "in a narrow lane between the Coliseum and St Clement's church." One of the earlier sources tells the story with a slightly different slant. She "disguised herself as a man and became, by her character and talents, a curial secretary, then a cardinal, and finally pope. One day, while mounting a horse, she gave birth to a child."

Following the birth, the narrative is muddled. Pope John VIII, who is actually Pope Joan, reigns for less than three years. But when she is found to be disguising herself as a man, there is no mercy. By one account she is tied by the feet and dragged over the cobblestones while citizens of Rome stone her to death. She is then buried at the very spot where she gave birth — the whereabouts of the baby unknown. She is not "placed on the list of the holy pontiffs, both because of her female sex and on account of the foulness of the matter." Another version suggests a more humane post-partum ending.

She is secreted away to an undisclosed convent, where she repents and raises her son, who grows up to become bishop of Ostia.

From the thirteenth century into the Renaissance, the report of *Pappess Joanna* is widely disseminated — in one instance to defend a pope who is a heretic. If being a woman does not disqualify one from being pope, so the argument goes, why should heresy? Although the church officially denied the account, the rumors persisted — one asserting that for a time there was a statue near the Lateran called "The Woman Pope with Her Child." Likewise, the church was rumored to be so nervous about the possibility of electing another woman pope that the chair used for the papal consecration was designed with a hole so that an inspector can verify gender with certainty. Sixteenth-century Reformers used the story to disparage the church. Since that time the account of the female pope has continued to resurface, but it is generally considered to be no more than a fascinating, albeit false, story.

## Anskar: Apostle to the North

The ministry of Anskar (801–865), like that of Boniface, is closely tied to military exploits. A French-born Benedictine monk, he risks his life to evangelize Scandinavia. Initially, he faces strong opposition in Denmark and welcomes an invitation from King Bjorn to relocate in Sweden. Successful as a diplomat, he is soon named archbishop of Hamburg for all Scandinavia and northern Europe. Conversions—often politically motivated—are numerous, but after fourteen years of arduous labor he is forced to flee. All the previous gains are lost with the Danish invasion of Sweden.

As military threats wane, he returns to his post and pours his life into spiritual formation rather than merely counting converts. A preaching, teaching monk who leads by example, he is troubled when he is heralded a saint and insists that his life story not be written until after he dies. Yet he knows his story will inspire others, and Rimbert, his biographer, faithfully records it, emphasizing his youthful conversion:

> When he had thus given himself up to boyish levity, he had a vision during the night in which he appeared to be in a miry and slippery place, from which he could not escape except with great difficulty; beside him was a delightful path on which he saw a matron advancing . . . followed by many other women clothed in white, with whom was his (deceased) mother. . . . The mistress [being] the Holy Mary, said to him: "My son . . . if you desire to share our companionship, you must flee from every kind of vanity. . . ." Immediately after this vision . . . his manner of life . . . suddenly changed.

Anskar is known for prayer and fasting but never at the expense of other duties. His monks are expected to be ever busy at work—taking a page from the Benedictine principle *ora et labora* (pray and work). When unable to do heavy manual labor, he is often seen knitting while he prays. Like many other medieval saints, Anskar is credited with countless miracles. He brushed aside such claims, insisting that "the greatest miracle in my life would be if God ever made a thoroughly pious man out of me." He died of natural causes, having been denied the martyr's crown for which he longed. In the years that followed, much of his religious realm reverted to paganism.

---

### SYNAGOGUE OF SATAN, ROMAN AMAZONS, AND PAPAL PORNOCRACY

The political disorder of Europe [in the tenth century] affected the church and paralyzed its efforts for good. The papacy itself lost all independence and dignity, and became the prey of avarice, violence, and intrigue, a veritable synagogue of Satan. . . . And what is worse . . . three bold and energetic women of the highest rank and lowest character, Theodora the elder . . . and her two daughters, Marozia and Theodora, filled the chair of St. Peter with their paramours and bastards. These Roman Amazons combined with the fatal charms of personal beauty and wealth, a rare capacity for intrigue, and a burning lust for power and pleasure. . . . They turned the church of St. Peter into a den of robbers, and the residence of his successors into a harem. And they gloried in their shame. Hence this infamous period is called the papal Pornocracy.

Philip Schaff, *History of the Christian Church*

## Gregory VII (Hildebrand): Proponent of Papal Supremacy

Hildebrand (c. 1020–1085), who reigned as Gregory VII for twelve years beginning in 1073, was the most honorable and most powerful pope in the centuries following Gregory I. Born in Soana, a village in southern Tuscany, he worked his way up the clerical ladder with the help of his uncle, a well-connected abbot. He was a powerhouse of managerial energy and was known as the "little monk" because he was small in stature and had been educated in a monastery in Rome. His competency attracted the attention of John Gratian (Pope Gregory VI), who in 1045 had purchased the papal office from his god-son Pope Benedict IX for a large sum. On assuming office, John Gratian assigned Hildebrand the job of eradicating the corruption and violence running rampant in all levels of the church.

But opposition is strong. A year later, in 1046, King Henry III of Germany deposes John Gratian along with two other competing popes and names a German bishop as Pope Clement II. Clement returns the favor by crowning Henry as Holy Roman Emperor, giving him the authority to appoint subsequent popes. Pope Gregory (John Gratian), flees to Germany for refuge, accompanied by Hildebrand. After Gregory dies, Hildebrand briefly returns to monastic life before being called back to Rome to become an aide to Pope Leo IX. When Leo dies, Hildebrand continues his administrative responsibilities under Pope Victor II, and two years later he is working in behalf of the soon-to-be-elected Pope Stephen IX. In 1059 he secures the papal throne for Nicholas II, and he is again at center stage in 1061 for the coronation of Pope Alexander II, whose reign extends for twelve years, during which time Hildebrand's star continues to rise.

While the funeral rites are being conducted in Rome for Alexander on a spring day in 1073, a sudden uproar is heard in the Lateran basilica: "Blessed Peter has chosen Hildebrand! Let Hildebrand be pope!" Hildebrand reportedly seeks to stifle the crowd, but when the ceremony is over, he accepts an escort, and with cheering crowds, goes to St. Peter's, where cardinals and other high-ranking clergy pronounce his election as pope. His detractors charge that the election is highly irregular and even illegal. It ignores the protocol set in place by his predecessor, Nicholas II, most specifically that papal elections must have the approval of the German emperor — in this case Henry IV. But he is the right man for the job. The rationale is enunciated the following day in the decree of election:

> A man mighty in human and divine knowledge, a distinguished lover of equity and justice, a man firm in adversity and temperate in prosperity, a man, according to the saying of the Apostle, "of good behavior, blameless, modest, sober, chaste, given to hospitality, and ruling his house well"; a man from his childhood generously brought up in the bosom of this Mother Church, and for the merit of his life already raised to the archidiaconal dignity.

Henry IV, informed of the decision, gives his consent. Hildebrand is consecrated pope in June, having been ordained a priest in May. Like popes before him, he claims great power, based in part on the eighth-century forged Donation of Constantine. Hildebrand, however, trumps the Donation with his own *Dictatus*, twenty-seven theses that confirm his power.

Old enough to be Henry's grandfather, Hildebrand seeks to take advantage of the king's youth. But opponents of the pope are numerous, particularly after he threatens to both excommunicate and depose Henry. Indeed, on Christmas night 1076, Hildebrand is ambushed and taken prisoner, only to be released the next day.

## GREGORY VII, *DICTATUS PAPAE* (1075)

1. That the Roman church was established by God alone....
9. That all princes shall kiss the foot of the pope alone....
12. That he has the power to depose emperors....
18. That his decree can be annulled by no one, and that he can annul the decrees of anyone.
19. That he can be judged by no one.
22. That the Roman Church has never erred and will never err to all eternity....
26. That no one can be regarded as catholic who does not agree with the Roman Church....

But weeks later, Henry calls a synod and, with the support of German clergy and ruling class, deposes the pope. Hildebrand promptly declares Henry not only deposed but also excommunicated. Henry shoots back with a memo accusing Hildebrand of being "no pope" at all, who must be replaced with "another who will not cloak violence with religion"—a "false monk" who dares to defy the one "anointed to kingship" by God. "Step down, step down, thou eternally damned."

The showdown has begun. At stake is who will control appointments to church office. This dispute, known as the Investiture Controversy, is considered by many scholars to be the most far-reaching conflict between secular and religious powers in medieval Europe. Henry underestimates German reverence for the pope—and his own low popularity ratings. German princes, recognizing an opportunity to enhance their own standing, side with Hildebrand and are prepared to elect a new king. Recognizing his situation, Henry journeys across the Alps to a castle at Canosa where the pope is residing. For three long January days, he stands barefoot at the gate in penitence. Finally, the Pope absolves Henry and revokes the excommunication.

The pope has prevailed, and the king is humiliated. But soon Henry is up to his old tricks, and Hildebrand excommunicates him again. Henry then deposes Hildebrand, and Clement III becomes antipope. Hildebrand, now a sickly old man, is exiled. But he fights back with words: "I have loved righteousness and hated iniquity, therefore I die in exile." He dies in 1085. Ten years later Henry is deposed for the final time by his own son and also dies in defeat.

For Hildebrand, however, glory comes some seven centuries later when he is canonized by Pope Benedict XIII in 1728. Considered by some to be one of the greatest pontiffs of all time, he fought corruption—with corruption, some would say—and helped clean up the moral sewer in which the church had been wallowing. His reign increased the power of the papacy and helped to establish a process whereby popes would be selected by the College of Cardinals.

## Pope Urban II: Clamoring for Crusades

Hildebrand's protégé, Urban II (c. 1035–1099), reigned as pope for more than a decade, from 1088 until his death, though opposition kept him in exile from Rome until 1094. He is most remembered for launching the Crusades. In 1095, at the Council of Clermont, he delivered a stirring address calling for an army of God to rescue the Holy Land from the Muslim invaders, a plea that had already been voiced by Alexius, emperor in the East. Rumors of Urban's anticipated Crusade sermon had spread, spurring thousands of people to congregate and

© 2010 Jupiterimages Corporation

Pope Urban II commissions the First Crusade

listen intently for marching orders. Priests and peasants, monks and military leaders pack the cathedral and push out into the surrounding fields as Urban gives a rousing appeal, speaking with force and conviction:

> From the confines of Jerusalem and from the city of Constantinople a horrible tale has gone forth ... an accursed race, a race utterly alienated from God ... has invaded the lands of those Christians and depopulated them by the sword, plundering and fire.... Recall the greatness of Charlemagne. O most valiant soldiers, descendants of invincible ancestors, be not

degenerate. Let all hatred between you depart, all quarrels end, all wars cease. Start upon the road to the Holy Sepulchre, to tear that land from the wicked race and subject it to yourselves.

As he enumerates unspeakable atrocities of torture and rape and murder committed by Turks against Christians, the frenzied crowd spontaneously shouts *"Deus vult!"* (God wills it!), which will become the rallying cry of the Crusades. In the months following the council, Urban persuades some of the most popular preachers of the day to offer their support. Peter the Hermit becomes the front man, stirring Christians of every social status in villages and towns to sacrifice themselves and their sons to this work of God.

Vast armies of Christians make their way to the East, utterly unprepared to fight as disciplined soldiers or to sustain themselves apart from foraging off the land and breaking into homes. Jews and Muslims are sometimes slaughtered indiscriminately. Yet these untrained soldiers are persistent, despite their losses. They are fighting under the sign of the cross; this is a holy war.

Jerusalem is captured in 1099, taken by an army of less than forty thousand, the remnant of a swarm ten times that size. An observer wrote that he had waded through corpses and blood up to his knees on his way to worship on the Temple Mount the following morning. No doubt this was an exaggeration, but it is awful enough to make the Muslims vow they will never forget such atrocities.

Urban dies after the "victory" but before the news reaches Rome. He will play no part in the joyous celebrations. Christian forces control Jerusalem for most of a century and set up four Crusader states before being overtaken by Muslim warriors. The Eastern Empire has made a treaty with the Turks, much to the chagrin of the Western church leaders and crusaders. More Crusades will follow.

## Pope Innocent III: Symbolic Sun

In the century following the death of Hildebrand, popes of varying capabilities come and go, but none have power and influence comparable to that of Innocent III (1160–1216). During his eighteen-year reign, he fashions the papacy into a multinational corporation such as never seen before. The pope, as he envisions the office, is the ruler of the universe, second only to God. Before he ascended the papal throne at age thirty-seven, he had analyzed the reign of six successive incompetent popes and had determined that he could be far more effective if he demanded for himself absolute power. So without wasting any time, he sealed his authority in the first year of his reign with a document boldly pronouncing himself the sun, in comparison to the temporal ruler, who was merely the moon.

Like many popes before and after, Innocent was born into a wealthy aristocratic family with clerical connections. Indeed, his pedigree was no less than Segni blueblood—a most prominent family that had, through the generations, given the church nine of its sons as popes. As a young man he had worked for his uncle, Pope Clement III. Armed with an excellent education, he went on to become one of the most scholarly popes of all times—and a wily politician as well. With sleight of hand, he turned rulers against each other for political advantage and excommunicated others, quickly naming their successors.

The most far-reaching test of his theory of power involved King John of England. The pope and king had previously crossed swords, their duel culminating in John's refusal to accept Stephen Langton as Innocent's nomination for archbishop of Canterbury. Innocent retaliated by placing England under interdict (a discontinuance of all church rites), published on Palm Sunday 1208. King John strikes back, confiscating church properties and levying heavy taxes on the clergy, sending his henchmen to break into their residences and kidnap the clerics' unlawful wives—wives who can be retrieved

## "THE MOON AND THE SUN"

The creator of the universe set up two great luminaries in the firmament of heaven; the greater light to rule the day, the lesser light to rule the night. In the same way for the firmament of the universal Church, which is spoken of as heaven, he appointed two great dignities; the greater to bear rule over souls (these being, as it were, days), the lesser to bear rule over bodies (those being, as it were, nights). These dignities are the pontifical authority and the royal power. Furthermore, the moon derives her light from the sun, and is in truth inferior to the sun in both size and quality, in position as well as effect. In the same way the royal power derives its dignity from the pontifical authority: and the more closely it cleaves to the sphere of that authority the less is the light with which it is adorned; the further it is removed, the more it increases in splendor.

Pope Innocent III, 1198

only by paying a fine. The interdict lasts more than six years. Some eight thousand churches and cathedrals are closed, and thousands of clerics are without jobs. Christmas and Easter services and all Masses are cancelled, as are marriages and funerals. England is in a mess.

King John finally relents after Innocent incites Frankish warlords who are eager to invade England. He agrees to make financial reparations and to return the church property. But the six-year religious recession has profound consequences. English barons, angry with their king, rebel. The Magna Carta is drafted, and John is forced to sign it. However, Innocent, now fearing parliamentary power, promptly condemns the document and threatens excommunication on anyone who seeks to enforce it.

But England is not the only brush fire Inno-

## TEN CRUSADES

The generations before and after the reign of Charlemagne witnessed a corrosion of papal decorum. But it was also an era during which time the Church consolidated its power against the state and launched Crusades against its enemies. Catholicism today is vastly different, and yet it draws deeply from the often muddy well of medieval times.

The number of the Crusades varies from seven to more than a dozen (if lesser crusades such as the Shepherds' Crusade are counted). The length of time is also disputed, the Seventh Crusade, for example, is sometimes calculated as two years rather than six. The success of the Crusades has been the most widely debated issue over the centuries, and they are often viewed today as dismal failures.

*First Crusade* (1096–1099): Initiated by Pope Urban II under the motto *Deus vault!* Joined by King Sigurd of Norway. Cheered on by Peter the Hermit and Walter the Penniless. Siege of Antioch and Jerusalem. Crusader States established.

*Second Crusade* (1147–1149): Instigated by Bernard of Clairvaux. Led by Emperor Conrad III and French King Louis VII. Jews are slaughtered; Lisbon is recaptured from Muslims.

*Third Crusade* (1187–1192): Initiated by Pope Henry VIII to mop up disasters of Second Crusade. Led by English King Richard I (the Lionheart), French King Philip II, and Emperor Frederick I. Jerusalem recaptured.

*Fourth Crusade* (1202–1204): Initiated by Pope Innocent III. Constantinople sacked and Crusader States re-established.

*Children's Crusade* (1212): Led by French teenage peasant Stephen (accompanied by 30,000 children) and by a German leader of 7,000 children. None reached Holy Land, and the event may be more legend that historical fact.

*Fifth Crusade* (1217–1221): Initiated by the Fourth Lateran Council. Led by Hungarian King Andrew II and Austrian Duke Leopold VI. Goal is recovery of Jerusalem with attacks on Egypt. Greater losses than victories.

*Sixth Crusade* (1229–1229): Led by Emperor Frederick II, who recovers Jerusalem and Bethlehem through diplomacy and makes peace with Egypt.

*Seventh Crusade* (1248–1254): Led by French King Louis IX and directed primarily against Egypt.

*Eighth Crusade* (1270): Led by French King Louis IX. Destination is Syria.

*Ninth Crusade* (1271–1272): Led by English Prince (later king) Edward I. Directed against the Sultan of Egypt and Syria.

cent is fighting. Fully aware of the bloodthirsty assaults in previous Crusades, he calls for a Fourth Crusade in 1198 (launched two years later). Although he is adamant that no Christian communities be attacked, unruly hordes sack the great city of Constantinople. Another target of the Crusade is a sectarian movement known as the Albigenses (or Cathars) in southern France. Refusing to acknowledge papal authority, they hold beliefs similar to those of the Manicheans, particularly a strong dualism of good and evil. Monks commissioned by the pope to set them straight are killed. Innocent declares war, suppresses the heresy, and confiscates their land.

Pope Innocent's crowning achievement is the Fourth Lateran Council in 1215, the largest council to date, with some fifteen hundred clergy in attendance. At this council there is further consolidation of church power. The Waldensians (followers of Peter Waldo) are condemned and later persecuted with the full force of the Inquisition, and the church's anti-Semitic stance is toughened. Jews are forcibly separated from Christians and required to wear badges identifying them as inferior to their countrymen. With

Innocent's endorsement, a Fifth Crusade is scheduled for 1217. But before it is launched, he dies.

Innocent's legacy is summed up in part by *On Heresy,* Canon 3 of the Fourth Lateran Council. It sets the tone for centuries to follow:

> We excommunicate and anathematize every heresy raising itself up against this holy, orthodox and catholic faith which we have expounded above. We condemn all heretics.... Let those condemned be handed over to the secular authorities ... for due punishment.... Catholics who take the cross and gird themselves up for the expulsion of heretics shall enjoy the same indulgence, and be strengthened by the same holy privilege, as is granted to those who go to the aid of the Holy Land.

The generations before and after the reign of Charlemagne witnessed a corrosion of papal decorum. But it was also an era during which time the church consolidated its power against the state and launched Crusades against its enemies. Catholicism today is vastly different, and yet it draws deeply from the often-muddy well of medieval times.

---

## What If ....

What if Charlemagne had devoted his energy to military might, to the exclusion of education and the arts? It is difficult to imagine the Renaissance without the earlier Carolingian Renaissance of the later Middle Ages, spurred by this one man.

What if Hildebrand (Pope Gregory VII) had not reformed the papacy, and the Catholic Church had continued on for generations mired in corruption? Might the Reformation have occurred much earlier? Or would the church have rotted and withered on the vine?

What if Urban II had not called for the First Crusade? Would the other Crusades have followed? The Crusades remain a sore point among Muslims today. How might Christian-Muslim relations be different were it not for the Crusades?

What if, centuries earlier, Charles Martel had not been victorious at the Battle of Tours, preventing the Moors from overrunning Europe? Would the Western world be Muslim today?

## Further Reading

Baring-Gould, Sabine. *Curious Myths of the Middle Ages: The Sangreal, Pope Joan, The Wandering Jew, and Others*. New York: Dover, 2005.

Boniface, Saint (Winfrid). *Letters of St. Boniface*. Translated by Ephraim Emerton. New York: Columbia University Press, 2000.

Boureau, Alain, and Lydia G. Cochrane. *The Myth of Pope Joan*. Chicago: University of Chicago Press, 2001.

Browne, G. R. *Alcuin of York*. New York: Hesperides Press, 2008.

de Joinville, Jean, and Geoffroy de Villehardouin. *Chronicles of the Crusades*. Translated and with an introduction by Margaret Shaw. New York: Penguin, 1963.

Gregory of Tours. *History of the Franks*. Translated and with an introduction by Lewis Thorpe. New York: Penguin, 1976.

Logan, F. Donald. *A History of the Church in the Middle Ages*. New York: Routledge, 2002.

Madden, Thomas F. *The New Concise History of the Crusades*. Lanham, Md.: Rowman and Littlefield, 2005.

Powell, James M. *Innocent III: Vicar of Christ or Lord of the World?* Washington D.C.: Catholic University of America, 1994.

Riche, Pierre. *Daily Life in the World of Charlemagne*. Translated by Jo Ann McNamara. Philadelphia: University of Pennsylvania Press, 1988.

Stark, Rodney. *God's Battalions: The Case for the Crusades*. San Francisco: HarperOne, 2009.

Williams, Rose. *The Lighter Side of the Dark Ages*. New York: Anthem, 2006.

Wilson, Derek. *Charlemagne*. New York: Doubleday, 2007.

# CHAPTER 8

# Medieval Theology

*Anselm to Aquinas*

*Illicit sex. Scandalous romance. Activities not typically associated with medieval theologians. Anselm and Aquinas and John Duns Scotus do not exude sex appeal. The same cannot be said, however, for Peter Abelard, theologian and teacher. He was the Brad Pitt of his day—handsome, intelligent, confident, and the ultimate ladies' man.*

*I first became acquainted with Abelard in college. I liked him for his outspoken challenging of his teachers, and I took for myself his motto: "The first key to wisdom is this constant and frequent questioning.... For by doubting we are led to question, by questioning we arrive at the truth."*

*My regard for Abelard began to erode, however, twenty years ago when I was researching my book* Daughters of the Church. *Reading about his love affair with Heloise, I became convinced that it was no love affair at all but a case of sexual abuse perpetrated on a minor. Perhaps he deserved what he got, I reasoned, when he was castrated.*

*Several years later I did further research when I was writing an article titled "Heloise and Abelard's Tumultuous Affair," and as I came to know these two individuals better, my thinking shifted again. At seventeen, Heloise, though nearly half the age of Abelard, was considered an adult. She may have seduced him as much as he did her—though he did later admit to having threatened her. After the castration, he repented and moved on, while she groveled in her undying love for him. They spent the rest of their lives separately serving in monasteries.*

*Since writing that article, however, I have again wondered about my assessment. How much of the love affair and subsequent letters can we really trust? Is this history or legend or some of both? So compelling is the story that it has been made into a Hollywood film,* Stealing Heaven. *Here the sexy scholar is portrayed with his enraptured student, who is gorgeous and gifted. The thousand years of distance easily vanishes.*

---

> History is, strictly speaking, the study of questions; the study of answers
> belongs to anthropology and sociology.
> W. H. AUDEN

When we consider theologians of the High Middle Ages, we find that history is in many respects the study of questions. The first key to wisdom, cries Abelard from the grave, is questioning. Abelard seeks answers, but what stands out in this era are the questions. Indeed, answers belong, if not to anthropology and sociology, to some discipline other than history.

Church history is often divided into theological periods. The patristic period, or study of the church fathers, extends from the apostolic age to approximately the time of the sack of Rome or as late as Pope Gregory I. In this period Augustine rises above all others. The early medieval period begins in the sixth or seventh century through the reign of Charlemagne to the eleventh or twelfth centuries. The education and thinking is associated with monastic schools. Here Boethius and Alcuin rise above others. There are then two centuries of intellectual decline. The third period—from the eleventh century to the mid-fourteenth century is labeled the High Middle Ages. Here we see the flowering of scholasticism, the system of theological speculation in the Latin West. Among the most prominent names of this era are Anselm,

Peter Abelard (and Heloise), Thomas Becket, Thomas Aquinas, Bonaventure, and William of Ockham.

The term *medieval* means "between times," in this case the era between the classical period of ancient Greece and Rome and the humanism of the Renaissance. This thousand-year span portrays life in every imaginable setting and psychological nuance. Among the shifting scenes in this panoramic "Age of Faith" is the study of theology and its twin, philosophy. Medieval philosophical speculation is all about God. The period begins with Anselm of Canterbury, considered the father of scholasticism, who puts forth his ontological argument for the existence of God. The times are marked by a slow shift toward Aristotelian philosophical foundations and away from Platonism and neo-Platonism, particularly that found in the writings of Augustine of Hippo.

Prior to the year 1000 there were only a handful of great philosophical thinkers. After that year the numbers grow by leaps and bounds. There are several reasons for this change, including the decline of barbarian invasions and significant population growth.

## PARADE OF HISTORY

As the parade of Christian history moves through the Middle Ages, we see an increasing number of robed scholars taking their place in the pompous processions. We also see a continued jockeying for position as grand marshal. Whether the king or the pope (or chief cleric) will prevail is never certain. When the scholarly Thomas Becket, after several years in exile, returns in 1170 to fill his post as archbishop of Canterbury, people line the parade route, throwing their cloaks before him and hailing him as the blessed one who comes in the name of the Lord. But the king's men quickly turn on him, making him a martyr — a martyr who calls forth an endless procession of pilgrims.

The frontier was pushed back as forests were cleared, paving the way for stable communities and more food production. These factors served to enhance political stability and foster economic growth, dynamics that contributed to leisure time activities such as art, music, and scholarship — activities no longer confined to the monastery.

Anselm represents monastic theology (with its emphasis on spiritual experience, that of heart over mind), while Peter Abelard (who later retreats to the monastery) is a man of the world. Abelard emerges early in this period as the thinker who will push philosophy — or theology — almost to the breaking point, at least in the eyes of church officials. Like Anselm, he regards the rational mind as a friend of *theology* (a term introduced largely through his writing). But unlike most of his predecessors, Abelard views theology — or philosophy — as an academic discipline to be studied by specialists. He is a teacher, and his dates correspond with the widespread rise of universities, when classical works of philosophy are being translated into Latin and thus made accessible to scholars.

Abelard's influence infiltrates the universities in the succeeding generations. Reason has now trumped tradition and religious authorities. His dialectical method (the disputation of yes and no) fosters a "negative theology" — a theology that seeks to discern God by what God *is not* rather that by what God *is* in light of God's so-called attributes. No longer are monastic schools the primary venues of education. Cathedral schools in large population centers offer a more well-rounded education and begin to flourish in the twelfth century. By the thirteenth century, the university is proliferating, often as an outgrowth of cathedral schools. The most prestigious is the University of Paris, complete with a charter and governing board.

## SAINT AUGUSTINE'S LONG SHELF LIFE

For more than a millennium after his death, Augustine was an authority who simply had to be accommodated. He shaped medieval thought as no one else did. Moreover, his influence did not end with the Middle Ages. Throughout the Reformation, appeals to Augustine's authority were commonplace on all sides.

Paul Vincent Spade, *Five Texts on the Medieval Problem of Universals*

Disciplines include not only theology but also law and medicine and liberal arts. Large faculties and facilities serve the growing student body and offer a wide variety courses.

Education is entering the modern world but not without church limitations and prohibitions. Thirteenth-century popes do not hesitate to put Aristotle on the banned-books list — at least for dissemination in university lectures. As translations proliferate, however, Aristotle is cited by all great scholars of the era, especially Thomas Aquinas.

Scholasticism of this era encompasses a wide range of perspectives. Indeed, there is bitter disagreement among the schoolmen. Some are Realists who gravitate to Platonic "ideas" or "universals" — "perfect forms." Others, including William of Ockham, are Nominalists (or Conceptualists) who see no reality in forms or universals. Ockham argues they "are not things other than names." A chair, for example, is a name for a piece of furniture. All pieces of furniture with a similar look are called chairs. There is no "universal" or "form" that is the *real* chair beyond the physical chair. How then do we know what we know? Ockham, considered by some to be the father of modern epistemology,

## Marriage and Family in Medieval Times

During the course of the Middle Ages marriage customs and laws were inconsistent and ever changing. Throughout the period clerics preached on morals and proper behavior in courting and marital relationships, but they had little authority to back up their words. Standards varied from region to region and among social classes. Life was disorderly and wild in the vast, lawless backwoods. In some areas kidnapping a woman and having sex with her (which in most cases was nothing short of rape) constituted marriage. Common-law marriage was the standard among peasants, most often sealed with a sexual rendezvous in a hayloft or forest refuge. Family and community acceptance cemented the relationship.

How Reymont and Melusina were betrothed and by the bishop were blessed in their bed on their wedlock

Among upper classes, despite church decrees, divorce was not infrequent, though it was a highly divisive issue. Marriages were typically arranged for economic and political gain, and thus when better opportunities arose such marriages were *un*-arranged. The justification for divorce was often the accusation of incest—the wife, for example, being a cousin within seven degrees of kinship, that being the church's own standard. Changes came in 1215 at the Fourth Lateran Council: Cannon 50 prohibits marriage to the fourth degree only; Canon 51 prohibits "clandestine marriages"; and Canon 52 prohibits hearsay evidence at divorce trials. With these new regulations the church had authority to threaten excommunication, but enforcement of such laws was uneven at best.

The purpose of marriage in the eyes of the church was procreation. Childbirth was a celebratory time unless things went wrong, as they often did. Midwives supervised birth in both castles and crude huts. They were experienced, and the best of them had impressive records of live births. Rudimentary sanitation was practiced

### A KISS AND A PROMISE

... beguile a woman with words;
To give her troth but lightly
For nothing but to lie by her;
With that guile thou makest her assent,
And bringest you both to comberment.

Robert Manning (1298 – 1338),
*Handling Synne*

alongside superstitious rituals such as opening cabinet doors and drawers and removing covers from jugs and jars. The odds of bringing a healthy baby into the world varied according to economic circumstances. Keeping the mother alive was equally challenging.

Aware of the risk, midwives were authorized to baptize an infant when a cleric was unavailable. If the baby was healthy, baptism was typically administered at the church the following day. The mother, weakened by the ordeal and considered too *unclean* to be present in the sanctuary, remained confined to bed. The father, accompanied by godparents, brought the infant to the church, where the ceremony

Typical country life

began on the porch and ended when the baby was immersed in the stone baptismal font, a shocking experience and only one hurdle on the difficult road to survival.

is an empiricist, believing that knowledge comes from the senses, not from some sort of innate understanding. These issues were the stuff of debate in the High Middle Ages.

But this age of philosophical thinking is not to be separated from the emerging monastic orders of friars who traverse the land begging, feeding the hungry, and stamping out heresy. Nor is it alienated from voices and visions, as Aquinas himself demonstrates. This *other* side of church life is featured in the next chapter.

## Anselm of Canterbury: Scholastic Theologian

As one of the early proponents of scholasticism, Anselm (1033–1109) exemplifies the theological mindset of the eleventh century. Even as he

develops his philosophical approach, he does not challenge the given wisdom of the age. Yet he is often heralded as the most influential theologian between Augustine and Aquinas. His monastic theology grows out of his spiritual underpinnings: "I believe in order to understand" was his motto, and his best-known philosophical writing—his ontological proof for God—is presented as a prayer.

Born into landed nobility in a mountainous region of northern Italy, Anselm remembers imagining God living in a palace perched high on a mountain. Encouraged by his mother, he is determined to become a monk at a nearby monastery—a calling delayed until he is twenty-seven because of his father's objections. Anselm blossoms at the Benedictine abbey of Bec in Normandy, under the scholarly leadership of

Virgin Mary appearing to Anselm of Canterbury

Lanfranc. At thirty he is selected to succeed Lanfranc, who transfers to another monastery.

The relationship between student and teacher often runs deep. Indeed, emotional bonds formed amid monastic living are often closer than family ties. In a letter written in his mid-forties, Anselm reveals pain comparable to that of a spouse forsaken by the other:

> Brother Anselm to Dom Gilbert, brother, friend, beloved lover ... sweet to me, sweetest friend, are the gifts of your sweetness, but they cannot begin to console my desolate heart for its want of your love. Even if you sent every scent of perfume, every glitter of metal, every precious gem, every texture of cloth, still it could not make up to my soul for this separation.... But you have gained from our very separation the company of someone else, whom you love no less — or even more — than me; while I have lost you, and there is no one to take your place. You are thus enjoying your

consolation, while nothing is left to me but heartbreak.

Despite such pain — or perhaps because of it — Anselm focuses his attention on God and on spiritual exercises and rigorous asceticism.

A medieval teacher leads his students

He effortlessly combines philosophical studies with spirituality, writing devotions and prayers and songs as a matter of course. His poetry captures visual images of God, especially as when he portrays Jesus as mother:

> Jesus, as a mother you gather your people
>> to you:
> You are gentle with us as a mother with her
>> children;
> Often you weep over our sins and our
>> pride:
> tenderly you draw us from hatred and
>> judgment.
> You comfort us in sorrow and bind up our
>> wounds:
> in sickness you nurse us,
> and with pure milk you feed us.

For Anselm, meditation and prayer are the key that opens minds to an understanding of God. "Being continually given up to God and to spiritual exercises," his contemporary biographer writes, "he attained such a height of divine speculation that he was able by God's help to see into and unravel many most obscure and previously insoluble questions."

The most difficult problem Anselm tackles is *Does God exist*? His ontological argument for the existence of God is still discussed today by theologians and philosophers alike. God's non-existence is inconceivable, he argues; therefore, God exists. He begins with a terse proverb, "The fool has said in his heart: There is no God." He insists that this is a contradiction. One cannot speak of God and then claim he does not exist. But his "proof," according to critics, is tangled in circuitous arguments. Almost immediately another theologian writes a response entitled "A Reply on Behalf of the Fool." Aquinas likewise rejects the argument, as do many philosophers of the Enlightenment and since. But Anselm's

---

## ONTOLOGICAL PROOF FOR GOD

This proposition is indeed so true that its negation is inconceivable. For it is quite conceivable that there is something whose non-existence is inconceivable, and this must be greater than that whose non-existence is conceivable. Wherefore, if that thing than which no greater thing is conceivable can be conceived as non-existent; then that very thing than which a greater is inconceivable is not that than which a greater is inconceivable; which is a contradiction.

So true is that there exists something than which a greater is inconceivable, that its non-existence is inconceivable: and this thing you are, O Lord our God!

Anselm, *Proslogion*

---

proof has had an astoundingly long shelf life, and a history of philosophy textbook would not be complete without it.

In 1092 Anselm journeys to England, following the footsteps of Lanfranc, who has been appointed archbishop of Canterbury. Anselm is named a bishop, and later he too is appointed archbishop of Canterbury, a position that pits him against King William Rufus in a church-state duel. He is subsequently exiled and travels to Rome, pleading his case with the pope. His exile allows him time to complete his writing on the atonement that is still widely referenced today. In *Cur Deus Homo* (Why a God-Man?), he argues that there is a rational explanation for the incarnation directly tied to Christ's death on the cross. He asks why it was necessary for God to send his son to die for sin. He answers that sin robs God of his honor, and for God's honor to be preserved there must be either satisfaction or punishment. Satisfaction for sin requires far more than an individual can render. But *man's* sin must be satisfied by a *man*. Thus, in the incarnation God-*man* offered satisfaction for *man's* sin.

Anselm also makes interesting contrasts and references to sin and redemption as he seeks to explain Christ's death on the cross:

> For it was fitting that, just as death entered into the human race by man's disobedience, so should life be restored by man's obedience. And, that, just as the sin that was the cause of our damnation had its beginning from woman, so the author of our justice and salvation should be born from woman. And, that the devil conquered man through persuading him to taste from the tree, should be conquered by man through the passion he endured on the tree.

Protestant Reformers drew on Anselm in explaining the atonement, although John Calvin emphasized God's holiness and justice over his honor. Other theories have been put forward, but the theory that drew the most attention was set forth by a young upstart more than forty years Anselm's junior, Peter Abelard, who was coming of age just as Anselm was finalizing his atonement theory.

After the death of King Rufus, Anselm returns to his post as archbishop. But the new king creates even more problems for him. Once again he journeys to Rome and is vindicated by the pope. Considered a saintly man in his lifetime, Anselm is still honored as a saint by both Catholics and Anglicans today.

## Peter Abelard: Scholar with Sex Appeal

Peter Abelard (1079–1142) was a freethinker by twelfth-century standards, not bound by the wisdom of archbishops or saints. He challenged philosophers and theologians, including Anselm and his theory of the atonement. Christ's death, he insisted, revealed his infinite love more than anything else. In his commentary on Romans, he argues:

> Our redemption through Christ's suffering is that deeper affection in us which not only frees us from slavery to sin, but also wins for us the true liberty of sons of God, so that we do all things out of love rather than fear—love to him who has shown us such grace that no greater can be found.... Indeed, how cruel and wicked it seems that anyone should demand the blood of an innocent person as the price for anything, or that it should in any way please him that an innocent man should be slain—still less that God should consider

---

### ABELARD'S MORAL INFLUENCE THEORY OF THE ATONEMENT

Abelard's formulation is the classic response to the Anselmic type of theory, though later expressions of the moral-influence view might vary according to the emphasis placed on Jesus' teaching, example, life of faith, or manifestation of God's love in His total ministry and epitomized in His death. But the fundamental rationale is the same in them all. Christ's death has no immediate and objective significance with reference to satisfying the offended honor or the broken law of a holy God. Rather, His life and death have an exemplary value, a moral influence, intended to awaken within man a responsive love and faith that become the immediate ground of God's gracious forgiveness.

Stanley N. Gundry, *Love Them In: The Life and Theology of D. L. Moody*

the death of his Son so agreeable that by it he should be reconciled to the whole world!

Abelard's views on the atonement are as controversial today as they were in his own day. Before Anselm's influential writing on the topic, the position put forth by Irenaeus in the second century was the standard view: sinners are ransomed through the price paid for their sin by Christ on the cross. To whom was this ransom paid? Origen, writing soon after, argues it was paid to Satan. Such arguments are unacceptable to Abelard.

Even as Anselm had combined theology and philosophy, so also did Abelard, who turned Anselm's motto — "I believe in order to understand" — upside-down. In his volume *Sic et Non* (Yes and No), he set forth his guiding principle: "The first key to wisdom is the constant and frequent questioning.... For by doubting we are led to question, and by questioning we arrive at the truth." Abelard's thought-provoking subject matter, his engaging teaching style, his confident and easy manner, and his good looks combined to transform him into a popular professor, at times drawing as many as a thousand students.

From his youth, Abelard had been an inquisitive student. Born into a noble French family, he enjoyed first-rate tutoring from his earliest years. When still in his teens, he became a wandering scholar, ever challenging the given wisdom of church tradition. He debated the best teachers of the day, turning academic rivalry into a sport. He is hardly modest as he recounts his brilliant jousting:

> I came at length to Paris, where above all in those days the art of dialectics was most flourishing, and there did I meet William of ·Champeaux, my teacher, a man most distinguished in his science both by his renown and

by his true merit. With him I remained for some time, at first indeed well liked of him; but later I brought him great grief, because I undertook to refute certain of his opinions, not infrequently attacking him in disputation, and now and then in these debates I was adjudged victor.

From rhetoric and debate Abelard moves on to theology. Soon he is challenging and besting his theology professor, and his reputation soars even higher. The peak of his teaching career comes in his late thirties, when he is invited to fill an academic chair at the Cathedral School of Notre Dame. His future looks to be brilliant — but for Heloise. Their story is one of romance, intrigue, violence, and repentance — all filtered through the curtain of the medieval church.

Canon Fulbert, uncle and guardian of Heloise, was Abelard's superior at Notre Dame. He may have set aside his own better judgment when

Heloise banished to a convent

placing his sparkling teenage charge under the tutorship of the handsome middle-aged teacher. Abelard concedes that he had more than dialectical discourses in mind when he contemplated moonlighting as a tutor. "I … decided she was the one to bring to my bed, confident that I should have an easy success, for at that time I had youth and exceptional good looks as well as my great reputation to recommend me."

Taking advantage of her eagerness to learn, he lays his snare: "Knowing of the girl's knowledge and love of letters, I thought she would be all the more ready to consent." Heloise resists, but Abelard is not easily dissuaded. "Under the pretext of study we spent our hours in the happiness of love," Abelard later confides. "Our kisses far outnumbered our reasoned words." Heloise soon discovers she is pregnant. Fulbert is outraged not only by her pregnancy but also by Abelard's dismissive response — that of putting Heloise in a convent while he carries on with his successful academic career. There follows negotiations and an apparent effort on both sides to resolve the situation. But the anger seething beneath the surface explodes. What happens next is best described in Abelard's own words: "Her uncle and his friends … wild with indignation … plotted against me, and one night as I slept … took cruel vengeance on me.… They cut off the parts of my body whereby I had committed the wrong of which they complained."

Abelard recovers from his terrible wounds and is seemingly able to put the past behind him. Indeed, he later reasons, what happened was a blessing in disguise. The assault was God's means of setting him aside as a monk. He enters the Abbey of Saint Denis. "Consider the magnanimous design of God's mercy for us," he writes to Heloise. God "made use of evil itself and mercifully set aside our impiety, so that by a wholly justified wound in a single

part of my body he might heal two souls." For Heloise, God's mercy is not nearly so evident. Although Abelard pleads with her to forget about him and "have compassion on Him who suffered willingly for your redemption," she cannot deny her love for him. He establishes her in her own convent, the Paraclete, and she goes on to become a highly acclaimed abbess. But she never fully comes to terms with her separation from Abelard.

Abelard finds the monastery "utterly worldly and in its life quite scandalous," and thus "departed thence to a certain hut." But try as he might, he could not live as a hermit: "such a throng of students flocked that the neighborhood could not afford shelter for them, nor the earth sufficient sustenance." Yet he continues to teach, using philosophy as bait to interest students in theology — "true philosophy." But his growing popularity only exacerbates the fury of his enemies. They charge him with heresy, especially in relation to his book on the Trinity, accusing him of claiming God "begat" himself. He is summoned before a council at Soissons in 1121. The meeting is stacked against him. Without specifying particular passages or allowing a defense, the council punishes him once again: "Straightway upon my summons I went to the council, and there, without further examination or debate, did they compel me with my own hand to cast that memorable book of mine into the flames." He is incarcerated at a monastery in Soissons.

On release he retreats to a remote area and builds his own rude hermitage, but again he is inundated with students. Fearing persecution from church authorities, he flees to another monastery. But he cannot escape the clutches of critics — the most vitriolic being Bernard of Clairvaux, a leading reformer of Cistercian monasticism, enthusiastically promoting ven-

## PETER LOMBARD AND THE FOUR BOOKS OF SENTENCES

The most widely read theology text of the Middle Ages was *Four Books of Sentences* by Peter Lombard (c. 1095–1160). Indeed, until the time of the Reformation it was considered the standard text, cited for its information on both theological and biblical topics. The four major divisions dealt with the nature of God, creation, Christ and redemption, and the sacraments, with a wide range of lesser topics interspersed. The sentences, or glosses, were short explanations of biblical words or verses or theological concepts referencing the writings of others. Based loosely on Abelard's *Sic et Non*, it covered the fine points of theology in a systematic arrangement, offering excerpts from the Bible as well as church fathers and later scholars. The timing was right. Abelard had raised the expectations, and Lombard filled the void. Having studied under both Bernard and Abelard, he established himself as a moderating influence. Lacking Abelard's razor-sharp wit and originality, he was primarily a compiler of theological wisdom.

eration of Mary. Widely known for his work *On Grace and Free Will*, Bernard is angered by Abelard's explanation of Christ's atonement. Writing to the pope, he insists it is not compatible with the gospel. "I was made a sinner by deriving my being from Adam. I am made just by being washed in the blood of Christ," he argues. "Such is the justice which man has obtained through the blood of the Redeemer. But this 'son of perdition' [Abelard] disdains and scoffs at it."

Through Bernard's persistence, the pope summons Abelard to appear at the Council of Sens in 1141, where his teachings on various matters are condemned. Abelard appeals the decision, but the sentence is upheld. On his way to Rome to further petition the pope, he is taken ill and dies soon afterward. His body is interred on the grounds of the Paraclete abbey, where the grave is tenderly watched over by the abbess, Heloise. Some two decades later she is buried beside him.

The grave is not the end of Abelard, however. Although his writings had been condemned by the church, there is no going back on his "liberal" methodology—methodology that had taken hold in the cathedral schools and universities and is today taken for granted. He, more than any-

one else, introduced questioning and doubting of the sources—even the church fathers, who had been presumed authoritative. Pointing to their inconsistencies and contradictions, he unleashed a mindset of distrust and urged a dependence on reason. If the Fathers did not agree on an issue, he argued, the solution is to think through the matter and let reason prevail.

Abelard's nemesis, Bernard of Clairvaux, desperately sought to hold the conservative line, ridiculing this new method as *stultilogia* (stupidology) but the current was too strong. Abelard's ideas would win the day in academia, while Bernard would go on to become a saint.

### Thomas Becket: Murder in the Cathedral

Another celebrated twelfth-century cleric who does not fit neatly as a theologian or monk is Thomas Becket (1118–1170). An archbishop of Canterbury and the most popular saint of the High Middle Ages, he is the reason for which people make pilgrimages to Canterbury—"the holy blisful martir for to seke." Without this saint, who from the tomb heals all varieties of diseases, the wonderfully earthy poetry of Chaucer's *Canterbury Tales* would not have been written. Thomas Becket, murdered in the cathedral, is loved and hated as both saint and traitor.

Through family wealth, good connections, and street smarts, Becket easily climbs the ladder of success. Reared as a gentleman, he rides and hunts and furthers his education by traveling abroad to Paris and other European cultural centers. He begins his career as an aide to the archbishop of Canterbury. Later he is appointed archdeacon of Canterbury and eventually Lord Chancellor in service of King Henry II, helping to maximize royal power over church office and land. But his tenure is not without tension. Taxing church property becomes a sore point, particularly for clerics whose incomes are diminished. As the king's right-hand man, Becket is perceived as the archenemy of the church. Moreover, he is far more than just an aide to the king. Twelve years his senior, he is a father figure to the young Henry, who is still in his twenties.

In 1162, to secure absolute authority over the church, Henry appoints Becket archbishop of Canterbury, a brilliant strategic stroke, he imagines. Becket is ordained a priest on Saturday and an archbishop on Sunday. However, unlike previous advancements, the promotion has a dramatic effect on Becket. Henry is no longer his superior—only God is. With this seemingly sudden conversion, he becomes a *servant* leader. In championing the church rather than the state, he takes a page from desert asceticism. He sets aside his ornate clerical wardrobe and dons a hair shirt and rags. Turning his back on the culinary delights and comforts of the court, he takes on the diet of a beggar. He daily washes the feet of lepers, and to atone for his sins he lashes his back with spiked fronds until his flesh is raw.

The king is not impressed. But there is more at stake than an archbishop flaunting his self-denial and long hours of prayer. Devoted to God and the church, Becket now opposes the king in matters of church property taxes and challenges church authority in general. He refuses to accede to the Constitutions of Clarendon that favor royal power. The tensions escalate to the point that Becket fears for his life. He flees to France in 1164, where he is welcomed by King Louis VII. But the story is complex. His motives and activities are questioned by friend and foe alike. He is at odds with his own bishops, whom King Henry II manages to ingratiate, and his dealings with both papal and state authorities are tangled and inconsistent.

He attempts to convince the pope to excommunicate Henry and to place an interdict on England—suspending all worship services and sacraments. Accusations are hurled from both sides. But in the end, Henry seems to back down. An interdict would be the kiss of death for the king. Under this threat, Henry promises Becket safe passage to England and restoration of his post as head of the English church.

On December 1, 1170, Becket, having spent some six years in exile, returns to a Palm-Sunday style entry: people line the roads, throwing their cloaks before him and hailing him: "Blessed is he that cometh in the name of the Lord." But Becket's enemies among clerics and court officials are numerous—and for good reason. He adamantly refuses to back down on his demand for independent power for the church. And more than that, he excommunicates all those who sided with the king. Henry is enraged. From his sickbed he moans a message, the exact words ever since debated. His closest aides understood him to ask: *Who will rid me of that troublesome priest?*

Before dawn on his fatal last day, Becket arises, officiates at the Mass, and confesses his sins. There is a sense of foreboding as he warns those close to him to flee. In the late, cold afternoon of December 29, 1170, four knights enter the cathedral during the vesper service and attack Becket as he is proceeding to the high altar. It is a grisly scene. According to an eyewitness, "The crown of his head was separated from the head in such a way that the blood, white with brain, and the brain no less red from the blood, dyed the floor of the cathedral."

Within minutes Becket has become the greatest martyr the English church had ever known. But the story of the veneration of Becket does not end with *Canterbury Tales* and generations of pilgrimages that follow. Nearly four hundred years after his death, during the reign of Henry VIII, Becket is charged with treason. His tomb is plundered and pilgrimages and festivals are outlawed. But not even Henry VIII could erase the devotion in the people's hearts. Today he is still revered as a martyred saint by both Catholics and Anglicans.

His contribution to the field of theology was most specifically in the discipline of ecclesiology. Through his influence, there was born in the English people a deep conviction that no king could ever stand between them and God.

## Thomas Aquinas: *Dumb Ox* for the Ages

Regarded today as the greatest theologian of the Middle Ages, Thomas Aquinas (c. 1224–1274)

was viewed with skepticism in his own day. Born of nobility in a castle situated south of Rome, he was educated at a local Benedictine school from age five. At sixteen he entered the University of Naples, planning to become a Dominican monk, much to the chagrin of his family. Becoming a respected abbot of a monastery would be acceptable, but the family is humiliated by the prospect of his joining a mendicant order, whose friars travel from town to town preaching and begging. They kidnap him, tempt him with a prostitute, and call on the archbishop of Naples for support. But after more than a year of captivity, they realize that their deprogramming efforts have failed. His mother intervenes and helps her strong-willed son to escape. Still a teenager, he joins the Dominicans.

His brilliant mind impresses his superiors, who arrange to have him study in Cologne with Albertus Magnus (c. 1200–1280), the greatest Dominican scholar of the day. During this time the hulking youth acquires the nickname, "Dumb Ox." Albertus, however, is quick to defend him, reportedly saying: "You call him 'a dumb ox,' but I declare before you that he will yet bellow so loud in doctrine that his voice will resound through the whole world." His influence on Aquinas is profound, especially in

---

### STRUGGLING WITH THE SEVENTH SON

For it had been long apparent to Count Landulf that nothing could be done with his seventh son Thomas, except to make him an Abbot or something of that kind. . . . He was a large and heavy and quiet boy, and phenomenally silent, scarcely opening his mouth except to say suddenly to his schoolmaster in an explosive manner, "What is God?" . . . So everything was smoothly arranged for Thomas Aquinas becoming a monk, which would seem to be what he himself wanted; and sooner or later becoming Abbot of Monte Cassino. And then the curious thing happened. . . . Thomas Aquinas walked into his father's castle one day and calmly announced that he had become one of the Begging Friars, of the new order founded by Dominic the Spaniard. . . .

G. K. Chesterton, *St. Thomas Aquinas: The Dumb Ox*

linking theology with science rather than viewing them as opposing disciplines. When Albertus transfers to Paris to study and teach, Aquinas accompanies him. After completing his studies in Paris, Aquinas returns to Cologne to teach and write.

For Aquinas, as was true in the early church, theology serves as an apologetic tool in the cause of mission outreach—in this case to Muslims and Jews. By the thirteenth century the works of Islamic and Jewish writers have been translated into Latin, and there is a lively exchange of scholarship. With this development Aquinas writes *Summa Contra Gentiles* (also known as *Manual Against the Heathen*). Depending heavily on Aristotle ("the philosopher"), he argues that the existence of God can be proved through reason and maintains that such an apologetic paves the way for the "heathen" to understand the Bible, particularly the Trinity and the incarnation.

Thomas Aquinas

After teaching at Cologne, Aquinas relocates to the University of Paris, where he continues to pursue his education and teaching. But he does not settle down for long. Beginning in 1260 and until his death in 1274, he travels throughout Europe, preaching and teaching and consulting. He performs service for the pope and for the Dominican Order. Amid his other duties, he writes obsessively, his works eventually filling some twenty large volumes. In addition to his apologetics manual, he turns out numerous biblical commentaries. But his magnum opus is *Summa Theologica*, the most comprehensive treatise on theology ever written, acclaimed more for its sheer volume and breadth than for its originality. Unlike Abelard, Aquinas is not venturing into uncharted terrain. Rather, he cites authorities and often seeks to harmonize contrasting views.

In part 1, Sacred Doctrine, for example, he deals with seven major topics (God, Trinity, creation, angels, matter, man, government). Under the topic of God, he lists several categories, including intellect and will, under which he includes predestination—a subject that merits a total of eight major questions. The first of these questions is: "Is predestination suitably attributed to God?" The third question is: "Does the reprobation of some men belong to God?" For each question he lists a series of objections and a series of replies, all referenced from sources, including Scripture, the church fathers, theologians, and philosophers.

> *"Hold firmly that our faith is identical with that of the ancients. Deny this, and you dissolve the unity of the Church."*
>
> Thomas Aquinas

Christian scholars would later come to cite Thomas Aquinas as "the theologian" as easily as Aquinas cited Aristotle as "the philosopher." More than presenting merely an objective encyclopedia of theological positions, Aquinas takes a solid stance (based on the arguments of others), and his work serves as a standard for correct doctrine. His conclusions are often less than profound, as on the topic of predestination. "It is fitting that God should predestine men," he writes. "For to destine, is to direct or send. Thus it is clear that predestination, as regards its objects, is part of providence." On reprobation he writes: "Therefore, as predestination includes the will to confer grace and glory, so also reprobation includes the will to permit a person to fall into sin, and to impose the punishment of damnation on account of that sin."

As knowledgeable as he was, Aquinas confessed that "the most man can know is that he does not know God." Yet one of his claims to fame is his formulation of his famous "Five Ways," proving the existence of God through natural theology. These "ways" are arguments drawn largely from Aristotle, summarized as follows:

1. Motion in the universe is the result of a Prime Mover, that being God.
2. Nothing can produce itself; everything has a Creator or Cause, that being God.
3. Things in the universe would not exist at all, but for a Planner, that being God.
4. Standards of excellence can only come from what is Perfection, that being God.
5. The universe is orderly, the work of an Intelligent Designer, that being God.

At times Aquinas seems to labor too hard to harmonize Aristotle's philosophy with the tenor of the Bible. For example, in discussing the providence of God he is dealing with two seeming opposites: Aristotle, who essentially maintains that God, the "Unmoved Mover," is not actively involved in the world; and the biblical portrayal of God. In attempting to harmonize this, Aquinas acknowledges that God is within his very being the ultimate cause and thus

---

## SUMMA THEOLOGICA

It is not possible to characterize the method of St. Thomas by one word, unless it can be called eclectic. It is Aristotelian, Platonic, and Socratic; it is inductive and deductive; it is analytic and synthetic. He chose the best that could he found in those who preceded him, carefully sifting the chaff from the wheat, approving what was true, rejecting the false. His powers of synthesis were extraordinary. No writer surpassed him in the faculty of expressing in a few well-chosen words the truth gathered from a multitude of varying and conflicting opinions.

*New Advent Catholic Encyclopedia*

---

knows everything, past and future, in that he exists outside of time. Thus as Unmoved Mover, God is the one who is always active in human affairs—a God made understandable in human terms through Scripture.

Because of his heavy dependence on Aristotle, Aquinas was strongly criticized after his death by certain other theologians, including William of Ockham and Duns Scotus, who recognized the inherent contradictions in revelation and reason. In 1277 the archbishop of Paris sought to have his work condemned by the church, but the effort was stopped before a trial began.

Lofty matters of metaphysics comprise only a portion of *Summa Theologica*. Among down-to-earth matters included in his tome is a lengthy discussion of sex, specifically as it relates to sin. Conceding that sex in marriage for procreation is not sin, he goes on to cover a wide range of related issues including:

Whether simple fornication is a mortal sin?
Whether fornication is the most grievous of sins?

Whether there can be mortal sin in touches
and kisses?

Whether nocturnal pollution is a mortal
sin?

Whether seduction should be reckoned a
species of lust?

Whether rape is a species of lust, distinct
from seduction?

Whether adultery is a determinate species
of lust, distinct from other species?

Whether incest is a determinate species of
lust?

Whether unnatural vice is a species of lust?

In discussing unnatural vice (masturbation, sodomy, and bestiality), Aquinas asks whether this is the greatest of such sins. His answer in the affirmative is perhaps not surprising in light of his marriage of theology and natural science. What is against nature is against God. "In every genus, worst of all is the corruption of the principle on which the rest depend," he argues. "Therefore, since by the unnatural vices man transgresses that which has been determined by nature with regard

to the use of venereal actions, it follows that in this matter this sin is gravest of all."

The range of topics that Aquinas addresses in his thousands of pages of writing is astounding. In fact, according to the testimony of one of his closest associates, he would sometimes dictate to as many as three or four secretaries at a time on different subjects, from memory rather than from notes or manuscripts. When stumped on a particular theological conundrum, he would

---

**AQUINAS AND THE REFORMATION**

Faith is higher than reason; but reason is higher than anything else, and has supreme rights in its own domain. That is where it anticipates and answers the anti-rational cry of Luther and the rest; as a highly Pagan poet said to me: "The Reformation happened because people hadn't the brains to understand Aquinas."

G. K. Chesterton,
*St. Thomas Aquinas: The Dumb Ox*

---

**REASON AND REVELATION STROLL HAND IN HAND**

During the three weeks when I submitted myself to the discipline of inhabiting Aquinas' thought, of seeing with his eyes and breathing through his nostrils, I came to understand how comfortable the worldview of the Church could be. "Just give your assent to a few little preliminary ideas," the Summa whispered, "and I will take care of everything else; I will settle all your questions, even the questions you don't know how to ask; I will order the world into a total structure, a magnificent architecture of hierarchically interconnecting ideas. Everything will be decided forever. Let me do it for you. Trust me." I could feel the satisfaction this kind of system provided; at least, for several pages I could feel it. There I was, standing in the downtown of Christian culture, with the great emporiums of belief lining the granite boulevards. Reason and Revelation strolled arm in arm beside me on a spring afternoon, window-shopping. All the floor-managers and salespeople patiently displayed their wares and answered us in the politest newspaper Latin. Somewhere, on some top floor, the Holy Spirit occupied His revolving chairmanship, on the lookout for safe investments. In every president's office of every building, God the Father leaned back in a leather chair, His ankles crossed on the desk, while in the room with the bare light bulb His Son added up figures for the final inventory.

Stephen Mitchell, *Meetings with the Archangel*

pause to go into deep meditation and prayer and then return to the topic with clarity. Some of his writing is drafted in his own difficult-to-decipher handwriting but with the same logical progression that typifies his dictation.

Aquinas, who proves the existence of God with "Five Ways," finds God most real in a vision. He had experienced visions earlier in life, but a vision near the end of his life affects him so profoundly that he sets aside his writing. His closest aide pleads with him to take up his pen again. "I cannot," he confides. "Such things have been revealed to me that what I have written seems but straw." The vision has physical consequences as well, causing some to speculate that he may have had a stroke or a mental breakdown. Some time later he is injured while riding a donkey to a church council and dies soon after.

Recognized as a great scholar during his lifetime, Aquinas continued to be revered after his death. His works were copied and housed in monastic and university libraries throughout Europe. In 1323 he was canonized a saint by Pope John XXII. Then in 1879 Pope Leo XIII declared that his writings represent official Catholic teaching, though not so authoritative as to be above challenge.

## Bonaventure: Monk of Good Fortune

Bonaventure (c. 1221 – 1274), like Aquinas, was both a philosopher and a monk. While studying at the University of Paris, he entered the Franciscan Order. Soon he became director of the Franciscan School in Paris, and at thirty-six he was named minister-general of the order.

Born John di Fidanza, son of Giovanni and Maria, he grew up in Italy near Rome. As an infant with a life-threatening illness he was taken to St. Francis and, according to legend, miraculously cured. Francis blesses him, *O buona ventura,* pronouncing good fortune on him.

Like Aquinas, his classmate at the University of Paris, Bonaventure is a bright scholar; but unlike Aquinas, he looks to Plato as *the* philosopher. His mystical spirituality blends with his philosophical and theological enterprise. Warm affection of the heart is superior to

### THEOLOGICAL DEFENSE OF THE IMMACULATE CONCEPTION

John Duns Scotus (c. 1265 – 1308), one of Ockham's teachers, is recognized as the first Western theologian to offer theological support for the immaculate conception of the Virgin Mary. So influential are his arguments that he is known as the "Marian Doctor." His devotion to Mary dates to his early childhood, when an apparent learning disability pegs him as a "pea-brained" boy. He pours out his heart to Mary, pleading for help, and is soon at the head of his class. Decades later, on Christmas night in 1299, Mary appears to him and places the baby Jesus in his arms, stirring him to concentrate his study and writing on the incarnation of Christ. But it is his focus on Mary's sinlessness for which he is most remembered. Praying for "strength against [his] enemies," he is assured by her that she will empower him. Convinced of her guidance, he presents his argument: Like everyone else, Mary needs to be redeemed through Christ's atonement on the cross. But had her redemption not occurred until he was crucified, she would have committed sins. So her sins are paid for through the crucifixion in advance, and she is thus born without sin. Duns Scotus further argues: "The Perfect Redeemer must, in some case, have done the work of redemption most perfectly, which would not be, unless there is some person, at least, in whose regard the wrath of God was anticipated and not merely appeased."

## COULD A DONKEY HAVE BECOME THE INCARNATE *CHRIST?*

Ockham contributed to the destruction of the scientific God ... by launching a process that led to the decoupling of the Christian God from the Greek philosophical idea of First Cause.... Ockham understood God's omnipotence to mean that God can do anything that God chooses to do. This emphasis formed a stark contrast to the implications inherent in the older metaphysic of essences, which suggested that God was governed by (and therefore, in Ockham's estimation, limited by) the eternal ideas of essences.... [This] is evident, for example, in his declaration that God could have chosen to become incarnate as an animal such as an ox or a donkey, rather than a human being. This seemingly crass statement articulates Ockham's conviction that the incarnation, like God's ways in general, is the product of an arbitrary act of divine will, rather than the outworking of a rational plan.... Ockham rejected the claim implicit in Thomism that divine and human reason are so close that if we were able to gain access to God's mind we could understand its operative logic. In Ockham's estimation, this assumption was tantamount to transforming the living God of the Bible into a "civilized Aristotelian."

Stanley James Grenz, *The Named God and the Question of Being*

intellectual reasoning. He lectures on Lombard's *Four Books of Sentences* and teaches philosophy, but his primary focus is spiritual formation. *The Soul's Journey into God* is written in Tuscany at the same spot where Francis had a profound visionary experience. In this spiritual manual he challenges the Christian to avoid seeking God merely through reasoning or study:

First, therefore, I invite the reader to the groans of prayer through Christ crucified, through whose blood we are cleansed from the filth of vice — so that he not believe that reading is sufficient without unction, speculation without devotion, investigation without wonder, observation without joy, work without piety, knowledge without love, understanding without humility, endeavor without divine grace, reflection without divinely inspired wisdom.... Therefore, man of God, first exercise yourself in remorse of conscience before you raise your eyes to the rays of Wisdom reflected in its mirrors, lest perhaps from gazing upon these rays you fall into a deeper pit of darkness.

## William of Ockham: The Merit of Simplicity

Born in the small town of Ockham in Surrey, England, William (c. 1288–1347) is perhaps best remembered for "Ockham's Razor," a philosophical method or principle that demands simplicity. One must cut through complicated ideas by identifying the basics and then pursuing the simplest hypothesis. Problem solving must not be unnecessarily complex. During his lifetime and since, the counter-argument is that the simplest hypothesis is not always true — that sometimes a complex and convoluted process is required. But for all students who struggle with problems that seem to be unnecessarily weighed down with complexity, Ockham is a hero. However, Ockham is far more than that. Deeply involved in church matters, he has been regarded by some as the first Protestant.

As a youth William joins the Franciscans and continues his schooling at Oxford, becoming a leading critic of scholasticism, a theological system he finds convoluted and often irrelevant. He also criticizes the church for its ostentatious wealth. As a Franciscan, he tangles with the pope and with his own religious order over Christ's call to poverty. Franciscan monasteries have acquired land, established educational institutions, and become rich — the rule of poverty long since abandoned. Critics, however, disparage what they deem pride in poverty. Popes living in luxury are caught up in the debate. Pope John XXII pontificates against the rule of poverty and in 1322 decrees that the Franciscans must own property. He likewise challenges the Franciscan "heresy" that Christ and the disciples lived a life of poverty, owning no property.

But Ockham's problems with the pope involve more than the matter of poverty. His teaching at the University of Paris has a profound impact on scholars and lay people who, like him, challenge the power of the papacy — particularly in this era of Avignon popes and antipopes. With his public censure of the pope, he is summoned to Avignon in 1324. During the four years that follow, he is held under house arrest while charges of heresy are investigated. He, in turn, charges the pope with heresy, and in 1328 he escapes to Germany. Here, with the head of the Franciscan order, he finds protection under Emperor Ludwig (Louis IV), who is also challenging papal authority.

Together, monk and emperor seek to overturn the authoritarian rule of Pope John and his successors, Benedict XII and Clement VI. Ockham's philosophical views on church and state would become foundational for Reformers and the conciliar movement, which sought to limit papal power in favor of councils. His demands are dangerously "liberal" for the late medieval church. Though hardly representative of modern democracy, his views pave the way for human rights advocacy in later centuries. Christians, right or wrong, he argues, have a right to hold and defend their opinions without threats from church or state. Other controversial stands he proposes include:

- Neither the pope nor church councils are infallible.
- A pope who propagates false teaching or infringes on the rights of Christians can be deposed.
- Secular states are not under the authority of the church.
- Secular authorities must honor the rights of citizens.
- A despot may be deposed.

One of the most daring of Ockham's proposals relates to women. In his *Dialogues,* he portrays the student interacting with the teacher. In one instance the disciple asks the master about women's involvement in church councils. The master responds: "In the new man there is 'neither male nor female '[Galatians 3:28]. And therefore, where the wisdom, goodness or power of a woman is necessary to the discussion of the faith (which is to be discussed especially in a general council), the woman is not to be excluded from the general council."

Ockham lived out his life at a monastery in Munich, challenging the church from afar. His influence on late medieval reformers was profound, and many of his views paralleled those of John Wycliffe and Jan Hus. In many ways he is the most modern — and perhaps the most admirable — of the great medieval theologians.

Medieval theology is not an abstract venture created in a vacuum devoid of emotion and personality. Scholars have long recognized *theology as biography* — that theological propositions are significantly formed by an individual's background and character traits. So it was in the Middle Ages.

## What If ...

What if Anselm had not written *Cur Deus Homo* (Why a God-Man?)? It is difficult to exaggerate the influence that manuscript has had on the theology of the atonement. Might Catholic and Protestant theology be different today without that slim volume?

What if Abelard had not sought out an opportunity to tutor the beautiful Heloise? Might his star power as a brilliant Christian philosopher have won the day, slanting church dogma in a very different direction?

What if Thomas Aquinas had followed his older brothers into a military career? Without his writings, the Catholic Church might have floundered in a maze of differing theological perspectives. Even early Protestant theologians would have been the poorer without his vast foundational landscape to either accept or reject and to challenge point by point.

What if William of Ockham had prevailed in his argument that in the "new man" there is neither male nor female and that women therefore should not be excluded in the highest levels of the church? Imagine how different the church might be today if women since the High Middle Ages had been welcomed in all levels of ministry and considered, as Ockham argued, "necessary to the discussion of the faith."

## Further Reading

Abelard, Peter. *Story of My Adversities*. Mineola, N.Y.: Dover Publications, 2005.

Barlow, Frank. *Thomas Becket*. Berkeley: University of California Press, 1990.

Chesterton, G. K. *Saint Thomas Aquinas: The Dumb Ox*. New York: Doubleday, 1974.

Clanchy, Michael. *Abelard: A Medieval Life*. Hoboken, N.J.: Wiley-Blackwell, 1999.

Cullen, Christopher M. *Bonaventure*. New York: Oxford University Press, 2006.

Evans, G. R. *The Medieval Theologians: An Introduction to Theology in the Medieval Period*. Hoboken, N.J.: Wiley-Blackwell, 2001.

Gilson, Etienne. *The Spirit of Mediaeval Philosophy*. Translated by A. H. C. Downes. Notre Dame, Ind.: University of Notre Dame Press, 1991.

Kenny, Anthony. *Medieval Philosophy*. New York: Oxford University Press, 2007.

Rosemann, Philipp W. *Peter Lombard*. New York: Oxford University Press, 2004.

Selman, Francis. *Aquinas 101: A Basic Introduction to the Thought of Saint Thomas Aquinas*. Notre Dame, Ind.: Ave Maria Press, 2007.

Southern, Richard W. *St. Anselm: A Portrait in a Landscape*. London: Cambridge University Press, 1992.

Spade, Paul Vincent. *Five Texts on the Mediaeval Problem of Universals: Porphyry, Boethius, Abelard, Duns Scotus, Ockham*. Indianapolis, Ind.: Hackett, 1994.

# CHAPTER 9

# Beyond the Cloistered Walls

*Monasticism, Mysticism, and Social Outreach*

*What most pleases God? Prayer and meditation or humanitarian service? This is an age-old, often unconscious issue facing Christians of every generation. Should our faith be weighted toward the contemplative or the active life?*

*More than a decade ago, after delivering a series of lectures at Whitworth College in Spokane, Washington, I was seated, on my flight home, across the aisle from a nun in full habit who was praying her rosary. My curiosity mounting, I waited to greet her until our lunch was served. I forget my "pick-up line," but within minutes we were engaged in a lively conversation. She had taken a vow of silence, but was able to talk while away from the convent with anyone who opened up a conversation. She was pleased that I had reached out to her.*

*Here was a one-time executive office manager who had left her promising career and gone through a marriage ceremony with Jesus. In fact, she showed me photographs of her wedding. She looked lovely in her elegant, lacy white gown.*

*Although she had taken a vow of silence, she was now being released to teach at an inner-city parochial school in Cleveland, Ohio. She was excited about this temporary opportunity for service. When I asked if she would like to be released to spend the rest of her life in such a service ministry, she expressed ambivalence. As exciting as this new venture was, she did not want to leave behind her life of contemplation.*

*As we consider monasticism in the Middle Ages, we see extremes of both the active and the contemplative life—not so much in one individual as in particular monastic systems. Is one way more spiritual than the other? We come to understand our own perspective on spirituality as we reflect on historical models.*

> Religions, which condemn the pleasures of sense,
> drive men to seek the pleasures of power.
> Throughout history power has been the vice of the ascetic.
> BERTRAND RUSSELL

It may seem difficult to imagine gentle Saint Francis or studious Saint Dominic or Saints Catherine or Hildegard with serious vices, having condemned the pleasures of sense. But a closer look confirms that power truly is the vice of the ascetic. In the name of God they wield authority. Ascetics rallied crusaders and led crusades. Dominican friars propelled the Inquisition. Cloistered nuns authenticated their authority through visions and supernatural powers. We fail to fully understand asceticism and monasticism if we do not recognize how closely the vice of power and the profession of godliness are linked.

Monastic movements had grown alongside the church hierarchy from the early centuries as parachurch organizations. Each had a specialty or uniqueness by which it was known, and they often spawned spiritual celebrities. Some of these saints, however, operated independently, outside the confines of the monastery. Among the household names of the High Middle Ages were Bernard of Clairvaux, Hildegard of Bingen, Francis of Assisi, Clare of Assisi, Dominic, Catherine of Siena, and Margery Kempe.

As the Middle Ages progress, the number of saints increases. In an age when the super-natural is easily meshed with superstition, miracle stories are the "reality shows" of the day. But for every miracle there are a dozen torments by the devil, sometimes attacking innocent people in the night and other times merely spoiling the milk. Life is difficult, with few comforts for the average family. Death and disease are ever-present realities. Nearly a third of children born healthy die before their mid-teens. Old age, however, is not uncommon. Every village honors the old ones who remember the stories of long ago.

By 1250 a robust population increase benefits the economy, and in some areas it reaches levels it will not see again until the nineteenth century. This trend is checked in the following centuries by a series of calamities, notably the Black Death but also numerous wars and economic stagnation. During the time of economic growth, several new religious orders are founded, including the Franciscans in 1209 and the Dominicans in 1216, both orders of preaching friars. But whether cloistered nuns or begging friars, monasticism is controversial. Among those who profess no faith, monasteries are a costly waste of time and energy. Even among

## PARADE OF HISTORY

As the Christian church continues to push northward into the whole of Western Europe, monastic leaders are in the front lines, often leading a parade of followers into the wilderness to establish new monastic sites. Bernard sometimes marches with as many as thirty men following dutifully behind him. So also does Francis of Assisi, a pied piper with a parade of disciples. Women are rarely part of the parades, though Margery Kempe wiled away many years annoying fellow travelers on her various pilgrimages.

## A FATAL DOUBLE STANDARD

Monasticism was represented as an individual achievement which the mass of the laity could not be expected to emulate. By thus limiting the application of the commandments of Jesus to a restricted group of specialists, the Church evolved the fatal conception of the double standard.... And so we get the paradoxical result that monasticism, whose mission was to preserve in the Church of Rome the primitive Christian realization of the costliness of grace, afforded conclusive justification for the secularization of the Church.

Dietrich Bonhoeffer, *The Cost of Discipleship*

Christians, monasticism has severe critics. Martin Luther protested loudly against monasteries and the vow of celibacy:

> If you are able to remain chaste and be pure by your own strength, why then do you vow to be chaste? Keep it, if you can, but it is a mere nothing that you should want to boast about your vow.... Do you want to know to whom you have vowed to keep chastity? I'll tell you: the miserable devil in hell and his mother.

Long before the preaching friars came on the scene, monastic communities had been located in remote desert areas and later in the mountains or forests of Europe. Monasticism meant being separated from the world, though wherever monasteries were located, the world found them. One of the trademarks of medieval monasticism was repeated renewal and reform. This reform typically meant going back to the basics — stricter rules, less worldliness, and more limitations on women religious. Monastic reform in the tenth and eleventh centuries was centered at the Monastery of Cluny with the aim of revitalizing the monastic system that had been severely weakened by military conflict.

In addition to its ornate churches, the most notable feature of Cluniac monasticism was its regimented daily cycle of worship. Monks rose before dawn to begin church services and private devotions and continued on through the day with alternating periods of work and worship. The benefactor of the convent was Duke William of Aquitaine, an old man who had committed a murder in his younger years. "I will provide at my expense for men living together under monastic vows," wrote William, "with this hope, that if I cannot myself despise all the things of this world, at least by sustaining those who despise the world ... I may myself receive the reward of the righteous."

The collapse of the Benedictine monastic monopoly in the late eleventh century coincided with the beginning of the period of rapid expansion of monasticism in Western society. The two most successful of the new orders were Augustinians and Cistercians, emphasizing two sides of the Benedictine tradition. The Augustinians, basing their rule on a letter written by Augustine of Hippo, relaxed the rigid Benedictine regulations. Augustine had counseled that the most

Monastery of Cluny

## EVERYDAY LIFE

## Medieval Medical Practices

Illness in the Middle Ages was far more mysterious than it is today. Without the benefit of x-rays, EKGs, MRIs, and a multitude of other tests, medicine was largely guesswork. Home remedies, including a wide variety of herbal potions, were less risky than bloodletting and other procedures provided by physicians. Astrological charts and other superstitions were used to diagnose illness.

Until the Black Death, leprosy was the most dreaded malady, inflicting large numbers of people with its insidious eating away of the flesh. There was no cure, and its victims were segregated in colonies, some two thousand colonies in France alone by the beginning of the thirteenth century. The Black Death, however, trumped leprosy as the most dreaded medieval killer. Spanning four years between 1347 and 1351, the European plague wiped out more than a third of the population.

The cause of the plague was often judged to be sin, as was true of other maladies, particularly mental illness. Found in every town and village, the mentally ill were divided into two categories: that observed in infancy or childhood (often referred to as *idiocy*), and that which struck an otherwise normal individual. Women frequently suffered from what today is diagnosed as postpartum depression brought on by a hormonal imbalance. It was not uncommon for mentally handicapped children and adults to be sent to convents, a practice that met with some resentment from the monks and nuns charged with their care.

Whether at home or in a convent, those who were difficult to control were bound in chains. In some instances they were ostracized from the community and forced to wander or live in caves. Demon possession was often presumed to be the cause of the malady. Priests using a standard liturgy were equipped to perform exorcisms. Testimonials, including those from Anthony and Gregory the Great, point to instances of demons fleeing from the one exorcized, thus authenticating the saint's reputation. Whippings and forced consumption of foul substances were sometimes used to aid the exorcism.

Medicine during the medieval period

When medical specialists treated mental illness, they looked for an imbalance in bodily fluids or humors: black bile, yellow bile, phlegm, and blood. Too much black bile, for example, was believed to cause depression. Various potions and prescribed courses were offered to decrease the flow of black bile. The earliest mental institution was founded in 1247 in London at Bethlem Royal Hospital. In exchange for care, property and other valuables were often confiscated by government officials. With primitive and often violent treatment, the Bethlem atmosphere was chaotic and frenzied; thus the term *bedlam* entered the English language.

effective rule was one that left "much to the imagination" so that "it could be developed in various ways." Augustinian monks were extensively involved in relief work among the poor and in rebuilding churches. With thousands of communities by the thirteenth century, the lowly Augustinians had a profound impact on medieval society.

Unlike the Augustinians, the Cistercians, founded in 1098, sought to strictly interpret the *Rule of Benedict*. Located in remote areas and with tightly regulated activities, they sought to remove themselves from the rough and tumble everyday village life of medieval Europe. Lay brothers did the dirty work of manual labor and farming, while the "White Monks" (named for their habits of unbleached fabric) read and meditated and prayed. Unlike the ornate Cluniac churches, the Cistercian churches and liturgy were plain. Overall, medieval monasticism allowed for a wide range of styles. Even within an order or a single monastic house, amid regulated days and hours, unique

Bernard of Clairvaux

personalities—often colorful and unconventional, if not insane—emerged.

## Bernard of Clairvaux: Preaching Christ Most Excellently

The most celebrated of the Cistercians monks and the leading reformer of the twelfth century, Bernard (1090–1153) was more than a monastic leader. He was a theologian, a papal confidant, a Crusader, and a hymn writer. Indeed, he was one of the few medieval Roman Catholics widely heralded by the Reformers. John Calvin regarded him as the premier proclaimer of truth in the centuries between Gregory the Great and the Reformation, and Martin Luther found him to be "superior to all the doctors in his sermons, even to Augustine himself, because he preaches Christ most excellently."

Born in a French castle where his parents "ruled in feudal glory," Bernard turned away from wealth and prestige to become a Cistercian monk in his early twenties. Like his

## A REFORMER REFLECTS ON BERNARD

Since the apostles' time, the Scriptures have remained so obscure.... Even the holy fathers ... have often fallen into error, and, because they were ignorant of the languages, they very seldom agree, but one says one thing, and another another. St. Bernard was a man of great genius; so much so that I would place him above all the eminent doctrinists, both ancient and modern. But yet, how often does he play upon the language of the Scriptures (albeit in a spiritual sense), thus turning it aside from its true meaning.

Martin Luther, *Letter to Maintain and Establish Schools*, 1524

six brothers and a sister, he was influenced by the deep faith of their mother, Aletha. According to his earliest biographer she, with her husband, "governed the household in the fear of God, devoting herself to deeds of mercy and rearing her children in strict discipline ... not so much for the glory of her husband as for that of God; for all the sons became monks and the daughter a nun." As a youth, Bernard was inflamed by the passion of the Crusades, even as his father had been—despite the fact that his father, like so many others, never returned home.

Bernard's decision to become a monk, according to his biographer, occurs suddenly. He is riding one day through a dense forest. Coming upon a roadside chapel, "he went in and there prayed, with flooded eyes, lifting his hands toward Heaven.... From that hour ... God had kindled [fire] in the heart of his servant." Bernard then seeks out a Cistercian monastery, bringing more than two dozen men with him. His early life of luxury is behind him, and three years later he is commissioned to take twelve monks and start a new

> "While I am in this life this more sublime philosophy will be mine — to know Jesus Christ, and Him crucified."
>
> Bernard of Clairvaux

community. They march northward through deep forests to a valley near the headwaters of the River Aube. Here he and his followers build the Abbey of Clairvaux.

For the next thirty-four years Bernard ministers in this region, preaching, praying, and reaching out to those in need in the surrounding areas. So compelling are his recruitment efforts that women reportedly warn their husbands and lovers and sons to stay away from his monastery because he has magical powers for turning men into monks. The story of his sister Humbelina—the one sibling who had refused to enter the cloister—sheds light on his power. She is married with children, but Bernard is not moved by her maternal instincts. When she turns away from his demands, he refuses to speak with her. Eventually he breaks her will, and she consents to leave her family and spend the rest of her life in seclusion.

A celebrated traveling wonderworker, Bernard leaves behind testimonies of healings—particularly of young boys suffering a variety of afflictions who then join his band of recruits. On one occasion thirty young men who are healed or witness a healing follow him back to the monastery. By the middle of the twelfth century the Abbey of Clairvaux has some seven hundred monks and seventy daughter houses under his strict discipline—all secluded cloisters. When a monk leaves for a pilgrimage to Jerusalem, Bernard appeals to the pope, demanding that he be returned. Propelled "by a spirit of frivolity," he argues, the monk might encourage others to leave.

Yet for all his insistence on curbing the travel and curiosity of his monks, Bernard abides by no such rule for himself. Engaged in the most critical debates of the era, he is tireless in his efforts to end a church schism in 1130, and he becomes the attack dog in the campaign against Abelard. With the same intensity, he promotes the Second Crusade, launched in 1145. Before he becomes involved, there is little excitement for another long march east. But then the "honey-tongued" recruiter aims his evangelistic arrows at those needed to liberate the Holy Land. "I opened my mouth," he testifies, "and at once the Crusaders have multiplied to infinity. Villages and towns are now deserted. You will scarcely find one man for every seven women. Everywhere you see widows whose husbands are still alive."

Bernard spends a year traveling from town to town, appealing for troops. But the early news of Crusader defeats, dampens his spirits. Surely, he reasons, God must be punishing the sins of the Crusaders. In the end, the Islamic armies prevail, and Jerusalem is taken. Despite setbacks, his popularity is high, and he is canonized a saint in 1174, barely two decades after his death.

## Hildegard of Bingen: Directed by Divine Light

A contemporary of Bernard, Hildegard of Bingen (1098–1179) left behind a large portfolio of writings that sheds light on her inner thoughts as well as the world around her. During the final decades of her life she reigned as the abbess queen over her spirited German convent—a bevy of women all eager to express their ideas in writing.

The tenth child born into an aristocratic family, Hildegard grows up sickly and saintly. When she is but a small girl she informs her nurse that a pregnant cow is carrying a white calf with black spots on its head, back, and feet. For her spot-on accuracy she is given the calf as a pet. Soon after, she is sent away to study with the celebrated

### SAINT BERNARD: THE MAN AND THE DOG

The beloved big, slobbery Saint Bernard dog is not named for Bernard of Clairvaux, but rather, for Bernard of Menthon, born more than a century and a half earlier in 923. A Benedictine monk, Bernard founded two monasteries in the Alps providing refuge for pilgrims trudging through dangerous mountain passes on their way to Rome. Sometimes travelers were caught in storms and monks rescued them with their faithful dogs. The most celebrated of these rescue dogs was Barry, who saved nearly one hundred pilgrims. Today Barry is stuffed and lives in the Natural History Museum in Berne.

## MISERABLE AND WORSE THAN MISERABLE WOMAN

Venerable Father Bernard . . . I am greatly troubled from this vision, which appears to me in the spirit of mystery, which I have never seen with my external physical eyes. I, a miserable and worse than miserable woman, from my infancy have seen great marvels, which my tongue could not proclaim, except that the Spirit of God teaches me.

Hildegard of Bingen to Bernard of Clairvaux (1146/47)

anchoress Jutta. Like other anchors of both sexes, Jutta lives in a small cell attached to a church. Nearby is a Benedictine monastery where Hildegard is exposed to church music and liturgy.

Like Jutta, Hildegard testifies to revelations and visions that begin in her pre-teens. Then, on the death of Jutta, she assumes the leadership of the young women who have now joined together in community. In her early forties she testifies that God has given her the ability to comprehend the true meaning of sacred texts and has commanded her to record the meaning that is given her through a continuous stream of visions. Seeking sanction as God's mouthpiece, she contacts Bernard of Clairvaux. He passes her request on to the pope, who encourages her to continue transcribing her visions. She takes this as papal support and begins publishing her visions under the Latin title *Scivias* (know the ways [of the Lord]), which is soon popular among both laity and clerics.

The revelations, according to Hildegard, do not come during a dream or a trance, "but watchful and intent in mind I received them according to the will of God." Directed by a divine light "more brilliant than the luminous air around the sun," she speaks with authority:

And it came to pass . . . when I was forty-two years and seven months old, that the heavens were opened and a blinding light of exceptional brilliance flowed through my entire brain. And so it kindled my whole heart and breast like a

flame . . . and suddenly I understood the meaning of expositions of the books. . . .

Yet when commanded by God to write down what she is seeing, she feels "wretched in my womanly condition" and an "unworthy servant":

Self-doubt made me hesitate. I analyzed others' opinions of my decision and sifted through my own bad opinions of myself. Finally, one day I discovered I was so sick I couldn't get out of bed. Through this illness, God taught me to listen better. Then, when my good friends Richardis and Volmar urged me to write, I did. I started writing this book and received the strength to finish it, somehow, in ten years. These visions weren't fabricated by my own imagination, nor are they anyone else's. I saw these when I was in the heavenly places. They are God's mysteries. These are God's secrets. I wrote them down because a heavenly voice kept saying to me, "See and speak! Hear and write!"

Soon Hildegard relocates her nuns to the Rhine River in Bingen. Here her reputation flowers as she and her nuns write on a wide variety of topics in a number of genres, including plays, letters, music, and scientific treatises. Throughout her ministry she criticizes corrupt clergy, warning people not to seek out priests for salvation, but to seek Christ and the Scriptures—or expect pain and punishment in the life to come:

I saw a well deep and broad full of boiling pitch and sulphur, and around it were wasps and scorpions.... And I saw a great fire, black, red, and white, and in it horrible fiery vipers, spitting flame; and there the vipers tortured the souls of those who had been slaves of the sin of uncharitableness.

On a more personal level she responds to the ordinary concerns as a *Dear Abby* or *Dr. Ruth* of the twelfth century, often serving as an advocate for children. As such she firmly counsels parents not to place children in convents without their consent. Nor is she prudish on the topic of sex, challenging the common belief that the woman is passive in the sex act and that pregnancy is a result of a mere deposit of the male *seed*. Indeed, the woman plays an active and manly role.

Hildegard is only one of many influential abbesses of this era. The convent of Hefla attracts the most attention for its mystical visions and accompanying writings, an atmosphere encouraged by Gertrude of Hackeborn, who reigns as abbess of Hefla for forty years. Most of the writings there are the work of Gertrude the Great, Mechtild of Hackeborn, and Mechtild of Magdeburg. The writings of Gertrude the Great are very specific, as she peers into purgatory and sees the souls coming and going. She confidently offers advice to priests and laity concerning when souls will be released on the basis of the prayers offered.

Sometimes visions give nuns the validation needed to strike out on their own and go out into surrounding towns to preach. Indeed, through these ecstatic experiences, nuns receive authorization to take on priestly functions, though not without opposition from clerics. More important, however, is their recognition as authentic saints. Near the end of her life, Gertrude testifies to receiving (several decades after a similar experience of Francis of Assisi) the most spectacular miracle of all—the *stigmata*. Although invisible to others, she sees and feels the bleeding nail prints in her hands and feet.

Along with visions are personal problems and struggles with demons. During Hildegard's long service as an abbess, a young nun, Richardis von Stade, becomes her beloved personal assistant. Due in part to an unexplained falling out (of which Hildegard writes that they both have sinned), Richardis arranges to move to another convent where, through the influence of her brother an archbishop, she will become abbess. Hildegard claims that God has told her Richardis should not go. To the archbishop she writes: "Your curses and your malicious and threatening words are not to be heeded." To Richardis, after she has departed, Hildegard writes: "Why have you forsaken me like an orphan? I loved you for your noble bearing, your wisdom, your purity, your soul and all your life!" Hildegard relentlessly battles for her "daughter" to return, demanding such in a

## WHEN A WOMAN MAKES LOVE....

When a woman is making love with a man, a sense of heat in her brain, which brings with it sensual delight, communicates the taste of that delight during the act and summons forth the emission of the man's seed. And when the seed has fallen into its place, that vehement heat descending from her brain draws the seed to itself and holds it, and soon the woman's sexual organs contract, and all the parts that are ready to open up during the time of menstruation now close, in the same way as a strong man can hold something enclosed in his fist.

Hildegard of Bingen, *Liber Subtilatum*

court of law. Richardis prevails, but the battle ends only at her death.

Unlike her cloistered sisters, Hildegard travels and preaches widely. In fact, despite her poor health, she conducts four preaching tours over a span of thirteen years, the final one completed during her seventy-fourth year. She visits monasteries and cathedrals, counseling and preaching to men more often than women. She corresponds with popes and bishops and heads of government as well as lesser clerics and laity. She also writes music and is now recognized as one of the great medieval composers.

## Francis of Assisi: Blessing Our Brothers, the Birds

The story of Francis of Assisi (c. 1181–1226), symbolized in a concrete garden statue of a robed monk with woodland birds and animals, is as beloved as it is familiar. The preeminent wanderer, Francis and his followers personified what Bernard forbade. His religious order, the Order of Friars Minor (Franciscans) paved the way for the preaching friars.

The son of Pietro di Bernadone, a wealthy Italian fabric merchant, Francis is one of seven children. From an early age, he gravitates toward his mother Pica's faith far more than his father's financial wizardry. His very name reflects different parental aspirations. His father away on business when he is born, Pica baptizes him Giovanni di Bernardone for John the Baptist. When Pietro

Francis of Assisi and scenes from his life

returns home, he objects to the name's significance and changes it to Francesco.

Young Francis finds little satisfaction in his father's business enterprise, nor is he interested in living a life of adventure as a knight. He sleeps late and loafs around during the day and then becomes a troubadour, a singer, and songwriter who wanders through markets presenting an appealing alternative to monks' Latin hymns. Nights are filled with rollicking fun and mischief. Perhaps realizing he will never become a star troubadour, he joins the military. But before he sees action, he is taken prisoner, during which time he is dazzled by a vision. He wonders if God is calling him to serve the poor. After his release he goes back to a life of leisure, only to face serious illness before returning again to the military. Obsessed with God's call, he leaves the military and goes home. But he no longer sings on the street corners and in the bazaars. A pilgrimage to Rome proves decisive. There he has another vision, this time while meditating on an icon of Christ on the cross. Three times the voice of the crucified speaks to him: "Francis, go and repair my house which, as you can see, is falling into ruins."

So ardent is his zeal that he becomes a virtual Robin Hood, stealing from his own father. How else, he reasons, is he going to acquire the money to repair God's house? His father is not amused. In fact, he is so outraged that he calls on the bishop to settle the matter. Francis is anything but repentant. Dressed for success, he appears before the bishop and hears the charges against him. He

Dante's *Paradiso* portrays Thomas Aquinas commemorating Francis:

> Let me tell you of a youth whose aristocratic father disowned him because of his love for a beautiful lady. She had been married before, to Christ, and was so faithful a spouse to Him that, while Mary only stood at the foot of the Cross, she leaped up to be with Him on the Cross. These two of whom I speak are Francis and the Lady Poverty. As they walked along together, the sight of their mutual love drew men's hearts after them. Bernard saw them and ran after them, kicking off his shoes to run faster.
>
> Dante, *Paradiso*

then steps behind a door and reappears naked, handing his clothes and his money to the bishop and makes an announcement: "Up to this time I have called Pietro Bernardone father, but now I desire to serve God and to say nothing else than 'Our Father which art in heaven.'"

In 1209, now in his late twenties, he hears the voice of God in a sermon from Matthew 10:9: "Preach, the kingdom of heaven is at hand, heal the sick, cleanse the lepers, cast out devils. Provide neither silver nor gold, nor brass in your purses." This becomes his rule of life.

> *"If you have men who will exclude any of God's creatures from the shelter of compassion and pity, you will have men who will deal likewise with their fellow men."*
>
> Francis of Assisi

He discards his purse and shoes, dresses in rags, and feels guilty if he meets someone who is poorer than he. He lives with lepers, washing their puss-filled sores and kissing their fingerless hands and stubbed feet. His father and his friends think he has gone mad. Initially, he is a loner. But then a follower comes along, and by the end of the year, with ten more disciples, the "Lesser Brethren," as mendicants, beg from house to house, spending nights out of doors.

In Rome Francis seeks the papal blessing. However, Innocent III is insulted by his apparent show of disrespect, reportedly telling him: "Go brother, go to the pigs, to whom you are more fit to be compared than to men, and roll with them, and to them preach the rules you have so ably set forth." But Innocent also sees something remarkably sincere in Francis. After putting him off, he later agrees to give provisional approval for a new religious order. Final sanction will come only after they have proven themselves worthy.

Poverty is not a new concept in monasticism, but Francis gives it greater prominence than others had. For Benedictines, obedience is emphasized over poverty. And previously, poverty had been associated with a rural, secluded life. But with Francis, urban poverty takes on a whole new meaning. He embraces poverty rather than separating from it as hermits and monks had done. The inward emphasis on personal self-denial is turned upside-down with an outward focus on the poor and needy living on the margins of society.

Although taking a vow of celibacy, he himself is married. He had boasted as a youth that his wife would be the most beautiful woman to be found. And now, as a wandering beggar, he finds her, recognizing her as his true love. He finds her on a mountaintop, "sitting on the throne of her neediness." She is Lady Poverty, informing him that she was with Adam in paradise but that after he sinned she was forced to become a homeless wanderer. She was married to

Jesus when he walked the earth. Since then she has sought refuge in one monastery after another but was always turned away. Revering her as "the mistress and queen of the virtues," Francis marries her and she comes to dwell with him.

Francis has another love in his life second only to Lady Poverty—Mother Nature. He stands out as the premier medieval environmentalist, his devotion to nature as sincere as his devotion to poverty.

So close was Francis to nature that he preached sermons to those he regarded as his companions: "Brother birds," he admonished, "you ought to love and praise your Creator very much. He has given you feathers for clothing, wings for flying, and all things that can be of use to you. You have neither to sow, nor to reap, and yet He takes care of you." An environmentalist before his time, he asked the emperor to enact laws to protect "our sisters, the birds."

For Francis, however, life is far from idyllic. For many of the less-committed friars, the love for Lady Poverty quickly dissipates. They rebel against what they perceive to be an evil stepmother. Having been stirred by the personal charisma and emotion-charged sermons of Francis, they have second thoughts about being on the bottom rung of society. Other monks, they observe, live the good life. Supported by clerics, angry friars replace Francis with a new leader while he is away on a mission trip. It is the most dramatic coup in monastic history. He returns to find a wealthy cleric in charge of the very ministry he has founded. He might have rallied his dedicated followers and led them away and begun anew. But this, he reasons, is not the way of humility. He accepts the stunning reversal as God's will. He tells his followers, "From henceforth I am dead for you. Here is brother Peter di Catana whom you and I will obey." He then prostrates himself before his new superior and directs the friars to follow in submission. His heart is broken, but there is no other course of action for this most singular saint.

Despite this turn of events, Francis is widely regarded as a saint, and his death in 1228 only increases his stock as a holy man. Church leaders from far and near, including Pope Gregory IX, bask in his popularity. In fact, the pope preaches at his funeral, lays the cornerstone for a church in his memory, and canonizes him as a saint. The miracle most associated with Francis is the stigmata, as testified by the vicar of the Franciscan order the day after Francis dies:

> Never has the world seen such a sign except on the Son of God. For a long time before his death, our brother had in his body five wounds which were truly the *stigmata* of Christ, for his hands and feet have marks as of nails, without and within, a kind of scars, while from his side, as if pierced by a lance, a little blood oozed.

## THE SAINTLY ENVIRONMENTALIST

The hymn ["Canticle to the Sun"] is a pious outburst of passionate love for nature. It soars above any other pastorals of the Middle Ages. Indeed Francis' love for nature is rare in the records of his age, and puts him into companionship with that large modern company who see poems in the clouds and hear symphonies in flowers. He loved the trees, the stones, birds, and the plants of the field. Above all things he loved the sun, created to illuminate our eyes by day, and the fire which gives us light in the night time, for "God has illuminated our eyes by these two, our brothers."

Philip Schaff, *History of the Christian Church*

## Clare of Assisi: Sequestered and Silent

Women played an important role in communal monasticism almost from the beginning. Some were placed in convents as children, but many devoted their lives to God, thus avoiding the drudgery and danger of childbearing. Like many who fell under the spell of Francis, Clare of Assisi (1194–1253) heard him preach early in his ministry and was determined (as was her brother) to join the new order. Born into a noble

Clare of Assisi saving a child from a wolf

family of Sciffi, she is only a teenager when she announces to her family that she will be taking a vow of poverty. Clare's mother, Ortolana, is a devout Christian who has taken pilgrimages to Rome and to the Holy Land. In view of their social status, however, she and her husband, the Count of Sasso-Rosso, are determined that Clare marry a worthy and wealthy nobleman.

Strong-willed, Clare flees, living under the protection of Francis, who is aware of her reputation for holy living. They meet often, and two years later, in 1212, she establishes the Order of the Poor Dames (later called Poor Clares), based on his rule. She commits herself to poverty and begins wearing a plain garment. Her distraught family soon loses another daughter when Agnes joins Clare. And later their mother also joins. Clare spends the rest of her life in the convent, her days spent in prayer and meditation as well as with menial tasks and supervising the women who join her. Unlike the friars,

### SAINT CLARE GOES TO CHURCH ON CHRISTMAS EVE

St. Clare was ... so ill that she could not go to church with the other nuns to say the Office on the night of the Nativity of Christ. All the other sisters went to Matins; but she remained in bed, very sorrowful.... But Jesus Christ, her Spouse, unwilling to leave her comfortless, carried her miraculously to the church of St. Francis, so that she was present at Matins, assisted at the Midnight Mass, and received the Holy Communion, after which she was carried back to her bed. When the nuns returned to their convent, the ceremonies being ended at St. Damiano, they went to St. Clare and said to her: "O Sister Clare, our Mother, what great consolations we have experienced at this feast of the Holy Nativity! Oh, if it had but pleased God that you should have been with us!" To this St. Clare answered: "Praise and glory be to our Lord Jesus Christ ... for by the intercession of my father, St. Francis, and through the grace of our Saviour Jesus Christ I have been personally present in the church of my venerable father, St. Francis, and with the ears of my body and those of my spirit have heard all the Office, and the sounds of the organ, and the singing, and have likewise received there the most Holy Communion."

*The Little Flowers of St. Francis of Assisi,* Chapter XXXV

she and her nuns are strictly cloistered, with no freedom to preach and serve the poor. Yet their only means of support is begging—sending out word of their needs. The rule of Clare does not even permit rich girls to enter with their dowries: "Let the sisters not appropriate anything to themselves.... Let them send confidently for alms. Nor should they be ashamed, since the Lord made Himself poor in this world for us."

## Dominic: Founder of the Dominicans

In many ways the polar opposite of Francis, Dominic of Osma (1170–1221) stands alongside Francis as the founder of another very influential order of friars. The Dominican order of Preachers was established less than a decade after Francis founded the Franciscans. Dante compared the two: "Francis filled the world with passion and love; Dominic ... filled the world with light." The latter emphasized preaching with scholarly rigor, especially to "heretics,"

urging them to come back to the fold. As with the Franciscans and other orders of friars, the Dominicans begged for alms and were largely located in urban settings.

Born in a Spanish castle, Dominic shares with many other medieval saints a noble heritage and a mother who profoundly influenced his spiritual vocation. Juana, long venerated by Dominicans as a saint, tells an extraordinary birth story. Before her son is born she has a dream of a dog jumping out of her womb with a torch fastened in its teeth. It is a prophecy that the child she is carrying will "set the whole earth on fire."

Well educated in theology and liberal arts, Dominic, the nephew of an archbishop, is reared in the shadow of the church. While he is completing his university training, famine devastates large regions of Spain and starving refugees flee the countryside. Selling his clothes and precious manuscripts, Dominic feeds the hungry. When friends admonish him to consider his

Stained glass showing the legend of Mary giving Dominic the rosary

## DOMINIC'S EARLY MINISTRY IN SPAIN

Dominic abode there alone with a few Christian men and Catholic, against the heretics, and denounced and preached the word of God firmly. And the adversaries of truth mocked him, and spit at him, and threw at him filth of the streets, and other right foul things, and ... he answered, without fear or dread: "I am not worthy to be martyred, nor I have not yet deserved that death by glory." And therefore he passed hardily by the way where they despised him, and sang, and went joyously. And they marveled and said to him: "Hast thou no dread of death? What wouldst thou have done if we had taken thee?" "I had prayed you," said he, "that ye should not have slain me suddenly, but little and little ye should have hewn member from member, one after another." ... He found a man that for the great poverty that he suffered was joined to the heretics, and S. Dominic, seeing this, ordained himself to be sold, and that the price of him should be given to the poor man to bring him out of his poverty. And this did he for to bring him [out] of the foul error he was in.

*The Golden Legend or Lives of the Saints*, 1275

own academic future, he reportedly responds: "Would you have me study off these dead skins, when men are dying of hunger?"

After leaving the university, Dominic travels widely, maintaining close connections with Rome. In Southern France he finds the Albigensian heresy flourishing. Distressed by their Manichean dualism that pits light against darkness and spiritual against material, he vows to devote his life to fighting heresy. Like Francis he makes a pilgrimage to Rome to beseech Pope Innocent III for permission to found a new order. The year is 1215. The event is the Fourth Lateran Council. Permission is granted, and the "Black Friars" are born.

Dominic's initial evangelistic strategy had been to convince heretics to repent through persuasive preaching — not by the power of Rome. "It is not by the display of power and pomp, cavalcades of retainers, and [decked-out horses], or by gorgeous apparel, that the heretics win proselytes," he adamantly insists. Rather, "it is by zealous preaching, by apostolic humility, by austerity, by ... holiness. Zeal must be met by zeal, humility by humility, false sanctity by real sanctity, preaching falsehood by preaching truth."

But in 1232, the work of the Inquisition is given to the Dominicans, and conversion by force becomes the preferred approach. Unlike most monastic leaders Dominic makes his headquarters in Rome. From there he and his friars spread out, recruiting followers and reclaiming hearts and minds from heresy. The luxury of Rome does not tempt him. He practices strict asceticism, wearing a heavy chain around his waist and a rough hair shirt, often walking long distances barefoot and sleeping outside in the elements. He fasts frequently, eats no meat, and observes a strict regimen of prayer and silence. Not surprisingly, his health fails and he dies before he reaches his fifty-second birthday.

As a dead saint, Dominic does not enjoy the popularity accorded Francis. The reason is the Inquisition. Reformers pointed to the Dominicans as theological thugs. Today the Inquisition — this Catholic arm of terror — is disdained by Catholics and "heretics" alike. But Dominicans were more than theological thugs. Their rapid growth within a century to some six hundred religious centers uniquely positioned them for mission outreach during the age of discovery and colonialism. Though the order was less than half the size of the Franciscans, they competed in the race for religious domination in the New World, India, and the Orient.

Like Francis, Dominic is credited with a wide rage of miracles, most notably raising people from the dead. In one story a worker employed to help construct a church is crushed when a wall caves in. Arriving on the scene, Dominic raises him to life. In another case, a cardinal's nephew falls from a galloping horse; several hours later Dominic brings him back to life with no sign of the injuries. In still another situation, a woman returns from hearing the saint preach only to find her son dead. She rushes back to Dominic with the child in her arms and he raises him from the dead. When Dominic died he remained dead. But twelve years later, during church renovation, his remains were moved and it is said that "a gentle aroma, like a sweet perfume, filled the air to the delight of all."

## Catherine: Saint on the Streets of Siena

More than a century after Dominic's death, Catherine of Siena (1347–1380), at age sixteen, joins the Third Order of St. Dominic. The First Order was comprised of friars, the second of nuns, and the third of laity. Unlike Clare, who lived out her life secluded in a convent, Catherine follows a course more closely associated with Francis himself. She spends her days nursing the poor—particularly lepers and victims of the plague.

The daughter of a prosperous fabric dyer, she is the third youngest of twenty-five children. (As was true of other very large families, mothers die in childbirth and fathers remarry.) She survives infancy despite the Black Plague that ravages Siena when she is but a toddler. From the age of four she meditates and prays, and at seven (the legal age of consent to marriage) she takes a vow of virginity. Against her parents' objections, she cuts her long hair so as to be unattractive to the man with whom marriage has been arranged. During these years she is sustained by visionary experiences. On one occasion, during a pre-Lenten carnival, demons tempt her with the feminine and marital joys she is denying herself. While friends and family and neighbors are in the streets eating and drinking and dancing—typical pleasures of a medieval community—she is in her dark cell. Suddenly Jesus and the Virgin and other saints appear. Jesus puts a gold ring on her finger, and Catherine becomes his bride.

From then on she holds to strict asceticism, wearing a hair shirt and pelvic chain and residing in a secluded cell. But she gradually moves out into the streets of Siena among lepers and the plague-infected. On one occasion, as she is kneeling over a woman and draining pus from the woman's putrid sores, she is overcome by the sickening stench. Guilt-stricken by her revulsion, she reaches for the bowl of pus, lifts it to her lips, and drinks it, later insisting that it was the sweetest taste she had ever known. That her sanity is questioned does not deter her. On another occasion she is caring for a man on the day of his execution. Through her comfort on previous visits, his violent ways have subsided. The execution, as she relates, is turned into their own private celebration:

> I was there at the place of execution, waiting and praying.... At length he came, like a meek lamb. When he saw me, he laughed and asked me to make the sign of the Cross over him. When I had done so I said: "Kneel down now, my sweetest brother. To the nuptials! In a moment you will have entered into life eternal." He knelt down gently and I bent over him and held him as he lowered his head,

reminding him of the blood of the Lamb. His lips murmured nothing but the names, Jesus and Catherine. I closed my eyes, accepting in the Divine Goodness the sacrifice, and as he was speaking I received his head into my hands.

While some consider Catherine mentally unstable, others are deeply moved by her selfless acts of service. Like other Catholics of her day, she was deeply troubled by the volatility of the papacy—and thus the church itself. In 1309, more than forty years before she was born, the papacy, prompted by carnage in Rome, had moved to Avignon. Opponents of the newly elected pope had threatened his life, so the French king kidnapped and secured him in France. His successors continued to live in Avignon for nearly seventy years—a period known as the Babylonian Captivity of the Church by those demanding that popes return to Rome. Critics rightly regard the Avignon papacy as a puppet of the increasingly powerful French regime, and not until 1377, did Pope Gregory XI return the papacy to Rome. His death, however, triggered the Great Schism in the Western church that lasted for four more decades. In this instance the cardinals, regretting their election of Urban VI, reversed the decision and elected Pope Clement VII. Two popes and more, supported by various factions, created turmoil until the schism ended with the Council of Constance in 1417.

Catherine of Siena

Catherine died in her early thirties, only two years after the Great Schism has begun, but years earlier she had sought to convince the pope to depart from Avignon, the "Babylon of the West." With some twenty devoted followers, she leads a march to Avignon. She is granted an audience with the pope but only after she is found by papal officials to be neither insane nor a heretic. She offers a ready-made solution: launch another Crusade. Gregory IX counters that the church must settle its internal strife before going to war, but Catherine persists in the age-old argument that the best way to solve the problems at home is to declare war on the enemy. That Catherine, according to one historian, "dominated Pope Gregory and to a lesser extent Urban VI" is an unwarranted conclusion. She was one among many who urged the pope to return to Rome. But her tenacity in serving the poor and challenging the hierarchy of the church solidified her fame.

Through revelations, she sought to confirm church tradition not clarified in Scripture. Medieval theologians from Anselm to Aquinas, for example, had argued that Mary was conceived sinless and remained so all her life, ever remaining a virgin. Aquinas had summed up the common belief: "As a virgin she conceived, as a virgin gave birth, and she remains a virgin forever." Through a vision, Catherine confirms the tradition and offers an additional detail: Mary was not perfected until three hours after her conception. But her revelation is trumped by theologian Duns Scotus, who insisted that Mary was perfected at the instant of conception.

Catherine was canonized by Pope Pius II in 1461. More notable, however, was her elevation by Pope Paul VI in 1970 to Doctor of the Church, along with Theresa of Avila, the first women to be so named. She was recognized again in 1999 by Pope John Paul II, who named her a patron saint of Europe.

## Margery Kempe: Unconventional Pilgrim

Not all medieval women who followed God's call were unmarried. Indeed, some of the most celebrated holy women practiced celibacy in marriage. In 1413, after twenty years of marriage and fourteen children, Margery Kempe (c. 1373–1438) convinced her husband to agree to sexual abstinence for the remainder of their lives. If Catherine of Siena seemed strange to many observers, Margery's idiosyncrasies were even more bizarre. For some two decades she traveled as a pilgrim to various sacred shrines, seeking an

audience with local churchmen, recounting to them her revelations and visionary experiences. To fellow pilgrims she was a nuisance and worse. Known for shrill moralizing, she was regarded by many as deranged, and they sought to escape her company.

Born into a middle-class family in Norfolk, England, Margery was the daughter of a wool merchant who also served as a local politician and member of Parliament. At twenty, she married John Kempe. Soon after the birth of their first child, she suffered a serious breakdown—one of the earliest such incidents described by the patient herself. In *The Book of Margery Kempe*, dictated to a scribe, she tells her story of being attacked by devils, often speaking of herself as "this creature." Hallucinations are so severe that she is restrained:

> For dread she had of damnation ... this creature went out of her mind and was wonderfully vexed and labored with spirits half year eight weeks and odd days. And in this time she saw, as her thought, devils open their mouths all inflamed ... sometime ramping at her, sometime threatening her, sometime pull-

## THE BLACK DEATH

I say, then, that the years of the beatific incarnation of the Son of God had reached the tale of one thousand three hundred and forty eight, when in the illustrious city of Florence, the fairest of all the cities of Italy, there made its appearance that deadly pestilence.... In men and women alike it first betrayed itself by the emergence of certain tumors in the groin or the armpits, some of which grew as large as a common apple ... and spread itself in all directions indifferently; after which the form of the malady began to change, black spots ... making their appearance in many cases on the arm or the thigh or elsewhere, now few and large, then minute and numerous.... Citizen avoided citizen ... kinsfolk ... never met, or but rarely; ... brother was forsaken by brother, nephew by uncle, brother by sister, and oftentimes husband by wife: nay, what is more, and scarcely to be believed, fathers and mothers were found to abandon their own children, untended, unvisited, to their fate, as if they had been strangers. Wherefore the sick of both sexes, whose number could not be estimated, were left without resource but in the charity.

Giovanni Boccaccio (1313–1375)

### JULIAN OF NORWICH

An anchoress living in a small cell attached to a church in Norwich, Julian (1342–1416) is regarded as one of the great English mystics of all times. She is known primarily for *Revelations of Divine Love*, visions that began at age thirty during a serious illness. Although she billed herself as "a simple unlettered creature" who was "lewd, feeble and frail," her writings show otherwise. Indeed, she is one of the most quotable and most quoted medieval mystics. From her pen come the oft-repeated lines: "All shall be well, and all shall be well, and all manner of things shall be well." Of Christ she writes: "He said not 'Thou shalt not be tempested, thou shalt not be travailed, thou shalt not be diseased'; but he said, 'Thou shalt not be overcome.'" She reflected on the Trinity in feminine images: "God is oure moder," "oure savyouure is oure very moder," "very moder Jhesu," and "oure moder, Christ."

ing her and hauling her both night and day the foresaid time. And also the devils cried upon her with great threatenings and bade her she should forsake her Christendom, her faith, and deny her God, his Mother, and all the saints in Heaven, her good works and all good virtues, her father, her mother, and all her friends. And so she did. She slandered her husband, her friends, her own self ... like as the spirits tempted her.... She bit her own hand so violently that it was seen all her life after. And also she [scratched] her skin on her body ... with her nails ... and worse she would 'a done save she was bound and kept with strength both day and night that she might not have her will.

Margery testifies that amid this suffering, while her guardians are out of sight, she suddenly experiences a profound vision of Jesus:

> Our merciful Lord Christ Jesus ... appeared to his creature.... "Daughter, why hast thou forsaken me, and I forsook never thee?" And ... as he had said these words she saw verily how the air opened bright ... and ... the creature was stabled in her wits and in her reason as well as ever she was before, and

prayed her husband as soon as he came to her that she might have the keys of the buttery to take her meat and drink as she had done before.

The fascinating story of this thirteenth-century English woman, regarded by some as the first autobiography written in the English language, demonstrates the profound role of religion in everyday life of the Middle Ages. As a pilgrim, Margery represents religious women who are among the freest in medieval society. They have been released—often through claims of visions—from the bonds of marriage and are under no one's "rule" but their own. Unlike nuns in convents, these pilgrim women live very geographically and socially and spiritually liberated lives. Medieval religion—and life itself—was as interesting and varied as it is today.

It is fashionable today to read the lives of medieval saints, quote their writings and imagine they are our spiritual sisters and brothers. And, of course, they are. But there is a chasm that separates us from them—a cultural chasm that can never be spanned by words alone. Their inner lives and outward actions belong not to us but to a distant medieval world.

## What if....

What if Francis, the troubadour, had continued composing and singing love songs regaling exploits of knights and helpless damsels instead of composing songs like his Canticle of the Sun?

What if Dominic had continued his softer response to heretics through persuasive preaching and had not commissioned the Dominicans to serve in the forefront of the Inquisition? Might the course of medieval church history gone in a different direction without the terrors of these preachers of orthodoxy?

What if the Catholic Church had denied medieval women the opportunity to pursue a religious vocation? Did Hildegard of Bingen, Clare of Assisi, and Catherine of Siena contribute significantly to the depth and richness of spiritual life in the Middle Ages? How have they influenced both men and women in the centuries since?

## Further Reading

Barter, James. *The Working Life: A Medieval Monk*. Chicago: Lucent Books, 2003.

Beebe, Catherine, *St. Dominic and the Rosary*. Ft. Collins, Colo.: Ignatius Press, 1996.

Brooke, Christopher N. L. *The Age of the Cloister: The Story of Monastic Life in the Middle Ages*. New York: HiddenSpring, 2003.

Cahill, Thomas. *Mysteries of the Middle Ages*. New York: Random House, 2006.

Collis, Louise. *Memoirs of A Medieval Woman: The Life and Times of Margery Kempe*. New York: Harper, 1983.

Flanagan, Sabina. *Hildegard of Bingen*. New York: Routledge, 1998.

Forbes, F. A. *St. Catherine of Siena*. Rockford, Ill.: Tan Books, 1999.

Hildegard of Bingen, *Selected Writings*. Translated and edited by Mark Atherton. New York: Penguin Classics, 2001.

Kempe, Margery, and Tony D. Triggs. *The Book of Margery Kempe: Autobiography of the Madwoman of God*. Liguori, Mo.: Liguori Publications, 1995.

Kennedy, Robert F., Jr., and Dennis Nolan. *Saint Francis of Assisi: A Life of Joy*. New York: Hyperion, 2005.

Kroll, Jerome. *The Mystic Mind: The Psychology of Medieval Mystics and Ascetics*. New York: Routledge, 2005.

Maddock, Fiona. *Hildegard of Bingen: The Woman of Her Age*. New York: Image, 2003.

McDermott, Thomas. *Catherine of Siena: Spiritual Development of Her Life and Teaching*. Mahwah, N.J.: Paulist Press, 2008.

Spoto, Donald. *Reluctant Saint: The Life of Francis of Assisi*. New York: Penguin, 2003.

Tamburello, Dennis. *Bernard of Clairvaux: Essential Writings*. New York: Crossroad, 2000.

# CHAPTER 10

# Renaissance Humanism and the Dawn of the Reformation

*Waldo to Wycliffe*

*The prelude to the Reformation was both positive and negative. On the positive side, there were many individuals demanding reform in the Church. On the negative side, corruption was rife—all manner of fraudulent rackets right in the belly of the Church itself. But amid the corruption, creative juices were flowing, most notably in art, architecture, and literature. This is particularly evident in Florence, the birthplace of the Italian Renaissance.*

*On a trip to Italy in 2006 my husband and I were among the teeming crowds of tourists visiting that wonderful city—the "Athens of the Middle Ages." Here one finds not only spectacular works of art, but also places of great historical significance—some of which tourists are unaware. The Piazza della Signoria is one such spot. To this square Girolamo Savonarola, the celebrated evangelist of his day, brought his followers in the spring of 1497. They joined in building a bonfire to burn "vanities"—everything from popular books and board games to ladies' gowns and works of art. The next year the evangelist himself was burned in that very piazza.*

*In that same piazza stands that grandest of all of Michelangelo's sculptures, David—high and lofty in all his naked youth and beauty—having not moved since he took up residence in the fall of 1504.*

*The Medici family of wealthy bankers (with its close ties to the papacy) also took up residence in this city. While patronizing the arts and music, they controlled money and much more to their own advantage. Machiavelli called this city his home, and that is where he wrote "The Prince," his political guide for rulers. Dante also hailed from Florence. Although his poetic writings were apparently not among the vanities Savanarola burned, they were surely considered burnable by popes and others whom he harshly attacked.*

*Strolling through the piazzas and across the bridges spanning the River Arno, my husband and I almost sensed the cobblestones crying out in a clamor of voices from the past. Though distant in time and culture, we were yet so near to those who once deliberated in the piazzas and walked the narrow streets.*

> "Historians have their method, just like anyone else,
> and they're jealous of it, but the 'Illiad' shames any history of Greece,
> and Dante stands supreme above the world's collected medievalists.
> Of course the medievalists don't know it, but everyone else does.
> As a way to arrive at the truth, exactitude and methodology are,
> in the end, far inferior to vision and apotheosis."
>
> ALESSANDRO IN MARK HELPRIN, *A SOLDIER OF THE GREAT WAR*

The historical approach to understanding any given period in our past ought not be disabused, but at the same time there is a way of arriving at truth that calls forth vision and grandeur as much as exactitude and methodology. Dante's *Divine Comedy* is a supreme example. Though wading through his seemingly endless lines of his poetry can be tedious, he offers glimpses of life through a historical lens that cannot be found in an academic tome. Dante's lines in the *Inferno* reflect on the decadence of the Catholic Church of his day, most specifically aimed at the corruption of Pope Boniface VIII and the selling of church offices. But his poetry also draws from the church's very foundation in the New Testament:

> Then tell me how, how much gold did our
>        Lord
> ask that Saint Peter give to him before
> he placed the keys within his care? Surely

the only thing he asked was "follow me." And Peter and the others never asked for gold or silver when they asked Matthias to take the place of the transgressing soul.

Dante was surely not alone in challenging the church to be faithful to its mission. In fact, he was one of many who found himself on the outside of a church that used its power to reward its friends and defeat its enemies. The motives of these reformers are mixed. Like the mystical miracle-working saints, canonized and otherwise, these individuals seeking to bring renewal to the Christian faith struggle with their own derelictions and demons. Among them are Peter Waldo, John Wycliffe, Jan Hus, Thomas à Kempis, Girolamo Savanarola, and Desiderius Erasmus.

What is sometimes referred to as the *Dawn of the Reformation* encompasses a complex mix of individuals and events. If there is one represen-

## PARADE OF HISTORY

As church history marches into the Renaissance and toward the Reformation, the drum beats are becoming louder as accusations against Rome accelerate. In the late twelfth century Peter Waldo, on a Sunday excursion in the town square, listens to the song of a traveling troubadour. His life is transformed and he turns against Rome. A parade-turned-charade occurs in 1414, when Jan Hus, with thirty bodyguards, makes his way to Constance, only to be ambushed, imprisoned and burned at the stake. But the biggest procession of this era is later in the century when Savonarola and his multitude of followers march to a popular piazza in Florence to burn their "vanities." Soon thereafter another parade of onlookers is gawking at the burning of the preacher himself.

## MEDIEVAL AND RENAISSANCE ART

The distinction between Medieval and Renaissance painting is not one of competency.... Medieval art was hierarchic. Figures were often ranked in size on a scale of ascending importance.... In such a scheme it was necessary that the most significant figure in the painting be the largest and that all other figures, according to their rank, be of diminishing size.... A religious event could be depicted in serial fashion so that all key episodes were presented.... The picture did not require natural surroundings or realistic panoramas.... In order to avoid any analogy to human experience and to enhance the other worldliness of the scene, medieval settings were deliberately shallow in depth. Further, the application of gold leaf to the background areas conveyed ... purity.... While the Middle Ages were concerned with the mysteries of God, [the] Renaissance ... painted world was a stage set for significant human action that took place in a world that matched the natural environment of man.... Harmony, proportion, and unity, which in Medieval art had been tied to the divine, were now applied to human figures and to the compositions in which they were placed. These terms, with their humanistic emphasis, were achieved visually, by using a single point perspective. This perspective related all parts of the composition to the human viewer and the human world depicted. Thus, God looks at Medieval art, man looks at Renaissance art.

Sandra Willard, "The Illusion of the Renaissance," Yale–New Haven Teachers Institute

tative story—probably more legend than reality—it might be the dying words of Jan Hus. As he is being burned at the stake for his attack on various church practices and beliefs, he reportedly says, through the voice of prophecy: "In a hundred years, God will raise up a man whose calls for reform cannot be suppressed." Hus died as a martyr to the cause in 1415. In 1517, Martin Luther nailed his famous Ninety-five Theses to the church door in Wittenberg. We are tragically missing the story of these generations, however, if we are only craning our necks, looking forward to the Reformation.

It is widely argued that the Reformation began long before that chilly day in Wittenberg, October 31, 1517, when an Augustinian monk posted a document challenging the church primarily on the matter of indulgences. That incident ignited a flame, but there were innumerable other sparks that had filled the night sky of the late Middle Ages. And they were not all religious in nature. Political and social factors

combined with religious impulses to make the Reformation virtually inevitable. The church was entering the modern age, and it is highly unlikely that such a transition or transformation could have been made without major turmoil.

What shape this reform would take, however, was most uncertain. Throughout the medieval period there had been renewal movements and theological disputes and challenges to the papacy—all of which culminated in widespread discontent in the fourteenth and fifteenth centuries. Adding to the general discontent over the wealth and corruption of the papacy was the relocation of popes to Avignon, followed by the Great Schism.

While there were those who separated from the church, the majority of late medieval reformers were loyal Catholics. They could not have imagined being numbered with the heretics. Their only desire was to bring about changes in the church that they held so dear. Indeed, most agreed with church dogma that there was no

## Crime and Punishment

From the perspective of Dante, the worst crimes committed in medieval times were committed by clerics, especially popes. Dante's criminals rarely got their due in life, but in death they went on to burn endlessly in hell. The sins Dante identifies come in three categories, from lesser to greater: self-indulgence, violence, and maliciousness. Hell is a cone-shaped realm ringed with nine concentric circles, each going deeper into perdition. The ninth circle is at the very center of the earth, where the likes of Judas Iscariot and Satan himself are housed. In circle eight Dante finds Pope Nicholas III, who condemns the two popes who follow him, Boniface VIII and Clement V, for selling church office to the highest bidder. Boniface, whom Dante does not find in hell because he is still alive (and will not die until

*Justice* by Pieter Bruegel, showing different methods of torture

Dante has already gone to the grave), will surely find his way to one of the lowest circles.

But there are many other rings of hell and many crimes of a non-clerical nature. Indeed, the Middle Ages could be described as a thousand years of lawlessness. The feudal system opened the door for violence, with less-than-chivalrous knights assuming responsibility to keep order and fight wars. Peasants rebelled through thievery. Bands of highway robbers roamed the countryside and wielded control over whole regions. The brutality of the Crusaders only aggravated an already violent society, though when so many were marauding their way to the Holy Land there were fewer at home to disturb the peace. Violence in the church was widespread—not only in Crusades and Inquisitions but also in the very inner sanctums of power, where murder was one means of handling administrative problems.

Among commoners, crimes were committed and punished routinely. Crime-solving, barely in its infancy, favored clever criminals. Punishment was designed as a deterrent and meted out by often-conflicting levels of law enforcement. On a local level, petty crimes

## RAPE IN THE MIDDLE AGES

The women involved were often the wives and daughters of day labourers or textile workers or servant girls.... Violence against women was ... part of the sexuality of young males in late medieval Venice. Rape in Venice tended to be regarded as serious if it involved children, the elderly or the upper classes, but rape between social equals was not regarded as too serious and in some cases almost as part of the courtship ritual.... The attitude of sexual bravado was not limited to any one class, but seems to have been the norm.

Jeffrey Richards, *Sex, Dissidence and Damnation*

merited public humiliation, while more serious offenses drew a jail term. The criminal was typically chained in a dungeon, and care was assigned to the family. Without such support, the accused often wasted away amid filth and vermin without provisions and medical aid. Friars and nuns like Catherine of Siena sometimes offered assistance, but local priests and their parishes were less inclined to become involved. Torture, frequently used to force confessions of murder or heresy, took the form of beatings, ripping out fingernails, and knocking out teeth, but could end in dismemberment and slow burning at the stake.

The most common crime reported in medieval times was theft of food, crops, and livestock. Punishment was typically no more than a fine to compensate for the value of the stolen property as determined by the town council. When the fine had been satisfied, the guilty person was absolved and life went back to normal. On repeat offenses, a person might be publicly held in stocks or whipped or imprisoned, or in the case of multiple thefts, the hacking off of a finger or hand. In the mid-fourteenth century some seventy percent of punishable crimes involved thievery. Murder was second at nearly twenty percent.

Rape was not uncommon, though rarely reported due to the strict class divisions of the day. Indeed, attitudes toward crime and morals typically reflected one's social status. In the twelfth-century advice book *The Art of Courtly Love,* Andreas Capellanus writes that a man should not be considered unfaithful to his wife in a moment of passion when "Venus is urging him on" and he encounters "a little strumpet or somebody's servant girl" and takes her down into the grass. "We can say without fear of contradiction," he continues, "that just for this a lover is not considered unworthy of the love of his beloved." The only issue in this case is how the wife will feel; there is no concern for the raped servant girl. Violence is a way of life in the Middle Ages, and women often find themselves the victims. Dante makes an allusion to such crimes in the *Inferno's* eighth circle: "With ... honeyed tongue and ... dishonest lover's wiles ... [they] left [women] pregnant and forsaken. Such guilt condemns [them] to such punishment."

salvation outside the church. Thus, a Reformation that would spawn Lutheran and Reformed churches would have been abhorrent.

Although this era encompasses far more than religious turmoil, religion is intermingled with every activity of life. At the same time, the Renaissance march toward the modern world is evident everywhere. This cultural and intellectual movement begins in the fourteenth century and affects virtually every aspect of society. *Humanism* is the key word. Originating in Florence, it quickly fans out through the burgeoning cities, with university professors and students eager to grasp all things new. *Man* is now the focus. The reign of scholasticism is ending. Monastic contempt of beauty and the physical body is being repudiated. As Greek sculpture is once again honored and reclaimed, so also are classical languages and literature.

Science also gains momentum. Perhaps no one more comprehensively represents the "Renaissance man" than does Nicolaus Copernicus (1473–1543). A cleric, military officer, and diplomat, he was also a scholar with specialties in linguistics, classical studies, art, medicine, economics, mathematics, and astronomy. Although astronomy was little more than a fascinating hobby for him, it is in this arena that he met both criticism and fame. By no means was he the first to maintain that the earth was not the stationary center of the universe, but he demonstrated it convincingly. His scientific calculations would foment what would become known as the Copernican Revolution when clerics denounced his system as contradicting Scripture.

There is no female counterpart to Copernicus—a "Renaissance woman." There were, to be sure, women who learned the ancient languages and studied the classics. They were patrons of the arts who sometimes established schools for girls. But the era of modern feminism was far in the future. Women had spoken with prophetic and visionary voices, but neither the church nor the humanism of the universities were prepared to let them sit at the table as equals.

The backdrop to this progression toward the modern world was the growth of urban centers. After several centuries of stagnation in once-thriving European commercial and cultural hubs, trade routes to the East begin to open up, especially in the thirteenth century. Italian cities that have developed into city-states are the most notable beneficiaries. By the fourteenth century, with the Crusades now history, commerce expands. Finance and banking also add to Italy's growing wealth, with its corresponding class of non-aristocratic merchants and bankers. With wealth comes building projects and patronage that turns Italian cities into extravagant cultural attractions. By the fifteenth century, this love of art and architecture becomes a passion, perhaps most notably among a succession of *secular* popes.

But any imagined picture of Italian cities as grand, easy-going artist colonies is entirely mistaken. Wars and invasions and hostilities of every description mark the era. Social instability and class conflict add to the volatility, as merchants and bankers surpass aristocrats in wealth and as workers lose out in the process.

## Peter Waldo and the Poor Men of Lyons

Three centuries before the Reformation, Peter Waldo (c. 1140–1218) challenged the validity of indulgences, purgatory, and prayers for the dead. A wealthy clothing merchant in Lyons, France, he "made himself much money by wicked usury," according to a contemporary account. Whether a banker who loaned money at high interest rates or a pawnbroker, he was involved in shady business dealings. But then one Sunday in 1173, he hears the song of a troubadour and is struck by the lyrics. The traveling storyteller had spun a tale of a saintly old man who died with his sins forgiven and the promise of life eternal. Realizing that his good fortune will be reversed in the life to come, Waldo vows to devote his life to ministry and informs his wife that he is leaving her behind, giving her half his assets—either his personal property or his real estate holdings.

Although distraught by the sudden turn of events, she chooses the real estate—"ponds, groves and fields, houses, rents, vineyards, mills, and fishing rights." Of his remaining wealth, he gives a "great part of it . . . to his little daughters, who, without their mother's knowledge he places in the convent of Font Evrard." What remains goes first to all those he had cheated and the rest to the poor and for funding Bible translation. With nothing left for himself, he goes from door to door begging. So humiliated is his wife that she hauls him before the bishop, and "seizing her husband by the throat," she shouts at him, "Is it not better, husband, that I should redeem my sins by giving you alms than that strangers should do so?" The bishop rules in her favor, and Waldo is not permitted to take food from anyone "except from his wife." But poverty is his rule, and he and his followers are known as the Poor Men of Lyons, later the Waldensians.

His aim is not to form a new sect but rather to influence the church to serve the poor and study the Scriptures. As the movement grows, opposition mounts. In 1179 he journeys to Rome, where he meets with Pope Alexander III and defends his work before three clerics. Itinerant evangelism and Scripture translation in "the vulgar tongue" are the sticky issues. He is denied official recognition, and the movement is con-

> ## SLAUGHTERED SAINTS
>
> Avenge, O Lord, thy slaughtered Saints, whose bones
> Lie scatter'd on the Alpine mountains cold;
> Even them who kept thy truth so pure of old
> When all our Fathers worship't Stocks and Stones,
> Forget not: in thy book record their groans
> Who were thy sheep, and in their ancient fold
> Slayn by the bloody Piedmontese that roll'd
> Mother with infant down the rocks. Their moans
> The vales redoubl'd to the hills, and they
> To heav'n. Their martyred blood and ashes sow
> O'er all th' Italian fields where still doth sway
> The triple tyrant: that from these may grow
> A hundred-fold, who having learnt thy way
> Early may fly the Babylonian woe.
>
> John Milton, "On the Late Massacre in Piedmont"

demned at the Third Lateran Council. In 1184 Waldo is excommunicated, and his views are again condemned in 1215 at the Fourth Lateran Council. In the meantime, he and his followers move from Lyons to more remote mountainous areas in France. His theological views are drawn from his Catholic heritage, including a strain of perfectionism. Those committed to poverty and celibacy are considered more saintly and on a higher rung of faith than others. Such perfectionism is found among those who take monastic vows, but he offers a two-tiered ranking for laity as well.

While some of his more educated followers translate the Bible, he and others commit passages to memory and go out two by two as peddlers, preaching sermons based largely on memorized Scripture. Described by a critic as "naked disciples of a naked Christ," he insists that he and his followers are living by the Sermon on the Mount. Encountering intense persecution and ordered not to preach, he defends his work with Scripture: "It is necessary to obey God rather than man; God commanded the Apostles to preach the Gospel to every creature."

Many of the early preachers are terrorized and martyred, hunted down not only by the Inquisition but also officials of the state. Some later merge with Reformed Christians in Geneva. The most atrocious attack against them is in 1655, known as "Piedmont Easter," when French military forces slaughter more than seventeen hundred, including women and children.

## John Wycliffe: English Bible Translator

Twenty-nine years after John Wycliffe (c. 1324–1384) died, his bones were dug up and burned, a retroactive rebuke to the "stiff-necked heretic." A contemporary, however, felt otherwise: "They burnt his bones to ashes and cast them into the Swift, a neighborhood brook running hard by. Thus this brook hath conveyed his ashes into Avon, Avon into Severn, Severn into the narrow seas, they into the main ocean. And thus the ashes of Wycliffe are the emblem of his doctrine, which now is dispersed the world over." At the time of his death, a Catholic leader had written a scathing indictment:

> That instrument of the devil, that enemy of the church, that author of confusion to the common people, that image of hypocrites, that idol of heretics, that author of schism, that sower of hatred, that coiner of lies, being struck with the horrible judgment of God, was

smitten with palsy and continued to live till St. Sylvester's Day on which he breathed out his malicious spirit into the abodes of darkness.

Who was this man who drew forth such vitriol? To later Protestants he would be hailed as "the Morningstar of the Reformation." Like Waldo, he committed himself to Scripture translation in the "vulgar" language and denied purgatory and the validity of indulgences. But Wycliffe went further than Waldo in articulating a theological framework that rejected the efficacy of the Mass and the dogma of transubstantiation. Unlike Waldo, he was a scholar and a trained theologian whose direct link to sixteenth-century Reformers is very clear. Born into a large landed family in Yorkshire, England, Wycliffe attended local schools, and by his early twenties was a student at Oxford, where he received a broad education in science, mathematics, philosophy, and biblical studies. A brilliant scholar, he quickly moved from student

John Wycliffe

to tutor to director of Canterbury Hall, and he became a Doctor of Theology in his early forties, lecturing and later serving as a parish priest in Lutterworth.

As would be true of later reformers, Wycliffe's demand for religious reform was intrinsically tied to politics and commerce as well as to foreign policy. English clerics as well as merchants and government officials deeply resented foreign interference. Indeed, why should they pay monetary tribute to a papacy residing in France, as was the case during the seven decades of seven popes residing in Avignon? It was no secret that France wielded considerable power and influence over its resident popes. In light of this, Wycliffe was one of many calling for the secularization of church lands in England. In fact, his first book (containing eighteen theses) argued that in temporal matters the king and parliament have authority over the church and its clergy, including the pope.

The new ideas create excitement among Wycliffe's students, and the movement spreads like wildfire. Opposing him, however, are monks and most of the English clerics, who are dependent on the papacy. His most illustrious opponent is Pope Gregory XI himself, who issues a bull against Wycliffe and his eighteen theses, denouncing the professor's dangerous teachings. The pope angrily lays out his case against him, warning Oxford to be rid of him:

> John de Wycliffe, rector of the church of Lutterworth, has fallen into such a detestable madness that he does not hesitate to dogmatize and publicly preach, or rather vomit forth from the recesses of his breast, certain propositions and conclusions which are erroneous and false. He has cast himself also into the depravity of preaching heretical dogmas.... He has polluted certain of the faithful ... and led them

... to the brink of perdition.... We command your University ... to arrest the said John.

Summoned to appear before leading bishops in Lambeth, Wycliffe arrives, accompanied by a boisterous parade of supporters, including Joan of Kent, the king's mother. He is ordered to desist teaching heresy, but he refuses to be silenced, finding the pen more powerful than the tongue. Insisting that Christ, not the pope, is head of the church, he argues that it is not "necessary to go either to Rome or to Avignon in order to seek a decision from the pope since the triune God is everywhere." He later equates the pope with the antichrist.

Wycliffe's crowning achievement is the English Bible. Like Waldo, he insists that the only way Christians can truly follow Christ is through reading Scripture in their own tongue. Such ideas, however, threaten orthodoxy. "The jewel of the clergy," clerics rail, "has become the toy of the laity." Distributing the newly translated Scriptures are barefoot itinerant "poor priests" scorned as *Lollards*. They are persecuted, and Bibles are burned. But the movement continues to spread. "Every second man that you meet," an observer comments, "is a Lollard!" Wycliffe is revered by his followers: "I indeed clove to none closer than to him, the wisest and most blessed of all men whom I have ever found," recalled William Thorpe.

Both large and small landowners support the secularization of church property, but when Wycliffe begins meddling with religious rituals and dogma, many are uneasy. Church tradition is centuries old in England. Messing with the Mass is simply not tolerated. But that is exactly what he does. In 1380, just prior to the peasants' rebellion (which he strongly opposes), he issues a provocative challenge to the doctrine of transubstantiation, attacking Thomas Aquinas for what he deems heresy—that the bread and wine are transformed into the actual body and blood of Christ. He likewise maintains that the church is the body of Christ, made up of elect only, all others being reprobate. Also rejected are merit for indulgences, penance, pilgrimages, and confession, since only Christ forgives sin.

England is not ready for such a thoroughgoing reformation, however. In 1382 Wycliffe is ordered to appear before a synod in Oxford. Poor health and lack of concern among members of parliament work in his favor. He is permitted to return to his parish, where he dies two years later. His followers, the Lollards, carry on as an underground movement.

## Jan Hus: Czech Reformer and Nationalist

To a friend, Jan Hus (1371–1415) once remarked that he wished his soul might be wherever the soul of Wycliffe was found. Like Wycliffe, he would never live to see a real reformation in the Christian church. Yet he gave his life for the cause—condemned to death at the Council of Constance. Marking the end of the Great Schism that followed the Avignon papacy, the Council was far more reactive than proactive. Maintaining the status quo and stopping a popular "heretic" dead in his tracks filled the agenda. Among Hus's deplorable doctrines was his claim that the papacy was invented by man, not by God.

Born in Bohemia (today part of the Czech Republic) into an impoverished peasant family, Hus vows to rise above such destitution: "I had thought to become a priest quickly in order to secure a good livelihood and dress and to be held in esteem by men." Moving up the clerical ladder, he earns a doctorate in theology and is ordained a priest in 1401. His parish is Prague's 3000-capacity megachurch, Bethlehem Chapel. While still in his early thirties, he is also named rector of the university. But amid his good fortune, he becomes troubled by church corruption and by the issues raised by Wycliffe, whose writings have been widely disseminated in Bohemia.

The matter of indulgences, however, rises above all other issues. During the Great Schism, when Pope John XXIII (technically an antipope) calls for a special sale of indulgences to fund a crusade against his rival, Hus is outraged. The pope, he insists, is exploiting the Czech people. Acting "through ignorance and the love of money," the pope has no moral authority. Christ is the head of the church, he asserts, and the Bible is the only true authority for Christians. The Czech people in large numbers rally to his cause. But the pope has the trump card. He excommunicates Hus and places Prague

---

### PLAGUE, HERESY, AND UNBELIEF

The plague accelerated discontent with the Church at the very moment when people felt a greater need of spiritual reassurance. There had to be some meaning in the terrorizing experience God had inflicted. If the purpose had been to shake man from his sinful ways, it had failed.... "When those who have the title of shepherd play the part of wolves," said Lothar of Saxony, "heresy grows in the garden of the Church." While the majority of people doubtless plodded on as before, dissatisfaction with the Church gave impetus to heresy and dissent, to all the movements for reform which were ultimately to break apart the empire of Catholic unity.

Barbara Tuchman, *A Distant Mirror*

## THE EXECUTION OF JAN HUS

Then he was commanded to come down to the execution of his judgment, and in his coming down, one of the seven bishops before rehearsed, first took away the chalice from him which he held in his hand, saying, "O cursed Judas, why hast thou forsaken the counsel and ways of peace?" … The place appointed for the execution was before the gate Gotlebian, between the gardens and the gates of the suburbs.… Then was the fire kindled, and John Huss began to sing with a loud voice, "Jesus Christ, the Son of the living God, have mercy upon me." … When all the wood was burned and consumed, the upper part of the body was left hanging in the chain, the which they threw down stake and all, and making a new fire, burned it, the head being first cut in small gobbets, that it might the sooner be consumed unto ashes. The heart, which was found amongst the bowels, being well beaten with staves and clubs, was at last pricked upon a sharp stick, and roasted at a fire apart until it was consumed. Then with great diligence gathering the ashes together, they cast them into the river Rhine.

John Foxe, *The Book of Martyrs*

under an interdict, discontinuing all church sacraments. Hus flees to a remote area, where he spends two years immersed in research and writing. But in 1414 he is summoned to the Council of Constance.

Guaranteed safe passage, he journeys to Germany with thirty bodyguards. Despite the promises, however, he is arrested and confined to a small dungeon cell, bound in chains for more than ten weeks. When he is finally brought before the council in chains, he is given no opportunity for a hearing. Thirty charges are brought against him. His only option to avoid execution is to recant. He refuses and is sentenced to death. His execution infuriates his followers, stirring a spirit of Bohemian nationalism. With their leader's death, many are radicalized — especially when they became targets of a Crusade in 1420 that continues for more than a dozen years.

In the last half of the fifteenth century, the Catholic Church offers various compromise solutions to bring the Hussites back into the fold. In the sixteenth century many of them support the Reformation. Like the writings of Wycliffe, the life and death and words of Hus

Burning Jan Hus at the stake

inspire Protestant Reformers. On reading his sermons, the monk Martin Luther is stunned. "I was overwhelmed with astonishment," he later recalled. "I could not understand for what cause they had burnt so great a man, who explained the Scriptures with so much gravity and skill."

## Thomas à Kempis: Imitating Christ

While other reformers of late medieval times challenged church dogma on indulgences, purgatory, and transubstantiation, Thomas à Kempis (c. 1379 – 1471) reverenced these Catholic traditions, considering them necessary for true spiritual formation. In his classic, *The Imitation of Christ*, he makes the doctrine of transubstantiation warm and approachable:

> Oh, how sweet and kind to the ear of the sinner is the word by which You, my Lord God, invite the poor and needy to receive Your most holy Body! Who am I, Lord, that I should presume to approach You? Behold, the heaven of heavens cannot contain You, and yet You say: "Come, all of you, to Me."

Thomas Haemerken was born in the village of Kempen, Germany, near where Luther was born a century later. His father, like Luther's,

Thomas à Kempis

was a metal worker. Both were educated by the Brethren of the Common Life and both became monks. But their personalities and writings and response to church corruption were poles apart. Leaving home at thirteen, Thomas followed his brother's example and journeyed to Holland, where he joined the Brethren of the Common Life, founded in 1374 by Gerard Groote, a wealthy Dutchman who turned away from his life of luxury to live in poverty. His followers took no lifelong vows and were not bound by celibacy. Groote died of the plague at forty-four but left behind a religious order that influenced thousands of followers, including Nicholas Cusa and Erasmas, as well as Luther and Thomas. Indeed, the movement that became known as *Devotio Moderna* was a significant aspect of reform within the church.

In Holland, Thomas copied manuscripts from the church fathers and medieval writers, including his hero, Bernard of Clairvaux. But his greatest influence was the Bible, having

---

### SPIRITUAL ADVICE FROM GERARD GROOTE

True obedience is obedience in matters that are contrary and difficult.

In all things, humble yourself, especially in the heart but also outwardly before others.

It is the highest of all learning to know that one knows nothing.

The more one perceives how far short he is of perfection, the closer he is to it.

The beginning of vainglory is to please one's self.

Seek ever to observe and think of something good about another.

Always put more hope in eternal glory than fear in hell.

One's thoughts in falling asleep are the same in waking; pray and read psalms before retiring.

## SPIRITUAL COMFORT

When God bestows Spiritual comfort, receive it with a grateful heart; but remember that it comes of God's free gift, and not of your own merit. Do not be proud, nor over joyful, nor foolishly presumptuous; rather, be the more humble for this gift, more cautious, and more prudent in all your doings, for this hour will pass, and temptation will follow it. When comfort is withdrawn, do not immediately despair, but humbly and patiently await the will of Heaven; for God is able to restore you to a consolation even richer than before.

Thomas à Kempis, *The Imitation of Christ*

copied the entire text four times. After some twenty years of copying manuscripts and serving the poor, he was ordained and served as a priest in Germany, where he completed his *Imitation of Christ*. "Thomas gave all his attention to God in church," recalled a monk. "While he chanted the Psalms, his eyes were ever raised towards Heaven, and he appeared to be filled with a Divine energy." He died at ninety-two, having lived out his own philosophy of life: "Love flies, runs, and rejoices; it is free and nothing can hold it back."

## Savonarola: Fundamentalist Preacher of Florence

Like Jan Hus, Girolamo Savonarola (1452–1498) met an untimely death at the hands of church authorities. Savonarola was an Italian reformer who abandoned his medical training to become a Dominican monk. A powerful and gifted preacher, he warned of the coming judgment of God. So popular was he that all of Florence reportedly thronged to hear him as he preached from the pulpit of the great Church of San Marco. Instead of enjoying the wealth and prestige associated with the position, however, he organized a lay monastic order. He and his followers soon began practicing a strict rule of poverty, living in tiny cells, renouncing all but the barest of food and clothing. The brothers quickly grew from a few dozen to over two hundred, all the while the prophet warning his burgeoning congregation of the apocalypse to come.

Through the power of his pulpit, Savonarola attained political leadership, and he wasted no time in introducing tax reforms and humanitarian programs for the poor. Nor did he stop there.

Determined to rid the city of its moral corruption, he condemns the pope as a false prophet

## A MEDIEVAL SERMON ILLUSTRATION ON THE "VANITY" OF PETS

There was [a] lady that had two "litell doggis," and loved them so that she took great pleasance in the sight and feeding of them: and "she made every day dress and made for them dishes with sops of milk, and often gave them flesh. But there was once a friar that said to her, that it was not well done that the dogs were fed and made so fat, and the poor people so lean and famished for hunger. And so the lady for his saying was wroth with him, but she would not amend it." So the lady came to a bad end, as she deserved. "And therefore here is a good ensample that ladies nor gentlewomen should not have their pleasaunce in such beasts, not give them that the poor people might be sustained with, that die for hunger, the which be God's creatures and made to his likeness."

Margaret Deanesley, *A History of the Medieval Church*

and rails against lax morals among clergy and laity. New laws are enacted. Worldliness no longer holds sway. In 1496, he organizes a "burning of vanities." His followers spread the word to rich and poor alike, calling all Christians to come to a great bonfire on the last day of the town's big carnival. They are to bring with them not only fuel for the fire, but also their worldly adornments and toys: cosmetics, wigs, hats, jewelry, trinkets, mirrors, dresses, musical instruments, cards, dice, chess pieces, pornography, and sexual paraphernalia. Even great works of art, including ones by Michelangelo, are reportedly thrown to the flames that shoot some sixty feet into the sky. All this is presided over by the great prophet, Savonarola himself.

## THE RENAISSANCE POPES

Nicholas V (1447–1455): The first of the Renaissance popes, he lavished church funds on the arts and ordered plans for a new Vatican Palace and the building of St. Peter's Basilica. As a patron of Renaissance painters, he initiated the Vatican's collection of priceless works.

Callixtus III (1455–1458): A member of the infamous Borgia family, he appointed nephews as cardinals, including Rodrigo, a future pope. He was the first pope to hail from Spain in more than a thousand years.

Pius II (1458–1464): Well-educated and a patron of the arts, he gained prestige as poet laureate for Holy Roman Emperor Frederick III. The father of illegitimate children, he appointed a "nephew" as cardinal, paving the way for him to become Pius III.

Paul II (1464–1471): Uneducated and uninterested in cultural advancement, he removed patronage for the arts in favor of a printing press for papal publications, though not without opposition. His cultured enemies were numerous and plotted against him.

Sixtus IV (1471–1481): A brilliant scholar, he was a devoted patron of the arts and architecture and watched over the construction of the Sistine Chapel. Pressured by greedy fortune-seeking relatives, he carried nepotism to a new high, appointing six "nephews" (some his own sons) as cardinals, one who would become Pope Julius II. He declared war on the powerful Medici family in Florence, sparking years of turmoil.

Innocent VIII (1484–1492): A compromise pope whose election was controversial, he was previously married and used his power and privilege to enhance the lifestyles of his children and other relatives. To increase his wealth he not only sold offices but also priceless treasures, including the papal crown.

Alexander VI (1492–1503): More commonly known as Rodrigo Borgia, he was reportedly the most corrupt and degenerate pope of all times. He openly flaunted his mistresses, including married women and teenage girls. His decade-long papal rule was bloodied with murders, political assassinations, and wars. His son Casare Borgia, appointed cardinal at age eighteen, killed his older brother and captured large tracts of land for himself.

Pius III (1303): Ill when he was elected pope in 1503, he died less than a month later.

Julius II (1503–1513): The nephew of Sixtus IV and groomed for pontiff as a youth, he sought unsuccessfully to unseat Pope Alexander VI, whom he accused of simony. Alexander's death was suspicious, since Julius was waiting in the wings to be enthroned. He was the Warrior Pope who led papal troops into battle and was hounded by French opposition throughout his term. He was a very active pope, particularly in foreign policy, but he was also a leading patron of art and architecture.

Savonarola's execution in the Piazza della Signoria, Florence

But when the Lord does not return and the local economy falters, some of Savonarola's supporters begin to sour on his campaign of righteousness. He is now looked upon as a tyrant. Restless antagonism begins with the town's rebellious youth, but soon large numbers of ordinary citizens join the opposition. They defy the laws and begin dancing and singing in the streets. The pubs open their doors and the dice roll again. Public opinion quickly turns against the great preacher, and Pope Alexander VI seals the popular disaffection with a bull of excommunication. Savonarola and his two closest disciples are imprisoned and tortured until they confess to heresy. The execution is straightforward. The three are taken to the central piazza, where they are hanged while a great bonfire roars beneath them. The prophet's last words are

## JACQUES LEFÈVRE: INFLUENTIAL RENAISSANCE HUMANIST

Theologian and humanist, Jacques Lefèvre d'Étaples (c. 1450–1536) paved the way for the Reformed movement in France. Although he never separated from the Church of Rome, he was forced into exile and several of his books and Scripture translations were condemned. Among his students was William Farel, who initiated the Reformation in Geneva. A hunted man, Lefèvre found protection at various times from King Francis I and Queen Marguerite of Navarre. John Calvin was profoundly influenced by him and reportedly spent time with him before fleeing from France.

Desiderius Erasmus

a prayer: "O Lord, a thousand times have you wiped out my iniquity. I do not rely on my own justification, but on thy mercy." Soon their bodies are consumed, even as the vanities had been.

Had he not been brutally executed at forty-six, Savonarola might have lived on for another two decades until another monk challenged the church — one who would also condemn the pope as a false prophet and worse. Martin Luther would look to Savonarola as a martyr, publishing the meditations on Psalms 32 and 51 that he had penned amid torture. To Luther they represented "a piece of evangelical testing and Christian piety."

## Desiderius Erasmus: Renaissance Humanist

A clever satirist and serious student of Scripture, Desiderius Erasmus (1466–1536) had a profound influence on the Reformation, but he does not easily fit into a religious category. Erasmus was a Renaissance humanist and a contemporary of Luther and Zwingli. Though his writings were a critical element in the success of the Reformation, he remained a Catholic his entire life.

The illegitimate son of a Dutch cleric and his mistress, Erasmus was born in Rotterdam and cared for by his parents until his teen years, when he and his brother were orphaned by the plague. He was educated in monastic schools, including one sponsored by the Brethren of the Common Life, where personal piety was emphasized. But the rigid rules, he insisted, served to break a scholar's spirit more than to encourage humility. In his mid-twenties he took vows to become an Augustinian monk, but he was unable to settle into a life of monastic asceticism.

After studying at the University of Paris, Erasmus travels as an independent writer and teacher. His scholarly reputation quickly spreads throughout the Renaissance world, and he is offered prestigious teaching posts. For a time he lectures at the University of Cambridge, but he severs those ties for the autonomy of an unsettled scholar. After residing in Italy, he moves to Switzerland, where he finds a supportive environment.

Erasmus spends many years studying Greek and preparing a Greek edition of the New Testament along with a new Latin translation that provides hundreds of corrections to Jerome's Vulgate version. Convinced that these are the foundation for his scholarship, he writes to a friend: "I cannot tell you, dear Colet, how I hurry on, with all sails set, to holy literature. How I dislike everything that keeps me back, or retards me." Though it is dedicated to Pope Leo X, his new Greek edition with study notes paves the way for the Protestant Reformation. Published in 1516, it serves as the source for many future translations. In the preface he emphasizes that his purpose is to lay the groundwork for the future. "Would that these were translated into each and every language," he writes. "Would that the farmer might sing snatches of Scripture at his plough and that the weaver might hum phrases of Scripture to the tune of his shuttle, that the traveler might lighten with stories from Scripture the weariness of his journey."

Although he is always claiming to be loyal to the Catholic Church, Erasmus is accurately accused of having "laid the egg that Luther hatched." He does not deny his role in the religious uprising but insists that he had anticipated "quite another kind of a bird!" Like other humanists, he scorns the inflexibility of medieval scholasticism. But at the same time he is convinced that Luther and other Reformers are creating a new form of dogmatism. On the matter of human freedom, for example, he challenges Luther's severe limitations of free will. Although he and Luther never meet in person, they correspond with each other and at times express more than qualified admiration for each other. But they are remembered for their differences.

The dispute between Erasmus and Luther on free will would erupt on a much wider scale not only among Catholics and Protestants but also among various Protestant factions. The debate goes directly to the core of soteriology—how humans are saved. Is one saved by God's sovereign grace alone, or does the individual have a part in gaining salvation? In *On the Freedom of the Will*, Erasmus defines free will as "a power of the human will by which a man can apply himself to the things which lead to eternal salvation or turn away from them." Salvation, he maintains, is a cooperative venture between God and the individual.

Yet Erasmus insists that God's grace trumps human free will: "It is not wrong to say that man does something yet attributes the sum of all he does to God as the author." God's grace and human free will combine "in such a way,

however, that grace is the principal cause and the will secondary, which can do nothing apart from the principal cause since the principal is sufficient in itself." Luther writes against Erasmus point-by-point, lashing out at his inconsistencies. If the individual truly has free will, Luther argues, then there is no need for grace. In short, Erasmus makes no sense. He makes his case "like a man drunk or asleep, blurting out between snores, 'Yes,' 'No.'" The dispute is not settled by the two men, nor has it been settled in the generations since.

> *"I doubt if a single individual could be found from the whole of mankind free from some form of insanity. The only difference is one of degree. A man who sees a gourd and takes it for his wife is called insane because this happens to very few people."*
> Desiderius Erasmus

Throughout his career, Erasmus is criticized from both sides. The Catholic Church bans his writings, while Luther accuses him of being like Moses, dying in the wilderness instead of moving forward and "entering the promised land." Erasmus had at one time praised Luther as "a mighty trumpet of gospel truth," though he desperately feared the schism Luther was creating. He pleads with leaders on both sides to come together in compromise. Although Protestants persistently court him, his mind is made up: "I am not so made as to fly in the face of the Vicar of Christ." Yet he is pained by the bitterness he sees on both sides: "I detest dissension because it goes both against the teachings of Christ and against a secret inclination of nature. I doubt that either side in the dispute can be suppressed without grave loss. It is clear that many of the reforms for which Luther calls are urgently needed." As time passes, tensions rise. "Had I

## POPE JULIUS II CHATTING WITH THE APOSTLE PETER

Julius: [T]he absolute power by virtue of which a pope on his own is far superior to a universal council. In fact, he cannot be deprived of his jurisdiction for any crime at all.

Peter: Not for murder?

Julius: Not for parricide.

Peter: Not for fornication?

Julius: Such language! No, not even for incest.

Peter: Not for unholy simony?

Julius: Not even for hundreds of simoniacal acts.

Peter: Not for sorcery?

Julius: Not even for sacrilege.

Peter: Not for blasphemy?

Julius: No, I tell you.

Peter: Not for all these combined in one monstrous creature?

Julius: Look, you can run through a thousand other crimes if you like, all more hideous than these. The Roman pontiff still cannot be deposed for them....

Peter: How lucky the pope would be, if he could make a law by which he could not merely cheat councils, but Christ himself! However ... against such a man it is obviously not a general council that is needed, but a rising of the people, armed with stones, to remove him publicly from their midst as a public nuisance to the whole world....

Desiderius Erasmus, *Julius Excluded from Heaven*

not seen it, nay, felt it myself," he laments, "I should never have believed anyone who said theologians could become so insane."

His efforts to play a role as mediator, however, do not satisfy either side: "My only wish is that now that I am old, I be allowed to enjoy the results of my efforts," he writes. "But both sides reproach me and seek to coerce me. Some claim that since I do not attack Luther I agree with him, while the Lutherans declare that I am a coward who has forsaken the gospel." At the end of the day, Erasmus clearly points to Luther as the premier provocateur.

> Even if I approved all of Luther's doctrine, I could not but condemn such obstinacy in making assertions, and the bitter imprecations that for him lie so ready to hand. Nor can I persuade myself that the spirit of Christ dwells in the bosom from which such acrimony gushes

forth. Would that my suspicion be wrong! The spirit of the Gospel has its own wrath, I understand, but of a different kind, for it never lacks the honey of charity to sweeten the bitter aloe of abjuration.

Erasmus is above all else a satirist, and his most biting lines mock the traditions of the Catholic Church in an effort "to correct the errors of those whose religion is usually composed of ... ceremonies and observances of a material sort and neglect the things that conduce to piety." In his hugely popular parody of religious ritual entitled *In Praise of Folly* (1511), he satirizes all things Catholic, from indulgences and images to monasticism and phony miracles. Even marriage is folly—particularly as seen in light of producing the church hierarchy: "What man would submit his neck to the noose of wedlock," he asks, if he truly weighed the consequences. "Or what woman is there would ever go to it did she seriously consider the peril of child-bearing or the trouble of bringing them up?" The answer is not merely folly, but folly's "follower, Madness." And what are the results? "For out of that little, odd, ridiculous May-game came the supercilious philosophers, in whose room have succeeded a kind of people the world calls monks, cardinals, priests, and the most holy popes."

*The Praise of Folly* quickly turns into a best-seller and is translated into French and German, going through several editions during Erasmus's lifetime. It is considered a key document that helps to spur the Protestant Reformation. The book is dedicated to his soul-mate, Sir Thomas More, whose dear friendship and wit and cleverness gives Erasmus "such delight" that he could say "let me perish if in all my life I ever met with anything more delectable." Unlike Erasmus, More has a wife and four children. An English lawyer and a leading Renaissance humanist, he is best known for his writing on statecraft. *Utopia* is the name he gives to his ideal society. But More lives in anything but an ideal society.

When he refuses to swear an oath of allegiance to the 1534 Act of Succession (making Elizabeth first in line to succeed her father) and to recognize king as head of the English Church, Henry VIII is not amused. More is beheaded in 1535.

"The world is full of rage, hate, and wars," Erasmus wails. "What will the end be if we employ only bulls and the stake? It is no great feat to burn a little man. It is a great achievement to persuade him." What had been hailed as the coming of a golden age, he laments, has turned into the "very worst century" since the time of Christ. During More's imprisonment in the Tower of London, Erasmus suffered with him vicariously. When he learned of his execution, something in him died also: "By his death I feel myself to be dead." He died the following year.

Was this Reformation era a golden age or was it the very worst century since Christ? Protestants easily look back and stamp it with a golden seal. But as we look at this age in its various facets of reform, we will see utterly unchristian behavior — violence and bloodshed often baptized in sanctimonious vindication.

---

## What if ...

What if Peter Waldo had backed down in response to his wife's objections to his conversion? What if he had renounced his beliefs in the face of persecution? Would Christianity today be different without Waldo in our heritage?

What if John Wycliffe had not gathered around him a devout band of followers and translated the Scripture? What if Jan Hus had not taken inspiration from his life and ministry and courageously vowed to conduct a similar ministry in Bohemia? Did they serve only as

forerunners of the Reformation, or do their lives stand alone, apart from later Reformers?

What if the Renaissance popes had faithfully served the church? Did their luxurious and scandalous lives pave the way for the Reformation?

What if the teaching of Thomas à Kempis had gained widespread support? What if devout Catholics like Savonarola and Erasmus and More had been able to inspire widespread reformation from within the church? How might church history be different today?

## Further Reading

à Kempis, Thomas. *The Imitation of Christ.* Translated by Joseph N. Tylenda. New York: Vintage, 1998.

Audisio, Gabriel. *The Waldensian Dissent: Persecution and Survival.* Translated by Claire Davidson. London: Cambridge University, 1999.

Caughey, Ellen. *John Wycliffe.* Uhrichsville, Ohio: Barbour Publishing, 2001.

Dallman, William. *John Hus: A Brief Story of the Life of A Martyr.* Whitefish, Mont.: Kessinger Publishing, 2006.

Erasmus, Disiderius, and Martin Luther. *Discourse on Free Will.* Translated and edited by Ernst F. Winter. New York: Continuum, 2005.

Erasmus, Desiderius. *In Praise of Folly.* Translated by John Wilson. New York: Cosimo Classics, 2007.

Jardine, Lisa. *Worldly Goods: A New History of the Renaissance.* New York: W.W. Norton, 1998.

Kettlewell, Samuel. *Thomas à Kempis and the Brothers of Common Life.* Whitefish, Mont.: Kessinger Publishing, 2007.

Manchester, William. *A World Lit only by Fire: The Medieval Mind and the Renaissance.* Boston: Little, Brown and Company, 1993.

Martines, Lauro. *Fire in the City: Savonarola and the Struggle for Renaissance Florence.* New York: Oxford University, 2006.

Plumb, J. H. *The Italian Renaissance.* New York: Houghton Mifflin, 2001.

Rabb, Theodore. *Renaissance Lives: Portraits of an Age.* New York: Basic Books, 2001.

Tuchman, Barbara W. *A Distant Mirror: The Calamitous 14th Century.* New York: Alfred A. Knopf, 1978.

# CHAPTER 11

# The German Reformation

## *Luther and Colleagues*

*I often wonder how I might have responded to the whirlwind of reform in sixteenth-century Germany. It is muddled and messy and mean-spirited, virtually devoid of the pious saints we imagine inspiring a reformation.*

*I sometimes play a little game with myself. What if I were not so different from who I am but living five hundred years ago in the German homeland? As an educated woman, I might have been a Roman Catholic nun. How then would I have responded to the Reformation? Would I have reacted like many nuns did and resisted any attempt to force "freedom" onto me? Would I have clung tightly to the bonded community of the convent? Or would I have conspired to escape in the dark of the night, hidden on a wagon designed to carry herring barrels?*

*So it was with Katherine von Bora—a nun who welcomed what she perceived to be freedom and biblical truth associated with Luther and reform. Like the feisty, outspoken Katie, might I have been the last one for whom a husband could be procured and have ended up married to Luther? Like her, might I have been more than a house frau and had a little farm of my own—entirely outside my famous husband's oversight? I think I would have enjoyed overseeing a manse with lively little ones underfoot and celebrated scholars and students coming and going. But being the house frau of Martin Luther would have been a most difficult role. Katie Luther holds my deepest admiration and sympathy.*

*So I ask myself: Would I have held true to tradition, courageously refusing to bow to this new "heresy," or would I have heralded a new day, thumbing my nose at the convent, never looking back? For me the answer is easy. On my father's side, I come from a long line of German Lutherans. I am in personality and in spirit and in heritage a true daughter of the Reformation. I would have relished being at the center of theological turmoil in the very foundational years of this momentous movement.*

*The influence Luther has had on my heritage and on that of all Protestants is enormous and difficult to exaggerate. Thus, I devote an entire chapter to his life and ministry and closest colleagues.*

> We desert historical experience whenever we ... abstract a moment
> in the historical world and think of it as the cause of the whole or any part
> of what remains. Thus, every historical event is necessary,
> and it is impossible to distinguish between
> the importance of necessities.
>
> MICHAEL OAKESHOTT

The posting by Martin Luther of his Ninety-five Theses to the church door in Wittenberg, on October 31, 1517, is for Protestants a most significant historical event. We desert historical experience, however, when we single out such a moment in the historical world and think of it as the *cause* of the Reformation. Does that date really rise above other moments? Are there not other seemingly random moments that are also necessary precursors to that one so-called big event? We must be cautious about singling out any one moment as a definitive marker in the course of history.

The sixteenth century encompassed much more than the Protestant Reformation. It is one important aspect in the centuries-long Renaissance that had begun in the late fourteenth century. The Renaissance provided a foundational worldview without which the Reformation might have faltered. Humanism opened the curtain of the Greek scriptures and the early church. Reform was an inevitable outcome. If Luther had not risen up, someone else would have. He stood above all others, yet he was surely no one-man show. Key individuals played significant roles alongside him in the German Reformation, including Katherine von Bora, Philip Melanchthon, Argula von Stauffer, and Katherine Zell.

There is a class difference between leading Reformers and medieval monastic leaders. One after another—from Francis and Dominic to Catherine and Hildegard—monastic leaders came from aristocratic backgrounds. The Reformers, on the other hand, rose out of peasant stock and the new mercantile or middle class, as in the case of Martin Luther. While retaining many medieval traits, Reformers were nevertheless children of the Renaissance. They did not accept the given wisdom of tradition without challenge, having more in common with Peter Abelard than with Bernard of Clairvaux and other monastic scholars.

Yet it is a mistake to imagine that the Protestant Reformation set the stage for modern man and heralded a new age. It did not. The Magisterial Reformation, as represented by Luther, Zwingli, and Calvin, holds fast to the Christen-

## PARADE OF HISTORY

The march toward Protestantism is not the only sixteenth-century parade in town. Indeed, the pomp and ceremony of the Catholic Church never slows. And provoking the need for reform are the likes of the Dominican friar Johann Tetzel, who parades through towns with fanfare and catchy jingles and good deals on indulgences. But the most momentous parade marking the Protestant movement is the twenty-mile procession from Wittenberg to Leipzig. Luther, accompanied by a regiment of armed students, goes head to head with the Catholic scholar, John Eck.

## LUTHER AND THE PRINTING PRESS

The question is impossible to answer, but that hasn't kept those who study religion and mass media from asking it: Would the Protestant Reformation have happened without the invention of moveable type?

While stopping short of directly linking Martin Luther and Johannes Gutenberg, members of the Religion Newswriters Association of America have selected the Protestant Reformation and the invention of the printing press as the top events in a poll to determine the top 10 religion stories of the Second Millennium.

"There were all kinds of reform movements before Martin Luther and there were other reformers hard at work all around him," said Lutheran scholar Martin Marty.... "But Luther is a dramatic leader who comes along and is in the right place at the right time. So, for a lot of reasons, it is the revolt of the junior faculty at the University of Wittenberg that gets the attention. Luther becomes the symbol of an entire era of change."

Terry Mattingly, "Luther Meets the Printing Press," newspaper column, 1999

dom of earlier centuries. The visible Christian church is viewed as being essentially the same as the surrounding society. A town resident is presumed a church member and a Christian. Old beliefs and values and medieval customs are ever present. In the 1540s witch burnings are conducted in Protestant Wittenberg, and more than forty women are executed in Calvin's Geneva. Indeed, religious persecution is rife in this medieval world of the sixteenth century. The Enlightenment is still far in the future.

The religious debates of the Reformation meld with matters of state. The church is far more than a religious entity, and if the church loses stability, so goes the state. If the pope is not supreme ruler over religious life, what authority does an emperor—or a landlord—possess? The sixteenth-century mind did not naturally separate religious matters from political, social, and economic issues. The church had wielded power over virtually every aspect of life. If the power of the church is broken, should not authority in general be challenged?

Luther was not interested in expanding the Reformation beyond religious or theological issues. He was a conservative, fearful of societal change. That peasants and other interest groups should imagine reform as changing their everyday lives was a natural assumption, however. Demands for social and political reforms interfaced with religious reform, all stimulated by easy access to printed materials. Any literate and intellectually curious individual could aspire to write a pamphlet proposing changes in economic conditions or biblical understandings. It was a heady—and dangerous—time.

With the sixteenth century came societal instability that had been a long time in the making. The interdependency of medieval life was unraveling in favor of budding individualism. Full-fledged capitalism was far in the future, but the competitiveness of a capitalist spirit was on the increase, while the old "honor" system was on the decline. Even the lowliest peasant contemplated working for himself, making a profit, and rising in social status.

In the two centuries prior to 1500, the population of Western Europe has increased by upwards of fifty percent. Towns have grown in size, as the aristocratic classes are shrinking in

## The Sixteenth-Century Book Business

The printing press with ingenious movable type was nothing short of a media revolution in Western Europe. Although it was first introduced to Europe (in part through ideas from China) in the 1440s, not until the sixteenth century did it begin to effect a large-scale societal transformation. At the same time paper production was becoming less expensive, and new and better formulas for ink were widely available.

Prior to 1500 there were approximately one hundred printed editions of the Bible. Most of the other books that had been printed were academic tomes. In the decade before 1517, German printers issued an average of forty books a year; in the years that followed, the number surged to some five hundred a year. Much of the credit for the rapid expansion of printing rightly goes to Johannes Gutenberg (1398–1468). He was an inventive and far-sighted goldsmith who used ideas of others and launched a new industry that spurred countless innovations in the decades that followed. His printing of the Bible was the pinnacle of his success. The Gutenberg Bible, a printed edition of the Latin Vulgate, will forever be associated with his name.

If a Latin Bible was now available in book form, why not an English Bible or a German Bible? The possibilities were endless. And why not the writings of the church fathers and

Sixteenth-century printing press in Germany

Aquinas and even Aristotle? The next step: Why not *my* writings? The first books consisted of the writings of others. But as one generation flows into another, ordinary monks like Martin Luther can write bestsellers. Indeed, Luther transforms the publishing business. He writes primarily in the vernacular (German rather than Latin) and publishes booklets (typically of 32 pages, including illustrations). He is far and away the most prolific writer of these *Flugschriften,* or flying writings, as they were called. But others catch on quickly, realizing there is money to be made. In fact, some of these booklets contain Luther's sermons that others have transcribed, thus denying him potential earnings. But there are no copyright laws governing such theft.

Printing booklets is only the first step in launching a bestseller. Marketing is a critical element. Prior to Luther's religious revolution, getting the word out was a difficult aspect of publishing. The Frankfurt Book Fair had its origins as far back as the eleventh century, but it had a slow start. By the third decade of the sixteenth century, it was rapidly gaining momentum, and Luther's books were quickly snatched up. Most of his writings, however, were peddled by booksellers. With word-of-mouth publicity, booksellers often ran out of stock within days or weeks — if not hours. Bookselling was a rapidly expanding business that never looked back. The early "bookstores" were covered wagons pulled by a donkey driven from town to town. Indeed, the donkey played an important role in the Reformation.

numbers, and wealth in the middle-class that consisted of artisans and merchants and farmers and academics is on the rise. Money is more readily accessible and gun powder has revolutionized warfare. Novelties are waiting to be invented by clever minds and skillful hands. Overseas discoveries and dreams of sailing to a promised land capture the imaginations of young men. There is an excitement in the air. The future is anything but predictable.

The time is ripe for the volcanic activity of the Protestant Reformation. The groundswell of public reaction against the church merges with a new sense of spiritual independence. As education and books become more readily available, ordinary individuals are eager to openly study and discuss and debate issues of faith. The "democratic" religion of Wycliffe and Hus — religion that offered "vulgar" Bible translations to the rabble — was shunned by church leaders. The Bible, they argued, belongs not to the people but to the parish priest. The spiritual secrets of Scripture, like the money given for indulgences, are hoarded by the church hierarchy. But all that changes with one very innocuous act by a little-known German monk. Within a decade, there is a mindset among vast numbers of people that religion is not simply a received tradition belonging only to the clerics. It requires thinking and choosing. It is as frightening as it is exhilarating.

## Martin Luther: Premier Protestant Reformer

Vast numbers of Christians during and following the Reformation viewed Martin Luther (1483–1546) as a heretic and worse. King Henry

VIII pronounced him the antichrist. Heinrich Bullinger, a Swiss Reformer and a contemporary, lamented his "muddy and swinish, vulgar and coarse teachings." In fact, "no one has ever written more vulgarly, more coarsely, more unbecomingly in matters of faith and Christian chastity and modesty and in all serious matters than Luther." To Pope Leo X, he was a wild boar and more. Jews and many poor peasants, for good reason, despised him.

Luther is an enigma. His own best friends and strongest supporters were troubled by his outrageous conduct, and since his death he has not attained a reputation for piety that Christians bestow on dead saints. Brash and vulgar, he possessed dogged faith and deep convictions, relentlessly pursuing the truth. He earned his rank as first among Reformers not because of his personality and lifestyle but because of his success in tackling the errors of the church. He was a warring soldier for whom Scripture was his sword.

Martin Luther

Luther was the first of seven children born to Hans and Grethe Luther of Eisleben. Having risen out of peasant stock, the family soon moved to the town of Mansfeld, where Hans supervised his own copper-mining operation and later served on the town council. With a large family, however, the living standard remained humble. At age five young Martin entered the local Latin school, and at fourteen he left home to attend Magdeburg, a nearby boarding school conducted by the Brethren of the Common life.

He later recalled his parents as strict disciplinarians, his father once beating him so badly that he ran away from home. I was so "embit-tered against him that he had to win me to himself again." Nor could he escape to his mother for protection. On one occasion, she "on account of [my stealing] an insignificant nut, beat me till the blood flowed, and it was this harshness and severity of the life I led with them that forced me subsequently to run away to a monastery and become a monk." At eighteen, he entered the University of Erfurt, where he excelled in studies, acquiring the nickname "Philosophus." He lived austerely, avoiding the "scent of wine, beer, and wenches" that were readily available. He relished the pomp and prestige of the academic life: "What a moment of majesty and splendor was that, when one took the degree of Master, and torches were carried before, and honor was paid one. I consider that no temporal or worldly joy can equal it."

Then suddenly, on a hot July day in 1505, the course of his life changed. The story—or legend—is familiar. On his way back to Erfurt, following a visit with his family, booming cracks of thunder terrify him. Then his worst nightmare occurs. A bolt of lightening strikes him to the ground. In a moment of fright, he cries out, "St. Anne help me! I will become a monk." Why pray to this legendary mother of the Virgin Mary? Perhaps because she is the patron saint of his father and all miners. But why in this instant at death's door does he vow to become a monk? One wonders if the ascetic life of the monastery is already on his mind.

Yet Luther's decision to enter a monastery is nothing short of radical. On his graduation only two months earlier, his anti-clerical father had given him a costly volume to help him prepare for a career in law. Now he turns away from any hope of success to pursue life as an ascetic—a contemptible monk. Nor does he move ahead half-heartedly. Of the twenty monasteries in Erfurt, he chooses the Augustinian cloister, known for its strict adherence to the rule. He reveals his resolution to friends and enjoys one last occasion to drink and sing with them before he enters the gate.

As a monk, he goes above and beyond the call of duty in prayers, fasting, self-scourging, and sacrifice—denying himself clothing and blankets in winter. "I was a pious monk, and so strictly observed the rules," he later recalled, "that if ever a monk got into heaven by monkery, so should I also have gotten there." After a year of probation he takes vows of poverty, chastity, and obedience; and the following year, in 1507, he is officially ordained to the priesthood. His first Mass affects him deeply. Reflecting on the eternal God, he nearly breaks down. "At these words I was utterly stupefied and terror-stricken," he remembered. "With what tongue shall I address such Majesty, seeing that all men ought to tremble in the presence of even an earthly prince?" He acknowledges his inadequacy. "Who am I, that I should lift up my

Market square in Wittenberg

eyes or raise my hands to the divine Majesty?" he wonders. "For I am dust and ashes and full of sin and I am speaking to the living, eternal and the true God."

In the following years he buries himself in books and teaches at the universities of Erfurt and Wittenberg, all the while preparing for and passing exams for his doctoral degree. But despite his striving, he cannot live up to the standard of holiness God requires. He goes to confession daily, sometimes straining the patience of his confessor, dredging up sins from long ago. He takes a pilgrimage to Rome, climbing Pilate's stairs on his knees, repeating the *Pater Noster* (Lord's Prayer) at every step, hoping to decrease his time in purgatory. He is shocked by

---

### JOHANN VON STAUPITZ: LUTHER'S CATHOLIC FRIEND AND MENTOR

One of the most neglected *saints* of the Reformation is Johann von Staupitz (1486–1543), whose years closely parallel Luther's. His position as the head of the German Augustinians is critical to Luther's early spiritual development. He recognizes the monk's brilliance and seeks to soften the sharp edges of his personality. Luther is grateful: "If it had not been for Dr. Staupitz, I should have sunk in hell." Even after Luther is in the thick of the battle, Staupitz shows deep concern: "The world hates the truth. By such hate Christ was crucified, and what there is in store for you today if not the cross I do not know." His deepest longing is for some sort of compromise between the two sides. "Do not denounce points of indifference which can be held in sincerity," he pleads. "We owe much to you, Martin." Though remaining a devout Catholic to his last breath, his own books — all with a devotional slant — are included on the Index of Prohibited Books in 1559.

## FINDING A GATE TO HEAVEN

I greatly longed to understand Paul's Epistle to the Romans and nothing stood in the way but that one expression, "the justice of God," because I took it to mean that justice whereby God is just and deals justly in punishing the unjust.... Night and day I pondered until I saw the connection between the justice of God and the statement that "the just shall live by his faith." Then I grasped that the justice of God is that righteousness by which through grace and sheer mercy God justifies us through faith. Thereupon I felt myself to be reborn and to have gone through open doors into paradise. The whole Scripture took on a new meaning, and whereas before the "justice of God" had filled me with hate, now it became to me inexpressibly sweet in greater love. This passage of Paul became to me a gate to heaven.

Martin Luther

the moral laxity and insincerity of priests and church leaders.

As an Augustinian monk, Luther carefully studies Augustine and his emphasis on original sin. "I was born," he writes, "indeed conceived and formed in the womb, as a sinner." Does such original sin make him any less guilty? Not at all. God's "fury or wrath toward ... sinners is ... immeasurable and infinite." But in 1515, now in his early thirties, while he is teaching at the University of Wittenberg, he begins to comprehend the doctrine of justification in a different light.

The strict monastic regimen and the new spiritual insights collide. He is living in a system that denies the very doctrine of justification by faith alone that Paul is teaching in Romans. It is a system further scandalized by the purchase of indulgences. His disgust with indulgences was prompted not only by his insights from Romans but also by the blatant hawking of them by the popular preacher Johann Tetzel. A Dominican monastic leader and an agent of the Inquisition, Tetzel deliberately appeals to the superstitious mentalities of the poorest and least-educated Christians. To them he is a celebrity. But even magistrates and monks fall under his spell. Indeed, as he enters towns, priests lead the procession to meet him, bells ringing and banners waving.

Forbidden by Frederick, Elector of Saxony, to make his sales pitch inside the gates of the city Wittenberg, Tetzel sets up shop outside town. His scheme is straightforward. He reminds his listeners that dear ones have passed on without their sins forgiven and are suffering in purgatory. His emotional plea is enhanced with catchy jingles: "As soon as the coin in the coffer rings, the soul from purgatory springs." For all his fanfare, Tetzel's role in the Reformation was a minor one. But to Luther, he exemplified what was wrong with the church.

On October 31, 1517, when Luther nailed his now-famous Ninety-five Theses to the Castle Church door in Wittenberg, he was a committed Roman Catholic, insisting he was being true to the church: "Nor do we believe we have said anything that is not in agreement with the Catholic church and the ancient doctors of the church." His actions were anything but a sudden outburst of provocation. Eight months earlier, in fact, he had delivered a message in the Castle Church condemning indulgences, a stance potentially affecting his own job security, since funds for the university come in part from indulgences sold by the Castle Church. The massive collection of relics was impressive, including a piece of bread blessed by Jesus at the

Last Supper and some twenty thousand other relics with the combined capacity for reducing time in purgatory by nearly two million years.

Some of Luther's Ninety-five Theses, such as thesis 36, appear mild: "Any truly repentant Christian has a right to full remission of penalty and guilt, even without indulgence letters." Others are strongly worded, as is thesis 32: "Those who believe that they can be certain of their salvation because they have indulgence letters will be eternally damned, together with their teachers." When he posted the document, he did not imagine it would become a pamphlet for the masses. Indeed, it might have been written differently had that been his intention. Rather, he composed it for the purpose of inviting scholarly disputation. But what initially belonged to him quickly became the possession of ordinary people. The presses could not print the document fast enough.

As the news of his protest spreads, warring camps quickly consolidate. Leading the support are those who resent the wealth and arrogance of the church. Opposing him are those who depend on the sprawling institution for their very livelihoods. Indeed, the opposition is fierce.

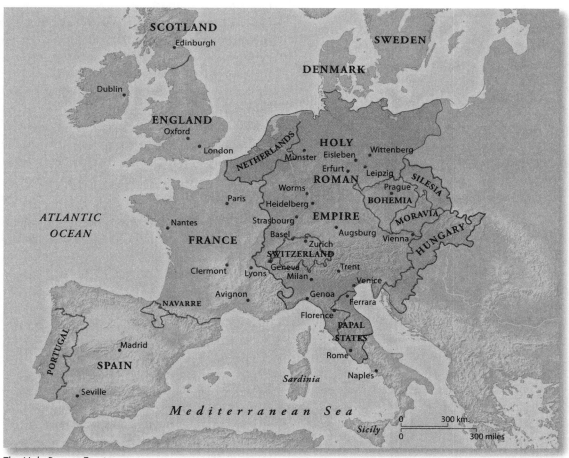

The Holy Roman Empire

The Dominican Tetzel vows to defeat Luther (half his age) by his own tactics. Within weeks after Luther posted his theses, Tetzel counters with *One Hundred and Six Anti-Theses* — a document Luther's supporters promptly burn in protest. The ferment only complicates Luther's already frenzied schedule.

> I could use two secretaries. I do almost nothing during the day but write letters. I am a conventual preacher, reader at meals, parochial preacher, director of studies, overseer of eleven monasteries, superintendent of the fish pond at Litzkau, referee of the squabble at Torgau, lecturer on Paul, collector of material for a commentary on the Psalms, and then, as I said, I am overwhelmed with letters. I rarely have full time for the canonical hours and for saying mass, not to mention my own temptations with the world, the flesh, and the Devil. You see how lazy I am.

In the months that follow, events move swiftly. Threats and rumors fly as scholars schedule debates and write treatises and counter-treatises. In April of 1518, Johann von Staupitz invites Luther to appear at the annual meeting of the German Augustinians. Here Luther challenges fellow Augustinians with biblical insights drawn in part from St. Augustine himself. Among those present at the gathering is Martin Bucer, who will later become the key Reformer of Strasbourg. In a letter to Luther, he writes that this was the first time he had ever heard "the theology of the cross." Later that year, Cardinal Cajetan, a Dominican acting as the pope's representative, orders Luther to appear before him, convinced the matter is of little significance and will quickly blow over. During the three days of meetings, they focus on what will become the key issue of the Reformation: Where does authority lie? Is the pope the supreme spiritual authority, or is Scripture? The meetings end when the cardinal orders Luther out of his presence. Luther returns to Wittenberg and remarks to his friends that the cardinal was "no more fitted to handle the case than an ass to play a harp."

In 1519, after being released from his Augustinian vows, Luther accepts a challenge to debate Professor John Eck from Ingolstadt University. The setting is Leipzig University. Tensions are running high. Multitudes are pouring into town. Luther arrives, protected by two hundred armed students. The debate focuses on purgatory, papal infallibility, and authority. As a biblical scholar, Luther emphasizes the lack of scriptural support for purgatory and indulgences. Does the pope err? Of course, just like the apostle Peter. For Eck the task of correlating centuries of church tradition with the Bible is most difficult. In the end, the two-week debate serves to heighten Luther's credibility and to inspire his followers. Among those who stand with him are fellow professors at Wittenberg, Philip Melanchthon and Andreas Karlstadt, the latter a fiery radical whom Luther describes as "hotter in the matter than I." Not so Melanchthon. Luther writes:

> I have been born to war, and fight with factions and devils; therefore, my books are stormy and warlike. I must root out the stumps and stocks, cut away the thorns and hedges, fill up the ditches, and am the rough forester to break a path and make things ready. But Master Philip walks softly and silently, tills and plants, sows and waters with pleasure, as God has gifted him richly.

Luther's "stormy and warlike" books add to his prestige among the German people and effectively communicate his evangelical faith.

1520 is a productive year. In August, he publishes *Address to the German Nobility,* arguing that reform will never come through the corrupt church hierarchy, but rather through Christian rulers. In October, he publishes *The Babylonian Captivity of the Church,* questioning the validity of the sacraments except for baptism and the Lord's Supper—and at this point in his ecclesiastical career, penance. He argues that transubstantiation and the sacrifice of the Mass (the priest's offering of Christ on the altar as a propitiation for sin) are false teachings. In November, he publishes *On the Freedom of the Christian,* insisting that the natural response to God's free grace is faith and loving service. The publication of these books and his continued defiance of papal authority prompts direct action from Pope Leo X, who issues a papal bull ordering Luther to recant or face excommunication. Accompanying this decree is Leo's rationale:

> Arise, O Lord, and judge the cause. A wild boar has invaded thy vineyard. Arise, O Peter, and consider the case of the Holy Roman Church, the mother of all churches, consecrated by thy blood.... Arise, all ye saints, and the whole universal Church, whose interpretation of Scripture has been assailed. We can scarcely express our grief over the ancient heresies which have been revived in Germany.... We can no longer suffer the serpent to creep through the field of the Lord. The books of Martin Luther which contain these errors are to be examined and burned.

The response is vintage Luther. Joined by his students and colleagues, he throws the bull into the flames. Weeks later, on a cold winter day in January of 1521, he is officially excommunicated. Following his excommunication, Emperor Charles V summons him to appear before the Diet of Worms. The emperor is in a precarious position. He does not wish to defend a "heretic" and anger the pope, nor does he wish to alienate Luther's growing list of supporters. Although there are other issues before this assembly of Germany's leading nobles and churchmen, this controversy takes center stage. "All Germany is up in arms against Rome," laments Jerome Alexander, the papal envoy. "I cannot go out in the streets but the Germans put their hands to their swords and gnash their teeth at me."

When Luther finally appears before the Diet nearly three months after it has convened, his nerves are frayed and he is tempted to recant, remembering the fate of Jan Hus. On the second day, however, when asked to recant, he boldly asserts that he would recant only that which could be proven contrary to the Bible. To this the Archbishop of Trier responds that heretics—including Wycliffe and Hus—have all used this excuse. Again he demands that Luther recant. Luther's response is memorable: "My conscience is captive to the Word of God. I cannot and I will not recant anything, for to go

---

### COUNSEL FOR THOSE FEELING ABANDONED BY GOD

If God hides himself in the storm clouds which brood over the brow of Sinai, then gather about the manger, look upon the infant Jesus as he leaps in the lap of his mother, and know that the hope of the world is here. Or again, if Christ and God alike are unapproachable, then look upon the firmament of the heavens and marvel at the work of God, who sustains them without pillars. Or take the meanest flower and see in the smallest petal the handiwork of God.

Martin Luther

against conscience is neither right nor safe. Here I stand. I cannot do otherwise. God help me. Amen." The exact wording has been debated but never the meaning. The die is cast. Institutionalized Christianity will never be the same again.

The church and the emperor respond with the Edict of Worms, condemning him as a heretic and pronouncing him an outlaw and a target for death on the spot. Luther's supporters rightly fear for his life. Under the cover of darkness, agents of Frederick the Wise (Luther's prince who had refused to sign the edict), kidnap him, jostling him away to a secure hideout at a castle in Wartburg. Here he is in safekeeping and finds much-needed time to translate the New Testament into German. He also battles boredom, physical maladies, and Satan, at whom he reportedly hurls an inkpot.

Despite this secure sabbatical Luther is frustrated. The translation is thorny and laborious: "I sweat blood and water in my efforts to render the Prophets into the vulgar tongue. Good God! What a labor to make those Jew writers speak German. They struggle furiously against giving up their beautiful language to our barbaric idiom. It is as though you would force a nightingale to forget her sweet melody and sing like a cuckoo." Finally, depressed and lonely for friends and colleagues, he can stand the enforced confinement no longer. "I had rather burn on live coals," he laments, "than rot here.... I want to be in the fray."

> "Next to the Word of God, the noble art of music is the greatest treasure in the world."
> Martin Luther

The "fray" that Luther is missing involves many whom he perceives as "radicals," including his friend Andreas Karlstadt from Wittenberg.

Peasants living a typical country life

Three years younger than Luther, Karlstadt is neither a monk nor a priest. Having received his doctorate in 1510, he had become the chancellor of Wittenberg University and awarded Luther his doctorate. He and Luther had traveled together to the Diet of Worms. But Karlstadt had returned to Wittenberg, and, while Luther is hiding out, he unfurls the Reformation flag. On Christmas Day 1521, he administers the Lord's Supper without Catholic ritual and meaning. Speaking in German, he offers both bread and wine to those present. Nor does he wear clerical vestments. Three weeks later at thirty-five he marries Anna, half his age. Identifying himself as "Brother Andreas," he repudiates his doctoral degree and dresses like a commoner.

When Luther returns from his confinement in Wartburg, he is stunned by the momentum of reform. Monks and priests are abandoning their vestments and vigils and vows of celibacy; hoodlums are wreaking havoc on churches, smashing images and altars. He rails against Karlstadt, publicly renouncing him as a dangerous sectarian. In the following years they carry on a love-hate relationship. While Luther's fame rises, Karlstadt, for a time, is serving drinks at a Wittenberg pub, only later returning to Basel and his vocation of preacher and professor of Hebrew.

Besides encountering vexing church matters, Luther confronts social unrest. Nicholas Storch and Thomas Müntzer, whom he regards as rabble-rousers, are stirring discontent among peasants. Luther takes the side of the landed nobles. Never mind that the impoverished peasants have toiled on the land for generations with no redress. In an impassioned tract entitled *Against the Plundering Murderous Hordes of Peasants,* he writes: "Therefore let everyone who can, smite, slay, and stab, secretly or openly, remembering that nothing can be more poisonous, hurtful, or devilish than a rebel.... For baptism does not make men free in body and property, but in soul."

In the midst of the turmoil swirling around him, Luther encounters a nun, Katherine von Bora (1499–1552). Born in poverty, she was reared in a tiny village near Leipzig. When she was five, her mother died, and soon after, her father remarried and sent her to a Benedictine convent to prepare for Holy Orders. Her early religious training is influenced by two aunts (one from each side of the family)—one who serves as Abbess of the convent where she takes her vows, and another who later escapes the convent with her.

Having moved to the Cistercian Convent of Nimbschem, Katie is one of forty cloistered nuns. Even relatives are not permitted to communicate except through a latticed window with the abbess close by. Silence is the rule. Friendships are forbidden. Yet despite strict supervision, Luther's ideas penetrate the walls. For the first time, Katie dares to dream of freedom. Luther's writings spur a

Katherine von Bora

conspiracy to escape. Duke George, a staunch enemy of the Reformation, controls the region. Kidnapping a nun is a capital offense. Despite the risks, the nuns send word to Luther of their plight. Knowing the potential consequences, he arranges for a merchant who sells smoked herring to make a delivery late at night and on his return trip to bring out nuns hiding in the empty—and no doubt smelly—herring barrels.

The strategy succeeds but only adds to Luther's problems. Some nuns return to their families, but those remaining require lodging. A cynical student in Wittenberg sums up the situation: "A wagon load of vestal virgins has just come to town all more eager for marriage than for life. May God give them husbands lest worse befall." Luther seeks to arrange marriage for Katie with eligible bachelors, including one Kaspar Glatz. But the feisty red-head spurns the suggestion. He is much older and has a reputation for being miserly. She arranges a meeting with a colleague of Luther's and angrily asserts that she will have nothing to do with Glatz, adding that she would be willing to marry Luther. Luther had already made his position clear to a friend: "Hitherto I have not been, and am not now inclined to take a wife. Not that I lack the feelings of a man (for I am neither wood nor stone), but my mind is averse to marriage because I daily expect the death decreed to the heretic."

In the following months, Luther, perhaps pressured by his parents, modifies his position. Then in the summer of 1525, without formal courtship, he takes the plunge. He is forty-two; Katie is twenty-six. He later wrote: "If I

*"Before I was married the bed was not made for a whole year and became foul with sweat. But I worked so hard and was so weary I tumbled in without noticing."*

Martin Luther

had not married quickly and secretly and taken few into my confidence, everyone would have done what he could to hinder me; for all my best friends cried: 'Not this one, but another.'" Secrecy prior to the marriage, however, does not extend into the marriage. Indeed, his first intimate moments with Katie are anything but private. Justus Jonas, Martin Luther's good friend, describes the scene the following day: "I was present yesterday and saw the couple on their marriage bed. As I watched this spectacle, I could not hold back my tears." Whether Katie could hold back the tears during this "spectacle" amid onlookers is not revealed. Patrick O'Hara, one of Luther's harshest critics, writing in 1916, blamed Luther, not custom, for "the vulgarity to lift the covers of the nuptial bed and disclose its sacred secrets to the gaze of others."

At the time of his marriage, Luther is wrestling with conflict and controversy far beyond that of clerical celibacy. The most bitter battles he wages concern the Lord's Supper. He has rejected transubstantiation in favor of his own construct of consubstantiation. He insists there is a *real presence* of Christ in the elements. Against Catholics, he argues that the bread and wine do not become Christ's body and blood through the priest's officiating of the sacrifice of the Mass. Rather, Christ's body and blood coexist in and with the bread and wine, which are unchanged. But Luther is not only going up against Catholics. His colleague Andreas Karlstadt had published three pamphlets in 1524 rejecting the real presence in the elements. Zwingli essentially agreed with Karlstadt and began publishing his own opposition to the *real presence*, insisting the words, "this is my body" and "this is my blood," mean the elements *signify* the body and blood.

Luther does not take the challenge lightly, suggesting in 1527 that Zwingli and others are tools of Satan. The controversy continues for more than a year, while Martin Bucer seeks to

## LUTHER'S CURIOUS BIBLICAL HERMENEUTICS

Luther read the New Testament in light of the Pauline message that the just shall live by faith and not by works of the law. That this doctrine is not enunciated through the New Testament with equal emphasis and appears to be denied in the book of James did not escape Luther, and in his preface to the New Testament of 1522 James was stigmatized as "an epistle of straw." . . . The conclusion was a hierarchy of values within the New Testament. First Luther would place the Gospel of John, then the Pauline Epistles and First Peter, after them the three other Gospels, and in a subordinate place Hebrews, James, Jude, and Revelation. He mistrusted Revelation because of its obscurity. "A revelation," said he, "should be revealing." . . .

If the New Testament was for Luther a Pauline book, the Old Testament was a Christian book. . . . The Old Testament foreshadowed the drama of redemption. Adam exemplified the depravity of man. Noah tasted the wrath of God, Abraham was saved by faith, and David exhibited contrition. The pre-existent Christ was working throughout the Old Testament.

Roland Bainton, *Here I Stand: A Life of Martin Luther*

mediate and Philip of Hesse calls for a compromise in an effort to form a Protestant coalition. At the invitation of Philip, Zwingli and Luther meet at Marburg in an effort to iron out their differences. The three-day Marburg Colloquy convened in October of 1529 produced fifteen articles, fourteen of which are supported by both sides. The fifteenth, which dealt with the Eucharist, however, is the sticking point. Both Luther and Zwingli refuse to budge.

Another theological issue that rears its head is free will versus the sovereignty of God. Luther's chief opponent is Erasmus, who argues that an individual's freedom to make choices and carry them out demonstrates free will. "The human will is like a beast between [God and Satan]," Luther asserts. "If God sits on it, it wills and goes where God wills to go.... If Satan sits on it, it wills and goes where Satan wills. Nor does it have the power to choose which rider it will go to or seek, but the riders struggle over which of them will have it or rule it." As with the Eucharist, Luther regards those who disagree to be agents of Satan.

As he settles into the routine of family life, Luther continues his career as teacher and pastor. In 1527, he could look back at a fast-paced decade. Beginning with his posting of his Ninety-five Theses, he had publicly debated and defended himself before church authorities; he had fought the Catholics, the radicals, the peasants, and fellow-reformers; he had written pamphlets and books and catechisms, translated the New Testament, begun composing a great hymn ("A Mighty Fortress"), married a nun, and welcomed his first son into the world. All this took its toll. By his early forties he was frequently ill, sometimes paralyzed by depression and doubt. "I spent more than a week in death and in hell," he confided. "My entire body was in pain, and I still tremble. Completely abandoned by Christ,

I labored under the vacillations and storms of desperation and blasphemy against God. But through the prayers of the saints God began to

## On Communion

If any one shall say that, in the most holy sacrament of the Eucharist, there remains the substance of bread and wine together with the body and blood of our Lord Jesus Christ; and shall deny that wonderful and singular conversion of the whole substance of the bread into the body, and of the whole substance of the wine into the blood, the species of bread and wine alone remaining, which conversion the Catholic Church most fittingly calls Transubstantiation, let him be anathema.

Council of Trent, 1551

---

Before I drink mere wine with the Swiss I shall drink blood with the pope.

Martin Luther

---

Every time Luther mentions the Lord's Supper he has in mind something that a butcher handles.

John Calvin

---

It is indeed true that this same grace is offered us by the gospel, yet as in the Supper we have more ample certainty, and fuller enjoyment of it, with good cause do we recognize this fruit as coming from it.

John Calvin

---

But when you come to the Lord's Supper ... and along with the brethren partake of the bread and wine which are the symbols of the body of Christ, then you eat him sacramentally, in the proper sense of the term, when you do internally what you represent externally, when your heart is refreshed by this faith to which you bear witness by these symbols.

Ulrich Zwingli

## First Dog of the Reformation

Luther's much beloved dog Tolpel is a household favorite among children and adult company and is often referred to by guests. Like many house dogs, Tolpel patiently waits for table scraps, behavior that Luther turns into an object lesson: "Oh, if I could only pray the way this dog watches the meat!"

have mercy on me and pulled my soul from the inferno below."

Despite such torment, the Luther parsonage is an invigorating center of activity. Here in a former monastery, students and seasoned scholars drink beer, debate theology, and deride the Church of Rome. Here the Luthers raise their boisterous brood of a half-dozen children whose laughter and scrapping fills the once-solemn halls. Family life is a source of pride for Protestants. Indeed, when first-born son Hans arrives in the summer of 1526, some celebrate it as a national event—as does Luther himself. "When I'm writing," Luther tells his students, "my Hans sings a little tune for me. If he becomes too noisy and I rebuke him a little for it, he continues to sing but does it more privately." When Katie was busy tending her brewery or traveling to oversee her farm, he baby-sits. On one occasion, he moaned: "Christ said we must become as little children to enter the kingdom of heaven. Dear God, have we got to become such idiots?"

In addition to their own children, the Luthers welcome many others, some of whom became permanent residents. An observer described the atmosphere to a German prince who was contemplating a visit to the Wittenberg parsonage:

> The home of Luther is occupied by a motley crowd of boys, students, girls, widows, old women, and youngsters. For this reason there is much disturbance in the place, and many regret it for the sake of the good man, the hon-

orable father. If but the spirit of the Doctor Luther lived in all of these, his house would offer you an agreeable, friendly quarter for a few days so that your Grace would be able to enjoy the hospitality of that man. But as the situation now stands and as circumstances exist in the household of Luther, I would not advise that your Grace stop there.

Luther is known for what are rightly labeled sexist remarks about women. "Take women from their housewifery," he quipped, "and they are good for nothing." Yet he frequently praised Katie, fondly referring to her as "King and dear lord and master, Katy, Lutheress, doctoress, and priestess, of Wittenberg." But he does not grow old gracefully. (Nor are his younger years graceful, as Eric Erickson graphically pointed out in a psychological study entitled *Young Man Luther*.) Friends stay away because, as one

## A Man of Disputations and Dirty Diapers

O God . . . I confess to Thee that I am not worthy to rock the little babe or wash its diapers, or to be entrusted with the care of the child and its mother. How is it that I, without any merit, have come to this distinction of being certain that I am serving Thy creature and Thy most precious will. O how gladly will I do so, though the duties should be even more insignificant and despised.

Martin Luther

reports, "hardly one of us can escape his anger and his public scourging." Even Melanchthon flinches and feels abused by his irate outbursts. During these years, Luther's vitriolic attacks against Jews are a major embarrassment.

Indeed, Luther's later writings on Jews are deplorable—words that centuries later helped prop up Adolf Hitler and offered justification for the Holocaust. Not so his early writings. His essay "That Jesus Christ Was Born a Jew," published in 1523, is devoid of his later seething acrimony toward Jews:

> If I had been a Jew and had seen such dolts and blockheads govern and teach the Christian faith, I would sooner have become a hog than a Christian. They have dealt with the Jews as if they were dogs rather than human beings; they have done little else than deride them and seize their property.... When we are inclined to boast of our position we should remember that we are but Gentiles, while the Jews are of the lineage of Christ.... If we really want to help them, we must be guided in our dealings with them not by papal law but by the law of Christian love.

Alas, this writing is not the document for which Luther's views on Jews are remembered.

His later writings are far more numerous and are those most associated with his name and ministry. Hardly a decade after this earlier work, Luther is successfully petitioning John Frederick, Prince of Saxony to enact laws forbidding Jews from conducting business, obtaining residency, or even traveling through Saxony. Seven years later, exasperated by Jews' refusal to convert to Christianity, Luther publishes his most rancid work, *On Jews and Their Lies*. His vicious language is calculated to arouse hatred. They are filled with the "devil's feces ... which they wallow in like swine." They are "poisonous envenomed worms" who should be banished from Christian lands or worse. Their homes, their schools, their synagogues should be burned. Jews, he rails, must be killed. Christians "are at fault in not slaying them."

Far better for the Protestant cause if Luther had been martyred or had died before he wrote such vitriol. But for Katie, he died too soon. With young children and few provisions for their care, she is left impoverished. Besides financial problems, she struggles to keep her family together. A government official rules that her sons be removed from the home for their schooling. She fights to keep them and prevails. In 1552, during an epidemic in Wittenberg,

## LUTHER AND THE SCANDAL OF BIGAMY

Did Luther approve the practice of bigamy? Philip of Hesse, a high-ranking German ruler and supporter of the Reformation, had sought the backing of Luther and other Reformers (including Philip Melanchthon and Martin Bucer) in his plan to take a second wife, pointing to Old Testament polygamy. Not wanting to risk the loss of his support, Luther sanctions the plan, insisting it be kept secret. How to keep a secret wife, however, was apparently not part of his counsel. As rumors spread, Luther tells Philip to "tell a good, strong lie." But the cover-up unravels. Bigamy is a capital offense and Philip fears for his life. In the end Emperor Charles V makes a deal with Philip, agreeing not to prosecute. But Philip loses power and influence in the process — including his support for the Protestant cause. And the reputations of Luther and his colleagues are sullied.

she flees the town, crashing her horse carriage. Badly injured, she dies some months later at fifty-three.

## Philip Melanchthon: Gentleman German Reformer

The body of Philip Melanchthon (1497–1560) appropriately lies buried beside that of Martin Luther in Wittenberg. He is considered the second man—the *gentle*man—of the German Reformation, faithfully working alongside Luther for nearly three decades. Orphaned at ten, Melanchthon lived with his grandmother until he enrolled at the University of Heidelberg at age twelve to study philosophy, astronomy, and rhetoric. At sixteen he pursued graduate studies in theology at the University of Tübingen. A student of Erasmus, he was a published author by the time Luther (fourteen years his senior) was posting his Ninety-five Theses.

VIVENTIS·POTVIT·DVRERIVS·ORA·PHILIPPI
MENTEM·NON·POTVIT·PINGERE·DOCTA
MANVS
1526

Philip Melanchthon

Melanchthon's opposition to scholastic theology prompts him to question Catholic dogma and traditions. At the same time he learns of Luther's insights. In 1518 he accepts a post at the University of Wittenberg, and the two scholars become life-long partners. Brilliant and popular, Melanchthon draws students much like Abelard did four centuries earlier. He is courted by other academic institutions, but with Luther and others playing cupid, he marries Katharina Krapp, daughter of the Wittenberg mayor.

One of Melanchthon's most important achievements was his contribution, at the behest of Luther, to the Augsburg Confession. These twenty-eight articles, written in both Latin and German, were presented to Emperor Charles V, who summoned a Diet at Augsburg in 1530 to settle the religious differences among the German princes and people. Melanchthon began with his usual conciliatory style, affirming twenty-one statements accepted by both Catholics and Reform-

### THE LIGHTER SIDE OF PROFESSOR MELANCHTHON

A visitor to the Melanchthon household one evening was surprised to see Philip reading from a book in one hand while rocking a cradle with the other, and promptly received a lecture on the duties of parenting. On a visit to Torgau for a conference among the learned, Melanchthon happened to see a woman, a deacon's wife, with three children. One, a baby, she was nursing at her breast. The other two stood before her while she said a morning prayer. At the same time, with her right hand she managed to cut bread for the children. Melanchthon delightedly told the assembly of divines of these "three holy deeds," these wonderful things and powerful prayers that he had seen and heard that day.... In 1529, now a married man with children, [he was spotted] dancing with the Provost's wife at a social function. Philip and Katherine Melanchthon loved to show hospitality both to visitors and students. In particular, Philip liked students to present dramas in his home.

John Schofield, *Philip Melanchthon and the English Reformation*

ers. The remaining seven articles focused on matters disputed with Catholics, all supported with Scripture. The Augsburg Confession established the German Reformation on justification by faith alone and serves today as a foundational document of Lutheran belief.

In the remaining years of his life, Melanchthon was embroiled in family and religious difficulties. Although he was considered by many to be Luther's successor, opponents challenged his loyalty to the Reformation cause, insisting he was too eager to compromise with Catholics. Harshly criticized in his own day, he has been admired in recent generations for his keen intellect and his careful scholarship as well as for his efforts to foster unity among Christians. He was ever the patient and kind Reformer, generous to a fault.

## Argula von Stauffer and Katherine Zell

One of Luther's most outspoken defenders was Argula von Stauffer (1492–1563). But in the eyes of Catholic opposition, she was an "insolent daughter of Eve." Born into landed nobility in Bavaria, she married a nobleman with whom she bore a daughter and three sons. For more than four decades she risked her life and the well-being of her family for the cause of the Reformation. She refused to be silenced, and in a letter to Catholic authorities, she demanded, "What have Luther and Melanchthon taught save the Word of God?" She taunted them for condemning him but not refuting him. In 1523, as a young mother, she boldly defended her views in a debate before the Diet of Nurnberg. The German princes, however, paid her little heed. "I am distressed," she lamented, "that our princes take the Word of God no more seriously than a cow does a game of chess."

Persecuted not only by state officials but also by her husband, whose political career and very livelihood are in jeopardy because of her activities, she is aware of the risk: "I understand that my husband will be deposed from his office. I can't help it. God will feed my children as he feeds the birds and will clothe them as the lilies of the field." Luther, writing to a friend, clearly recognizes her sacrifice:

> The Duke of Bavaria rages above measure, killing, crushing and persecuting the gospel with all his might. That most noble woman, Argula von Stauffer, is there making a valiant fight with great spirit, boldness of speech and knowledge of Christ.... Her husband, who treats her tyrannically, has been deposed from his prefecture.... She alone, among these monsters, carries on with firm faith, though, she admits not without inner trembling. She is a singular instrument of Christ.

Her heroes are Old Testament women like Deborah and Esther, but she does not dismiss apparent New Testament constraints: "I am not unacquainted with the word of Paul that women should be silent in church," she concedes, "but, when no man will or can speak, I am driven by the word of the Lord when he said, 'He who confesses me on earth, him will I confess and he who denies me, him will I deny.'" She breaks civil law by repeatedly conducting religious meetings in her home and officiating at clandestine funerals. She faithfully carries on Luther's reform, outliving him by nearly two decades. The "old Staufferin," as the Duke cynically describes her, is twice imprisoned, the last time shortly before her death at age seventy.

Another Reformer who boldly challenged the religious establishment—and sometimes her fellow Reformers—was Katherine Zell (1497–1562). "Ever since I was ten years old I have been a student and sort of church mother, much given to attending sermons," she later recalled. "I have loved and frequented the company of learned men, and I conversed much with them, not about dancing, masquerades, and worldly pleasures but about the kingdom of God."

Her decision to marry Matthew Zell, a priest-turned-Reformer, corresponds with the Reformation focus on the family. She defends the marriage, insisting it diminishes the frequent priestly sins of lust and fornication. As a minister's wife in Strasbourg, she works with refugees fleeing persecution, providing shelter to hundreds of homeless exiles. During the Peasants' War of 1525, she directs a vast relief program, serving some three thousand who seek refuge in Strasbourg. The Zell home is also open to some of the most celebrated Reformers of the era, including Zwingli and Calvin. But she is not star-struck by fellow Reformers. "Why do you rail at Schwenckfeld?" she demands of a Lutheran leader. "You talk as if you would have him burned like the poor Servetus at Geneva" (a swipe at Calvin). She laments that the Anabaptists—good Christians "who accept Christ in all the essentials as we do"—are "pursued as by a hunter with dogs chasing wild boars."

Accused of becoming "Dr. Katrina" and taking over her husband's pulpit at his death, she angrily reacts, insisting that "instead of spending my time in frivolous amusements I have visited the plague infested and ... those in prison and under sentence of death," often without eating or sleeping. She writes evangelistic tracts and devotionals as well as materials on religious education, civic reform, pastoral care, apologetics, and theology. In her spare time, she edits a hymnbook, writing:

> This is not just a hymn book but a lesson book of prayer and praise. When so many filthy songs are on the lips of men and women and even children, I think it well that folk should with lusty zeal and clear voice sing the songs of their salvation. God is glad when the craftsman at his bench ... the farmer at the plough ... the mother at the cradle break forth in hymns of prayer, praise, and instruction.

In her final act of selfless ministry, she officiates a funeral service for a woman regarded as a "radical"—a Reformation heretic. She crawls out of her sickbed at dawn to minister at the grave-side service. When the city council hears of it, they resolve to reprimand her when she recovers. But she dies before they can officially condemn her one final time.

The German Reformation was softened by the likes of Staupitz, Melanchthon, and Katherine Zell. But Luther's personality, for better or for worse, overpowered them all and made its indelible mark on the Reformation as a whole. Without the peculiarities of this larger-than-life man, the Reformation would not have been nearly so spellbinding—and might never have succeeded at all.

## What If ...

What if the Catholic Church had nipped the Reformation in the bud and Martin Luther were one more martyr following after Jan Hus? Other heretics were burned. Why not Luther?

What if Luther had recanted at the Diet of Worms? Would someone else have stepped up and taken his place? Or would the 1520s be remembered as just another futile attempt at reformation of the church?

What if the wagonload of nuns had been stopped by local law enforcement and sent back to the convent? Luther would not have married Katherine von Bora, and the Reformation focus on the family might have been dimmed.

What if Luther had maintained his early positive approach to Jews? How might that have changed his own legacy and world history?

What if Melanchthon's position of compromise had won the day? What if Argula von Stauffer and Katherine Zell had minded their own business and not stepped out in ministry? Would the texture and tone of the Reformation have been different without them?

## Further Reading

Bainton, Roland. *Here I Stand: A Life of Martin Luther*. New York: Hendrickson, 2009.

Bainton, Roland. *Women of the Reformation in Germany and Italy*. London: Academic Renewal Press, 2001.

Cameron, Euan. *The European Reformation*. New York: Oxford University, 1991.

Erikson, Erik H. *Young Man Luther: A Study in Psychoanalysis and History*. New York: W.W. Norton, 1962.

Friedenthal, Richard. *Luther: His Life and Times*. Translated by John Nowell. New York: Harcourt Brace Jovanovich, 1970.

Kittelson, James M. *Luther the Reformer: The Story of the Man and His Career*. Minneapolis: Augsburg, 1986.

Kleinhans, Theodore J. *Martin Luther: Saint and Sinner*. London: Marshall, Morgan & Scott, 1959.

Luther, Martin. *Martin Luther: Selections from His Writings*. Edited by John Dillenberger. Harpswell, Me.: Anchor, 1958.

Marius, Richard. *Martin Luther: The Christian Between God and Death*. New York: Harvard University Press, 2000.

McKee, Elsie A. *Katharina Schutz Zell: The Life and Thought of a Sixteenth-Century Reformer*. Leiden: Brill, 1999.

Markwald, Rudolf K. *Katharina Von Bora: A Reformation Life*. Moorhead, Minn.: Concordia College, 2002.

Marty, Martin. *Martin Luther: A Life.* New York: Penguin, 2008.

Nichols, Stephen J. *The Reformation: How a Monk and a Mallet Changed the World.* Wheaton: Crossway, 2007.

Ozment, Steven. *When Fathers Ruled: Family Life in Reformation Europe.* New York: Harvard University Press, 1985.

Schwiebert, E. G. *Luther and His Times.* St. Louis, Mo.: Concordia Publishing House, 1950.

# CHAPTER 12

# The Swiss Reformation

*Zwingli, Calvin, and Company*

*I consider myself part of the Reformed family of faith. For good or for ill, John Calvin is the recognized "father" of this movement. His influence, however, goes far beyond the tens of millions of Reformed Christians worldwide found in such diverse places as France; Scotland; Korea; South Africa; Orange City, Iowa; and Grand Rapids, Michigan. And Calvinists are found in Baptist and Bible and Pentecostal churches as well.*

*Calvin's ideas also permeated secular culture. The Pilgrims and Puritans were largely descendants of Calvin. The Geneva experiment was carried to the American colonies, and even today American culture cannot fully escape the influence by Calvin.*

*The five-hundred-year anniversary of Calvin's birth in 2009 drew attention to his important place in religion and culture. It also drew light-hearted reflections on this most serious Reformer—humor that reminded me of a spoof years ago in the Calvin College student publication. A popular party game was "Servetus," named for the well-known heretic burned at the stake in Geneva. The object was "to think of a new excuse why JC was justified in giving Servetus the torch. . . . If you give a reason that is ethically equivalent to saying 'everyone in the 16th century was doing it' then the whole table has to drink a shot of tequila. . . . That's the party equivalent of a home run."*

*In honor of Master Calvin's big 500, I added my own attempt at humor with a rewrite of a familiar nursery rhyme that begins with an allusion to the Heidelberg Catechism, which is still widely used today:*

*Heidel, diddle diddle*
*The catechism and the Bible;*
*Old Calvin jumped over the flames.*
*Servetus scowled to see such sport,*
*Simultaneously dissed and mooned.*

*A touch of humor perhaps to disguise shame I bear when I look back at my Reformed heritage.*

Books are the carriers of civilization.
Without books, history is silent,
literature dumb, science crippled,
thought and speculation at a standstill.
BARBARA TUCHMAN

For anyone who reads and wonders about times gone by, it is difficult to imagine an era without books. Books are indeed the carriers of civilization, and they paved the way for religious reform in the sixteenth century. Among all previous reform movements there was no similar opportunity to make use of the printing revolution. The printed page allowed religious opinions to be circulated much more rapidly in the marketplace of ideas. Controversies caused a whirlwind of excitement that pressed toward the future while drawing from the deep well of the past.

While Martin Luther is the Reformer most associated with the printing revolution, the sixteenth-century book that made the greatest impact on the period and the succeeding generations was John Calvin's *The Institutes of the Christian Religion* (1536).

Calvin stands out among Reformed churchmen, but before he rose in stature others, including Ulrich Zwingli and Heinrich Bullinger, had laid the groundwork. His work also interfaced with the ministry of women such as Renee of Ferrara.

The Swiss Reformation was also influenced by Luther and his colleagues. With the success and staying power of Luther's challenge to the church—unlike that of Wycliffe and Hus—reform was encouraged elsewhere, each successive development with its own theological slant. Issues relating to the Lord's Supper and baptism took center stage in the sixteenth century, much as debates about the Trinity were critical in the fourth century, and biblical authority and women's ordination in the twentieth century. The nature of the church was also a key matter of doctrine for Reformers. Should the church be sanctioned by the state, or is it to be entirely separate and free from government oversight?

By the time Calvin came to the fore, the first generation of Reformers had laid the theological foundation. Thus his work was largely that of consolidation. His grappling with what constitutes the church and its role in society, however, had a significant impact on others. Likewise his

---

PARADE OF HISTORY

As the parade of the Reformation winds its way through Switzerland, it picks up Ulrich Zwingli, John Calvin, and others who add to the color and texture of the developing Protestant mind. But Zwingli at forty-five marches into battle and returns in a body bag. Fearing not enemy soldiers but Geneva citizens and council members, Calvin, after having been coerced into settling in Geneva in the first place, marches out of the city gates in a huff on his way to Strasbourg. But three years later, persuaded by perks and by contrite council members, he returns. Soon thereafter, a messenger of state is dispatched to escort his wife, Idelette, in a horse-drawn carriage fit for a princess. As the parade approaches Geneva, officials and townspeople alike give her a royal welcome.

concerns for practical everyday matters of Christian living were critical. Geneva was his laboratory, and what transpired there had implications for succeeding generations.

Unlike the German Reformation, the Swiss Reformation was not marked by a larger-than-life fiery personality. But like the German Reformation, it has its own claim to shame. Luther's verbal attacks on Jews were equaled by Zwingli's involvement in the execution of Anabaptists and Calvin's tacit approval of the burning of Servetus and others. Yet, amid the agitation of executions and theological disputations, Swiss Reformers, like their German counterparts, focused on the family and spiritual formation.

But the second phase of the Reformation, as represented by Calvin, also exhibited a pragmatic flare in the economic realm. Max Weber's famous thesis argued that the Protestant ethic was a key factor in the rise of capitalism. Although his ideas have been largely discredited by scholars in recent years, there remains some truth to the theory. Calvin was more open and attuned than Luther to ownership of private property and economic development—early concepts of a free-market economy. He did not condemn lending institutions as dishonest promoters of usury, as some had, provided there were ethical standards in place. He likewise emphasized the honor of work, identifying any "calling," be it ministry or farming or woodworking as respectable God-ordained labor. All spheres of activity, he said, are vocations by which an individual can fully serve God.

## Ulrich Zwingli: Swiss Soldier and Reformer

A contemporary of Luther, Ulrich Zwingli (1484–1531) was overshadowed by the giant from Wittenberg. He is often referred to as the

Ulrich Zwingli

third man of the Reformation behind Luther and Calvin. Zwingli fought bitterly against Luther over the issue of the Lord's Supper, viewing it as a symbolic meal, a position later adopted by a large segment of Protestantism. In other areas his legacy is more dubious. His brutal hostility toward the Anabaptists resulted in the death penalty by drowning—"the cruelest joke of the Reformation."

Born in a small village in a Swiss mountain valley, one of nine children, Zwingli was just seven weeks younger than Luther. From his early schooling through his university training, his most influential teachers are Renaissance humanists. Erasmus is to him "the greatest philosopher and theologian"—a man whose books he reads every night before retiring. In 1506, at the age of twenty-two, he is ordained and appointed priest in the city of Glarus, reportedly having had to pay for the position. He is initially known as a humanist and statesman

## Sixteenth-Century Christian Music

Music is as old as recorded history, though always marked by differences across cultures and centuries. Religious themes often predominate even in what is viewed as "secular" music. In late medieval times amateur guilds of singers arose in Germany—guilds that performed in monthly competitions. The songs typically featured a religious or moral topic with a more wholesome set of lyrics than those which might be sung in bars or on the street. The

Village dance

most celebrated *Meistersinger* was Hans Sachs, who became a follower of Luther and dedicated his talents to the Reformed cause.

Antiphonal singing was standard in the early church, but as harmony, rhythm, melody, and Latin lyrics became more complicated, the role of music-making fell to professional musicians. The rebirth of congregational singing was one of the marks of the Reformation. Luther wrote his great hymn "A Mighty Fortress is our God" (Psalm 46) for congregational singing. Indeed, this was a time when devotional singing was encouraged, at home and in church.

Ulrich Zwingli was one of the most musically inclined Reformers. Known for his instrumental prowess, he entertained both children and adults, though never during a worship

### MUSIC AS PUBLIC PRAYER

As to public prayers, there are two kinds: the one consists of words alone; the other includes music. And this is no recent invention. For since the very beginning of the church it has been this way, as we may learn from history books. Nor does St. Paul himself speak only of prayer by word of mouth, but also of singing. And in truth, we know from experience that song has a great power and strength to move and inflame the hearts of men to invoke and praise God with a heart more vehement and ardent.... For even in our homes and out of doors let it be a spur to us and a means of praising God and lifting up our hearts to Him, so that we may be consoled by meditating on His virtue, His bounty, His wisdom, and His justice. For this is more necessary than one can ever tell.

John Calvin

service. He played the harp, violin, dulcimer, flute, and hunting horn. His performances delighted the children, but critics ridiculed him as "the evangelical lute-player and fifer." Yet he stood firm in his opposition to church music. The organist reportedly wept when the grand organ, with his sanction, was destroyed. Organ music, and professional music of any form, he argued, distracted people from their worship of God. Antiphonal psalms, however, were permitted.

John Calvin more than other Reformers promoted singing as the proper way to pray and worship God. The Genevan Psalter was first published under Calvin's supervision in 1539. Using the Psalms as the lyrics, appropriate tunes were composed for congregational singing in unison. Complicated harmony was considered distracting embellishment that did not aid the Christian in worshiping God. The complete Psalter, offering a different tune for every one of the one hundred fifty psalms, was published in 1562. After many translations and revisions Genevan texts and tunes are still sung today.

more than as a religious scholar. His conversion is a slow process that began while he was ministering in Glarus, coming to full flowering during his early pastoral ministry in Zurich. His change of heart is prompted in part by a scandal that surfaces when he is being considered as the preacher of the prestigious cathedral in Zurich.

Rumors are rife that he had seduced the daughter of a prominent official. It is widely known that Renaissance popes had mistresses and children and that the Swiss Bishop of Constance earned hundreds of florins a year by fining his priests four florins for every child they fathered. Yet the leaders at Zurich are disinclined to extend a call to a preacher whose moral life is the subject of gossip. In response to their questions, Zwingli frankly admits his lapses, but he emphasizes that "shame always restrained me within certain limits and … I did it so secretly that even my intimates noticed practically nothing." He further emphasizes: "My principle was to inflict no injury on any marriage … and not to dishonour any virgin nor any nun." Indeed,

he has proof: "I can call to witness all those among whom I have lived."

Zwingli stresses that he is remorseful and that he had made a pledge in 1515 to abide by Paul's admonition "not to touch women." He upheld the vow for more than a year, but then he became entangled with a young woman—not a virgin, as was alleged—who had previously brought disgrace on herself. "I have fallen again," he lamented, "and am become like the dog of which the apostle Peter speaks, returning to his own vomit." The guilt that Zwingli suffers is largely due to his increasing regard for Scripture: "In the year 1516," he later remembered, "I began to preach in such wise that I never mounted the pulpit without taking personally to heart the Gospel for the day and explaining it with reference to Scripture alone."

Despite misgivings, the leaders in Zurich invite him to be their preacher. When they discover that the other candidate they were considering has six children, his sins do not seem so glaring. He begins in 1518 and continues until

## BLACK DEATH: THE PLAGUE HYMN

Help me, O Lord,
My strength and rock;
Lo, at the door
I hear death's knock.
Uplift thine arm,
Once pierced for me,
That conquered death
And set me free.
Yet, if thy voice,
In life's midday
Recalls my soul,
Then I obey.
In faith and hope
Earth I resign,
Secure of heaven
For I am Thine....
Lo! Satan strains
To snatch his prey;
I feel his grasp;
Must I give way?
He harms me not,
I fear no loss,
For here I lie
Beneath thy cross....

his death twelve years later. "Though I was young, ecclesiastical duties inspired in me more fear than joy because I knew, and I remained convinced, that I would have to give account of the blood of the sheep which would perish as a consequence of my carelessness."

The event that initiates the Swiss Reformation is often referred to as the "Affair of the Sausages." It occurred in 1522 during the Lenten season (when meat eating is forbidden). A local printer who is preparing Zwingli's manuscript on Paul's epistles invites him to his home for dinner. The main course is sausage. Zwingli reportedly does not partake, but for his part in hosting the dinner, the printer is arrested.

Zwingli, however, would have the last word. He preaches a sermon the following Sunday entitled "On the Choice and Freedom of Foods." Here he takes the side of freedom. Sausage is Zwingli's ninety-five theses.

During his first year of his ministry in Zurich, the plague strikes, leaving a third of the population dead. Away at the time, Zwingli hurries back to serve the sick and dying. He contracts the illness himself and is not expected to live. When he arises from his deathbed and continues his ministry of preaching and service, he is hailed with great affection.

Following in the footsteps of Luther, Zwingli also draws up theses—sixty-seven in his case—that denounce purgatory, indulgences, the Mass, prayers to saints, celibacy, and monasticism. The theses are straightforward and direct, as the eighteenth illustrates: "Christ, Who offered Himself once on the cross, is the sufficient and perpetual sacrifice for the sins of all believers. Therefore the Mass is no sacrifice, but a commemoration of the one sacrifice of the cross."

Within a few years Zwingli and his supporters give Zurich a makeover. Monasteries are closed, images destroyed, pilgrimages banned, and relics and rituals outlawed. In fact, those who attend Mass are punished with a fine. Another law requires citizens to eat meat rather than fish on Friday—again, enforced by a fine. Preaching against enforced celibacy comes natural to Zwingli, and through his persistent petitioning, permission is granted in 1522 by a church official in Lucerne for priests to marry. Zwingli himself keeps house with Anna Reinhart, a widow with three children, and secretly marries her before the birth of their own child. He tries hard to avoid scandal, but the story gets out and critics howl.

In Zurich he presides over a theocracy of sorts, similar to that which Savonarola sought to establish in Florence and Calvin would institute in Geneva. Adulterers and fornicators pay fines, as do those committing other sins. City offices are reserved for Protestants only. In fact, simply being a Catholic is enough to warrant a fine, and so is staying home from church on Sunday. But Zwingli does not focus on negatives only. He delivers lively sermons, and his preaching more than anything else advances the cause of reform in Zurich. Many priests had virtually dispensed with the sermon in favor of the Mass, but Zwingli makes his expository sermons the showpiece of the worship. His sermons sometimes extend to an hour, but surely not before a sleeping crowd. He is the best entertainment in town. He speaks fast and embellishes the text with his natural humor and homespun anecdotes.

Zwingli finds himself defending the faith on three fronts. Not only does he struggle to identify the reform against the Catholics on the right and Anabaptists on the left, but against Luther, with whom his reform is most often associated. "Why don't you call me a Paulinian since I am preaching like Saint Paul," he demands of a critic. "I do not want to be labeled a Lutheran

by the Papists, as it is not Luther who taught me the doctrine of Christ, but the Word of God. If Luther preaches Christ, he does the same thing as I do. Therefore, I will not bear any name save that of my chief, Jesus Christ, whose soldier I am." Although Luther accuses him of sympathizing with the radicals, Zwingli upholds the concept of a state church, arguing that separation is not the solution to the spiritual and moral corruption within the church. In Zurich, however, there are many so-called radicals who want no part of a marriage between church and State.

Closely tied to the issue of a "pure church" separated from the world is that of infant baptism. The so-called Radical Reformers — more properly identified as Anabaptists — insist that only true believers should be baptized. Zwingli initially seeks to persuade them of their errors through argument, but when that method fails, he turns to more drastic measures. Leading Anabaptists are arrested and warned by officials that if they do not turn from their "heresy" they will face death by drowning — "He who dips, shall be dipped." Six men are bound and thrown into the river. Zwingli himself does not carry out the executions, but neither does he prevent them.

## PREACHING ON "ALL CREATURES GREAT AND SMALL"

But man is not alone the offspring of God; all creatures are so.... They are by birth of God and in God.... Do not the creatures of the species of rodents proclaim the wisdom and providence of the Godhead? The hedgehog when with its spines he most cleverly carries a large quantity of fruit to its dwelling place, by rolling over the fruit and planting its spines in it. Alpine rats or marmots, which we now call the mountain rats, station one of their number upon an elevation, that, as they run about intent upon their work, no sudden danger may fall upon them without his timely cry of warning, while meantime the rest of the band carry off the softest hay from all around. And since they have no wagons, they turn themselves into wagons by turns, one lying upon his back and holding fast with all his feet the hay loaded upon his stomach and chest, while another seizes by the tail his comrade thus transformed into a wagon, and drags him with the plunder to their dwelling place to enable them to sleep through the inclemency of the harsh winter season.

Ulrich Zwingli, "On the Providence of God"

## ULRICH ZWINGLI'S PROTESTANT DEATH

On the battlefield, not far from the line of attack, Mr. Ulrich Zwingli lay under the dead and wounded. While men were looting ... he was still alive, lying on his back, with his hands together as if he was praying, and his eyes looking upwards to heaven. So some approached who did not know him and asked him, since he was so weak and close to death (for he had fallen in combat and was stricken with a mortal wound), whether a priest should be fetched to hear his confession. Thereat Zwingli shook his head, said nothing and looked up to heaven. Later they told him that if he was no longer able to speak or confess he should yet have the mother of God in his heart and call on the beloved saints to plead to God for grace on his behalf. Again Zwingli shook his head and continued gazing straight up to heaven. At this the Catholics grew impatient, cursed him and said that he was one of the obstinate cantankerous heretics and should get what he deserved. Then Captain Fuckinger of Unterwalden appeared and in exasperation drew his sword and gave Zwingli a thrust from which he at once died. So the renowned Mr. Ulrich Zwingli, true minister and servant of the churches of Zurich, was found wounded on the battlefield along with his flock (with whom he remained until his death).

Heinrich Bullinger

Despite such atrocities, Zwingli's success in Zurich is remarkable. By 1524 the Reformation in that city is far more complete than it is in Luther's Wittenberg. This achievement inspires him to move beyond Zurich to other Swiss cantons in the hope of igniting the Reformation there. Some of the cantons follow him, but others form a Catholic League in opposition. He sends missionaries to these cantons, and when one of the missionaries is burned at the stake, the Zurich city council declares war. A temporary peace is negotiated, but in 1531, after Protestants declare an economic blockade, Catholic armies march against them. Outnumbering them by more than five to one (8,000 to 1,500), the Catholics forces quickly overwhelm their opponents, and Zwingli is one of the five hundred Protestants killed in battle.

The city of Zurich mourns the loss of lives in battle, particularly the loss of their beloved pastor. He is succeeded by Heinrich Bullinger, who recognizes his predecessor as the founder of the Swiss Reformation and as a heroic martyr. But Luther proclaims "good riddance." It is

God's will that his theological enemy should be silenced once and for all.

### Heinrich Bullinger: More Calvinistic than Calvin

Following Zwingli's death, Heinrich Bullinger (1504–1575), leaves the monastic school in Cappel where he has been studying and relocates in Zurich to carry on with reform. Like many others, he enters the Reformed ministry having served as a Catholic cleric. He is also the son of a priest who had grown up in a rectory with four boisterous brothers. Under the lenient rules of some Swiss bishops, married priests merely pay fines to maintain family life. His father would remain a loyal Catholic until old age, when he too confessed the Reformed tenets his son is preaching.

Like Erasmus and Luther and Thomas à Kempis, Bullinger is educated by the Brethren of the Common Life, and like Luther he earns his keep by singing. Moving on to the University of Cologne, he studies scholastic theology but soon gravitates to the church fathers and to Scripture itself. At the same time, he is intrigued with Luther's teachings. With a master's degree, he returns to his homeland at age eighteen to teach at the monastic academy at Cappel. But realizing his weakness in Greek and Hebrew, he travels to Zurich to study under Zwingli. In the tradition of his father, he marries and pays his fines. His wife Anna, a former nun, makes a smooth transition as minister's wife, raising sons who will follow their father into ministry.

In Zurich, Bullinger preaches seven times a week and ministers to those afflicted by the recurring plague. He also serves as the chief administrator of the local schools and seminary and helps formulate the Helvetic Confessions adopted by Swiss churches. To a friend he writes: "I almost sink under the load of business and care, and feel so tired that I would ask the Lord to give me rest if it were not against his will." Yet the Bullinger household (which now includes Zwingli's widow and children) welcomes refugees and is known for its good times.

Challenging Calvin, Bullinger strongly objects to double predestination. "For we must not imagine that in heaven are laid two books, in the one whereof the names of them are written that are to be saved, and so to be saved, as it were of necessity, ... and that in the other are contained the names of them which ... cannot avoid everlasting damnation." In fact, his issues with predestination go further. To Calvin, he writes: "However many men are saved, they are saved by the pure

John Calvin

grace of God the saviour; those who perish do not perish by fated, compelled necessity, but because they willingly reject the grace of God. For there is not any sin in God; that the blame of our damnation inheres in us." But Bullinger flip-flops under pressure. In order to keep peace among various factions, he agrees to sign on to Calvin's definition of predestination. But he soon takes it back, insisting God desires that all will be saved.

In 1565, ten years before his own death, his wife and three daughters are cut down by the plague. His final years are wracked with ill health and loneliness, but he carries on his conciliatory efforts to the very end.

## John Calvin: Reform Far Beyond Geneva

After five centuries, John Calvin (1509–1564) remains an enigma. By nature he tended to be a timid and less-than-commanding figure. Over the centuries, however, he has acquired the reputation of a harsh authoritarian bent on stern discipline. Quiet and unassuming, he was described by friends and enemies alike as scholarly, melancholy, fastidious, and old before his time.

At the time of Calvin's birth in 1509, Luther and Zwingli are both well on their way to establishing their careers. Young "Jean" grows up in a strict Roman Catholic environment in Noyon, France, the youngest of four sons. His mother dies when he is very young. His father, an official in the local cathedral, sends him away for schooling. In his teens he enrolls at the University of Paris, where he studies law. After his father's death in 1531, he shifts to classics and biblical languages and devours the humanist teachings of Erasmus.

Although initially alarmed by the deep rift Luther has created in the church, Calvin is himself converted to the cause: "God himself produced the change. He instantly subdued my heart to obedience." Through Scripture he finds the true essence of salvation. "Only one haven of salvation," he writes, "is left open for our souls and that is the mercy of God in Christ. We are saved by grace — not by our merits, not by our works."

The humanist influence in France briefly opens the way for new ideas. But any attack on the church quickly brings down the wrath of the state. On All Saints Day, November 1, 1533, Nicolas Cop, the newly elected rector of the University of Sorbonne, delivers his inaugural address. A close friend of Cop, Calvin helped prepare the address, denouncing theologians who "teach nothing of faith, nothing of grace,

nothing of justification." University and government officials respond with threats of severe punishment, and Cop and Calvin flee town. Calvin reportedly escapes through an upstairs window by tying bed sheets together. Disguising himself as a peasant, he passes through the streets unnoticed.

He returns to Paris the following year only to face even greater danger. Posters denouncing the "horrible, great, intolerable abuses of the popish Mass" begin appearing in public places, and one finds its way into the very chambers of King Francis I, who is so incensed that he orders mass imprisonments and executions. Burning at the stake is not severe enough. Those accused are slowly suspended and raised in the flames to prolong the torture. Some two dozen Protestants are publicly executed. Fearing for his life, Calvin flees to Strasbourg.

The exile from his homeland affords him time to write and think. The result is his masterpiece of theology, *The Institutes of the Christian Religion*, which would stand for centuries as an enduring monument to the Protestant Reformation. His motivation is straightforward: "to lay down some elementary principles, by which inquirers on the subject of religion might be instructed in the nature of true piety." Quickly recognized as a Protestant standard of faith, it becomes a second bible to some and is burned by others. The first edition sells out within a year, and succeeding editions are expanded, the final one exceeding one thousand pages.

As a second generation Protestant, Calvin depends heavily on Luther: "I have often said that even though he were to call me a devil, I would nevertheless hold him in such honor that I would acknowledge him to be a distinguished servant of God." He is not, however, above criticizing his hero. To Bucer he writes that although he is "perfectly convinced of Luther's piety," he disdains his "haughty manner and abusive language," his "ignorance and most gross delusions," and his "insolent fury." He also criticizes Luther's sloppy scholarship, a factor that does not escape the meticulous Frenchman.

During this time Calvin, disguising himself and going under an assumed name, is also traveling. In 1536 he arrives in Geneva— an unscheduled visit that changes the course of his life. Here William Farel, a Reformer twenty years his senior whom he much admires, is striving to plant the evangelical faith. He needs assistance, as Calvin later relates:

Guillaume Farel

> Farel, who burned with an extraordinary zeal to advance the gospel, immediately strained every nerve to detain me. And after having learned that my heart was set upon devoting myself to private studies, for which I wished to keep myself free from other pursuits, and finding that he gained nothing by entreaties, he proceeded to utter an imprecation that God would curse my retirement and the tranquility of the studies which I sought, if I should withdraw and refuse to give assistance when the necessity was so urgent. By this imprecation I was so stricken with terror that I desisted from the journey I had undertaken.

In 1535, a year before his arrival, city officials had banned Catholic worship. Statues were removed from churches, and monasteries were closed. Farel had initiated the changes, but he now needs Calvin to administer the reform. Calvin reluctantly agrees, but he faces stiff opposition. Many townspeople defy his efforts to control their social life and religious activities. After an explosive council meeting, an angry mob gathers outside his residence and shouts obscenities. That night he awakes to gunshots and pounding on his door. As the months pass, the situation worsens. When he refuses communion to the troublemakers on Easter Sunday in 1538, the die is cast. He and Farel are ordered out of town. "Well and good," is Calvin's parting retort.

After leaving Geneva, he returns to Strasbourg, settling into ministry and pondering his single status. "I am none of those insane lovers who embrace also the vices of those with whom they are in love, where they are smitten at first sight with a fine figure," he writes to Farel. "This only is the beauty which allures me, if she is chaste, if not too fussy or fastidious, if economical, if patient, if there is hope that she will be interested about my health."

Although he is widely respected for his intellect and leadership capabilities, Calvin is not the Reformation's most eligible bachelor. He has a particular woman in mind—a wealthy supporter from Germany whose brother is the go-between. To Farel he writes, "We look for the bride to be here a little after Easter." Her financial status, he concedes, is a mixed blessing. "I cannot call a single penny my own. It is astonishing how money slips away." But he has apprehensions. "You understand, William, that she would bring with her a large dowry, and this could be embarrassing to a poor minister like myself. I feel, too, that she might become dissatisfied with her humbler station in life." Because of these and other factors, the plan fizzles.

Farel suggests another woman, but Calvin is not willing to consider a wife fifteen years older than he. With another new prospect in mind, he asks Farel to arrange someone to officiate at his marriage not "beyond the tenth of March," fearing for the worst. "I make myself look very foolish if it shall so happen that my hope again fall through." But again his efforts are thwarted.

Disheartened, he laments to Farel, "I have not found a wife and frequently hesitate as to whether I ought any more to seek one." Then one day he notices a woman in his own congregation, Idelette de Bure, a young widow with two children who, with her husband, converted from Anabaptist beliefs under his preaching. In the spring of 1540, while Calvin was still seeking a wife, her husband had died of the plague. Shortly thereafter, Calvin marries her. He had hoped that marriage might improve his financial status, but Idelette's children are her only "fortune." Married life is filled with complications and frustrations. In addition to his duties as a pastor in Strasbourg, Calvin is a teacher and houseparent at his own boarding school. Home for Idelette and her children thus becomes the hectic life of a boarding school. To make matters worse, both suffer ill health.

During his absence from Geneva disorder reigns in the streets and in the city council. In fact, the four council members responsible for expelling Calvin and Farel are all involved in criminal activity—one arrested on a capital charge of murder. In the midst of this disarray, the reorganized council sends a plea for Calvin to return. Life is relatively peaceful in Strasbourg, and Calvin is adamant: "Rather would I submit to death a hundred times than to that cross, on which one had to perish daily a thousand times over." But the pressure from Farel and others mounts. In 1541, three years after he was expelled, he returns to Geneva on a trial basis, leaving Idelette and the children behind.

With his return, the council sweetens the deal with gifts, including a fur-trimmed black velvet robe. They promise help in relocating Idelette "and her household," escorting her in a two-horse carriage with the honor accorded royalty. Their residence is the abbey on Rue de Chanoines overlooking Lake Geneva with a backdrop of the towering Alps. He succumbs to their pleas, but he has no time for lightheartedness. If townspeople had expected him to make references to his absence, they were mistaken. Although he has been away for three years, he methodically begins his expository preaching precisely where he left off.

Calvin's most bitter enemies in Geneva continue to be Libertines who oppose his strict regulations. What right does he have to interfere in their personal lives? They are not lawless. "In

## THE PROPHET JEREMIAH AND IMPIOUS POPISH BLASPHEMY

Here [in Jeremiah] is the refutation of that impious popish blasphemy which prattles that not only the law but even the gospel is obscure. But Paul claims that the gospel is plain *except to those who are perishing* (2 Cor. 4:3); over them a veil is thrown because they deserve to be blind (2 Cor. 3:14–15). But, as we see, Jeremiah here affirms that the law, even though it is less clear than the gospel, is set plainly before the eyes of all, and that all may learn from it exactly what pleases God and what is right.

John Calvin, *Commentary on Jeremiah*

short, everyone who maliciously and voluntarily hurts another deserves to be punished," Jacques Gruet argues. "But suppose I am a man who wants to eat his meals as he pleases, what affair is that of others? Or if I want to dance, or have a good time, what is that to do with the Law? Nothing." Gruet's resistance to the new laws, his petitioning the king of France to intervene, and his unorthodox beliefs result in his execution in 1547.

The most publicized execution in Geneva during Calvin's tenure is that of Michael Servetus. A brilliant Spanish physician who is also educated in mathematics and law, Servetus thrives on theological disputations. In *Errors About the Trinity* he defends his thesis with Scripture. But such issues are not open to debate. Both Catholics and Protestants consider him a heretic. In fact, before he visits Geneva, Catholic officials have judged him guilty *in absentia* and sentenced him to burn at the stake. Considering the consequence of promoting heresy, he appears to have been brazenly taunting Calvin by coming to Geneva. Arrested in the fall of 1553, he is burned at the stake. Such punishment, according to Calvin, is necessary to uphold God's honor:

> Whoever shall maintain that wrong is done to heretics and blasphemers in punishing them makes himself an accomplice in their crime and guilty as they are. There is no question here of man's authority; it is God who speaks.... Wherefore does he demand of us a so extreme severity ... so that we spare not kin, nor blood of any ... when the matter is to combat for His glory.

Religious toleration is not in vogue in the sixteenth century, but there are dissenting voices, and some of the most outspoken are women. Katherine Zell renounces the burning of the

### CALVIN'S SUNDAY SPORT

Although many straight-laced Reformed Christians in the generations after Calvin held to tight Sunday restrictions on leisure-time activities, he often engaged in lawn bowling — even on Sundays!

"poor Servetus." And Renee of Ferrara strongly opposes carnage against religious dissenters.

Throughout his life, Calvin maintains an active correspondence with dozens of religious and political leaders, staying abreast of reform in France and Germany and Italy. During his second tenure in Geneva he lectures and preaches daily sermons and is involved in church discipline, administration, and writing, aided by secretaries who take dictation and help prepare commentaries and other manuscripts for publication. His busy life often leaves him no more than four hours of sleep.

After less than a decade of marriage Idelette dies, leaving him to rear her own children. None of her children by Calvin came to full term or survived infancy. "Although the death of my wife has been bitterly painful to me, yet I restrain my grief as well as I can," Calvin writes to a friend. "I have been bereaved of the best companion of my life.... As long as she lived she was the faithful helper of my ministry." He vows "to henceforth lead a solitary life," concerned about an affliction that would make him unsuitable for marriage: "I know my infirmity, that perhaps a woman might not be happy with me."

Like Luther, Calvin struggles with doubt. Indeed, for Calvin "doubt and anxiety are thus the most terrible adversaries of every Christian, even the most faithful," including himself: "Every one of us knows only too well, from his own experiences, our difficulty in believing,"

## PREACH PREDESTINATION

Scripture is the school of the Holy Spirit, in which as nothing useful and necessary to be known has been omitted, so nothing is taught but what it is of importance to know. Every thing, therefore delivered in Scripture on the subject of predestination, we must beware of keeping from the faithful, lest we seem either maliciously to deprive them of the blessing of God.

John Calvin, *The Institutes of the Christian Religion*

he observed. "Everyone's weakness certainly witnesses to many doubts that steal upon us." The most committed Christians, in fact, "frequently stagger in unbelief." Faith is constantly attacked by Satan's stirring "many occasions for incredulity."

Most people know Calvin more for his theology than for his exegesis, but the two disciplines come as a package. The Bible is the foundation for his theology, and his theology informs his biblical commentaries. Having studied both Greek and Hebrew and having read widely among the church fathers and later commentators, he is an impressive scholar, and his work has stood the test of time. Rejecting the allegorical method, he wrote:

> I acknowledge that Scripture is a most rich and inexhaustible fountain of all wisdom, but I deny that its fertility consists in the various meanings which any man at his pleasure may put into it. Let us know, then, that the true meaning of Scripture is the natural and obvious meaning; and let us embrace and abide by it resolutely.

With Paul and Augustine, he affirms God's sovereignty, original sin, and saving grace

bestowed on the elect. Indeed, the doctrine of predestination, or election, becomes the doctrine for which he is most associated. Only those elected by God will enjoy eternal bliss in the life hereafter. All others are doomed to eternal suffering in hell. This perspective is laid out in book 3 of the *Institutes.* Here he argues that those who are Christians are regenerated by the Holy Spirit, chosen before creation — before the *foundations of the world.* Salvation comes not by works or by choice but solely by the grace of God. Good works demonstrate who the saved likely are, and in Calvin's theological system they seek to transform the world — thus the experiment in Geneva of the elect in community showing forth godly living.

Calvin's later years are filled with loneliness and difficulties, including scandal in his own family. Several years after Idelette's death his stepdaughter is convicted of adultery. So humiliated is Calvin that he remains behind closed doors for days. He suffers from painful headaches, kidney stones, gout, and pulmonary hemorrhaging. Yet he continues preaching, sometimes being carried into church and other times lecturing while students surround his bed. Why not just retire, his friends ask. "What!" he snaps. "Would you have the Lord find me idle when he comes?"

### Renee of Ferrara: Friend of Calvin

Daughter of King Louis XII of France, Princess Renee of Ferrara (1510 – 1575) was Calvin's staunchest supporter in Italy. As a girl she had been influenced by Marguerite of Navarre (sister of King Francis I), nearly twenty years her senior. Marguerite was a Protestant in all but name. Having read Jacques Lefevre's commentary on Paul's epistles she held to justification by faith alone. Her views on women were controversial among both Catholics and Protestants. "Do not follow the opinion of wicked men who take a passage of Scripture for themselves," she warns her readers. "If you have read St. Paul all the way to the end, you will find that he recommends himself to the ladies who have worked very hard with him in the Gospel."

Having read both the apostle Paul and Marguerite, Renee had similar issues with those who sought to interpret Paul negatively on women's roles. She recognized early her second-class status in the royal family. Indeed, gender made all the dif-

Renee, Princess of Ferrara, daughter of King of France Louis XII

ference. Her words are biting: "Had I had a beard I would have been the king of France. I have been defrauded by that confounded Salic Law" (denying women succession to the throne). Born in 1510, Renee was a year younger than Calvin. Her father was a devout Catholic, known as "the Father of the People" for his tax and legal reforms. Her mother, Anne the Duchess of Brittany, was a shrewd administrator, a devoted mother, and the richest woman in Europe. She intended for Renee to succeed her but died before Renee turned four, and Brittany came under French control.

---

## CALVIN'S COLLEAGUES

**William Farel** (1489–1565): More than any other Reformer, Farel wielded persuasive power over Calvin, convincing him with threats and curses to initially join him in Geneva and later to return after they had been driven out. A fellow Frenchman and fiery preacher, Farel was one of the first Protestants brought into the fold by the biblical teaching of Jacques Lefever d'Etaples, who remained a priest and Catholic Reformer.

**Martin Bucer** (1491–1551): Converted to Reformed teachings while listening to Luther debate at Leipzig, the French-born Dominican monk Martin Bucer (also spelled Butzer), had a major impact on Calvin. He emphasized the continuity between the Old and New Testaments, harmonized by Christology, and insisted the Mosaic law was not abolished altogether, giving Calvin a very different biblical perspective from that of Luther. He succeeded Mathew Zell as the leading Protestant minister in Strasbourg.

**Theodore Beza** (1519–1605): A disciple of Calvin, Beza also hailed from France. More than anyone else, he supplemented Calvin's writing during his lifetime and for four decades after his death. He has been accused of making Calvin's theology more Calvinistic than Calvin himself did — particularly on the matter of predestination. He edited the first compilation of Calvin's letters and defended him on controversial matters, including Geneva's church polity and the burning of Servetus. In addition he wrote theological and political treatises, an annotated Greek New Testament, and a Greek grammar and still had time for satires, dramas, and devotional works. After his friend died, he wrote, "Now that Calvin is dead, life will be less sweet and death less bitter."

Renee has every reason to be miffed by the Salic Law that makes her third cousin, Francis, king after her father dies. Since none of her father's three wives bore a son, his nephew inherits the throne. But the value of a daughter is nevertheless significant. In foreign policy, Louis XII was an expansionist, and Renee, by her arranged marriage to an Italian duke, is a prized pawn. The process of matchmaking had begun when she was a young girl. At seventeen she was married to Ercole II, the son of Lucrezia Borgia, the *femme fatale* of the Italian Renaissance. Lucrezia, however, had died in 1519 when Renee, living in France, was only nine. Nevertheless, Renee surely must have been aware of the gossip surrounding this most celebrated and scandalous woman whose life has since been widely portrayed in art and literature and films.

When Renee arrived in Ferrara to marry Duke Ercole, she entered Renaissance high culture. The refinement of Ferrara features not only palatial living, dazzling dresses, and jewels but also the finest art and music the Renaissance has to offer. Ercole's family is a premier patron of music, art, and architecture.

Portrayed by contemporaries as strong-willed, Renee vigorously challenges the authority of her husband, and religious beliefs quickly become a serious source of contention. Back in France the news — perhaps conveyed by her friend and cousin Marguerite of Navarre — is alarming. Protestants are being hunted down, some fleeing to Ferrara to find refuge. Among these heretics is none other than John Calvin (in disguise and using the alias Charles d'Espeville). He arrives in the spring of 1536 and stays for a month. By the time he leaves, Renee is even more committed to Reformed teachings, though she will never be a submissive student of Calvin or anyone else. Yet from his correspondence it is clear that a budding friendship has developed.

## JOHN CALVIN AND GENDER ISSUES

For both sexes were created according to the image of God.... But when he [Paul] is speaking about image here, he is referring to the conjugal order. Accordingly, it has to do with this present life; it does not pertain to the conscience. The straightforward solution is this, that Paul is not dealing here with innocence and holiness, which women can have just as well as men, but about the pre-eminence which God had given to the man, so that he might be superior to the woman.

John Calvin, Commentary on
1 Corinthians 11:7

"If I address you, madam," he writes, "it is not from rashness or presumption, but pure and true affection to make you prevail in the Lord."

Indeed, Calvin seems to have been somewhat awed by his newfound connections at court. "When I consider the pre-eminence in which He has placed you," he writes to Renee of Ferrara, "I think that, as a person of princely rank, you can advance the kingdom of Jesus Christ." He goes on to praise her spiritual maturity: "I observe in you such fear of God, and such a real desire to obey Him, that I should consider myself a castaway if I neglected the opportunity of being useful to you."

But when Renee continues to give the public pretence of being a faithful Catholic, Calvin is incensed. "I have heard that your domestics have been scandalized by the word of a certain preacher who says that one may go both to Mass and to the Lord's Supper," he writes, alluding to her as well. "I cannot suffer a wolf in sheep's clothing. I esteem the word of this preacher no more than the song of a jackdaw. The Mass is an execrable sacrilege and an intolerable blasphemy."

But the Catholic side is no less adamant. In 1544 King Henry II of France writes to his "only aunt," whom he "loved and esteemed." He expresses his grief in learning of her apostasy and begs her to be "restored to the bosom of our holy mother church, cleansed and purified from those cursed dogmas and reprobate errors." He tells her that he will be sending the Inquisitor Ori to counsel and teach her and threatens that if this does not work he will bring her "to reason by severity." A letter is also sent to her husband, Ercole, who now discovers how deep her religious convictions are. On September 17, 1544, she is forcibly placed under house arrest away from the palace in solitary confinement with her attendants. Her daughters Lucrezia and Leonora are placed in a convent. She is distraught, and in less than a week sends for a priest in order to confess and take communion. With this she gets what she most wants—her girls back under her own care.

When Calvin hears the news, he is deeply offended, perhaps conveniently forgetting that he himself had gone into hiding and then fled France amid persecution. "I fear you have left the straight road to please the world," he writes her. "And indeed the devil has so entirely triumphed that we have been constrained to groan, and bow our heads in sorrow." He admonishes her to humble herself before God and come back to the faith—and, we may presume, to give up her daughters to the convent. The letter is signed "Your very humble servant, Charles d'Espeville." The correspondence continues in the succeeding years.

When Duke Ercole dies in 1559, his son Alfonso succeeds him. Renee thinks she can now practice her Reformed faith more openly, but her

The Saint Bartholomew's Day Massacre

son threatens to exile her. Soon after that she returns to France. The poor and needy of Ferrara reportedly weep at her departure for she is known as a generous benefactor to the dispossessed. In France, prodded by Calvin, she defends Reformed "heretics." As in the past, however, she stands up to him. When her son-in-law is assassinated, she grieves, feeling she must defend her sorrow to Calvin, whom she accuses of consigning him to hell. She also complains to Calvin's agent, Francois Morel, about not being given a role in church decision making. Morel writes to Calvin: "Renee wants to attend the meetings of the synod.... But if Paul thought that women should be silent in the church, how much more should they not participate in the making of decisions. How will the Papists and the Anabaptists scoff to see us run by women!"

Renee is not amused by Morel's arguments, but her biggest concern is for Catholics who are enduring terrible atrocities perpetrated by Reformed Christians in France: "Monsieur Calvin, I am distressed that you do not know how the half in this realm behave. They even exhort simple women to kill and strangle. This is not the rule of Christ. I say this out of the great affection which I hold for the Reformed religion." Calvin places the blame on others. Among his final letters are ones to Renee. She lives on for more than a decade, during which time Protestants of France suffer unspeakably, especially in the St. Bartholomew's Day Massacre of 1572. A plot to kill Protestants, believed to have been hatched by Catherine de' Medici (a staunch Catholic and mother of the king), is carried out during a celebration following the marriage of the king's sister to Henry III of Navarre, a Protestant. The initial attacks are aimed at prominent aristocrats, but in the end thousands are dead and the Protestant cause in France has been dealt a severe blow.

Old and perhaps in seclusion, Renee survives. When she dies, there is little to show for her sacrifices to the Reformed faith; none of her children confess the beliefs they had learned as little ones under her supervision.

Renee was not the only French princess courted by Calvin and his successors. Jeanne d'Albret (1528 – 1572), daughter of Marguerite of Navarre, was eighteen years younger than Renee. In 1560, in her early thirties, she publicly professed her allegiance to the Reformed faith. Unlike Renee, she was in the thick of religious violence in France. Her unflagging support of the Huguenots (Reformed Protestants in France) so infuriated her husband that he locked her up and took full custody of their eight-year-old son. Church officials — including her cousin Cardinal d'Armagnac — railed against her. You are "being misled by evil counselors who seek to plant a new religion," he fumed. They are inciting "subjects to take up arms against kings and princes."

She responds with resolve: "I am not planting a new religion but restoring an old one." As to "evil counselors," she is firm: "I follow Beza, Calvin and others only in so far as they follow Scripture." Unlike Renee, who had called for religious toleration, Jeanne imposes restrictions on Catholics and rallies the troops to fight against the Catholic forces. Indeed, when a Huguenot general is killed in battle, she rides into the field to rally the troops. She dies several months before the St. Bartholomew's Day Massacre. Her son turns away from his mother's Reformed faith when he ascends the throne, but as Henry IV he is remembered for signing the Edict of Nantes (1598), granting religious toleration to the Huguenots for nearly a century.

The Swiss Reformation extended far beyond the borders of Switzerland. It naturally captured hearts and minds in France, Calvin's homeland. But it also quickly made its way into the Netherlands and what is today Hungary and Romania and would have permeated Italy but for fierce opposition. In a matter of generations this Calvinist faith would find its way to the New World through English Puritans, Scottish Presbyterians, French Huguenots, and Dutch Reformed — and today is a worldwide branch of Protestantism.

## What if . . . .

What if Ulrich Zwingli had reached out a hand of reconciliation toward his Anabaptist students and colleagues rather than participating in that "cruel joke" of drowning them?

What if John Calvin had been arrested before he fled France in the face of persecution? Other Frenchmen identified with the Reformed views of Luther were tortured and burned alive. How different would Protestantism be today were it not for John Calvin's conversion to the Protestant cause?

What if Renee of Ferrara and her aunt Marguerite and cousin Jeanne had remained faithful Catholics like the French male royals? They were strong and determined women whose influence went far beyond France. Had Renee been permitted by law to ascend to the throne in France, might the future of the French church have gone in a very different direction?

## Further Reading

Bainton, Roland H. *Women of the Reformation in Germany and Italy*. Minneapolis: Augsburg, 1971.

Bouwsma, William J. *John Calvin: A Sixteenth-Century Portrait*. New York: Oxford University Press, 1988.

Calvin, John. *Institutes of the Christian Religion*. Translated by Henry Beveridge. Peabody, Mass.: Hendrickson, 2008.

de Greef, Wulfert. *The Writings of John Calvin, Expanded Edition: An Introductory Guide*. Translated by Lyle D. Bierma. Louisville: Westminster John Knox, 2008.

Estep, William Roscoe. *Renaissance and Reformation*. Grand Rapids: Eerdmans, 1986.

Gordon, Bruce, and Emidio Campi, eds. *Architect of Reformation: An Introduction to Heinrich Bullinger, 1504–1575*. Grand Rapids: Baker, 2004.

Harkness, Georgia. *John Calvin: The Man and His Ethics*. Nashville: Abingdon, 1958.

Hyma, Albert. *The Life of John Calvin*. Grand Rapids: Eerdmans, 1943.

Parker, T. H. L. *John Calvin: A Biography*. Philadelphia: Westminster, 2007.

Piper, John. *John Calvin and his Passion for the Majesty of God*. Wheaton, Ill.: Crossway, 2008.

Rilliet, Jean. *Zwingli: Third Man of the Reformation*. Translated by Harold Knight. Philadelphia: Westminster, 1959.

Stjerna, Kirsi. *Women and the Reformation*. Hoboken, N.J.: Wiley-Blackwell, 2008.

Van Halsema, Thea B. *This Was John Calvin*. Grand Rapid: Baker, 1981.

Witte, John, and Robert M. Kingdom. *Sex, Marriage, and Family Life in John Calvin's Geneva*. Grand Rapids: Eerdmans, 2005.

# PART II

## Sixteenth-Century Anabaptism to the Twenty-first Century

# CHAPTER 13

# The Anabaptists

## *Separation of Church and State*

*In addition to speaking, teaching, and writing, I have for more than a dozen years operated Carlton Gardens, a gift shop featuring art, antiques, floral furniture, birdhouses, chimes, and much more. Lyle, my supplier for arbors, swings, and benches, is an Amish artisan from northern Indiana. His lifestyle is as simple as it is complex.*

*The Amish, known for plain living, actually conduct their lives under a system of complicated rules and restrictions. For example, Lyle has a toll-free phone number, but he must travel three miles each morning in his horse and buggy to access his messages. There is no electricity on his farm—only a large generator that powers his very sophisticated woodworking tools.*

*Why is he permitted to have such tools but not allowed to drive a truck? Why can he use a generator to make furniture, while his wife washes clothes by hand and lights lanterns to illuminate the rooms at night? It all makes perfect sense to Old Order Amish communities who each have their own variants of the given rules. Maintaining a plain lifestyle is the critical element in determining how modern implements and technology can be used. If a toll-free phone and power tools do not impinge on lifestyle, leaders of the local congregation may permit their use.*

*Because his religion does not permit him to own or drive a vehicle other than his horse-drawn buggy, Lyle teams up with Mennonite neighbors who deliver his furniture. Mennonites are spiritual cousins of the Amish, some of whom are still known for their distinctive lifestyles and separation from the world. A young man and his "spoken-for" girlfriend, neither out of their teens, delivered one of my orders. They were a striking pair—he in a white shirt, black hat, pants, and suspenders; she in a light blue ankle-length dress, white sneakers and socks, her hair pulled back in a bun and covered with a small white head-covering. She worked alongside her future husband as they unloaded the truck.*

*I talked with them as I have often talked with Lyle. They are at ease in their separation from the world, enjoying a sense of security and community that few of us in the hustle of our fast-paced lives will ever fully realize. They draw heavily on a spiritual and cultural Anabaptist heritage that arose in the sixteenth century—a tragic time of martyrdom at the hands of so-called Christians—Catholic and Protestant alike.*

> History is a jangle of
> accidents, blunders, surprises and absurdities,
> and so is our knowledge of it,
> but if we are to report it at all
> we must impose some order upon it.
> HENRY STEELE COMMAGER

The history of sixteenth-century Anabaptists, like all history, is "a jangle of accidents and blunders and surprises." The German and Swiss contours of the Magisterial Reformation have long ago been set in some semblance of order by historians, but the various strands of Anabaptism have been less identified. Among those labeled Anabaptists—or "Radicals"—are some promoting polygamy and a militaristic kingdom of God on earth. Others want nothing more than to live in peace and spread the gospel. Most bizarre of all is that Reformers—those who risked their lives in breaking away from the Catholic Church—are the very ones torturing and executing these peaceful Christians. Their "heresy" is not the denial of the Trinity or the infallibility of Scripture. Their crime is the practice of believers' baptism and separation from the world. How then do historians impose order on such a jangle of absurdity?

A critical question asked by Reformers was *How are we saved?* Catholics, with such accoutrements as relics and indulgences, maintained that salvation is through faith plus works. Luther insisted on faith alone—*sola fide*. He denounced the Catholic Church as diseased and in need of serious surgery. But while performing such surgery, he failed to remove the cancerous connection to the state. If Protestants controlled a particular realm, then all residents were regarded Protestant. Such was the case also with Calvin in Geneva. Anabaptists, however, saw Protestants as behaving no better than Catholics. Neither demonstrated true discipleship. Neither showed signs of having been saved by following Christ in separation and sacrifice and service—and believers' baptism. Among these so-called heretics defending their faith were Conrad Grebel, Felix Manz, Balthasar Hubmaier, Michael Sattler, Menno Simons, and Elizabeth Dirks.

The term Anabaptist means *baptize again*. When used in the sixteenth-century context it was a broadly inclusive term that encompassed many groups—some unrelated to others. Like

---

### PARADE OF HISTORY

The Reformation procession takes a sharp turn as it veers into Anabaptism. No longer will the Christian parade comprise the state church. Rather, it will include only a called-out few. Those marching to glory are separated from the world and profess a conversion experience marked by believers' baptism. The notorious parade that gives Anabaptists a bad name is the march to Münster—pilgrims in wagons and on foot joining in a procession to the city where the millennial kingdom will be proclaimed. Arriving in Münster, they find like-minded locals parading in the streets, including women participating in frenzied dances and tearing off their clothes until they are "half-naked."

the early Christians, they were separated from the world and its government. If the church was composed of all those living in a given area or all generations of a family or community, then infant baptism would make sense. But if the church is made up of only those who testify to a conversion experience and who commit to living a different life from the rest of the world, then believers' baptism, symbolizing the "new birth," is appropriate. As a pilgrim church seeking to follow the precepts of Jesus, Anabaptists stand out among all other Reformers.

For a time Zwingli himself contemplated a separated church that pushed the boundaries of reform further than Luther could have anticipated. But such an ecclesiastical stance was far more radical in the sixteenth century than it would be today. He quickly pulled back. His enthusiasm for offering Bible studies to eager students, however, led to biblical interpretations that carried reform far beyond what the Magisterial Reformers had in mind. Soon Anabaptist house churches were forming right under his nose. Spurred by their commitment to lay evangelism, they quickly spread the gospel message—so rapidly in fact, that many Reformers, particularly in Switzerland, feared that whole regions might be swept away. "The people are running after them as though they were living saints," lamented Heinrich Bullinger. Another warned that "there was reason to fear that the majority of the common people would unite with this sect." Still another reported that they "spread so rapidly that their teaching soon covered the land as it were," having "gained a large following, and baptized thousands."

While it is true that some cell groups expanded into congregations, most Anabaptist groups were independent from one another, and there was no one charismatic leader to unite them all into a threatening political force. Besides, most Anabaptists were pacifists who had no interest in upending the ruling powers. True, certain segments of the movement were mesmerized by authoritarian figures, but they were the exception to the rule. One such group arose in Münster. Here the rule of God was established under a self-identified king; militant followers took up arms against their oppressors, seeking to institute common property, polygamy, and other practices viewed as dangerous.

Catholic authorities were brutal in stamping down such insurrection and in their persecution of peaceful Anabaptists. But it was Zwingli who

## ANABAPTIST INFLUENCE ON CHURCH AND STATE

Judged by the reception it met at the hands of those in power, both in Church and State, equally in Roman Catholic and in Protestant countries, the Anabaptist movement was one of the most tragic in the history of Christianity; but, judged by the principles, which were put into play by the men who bore this reproachful nickname, it must be pronounced one of the most momentous and significant undertakings in man's eventful religious struggle after the truth. It gathered up the gains of earlier movements, it is the spiritual soil out of which all nonconformist sects have sprung, and it is the first plain announcement in modern history of a programme for a new type of Christian society which the modern world, especially in America and England, has been slowly realizing — an absolutely free and independent religious society, and a State in which every man counts as a man, and has his share in shaping both Church and State.

Rufus M. Jones, *Studies in Mystical Religion*

## Sixteenth-Century Fashion

Anabaptists in all their various forms did not stand out in sixteenth-century society as they have since then. Their plain and simple dress was similar to that of the lower classes, and in some cases it has changed very little. In fact, today Amish and certain Mennonites appear to have walked straight out of the sixteenth century. Anabaptists considered fashionable clothes dishonoring to God, a sign of "worldliness."

Renaissance paintings function like a fashion catalog for us. Men's, women's, and children's clothing appear in full color, from top-of-the line ball gowns to laborers' work clothes. We glimpse into the lives of the rich and famous as well as those of nameless peasants toiling in the field. Women selling and buying in the market, whose husbands might have been working behind a plow or in a cobbler's shop, are often shown with colorful dresses that feature interesting layered designs. The collars are sometimes open, betraying more bosom than Calvin would have approved. An apron covering the skirt is a common feature worn both in the home and in the market. Headscarves, veils, and bonnets frequently cover the hair, and hats are common for both men and women.

Working men's clothing is typically much simpler than that of their wives. Shirts are rarely collared and are often worn under a vest or an outer shirt. Trousers are straight and full, held up with a rope tied around the waist. Short pants and leggings are also worn,

### STYLISH FASHION IN GENEVA

Men and women were dressed to a tee. They all wore the latest fashions which featured an abundance of lace and fur and splashes of loud colors.... The year was 1540. The town was Geneva, Switzerland. The minister was John Calvin. Pastor Calvin mounted the twelve steps that led to his pulpit in the stately St. Pierre Church.... "Just look at yourselves," he began, pausing for effect. "Men dress up as young women as though they grieve over the fact that God has not made them women. And women dress as glorious rainbows, trying to catch the glances of men...."

"Tell us, Sir. How should we dress?" The voice was that of a shop-keeper....

"In clothing that simply protects you from the cold and heat," shot back Calvin. The congregation fell silent. What sort of standard was that for the fashion-conscious? Had this Calvin no sense of fabric or texture?... Calvin was reacting to the secular spirit which pervaded 16th-century Geneva. He was living among a stubborn, worldly bunch who resisted the will of God.

Adrian Dieleman, "John Calvin on Clothing," sermon, June 22, 2003

perhaps more often by men on the make. Lower-class families have only one or two sets of clothing per person; washing is arduous and infrequent.

Prosperous women employing professional dressmakers typically wear full skirts, billowy sleeves, and ruffles. A low, square neckline is a popular style that displays an assortment of jewelry. For those who can afford it, a long floor-length cape completes the look for a social function. The fashion of middle-class men is more varied and fluid than it is today. A knight might wear a short skirt-like tunic with tights; "blouses" with puffy sleeves are popular. Professors and anyone else with academic standing wear robes and an appropriate hat.

Kings and princes are often painted in heavy robes, sometimes lined in fur and accessorized with heavy jewelry, and a crown or fashionable hat. Beneath the robe are shirts with high pleated collars. Tights and fancy pointed shoes can be spotted behind the folds and hem of the robe.

Ornate hats, gowns, and jewelry are the fashion for aristocratic women. In lieu of hats, very elaborate hairstyles often served to crown the lady's attire—a high up-do held by jewel-encrusted combs. Silk, imported from the East, is a favorite fabric. Underneath the gown a variety of underwear effects serve to cinch the waist and increase the bustline. Stuffing of various materials also enhance the lady's figure.

Fashions varied from region to region, and for both men and women of any social status there is an amazing variation of styles. Indeed, with the onset of the Renaissance, fashion has become not only a critical status symbol but also an art form. It is this fashion-conscious mentality that prompted Savonarola to call for gowns to be thrown into the fire along with other "vanities" such as frivolous hats, jewelry, and makeup. John Calvin also has harsh words for those who used adornment as a status symbol.

Children are rarely shown wearing clothing designed specifically for youngsters. Rather, whatever their social status, they tend to reflect their superiors in fashion, making them appear as miniature grownups.

---

is most associated with what has been termed "the cruelest joke of the Reformation." One would suppose that those who have endured persecution themselves would be less likely to persecute and torture others, yet history demonstrates otherwise. The execution of scholarly and peaceful Anabaptist theologians and lay people defies imagination. Many of them had once been Zwingli's friends and colleagues, making his brutality even more difficult to comprehend.

An authoritarian leader, Zwingli is determined to nip in the bud what he deems heresy.

Several of his followers have begun calling for separation of church and state. To them believers' baptism goes hand in hand with a "called-out" body of believers. Zwingli is not convinced. When Felix Manz and Conrad Grebel begin holding their own Bible study groups, Zwingli calls for a disputation. Manz and Grebel insist that the Scripture alone determines doctrine—

that the church fathers and church tradition often veer far away from biblical teaching. When the city council bans voluntary church congregations and requires that all babies be baptized, the two sides are at loggerheads. Manz and Grebel are ordered into exile. They ignore the order, and, with more than a dozen followers, organize a free, independent church. The Anabaptist movement is born.

## Conrad Grebel: Father of Anabaptism

The son of a well-respected iron merchant, Conrad Grebel (c. 1498–1526) is considered the father of the Anabaptist movement. He was, according to Zwingli, "the ringleader" of Zurich's Anabaptists. One of six children, he grew up in Grüningen, the son of Dorothea and Junker Jakob Grebel. He attended Latin school in Zurich, and through his father's aristocratic connections, took further studies at the University of Vienna and the University of Paris. But he squandered his first-rate education and spent his best years in drinking and brawling. Learning of his son's behavior, his furious father called him home. After some six years of higher education he was still without a degree.

Back in Zurich in 1521, in his early twenties, Grebel joins Zwingli, Felix Manz, and other young scholars to study the Bible in Greek and Hebrew. The following year he testifies to a profound conversion experience and a call to ministry. At the same time, his devotion and loyalty to Zwingli deepens and he becomes one of his most trusted followers. But then, through his studies and his friendship with Manz, he becomes convinced that Zwingli is disobeying Scripture by continuing to perform the Mass—a practice that continues until 1525. The resulting break with Zwingli is painful. The issue creating the most serious rift between Zwingli and his students is believers' baptism. Grebel, Manz, and others insist that infant baptism is invalid. They debate Zwingli in a public forum in 1525, and the town council sides with Zwingli. But Grebel has a baby daughter whom he refuses to baptize. The debate is now very personal.

In the weeks and months that follow, a "free" congregation—the Swiss Brethren—emerges in Zurich. While meeting in the House of Felix Manz, one of the men, after making confession of faith, requests baptism from Grebel. Others follow suit. There is no turning back. Grebel, leaving the oversight of the tiny congregation to others, sets off as an itinerant evangelist. As people listen to his persuasive preaching, some five hundred "converts" are baptized (or *re*-baptized) by immersion, often in a nearby stream. Others join in the evangelistic outreach.

In the fall of 1525 Grebel is incarcerated, during which time he writes a biblical defense of his beliefs that is published after his escape the following spring. But his ministry is cut short. He falls ill of the plague and dies before the age of thirty. Nevertheless, his ministry of less than four years is foundational to the Anabaptist cause. Though he is a very persuasive evangelist, his desire to convert his father and to convince him to abandon Zwingli does not lie within his reach. His own children are reared by relatives in the Reformed faith of Zwingli.

## Felix Manz: Execution in Icy Waters

A student of Zwingli and a good friend of Grebel, Felix Manz (1498–1527) was cofounder of the first congregation of Anabaptist Swiss Brethren. The son of a Catholic cleric, Manz, like Grebel, had a well-rounded sixteenth-century humanist liberal arts education that included Latin, Greek, and Hebrew. Like Grebel, he was imprisoned for preaching his new-found faith and for

## Anabaptist Beliefs on Pacifism and Baptism

Moreover, the gospel and its adherents are not to be protected by the sword.... True believing Christians are sheep among wolves, sheep for the slaughter. They must be baptized in anguish and tribulation, persecution, suffering, and death, tried in fire, and must reach the fatherland of eternal rest not by slaying the physical but the spiritual. They use neither worldly sword nor war, since killing has ceased with them entirely, unless indeed we are still under the old law, and even there (as far as we can know) war was only a plague after they had once conquered the Promised Land. No more of this.... On the subject of baptism ... the Scriptures describe ... that it signifies the washing away of sins by faith and the blood of Christ (that the nature of the baptized and believing one is changing before and after), that it signifies one has died and shall (die) to sin and walks in newness of life and Spirit and one will surely be saved if one through the inward baptism lives the faith according to this meaning....

Conrad Grebel, Letter to Thomas Müntzer

challenging the Zurich city council on the matter of believers' baptism.

In March of 1526, only months before Grebel's death of the plague, the Zurich city council had enacted a law making believers' baptism (rebaptism) a capital offence punishable by drowning. Manz would become the first Anabaptist martyred for this offence. Insisting that he was not seeking to prevent Reformers from baptizing infants, he argued that his only motive was "to bring together those who were willing to accept Christ, obey the Word, and follow in His footsteps, to unite with these by baptism, and to leave the rest in their present conviction." But Zwingli and the city council were determined to make Manz's death a deterrent. Just two days before his drowning, Zwingli wrote to a fellow Reformer: "The Anabaptist, who should already have been sent to the devil, disturbs the peace of the pious people. But I believe, the axe will settle it."

But Manz would not be axed to death. Rather, officials execute him by his own baptismal prescription — immersion of an adult believer. His death is ridiculed as the third baptism: infant, believers, and drowning — "He

who dips shall be dipped!" The story is chilling. Bullinger describes the scene: On a bitterly cold Saturday afternoon in January of 1527, "Manz was taken out of the Wellenberg prison and led to the fish market there by the Limmat [River]. There his death sentence was read. He was taken to the butcher shop, and then forced into a boat, in which the executioner and a pastor were standing." A crowd of onlookers, including his mother and brother, had accompanied him. Offered an opportunity to recant, he publicly proclaims his faith, encouraged by his family

Anabaptist rescuing his captor from the river

and other supporters. He is then rowed some distance from shore, where he is pushed into the icy water, declaring his faith in Christ until the water engulfs him. Among the writings that he leaves behind is a hymn, the first lines offering his own testimony:

> With gladness will I now sing;
> My heart delights in God,
> Who showed me such forbearance
> That I from death was saved
> Which never hath an end.
> I praise Thee, Christ in heaven
> Who all my sorrow changed.

In the weeks and months that follow, six more Anabaptists suffer a similar fate.

## Thomas Müntzer: Prophet of the Peasants' Uprising

It is inaccurate to suppose that the Reformation was religious in nature only. Many leaders and their followers were influenced by social and political factors as well. Thomas Müntzer (c. 1488–1525) was a radical reformer whose philosophical and religious perspectives soundly clashed with most Anabaptists as well as with Catholics and Magisterial Reformers. Though often lumped with the Anabaptists, he does not easily fit that label, and he predates the broader Anabaptist movement. Born in a small village in Germany, he was raised a devout Catholic and was a monastic leader by the age of twenty-one. But motivated by the writings of Luther, he left the monastery behind for university studies and political activism.

In 1520, Müntzer accepts a call to serve as minister in a church in Zwickau, a town that had gained a reputation for radicalism as the home of the Zwickau prophets. Some of these prophets had relocated in Wittenberg and cre-

ated problems for Luther. Müntzer has barely begun his ministry when his church sends him packing. He is too radical for their tastes. Moving on to Prague, he is welcomed as a reformer in the tradition of Luther. There he writes the "Prague Manifesto," denouncing Catholic clerics and prophesying the reign of Christ. Luther renounces him as a *Schwärmer* (fanatic), as do secular rulers. By 1523, he is back on German territory, ministering in the village of Allstedt. He remains long enough to marry Ottilie von Gerson, a former nun. Fearing the wrath of authorities, he moves on and becomes an instigator in the peasants' uprising, using as his rallying cry, *Omnia sunt communia* (all things in common). Indeed, some scholars view him as a precursor to modern socialism. But his views change as often as does his place of residence.

Settling down in Mühlhausen in 1525, he stirs the citizens to overthrow the city council and institute his "Eternal League of God." At the height of his popularity he leads some one thousand followers in an independent religious community, identifying himself as an interpreter of dreams in the tradition of the Old Testament prophet Daniel. But more important than the Bible is his direct revelation from God. "These villainous and treacherous parsons are of no use to the church in even the slightest manner," he thunders, "for they deny the voice of the bridegroom, which is a truly certain sign that they are a pack of devils. How could they then be God's servants, bearers of his word, which they shamelessly deny with their whore's brazenness? For all true parsons must have revelations, so that they are certain of their cause."

Unlike Anabaptists, Müntzer does not administer believers' baptism, nor is he a pacifist. In fact, he leads thousands of ill-equipped peasant soldiers in the final battle of the Peasants' War in the spring of 1525. Government troops had agreed to a truce, but the next day they attack in full force, slaughtering the unsuspecting peasants. Müntzer is arrested and tortured to the point that he recants and submits to the Mass. Any hope for leniency, is dashed, however. He is beheaded, and his head is publicly displayed to serve as a deterrent to future radicalism.

## John of Leiden: Prophetic Revelations and Bible Burning

Not to be confused with Thomas Müntzer, John of Leiden (c. 1509–1536) reigned as self-proclaimed king for more than a year in the German town of Münster. Like Müntzer, he is often labeled an Anabaptist. But he fits the category only in his practice of re-baptizing. Born in the Dutch town of Leiden to an unmarried woman, he was reared in poverty. Unlike other religious leaders of this era, his schooling was meager and he worked as a tailor as well as an innkeeper, having neither a monastic nor university education.

In his mid-twenties, John encounters Jan Matthys, an Anabaptist lay-evangelist who has baptized thousands of converts. Captivated by his message, he soon becomes his chief lieutenant. As he is traveling and preaching, he comes to Münster, a city ripe for his message. With the help of local merchants, he takes control of the town council and calls on Matthys for help. Matthys pronounces Münster the "New Jerusalem," and with his followers they usher in the kingdom of God.

Melchior Hofmann, another lay preacher, had sought to establish a similar New Jerusalem in Strasbourg, a crime for which he was sentenced to life in prison. Blaming Hofmann for his own failure, Matthys is convinced God has given him prophetic powers that will guarantee his success. His take-over of Münster in February of 1534 comes at a heavy cost to local residents, who flee in the face of violent persecution. Those who remain are forced to submit to re-baptism. At the same time, Matthys's out-of-town followers are flocking to the city. He distributes the possessions of the "godless" to the newcomers as "communism" is instituted. In March he demands that all Bibles or portions thereof be brought to the cathedral square, where he presides over their burning, solidifying himself as the sole authority.

But a month later on Easter Sunday 1534, Matthys is fatally wounded in a failed military campaign. Despite this setback, within months John of Leiden gains the upper hand, pronouncing himself King of Münster, King David's successor. He begins his reign by jogging through the streets naked, after which he falls into a three-day trance. When he regains his senses, he sets up a new government patterned after the Twelve Tribes of Israel, each with its own judge. "Now God has chosen me to be king over the entire world," he declares. "What I do, I must do, because God has ordained me."

To demonstrate his power, he micromanages every aspect of life from renaming streets and days of the week to minting coins and regulating family activities. He and his henchmen execute dozens of those who challenge or disobey his rules. With many of the men soldiering and dying, he introduces polygamy and reportedly takes some dozen wives, executing one for disobedience, beheading her in the public market. But such a dictatorship cannot last. Two guards escape and aid outside Catholic forces in taking military control of the city. In late June of 1535, the reign of terror in Münster comes to an end. After interrogation and indescribable torture, John is executed.

A significant outcome of the Münster episode was its negative effect on the larger Anabaptist movement, which, contrary to John's

## ANABAPTIST INFLUENCE ON AMERICAN DEMOCRACY

There can be no question but that the great principles of freedom of conscience, separation of church and state, and voluntarism in religion, so basic in American Protestantism and so essential to democracy, ultimately are derived from the Anabaptists of the Reformation period, who for the first time clearly enunciated them and challenged the Christian world to follow them in practice. The line of descent through the centuries since that time may not always be clear, and may have passed through other intermediate movements and groups, but the debt to original Anabaptism is unquestioned.

Harold S. Bender, *The Anabaptist Vision*

radical teaching, rejected military and political entanglements and revered Scripture.

### Balthasar Hubmaier: Anabaptist Theologian

One of the most highly educated and respected theologians among Anabaptists was Balthaser Hubmaier (c. 1480–1528). Born in Bavaria, he taught school while earning his doctorate from the University of Ingolstad in 1512. So respected was his scholarship that he was invited to stay on as a rector at the university.

In 1516, a year before Luther posted his Ninety-five Theses, Hubmaier accepts a call to a church in Regensburg, where he is widely hailed as a superb preacher. In the years that follow, he interacts with Erasmus and Conrad Grebel. Then, in 1523, he meets Zwingli for a disputation; he argues that there is no biblical precedent for infant baptism. Two years later, he and dozens of his parishioners—soon to be followed by some three hundred more—are re-baptized by an Anabaptist leader.

Balthasar Hubmaier

Hubmaier is well aware of the cost of being an Anabaptist. In 1524 he had written *Heretics and Those Who Burn Them*, and the following year—almost baiting authorities—he writes *The Christian Baptism of Believers*. He makes a strong case for religious toleration, arguing against the criminalization of heresy or unbelief. "It is well and good that the secular authority puts to death the criminals who do physical harm to the defenseless (Romans 13)," he asserts. "But no one may injure the atheist who wishes nothing for himself other than to forsake the gospel."

Threatened by Catholic authorities in Austria, Hubmaier escapes to Zurich. But Zwingli shows no sympathy and promptly has him arrested. He is permitted to defend his views on believers' baptism, using some of Zwingli's earlier statements. Zwingli denies having ever seriously considered such statements, though others remember him counseling that children should be instructed before being baptized.

Fearing for his life, Hubmaier agrees to recant, but

then, speaking before a larger congregation, he takes back his recantation: "Oh what anguish and travail I have suffered this night over the statements which I myself have made. So I say here and now, I can and I will not recant." Going on to defend the practice of believers' baptism, he is immediately arrested and returned to prison, where under torture he once again recants. With his second recantation and release, he hastens to get out of town. He journeys to Nikolsburg, a tolerant town in Germany. Once again wracked by guilt—as is evidenced in his *Short Apology* of 1526—he confesses: "I may err—I am a man, but a heretic I cannot be because I ask constantly for instruction in the word of God.... But faith is a work of God and not the heretic's tower, in which one sees neither sun nor moon, and lives on nothing but water and bread.... O God, pardon me my weakness."

A free man, Hubmaier reportedly baptizes some six thousand followers in the space of a year. He also clarifies the distinct theology of the Anabaptists in tracts and treatises and promotes their wide distribution. Here he develops his stance on the sacraments as well as on salvation, which is marked by a new birth as a requisite for entrance into heaven. The Christian life consists of good works and evangelism—especially to "Jews and pagans," who are to be warmly received "so that they might be drawn by a Christian example to faith in Christ." He criticizes Luther's reform as

Anabaptists tortured

permissive of moral laxity. The biblical solution is to be a part of a confessing community of believers set apart from the world.

Some of Hubmaier's followers are influenced by those who insist on a socialist sharing of possessions and on avoiding sinful allegiance to the state. Hubmaier, however, argues that secular governments are legitimate and that Christians should be involved in policy making. Unlike most Anabaptists, he likewise maintains that that there are occasions to take up arms.

Although Hubmaier seeks to avoid stirring up controversy with government and church officials, his months of preaching and writing come to an abrupt halt as the political landscape changes. The following year he relocates to Austria, where officials arrest him along with

## ANABAPTISTS TURN BACK TO BIBLICAL BASICS

The Reformers aimed to reform the old Church by the Bible; the Radicals attempted to build a new Church from the Bible. The former maintained the historic continuity; the latter went directly to the apostolic age, and ignored the intervening centuries as an apostasy. The Reformers founded a popular state-church, including all citizens with their families; the Anabaptists organized on the voluntary principle select congregations of baptized believers, separated from the world and from the State.

Philip Schaff, *History of the Christian Church*

## AN ANABAPTIST PRAYER FOR COURAGE AMID TORTURE

O holy God, O mighty God, O immortal God, that is my belief, which I confess with heart and mouth and have witnessed before the church in water-baptism. Faithfully, graciously, keep me in that till my end, I pray thee. And though I be driven from it by human fear and terror, by tyranny, pangs, sword, fire or water, yet hereby I cry to thee, O my merciful Father: Raise me up again by the grace of thy Holy Spirit, and let me not depart in death without this faith. This I pray thee from the bottom of my heart, through Jesus Christ, thy best-beloved Son, our Lord and Saviour. For in thee, O Father, I hope; let me not be put to shame in eternity. Amen.

Balthasar Hubmaier

An Anabaptist woman being drowned

---

his wife. He remains in prison until his execution date in the spring of 1528. He is convicted of being a heretic—the very label he denies so vehemently. With his wife pleading with him not to again recant, he is burned in the Vienna town square. Three days later she is executed in true Anabaptist fashion. Fastened to a large rock, she is cast into the Danube.

Hubmaier left behind writings that inspired the Anabaptist movement for generations. Indeed, so influential was his preaching ministry and his many written works that he was condemned as a heretic in 1545, by the Catholic Council of Trent along with the three most prominent Magisterial Reformers, Luther, Zwingli, and Calvin.

### Michael and Margaretha Sattler: Faithful to Death

Born in the German village of Staufen, Michael Sattler (c. 1490–1527) enrolled at the University of Freiburg at a young age and then took vows as

a Benedictine monk, serving at a monastery in the Black Forest. His schooling included a broad theological education as well as biblical studies in Latin, Greek, and Hebrew. Highly regarded by the Benedictines, he was elected to the position of prior.

While yet in his twenties, he becomes engrossed in Reformation ideas. Though living in relative seclusion in a monastery, he is influenced by the new religious ideas swirling around him. As an avid student of Scripture he is most interested in Luther's examination of Paul's epistles. His studies convince him that monasticism is not the path to true righteousness, but his first personal face-to-face encounter with the new teachings comes through Anabaptists, specifically through peasants with both a social and spiritual agenda. During the Peasants' War of 1525, while living in the Black Forest region, Sattler is converted to the Anabaptist cause.

Turning away from his monastic vows, he marries Margaretha, a former nun who has also converted to Anabaptist beliefs. Later that year he defends his position biblically in a series of disputations in Zwingli's Zurich. In hindsight, the outcome for any such public debate is fixed: that an Anabaptist would lose is obvious. But one after another of the young Anabaptist theologians take the bait, only to be caught in the tangle of political determinism. Sattler is arrested and threatened with torture until he recants and promises not to return to Zurich. His expulsion, like the expulsion of first-century Christians from Jerusalem, only serves to spread the message. He journeys as a missionary in exile and baptizes converts along the way. Unlike other early Anabaptist leaders, he maintains close contact with Magisterial Reformers, interacting on controversial theological issues with Martin Bucer and others in Strasbourg.

By 1527 he is one of the recognized leaders of the movement and helps to formulate the Schleitheim Confession, which outlines Anabaptist beliefs, including the concept of a called-out community of believers separated from the world. The confession also lays out a pacifist position, clearly taking issue with the more radical militants. So significant is this document among the growing movement of Anabaptists that Zwingli caustically concedes: "There is almost no one among you who does not have a copy of your so well founded commandments." Not long after drafting the confession, Michael and Margaretha are arrested by Catholic authorities led by Austrian regent Ferdinand. Ferdinand regards the crime of a monk converting to Anabaptism so heinous that he argues Sattler should be drowned without the courtesy of a trial. But other officials, conscious of public opinion, are determined to at least go through the motions of a court interrogation.

Other Anabaptists are arrested along with Sattler, but he alone is charged with abandoning his vows as a monk and marrying a nun. Among the other charges are denial of transubstantiation, rejection of infant baptism, corruption of the Lord's Supper, failure to properly honor the Virgin Mary, and refusal to take oaths. The matter of pacifism also draws criticism; anyone unwilling to fight invading Turks is deemed a traitor. He responds to the charges with biblical evidence, but the judges are not in the mood for a debate. Their verdict leaves no room for compromise:

> Michael Sattler shall be committed to the executioner. The latter shall take him to
> the square and there first cut out his tongue, and then forge him fast to a wagon
> and there with glowing iron tongs twice tear pieces from his body, then on the
> way to the site of execution five times more as above and then burn his body to
> powder as an arch-heretic.

Eyewitness reports claim that even after his tongue is cut out, Sattler continues praying for his enemies to the very end. The following week Margaretha is executed by drowning in the Necker River. The multiple martyrdom of Sattler, his wife, and several followers only serves to spread the word and bring greater attention to the Anabaptist confession that is read and studied in households and conventicles all over Europe.

## Menno Simons: Father of the Mennonites

Recognized as the father of the Mennonites, Menno Simons (1496–1561) represents the Dutch faction of the Anabaptists, though he traveled widely to other regions of Western Europe. He was raised in a peasant family and as a young boy was sent to a monastic school to train for the priesthood. His education included

> *"Out of the ashes of Münster, a new Anabaptist group emerged, led by Menno Simons."*
>
> John D. Roth, Historical Committee & Archives of the Mennonite Church

philosophy, Latin, and Greek. In his late twenties, he was ordained a priest and assigned a parish near his childhood home. In 1531 he accepted a call to the parish in Witmarsum where he had been baptized as an infant. By his own testimony, he spent much of his time in "playing cards, drinking, and frivolities of all sorts."

By the time Menno is transferred to Witmarsum, the Reformation in Germany and Switzerland is well underway. He had studied the writings of the Reformers as well as those of Erasmus, but his study of the Bible, more than anything else, spurs spiritual renewal. His initial concerns relate to transubstantiation, but as he digs deeper he begins to study the Bible and Anabaptist writings on baptism. Infant baptism, he concludes, is not the biblical way. By the late 1520s, he is preaching an evangelical gospel while remaining a Catholic priest.

Menno Simons

Like other Anabaptists, Menno emphasizes the necessity of a conversion experience—an experience of saving faith that is a prerequisite to baptism. His own transformation comes in stages, beginning with his ministry as a priest. In 1525, as he is officiating the Mass, he begins to question whether the bread and wine are actually the body and blood of Christ. Initially fearing that the devil is tempting him, he later becomes convinced the doctrine is man-made. But his actual evangelical conversion comes a decade later.

Menno is not the first of the Dutch Anabaptists. Some of those preceding him were social radicals who gave Anabaptism a bad name. He simply wants to preach what he is discovering in the Gospels and shift the Reformation in a different theological direction. Luther had placed the emphasis on justification by faith alone. Menno, like other Anabaptists, focuses more on the ministry of Jesus—on outward deeds and inner holiness.

In 1531 Menno is forced to decide whether he will continue his Anabaptist preaching or turn back. He is well aware of the Swiss Brethren who have been drowned in Zurich and others who have been executed at the hands of Austrian Catholic officials. Some had openly defied the law. But now he is confronted with a different situation. In a nearby village a "God-fearing, pious hero," Sicke Freeriks Snijder, is executed for the crime of having been re-baptized. Menno realizes that if he does not stop preaching his evangelical gospel he may be the next preacher to be killed. So, although convinced that there is no biblical support for infant baptism, he nevertheless continues to carry out his duties as a priest.

In the meantime, certain groups of Anabaptists are adding authoritarian militarism, visions and voices, and apocalyptic drama to their message. It is this radicalism that brings Menno into the movement, defending Anabaptist beliefs while insisting that the extremists are not true followers of Christ. John of Leiden is the most extreme of these radicals. Revolutionaries in a town close to where Menno serves as priest are drumming up support for John and his kingdom in Münster. Their involvement comes even closer to home for Menno when members of his own congregation, including Peter Simons, his brother, are killed in the uprising. Menno denounces the violence and the claims of revelations and visions, insisting that becoming a disciple of Jesus is above all a pilgrimage of peace and willingness to suffer. With the fall of Münster and its outlying supporting towns, Menno vows to bring stability to an Anabaptist movement.

The decision is difficult: "Pondering these things my conscience tormented me so that I could no longer endure it," he recalled. "If I through bodily fear do not lay bare the foundation of the truth ... oh, how shall their shed blood, shed in the midst of transgression, rise against me at the judgment of the Almighty and pronounce sentence against my poor, miserable soul!" During this time he prays to God "with sighs and tears that He would give to me, a sorrowing sinner, the gift of His grace, create within me a clean heart, and graciously through the merits of the crimson blood of Christ, he

---

### CALLED TO BE A CHURCH OF PEACE

The Prince of Peace is Jesus Christ. We who were formerly no people at all, and who knew of no peace, are now called to be ... a church ... of peace. True Christians do not know vengeance. They are the children of peace. Their hearts overflow with peace. Their mouths speak peace, and they walk in the way of peace.

Menno Simons,
*Reply to False Accusations*

---

would graciously forgive my unclean walk and unprofitable life."

His forthright stance brings threats against him, and he realizes he can no longer appear in the pulpit. After more than a decade of struggle, he commits himself to the cause, resigns his ministry, and goes into hiding. In January of 1536, he leaves behind his salary and security. "Without constraint," he later reflected, "I renounced all my worldly reputation, name and fame, my unchristian abominations, my masses, my infant baptism, and my easy life, and I willingly submitted to distress and poverty under the heavy cross of Christ."

---

### A TRACT ON THE NEW BIRTH

Do you suppose, dear friends, that the new birth consists of nothing but in that which the miserable world hitherto has thought that it consists in, namely, to be plunged into the water; or in the saying, "I baptize thee in the name of the Father and of the Son, and of the Holy Ghost?" No, dear brother, no. The new birth consists, verily, not in water nor in words; but it is the heavenly, living, and quickening power of God in our hearts which flows forth from God, and which by the preaching of the divine Word, if we accept it by faith, quickens, renews, pierces, and converts our hearts, so that we are changed and converted from unbelief to faith, from unrighteousness to righteousness, from evil to good, from carnality to spirituality, from the earthly to the heavenly, from the wicked nature of Adam to the good nature of Jesus Christ.

Menno Simons

---

### ANABAPTIST MOTHER'S LAST WORDS TO HER BABY DAUGHTER

My dear little child, I commend you to the Almighty.... Hence, my dear lamb, I who am imprisoned and bound here for the Lord's sake, can help you in no other way; I had to leave your father for the Lord's sake, and could keep him only a short time. We were permitted to live together only half a year, after which we were apprehended, because we sought the salvation of our souls.... I had to remain ... and give birth to you here in prison, in great pain, they have taken you from me. Here I lie, expecting death every morning.... I must through these lines cause you to remember, that when you have attained your understanding, you endeavor to fear God, and see and examine why and for whose name we both died; and be not ashamed to confess us before the world, for you must know that it is not for the sake of any evil. Hence be not ashamed of us; it is the way which the prophets and the apostles went, and the narrow way which leads into eternal life, for there shall no other way be found by which to be saved. Hence, my young lamb ... read the Scriptures ... concerning the cross of Christ.

Janneken Munstdorp, Antwerp,
"Letter to Her Daughter," 1573

---

Within a year, Menno is ordained an Anabaptist minister, and he soon realizes how heavy the cross will be. There is a reward of five hundred guilders for his capture, but his greatest anguish is that of putting others in harms way. Tjard Reynders, for example, is executed for giving him shelter and taking him downriver to his next hiding place. He travels as an evangelist, seeking to bring together the scattered and suffering believers. Dutch officials are on his trail, but he eludes them. One story in Mennonite lore has Menno seated on top of a stagecoach next to the driver. Armed troops approach and demand to know if the hunted outlaw is hiding in the carriage. Menno leans over and looks down and asks if he is there. The armed men verify the negative response by looking inside, and when they are satisfied that he is not there they ride off.

How he manages to keep eluding the authorities is nothing short of a miracle — at least in the eyes of his followers. After all, he is not traveling alone. His wife Gertrude and three children travel with him. And he stays in one spot long enough to write lengthy tracts defending various Anabaptist beliefs — writings easily understood by artisans and peasants. But the five of them are constantly on the move. Eight years after leaving his parish, he protests that he "could not find in all the countries a cabin or hut in which [we] could be put up in safety for a year or even a half a year." Two of his little ones die while they are on the run, and then Gertrude also dies. Menno continues on in poor health.

His situation becomes even more precarious when authorities rule that anyone charged with even reading one of Menno's tracts is guilty of a criminal offense. Yet his tracts continue to be widely circulated.

Menno's most noteworthy writing is his *Foundation of the Christian Doctrine* (1540). Written on the run, it defines Dutch Anabaptism; and within a few years his followers are being called Mennists or Mennonites. Despite being hunted by authorities, he continues his ministry and dies a natural death at sixty-five, a quarter-century after he left the priesthood.

## Elizabeth Dirks: Teacher, Preacher, and Deaconess

Born into Frisian nobility, Elizabeth Dirks (d. 1549) was reared in a convent. Yet in adolescence, she learns about the courageous martyrdom of Anabaptist Christians and wonders what beliefs would inspire such risk. As she studies her Latin Bible and learns more, she begins to question the validity of monasticism. When her ideas become known, she is charged with heresy and placed under convent arrest. Disguised as a milkmaid, she escapes and finds refuge in an Anabaptist home in Leeuwarden. Here she functions as a teacher and preacher and reportedly serves as the first Mennonite deaconess.

When she is discovered and arrested by Catholic officials in the winter of 1549, her reputation as a leader in the movement has preceded her. Indeed, she is presumed to be the wife of Menno Simons, which she denies, insisting that she has never been married. She is locked in prison, and the authorities demand to know who baptized her and who her teachers and associates are. She refuses to answer, willing only to respond to questions about her beliefs. Interrogated by Catholic clerics, she responds to their questions, often quoting biblical texts in Latin.

"What do you hold concerning our mass?," they demanded: "My lords, of your mass I think nothing at all; but I highly esteem all that accords with the Word of God." And what of the holy sacrament? "I have never in my life read in the holy Scriptures of a holy sacrament, but of the Lord's Supper," to which they responded: "Be silent, for the devil speaks through your mouth." And, what about infant baptism—and your own re-baptism? "No, my lords, I have not been rebaptized. I have been baptized once upon my faith; for it is written that baptism belongs to believers." Are children then damned because they are baptized? "No, my lords, God forbid, that I should judge the children." Is not salvation assured in baptism? "No, my lords, all the water in the sea could not save me; but salvation is in Christ." Do not priests have the authority to forgive sins? "No, my lords; how should I believe this? I say that Christ is the only priest through whom sins are forgiven."

Again they demand, under threat of torture, to know who has baptized her. When she refuses, Hans, her tormenter, employs the screw torture to her fingers and thumbs until her fingernails are spurting blood. As she cries out to God for mercy, he applies the screws to her shins until she is unconscious. When they realize that she is not yet dead, they revive her and tie her to a weight and throw her in the water to drown on a cold spring day in 1549.

The story of sixteenth-century Anabaptists is one of the most appalling chapters in church history. The viciousness meted out to them by Protestants and Catholics alike was beyond the pale. Katherine Zell's words ring down through the centuries: They "accept Christ in all the essentials as we do"; yet they are "pursued as by a hunter with dogs chasing wild boars." Shame. Shame. Shame.

## What if ...

What if Zwingli had been attuned to the Sermon on the Mount and the cry of Katherine Zell for religious toleration and had allowed Anabaptists to go their own way? Did the drowning of these innocent Christians in Zurich give fuel to the fire of the Anabaptist movement? Might evangelical faith look different today if this "cruelest joke of the Reformation" had never occurred?

What if men like Thomas Müntzer and John of Leiden had kept their wits about them and had subscribed to pacifism as did most Anabaptists? Would we even know the term Radical Reformation? Would Menno have felt compelled to join the cause in order to rescue the reputation of the movement? Or, without the burden of being associated with radicalism, might Anabaptists have grown more rapidly?

What if Elizabeth Dirks had recanted and gone back to the convent? Her name is now barely a footnote in history. But her martyrdom in 1549 (four years before Servetus was burned in Geneva), though serving as a deterrent to some, spurred on the movement and inspired others to leave convents and careers behind and join with these persecuted pilgrims.

## Further Reading

Augsburger, Myron S. *The Fugitive: Menno Simons.* Scottdale, Pa.: Herald Press, 2008.

Baylor, Michael G. *The Radical Reformation.* London: Cambridge University, 1991.

Bender, Harold S. *Anabaptist Vision.* Scottdale, Pa.: Herald Press, 1944.

Bender, Harold S., and John Horsch. *Menno Simons' Life and Writings.* Eugene, Ore.: Wipf & Stock, 2003.

Dyck, Cornelius J. *An Introduction to Mennonite History: A Popular History of the Anabaptists and the Mennonites.* Scottdale, Pa.: Herald Press, 1993.

Estep, William Roscoe. *The Anabaptist Story: An Introduction to Sixteenth-Century Anabaptism.* Grand Rapids: Eerdmans, 1996.

Jackson, Dave. *On Fire for Christ: Stories of Anabaptist Martyrs, Retold from Martyrs Mirror.* Scottdale, Pa.: Herald Press, 1989.

Sattler, Michael. *The Legacy of Michael Sattler.* Compiled by John Howard Yoder. Scottdale, Pa.: Herald Press, 1973.

Snyder, C. Arnold, and Linda A. Hubert Hecht, eds. *Profiles of Anabaptist Women: Sixteenth-Century Reforming Pioneers.* Toronto: Canadian Corporation Studies in Religion, 1996.

Williams, George Huntston. *The Radical Reformation,* 3rd ed. Kirksville, Mo.: Truman State University, 2000.

# CHAPTER 14

# The Catholic Reformation

## Doctrine Defined and Mission Worldwide

*On a recent trip to Chicago my husband and I were exploring the city on a Sunday morning and happened on the Madonna Della Strada Chapel—an impressive structure on the Lake Michigan shore of Loyola University. Appropriately named, this particular Madonna had inspired Ignatius Loyola.*

*What I found most fascinating about the chapel is its stained-glass recognition of dozens of church notables, including more than twenty Jesuits, not the least of whom is Ignatius Loyola himself, and the most well-known missionary of the movement, Francis Xavier. But also in the stained glass are the four great Latin Fathers (Ambrose, Jerome, Augustine, and Gregory the Great) and the four great Greek Fathers (Gregory Nazianzen, Basil the Great, Athanasius, and John Chrysostom). In another area of stained glass are depictions of other well-known saints, including Thomas Aquinas, Thomas More, and Vincent de Paul. Here in one chapel is a virtual hall of fame of church history—featuring Jesuits to be sure, but giving a nod to Dominican scholar Thomas Aquinas.*

*Also depicted in stained glass are three nameless Japanese Catholic converts representing thousands of sixteenth and seventeenth-century martyrs. They, together with European missionaries, were killed by rulers suspicious of Christian priests and their religion.*

*As I looked in silence at the windows that Sunday morning, I was reminded of Shusaku Endo's powerfully written novel* Silence, *a story of seventeenth-century Catholic missionaries set in Japan. News that his mentor, a Portuguese priest, has apostatized prompts Father Rodrigues to search him out. In the process he too apostatizes: he tramples on a* fumie *(an image of Christ) to save the lives of Japanese Christians being slowly tortured to death. Where is God in the midst of such suffering? he wonders, overwhelmed with "the feeling that while men raise their voices in anguish God remains with folded arms, silent."*

*For all of us who have known the silence of God, this profound story offers less consolation than understanding.*

> Real history — as opposed to anachronistic morality tales —
> is always more complex than the simple motives we project
> back onto figures quite different from ourselves.
> ROBERT ROYAL

Real history is indeed complex, and we are tempted to simplify it with sentimental anecdotes of great heroes. The story of America's first president, George Washington, is replete with morality tales, as are stories of the saints. And new versions of these tales are offered in this age of political correctness, especially when we project simple motives back onto figures quite different from ourselves. From the apostle Paul and Augustine to Aquinas and Ignatius Loyola, we easily offer anachronistic constructs.

*In fourteen-hundred and ninety-two, Columbus sailed the ocean blue* introduces a long-cherished morality tale. The hero, Christopher Columbus, discovered the New World. For that, Americans celebrate a holiday. Never mind that native peoples had inhabited the land for thousands of years and that Vikings and others arrived before this Italian did. Nevertheless, Columbus is the figure we remember. A more recent morality tale, however, views Columbus as perpetrating a holocaust on the native Indians of the New World. Both tales fail to capture the complexities of Columbus and the age of discovery and conquest he represented. A key figure in the Catholic Reformation, Columbus paved the way for Jesuits and other religious orders to expand worldwide, an element of reform that overshadows other aspects of Catholic renewal. From a western European base the faith spread around the globe. Catholic Reformers in this age of discovery include Bartholomew de Las Casas, Ignatius Loyola, Francis Xavier, Teresa of Avila, and Menocchio Domenico Scandella.

The Catholic Reformation entailed more than "countering" Protestants by affirming traditional dogma and practice. It encompassed renewal and reaffirmation of spirituality, particularly the form of piety represented by holy martyrdom as had not been seen since the early centuries. Missionaries to the New World as well as those who ventured to the Far East and Africa and the South Sea Islands accepted (if not welcomed) the opportunity to follow their Savior in dying to save others. But Catholic Reformation piety was also seen in the mysticism of Saint Teresa and John of the Cross.

In its reform, the Catholic Church was looking to the future. Seeking to move beyond the scandals of the late medieval papacy this was a

---

## PARADE OF HISTORY

With the Catholic Reformation, we see a reaffirmation of church tradition and a procession of missionary monks, merchants, and soldiers sailing to outposts beyond the seas. But this is anything but a glorious parade. In one region after another, converts were slaughtered or decimated by disease and military might. In many respects the devout Catholic Christopher Columbus symbolizes this era. He set the stage for the marriage of missions and colonialism. Today, with virtually no religious reflection, Columbus Day parades are celebrated on October 12 across America.

time for advance. The medieval mindset, to be sure, was alive and well as was evident in the torture and tyranny often associated with the Inquisition and the Index of Prohibited Books that severely curbed intellectual curiosity. But a renewed church built on missionary outreach and worldwide multicultural expansion was the wave of the future. This multifaceted Catholic renewal was underway before Luther proffered his Ninety-five Theses. Growing numbers of faithful Catholics had been calling for changes in the church for generations. With the accession of Pope Paul III in 1523, the path to reform was officially open, though the beginning of this Reformation is often dated at 1560 with the reign of Pope Pius IV, extending to 1648 with the end of the Thirty Years' War. In the years leading up to the Council of Trent, many Catholic officials continued to hold out hope that Humpty-Dumpty could be put back together again — the Western Church united under the banner of Rome. This hope was accompanied with threats and the heavy hand of the Inquisition.

The Inquisition was a Catholic tribunal that investigated those who broke church laws. The most general offenses consisted of openly challenging church dogma, such as the doctrine of transubstantiation, and refusing to recognize the pope as authoritative head of the church. The accusation of heresy was common, though adding local superstitions to one's belief system would typically not cause consternation. Earlier Inquisitions were carried out in medieval times with Dominicans largely in charge. But faced with the Protestant Reformation, Paul III instituted the Supreme Sacred Congregation of the Roman and Universal Inquisition, supervised by cardinals who carried out the duties of investigating and punishing heresy well into the twentieth century.

The Spanish Inquisition, initiated by Ferdinand and Isabella in 1478, more than a generation before the Protestant Reformation, is remembered for the terror it inflicted on citizens, particularly Jews. The first Inquisitor General, the infamous Dominican Tomás de Torquemada (1420–1498), was so ruthless and hated that he reportedly traveled with fifty mounted bodyguards. His name has since become synonymous with fanatical cruelty in the name of the church. Heresy was hunted down, and rumors of such were enough to convict. Death sentences were carried out without the benefit of an advocate or the identity of the accuser. From the late fifteenth to the early nineteenth centuries, more

## THE COUNCIL OF TRENT AFFIRMS SAINTS AND RELICS

The holy Synod enjoins on all bishops, and others who sustain the office and charge of teaching, that ... they especially instruct the faithful diligently concerning the intercession and invocation of saints; the honour (paid) to relics; and the legitimate use of images: teaching them that the saints, who reign together with Christ, offer up their own prayers to God for men; that it is good and useful suppliantly to invoke them, and to have recourse to their prayers, aid, (and) help for obtaining benefits from God, through His Son, Jesus Christ our Lord, who is our alone Redeemer and Saviour.... Also, that the holy bodies of holy martyrs, and of others now living with Christ — which bodies were the living members of Christ, and the temple of the Holy Ghost, and which are by Him to be raised unto eternal life, and to be glorified — are to be venerated by the faithful....

Council of Trent, Session 25

## Sailing the Seas

Most sea voyages prior to the era of discovery were across inland seas such as the Mediterranean or along the coasts of continents. With Columbus came trans-Atlantic travel for merchants, monks, military personnel, and ordinary people fleeing persecution. His remarkable success does not diminish the dangers seafarers faced. Having no knowledge of weather patterns, much less distance or destination or safe harbors, he fearlessly set sail for India, on a westward voyage with three small ships, including the flagship *Santa Maria* and 104 crewmen. After a stop in the Canary Islands, the ships sailed on uncharted seas.

Time was calculated with an hourglass and direction with a compass, both part of navigation necessities for centuries. Speed was gauged by the use of a chip log with a knotted line, thus measurement of speed in knots. The ships' speed averaged slightly more than a jogging rate of six miles an hour. But at 150 miles a day, the voyage took little over a month. The crew worked four-hour shifts. Sleeping quarters were cramped

The Santa Maria

Columbus and the discovery of America

### SEA SERPENTS THAT SWALLOWED SHIPS

Life for the common seaman aboard the Columbus voyages of discovery was fraught with peril and hardship, both real and imagined.... Sailors of that day also feared attacks by sea serpents that could swallow ships whole, whirlpools from which there would be no return and, a far more earthly and likely threat, running out of water and food before land could be reached. In fact, had there been no New World on the way to the East, which was Columbus' original objective, his crew would probably have run out of provisions before reaching their destination, the distance of the East being far greater than had been estimated by Columbus.

Henry Ramsager,
"Early Ocean Voyages"

## A Boy and a Palm Sunday Parade

Christopher Columbus arrived in Seville on Palm Sunday, March 31, 1493. In his entourage marched seven Taino Indians captured in the Caribbean. Dressed in their native feathers and fishbone and gold ornaments, they drew curious stares from the gawking onlookers, as much impressed by the parrots as the strange "Indians." Young Bartolomé de las Casas, then eight years old, witnessed the procession into the city. It was the most exciting event of his life.... Change came about slowly in the medieval world. But the first voyage of Columbus detonated an explosion of knowledge that would transform the world. And young Bartholomew was there.

Lawrence A. Clayton, "The Boy in Seville"

except for a small private cabin for Columbus, though he often went for days without sleep. Indeed, life aboard ship was grim, storms and disease being the greatest dangers. Feeding the crew was a challenge. After the supply of fresh fruit was consumed, the one hot meal a day consisted of salted meat, cheese, dry biscuits, and occasionally fresh fish. Except for rainy days, the cook and his crew prepared the meal on deck over an open fire secured in a box of sand.

While some captains paid little heed to religious services, Columbus was not one of them. He insisted that the day begin with recitation of prayers and hymns and that the day also close with a religious service.

than three hundred thousand were burned at the stake and hundreds of thousands more were imprisoned and tortured.

Closely connected with the Inquisition was the Index of Prohibited Books — first issued by Pope Paul IV in 1559 to designate books that Catholics were forbidden to read. The list was long and included some seventy-five percent of the books being printed at the time, many of which were written by Protestants. It is no surprise that their forbidden status made them all the more sought after by many Catholic readers.

The Council of Trent, extending nearly two decades (1545–47, 1551–52, 1562–63), officially sanctioned the Catholic Reformation, turning it into a *counter* Reformation. Convened in northern Italy, this nineteenth ecumenical council of

the church stands out as one of the most significant councils, especially in its clarification of Catholic doctrine in light of the Protestant Reformation. Calling such a council had been in the works for decades. But there were pockets of resistance among both government and church factions, most notably papal supporters who feared a pope's authority might be undercut by a council. The question had long been debated in the church: who prevails, a council or a pope? Convening a council, many argued, enhanced the authority of such a body. But if a pope managed to control a council, his power and prestige would rise. So volatile was the issue that fistfights sometimes broke out among delegates.

The decades-long call for reform also focused on curtailing the practice of bestowing church offices to individuals and families for financial gain. In the same vein, the spiritual life of the church was made a priority, with greater emphasis on seminary education for priests. But doctrinal matters were at the forefront. Despite calls by Catholic Reformers to seriously consider theological and biblical matters raised by Protestants, the council took a hard line and strongly reiterated the beliefs most challenged by Reformers: transubstantiation, purgatory, justification by faith plus works, the legitimacy of seven sacraments, and the ranking of tradition alongside Scripture. The council also upheld various practices Protestants rejected: monasticism, clerical celibacy, veneration of saints (especially Mary), and the merit of relics and indulgences—though abuses in the sale of indulgences was censured. Likewise, the papacy retained its power, rejecting demands from the Conciliar Movement that favored council authority and curbing papal power.

During the second series of meetings, Protestants were in attendance at the insistence of the Holy Roman Emperor. However, they were not permitted to vote, a snub that kept the big names away. In the end the Protestant presence made little difference. When the third series of meetings confirmed traditional Catholicism, all hope for reconciliation between the two sides vanished.

The Council of Trent and its affirmation of Catholic tradition is *the* theological event of the Catholic Reformation. But the most far-reaching impact was the worldwide spread of the church's authority. As was true of the later British Empire, the sun never set on the Roman Catholic Church. Protestants were largely confined to land-locked countries; thus, in the sixteenth century the Protestant Reformation had little correlation with colonialism and missions.

The discovery of the New World was viewed in apocalyptic proportions—particularly for the expansion of the Catholic faith. Catholic nations controlled the seas, and every new "discovery" was God's open door for missionaries to pass through. The singular happening of 1492, according to an early Catholic historian and observer, was "the greatest event since the creation of the world (excluding the incarnation and death of Him who created it)."

It is appropriate that Columbus should be credited with this great event that rivaled creation. He was, in fact, a very devout Catholic whose interests later veered toward apocalyptic speculations, as evident in his *Libro de las profecías* (Book of Prophecies). But expanding Mother Church was his early obsession. In correspondence with Ferdinand and Isabella he wrote: "With a hand that could be felt, the Lord opened my mind to the fact that it would be possible to sail from here to the Indies, and He opened my will to desire to accomplish this project. This was the fire that burned within me when I came to visit your Highnesses."

Setting foot on the New World and encountering native peoples confirmed for him the imprint of the hand of the Lord. "As I saw that they were very friendly to us, and perceived that they could be much more easily converted to our holy faith by gentle means than by force," he wrote on October 12. "I presented them with some red caps, and strings of beads to wear upon the neck, and many other trifles of small value, wherewith they were much delighted and became wonderfully attached to us.... I am of the opinion that they would very readily become Christians, as they appear to have no religion." Again, writing to Ferdinand and Isabella, he pleaded for missionaries to come and teach the Native Americans so that the King and Queen might atone for the extermination of the Moors,

North African Muslims who had invaded Spain generations earlier:

> I have no doubt ... that were proper devout and religious persons to come among them and learn their language, it would be an easy matter to convert them all to Christianity, and I hope in our Lord that your Highnesses will devote yourselves with much diligence to this object, and bring into the church so many multitudes, inasmuch as you have exterminated those who refused to confess the Father, Son and Holy Ghost [referring to Moors], so that having ended your days (as we are all mortal) you may leave your dominions in a tranquil condition, free from heresy and wickedness, and meet with a favourable reception before the eternal Creator, whom may it please to grant you a long life and great increase of kingdoms and dominions, with the will and disposition to promote, as you always have done, the holy Christian religion, Amen.

Following his famous crossing in 1492, Columbus made four more major voyages and went on to live a life of accomplishment and controversy until his death in 1506—more than a decade before the tumultuous religious upheaval of the Reformation. He died with his dream of converting the natives unfulfilled, but a quarter-century after his death an image materialized on a Mexican peasant's cape—the Virgin of Guadalupe, a fitting symbol of the appeal of Catholicism among indigenous peoples of the world.

## Bartholomew de Las Casas: Missionary and Humanitarian

Considered by some to be the father of liberation theology (championing justice for the oppressed as central to the gospel), Bartholomew de Las Casas (c.1484–1566) became the greatest defender of the native peoples during the Spanish colonial period. The son of a merchant who had sailed with Columbus on his second voyage, Las Casas received from his father a native boy for a servant. After studying law, he sailed to the island of Hispaniola to serve as the governor's legal advisor. Settling into the affluent lifestyle of the colonists and readily accepting the conventional disdain for the natives, he participated in raids and enslaved them on his plantation. But amid his prosperity and success a change began to occur. His conscience was seared by the decimation of the native population in Cuba. "I saw here cruelty on a scale no living being has even seen or expects to see."

Then, in 1511, he hears a Dominican friar preach against the colonists' cruel treatment of the natives, suggesting that such tyrants dare not call themselves Christian. His words, as Las Casas remembered them, are severe:

> You are in mortal sin ... for the cruelty and tyranny you use in dealing with these innocent people. Tell me, by what right or justice do you keep these Indians in such a cruel and horrible servitude? On what authority have you waged a detestable war against these people? ... Why do you keep them so oppressed? ... Are not these people also human beings? ... Be certain that in such a state as this you can be no more saved than a Moor or a Turk....

While others revile the preacher, Las Casas senses his calling. Joining the Dominicans, he begins advocating for the natives. In that role, he travels to and from Spain, pleading their cause with government officials, sometimes presenting a naïve description of the "noble savage":

> God created these simple people without evil and without guile. They are most obedient and faithful to their natural lords and to the

## CRIMES AGAINST NATIVE AMERICANS

First, all the wars usually called conquests were and are unjust and tyrannical.

Second, we have illegally usurped all the kingdoms of the Indies.

Third, all encomiendas [land grants utilizing forced native labor] are iniquitous and tyrannical.

Fourth, those who possess them and those who distribute them are in mortal sin.

Fifth, the king has no more right to justify the conquests and encomiendas than the Ottoman Turk to make war against Christians.

Sixth, all fortunes made in the Indies are to be considered as stolen.

Seventh, if the guilty of complicity in the conquests or encomiendas do not make restitution, they will not be saved.

Eighth, the Indian nations have the right, which will be theirs till the Day of Judgment, to make just war against us and erase us from the face of the earth.

Las Casas, letter to Royal Council of Indies

Christians whom they serve. They are most submissive, patient, peaceful, and virtuous. Nor are they quarrelsome, rancorous, querulous, or vengeful. They neither possess nor desire to possess worldly wealth. Surely these people would be the most blessed in the world if only they worshipped the true God.

As part of his humanitarian outreach, he proposes the establishment of a safe haven for native Indians in Venezuela, with agricultural tracts, churches, and hospitals. Here native people would work alongside colonists at fair wages. But the publication of his plan backfires, and his opponents become even more militant in their aggression. Yet he perseveres in his evangelistic outreach, and his legal battles in support of the native peoples result in the New Laws enacted for their protection.

In 1544 he is appointed Bishop of Chiapas, an impoverished region in southern Mexico. Most of the Spanish planters there blame him for the New Laws, convinced they will ruin the plantation economy. When they ignore the laws, he orders his priests to deny them absolution. The battle lines are drawn. In fact, many of his own priests defy him, and his life is threatened. After three years he gives up his bishopric, discouraged and defeated. He returns to Spain never again to sail to the New World.

But the New World is ever on his mind as he fights battles in court and as he writes his *History of the Indies.* For four decades this six-volume tome is his obsession, but it remains unfinished at the time of his death. His purpose is to write the truth of the horrors of colonial exploitation of the native peoples, refuting the false accounts of others. In his eighties, shortly before his death, he writes a letter to Pope Pius V, condemning the ill-treatment of the indigenous people, one last time pleading their cause.

## Ignatius Loyola: Founder of the Jesuits

A small boy when Columbus first set sail, Ignatius Loyola (1491–1556) grew up in a world filled with possibility and exploding with geographical and mechanical discoveries. As the founder of the Society of Jesus—known simply as the Jesuits—he was one of the premier figures of the sixteenth century. Others had formed religious orders before, but his was a militaristic missionary organization demanding strict discipline and loyalty. He set the pace for Catholic outreach worldwide, and before he died there were Jesuits scattered across Europe and serving in outposts as remote as India, Japan, and Brazil.

Born into nobility in the Basque country of Spain, Loyola was schooled in the Spanish court and steeped in military training and the art of chivalry and courtly love. In his free time, he gambled and caroused with friends: "[I was] a man given to the vanities of the world, whose chief delight consisted in martial exercises, with a great vain desire to win renown." But the excitement of training soon turned into the horrors of war. Spanish troops were called up to defend Pamplona against French invaders. He is caught in the crossfire, and his shin is shattered by a cannonball. He endures excruciating primitive surgery with no anesthetic, leaving him with constant pain and a lifelong limp.

Now in his early thirties, he spends his time while recuperating reading biographies, including *Stories of the Saints* and *Life of Christ*. He is particularly impressed by the lives of two monastic leaders who founded religious orders. "What if I should do great things for God like St. Francis and St. Dominic?" he wonders. He vows to become a soldier of Christ, living a life of holy chivalry devoted to the Virgin Mary. To confirm his calling, he takes a pilgrimage to religious shrines that ends in a remote village. There he lives in seclusion—tempted, as he later relates, to take his own life. Yet he continues to seek God, retiring to a cave where he prays for hours and experiences visions that reassure him in his faith.

His fame, like Luther's, spreads through his writing, particularly his still-influential *Spiritual Exercises*. Here he lays out a path to piety, reflecting on his own spiritual life and the necessity of absolute obedience to Christ. The exercises begin to take shape in 1522 while he is meditating by the Cardoner River. Speaking of himself in third person, he writes, "The eyes of his understanding began to open and, without seeing any vision, he understood and knew many things, as well spiritual things as things of the faith."

*Spiritual Exercises* does not offer a warm and fuzzy spirituality—and for good reason. Its purpose is to lay the groundwork for devout and disciplined discipleship. The subject matter is designed to fit a four-week retreat, focusing first on sin, followed by Christ's earthly kingship, his passion, and his reign as risen Lord. Exercises challenge the Christian to avoid such sins as idle talk. Also prescribed is meditation on "the length, breadth and depth of Hell," while asking for a "sense of the pain which the damned suffer" and to imagine "the great fires and the souls as in bodies of fire." The exercises are designed not only for those who would become Jesuits but also for lay people.

> "Let me look at the foulness and ugliness of my body. Let me see myself as an ulcerous sore running with every horrible and disgusting poison."
>
> Ignatius Loyola

In the following years he travels and spends time studying theology at various universities, including the University of Paris. Collecting a band of followers, he stirs suspicions and is questioned by the Inquisition. In fact, he is twice briefly imprisoned. In 1534 he and six companions unite together and take vows of poverty, chastity, and obedience to the pope. They intend to evangelize Muslims in Palestine but are stymied by military engagements in the region.

## TWO KEY CHURCHMEN OF THE COUNTER REFORMATION

**Gasparo Contarini** (1483–1542): Like Erasmus, Contarini was a Christian humanist whose goal was to reform the Catholic Church. He worked closely with Philip Melanchthon on a compromise that would bring Catholics and Protestants back together — especially at the Colloquy of Regensburg in 1541. They found points of unity on justification by faith but were unable to agree on the Lord's Supper and papal authority. Even when they could agree, however, colleagues on each side opposed their efforts. Charged with heresy following the Colloquy, he died the next year before any action against him could be taken.

**Pope Paul III:** A reformer pope, he reigned from 1523 to 1534, establishing a reform commission headed by Contarini to shore up the morals of the papacy and the College of Cardinals. The commission sought to stamp out abuses relating to the sale of indulgences, prostitution, bribery, and other corruption that had infiltrated the church.

In 1539 they travel to Rome and receive the blessing of the Pope Paul III, who officially sanctions the Society of Jesus with a bull, *Regimini militantis ecclesiae* (To the Government of the Church Militant). Their absolute obedience to the pope comes in a "special vow" that Jesuits, unlike other orders, are required to obey — vowing to "take upon ourselves, beyond the bond common to all the faithful, a special vow ... meant so to bind that whatsoever the present Roman Pontiff and his successors may command us concerning the advancement of souls and the spreading of the faith, we shall be obliged to obey instantly."

Above all, Loyola is a devoted churchman. Right or wrong, the church is not to be questioned: "We should always be disposed to believe that that which appears white is really black, if the hierarchy of the Church so decides." Distinct from most other religious orders, the Jesuits do not require a monk's cowl or any other religious uniform, nor are daily liturgies or fasting or penance part of the religious routine. They follow the *Spiritual Exercises*, with its focus on an intense period of prayer and meditation. Unlike Francis and Dominic, Loyola does not establish an order for women, even though they are clamoring for one. He does, however, donate money for the establishment of the House of St. Martha, which helps prostitutes leave their profession and reunite with their families or join in the ministry.

Missionary outreach becomes the hallmark of the Jesuits as they spread out across the globe from India and Japan to South America, Africa, and French Canada. Loyola serves as Superior General, heading up the vast administrative duties from his office in Rome. Before he dies, he drafts the *Constitutions*, a lengthy and detailed rulebook that clearly differentiates Jesuits from the other monastic orders that require a strict ascetic life style. Mobility is the key to Jesuit effectiveness. As the church militant, cloistered monasticism simply is not their way of serving Jesus. By the time of his death in 1556, there are more than a thousand Jesuits, and within decades the membership exceeds ten thousand.

### Francis Xavier: Jesuit Missionary Hero

The most ardent follower of Ignatius Loyola and one of his first six companions was Francis

Xavier (1506–1552). Known primarily through his letter writing, he served as a missionary in India and later in the Far East, where his ministry in Japan met with harsh resistance. Like his mentor, he was born into Basque nobility. Unlike Ignatius, however, he associated for a time with a small group of Protestants who were risking their lives to spread the Reformation message. He contemplated joining them—that is, until he encountered the dynamic personal magnetism of Loyola. Soon Xavier joined with Loyola, turning his back not only on the Protestants but also on his family's wealth and the promising career he might have had as a church administrator.

His assignment to serve in cross-cultural evangelism came when he was singled out to replace another Jesuit who had become ill. Arriving in the port of Goa in India in 1542, he was astonished by the European corruption that permeated the city. Yet he and his companions, with no language training, visited prisons and leper colonies and recited the most basic tenets of the gospel. Ringing a bell as they walked the streets, they announced their services while singing their message in catchy tunes. But few showed interest. Xavier soon realized that the best way to evangelize was to focus on children who are more easily swayed than their elders.

But Goa, he is convinced, is not a suitable location for a mission. The corrupt westernized society with its mix of Muslims and Jews is too much like back home. When his preaching fails to stir the hearts of his hearers, he sends word to the King of Portugal, pleading that the strong arm of the Inquisition force the people to become good Catholics. Frustrated by the hopelessness of the situation, he leaves the area: "I want to be where there are . . . out-and-out pagans." He finds his "out-and-out pagans" among the impoverished Hindu pearl fishermen

Miracles of St. Francis Xavier

further south along the coast. Their response to Christianity depends primarily on caste. High-caste Brahmans, enjoying wealth and cultural superiority, are antagonistic. But low-caste Paravas and outcastes are open to any change that might benefit them. Soon there are crowds of people listening to simple messages and recitation of creeds. Baptisms are so numerous that he complains of being so exhausted from performing the sacrament that he can barely lift his arms.

Pleading with Ignatius for more missionaries he writes, "In these heathen places the only education necessary is to be able to teach the prayers and to go about baptizing little ones who now die in great numbers without the Sacrament because we cannot be everywhere at once to succor them." His focus on children is

## COMMISSIONING CHILDREN FOR MINISTRY

I told the children who memorized the Christian doctrine to betake themselves to the homes of the sick, there to collect as many of the family and neighbors as possible, and to say the Creed with them several times, assuring the sick persons that if they believed they would be cured.... In this way I managed to satisfy all my callers, and at the same time secured that the Creed, the Commandments, and the prayers were taught in the people's homes and abroad in the streets.

Francis Xavier

a two-pronged strategy: salvation and service. "I earnestly recommend to you the teaching of the children and be very diligent about the baptism of newly born babies," he counsels another missionary. "Since the grownups have no hankering for Paradise, whether to escape the evils of life or to attain their happiness, at least let the little ones go there by baptizing them before they die."

Far more fun for the youngsters than reciting creeds, however, are other activities he assigns. "They detest the idolatries of their people and get into fights with them on the subject," he reports. "They tackle even their own parents, if they find them going to the idols, and come to tell me about it. When I hear from them of some idolatrous ceremonies in the villages ... I collect all the boys I can, and off we go

together.... The little fellows seize the small clay idols, smash them, grind them to dust, spit on them and trample them underfoot." But his missionary outreach in India is severely limited by language barriers. After three years among the pearl fishermen, he still has great difficulty with the complex Tamil tongue. Religious services are ritualistic and repetitious, as his own account shows:

On Sundays I assemble all the people, men and women, young and old, and get them to repeat the prayers in their language.... I give out the First Commandment, which they repeat, and then we all say together, Jesus Christ, Son of God, grant us grace to love thee above all things.... [Then] we recite the Pater Noster together, and then cry with one accord, Holy Mary, Mother of Jesus Christ, obtain for us grace from thy Son to enable us to keep the First Commandment. Next we say Ave Maria, and proceed in the same manner through each of the remaining nine Commandments. And just as we say twelve Paters and Aves in honour of the twelve articles of the Creed, so we say ten Paters and Aves in honour of the Ten Commandments.

He is an evangelist at heart—always eager to win a convert. He reports one such opportunity while ministering on the coast of India: "I encountered a merchant who had a ship with

Jule_Berlin/www.flickr.com

Xavier family castle

wares. I spoke to him about the things of God, and God gave him to realize within himself that there are other wares in which he had not traded." The man leaves behind his ship and wares and becomes Xavier's traveling companion. "He is thirty-five years old. A soldier of the world for all his life, he is now a soldier of Christ. He heartily commends himself to your prayers. His name is Joao d'Eiro."

A trailblazer more than a church-planter, Xavier is eager to expand ministry in other regions. From India he travels to Malacca on the Malay Peninsula, where he establishes a mission post. But his sights are set on Japan with the hope of planting the church there. While ministering in Goa in 1548, he had met a Japanese citizen who was certain he would be welcomed in his homeland: "The king, the nobility, and all other people of discretion would become Christians, for the Japanese, he said, are entirely guided by the law of reason."

Arriving in Japan in 1549, Xavier realizes the incredible obstacles he is confronting, not the least of which is the language barrier: "We are like so many statues amongst them, for they speak and talk to us about many things, whilst we, not understanding the language, hold our peace." But within months he reports that people are glad to hear his words, "chiefly when they understand them." When he departs after two years, he identifies dozens of converts. In the succeeding years, missionaries witness even greater results. Within a decade, tens of thousands have been baptized, and by the end of the century the Japanese church numbers in the hundreds of thousands. But storm clouds are on the horizon. Christians begin to face severe persecution, and the church goes underground.

After leaving Japan, Xavier returns to Goa, where he makes plans to establish the Catholic faith in China. But while waiting for permission to enter, he becomes ill and dies barely a decade into his missionary career.

## Teresa of Avila: Carmelite Reformer

The Society of Jesus was not the only new religious order established in the sixteenth century. The Capuchins (named for their unique headgear), a mendicant order founded in Italy in the 1520s, sought to return to the way of St. Francis.

---

### JESUIT MISSIONARIES AROUND THE WORLD

#### Matthew Ricci

Following the footsteps of Xavier, Matthew Ricci journeyed to Goa, where he was later joined by thirteen other missionary monks. After four years they sailed to the Portuguese port city of Macao on the coast of China. Dressing as a Confucian scholar, Ricci identified with the educated classes. Much to the chagrin of Dominican and Franciscan missionaries also ministering in China, he was convinced that Confucianism was compatible with Christianity. In 1601, at the invitation of government officials, he relocated in Peking (present-day Beijing), where he carried out mission work in the shadow of the emperor's palace, supported by a government stipend. He died a decade later, having converted several palace officials. "It is a miracle of the omnipotent hand of the Most High," Ricci reflected, and "the miracle appears all the greater in that not only do we dwell in Peking, but we enjoy here an incontestable authority."

#### Robert de Nobili

While Ricci was seeking to contextualize the Christian faith in China, Robert de Nobili (1577–1656), was conducting a similar ministry in India — becoming a Brahmin to reach that caste with the message of the gospel. He separated himself from the already-existing Christian community in the region and began observing the laws and wearing the garments of the Brahmin caste. Like Ricci, however, his methods were very controversial. Some critics accused him of turning Christianity into just another Hindu sect.

#### Jean Brèbeuf

French Jesuits, under the leadership of Jean de Brèbeuf (1593–1649), entered Canada in the 1630s and began working among the Huron tribe. True to Jesuit mission strategy, they studied and appreciated the worldview of the natives. They modified their theology, avoiding reference to eating the body or drinking the blood of Christ (the very essence of the Mass) so as not to further encourage native cannibalism and blood drinking. Because of the Hurons' positive association with the color red, Jesuits used it freely — especially for the cross. Jesuits interpreted the Hurons' dreams as the Great Spirit's desire for them to convert. According to a grisly story related to a priest by Huron natives, Brèbeuf died at the hands of the enemy Iroquois. After beating him and burning him with coals, they tore out his nails. "To prevent him from speaking they cut off his tongue and both his upper and lower lips. After that, they set themselves to strip the flesh from his legs, thighs, and arms, to the very bone; and then put it to roast before his eyes, in order to eat it." Impressed by his great courage to the moment of death, they drank his blood to absorb his bravery.

The Ursulines were women religious who lived by the rule of St. Augustine while conducting charitable work and fostering education for girls. The Discalced (barefoot) Carmelites arose in an effort to bring renewal to the Carmelites, who had turned away from their heritage of poverty. Teresa of Avila (1515–1582) is the most noted of the Discalced Carmelites and the most celebrated woman of the Catholic Reformation. Like Loyola, she was regarded with suspicion and treated as a heretic by church officials. Yet she was a tireless reformer and mystic whose writings have inspired generations of religious seekers—both Catholic and Protestant.

Catholic Spain in the sixteenth century specialized in spirituality. Religion out-ranked all other facets of life. For Teresa, the Christian faith was as natural as breathing. There were those of her family, however, with questionable Christian credentials. Her Jewish grandfather, pressured to convert to Christianity, continued to hold to his Jewish beliefs and was later condemned by the Spanish Inquisition. Her father assimilated easily into the Christian community; her mother, Beatriz, a devout Christian, passed her piety on to her daughter.

Growing up in good times, she was a lively and fun-loving Spanish lass. A daughter of privilege, she enjoyed dancing, horseback riding, chess, and especially romance novels of chivalry. "So excessively was I absorbed in it that I believe, unless I had a new book, I was never happy," she writes in her autobiography. "I began to deck myself out and to try to attract others by my appearance, taking great trouble with my hands and hair, using perfumes and all the vanities I could get." But she also fanaticized about dying as a martyr preaching to the Turks in Palestine. In fact, at age seven she had run away with her brother to seek martyrdom, only to be spotted by an uncle and brought back home.

Teresa of Avila

Teresa's teen years were marked by the trauma of her mother's death and her own illness, which prevented her from finishing her education with nearby Augustinian nuns. She strived for piety, floundering until she read a copy of Jerome's *Letters*, a volume that affirmed women in monasticism. Determined to keep that tradition alive, she left home at twenty to join a local Carmelite convent. Poor health continued to plague her, however, and during her first decade as a nun she was filled with doubts: "I went through a life of the greatest conflict. On the one hand, God called me; on the other, I followed the world." Following the world, in her mind, was failure to live up to the strictest standards of asceticism. She lamented Carmelite slackness, determined to demonstrate her own devotion to God. She refused to see visitors and reportedly lashed herself "until the walls of her cell dripped with gore."

Her "conversion" comes at age forty. One day while participating in the liturgy, she suddenly comprehends for the first time the suffering Jesus, wounded and dying. "So great was my distress when I thought how ill I had repaid Him for those wounds that I felt as if my heart was breaking, and I threw myself down beside him."

> "When I started reading the [Augustine's] Confessions it seemed to me that I was seeing my own self right there. When I got as far as his conversion and read how he heard that voice in the garden, it was just as if the Lord gave it to me."
>
> Teresa of Avila

In the following years she continues to struggle with poor health. At the same time, however, she experiences ecstatic visions. "Having spent the day in prayer and begging the Lord to help me," she later recalled, "I began the hymn; and while I was reciting it, a rapture came on me, so sudden that it snatched me out of myself.... It was the first time the Lord had given me the grace of raptures. I heard these words: 'Now I want you to talk no longer with men, but with angels.'" The raptures occur with more frequency, and some fear that she has gone mad or is demon possessed. In fact, she wonders if the ecstasies are the result of a "troublesome disease." But she is eager that others find this same mystical union with God by following her meditation program—four stages described as tranquility, union, ecstasy, and spiritual marriage.

The rapture most associated with Teresa is an erotic experience of the love for God. In her *Life*, she testifies of how a seraphim plunged a fiery spear into her heart—to the very core of her being. This leaves her enflamed with love for God. But true love for God is something else: "Let everyone understand that real love of God does not consist in tear-shedding, nor in the sweetness and tenderness for which we usually long, just because they console us, but in serving God in justice, fortitude of soul and humility." Her ideal of justice, fortitude, and humility corresponds with her determination to reform Carmelite houses and to establish new ones throughout Spain. No more laxity and easy living for the nuns. Aided by her strong will and charismatic personality, she gains a following; and in less than twenty years she establishes fifteen new houses.

But her success is met with suspicion. A papal thug sent to investigate concludes that she is not acting properly for her gender. She is a "restless gadabout, disobedient, contumacious woman who promulgates pernicious doctrine under pretence of devotion." More than that, "She leaves her cloisters against the orders of her superiors, contrary to the decrees of the Council of Trent." Worse yet, "she is ambitious and teaches theology as if she were a doctor of the church in spite of St. Paul's prohibition."

## A GARDEN FOR THE LORD

A beginner in prayer must look on himself as one setting out to make a garden for his Lord's pleasure on most unfruitful soil which abounds in weeds. His Majesty roots up the weeds and will put in good plants instead. Let us reckon that this is already done when a soul decides to practice prayer and has begun to do so. We have, then, as good gardeners, with God's help to make these plants grow, and to water them carefully so that they will not die, but produce flowers which give out a good smell, to delight this Lord of ours. Then he will often come to take his pleasure in this garden and enjoy these virtues.

Teresa of Avila, *The Interior Castle*

## JOHN OF THE CROSS

A Carmelite reformer, John of the Cross (1542–1591) was in his twenties when he came under the sway of Teresa, who was then old enough to be his mother. Opposition to his efforts to reform the Carmelites led to his arrest, and with no trial he was held in a dungeon and tortured until he escaped several months later. One step ahead of Inquisitors he carried on with the work. He is most known for *The Dark Night of the Soul*, identifying various depths of darkness that lead to perfect union with God. A painful journey, this "spiritual night is the portion of very few." It is not available to the spiritually lazy or those who do not truly seek it and for good reason. The danger is so extreme that the seeker might in the process deny the faith: "Thinking that they are spiritually ruined, and that God has forsaken them … [they may] fall away, and abandon the right road." The key to finding God in darkness is detachment from possessions, family, education, and any interests that distract from total emersion in God.

Teresa feared she would be imprisoned even as her dear friend John of the Cross had been, but the pope rules in her favor and she is permitted to continue her itinerant work of reforming convents. The pope is particularly impressed with her work in reclaiming Protestants to the Catholic faith — ridding Spain of the "mischief and ravages those Lutherans had wrought in France." She regards the Protestant Reformation as a grave threat to true religion: "Had I a thousand lives," she vows, "I would give them all to save a single one of the many souls which were going to perdition."

Teresa's legacy involves more than her active public ministry. In 1562 she published her *Life*, a spiritual autobiography; and three years later, *The Way of Perfection*, written primarily for her nuns encouraging them to continue their struggle against the Protestant heresy. Her most important work, *The Interior Castle*, was not published until a few years before her death in 1582. The castle is the soul, and there are seven apartments representing seven stages of growth through prayer, the final and innermost apartment culminating in complete union with God.

Despite having to face the Inquisition and accusations of mental instability, Teresa's reputation was secure at the time of her death, and just four decades later she was canonized. Five years earlier she had been named Patroness of Spain. In 1970 Pope Paul VI bestowed upon her (with Catherine of Siena) the title Doctor of the Church, the first women to be so named. She was specifically honored as the Doctor of Prayer.

## Menocchio: Astrologer, Philosopher, and Prophet

Sixteenth-century religious turmoil is easily associated with well-known popes and bishops and monks and martyrs. But this era also found ordinary lay people jumping into the fray. Literacy was on the rise, and speculation on religious and scientific topics tempted amateur philosophers. Menocchio Domenico Scandella (1532–1599) was one such thinker. In biblical terms, he would not even rank as a minor prophet, but his life adds color to the tapestry of sixteenth-century religion.

His story is told by Carlo Ginzburg in *The Cheese and the Worms: The Cosmos of a Sixteenth-Century Miller*. Living in a village near Pordenone, Italy, Menocchio is a "very poor" laborer by his own testimony. His wife has given birth to eleven children — only seven of whom survive. While plying his trade, he serves for a time as town mayor, ever struggling to support his "poor family." Unlike many of his neighbors, however, he is literate and loves to ponder the great questions of life. And he is not alone: "The porter, the maidservant, and the bondsman," writes an observer, "dissect free will and make hash of predestination." Menocchio debates issues with traveling peddlers, particularly those hawking relics and religious paraphernalia. His beliefs are an amalgamation of biblical stories, pagan lore, astrology, and elementary science.

The Miller

Fascinated by the origin of the universe, he is an evolutionist before his time—and, some charge, an atheist. His basic question is: how did matter arise, and where did human—and divine—life come from? A neighbor testifies: "I heard him say that in the beginning this world was nothing, and that it was thrashed by the water of the sea like foam, and it curdled like a cheese, from which later great multitudes of worms were born, and these worms became men, of whom the most powerful and wisest was God." Boasting that he will gladly present his beliefs to authorities, he gets his chance in 1584. He is hauled off to prison and brought before an Inquisitor. A neighbor testifies: "He is always arguing with somebody about the faith just for the sake of arguing—even with the priest." For his part, Menocchio tells the court:

I have said that, in my opinion, all was chaos, that is, earth, air, water, and fire were mixed together; and out of that bulk a mass formed—just as cheese is made out of milk—and worms appeared in it, and these were the angels. The most holy majesty decreed that these should be God and the angels, and ... Lucifer sought to make himself lord equal to the king, who was the majesty of God, and for this arrogance God ordered him driven out of heaven with all his host and his company; and this God later created Adam and Eve and people in great number to take the places of the angels who had been expelled. And as this multitude did not follow God's commandments, he sent his Son, whom the Jews seized, and he was crucified.

To suggest that God, angels, and the devil had emerged out of the swirl of matter is

---

## JESUS RETURNS AND IS ARRESTED BY THE GRAND INQUISITOR

He comes silently and unannounced; yet all — how strange — yea, all recognize Him, at once! The population rushes towards Him as if propelled by some irresistible force.... He extends His hands over their heads, blesses them, and from mere contact with Him, aye, even with His garments, a healing power goes forth.... A terrible commotion rages among them, the populace shouts and loudly weeps, when suddenly, before the cathedral door, appears the Cardinal Grand Inquisitor himself.... Slowly raising his finger, he commands his minions to arrest Him....

Fyodor Dostoevsky, *The Brothers Karamazov*

controversial. The Inquisition takes him seriously, fearing that he might influence others. Nor is his cosmology his only heresy: "I said that if Jesus Christ was God eternal," he testifies, "he should not have allowed himself to be taken and crucified ... and so I suspected that since he was crucified, he was not God."

As the Inquisition progresses, he tempers his remarks and backtracks: "I have never associated with anyone who was a heretic," he insists, "but I have an artful mind, and I have wanted to seek out higher things about which I did not know." But languishing in prison, he retracts his beliefs: "I have held opinions that were wicked, but the Holy Spirit has enlightened me." Then comes his final plea: "I ask forgiveness and mercy of the most Holy Trinity ... the glorious Virgin Mary ... and also of your most holy and most reverend and most illustrious justice, so that you will want to pardon me and have mercy on me." Yet he is confined to his prison cell for nearly two years.

Finally a free man and back in business as a miller, he serves as a church administrator overseeing parish funds. Unable to keep his opinions to himself, however, he reportedly asks a neighbor: "Who do you think makes the Gospels if not the priests and monks, who have nothing better to do? They think up these things and write them down one after another." This time the Inquisitors do not give him a second chance, and Pope Clement VIII fears he is a dangerous heretic. At sixty-seven, he is found guilty and is burned at the stake.

The Catholic Reformation, like its Protestant counterpart, was beset with infighting and controversy. Like the Reformers, Catholics met opposition with brutal force and left behind a mixed legacy. Missionaries sacrificed their lives to carry the faith around the world while church officials banned books and the heavy hand of the Inquisition burned heretics.

## What if ...

What if Columbus had met with disaster and other European sailors met with the same fate? Might the Muslims been the ones to "discover" America? Might they have been more humane toward the natives? How different might the Americas be today under Islamic rule?

What if Ignatius Loyola had not been wounded in battle? He was aiming for a successful and chivalrous military career. How different would Catholic missions around the world be without the Jesuits?

What if Francis Xavier had converted

to the Protestant cause? Might his name today be listed as one of the great Protestant Reformers?

What if Pope Paul III or Gaspero Contarini and their Protestant counterparts had made further compromises? Would they have been able to bring the two sides together?

What if Teresa of Avila and John of the Cross had backed down or been executed before they carried out their reforms and wrote their mystical literature? Have their lives made a difference in the arena of Christian spirituality?

## Further Reading

Brockey, Liam Matthew. *Journey to the East: The Jesuit Mission to China, 1579–1724.* Cambridge, Mass.: Harvard University, 2007.

Broderick, James Patrick. *The Origin of the Jesuits.* Chicago: Loyola University, 1986.

Donnelly, John Patrick. *Ignatius of Loyola: Founder of the Jesuits.* West Plains, N.Y.: Longman, 2003.

Ginzburg, Carlo. *The Cheese and the Worms.* Translated by John and Anne Tedeschi. Baltimore: Johns Hopkins University, 1992.

Gutierrez, Gustavo. *Las Casas: In Search of the Poor of Jesus Christ.* Translated by Robert R. Barr. Maryknoll, N.Y.: Orbis, 1993.

Hardy, Richard P. *John of the Cross: Man and Mystic.* Boston: Pauline Books and Media, 2004.

Jones, Martin D. W., ed. *The Counter Reformation: Religion and Society in Early Modern Europe.* New York: Cambridge University, 1995.

Macnutt, Francis Augustus. *Bartholomew De Las Casas: His Life, His Apostolate and His Writings.* Charleston, S.C.: BiblioBazaar, 2008.

Malone, Mary T. *Women and Christianity: From the Reformation to the 21st Century.* Maryknoll, N.Y.: Orbis, 2003.

Meisner, William W. *Ignatius of Loyola: The Psychology of a Saint.* New Haven: Yale University, 1992.

Starr, Mirabai. *Teresa of Avila: The Book of My Life.* Bel Air, Calif.: New Seeds, 2008.

Xavier, Francis. *The Letters and Instructions of Francis Xavier.* Translation and introduction by M. Joseph Costelloe. St. Louis: Institute of Jesuit Sources, 1992.

# CHAPTER 15

# The English Reformation

## *Royalty Exploiting Religion*

*The English Reformation set the stage not only for the establishment of the Church of England but also for the Church of Scotland and the Puritan movement in its various guises. The era exploded with turmoil and excitement. Today religion in England almost seems to be a relic of the past. In fact, as we traveled through the English countryside a few years ago, my husband and I wondered at times if the Anglican Church might be classified as a vast museum.*

*Our vacation doubled as a speaking and study tour. As part of my research we visited dozens of old Anglican churches in urban settings as well as in small towns and rural areas. We were struck by their beauty — beauty often tempered by disrepair.*

*In London we wandered in the late afternoon to St. Paul's Cathedral for evensong and stayed on for the weekly lecture. In spite of its being presented by Rowan Williams, the archbishop of Canterbury, once a position of great power and prestige, no more than a few dozen worshippers were scattered throughout the vast sanctuary.*

*Our travels also took us to Scotland, where the once-vibrant Church of Scotland has now lost much of its fervor. Founded by John Knox, a sixteenth-century Reformer, its nineteenth-century mission outreach was second to none. I was curious to get a closer look at this fiery preacher — in some ways a male chauvinist of the first order — but we were disappointed to find the Knox home in Edinburgh closed for repair. I have since wondered how present-day Presbyterians feel about their founder.*

*Two miles away from my office in Grand Rapids, Michigan, is the John Knox Presbyterian Church, one of many churches so named. This morning I called Rick, the interim minister, asking him about the man for whom the church is named. Does anyone ever clamor to have the church otherwise identified, I asked, considering Knox's attitude toward women? His response did not surprise me. "I don't think anyone knows anything about him."*

*If you want to study the social and political history of modern nations, study hell.*
THOMAS MERTON

Studying hell is not a bad place to start in seeking to understand the English Reformation. It is a study of social and political history as much as a study of religion. And surely there must be a special place in one of the circles of Dante's *Inferno* for King Henry VIII and others who used the Christian faith as an excuse for just plain wickedness.

The English Reformation is often dated with the decision of Henry VIII to split with the Church of Rome. But nearly two centuries earlier John Wycliffe had laid the foundation for reform in the hearts and minds of the English people. His followers, called Lollards, kept the movement alive, albeit underground. But they were routed out and persecuted and burned at the stake. One of the last, Thomas Harding, was executed in 1532. Earlier, in the 1520s, Luther's writings had penetrated the British Isles as did the writings of Zwingli and other Reformers. Calvin's *Institutes* would also have a major influence on the English church. But the English (and Scottish) Reformation came clearly into focus with the work of William Tyndale, Thomas Cranmer, John Knox, and John Foxe, all of whom were at times both aided and impeded by royals.

The English Reformation, more than other sixteenth-century reform movements, cannot be understood apart from political alliances and court intrigue. Henry VIII captured center stage, but he was not first in the order of accession. Had he lived, Arthur, Henry's brother, would have been king and the English Reformation might have taken an entirely different course. But fifteen-year-old Arthur, Prince of Wales, died in 1502 of a mysterious virus. Married early to solidify political alliances, the young widow was none other than Catherine, daughter of Europe's power couple, Ferdinand of Aragon and Isabella of Castile, whose marriage had united these two principalities into the now powerful Spain.

Ten-year-old Henry attended the wedding in the fall of 1501, after which the newlyweds took up residence in Wales. Then some four months later Arthur was dead. Although Catherine later claimed the marriage had not been consummated, the pope stepped in and abrogated the law of Leviticus ("If a man marries his brother's wife it is an act of impurity.... They will be childless," 20:21), granting Henry a dispensation to marry the widow, now sixteen. How eleven-year-old Henry felt about this arrange-

## PARADE OF HISTORY

A parade marked the beginning of the English Reformation — that is, more specifically, the birth of the Church of England. Thomas Cranmer described the pageantry accompanying the coronation of Anne Boleyn, now the wife of Henry VIII: "All the [water]crafts of London" and "several barges decked after the most gorgeous and sumptuous manner," each featuring "diverse pageants," waited "for the Queen's coming to her barge" and then followed after "unto the Tower," while "trumpets, shawms, and other diverse instruments" were "making great melody" — pageantry so grand, "never was like in any time nigh unto our remembrance."

ment is unknown, but due to wrangling over money on both sides, his marriage to Catherine did not take place until he ascended the throne at seventeen, a mature groom by family standards.

Considering the circumstances, the marriage had incredible longevity—twenty-four years—though Catherine is out of favor long before, largely because she does not produce a male heir who survives infancy. To solve the problem, Henry finds another woman, Catherine's lady-in-waiting, Anne Boleyn. For the next several years he connives to have his marriage to Catherine annulled. His closest aide

Henry VIII

and chancellor, Cardinal Thomas Wolsey, seeks the blessing of Clement VII. But the pope balks, in part because he is a virtual lackey of Emperor Charles V, nephew of Catherine. For his failure in persuading the pope, Wolsey is stripped of his titles.

At the same time, Anne Boleyn is becoming increasingly impatient, refusing to become merely the king's mistress as her sister Mary had been. "Did I not tell you that when you disputed with the queen she was sure to have the upper hand?" she angrily wrote to King Henry. "I see that some fine morning you will succumb to her reasoning, and that you will cast me off. I have been waiting long and might in the meantime have contracted some advantageous marriage.... But alas! Farewell to my time and youth spent to no purpose at all."

With the help of his legal expert, Thomas Cromwell, and theologian Thomas Cranmer, Henry finally rids himself of Catherine. His rationale is that he had breeched the Levitical law when he married Catherine in the first place. Cranmer, a student of Scripture, an admirer of Luther, and a chaplain to Anne, is also a man of ambition who knows how to impress the king. He had contacted Henry as early as 1529, suggesting that divorce should be dealt with by theologians like himself, not by canon lawyers.

## THE ENGLISH REFORMATION AND DOGS

*Pawprints of History* [by Stanley Coren] is not just a story; it is an homage. Historians must look carefully, in the crannies of the past, to find the dogs of yore.... Still, whether or not dogs have their own history, there is no question that they have left their pawprints on ours. Had it not been for timely canine intervention ... Henry VIII might never have founded the Church of England.... [He] wanted the Pope to annul his marriage to Catherine of Aragon, so he sent Cardinal Wolsey to the Vatican to negotiate. Everything was going fine, the story goes, and Wolsey kneeled to kiss the Pope's toe, but, just then, Wolsey's greyhound, Urian (whom Wolsey had, oddly, brought with him), charged forward and bit down hard on the papal foot. This injury put an end to the negotiations, Henry was not granted his divorce, and the English Reformation followed shortly afterward.

Larissa MacFarquhar, "Bark," *The New Yorker*

The king is pleased, and in 1533 Cranmer is named archbishop of Canterbury.

In 1533 Henry passes the Act of Supremacy, declaring himself head of the English Church. All the while, Cranmer is working behind the scenes preparing divorce (more accurately, annulment) papers, even though Henry had, months earlier, already secretly married the pregnant Anne Boleyn. Cranmer informs Catherine in a memo:

> It was thought convenient by the King and his learned Council that I should repair unto Dunstable ... where the said Lady Catherine keepeth her house, and there to call her before me, to hear the final sentence in this said matter. Notwithstanding she would not at all obey thereunto, for when she was ... cited to appear ... she utterly refused the same, saying that inasmuch as her cause was before the Pope she would have none other judge.

Catherine had overlooked Henry's affairs in the past, but an annulment and remarriage would risk their daughter Mary's chance of becoming queen. As it turned out, Mary (later saddled with the label "Bloody Mary") would indeed become queen, her reign sandwiched between those of two younger half-siblings, Edward and Elizabeth. Henry would go on to rid himself of one wife after another. Anne Boleyn, too wily to be merely exiled from court, was beheaded. But her daughter Elizabeth would go on to set apart the English Church as truly distinct from Catholicism.

With Henry's break from Rome, the English

## THE ANGUISH OF A SCORNED WIFE

My tribulations are so great, my life so disturbed by the plans daily invented to further the king's wicked intention, the surprises which the king gives me, with certain persons of his council, are so mortal, and my treatment is what God knows, that it is enough to shorten ten lives, much more mine.

Catherine of Aragon to
Charles V, November 1531

Reformation was officially underway. But he remained a Catholic at heart. In fact, much earlier Pope Leo X had given Henry the title "Defender of the Faith" for his fierce attacks on Luther. It would be left to Elizabeth to bring about the English Reformation. While retaining much of Catholic high-church ritual and tradition, the Church of England adopted doctrinal changes introduced by Protestant Reformers. There had long been disenchantment with the Roman Church in England. In a popular pamphlet of the day, "The Supplication of the Beggars" (1529) by Simon Fish, the clergy are described as parasites. So in the minds of many there is a feeling of "good riddance" to Rome. But the English Reformation would not progress without pain. Persecution, execution, and ferocious fighting among Catholics and Protestants would be the distinguishing mark of this most political Reformation.

Anne Boleyn

## Sixteenth-Century Divorce

The Reformation influenced every aspect of life in Western Europe. Matters that were once routinely determined by canon law were disputed as Protestants severed ties with the Catholic Church, which had once reigned supreme. The dissolution of marriage was one such matter—one that changed the course of English history when Henry VIII ended his marriage with Catherine.

The ancient Romans under Augustus had made marriage and divorce a matter of government regulation. Before that, such issues were left solely to the family, without state interference. In the generations after Constantine, marriage and divorce were deemed church affairs, and canon law disallowed divorce. Some marriages were annulled for various financial reasons, especially among the wealthy and well connected. Typically, the justification for such a claim was that the spouse was a blood relative. But the church regarded marriage as a sacrament that could not be undone except in certain cases of adultery, and even then there could be no remarriage.

With the Protestant Reformation, however, the rules changed again. Protestants had freed themselves from canon law and did not regard marriage as a sacrament. Martin Bucer, a Reformer from Strasbourg, was the most articulate spokesman against the Catholic position. He wrote a lengthy treatise presenting legitimate grounds not only for divorce but also for the right to remarry:

> The Papists ... oppose themselves to God when they separate [couples] for many causes from bed and board and yet have the bond of matrimony remain, as if this covenant [of marriage] could be other than the conjunction and communion not only of bed and board, but of all other loving and helpful duties.... God requires of [both spouses] so to live together and to be united in body and mind with such an affection as none may be dearer and more ardent among all the relations of mankind.... The proper and ultimate end of marriage is not copulation or children ... but ... the communicating of all duties, both divine and humane, each to the other with utmost benevolence and affection.

John Calvin was likewise open on the matter of divorce and was personally involved in two cases in Geneva. Pierre Ameaux sought a divorce from Benoite, his wife of three years. The matter came before the Geneva consistory (a committee of pastors and lay people). When Benoite boldly claimed to have had many adulterous affairs, the consistory members were not convinced of her truthfulness and judged her mentally unstable. She was twice incarcerated, and Pierre was counseled to work things out with her. After more than a year when he again appealed to the consistory, he was granted the divorce and the right to remarry, with the support of Calvin. The second case involved Calvin's brother, who accused his wife of adultery. For her alleged sin, she was ordered to leave town, and her husband was given custody of the four children.

The allowance for divorce in Protestant realms did not open the floodgates for the dissolution of marriages. Indeed, until the twentieth century divorces would remain very rare. The difference between the Protestant and Catholic positions is that Catholic dissolution of marriage by annulment declares the union void, while Protestant allowance for divorce accepts the fact that a legitimate marriage has been severed. For both Protestants and Catholics marriage rarely rose to the standard Bucer called for.

## William Tyndale: Father of the English Bible

Remembered as the father of the English Bible, William Tyndale (c. 1494–1536) was a scholarly cleric who sacrificed his career and his life for the cause of the Reformation. Cambridge educated, he sought to bring knowledge of the Bible to his fellow Englishmen, most of whom were utterly ignorant of its content. The Catholic Church insisted that only clerics could be trusted with Scripture, but they, according to Tyndale, were not preaching it to their parishioners. "If God spare my life, ere many years pass," he warned a priest, "I will cause a boy that driveth the plough [to] know more of the Scriptures than thou dost." He was convinced that biblical faith would be dispersed more effectively by laity than by those trained in theology. Indeed, he had no confidence in the theological education of his day: "In the universities they have ordained that no man shall look on the Scripture until he be nozzled in heathen learning eight or nine years, and armed with false principles with which he is clean shut out of the understanding of the Scripture."

The *Wycliffe Bible*, translated into English from the Latin Vulgate, was available, but only in scarce hand-copied editions distributed against the law by the Lollards. Tyndale was determined to translate the New Testament from the Greek text and distribute it widely, ideally with the blessing of the church. He would be stymied, however, by Henry's fear of Lutheranism, "the German plague."

When authorities began to harass him, Tyndale in 1524 moved his translation project to Germany. With help from others he completed the New Testament translation in 1525, the first to be printed in English. The first six thousand copies were then smuggled back into England. So threatened were church officials that they confiscated as many copies as they could find and burned them in a public ceremony at St. Paul's Cathedral, at the same time turning the hidden copies into priceless treasures. Realizing that he had been outsmarted, the archbishop of Canterbury devised a new plan. He would purchase copies before they were publicly sold and immediately destroy them—a financial windfall for Tyndale, who used the money to fund a corrected revision.

Tyndale published the first five books of the Old Testament in 1530 and planned to follow through with the rest of the Old Testament. In 1529, Lord Chancellor Sir Thomas More attacked Tyndale, accusing him of heresy.

Besides criticizing his translation for bad word usage, he resorted to name-calling, describing Tyndale as a devil, a fraud, and one "puffed up with pride and envy." Tyndale responded publicly on specific doctrinal issues, including justification by faith:

> In this you see what faith it is that justifies us: The faith in Christ's blood, of a repenting heart toward the law alone justifies us, and not just any kind of faith. You must understand this therefore, so that you may see to come out of More's blind maze: that there are many faiths and all faiths are not the same faith. There is a historical faith, without feeling in the heart, through which I may believe the whole history of the Bible, and yet not set my heart earnestly to apply it.... And the faith through which a man does miracles is different than the faith of a repenting heart, to be saved through Christ's blood, and the one is no relation to the other, though Mr. More would have them seem so.

On orders of Henry VIII, Tyndale becomes a hunted man. Thomas More, the legal scholar, argues for his burning at the stake. While hiding out in Belgium, Tyndale is turned over to authorities by a fellow Englishman who had feigned friendship. Arrested and incarcerated in a prison near Brussels for more than a year, he pens a plea for mercy from the governor:

> I believe, right worshipful, that you are not unaware of what may have been determined concerning me. Wherefore I beg your lordship, and that by the Lord Jesus, that if I am to remain here through the winter, you will request the commissary to have the kindness to send me, from the goods of mine which he has, a warmer cap; for I suffer greatly from cold in the head, and am afflicted by a perpetual

William Tyndale

catarrh [runny nose], which is much increased in this cell; a warmer coat also, for this which I have is very thin; a piece of cloth too to patch my leggings. My overcoat is worn out; my shirts are also worn out. He has a woolen shirt, if he will be good enough to send it. I have also with him leggings of thicker cloth to put on above; he has also warmer night caps. And I ask to be allowed to have a lamp in the evening; it is indeed wearisome sitting alone in the dark. But most of all I beg and beseech your clemency to be urgent with the commissary, that he will kindly permit me to have the Hebrew Bible, Hebrew grammar, and Hebrew dictionary, that I may pass the time in that study.

Above all else he desires to finish the translation of the book he so loves. That wish does not come true. He is put on trial, found guilty, and strangled, his body burned at the stake. His last words reportedly are: "Lord, open the king of England's eyes." Thomas More, his nemesis,

## CRIMINAL CHARGES AGAINST WILLIAM TYNDALE

First, he had maintained that faith alone justifies.

Second, he maintained that to believe in the forgiveness of sins, and to embrace the mercy offered in the gospel, was enough for salvation.

Third, he averred that human traditions cannot bind the conscience, except where their neglect might occasion scandal.

Fourth, he denied the freedom of the will.

Fifth, he denied that there is any purgatory.

Sixth, he affirmed that neither the Virgin nor the Saints pray for us in their own person.

Seventh, he asserted that neither the Virgin nor the Saints should be invoked....

had been beheaded a year earlier in 1535 because he had opposed Henry's divorcing Catherine and had refused to swear allegiance to the Act of Succession, making Elizabeth rather than Mary heir to the throne.

## Thomas Cranmer: Theologian and Martyr

Considered the premier leader of the English Reformation, Thomas Cranmer (1489–1556) ranks alongside Luther in Germany, Calvin in Switzerland, and Knox in Scotland as a national religious figure of the sixteenth century. As the archbishop of Canterbury, he played a key role in making liturgy and doctrine conform more closely to Scripture. The *Book of Common Prayer* was largely his project, as were the Forty-two Articles, later reduced to thirty-nine.

Cranmer was born in Nottingham to a landed family, but his future lay outside the ranks of the country gentry. His older

Thomas Cranmer

brother would inherit the land, while he and his younger brother would become clerics. Awarded a fellowship at Cambridge in 1510, he lost funding when he married a tavern-keeper's daughter. However, her death in childbirth brought him back into the good graces of the school officials, and he was readmitted to prepare for clerical ordination. Completing his studies in the lower quartile academically, he was nevertheless appointed a university priest. In this capacity, he was introduced to the writings of an audacious monk from Wittenberg. It was an exciting time. Disputes and discussions broke out spontaneously, especially at the White Horse Tavern, labeled "Little Germany."

Unlike Tyndale, who, in the 1520s was taking a lead in English Reformation, Cranmer's "conversion" was slow in coming. During this decade, Cranmer was ordained to the priesthood and completed his doctorate of divinity at Cambridge. In 1532, because of his close connection with the Boleyns and his scriptural support of annulling the King's marriage to Catherine, Henry appoints him archbishop of Canterbury.

That Cranmer would support the king in his marriage to Anne Boleyn is difficult to understand apart from his being the Boleyn family chaplain. But that he would remain loyal to Henry after Anne was executed is astonishing, were it not for the fact that he might well have been beheaded along with her. When he is first told of the charges of adultery and incest (with her brother), he is incredulous, convinced the accusations are untrue. Yet he does the king's bidding by declaring the marriage to her invalid, as Catherine's had been, and he makes no outward effort to save her life, though he reportedly wept uncontrollably on the day she died. The king, however, is betrothed to Jane Seymour and marries her less than two weeks later. After she bears him a son (Edward) and dies shortly thereafter, Henry marries and divorces Anne of Cleves, then marries and executes Catherine Howard, and then finally marries Katherine Parr.

During Henry's lifetime, Cranmer remained loyal and alive, fearing to speak out against the king's wickedness. But on other matters he was

## THE EVENTFUL YEAR OF 1533

| | |
|---|---|
| January 25 | Henry VIII marries Anne Boleyn in secret |
| March 30 | Thomas Cranmer is appointed archbishop of Canterbury |
| May 23 | Cranmer pronounces Henry's marriage to Catherine null and void |
| June 1 | Anne is crowned Queen |
| June 25 | Henry publicly marries Anne at Whitehall |
| September 7 | Anne gives birth to Elizabeth I |

sometimes his own man. When Henry brought his Six Articles (upholding transubstantiation, clerical celibacy, and other Catholic dogma) before the Parliament, Cranmer initially argued against them. Indeed, he had a very personal stake in the matter of clerical celibacy. The previous year he had married Margaret, the niece of Andreas Osiander, a prominent Lutheran Reformer. She remained in Germany, and the marriage was kept secret—so secret that those who knew he was married joked that he traveled

## A PLEA TO JOHN CALVIN FOR A PROTESTANT "COUNCIL OF TRENT"

Our adversaries are now holding their councils at Trent for the establishment of their errors; and shall we neglect to call together a godly synod, for the refutation of error, and for restoring and propagating the truth? They are, as I am informed, making decrees respecting the worship of the host; wherefore we ought to leave no stone unturned, not only that we may guard others against this idolatry, but also that we may ourselves come to an agreement upon the doctrine of this sacrament. It cannot escape your prudence how exceedingly the Church of God has been injured by dissensions and varieties of opinion respecting the sacrament of unity.... I could wish for an agreement in this doctrine.... You have now my wish, about which I have also written to Masters Philip [Melanchthon] and Bullinger; and I pray you to deliberate among yourselves as to the means by which this synod can be assembled with the greatest convenience. Farewell.

Your very dear brother in Christ,
Thomas Cranmer

March 20, 1552

with her in his suitcase. But when Parliament voted to approve Henry's Six Articles, Cranmer backed down. Despite enemies in the court, however, Cranmer managed to remain in the good graces of the king, and he stood at Henry's bedside during his final moments.

With Henry's son Edward VI on the throne, Cranmer enjoys greater freedom to follow his

## ENGLISH ROYALTY AND THE REFORMATION

**Henry VIII** (1491–1547) defended the church against Reformation ideas so adeptly that the pope named him "Defender of the Faith." Yet he was responsible for separating the Church of England from the Church of Rome. With the help of Thomas Cromwell, he shut down monasteries and confiscated their property. During his reign, both Catholics and Protestants who were deemed disloyal were executed. Also ordered executed were two of his six wives.

**Edward VI** (1537–1553) ascended the throne at nine years of age when his father Henry VIII died. He was influenced by Lord Protector Edward Seymour to turn the direction of the Church of England toward Protestantism. He died of tuberculosis before he reached his sixteenth birthday, leaving a will (believed to have been written by the Duke of Northumberland) excluding his half-sisters Mary and Elizabeth from ascending the throne. Rather, his successor would be Lady Jane Grey (a distant cousin who had lived in the royal court before his father's death), who just happened to be the new bride of the Duke's son. The "conspiracy" to make her queen failed. She reigned for only nine days.

**Lady Jane Grey** (1537–1554) was the same age as Edward VI and grew up in court with him under the supervision of Katherine Parr, his father's last wife. Like Edward, she held to Protestant convictions and would have carried on with the Reformation had she not been unseated by Edward's half-sister, Mary. Forsaken in the end even by her father, she was imprisoned in the Tower of London and beheaded at sixteen, on orders of Mary.

**Mary I** (1516–1558) was the daughter of Henry's first wife Catherine of Aragon. She was twenty years older than her stepbrother and predecessor, Edward VI. Unseating her hated rival Lady Jane, she claimed the throne in 1553, and the following year married Philip II of Spain. A stanch Roman Catholic, she not only reversed the Reformation but also restored papal supremacy. Persecution of Protestants was her pastime. Indeed, there were so many executions that she was labeled "Bloody Mary." On her death from natural causes, Elizabeth I, her half-sister, succeeded her.

**Elizabeth I** (1533–1603) ruled for forty-five years. Daughter of Henry VIII by Anne Boleyn, she reversed Mary's Catholic restructuring and established once and for all the Church of England in a way that offered a balance between Reformed Protestantism and Roman Catholicism. Like her predecessor, she was known for executions, most notably that of Mary Queen of Scots in 1587. In 1588 she led her nation to victory over the Spanish Armada. Any concerns that her father and others may have had about a woman being incapable of wielding power were put to rest during her reign. She expanded the British Empire through commerce and exploration and also encouraged cultural development in literature and the arts. Courted by European royalty, she played the game to enhance her power but did not succumb to the offers of marriage.

instincts and develop a more Protestant-oriented liturgy and theology, particularly through the *Book of Common Prayer.* The first version, appearing two years after Edward ascended the throne, presented a mild Protestant stance. But three years later, in 1552, the volume demonstrated an even greater separation from Rome. The Forty-two Articles, which would become known as the Thirty-nine Articles, also held an unapologetic Protestant slant. Yet his theology offered a balanced perspective on such issues as predestination, accepting the Augustinian view of God's providence in salvation while adding a warning that it not be used to sanction sin or to despair of being elect. God leads and directs, according to Cranmer, but the individual has freedom of choice.

The future looks bright for Cranmer until the death of the young King Edward in 1553, followed by the nine-day reign of Lady Jane Grey.

## THE "GREAT BIBLE"

As archbishop of Canterbury, Thomas Cranmer, with the blessing of King Henry VIII, employed Myles Coverdale in 1539 to publish the first authorized English Bible. Known as the "Great Bible," it was a very large volume that was chained to the pulpit of every church. A key victory for the Reformation, it debuted three years after the martyrdom of Tyndale, who is remembered as "father of the English Bible."

But when Edward's older sister Mary ascends the throne, Cranmer's standing in court quickly changes. He is the one, after all, who declared Henry's marriage to Mary's mother void, making her technically a bastard. Mary had endured an unhappy childhood, and she is not in the mood for forgiveness. A devout Catholic, she is

## RIDLEY AND LATIMER

Along with Cranmer, Ridley and Latimer were the most renowned churchmen burned at the stake by Queen Mary I. Nicholas Ridley (c. 1500–1555) was priest and later a professor at the University of Cambridge, where he had received his master's degree. He argued that the English Church should not be ruled by Rome — that a pope had no more authority than any foreign bishop would have. He later served as one of the chaplains for Henry VIII, and in 1547 he was appointed Bishop of Rochester. In that post he directed churches to discontinue the Mass and replace it with the Lord's Supper. He also worked with Cranmer on the *Book of Common Prayer.* In the early 1550s he argued against John Hooper in a long debate (the Vestment Controversy), taking the stand that vestments were proper wear for churchmen and did not signify unnecessary uniformity with Rome. A more pressing concern was the matter of the impoverished conditions of London's homeless, particularly women and their children. Ridley is also remembered for his encouraging a daily program of Bible memory and family Bible reading. His support of Lady Jane Grey on the death of Edward VI was not forgotten by the new queen. He was sentenced to death.

Hugh Latimer (c. 1485–1555), also educated at Cambridge, is remembered as one of the most celebrated ministers during King Edward's reign. As Bishop of Worcester, he encouraged other ministers to hone their preaching skills and to make Sunday services a meaningful worship experience. He had been imprisoned in the Tower of London as a Protestant heretic in the waning months of Henry's reign. His preaching fame grew during the reign of Edward VI, but after Mary ascended the throne he was burned at the stake along with Ridley on October 16, 1555.

## PRAYERS OF CONFESSION AND CLEANSING

Almighty and most mercyfull father, we have erred and strayed from thy wayes, lyke lost shepe. We have folowed too much the devises and desyres of oure owne hearts. We have offended against thy holy lawes. We have left undone those things whiche we oughte to have done, and we have done those thinges which we ought not to have done, and there is no health in us: but thou, O Lord, have mercy upon us miserable offendors. Spare thou them, O God, which confesse theyr faultes. Restore thou them that be penitent, according to thy promyses declared unto mankynde, in Christe Jesu oure Lorde. And graunt, O most merciful father, for his sake, that we may hereafter live a godly, righteous, and sobre life, to the glory of thy holy name. Amen.

Thomas Cranmer, 1552 *Book of Common Prayer*

determined to reverse the English Reformation and restore the Catholic Church.

When Mary brings back the Old Latin Mass and sets aside the *Book of Common Prayer*, Cranmer strongly protests. He is arrested, tried, and sentenced to death. But executing him is too easy. He languishes in prison and lives on to agonize over the burning of his fellow Reformers, Nicholas Ridley and Hugh Latimer. Mary and the Catholic clerics are seeking a public recantation. Indeed, so important is his reconversion to Catholicism that he is visited regularly by clerics seeking to wear him down. The tactics work, and Cranmer recants his Protestant faith — not once but a total of five times. He signs a six-point document that denounces the tenets of the Reformation. And even though he gives his allegiance to the "Pope and vicar of Christ, to whom all the faithful are bound subject," it is not enough to save him. It is enough, however, to thoroughly humiliate him, which is exactly what his opponents desire. He is sentenced to be burned at the stake.

On March 21, 1556, after giving multiple copies of his signed recantation to the prison warden, Cranmer is led out to make a final public confession of his Catholic faith. But perhaps realizing the execution would not be stopped no matter what he says, he confesses his sins — particularly the grave sin of recanting the gospel message that he truly believes. He admits that the recantations were signed "for fear of death."

## THE EXECUTION OF ARCHBISHOP CRANMER

Then was he carried away; and a great number, that did run to see him go so wickedly to his death, ran after him. . . . Coming to the stake with a cheerful countenance and willing mind, he put off his garments with haste, and stood upright in his shirt. . . . Then the [Catholic] bishop . . . yet required him to agree to his former recantation. And [Cranmer] answered, (showing his hand), "This was the hand that wrote it, and therefore shall it suffer first punishment." Fire being now put to him, he stretched out his right hand, and thrust it into the flame, and held it there a good space, before the fire came to any other part of his body; where his hand was seen of every man sensibly burning, crying with a loud voice, "This hand hath offended." As soon as the fire got up, he was very soon dead, never stirring or crying all the while.

Anonymous bystander, March 21, 1556

With those words Cranmer goes down in the history books as a martyr to the Protestant faith. He is taken to the stake and the fire is lit. His final moments are memorable. He reaches into the flames with his right hand. "As my hand offended," he confesses, "writing contrary to my heart, my hand shall first be punished." (Another version of the account suggests that he was forced by his executors to burn first the hand that had falsely signed the recantation.) It was a slow, agonizing death as it had been for others—both Protestant and Catholic—who were sacrificed to the flames of religious intolerance.

## John Knox: Fiery Scotsman

Remembered as the founder of the Presbyterian Church, John Knox (1514–1572) was the leader of the Scottish Reformation. By his own account, he was born into a "base" environment near Edinburgh, Scotland. Orphaned when young, he and his brother were taken in by a prosperous family and provided with educational opportunities. In his mid-teens he enrolled at the University of St. Andrews to study for the ministry. It was an invigorating environment. Lutheran tracts smuggled in from the Continent circulated among students and professors. Debates were often heated. Church officials sought to suppress the new heresy with force, executing a Protestant convert during Knox's tenure as a student.

After graduation Knox found employment as a tutor and notary at the Catholic diocese of St. Andrews. But his heart is with the new Protestant movement, and he volunteers to serve as bodyguard for George Wishart, the most outspoken Protestant preacher in the region. Fiery passion drives him as he travels with the preacher, ever ready to defend him with his "two-handed sword." The evangelistic tour comes to a sudden end in December of 1545, when Wishart is arrested and executed a month later. Knox eulogizes his hero: "A man of such graces as before him were never heard within this realm, yea, and are rare to be found yet in any man."

Despite the obvious dangers, Knox is determined to pick up the mantle and carry on with reform. Banned from preaching on Sunday mornings, he offers lectures during the week and soon has a loyal—and angry—following. The execution of Wishart is not quickly forgotten. Indeed, two months after his death Protestant sympathizers attack St. Andrews Castle and murder Cardinal David Beaton, mutilating and hanging his body from a castle window for the crowds to see. Knox claims he was unaware of the conspiracy but insists the slaying is sanctioned by God to punish evil. The attackers barricade themselves in the castle, and

John Knox

Knox, having gone into hiding, soon joins them. Impressed with his courage and his commitment, the attackers invite him to serve as their minister, and he becomes the de facto leader of the Scottish Reformation.

But in 1547 the French Navy forces the rebels holed up in the castle to surrender. Knox and the others are taken captive and incarcerated as galley slaves. Chained at the neck and forced by the whip to row twelve hours a day, he survives despite lean rations and filthy sleeping conditions. But for rescue by the forces of King Edward VI, he might have perished. Knox later reported that during a religious service on board he was ordered to kiss a painted image of the Virgin Mary. He grabbed the "idol accursed" and hurled it into the water as he cried out, "Let our Lady now save herself." Assuming the account is true, it is surprising that he was not hurled into the high seas himself.

After his release Knox moves to England, where he serves in the royal chaplaincy and travels as an itinerant preacher. When young King Edward dies in 1553, however, he is suddenly out of favor at court. Queen Mary, whom he had labeled the "wicked English Jezebel," has ascended the throne. Fearing execution, he flees to France and then to Geneva, where he spends time with John Calvin. From Geneva he moves to Frankfurt to minister to English exiles. In this role he contemplates matters of church liturgy and sets aside the *Book of Common Prayer* (1552) in favor of a new guide, the *Book of Common Order*, a liturgy guide that would become standard for the Church of Scotland.

Not all of the church members approve of this liturgical change, however. Sharp dissension arises, and less than a year later, he departs for Geneva and then back home to Scotland, where he forms a congregation. But fearing a political backlash, he again goes into exile in Geneva, where he spends his time writing tracts against the British monarchy. Calvin wants no part in stirring up a revolution, but Knox is undeterred. He lashes out at the "iniquity and cruelty" of the Catholic rulers. Against Mary Tudor he writes his most vitriolic tract, *The First Blast of the Trumpet Against the Monstrous Regiment of Women* (1558). Comparing her to the biblical Queen Jezebel, he rails: "How abominable before God is the Empire of Rule of a wicked woman, yea of a traiteress and bastard."

The tract backfires. "My first Blast," he concedes, "hath blown from me all my friends in England." Nor could he have imagined that hardly before the ink had dried, Mary Tudor would die. Elizabeth ascends the throne. She is favorable to Protestants generally, but she despises Knox, whom she considers, among other things, a surly misogynist. She refuses to grant him safe passage through England, forcing him to make a longer journey on his way

---

## A BLAST THAT BACKFIRED

For who can denie but it is repugneth to nature, that the blind shall be appointed to leade and conduct such as do see? That the weake, the sicke and impotent persons shall norishe and kepe the hole and strong? And finallie, that the foolishe, madde and phrenetike shal governe the discrete and give counsel to such as be sober of mind. And such be al women, compared unto man in bearing of authoritie. For their sight in civile regiment is but blindness; their strength, weaknes; their counsel, foolishnes; and judgment, phrensie, if it be rightlie considered.

John Knox, *The First Blast of the Trumpet Against the Monstrous Regiment of Women*

home. He returns to a Scotland now ruled by the Regent, Mary of Guise, who is French and Catholic. She is anxious about the growing Protestant influence and is convinced — perhaps rightly so — that Knox and others are motivated by a political more than a religious agenda. Fearing they will be banished, Knox and supporting nobility storm St. John's Kirk, where he lashes out against Catholic idolatry. The church and nearby monasteries are trashed by mobs.

This is one more step toward a victorious Reformation in the eyes of Knox. Mary of Guise is forced to back down, but for Knox revenge has just begun. Increasing mob violence prompts the Regent to call for French reinforcements. When the English throne becomes involved in diplomacy, Knox is not permitted at the peace table. Yet his bitter venom continues. Mary of Guise is at death's door, suffering from dropsy (severe swelling due to accumulation of fluids), though safely ensconced in Edinburgh Castle. Knox responds to the news: "Her belly and loathsome legs [were caused] to swell, and so continued till God did execute his judgment upon her." Soon after her death, the Treaty of Edinburgh is finalized, followed by Acts of Parliament that seal Protestantism as the official religion of Scotland.

Knox quickly assumes ecclesiastical leadership through his preaching and writing and connections with well-placed nobility. But the political fighting continues, especially when the nearly six-foot-tall Mary Queen of Scots (daughter of Mary of Guise) leaves her exile in France and comes to Scotland in an effort to re-establish Catholic rule. But she is opposed by many of her subjects as well as by her cousin, Queen Elizabeth I, in England. Recognizing the situation for what it is, Mary reaches out to the Protestants. She rules amid turmoil and court intrigue until she is forced to abdicate the throne in 1567, having survived husbands

and lovers who died or were murdered. After a lengthy series of house arrests, she is executed in 1587 on the order of Elizabeth — a guarantee that she would never succeed Elizabeth as queen of England.

A contentious figure in public life, Knox is no less controversial in his personal affairs. A decade earlier, when he was preaching in England, he had become a close friend of Elizabeth Bowes. Though a Catholic and married to a staunch Catholic, she contributes to his ministry and corresponds with him regularly on personal and religious matters. "Since the first day that it pleased the providence of God to bring you and me in familiarity," he writes, "I have always delighted in your company." In fact, so intimate is their relationship that it creates scandal. She frequently follows him as he preaches in various places, bringing her teen-age daughter Marjorie with her. A few years later, she and Knox arrange for Knox to marry Marjorie, despite her husband's strong objections.

In the following years, Elizabeth is the one in whom he confides, the one to whom he pours out his heart and shares his struggles. When they are separated, he writes to his "Dearly Beloved Mother.... There is none with whom I would more gladly speak." He addresses her as "dear mother and spouse"; while to his young wife he writes, "Most dear sister ... Be sure I will not forget your company." Elizabeth abandons her husband to accompany Knox and her daughter to Geneva, and when they are separated he expresses his devotion in writing. When Marjorie dies in 1560, he is left with two young children and a mother-in-law who continues to live with him and care for the children. But Elizabeth Bowes is not the only love of his life. The married Anne Locke, mother of two children, also becomes a close confidante as letters indicate: "You write that your desire is earnest to

## PRINTING AND THE REFORMATION

The Lord began to work for his Church not with sword and target to subdue His exalted adversary, but with printing, writing and reading.... How many printing presses there be in the world, so many blockhouses there be ... so that either the pope must abolish knowledge and printing or printing at length will root him out.

John Foxe

see me. Dear Sister, if I should express the thirst and languor which I have had for your presence, I should appear to pass measure."

Four years a widower, he marries again at past fifty. His bride, seventeen-year-old Margaret Stuart, is the daughter of another ardent admirer, a woman who keeps a "prophet's chamber" for him in her home. At his death at fifty-nine, he leaves behind three young daughters and a widow in her twenties.

The legacy of John Knox lies primarily in his foundational ministry in securing the Scottish Reformation. His courage and outspoken support of Reformed doctrine challenged others to follow his example and carry on with the work he left unfinished when he died in 1572. As a preacher he systematically expounded the Scripture for the first thirty minutes, and then made application to the Scottish situation. Known as the "thundering Scot," he was so "active and vigorous" in pounding the pulpit that one parishioner confessed he could hardly take notes: "He made me so to ... tremble, that I could not hold pen to write."

Through his influence the Church of Scotland became more closely aligned

John Foxe

doctrinally with Calvin and the Reformed churches on the Continent than with the Church of England. Like Puritans of New England, the church prohibited secular activities on the Sabbath and Christmas and saints' day celebrations. In the nineteenth century the Church of Scotland sponsored overseas missions, with dozens of renowned missionaries on its roll, including David Livingstone, Mary Slessor, and Thomas Chalmers.

### John Foxe: Documenting Persecution and Martyrdom

The most influential and inspirational book arising out of the flames of the Protestant Reformation was *Foxe's Book of Martyrs*. This book, second only to the Bible in popularity, should be found, according to John Wesley, in every minister's library.

Born in Boston, England, John Foxe (1517 – 1587) grew up in a family of modest wealth and prominence. He began his studies at Oxford at the age of sixteen and completed theological studies with a master's degree nine years later, prepared to become a lecturer in logic, an academic career that would require priestly ordination and celibacy. However, his acquaintance with William Tyndale, Hugh Latimer, and other Reformers as well as his theological and biblical studies turned him away from his Catholic heritage.

Without a clerical position, Foxe struggled to support his bride, Agnes Randall. But with the death of Henry VIII and the ascension of Edward VI to the throne, his prospects improved. Protestant sympathizers were eager to support his ministry of teaching and writing. The Duchess of Richmond served as his patron and for a time provided housing in her castle. She introduced him to other leading Reformers of the day, including Nicholas Ridley, who presided over his ordination in 1550. But when Edward VI died and Mary ascended the throne, the good times for Foxe, his patron, and his fellow Reformers were over. Fearing for their lives, he and his pregnant wife left for Holland and then moved on to Frankfurt and Strasbourg.

Although united by a fear of Catholic rulers back home, the English exiles were unable get along among themselves. From Strasbourg,

## ORIGINAL TITLE FOR *FOXE'S BOOK OF MARTYRS*

*Actes and Monuments of these latter and perillous Dayes, touching matters of the Church, wherein are comprehended and described the great Persecution and horrible Troubles that have been wrought and practised by the Romishe Prelates, speciallye in this Realme of England and Scotland, from the yeare of our Lorde a thousande to the time now present. Gathered and collected according to the true Copies and Wrytinges certificatorie as well of the Parties themselves that Suffered, as also out of the Bishop's Registers, which were the Doers thereof.*

Foxe returned to Frankfurt as the minister of an English church. But soon the matter of liturgy caused the members, in his words, to fall into "the violence of warring factions." Some, influenced by Knox, insisted on following Calvin's church order, while others demanded the continued use of the *Book of Common Prayer*. Though a friend of Knox, Foxe, like most Reformers, was deeply troubled by Knox's "rude vehemency" toward Queen Mary.

## FIVE MARTYRS OF THE ENGLISH REFORMATION

These five martyrs suffered together, January 31, 1556. John Lomas was a young man of Tenterden. He was cited to appear at Canterbury.... His answers being adverse to the idolatrous doctrine of the papacy, he was condemned.... Agnes Snoth, widow, of Smarden Parish, was several times summoned before the Catholic Pharisees, and rejecting absolution, indulgences, transubstantiation, and auricular confession, she was adjudged worthy to suffer death, and endured martyrdom, January 31, with Anne Wright and Joan Sole, who were placed in similar circumstances, and perished at the same time, with equal resignation. Joan Catmer, the last of this heavenly company, of the parish Hithe, was the wife of the martyr George Catmer ... four women ... led to execution, whose lives were irreproachable.... The above five persons were burnt at two stakes in one fire, singing hosannahs to the glorified Savior, until the breath of life was extinct. Sir John Norton, who was present, wept bitterly at their unmerited sufferings.

John Foxe, *Book of Martyrs*, Chapter XVI

## HISTORY THAT NEVER HAPPENED

[Had Lady Jane Grey prevailed] England would have become the most powerful political player in the Reformed camp, with Cranmer a cordial if geographical distant partner with John Calvin. There is a potent symbolism in the fact that it was Cranmer's son-in-law who translated Calvin's *Institutes* into English, and Cranmer's veteran printer who published it. With a Cranmer-Calvin axis, the profile of Reformed religion across the whole continent would have been changed, and with the help and encouragement of Bishop Knox, the Reformation in Scotland might have followed a close path to that of the Reformed Church of England.

That is the history that never happened. Instead, in 1558 Queen Elizabeth had to cope with the consequences of Mary's steadily more successful effort to integrate a traditionalist comeback with the new dynamism of the Counter Reformation....

Elizabeth's solution to her dilemmas was remarkable: quite deliberately, she established a version of the Edwardian Church which proved to be a snapshot, frozen in time, of the church as it had been in September 1552, ignoring the progress made in further changing of the Church of England after that date.

Diarmaid MacCulloch, *Thomas Cranmer: A Life*

With the death of Queen Mary in 1558, Foxe, like many of his fellow English exiles eagerly returned to his homeland. But never again would he enjoy the luxurious patronage of his earlier years. Yet he continued writing and publishing, focusing on the history of persecution and martyrdom from the time of the early church to his own day. In 1563 he published the first edition of his *Book of Martyrs*, which became an immediate bestseller (though it never made him a rich man). His writing, based on trial records, journals, letters, and eyewitness accounts, served as a powerful defense of the Protestant cause while at the same time exacerbating the hostility between Catholics and Protestants. He exonerated Protestants while recording every account of Catholic brutality that came his way. But the book stood as a monument to faith and courage amid persecution, bringing consolation to Christians worldwide.

Although a religious partisan, Foxe was known for a spirit of religious toleration unusual in his era. He petitioned Queen Elizabeth to grant reprieve to several Anabaptists who had been sentenced to death, and some years later he pleaded for the lives of Jesuits awaiting execution.

The English Reformation would continue on into the late seventeenth century with the Puritans and their profound influence on religion in America. The dissatisfaction with the Anglican Church and its failure to carry out reform as Calvin had in Geneva spurred many English Christians to call for purity and separation, thus the terms Puritans and Separatists.

## What If ...

What if Catherine of Aragon had submitted to the demands of her husband to have their marriage annulled? Had she done so, Henry VIII might never have separated from the Church of Rome. Without this first step in the English Reformation, the history of England and America would be very different today.

What if Edward had not died so young, or if Lady Jane Gray's ascension to the throne had not been dismantled? Would the English Reformation have emerged along the lines of the Reformation in Geneva?

What if Queen Mary I ("Bloody Mary") had lived to old age rather than dying of apparent stomach cancer and her hated half-sister Elizabeth had not become Queen? There would be no Anglican Church worldwide, as we know it today. The English "Reformation" might be remembered as a brief failed attempt to separate from Rome.

What if John Foxe had cared more about earning money than spending his days writing his *Book of Martyrs?* Next to the Bible, that book has had a profound influence, particularly on Methodist circuit-riding evangelists and early overseas missionaries.

## Further Reading

Collinson, Patrick. *The Sixteenth Century: 1485–1603.* New York: Oxford University, 2002.

Daniel, David. *William Tyndale: A Biography.* New Haven: Yale University Press, 2001.

Foxe, John, and John N. King. *Foxe's Book of Martyrs: Select Narratives.* New York: Oxford University Press, 2009.

George, Margaret. *The Autobiography of Henry VIII: With Notes by His Fool, Will Somers.* New York: Macmillan, 1998.

Kyle, Richard G., and Dale W. Johnson. *John Knox: An Introduction to His Life and Works.* Eugene, Ore.: Wipf & Stock, 2009.

Loades, David M. *John Foxe and the English Reformation.* Menston, England: Scholars Press, 1997.

MacCulloch, Diarmaid. *Thomas Cranmer: A Life.* New Haven: Yale University Press, 1998.

Marshall, Rosalind K. *John Knox.* Edinburgh, Scotland: Birlinn Publishers, 2008.

Porter, Linda. *The First Queen of England: The Myth of "Bloody Mary."* New York: St. Martin's, 2008.

Selderhuis, Herman J., John Vriend, and Lyle D. Bierma, trans. *Marriage and Divorce in the Thought of Martin Bucer.* Kirksville, Mo.: Truman State University, 1999.

Thomas, Jane Resh. *Behind the Mask: The Life of Queen Elizabeth I.* New York: Clarion Books, 1998.

Weir, Alison. *Six Wives of Henry VIII.* New York: Grove, 1991.

Wilson, Douglas, and George Grant. *For Kirk and Covenant: The Stalwart Courage of John Knox.* Toronto: Cumberland House, 2000.

# CHAPTER 16

# Puritans in England and America

*Theologians and Preachers*

*Puritans. Love 'em or hate 'em. When the term is used as an adjective ("She's so puritanical!") it has negative connotations—though in this permissive age such a stigma can be refreshing. On matters of religion, Puritans truly were capable of being insufferable and priggish. They bemoaned and belabored the sinfulness of others, readily admitting their own faults and failures as well. Today many Christian leaders exhibit a façade of perfection. Not so the Puritans.*

*There was a time years ago when I took a page out of Puritan disciplines and kept a daily spiritual diary. I wanted to be hard on myself and my own sinfulness. Recently, I reviewed some of those entries:*

*February 14, 1981: "Well, here begins a week of a Puritan diary that I assigned for my American Church History class. . . . The study of the Puritans has been good for me. They were highly organized and wasted little time. I need that. Also, they seemed to accept their faith almost blindly, without philosophical doubts. . . . The Puritans were to a degree mystics, with their emphasis on meditation. I think this is more of what I need. . . . One of the strong points of the Puritans was their continual self-analysis which led to self-improvement. . . . If I can do that this week (and the rest of my life), this diary will be a success."*

*My plan to become a Puritan in a week was cut short by a severe case of strep throat. Nevertheless, I continued to keep a daily record of my sins, believing Puritan parameters ought to be mine. Like the Puritans I tend to be hard on myself—beating myself up even when it is unwarranted. Yet I have come to wonder if the continual striving to be more spiritual can at times be little more than self-absorption.*

*I eventually gave up on my Puritan diary, convinced I simply was not and never could be like they were. I smile today when I look back at this period in my life. Unlike some church leaders today who regard the Puritans as spiritual giants, I do not. Their positive attributes were offset by negative ones. We deceive ourselves when we idealize individuals or groups of individuals. Whether Moses or King David, Paul or Augustine, or Puritan divines, the heroes of the faith have feet of clay.*

*One cannot be a good historian of the outward, visible world without giving
some thought to the hidden, private life of ordinary people;
and on the other hand, one cannot be a good historian of this inner life
without taking into account outward events.*
VICTOR HUGO

One cannot be a good historian or even begin to understand the Puritans without giving some thought to the hidden, private lives of ordinary individuals. Nor can one understand them without taking into account outward events. They find honor in work and relish active involvement in the public square. Prosperity is not a dirty word. Community and family life operate like a well-oiled machine. But their private thoughts — particularly as revealed in diaries and letters — show them to be far more than outwardly pious practitioners of religion. They are introspective and believe that their hidden transgressions — known only to God — are as appalling as their public sins.

But Puritans are concerned not only for their own inner lives but also for the sins and private lives of their neighbors — thus their well-earned reputation as nosey busybodies, sniffing out sin. They would not have understood the current convention of looking the other way when the man next door entertains a lady in his apartment while his wife is in the hospital. They take others to task, while reviling their own "manifold sins." Outward appearance is of utmost importance — as their rules and regulations indicate — but purity of the heart is never to be neglected. The Church of England, they insist, is pure neither outwardly nor inwardly; thus the label *Puritans*. Among the most notable Puritans are John Owen, Richard Baxter, John Bunyan, and Cotton Mather.

The era of English Puritanism is generally considered to be the century between 1560 and 1660. This was also the era of William Shakespeare (1564–1616) and the era of the Pilgrims' Mayflower landing on Plymouth Rock (1620). In New England the Puritan period extends to the end of the sixteenth century and beyond, but it had seen its better days long before the death of its last great patriarch, Cotton Mather, in 1728.

As religious reformers, the Puritans are colorful characters. Like their spiritual sage John Calvin, they are consumed with theological matters, though never at the expense of practical piety and daily living. As with Calvin, there is much to commend but also much to censure. When in power, they banish and persecute and execute with the speed and ease of their own

## PARADE OF HISTORY

As church history winds its way into the seventeenth century, the most illustrious parade is the pilgrimage of Christian to the Celestial City, barely escaping the City of Destruction. Bunyan's *Pilgrim's Progress* turns the Christian life into a pilgrimage. The era also features the parade of Puritans — in the wake of persecution — to the New World. Bedtime reading includes *Foxe's Book of Martyrs*. But Puritans, known for their "puritanical" regulations, ban actual parades, which have been a part of popular culture since ancient times.

persecutors. Sin and guilt and self-righteousness are mixed with stories of scandal and intrigue. Selectmen's minutes are filled with petty gossip about local "scolds" who smear each other's reputations. But the gossip turns deadly when reports of witchcraft surface as in the case of Salem in the 1690s.

Puritans are community and family oriented, related by blood and by religious faith. Family activities are the business of the neighborhood as well as the business of the church. The purpose of the family, according to the Puritan divines, is first and foremost to glorify God. God established the family at creation, and the husband and wife are to carry out God's purpose by, in the words of Isaac Ambrose, "erecting and establishing Christ's glorious kingdom in their house." The home, then, is the foundation for all other institutions, and without a well-ordered home, there is no well-ordered society. The family is "a school wherein the first principles and grounds of government and subjection are learned"—a "true image of the commonwealth." Richard Baxter offers a slightly different slant: "A Christian family ... is a church ... a society of Christians combined for the better worshipping and serving God."

The Puritan "focus on the family" sounds like a modern Christian concept. But the severity with which Puritans dealt with disciplinary matters would not be tolerated today. Teachers regularly disciplined scholars by beating them, and severe punishment was routine in the home. In *Help for Distressed Parents*, Cotton Mather counseled parents that "children were better whipt, than Damn'd," though elsewhere he speaks against corporal punishment. A godly family, headed by the father, is one that prays and reads the Bible together and makes religion a natural part of everyday life, punishing sin and praising God.

In comparison to their religious predecessors, Puritans are not necessarily "puritanical" on matters of sex. The Roman Catholic perspective on sex had developed from the teachings of the church fathers, essentially viewing it as an act of the flesh that is sinful except for procreation. This view is challenged by Reformers and Puritans, who shift the focus from procreation to companionship. Sexual intercourse is to be part of the very family life that glorifies God. Indeed, they censure the Catholics, who, according to William Perkins, "hold that the secret coming together of man and wife cannot be without sin unless it be done for procreation of children," insisting rather that sex is not only legitimate but is "meant to be exuberant." Married couples are encouraged to engage in lovemaking "with good will and delight, willingly, readily, and cheerfully."

But their very modern outlook ends on Saturday nights. When Captain Kemble "lewdly" kissed his wife "publicquely" on the "Lord's Day noon," he was humiliated by being locked in stocks. Sarah Chapman and John Lewis enjoyed a Sunday afternoon sitting under an apple tree until they were caught and arrested. Indeed, men are not even permitted to "salute" their wives on the Lord's Day. Babies born on the Sabbath are widely rumored to have been conceived on that day of the week, but there is no punishment aside from raised eyebrows and whispers. Women who give birth out of wedlock are not so fortunate. The letter "A"—a badge of shame designating adultery—marks a fallen woman.

"Unnatural" sexual acts are the most severely punished. In 1646 William Paine of New Haven was executed for having "corrupted a great part of the youth ... by masturbations." Four years earlier, sixteen-year-old Thomas Granger of Plymouth confessed to buggery "with a mare, a cow, two goats, five sheep, two calves and a

## Games, Sport, and Leisure

Among Puritans there were mixed messages on the subject of pastimes, leisure, and enjoyment of life. God is the author of all things, thus even the enjoyment of sexual intimacy in the marriage bed is recognized, if not celebrated. But work—often the hard work of manual labor—is also encouraged and honored. In an era without modern conveniences, time that is not devoted to work is devoted to God, whether in church and community service or in prayer and private devotions. Highly literate, Puritans also spent leisure time reading devotional or theological literature. The romance fiction that Teresa of Avila enjoyed in her youth was forbidden.

But boys and men managed to steal an hour or two now and then for games and sports. Fishing and hunting, both for food and for pleasure, were common pastimes. Also popular were versions of soccer and cricket as well as foot racing, marksmanship, wrestling, and swimming. Table games included checkers, chess, and backgammon. Such activities were not permitted on the Sabbath, however. And Sabbath breaking came with the harshest penalty. A 1671 volume, *Divine Examples of God's Severe Judgment Upon Sabbath Breakers*, includes an illustration of drowning boys—boys who had been playing kickball on the Sabbath near a body of water.

Girls were rarely involved in active outdoor sports. They worked on the farm and in the gardens, but leisure activities—whether playing with dolls or crocheting doilies—related to the domestic side of life. A girl could play on a swing suspended from a tree limb in the backyard but did not have the proper attire to join her brothers climbing in the branches above.

Although card playing in some circumstances was permitted (though not among women), any connection with gambling was a serious affront to God. Nevertheless, gambling of all

### CARD-PLAYING IN CALVIN'S GENEVA

[Francois] Bonivard was widely known to be a passionate devotee of card-playing.... Bonivard's card games, in fact, had led to his own appearance before the consistory.... Bonivard had been accused of organizing card parties to which ministers had been invited. He had defended himself before the consistory by pointing out that there was as yet no general law against card-playing, only a rule against card-playing by the clergy, and he certainly had never invited Calvin or any other clergymen to his card parties. He added that he needed to play cards. He had reached such a ripe and decrepit old age (actually about fifty) that he was no longer capable of the amusements of younger men. All that was left for him was card-playing, and he did not intend to give it up.

Raymond Mentzer, *Sin and the Calvinists*

varieties, including the lottery, found its way into Puritan communities. In fact, Cotton Mather railed against lotteries as "scandalous games," as well as any activity with "popish origins," such as certain kinds of card playing. Throwing dice and huzzle-cap (hurling pennies at a wall) were likewise considered improper entertainment for a good Christian man. Even shuffleboard and billiards were outside the realm of godly, gentlemanly behavior, typically resulting in a fine for those who were caught.

Cockfighting and horse racing were common underground activities among sailors and hooligans, though absolutely forbidden among Puritans. So also was bearbaiting (setting vicious dogs onto a chained bear), a spectator sport enjoyed by Queen Elizabeth I. Her successors, particularly James I, argued that sports made young men fit for battle in the defense of the nation. He issued the *Book of Sports* (1618), instructing them to play ball games and other forms of competition on Sunday afternoons—perceived as a direct challenge by Puritans who insisted on Sabbath rest.

Oliver Cromwell was a great college athlete, according to a contemporary: "During his short residence [at Cambridge University] … he was more famous for his exercises in the fields than in [academics] … being one of the chief matchmakers and players of football, cudgels, or any other boysterous sport or game." Though a Puritan, Cromwell was not nearly as rigid on the matter of sports as most Puritans were. But even the most puritanical church leaders enjoyed their own special leisure-time activities. In sixteenth-century Geneva, Calvin was known to be a bowler—on Sunday, no less. And both Increase and Cotton Mather spent leisure time in Lynne, Massachusetts, at a well-known mineral bath.

turkey." He was put to death, as were the animals. Such "unnatural & horrid" acts demand the ultimate punishment.

Like their earlier sixteenth-century religious predecessors, the Puritans in England are intricately tied to the state, whether governed by a king or queen or lord protector. Their progress and setbacks ebb and flow with the royal line of succession from James I to James II (1603 to 1688), with Charles I and II in between. And sandwiched between these four kings is Lord Protector Oliver Cromwell, dubbed by some the Puritan Moses.

A member of Parliament, as was his father, Oliver Cromwell (1599–1658) commands troops on the side of the Parliamentarians against the Royalists in the Civil Wars stretching a decade from 1642 to 1651. Determined to choose only "godly, honest men" as his soldiers, he is a harsh disciplinarian and an imposing military leader—perhaps best remembered for his 1649 assault on Drogheda in Ireland. Vastly outnumbering the opposition, his forces bombard the well-fortified town and slaughter both soldiers and civilians, including Catholic clerics. By his own testimony, "in the heat of the action" he "forbade" his soldiers "to spare any that were in arms in the town." To his credit, he had sent a message to the royalist governor the day before, demanding surrender: "Sir, having brought the army of the Parliament of England before this place to reduce it to obedience, I thought fit to summon you to deliver the same into my hands to their use. If this be refused, you will have no cause to blame me."

Following the massacre, Cromwell justified his actions as "the righteous judgment of God on these barbarous wretches, who have imbued their hands with so much innocent blood." But the Irish who in 1641 had killed English and Scottish Protestants were not from Drogheda.

A few months before the Drogheda assault of 1649, the Commonwealth had been instituted, headed by the Long (or Rump) Parliament, and in 1653 the Protectorate was launched, under the dictatorship of Cromwell, lasting until 1659 — all of which serves as a backdrop for Puritanism. Although he had no love for Catholics and the "popish" ways of the Church of England, Cromwell was a strong supporter of religious toleration and initially argued for the freedom of groups as diverse as Jews and Quakers as well as adherents of other so-called Civil War sects. He tolerated divergent beliefs but not behavior such as Quaker interruptions of Anglican worship services.

## John Owen: Theologian, Military Chaplain, and University Dean

Considered by many to be the greatest preacher and theologian among the English Puritans, John Owen (1616–1683) is a hero to neo-Puritan Calvinists today, and his books continue to be widely read among that subculture. A man of moderation and religious toleration, he did not suppress Anglican forms when he had the opportunity to do so as others in high positions had done. He preached against persecuting people on religious grounds and wrote tracts, including "Indulgence and Toleration Considered," making a case for broadmindedness within orthodoxy.

One of five children, Owen was born in a village near Oxford, the son of a Puritan minister of whom he wrote: "I was bred up from my infancy under the care of my father, who was a Nonconformist all his days, and a painful laborer in the vineyard of the Lord." A workaholic from childhood, Owen was driven by a sense of responsi-

> "I owe more to John Owen than to any other theologian, ancient or modern."
>
> J. I. Packer

bility to present what he perceived to be the true gospel. He entered Queen's College, Oxford, at twelve and often studied so far into the night he had few hours left for sleep. Before he was twenty he had earned both a bachelor's and a master's degree. In the midst of his theological study, however, his insecurities boiled to the surface, and he found himself doubting whether he was in fact a sincere Christian.

Then, in his mid-twenties, Owen hears a sermon that changes his life. The text is Matthew 8:26: "Why are ye so fearful, O ye of little faith?" His conscience is pricked and he becomes a convinced Puritan. As such, he is no longer esteemed by clerics in the Church of England. Leaving Oxford before his divinity studies are completed, he accepts a call in 1643 to serve as a minister in the town of Fordham. That same year he publishes his first book, a treatise against the Arminian denial of predestination, arguing that this warmed-over Pelagianism denies the sovereignty of God. In 1646 he moves on to serve a congregation in Coggeshall, where he institutes congregational government.

His life now begins to move in a different direction. While serving his local congregation, he is invited to preach before the House of Commons at a critical time — one day after the execution of

King Charles I. His reputation as a great Puritan preacher soars, though he remarks that he would gladly exchange his sermons for the plain preaching of John Bunyan (a dozen years his junior). A second invitation to preach before Parliament catches the attention of Oliver Cromwell. As an astute theologian, Owen is asked to offer theological support for Cromwell's politics and to serve as chaplain for more than ten thousand psalm-singing soldiers assigned to duty in Ireland and Scotland. His assignment includes ministry during the bloodbath at Drogheda, causing him such anguish that he pleads with Parliament to stop the carnage. All the while he remains true to Cromwell.

John Owen

One promotion follows another until he is appointed dean and then vice chancellor of Christ Church College at Oxford University. In this capacity he serves as the campus spiritual leader, preaching long sermons, always with a Reformed slant. Students are required to take careful notes and then preach the sermon to others. Compulsory daily prayers with tutors are also part of the schedule. As dean, he is the chief disciplinarian, calling for an end to fist fights, rowdiness, and general unseemliness.

On one occasion two young Quaker women come to campus, preaching their message of the inner light of the Holy Spirit. When mocked by students, one of them, in good prophetic tradition, begins to disrobe, throwing her garments down and parading through campus proclaiming God's judgment. Doused with water and mocked by students, the women depart, only to return the following Sunday to disrupt the morning service. Owen orders them whipped and forcibly removed from town.

In addition to preaching, teaching, and writing, he continues to be on call with Cromwell and frequently travels to London to handle government affairs. After six years, due to poor health, he resigns his university post. With no pretence of modesty, he sums up his accomplishments at a convocation service:

> Behold your ship, the University, tossed by mountainous billows, is now safe and sound.... Professors' salaries lost for many years have been maintained.... The treasury is tenfold increased.... Reformation of manners has been diligently studied despite the grumbling of profligate brawlers; [my] labours have been numberless; besides submitting to enormous expense, often when brought to the brink of death on your account, I have hated these limbs and this feeble body which was ready to desert my mind; the reproaches of the vulgar have been disregarded; the envy of others has been overcome: in these circumstances I wish you all prosperity and bid you farewell.

In the following years he fills a lesser role at Oxford until 1660, when Charles II ascends the throne and makes life miserable for Nonconformists. Even before this, he had lost favor with Cromwell when he took issue with Cromwell's aspirations of becoming king. Not until Cromwell's son Richard succeeded his father, however, were Puritan Congregationalists (with independent churches) removed from high government positions to make way for Presbyterians.

## SEVENTEENTH-CENTURY ENGLISH ROYALTY

### James I (1603–1625)

Reigning for more than two decades, he succeeded Elizabeth I, the "Virgin Queen," who left no heirs. He was James VI of Scotland before he became the first to identify himself "King of Great Britain" (not merely England), whose unquestioned power was a "divine right," though Parliament challenged him on many points. He is most remembered for sponsoring the translation of the "King James Bible."

### Charles I (1625–1649)

The reign of Charles I was two years longer than that of his father, James I, though it was cut short when he was beheaded by the Roundheads (those who did not wear wigs). Struggling with Parliament over religious issues and taxation, he dissolved that body four years after he ascended the throne. Married to a Catholic (daughter of Henry IV of France), he vented his religious anxieties on the Puritans, many of whom emigrated or were imprisoned during his reign. In 1642 the Civil War broke out between the Cavaliers (the king and nobility, mostly Anglicans and Catholics) on one side, and the Roundheads (Parliament and middle and lower classes, mostly Puritans and other Nonconformists) on the other side. Battles between the Cavaliers and the Roundheads were waged for nearly a decade. The Roundheads, under the leadership of General Oliver Cromwell, prevailed, and Charles was beheaded in 1649.

### Oliver Cromwell (1648–1658)

Though paving the way for a republic, Cromwell's dictatorial rule exceeded that of his royal predecessors. He slaughtered his political and military opponents and dispensed with the Magna Carta. The "Rump Parliament" propped him up until he dismissed its members in 1653, leaving no one in government to challenge him. On his death in 1658, a decade after he came to power, he was accorded a state funeral in Westminster Abbey. But with the restoration of the monarchy in 1660, his body was dug up and beheaded, his head hoisted high on a pole in front of Westminster Hall.

### Charles II (1660–1685)

The Restoration came when Charles II, the son of Charles I, ascended the throne, marking the return of the Stuart line. Charles supported religious freedom and enjoyed popularity with all classes. He is remembered by some as the "Merry Monarch."

### James II (1685–1688)

Unlike the previous Stuart monarchs, who had reigned for more than two decades, James II, the son of Charles II and a Catholic, was removed from the throne only three years into his reign. Anglicans and Catholics had together opposed Cromwell, but England was not prepared for a Catholic king (which also ruled out his Catholic son as a successor). His daughter Mary, however, was a Protestant. Parliament stepped in and offered the crown to Mary, who was married to William of Orange. This "Glorious Revolution" was a peaceful transition of power but surely not glorious for the Catholics. Yet it was a critical era in British history, an era during which Parliament gained the considerable power it still wields today.

With the Restoration of 1660, Owen is further demoted, though he continues to preach to students. His mentor and friend John Cotton had earlier requested that he come to New England, but he had declined. Several years later he is invited to serve as president of Harvard, but again he turns down the offer. Although he never makes the trans-Atlantic voyage, his keen interest in the English colonies never wavers. In fact, he writes a strong discourse against the intolerance and persecution perpetrated by the Congregationalists of New England.

In the mid 1660s, with the Restoration in full swing, Owen is accused of conducting illegal private church meetings in his home, but unlike many others he evades imprisonment. In poor health due to gallstones and asthma, he returns to minister in London in 1665 during the Black Death and remains to serve there in the aftermath of the Great Fire of 1666.

With the reinstitution of the Conventicle Acts in 1670, independent meetings of Dissenters (all those dissenting against the Church of England, also termed Nonconformists) are forbidden. He strongly protests the action, and in 1672 Charles II publishes his Declaration of Indulgence, which grants Puritans and other Dissenters greater freedom. Owen begins offering weekly lectures in an effort to bring together Congregationalists and Presbyterians. He actively courts both Charles II and James II and opens lines of communication between Nonconformists and the king. In fact, Charles II offers significant funds for relief of ministers and others who suffered under laws against Dissenters. Now, enjoying more political freedom, Owen is openly preaching in an independent congregation in London.

In his late twenties, Owen had married Mary Rooke, who gave birth to eleven children, all but one dying in infancy. After Mary's death in 1675 he remarried, and he continued writing to his very last days. "I am going to Him whom my soul has loved, or rather who has loved me with an everlasting love—which is the whole ground of my consolation," he wrote to a friend the day before he died. "I am leaving the ship of the church in a storm; but whilst the great Pilot is in it, the loss of a poor under-rower will be inconsiderable. Live, and pray, and hope, and wait patiently, and do not despond; the promise stands invincible, that He will never leave us, nor forsake us." He left behind a great repository of writings, challenging Arminianism and setting forth his own slant on Calvin's theology of original sin, free will, the atonement, and predestination. Many of these topics were included in his catechism (1667) and developed more fully in his massive volume on historical theology, *Theologoumena Pantodapa* (Biblical Theology).

## Richard Baxter: Small-Town Preacher

As a small-town pastor and writer, Richard Baxter (1615–1691) is remembered as one of the leading Puritan preachers of the seventeenth century. Born in a village in the English countryside, his early education was primarily under the direction of poorly educated clerics. His break came when he was sent to a school directed by John Owen, whose teaching transformed his

*"Oh what a prize: Baxter's Reformed Pastor fell into my hands this morning."*
Francis Asbury, August 19, 1810

theological outlook. At age twenty-three he was ordained, and soon after he is called to serve as an Anglican minister in the village of Kiddermister. Here he crafts sermons that resonate with his congregation of poor loom workers. In fact, church attendance soars, and additional

## SPIRITUAL RENEWAL IN KIDDERMINSTER

To the praise of my gracious Master . . . the church at Kidderminster became so full on the Lord's Day that we had to build galleries to contain all the people. Our weekday meetings also were always full. On the Lord's Day all disorder became quite banished out of the town. As you passed along the streets on the Sabbath morning, you might hear a hundred households singing psalms at their family worship. In a word, when I came to Kidderminster, there was only about one family in a whole street that worshipped God and called upon His name. When I left, there were some streets where not a family did not do so. And though we had 600 communicants, there were not twelve in whose salvation I had not perfect confidence.

Richard Baxter, *Autobiography*

galleries are added as the numbers grow. Preaching "as a dying man to dying men," he has no patience for lackluster sermons. "How few ministers preach with all their might!" he grumbles. "There is nothing more unsuitable to such a business than to be slight and dull. What! speak coldly for God and for men's salvation! Let the people see that you are in earnest. Men will not cast away their dearest pleasures upon a drowsy request." Nor did he neglect home visitation: "We should know every person that belongs to our charge, for how can we 'take heed to the flock of God,' if we do not know them?"

Believing that such visitation was too time-consuming and intrusive, he was initially reluctant to call on families. But after initiating the program he wrote, "I find the difficulties to be nothing to what I imagined, and I experience the benefits and comforts of the work to be such that I would not wish to have neglected it for all the riches in the world. I cannot say that one family hath refused." In the following years he scheduled yearly visits to each of the some eight hundred homes in the parish. With his assistant, he offered catechism to dozens each week, using a standard question-answer format for continued use within the family. Approaching fifty, the bachelor preacher married a woman in her early twenties who heartily joined in the work. When she died

nineteen years later, he wrote: "I never knew her equal." She was "better at resolving a case of conscience than most Divines that ever I knew."

Baxter was twice incarcerated for his Nonconformist beliefs, but he refused to be intimidated and remained active in political affairs. Also high on his agenda was ecumenical unity, a stand that placed him virtually alone among Puritans in his desire to join with all those who subscribed to the Apostles' Creed. A prolific writer, he produced massive volumes, including his *Christian Directory* (1673) on Christian conduct, which ran some one million words. Most often quoted is his classic volume, *The Reformed Pastor*, but he was first and foremost an evangelist, as expressed in *The Saint's Everlasting Rest, A Call to the Unconverted*. Two years before his death at seventy-six, William and Mary introduced the Toleration Act of 1689, protecting him and his fellow Nonconformists from persecution.

### John Bunyan: A "Tinker" of Souls

John Bunyan (1628–1688) is best remembered as the author of the beloved Christian classic *Pilgrim's Progress*. A Baptist minister, he would become one of England's most celebrated prisoners. He was born in Bedfordshire, the son of a tinker who went from house to house repairing broken items. Bunyan later recalled living in abject poverty, his being the "meanest and most despised of all the families in the land." With little formal schooling and "without God," he was an unruly child. "I had but few equals ... both for cursing, swearing, lying, and blaspheming the holy name of God." Indeed, so "wicked" is the young Bunyan that he is afflicted with "fearful dreams" and "dreadful visions ... of devils and wicked spirits," tormented by "thoughts of the day of judgment" and "hell fire."

Later, while serving three years in the parliamentary army, he senses God singling him out for protection, while other soldiers around him die in battle. On leaving the military, still a teenager, he takes up his father's trade and becomes an impoverished tinker. When he marries Mary at twenty-one, he writes: "We came together as poor as poor might be, not having so much household-stuff as a dish or spoon betwixt us both"—except for two critical books belonging to Mary: *The Plaine Man's Path-way to Heaven* and *The Practice of Pietie*. Convicted of his sinful life of worldliness—particularly dancing and sports—he begins attending church. But he is soon "fiercely assaulted with this temptation, to sell and part with Christ." The words "Sell him, sell him, sell him, sell him" keep running through his mind—words, he is convinced, that are coming straight from the mouth of Satan.

Then one day he is startled when he overhears "three or four poor women sitting at a door in the room, and talking about the things of God." He later sees this incident as a turning point in his life: "I thought they spoke as if joy did make them speak; they spoke with such pleasantness of Scripture language and with such appearance of grace in all they said, that they were to me as if they had found a new world." In 1653, at the age of twenty-five, he is baptized and licensed to serve as a lay preacher.

But he is still assaulted by Satan, often through intellectual doubts:

> The tempter would also much assault me with this, How can you tell but that the Turks had as good Scriptures to prove their Mahomet the Saviour, as we have to prove our Jesus is? And, could I think, that so many ten thousands, in so many countries and kingdoms, should be without the knowledge of the right way to heaven; if there were indeed a heaven, and that we only, who live in a corner of the earth, should alone be blessed therewith? Everyone doth think his own religion rightest, both Jews and Moors, and Pagans! and how if all our faith, and Christ, and Scriptures, should be but a think-so too?

But more than doubts, he is plagued with sinfulness—sinfulness deep within his soul: "I remember that one day, as I was travelling into the country and musing on the wickedness and blasphemy of my heart.... At another time, as I sat by the fire in my house, and musing on my wretchedness...." Fortunately for him, a local Nonconformist minister comes to his rescue: "At this time, also, I sat under the ministry of holy Mr. Gifford, whose doctrine, by God's grace, was much for my stability."

With Mary's death six years into their marriage, Bunyan is left alone with four little children. Moving to Bedford, he remarries and begins his preaching ministry. His is a simple style of biblical storytelling, but he is soon drawing crowds, some coming from great distances to hear him. However, the timing corresponds with the Restoration of Charles II in 1660, following the death of Cromwell. After twenty years of freedom of worship, Nonconformist services are banned, and ministers are rounded up and arrested. Thus begins Bunyan's dozen years of prison. His second wife, Elizabeth, only seventeen when they marry, is now alone with young children. Yet she becomes his strongest defender and advocate, going before judges and magistrates and pleading his cause. At the same time, he is distraught:

> The parting with my wife and poor children hath oft been to me in [prison] as the pulling the flesh from my bones ... especially my poor blind child [Mary], who lay nearer my heart than all I had besides; O the thoughts of the hardships I thought my blind one might go under, would break my heart to pieces. Poor child, thought I, what sorrow must thou have for thy portion in this world?

Mary dies before reaching her thirteenth birthday while he is still in prison. Her death inspires the grief-stricken father to begin writing *The Resurrection from the Dead*. Besides writing, he supports his family by making "many hundred gross of long tagg'd [shoe] laces," but the earnings fall far short, forcing his family to depend on "the charity of good people." He could have freed himself by promising not to preach, but he refuses. He tells local magistrates that he would rather remain in prison until "moss grows on his eyelids" than fail to do what God has commanded him to do. Unlike many seventeenth-century incarcerations, his time behind bars is not all misery. In fact, guarded by a friendly small-town jailor, he is permitted some nights at home, and visitors are welcome. Most astonishingly, on occasion he is allowed to preach to those gathered in "unlawful assemblies." But the most precious freedom he enjoys is time for reading and writing.

*Grace Abounding to the Chief of Sinners*, his spiritual memoir of his early life and ministry, is a treasured piece of Puritan writing. With a simple straightforward style, he records events and relationships without overstated religious piety. He confesses temptations even during his Sunday sermon. "When I have been preaching, I have been violently assaulted with thoughts of blasphemy, and strongly tempted to speak the words with my mouth before the congregation." Besides inner struggle, he confronts community gossip: "It began ... to be rumoured ... that I was a witch, a Jesuit, a highwayman, and the like." But more devastating were rumors of sexual impropriety. "To all which, I shall only say, God knows that I am innocent," insisting he was not "guilty of having carnally to do with any woman save my wife."

Bunyan's final years in jail are devoted primarily to writing *Pilgrim's Progress*, the book for which he became famous. He is released, however, before the volume is finished. When Charles II issues the Declaration of Indulgence, freeing Nonconformists from their prison cells, Bunyan wastes no time

John Bunyan in Bedford Jail, 1677

## John Bunyan Discovers Martin Luther

I did greatly long to see some ancient godly man's experience, who had writ some hundreds of years before I was born.... Well, after many such longings in my mind, the God in whose hands are all our days and ways, did cast into my hand, one day, a book of Martin Luther; it was his comment[ary] on the Galatians — it also was so old that it was ready to fall piece from piece.... I found my condition, in his experience, so largely and profoundly handled, as if his book had been written out of my heart.... I do prefer this book of Martin Luther upon the Galatians, excepting the Holy Bible, before all the books that ever I have seen, as most fit for a wounded conscience.

John Bunyan, *Grace Abounding*

in getting back into regular ministry. But he soon finds himself back in jail when Nonconformity is again made illegal. The six-month confinement affords more time for writing.

*Pilgrim's Progress*, quickly regarded as a literary masterpiece, is an allegory that touches the emotions like few other books have, spanning every social class and religious identity. By the time of his death there are nearly a hundred thousand copies in print. Though the book is hardly a page-turner by today's standards, the opening lines pull the reader into the story:

> As I walked through the wilderness of this world, I lighted on a certain place where was a den, and I laid me down in that place to sleep: and, as I slept, I dreamed a dream. I dreamed, and behold, I saw a man clothed with rags, standing in a certain place, with his face from his own house, a book in his hand, and a great burden upon his back. I looked, and saw him open the book, and read therein; and, as he read, he wept, and trembled; and, not being able longer to contain, he brake out with a lamentable cry, saying, What shall I do?

While his fame is spreading, Bunyan continues to preach as an itinerant evangelist. Indeed, he travels so much that he is dubbed "Bishop Bunyan." He also serves as chaplain to the mayor of London. All the while he continues writing, producing in 1680 what some have regarded the first English novel: *The Life and Death of Mr. Badman*. He also writes theologically oriented treatises, including *Differences in Judgement about Water-Baptism no Bar to Communion*. Here he argues that "the Church of Christ hath not warrant to keep out of the communion the Christian that is discovered to be a visible saint of the word, the Christian that walketh according to his own light with God." Baptism, he insists, must not become an "idol."

Amid his growing fame, Bunyan found time for pastoral care, often going beyond the call of duty. In the summer of 1688, he responded to a plea from a young man who was seeking reconciliation with his father. Though having been seriously ill from the "sweating sickness," he nevertheless journeyed to London to serve as a mediator. He was able to bring about the hoped for resolution, but returning home in inclement weather he died at the home of a friend.

## Cotton Mather: Powerhouse of American Puritanism

A fussy, fastidious, and often self-loathing Puritan divine, Cotton Mather (1663 – 1728) represents the third generation of Mathers to play a formative role in colonial New England. Far more than a cleric, he is not only a preacher and theologian but also a scientist, child psychologist, and historian. He is particularly remembered for his involvement in the Salem witch trials. Born in Boston, the son of Increase Mather and grandson of Richard Mather, he has irrefutable Puritan credentials. Richard, like many other Nonconformists, had lost his parish in the midst of English persecution. In 1635 he and his wife Catherine sailed to New England, where he served as a church planter in Dorchester. Here Increase was born and raised.

At twenty-three, Increase married Maria Cotton, daughter of well-known minister John Cotton, who had also fled persecution. Increase later became a Congregational minister at Old North Church in Boston, continuing until his death nearly sixty years later. For some fifteen years, he also served as the president of Harvard College and as the Bay Colony agent to England.

Cotton Mather, named for his maternal grandfather, is given the best schooling New England can offer. Sickly and afflicted with a speech impediment, he learns Latin and Greek as he is learning English. From his "pious, loving, and tender" mother, he learns the spiritual disciplines of prayer, fasting, and daily Bible reading. Twice a year she reads the whole Bible aloud to her nine children. He enrolls at Harvard at age twelve, graduates at sixteen, and three years later completes his master's studies.

His decision to follow his father and grandfathers into the ministry is a difficult choice, considering his stutter, but the sense of calling persists. The first test comes when he is seventeen. His grandfather, the presiding minister, is as nervous as he is. But when he speaks without stammering, he is convinced it is a sign from

## COLONIAL NEW ENGLAND TIMELINE

| | |
|---|---|
| 1620 | The Mayflower lands at Plymouth Rock |
| 1626 | The Dutch purchase Manhattan Island from Native Americans for $24 |
| 1630 | Winthrop and a thousand Puritans arrive in Salem |
| 1635 | Roger Williams, driven from Bay Colony, institutes religious toleration in Rhode Island |
| 1636 | Harvard College is founded |
| 1637 | Pequot War is waged between Puritans and Native Americans |
| 1638 | Anne Hutchinson is banished from the Massachusetts Bay Colony |
| 1639 | John Wheelwright, driven from Boston, founds a colony in New Hampshire |
| 1640 | *Bay Psalm Book*, the first book printed in North America, is published |
| 1650 | The population of the colonies reaches some 40,000 |
| 1665 | An estimated 70,000 in London die of the Black Death |
| 1666 | Much of London burns in the Great Fire |
| 1675 | King Philip's War wreaks havoc on New England, destroying thirteen towns, killing some six hundred settlers and thousands of Indians |
| 1688 | James II consolidates the separate colonies in the Dominion of New England |
| 1689 | The "Glorious Revolution" of William and Mary deposes James II |
| 1691 | Massachusetts Bay and Plymouth unite, the Dominion of New England is disbanded, and the colonies once again maintain separate governments |
| 1692 | Witchcraft hysteria breaks out in the village of Old Salem |

God. Within months he is installed as assistant pastor at his father's church, serving there for the remainder of his life. Having always played second fiddle to his father, he comes into his own amidst divisive circumstances while his father is in London. The occasion is a reported out-break of witchcraft in his neighborhood. Four children from the same family sud-denly exhibit "strange fits." Martha, the most vocal, accuses her mother, who is tried and sentenced to death. So consumed is Mather with the phenomenon that he interviews the condemned woman in the jail before her execution and later brings Martha to live at his home for several months, during which time she is "cured."

Cotton Mather

A few years later, in 1692, ominous reports of witchcraft in Salem Village reach Boston. Regarded as an expert on the subject, Mather is called upon for counsel. Once again children are the accusers and the targets are primarily older women—sometimes village "scolds." The court accepts as fact spectral evidence, that is, testimo-nies of ghostly apparitions in human form and voice. Young girls give fanciful stories of being hounded by witches who demand that they do wicked things. Coerced to confess, some of the accused do so, only adding to the certainty that witches are plaguing Old Salem. By the time the ordeal ends, nineteen of the accused are convicted and hanged. The judge and jurors later acknowledge their rush to judgment and ask the pub-lic for forgiveness.

Cotton Mather, though not directly involved, is accused of fanning the flames. His account, *The Wonders of the Invisible World*, accepts testimonials of witchcraft at face value and sees witches as Satan's agents in an effort to "overturn this poor plantation, the Puritan colony." Although opposed to the death penalty and the use of spectral evidence, he is nevertheless blamed for his role as an expert witness and his part in increasing the hysteria.

For Mather, spiritual formation is every-thing. As a youth he had written prayers for his schoolmates and challenged them to cultivate lives of prayer. He fasted and prayed regularly and recorded progress and pitfalls in his diary. As an adult, he carries out a daily routine of self-examination, beginning the morning by asking himself, "What good may I do this day?" He contemplates a different topic each day. On

---

### SATAN IN OLD SALEM

An Army of Devils is horribly broke in upon the place … and the Houses of the Good People there are fill'd with the doleful Shrieks of their Children and Servants, Tormented by Invisible Hands.… These our poor Afflicted Neighbours, quickly after they become Infected and Infested with these Daemons.… Yea, more than … Twenty have Confessed that they have Signed unto a Book, which the Devil show'd them, and Engaged in his Hellish Design of Bewitching, and Ruining our Land.

Cotton Mather, *The Wonders of the Invisible World*, 1692

## A PURITAN WOMAN'S DOUBTS

Anne Bradstreet was Colonial New England's most noted female poet. The daughter and wife of prominent Massachusetts Bay Colony governors, she was the mother of eight children. In a letter to her children she confesses her struggle with doubt and unbelief: "Many times hath Satan troubled me concerning the verity of the Scriptures, many times by Atheisme how I could know whether there was a God; I never saw any miracles to confirm me, and those which I read of how did I know but they were feigned. That there is a God my Reason would soon tell me by the wondrous workes that I see.... But how should I know he is such a God as I worship in Trinity, and such a Saviour as I rely upon?"

Sunday, for example, his focus is the church; on Monday, his family. Every event in life, no matter how inconsequential, is ripe for a spiritual analogy. Washing reminds him of the washing of regeneration; rising from bed in the morning reminds him of the resurrection; feeding chickens reminds him of God's provisions. His prayers follow his daily activities. If he meets a neighbor along the way, he prays for her. When he sees adolescents grouped together, his prayer is "Lord help these persons to remember their Creator in the days of their youth." Guided by a signed covenant, he strictly regulates his life:

> I renounce all the vanities and cursed idols and evil courses of this world ... and wherein I find myself to fall short, I will ever make it my grief and my shame; and for pardon, betake myself to the blood of the everlasting covenant. Now humbly imploring the grace of the Mediator to be sufficient for me, I do, as a further solemnity, subscribe my name, with both hand and heart, unto this instrument.

The Mather dynasty—including John Cotton—had long wielded power in colonial New England, but times are changing. Cotton Mather, in the shadow of his influential father, observes his father losing favor toward the end of his life. The "liberals" are on the ascendant, and Increase is asked to step down as president of Harvard.

Much to the chagrin of the Mathers, the Puritans are slackening their standards. A conversion experience, once a critical rite of passage, almost seems optional. The "Half-way Covenant," promoted by Solomon Stoddard (grandfather of Jonathan Edwards), allows young adults to have their children baptized even though they themselves have made no profession of faith. Stoddard, an influential minister from western Massachusetts, sees revivals as the key to church growth. The accompanying enthusiasm is suspect to the more staid and traditional Mathers.

Yet Cotton Mather is in some respects ahead of his time. His curiosity about scientific discoveries and medicine is enormous. He incorporates the latest inventions and discoveries into his sermons, illustrating his message while educating the congregation. Widely heralded for his brilliance, he is awarded an honorary doctorate of divinity in 1710 by the University of Glasgow. Three years later he is honored with election to the Royal Society of London. He is particularly fascinated by psychology and child-rearing theory, an interest growing out of his experience as a father and a minister. His three wives gave birth to more than a dozen children, most of whom did not survive childhood. A loving and devoted father, he showered his children with affection.

In his early twenties he had begun contemplating marriage. A diary entry shows he had prayed to "seek for the guidance and blessing of God in what concerns the change of my condition in the world from single to married." Abigail Phillips, the "Desire of His Eyes" and a "Lovely Consort," becomes his first wife. Baby Abigail, their first child, "one of the loveliest infants that has ever been seen in the world," dies less than two weeks after birth. Five other little ones die in infancy. The anguished pain of losing a child is only exceeded by the loss of Abigail after sixteen years of marriage.

Hardly has the bell tolled for Abigail when the widowed minister becomes the most eligible

> "My ancestors were Puritans from England, They arrived here in 1648 in the hope of finding greater restrictions than were permissible under English law at the time."
> Garrison Keillor

bachelor in town. He has a reputation for being a devoted husband, and marrying a minister means upward mobility in Puritan social circles. So it is that Prudence Prynne seeks to snare Mather in what could be termed a "fatal attraction." Writing of her long-time affection for him, she declares her love for him two months after Abigail is buried and requests an interview. He is attracted to this young woman barely half his age, but he fears the devil is tempting him. "Her reputation has been under some Disadvantage," he writes in his diary. "She has gott a bad Name among the Generality of the People." But he cannot resist her. He welcomes her visits until neighborhood gossip gets back to him. Though smitten, he cannot risk his good reputation. "I sett myself to make unto the Lord Jesus Christ, a Sacrifice of a Person, who, for many charming Accomplishments, has not many equals in the English America," he painfully writes. "I struck my Knife into the Heart of my Sacrifice by a Letter to her mother."

But Prudence and her mother are not so easily dissuaded. "In my absence, the young Gentlewoman to whom I have been so unkind," he writes, "comes to my Father, and brings her good Mother with her and charms the Neighbors into her Interests; and renews her Importunities that I would make her mine." Apparently, she is telling others that he had made advances toward her and thus should marry her. Mather insists that she must put in writing that "I have never done any unworthy Thing." But some weeks later, when Prudence learns that Mather is courting Elizabeth, a young widow, she is enraged. According to Mather, she threatens "that she will be a Thorn in my Side, and contrive all possible Wayes to vex me, affront me, disgrace me, in my Attempting a Return to the married state with another Gentlewoman." Nevertheless, he marries Elizabeth in 1702, eight months after Abigail's death.

Elizabeth gives birth to six more Mather children, though only two survive infancy. After she dies in 1713, the widower of fifty-one decides to remain single, praying for "purity in the widowhood." Soon lamenting his single state, however, he marries a third wife, this time enamored with the much-younger Lydia George, widowed six months earlier. He is convinced that she is the love of his life, but she proves to be unstable, becoming violently hostile and leaving home for long periods of time.

As one of the most prodigious diarists of the era, Mather's personal struggles are recorded for posterity. During his first marriage we find him reflecting on the "manifold filthiness of my heart and life, and the horrible aggravations of that filthiness." When his uncle, the minister of Plymouth is driven from his pulpit for fornication in 1697, Mather is very fearful that God's judgment might also light on him for similar sins. At fifty-seven, years after he had married for the third time, he is still lamenting his "former pollutions."

After a brief illness Mather dies at sixty-five, having outlived his father by five years and having served in Old North Church for more than four decades. A brilliant scholar, he knew eight languages, including the very difficult Algonquin tongue. He left behind a mixed reputation as well as some four hundred published papers and books including works of science, history, biography, poetry, and fiction as well as theology, sermons, and devotional material. One of his most popular books, *Essays to Do Good*, offered pithy advice on proper behavior. Ben Franklin identified it as one of the formative books of his youth. The work for which he is most remembered, however, is *Magnalia Christi Americana*, a historical overview of New England.

During his lifetime, New England changed dramatically. He wanted to believe that God was continuing to do a great work in this new Israel, but the church no longer held a place of honor as it once had. Individualism was on the increase even as the younger generation ventured into the frontier. Obtaining property and earning a living trumped church-going and theological debates. Revivalism and rationalism were the twin enemies that threatened old-fashioned Puritan orthodoxy. The Mather dynasty had come and gone.

Eager to move beyond their Puritan past, many Americans, both religious and secular, scored their forebears in England and America for their priggishness and painstaking spirituality. But in recent generations, the reputation of Puritans has risen, The Puritan worldview with its focus on the family, the community, and hard work provided a stable foundation for later religious, social, and political developments

## What if ...

What if Oliver Cromwell had not died five years into his reign as Lord Protector? Might Puritan belief and culture have gained a strong foothold in Old England?

What if John Owen and Richard Baxter had backed down in the face of threats and persecution? What would the Christian church have lost without their Puritan writings and ministries?

What if John Bunyan had not been imprisoned? Would he have had time to write his autobiography and his classic *Pilgrim's Progress*? How would their absence have affected later generations?

What if English kings had not persecuted Puritans? Would the immigration to the American colonies had not had a religious component? How would that have affected the progress of American history? What would modern America be like without the profound influence of the Mathers and other Puritan leaders?

## Further Reading

Beeke, Joel R., and Randall J. Pederson. *Meet the Puritans: With a Guide to Modern Reprints*. Grand Rapids: Reformation Heritage Books, 2006.

Beougher, Timothy K. *Richard Baxter and Conversion: A Study of the Puritan Concept of Becoming A Christian*. Dublin, Ireland: Mentor, 2008.

Bunyan, John. *Grace Abounding to the Chief of Sinners: A Faithful Account of the Life and Death of John Bunyan*. New York: Cosimo Classics, 2007.

Daniels, Bruce C. *Puritans at Play: Leisure and Recreation in Colonial New England*. New York: Palgrave Macmillan, 1996.

Lovelace, Richard F. *The American Pietism of Cotton Mather: Origins of American Evangelicalism*. Eugene, Ore.: Wipf & Stock, 2007.

Mather, Cotton. *On Witchcraft*. Mineola, N.Y.: Dover, 2009.

Middlekauff, Robert. *The Mathers: Three Generations of Puritan Intellectuals, 1596–1728*. Berkeley: University of California, 1999.

Miller, Perry, and Thomas H. Johnson, eds. *The Puritans: A Sourcebook of their Writings*. Mineola, N.Y.: Dover, 2001.

Norton, Mary Beth. *In the Devil's Snare: The Salem Witchcraft Crisis of 1692*. New York: Vintage, 2003.

Packer, J. I. *A Quest for Godliness: The Puritan Vision of the Christian Life*. Wheaton, Ill.: Crossway. 1994.

Ryken, Leland. *Worldly Saints: The Puritans as They Really Were*. Grand Rapids: Zondervan, 1990.

Silverman, Kenneth. *The Life and Times of Cotton Mather*. New York: Welcome Rain Publishers, 2001.

Thomson, Andrew. *John Owen: Prince of the Puritans*. Fearn, Scotland: Christian Focus, 2004.

Trueman, Carl R. *John Owen: Reformed Catholic, Renaissance Man*. Surrey, England: Ashgate, 2007.

# CHAPTER 17

# Sectarian Movements in Europe and America

## *Visions and Voices*

*One of my most memorable stops during a ten-day trek through the English countryside some years ago was at the Swarthmoor Hall in the Lake District. Built in 1586 by George Fell, the estate was passed down to his son Thomas, who bequeathed it to his wife, Margaret Fell, the "mother of Quakerism." Throughout her lifetime Swarthmoor Hall became the command center for the Society of Friends.*

*Now a religious retreat and conference grounds, the estate was closed the Monday morning my husband and I visited; however, a kindly caretaker agreed to take us through the home: kitchen, dining room and parlor, and up the stairs to the bedrooms. He told stories and answered questions in a wonderfully homespun way. Then he let us roam the gardens and fields at our leisure. What a memory-filled sunny morning it was. Whether wandering through the dewy grass or poking around her kitchen, I sensed the spirit of Margaret still lingering from centuries ago.*

*Our time there reminded me of a comment made by a colleague, a professor of church history. He remarked to his students in class that Margaret Fell is famous only because she married George Fox, the founder of the Quakers. "This is one way you women can make a name for yourselves," he joked.*

*I find it interesting, and perhaps mystifying, that the highborn Margaret Fell married the rag-tag, smelly, eccentric, wandering prophet George Fox. But it surely was not to gain fame. She outlived him by more than a decade, and her singular accomplishments in many ways outranked his own. She helped to put the Quakers on a more solid scriptural footing; she set the stage for gender equality; and she paved the way for pacifism to become a key element in Quaker belief.*

*As a wealthy widow, she might have lived out the rest of her life in ease on that magnificent estate. Instead, she sacrificed her wealth and time and freedom for a higher cause.*

Almost always schism begets schism; once the instinct of discipline is lost,
the movement breeds rival prophets and rival coteries. . . .
Always the first fervors evaporate;
prophecy dies out and the charismatic is merged in the institutional. . . .
It is a fugal melody that runs through the centuries.
RONALD A. KNOX

The fugal melody of schism that runs through the centuries picks up steam following the Reformation as printing presses start humming and Bible translations begin to proliferate. The established church can no longer control the story. Prophets rise up and give birth to movements that breed rival prophets. When the fervor evaporates and the prophecy dies out, the movement is merged into the institutional church, and it persecutes the prophets in its wake. And the fugal melody with all its various voices plays on.

This scenario is best seen in the sixteenth century as Reformation schismatics become institutionalized and persecute Anabaptists, and as the Church of England schismatics persecute Puritans, who will in turn persecute Quakers. In each case the initial fervor evaporates as the schismatic movement evolves into an established church. These sectarian movements are present in every age, but they particularly flourished in England in the mid-seventeenth century. As individuals and groups fled persecution, the sects spread—sometimes to the New World where they bred new prophets or prophetesses. Women, seeing visions and hearing voices like their male counterparts, were prominent in these new movements. Among the prophets and prophetesses were Anne Hutchinson, Roger Williams, George Fox, and Margaret Fell.

The Conventicle Act of Parliament in 1664, ordered by King Charles II, might seem like an over-reaction. Why should the king and Parliament feel threatened if a dozen people are meeting together, for example, to read the Bible? The rationale for the law restricting the number to five was more than merely an effort to keep the peons in their place. Since the time of Constantine, church unity was presumed to foster national unity. The tight church-state relationship in medieval times constituted an arranged marriage beneficial to both sides. When German princes courted Reformers and visa versa, it was an effort to strengthen both sides. So also in England. The Church of England, beginning with Henry VIII, served to strengthen the state.

## PARADE OF HISTORY

The parade of sectarian prophets is one of the more colorful processions of church history. In 1636 Lady Eleanor, accompanied by several women companions, parades into Litchfield Cathedral, sits on the bishop's throne, and declares herself primate over the Church of England, identifying herself as "the Lamb's wife." But George Fox, founder of the Quakers, leads the noisiest parade into Litchfield. Barefoot and donned in a leather suit, this strange prophet marches into the city on market day two decades later, crying at the top of his lungs, "Woe unto Litchfield, thou bloody city!"

Thus ordinary individuals, meeting in conventicles, or small groups, were seen as potentially seditious. Who knows what might happen? A prophet might rise up right in their midst.

Students of church history sometimes imagine that the sixteenth century did not really begin until Luther nailed his Ninety-five Theses to the church door, and that all other important events of the century centered around that incident. True, Luther let the genie out of the bottle and the Christian religion would never be the same. But the sixteenth century was more broadly a time of political and social upheaval as well as a time of cultural advance. Renaissance literature, art, and music rivaled scientific and geographical discoveries. Similar circumstances were evident in the seventeenth century, as the religious revolution encountered what has been called the Age of Reason. In the 1640s, as George Fox was traveling on foot from town to town uttering prophetic messages from God and claiming perfection greater than that of Adam, Descartes was giving birth to Rationalism with his sudden notion of *Cogito ergo sum*—I think, therefore I am.

Every age has its own religious peculiarities and concerns. The Reformation challenged church authority with its emphasis on the Bible, while seventeenth-century religious renewal related more to the matter of church purity. The Puritans symbolize that emphasis, but the full flowering of this emphasis on purity came with the prophetic sectarian movements that arose alongside Puritanism. Puritans harked back to the *sola scriptura* of the Reformation—and particularly to the writings of Bucer, Calvin, and Bullinger. These three, more than Luther, had set forth a new pattern for the church, the home, and society. Medieval rituals and priestly traditions were scorned. Simplicity was prized. From celibacy and the confessional to the number of sacraments, the Bible ruled. There was no place for a pope—or a prophet.

It is in the prophetic realm that the sectarian movements differed from what might be broadly identified as Protestant orthodoxy. Prophetic movements had arisen in medieval times and among Anabaptists of the sixteenth century. But in the seventeenth century they flourished. In the British Isles many of these groups were identified as Civil War sects because of their prominence during the English Civil Wars. The Ranters, for example, considered themselves above the admonitions of Scripture in their perfectionism. They held that the true believer is a holy one, free of sin and the biblical laws.

The Fifth Monarchists, another sectarian movement, was a radical millenarian group that prophesied that it would usher in the reign of Christ as the fifth monarchy (following after the Assyrian, Persian, Macedonian, and Roman monarchies). Under the rule of Christ, this new kingdom would eliminate class and sex barriers. They formed "gathered congregations" and separated themselves from "non-elect." Itinerant

## PROPHET AS LONELY MADMAN

A genuine first-hand religious experience ... is bound to be a heterodoxy to its witnesses, the prophet appearing as a mere lonely madman. If his doctrine prove contagious enough to spread to any others, it becomes a definite and labeled heresy. But if it then still prove contagious enough to triumph over persecution, it becomes itself an orthodoxy; and when a religion has become an orthodoxy, its day of inwardness is over: the spring is dry; the faithful live at second hand exclusively and stone the prophets in their turn.

William James, *The Varieties of Religious Experience*

## Plain Speech vs. Politeness

Seventeenth-century England, as was true of other societies, was in many respects rigidly class conscious and preoccupied with cultural forms of honor (and dishonor). Deference was due individuals of higher social status, and that deference was evident in lifestyle, dress, behaviors, and speech. Among sectarian movements, however, such niceties were often scorned. All were equal before God—except, of course, for the leader or prophet. Such was especially the case among Quakers. In a concern for being truthful, they emphasized plain (truthful) dress, lifestyle, and speech. The plain dress was easily identified by the gray color and the flat hats worn by men. Plainness was also the rule in theology and church order. The "plain and simple truth" required no creeds or confessions; church meetings were spontaneous. But it was in the realm of plain speech that Quakers were most vilified, largely because of the implied disrespect.

George Fox initiated this approach in the beginning of his ministry: "For the Lord showed me, that though the people of the world have mouths full of deceit, and changeable words, yet I was to keep to Yea and Nay in all things; and that my words should be few and savoury, seasoned with grace." When addressing another individual, he insisted that honorary titles must be rejected. Catholic honorary terms for clergy were particularly odious, as were such terms that were used in the Church of England and Protestant bodies. The same rule applied when addressing kings and heads of state and members of the House of Lords—and political titles in general. "Yes, sir" or "No, your honor" were not permitted. Even the use of "Mr." or "Mrs." was deemed as conveying too much honor. This rule also held true for children. A five-year-old boy would be expected to address the elderly neighbor as Margaret rather than Mrs. Fell. There were no "ladies" and "gentlemen" among Quakers.

Though people living in the twenty-first century find it difficult to understand, pronouns became a major matter of dispute as well. The early Quakers may have been nitpicking, but they were not uneducated fools. In 1666 they published a grammar book that was based on a study of forty languages to prove that the pronoun *you* could not be used properly in the singular and blaming Catholics for the incorrect and damnable usage:

> You to Many and Thou to One: Singular One, Thou; Plural Many, You.... You to One came first from the Pope.... But to say the Plural in the Singular's place, you, for thou, this pleases our Priests, and School-masters, and peevish Magistrates: Thou's thou me, Cry they: and thus they have forgotten their Accidence [traditional grammar].

Why the debate over pronouns? Seventeenth-century usage set forth the polite plural forms *ye* and *you* when speaking to a single individual of high rank. Thus commoners were expected to use this form when addressing an upper-class lady or gentleman. Those of inferior status were to be addressed with *thou*. Fox, however, insisted that language must be plain and thus truthful. To refer to one individual as *you*—the plural form—would be the same as if a person claimed she had two pennies when she had only one. She would be untruthful. A form of untruthfulness was pride, and an aspect of Quaker ministry was to attack pride wherever it could be found. The use of *thou* and *thee* to an individual of rank was, according to Fox, "a fearful cut to proud flesh and self-honor."

women preachers, including Mary Cary and Anna Trapnel, were common. Cary's prophecies included eschatological utterances, theological pronouncements, and counsel for everyday living.

Trapnel, a woman of financial means, ranked high as a prophetic visionary, often taking on political leaders. In 1654, after spending days in a trance, she prophesied against Lord Protector Oliver Cromwell. God was about to "batter" him and his political cronies. Authorities were not amused, and she was arrested for subversive behavior. Such prophetic activity was not confined to the sects, however. Lady Eleanor Davis, daughter of the Earl of Castlehaven, considered herself a faithful Anglican. In 1625 she testified that she had "heard early in the morning a Voice from Heaven, speaking as through a trumpet these words: 'There is nineteen years and a half to the Judgment Day.'"

For twenty-five years she publicized her prophecies through writing and speaking. Her commentary on the Old Testament book of Daniel prophesied a dire end for Archbishop Laud and King Charles I. For such brazen pronouncements, she was sentenced to prison and required to pay a hefty fine. Described variously as insane, hysterical, and eccentric, she was unquestionably a colorful character. When she brazenly entered Lichfield Cathedral, she not only proclaimed herself the head of the church

but also desecrated the altar hangings. Despite her reputation for eccentricity, she had many followers, some in high places. She wrote some forty widely distributed tracts.

Charismatic, apocalyptic, and perfectionist sectarians were certainly not confined to England. Prophetic movements rose up on the Continent, particularly in France following the revocation by Louis XIV of the Edict of Nantes (making Protestantism illegal) in 1685. A Huguenot resistance group known as the Camisards, or Cevenal Prophets, arose in the Cevennes Mountains. Both leaders and followers claimed direct revelation from the Holy Spirit resulting in extraordinary physical affects. According to one observer, some "fell on their Backs" and "remained a while in Trances, and coming out of them with Twitchings, they utter'd all that came into their Mouths." There were instances of young children who were said to have given prophecies while speaking in tongues. Indeed, there were fantastic stories of babies bursting forth in fluent French, calling their elders to repentance.

Often authorities ignored what they deemed to be no more than routine rantings of religious eccentrics. But if the "crazy" man or woman took on the role of a prophet with a loyal following, the remedy of the day was severe persecution. Sometimes citizenry took matters into their own hands and pelted the annoying street preacher with rocks. But the heavy hand of the law was never far behind. Imprisonment and execution of heretics was a centuries-old tradition conducted by Christian regimes both Catholic and Protestant alike. There was no such thing as religious freedom, except, some imagined, in the New World. But the New World—and especially New England—was anything but a haven for religious dissenters. As was often true on the Continent and in England, the once-persecuted minority turned into persecutors as soon as their own brand of religion was in vogue. This is precisely what Ann Hutchinson and Roger Williams discovered after they immigrated to New England.

## Anne Hutchinson: New England "Heretic"

She was considered a dangerous woman, a much greater threat to the community than the ordinary "gossip" or "scold" who often found her way into the Massachusetts Bay Selectmen's Minutes. She was intelligent and articulate and commanded a hearing that few others enjoyed.

Born in Lincolnshire, England, Anne Marbury Hutchinson (1591–1643) was the daughter of an Anglican cleric who was twice imprisoned for his dissenting beliefs and his criticism of the incompetence of the clergy. Yet he managed to maintain a religious equilibrium that allowed him to continue serving in Anglican parishes. Young Anne was home-schooled in her father's library, and like him she challenged the authority of the Church of England. In 1612, the year after her father died, she married William Hutchinson, an up-and-coming merchant.

For the next twenty-two years she and her husband remained in England, where she mostly had babies and studied the Bible. Her mentor was her minister, John Cotton, who would become one of the leading Puritan divines of New England. When he sailed for the Bay Colony in 1633, she was devastated. It became "a great trouble to me," she confessed. "I could not be at rest but I must come hither."

Cotton is no doubt pleased when the Hutchinson family arrives in Boston. Referring to her early years in New England, he later praised her spiritual maturity and lay ministry:

> Shee did much good in our Town, in womans meeting at Childbirth-Travells, wherein shee was not onley skillful and helpfull, but readily fell into good discourse with the women about their spiritual estates … By which means many of the women (and their husbands) were … brought to enquire more seriously after the Lord Jesus Christ.

Middle-aged and the mother of fifteen children, Hutchinson has a keen mind and is highly respected in the community. Her "heresy" is to challenge the religious establishment, especially on the issue of liberty of conscience. But her challenge is also related to gender, though she is not a seventeenth-century feminist, as some writers have suggested.

The Puritan establishment, far more than sectarian movements, was by its very nature deeply entrenched in a highly organized system that championed the rule of law. Orderliness was prized. Within a century, however, that system would start to unravel with a more feminine slant to spirituality and Hutchinson was in the forefront. Initially, her activities do not create controversy. She holds weekly meetings in her home with neighborhood women, offering advice on childcare and homemaking and making comments on the Sunday sermon. Soon word spreads and more women attend—so many that they cannot be accommodated in her home without scheduling extra meetings. Women return home and tell their husbands, and the men begin to attend as well, fulfilling the fears of the authorities that she would "as by an Eve catch their husbands also." In fact, she had so many followers that they were dubbed "Hutchinsonians."

The authorities have good reason to oppose her. She is critical of the Boston ministers, spreading the word that the only ones who are truly elect are John Cotton and her brother-in-law, John Wheelwright. In her mind, the Puritan "covenant of works" represents no more than a man-made code of legal requirements that has no place in true religion, which, she insists, is a "covenant of grace" as one is guided by the Spirit through one's conscience. "As I do understand it, laws, commands, rules and edicts ["covenant of works"] are for those who have not the light which makes plain the pathway. He who has God's grace in his heart cannot go astray." Indeed, anyone can communicate directly with God. She testifies to special revelations from God, revelations that Puritans simply cannot tolerate. "If they be allowed in one thing [they] must be admitted a rule in all things," admonishes governor Winthrop, "for they being above reason and Scripture, they are not subject to control." She likewise challenges the doctrine of original sin.

That she would make such claims is serious offense, but that she has a following who fill her house at weekly meetings calls for court action. Indeed, the dozens of people who crowd into her home to listen to her sermon critiques and biblical expositions include, according to a contemporary observer, "some of the magistrates, some gentlemen, some scholars and men of learning."

By 1637, only three years after arriving with her family, Hutchinson is branded a "Jezebel" who is spreading "abominable" teachings, a "thing not tolerable nor comely in the sight of God, nor fitting for [her] sex." She testifies to Governor Winthrop that "upon a Throne of Justice," the Lord revealed that "I must come to New England, yet I must not fear nor be dismayed." Winthrop shoots back: "I am persuaded that the revelation she brings forth is delusion." That same year, at age forty-six and several months into her fifteenth and final pregnancy, she is called before the General Court of Massachusetts. She might have been intimidated by their charges of insubordination, but she stands her ground. "You have no power over my body, neither can you do me any harm," she responds. "I fear none but the great Jehovah, which hath foretold me of these things, and I do verily believe that he will deliver me out of your hands."

The court issues a sentence of banishment, but she is permitted to remain in Boston under house arrest until spring. By that time she may have thought better of being banished, for she

## FEAR OF FANATICISM

Generations after her death, Anne Hutchinson was often cited as the premier example of religious fanaticism. In 1743 Puritan leaders in Westfield, Massachusetts, were distressed by the activities of Bathsheba Kingsley, who admitted to "stealing a horse [and] riding away on the Sabbath with[ou]t her husband's consent." What were they to do with such women? She spent most of her days in outlying villages, "wandering about from house to house under a notion of doing Christ's work and delivering messages" — messages that often included condemnation of local clerics. Charles Chauncey, an opponent of the excesses of the Great Awakening, argued that such fanaticism was reminiscent of the days of Anne Hutchinson.

is ready to make concessions when court representatives interview her. The meeting continues until well after dark, by which time John Cotton, no longer her friend, "pronounced the sentence of admonition with great solemnity, and with much zeal and detestation of her errors and pride of spirit." The following day, March 22, 1638, she appears again and makes further concessions, including an admission of saying "rash and ungrounded" things against the magistrates. Winthrop recalled being surprised by her change of heart, for "this gave the church good hope of her repentance." But after further questioning and wrangling, the effort to "bring her to see her sin" was "all in vain, [and] the church, with one consent, cast her out." With her excommunication, "her spirits, which seemed before to be somewhat dejected, revived again, and she gloried in her sufferings, saying, that it was the greatest happiness, next to Christ, that ever befell her."

On March 28, under the orders of Governor Winthrop, Hutchinson left Boston for Providence, where her husband had purchased land from the Indians. For the Puritan leaders, however, banishment was not enough. They went

Quaker Mary Dyer led to execution on Boston Common, 1 June 1660. (By an unknown 19th-century artist)

to great lengths to besmirch her reputation. Following an agonizing miscarriage soon after her exile, a minister alleged she had not merely miscarried but rather had brought forth "20 monstrous births or thereabouts, at once, some of them bigger, some lesser, some of one shape, some of another," none of them "of human shape." John Cotton, her one-time minister and defender, joined in the malicious rumor and reported to an assembly in Boston that because of God's judgment she had delivered "twenty-seven . . . lumps of man's seed, without any alteration or mixture of anything from the woman, and thereupon gathered that it might signify her error in denying inherent righteousness."

But if a miscarriage was not enough to prove her reprobation, her untimely death was. After she and her family had moved to Long Island, word came back to Boston vindicating her detractors and warning any other would-be heretics:

> The Indians set upon them, and slew her and all the family . . . [and] did burne her to death with fire, her house and all the rest named that belonged to her. . . . I never heard that the Indians in those parts did ever before this, commit the like outrage . . .; and therefore God's hand is the more apparently seene herein, to pick out this wofull woman, to make her . . . an unheard of heavie example of their cruelty above al others."

In actuality, the Hutchinson deaths were part of a more widespread annihilation of both Dutch and English families by Indians on Long Island.

There would be other women who tested the Boston authorities, including Mary Dyer, who followed the teachings of Hutchinson but later, on a visit to England, joined the Quakers. Knowing that returning to Boston would spell trouble, she boldly entered the town and testified to her new-found faith. Dyer was banished, only to return, at which time she was sentenced to hang. But even the Bay Colony Puritans winced at hanging a woman—at least prior to the witch trials of 1692. Just before the execution she was given a reprieve and told in no uncertain terms that they would not be so lenient next time. Thus when she returned in the spring of 1660, she was hanged. That she was a woman preacher was not a critical factor in her execution; that she was not abiding by Puritan rules was. The same was true of Roger Williams, though he was able to get out of town before a worse fate befell him.

## Roger Williams: Proclaiming Separation of Church and State

Heralded as one of the founders of American liberty whose influence is seen in the Bill of Rights, Roger Williams (1603–1683) is an enigmatic figure whose lack of theological clarity illustrates a significant element in seventeenth-century Christianity. The Puritans, the Separatists, the Quakers, the Baptists—though often at odds among themselves—typically hold strong beliefs that are set forth by a theologian or prophet. Williams represents the religious critic who is more concerned with challenging the establishment than with formulating doctrine or developing a new movement.

Growing up in London, Williams witnessed the hard hand of the law in religious persecution. But more significant for his future develop-

Roger Williams

ment were the hours he spent in court observing cases against religious dissenters. Years later the daughter of a noted judge recalled that the young Williams "would in a short hand take sermons and speeches in the Star Chamber, and present them to my dear father." After schooling at Charterhouse and graduation from Cambridge in 1627, he was appointed an Anglican chaplain and married the daughter of an Anglican minister. But his inclinations are more in line with Puritanism.

In 1630 he and his wife sail for New England, where he is welcomed by John Winthrop and described as a "godly minister." But within weeks after his arrival, he moves to Salem to serve in a Separatist congregation, a church demanding complete separation from the Church of England.

In his espousal of Separatist beliefs and his criticism of the Boston establishment, Williams is now *persona non grata* in the Bay Colony. Under pressure from Boston, he is forced to leave Salem (amid rumors of his "heresy of Anabaptism"). He moves on to Plymouth, where he makes contact with local Indians. Soon he is accusing the Puritan authorities of employing an invalid charter issued by the king, who has no right to native lands. His ideas on religious toleration only exacerbate matters. He argues that "no human power has the right to intermeddle in matters of conscience and that neither church nor state, neither bishop nor king, may prescribe the smallest iota of religious faith." Further, he insists that no one should be required to financially support

*Detroit Publishing Co., 1949*

any church because "man is responsible to God alone." In 1635, the General Court issues an ominous order:

> Whereas Mr. Roger Williams, one of the Elders of the church of Salem, hath broached and divulged new and dangerous opinions against the authority of magistrates, as also written letters of defamation, both of the magistrates and churches here, and that before any conviction, and yet maintaineth the same without any retraction; it is, therefore, ordered that the said Mr. Williams shall depart out of this jurisdiction within six weeks now next ensuing.

Refusing to be stifled, Williams continues to hold meetings and seeks to convince others of his ideas. Many people are "taken with an apprehension of his godliness." In fact, they are whispering about plans to set up their own colony. The court then decides to rid itself of the troublemaker by shipping him back to England. But warned by Governor Winthrop of this impending turn of events, he flees into the wilderness, leaving his wife and infant behind. "I was unmercifully driven from my chamber to a winter's flight, exposed to the miseries, poverties, necessities, wants, debts, hardships of sea and land in a banished condition," he later wrote. "I was sorely tossed for . . . fourteen weeks in a bitter winter season, not knowing what bed or bread did mean."

Williams had already become familiar with the Indians, having earlier inquired of their social traditions and trading customs. He purchases land from the celebrated native chief Massasoit, but due to claims on the land by the Plymouth Colony, he moves away and establishes Providence Plantation, acknowledging the providence of God in his good fortune. News of his survival through the winter and his plans to establish his own colony bring family members and like-minded freethinkers south to join him in the spring.

For a man in his era, he is unusual in his esteem for Native Americans. He becomes convinced that the Indians are in many ways more noble than are the Puritan invaders. "For the temper of the braine in quick apprehensions and accurate judgements," he insists, "the most high and sovereign God and Creator hath not made them inferior to Europeans. . . . The same Sun shines on a Wilderness that doth on a garden." He strongly expresses his views in correspondence, essays, and books (including a Narragansett dictionary), as well as in verse that cuts to the heart of the matter:

> I've known them to leave their house and
>     mat
> To lodge a friend or stranger
> When Jews and Christians oft have sent
> Jesus Christ to the Manger
> Oft have I heard these Indians say
> These English will deliver us
> Of all that's ours, our lands and lives
> In the end, they'll bereave us.

Williams's religious ideas are in a constant state of flux and progression toward pluralism. He had come to the Bay Colony with evangelistic zeal. Like other Puritans, he had expressed "longing after the natives' soules." But as time passes, his philosophy of "soule liberty" develops to the point that he believes that conversion of the native people is not a priority, or even advisable. Like others, he acknowledges that native tribes fight each other and are known for terrible torture, but their battles are never over religious issues as are those of his fellow Englishmen and of Europeans in general. His stance on religious toleration is the exception to the rule, though one contemporary observer suggests that his views are widespread: "Under the pretence of liberty of conscience, about these parts, there come to live all the scum and the runaways of the country."

In the spring of 1636 word reaches Williams that the Pequots and their allies are on the verge of attacking the Puritan towns and ridding the region of the European settlers once and for all. The greatest fear is that the Narragansetts, with tens of thousands of fighting men, might join in the battle against them. Accompanied by a native runner, Williams makes great speed to meet with the Narragansetts in their territory. Battered by a storm, he arrives at their principal settlement some thirty miles away to plead the cause of the colonists. With his reputation for honesty, he negotiates a treaty between Massachusetts officials and the Narragansetts — and later with other tribes who might have joined in the attack.

Without the help of other tribes, the Pequot War (1634–1638) does not realize its goal of ridding the land of white men. Indeed, the colonial militia prevails and takes terrible revenge on any natives deemed complicit, much to the sorrow and chagrin of Williams. The final battle of the war comes when the colonial troops set fire to a large thatched building, trapping several hundred native warriors along with women and children — all of whom are burned to death. "It was a fearful sight," Puritan leader William Bradford observed, "to see them thus frying." Williams is sickened when he hears about the horrific inferno.

As time passes, his reputation grows. In spite of his heresies, he is looked upon with high regard by many Bay Colony leaders. In fact, Governor Endicott later welcomes him back. But he refuses the invitation. "I feel safer down here among the Christian savages along Narragansett Bay," he seethes, "than I do among the savage Christians of Massachusetts Bay Colony."

Among those who settle in Providence Plantation are Baptists, who do not find a warm welcome in the Bay Colony. In Providence, some keep the seventh-day Sabbath, while others do not. For a short time, Williams preaches to a joint gathering of Baptists and thus is considered by many to be the founding minister of the first Baptist church in America. But he is far too independent in his religious beliefs to be properly deemed a Baptist.

The colony of Rhode Island is not officially chartered until 1644, while he is back in England. That same year he publishes *The Bloody Tenent of Persecution for Cause of Conscience*, in which he presents his philosophy of toleration through a dialogue between Peace and Truth. The book is controversial — and popular. Liberty of conscience is a threat to the religious system, whether in England or America. John Cotton responds in 1647 with his own volume, *The Bloody Tenent washed and made White in the Blood of the Lamb*. But Williams has the final word. In 1652, he further challenges Cotton and his ilk with *The Bloody Tenent made yet more Bloody by Mr. Cotton's Endeavor to wash it White*.

Providence Plantation is anything but a utopian community. Though seeking peace and toleration from the intolerant Bay Colony, the settlers quickly find many things to fight about. Some join together to buy large tracts of land, thus preventing new arrivals from farming their own property. In a letter of 1654, Williams expresses his disappointment: "I have been charged with folly for that freedom and liberty which I have always stood for — I say, liberty and equality in both land and government." In the following years, land becomes a major focus as he seeks to mediate disputed claims.

Although known for toleration, Williams is not without his own prejudice. He despises Quakers, in part because of their claims to

## A LONELY PROPHET

I fasted much, walked abroad in solitary places many days, and often took my Bible, and sat in hollow trees and lonesome places until night came on; and frequently in the night walked mournfully about by myself; for I was a man of sorrows in the time of the first workings of the Lord in me.

During all this time I was never joined in profession of religion with any, but gave up myself to the Lord, having forsaken all evil company, taking leave of father and mother, and all other relations, and traveled up and down as a stranger on the earth . . . for I durst not stay long in a place, being afraid both of professor and profane, lest, being a tender young man, I should be hurt by conversing much with either. For which reason I kept much as a stranger, seeking heavenly wisdom and getting knowledge from the Lord. . . . As I had forsaken the priests, so I left the separate preachers also, and those called the most experienced people; for I saw there was none among them all that could speak to my condition. . . . When I was in the deep, under all shut up, I could not believe that I should ever overcome; my troubles, my sorrows, and my temptations were so great that I often thought I should have despaired, I was so tempted.

George Fox, *An Autobiography*

true-church purity and their subjective claim of inner light. Desiring to go straight to the source, he challenges the visiting George Fox to a debate. Fox ignores the dare, but local Quakers agree to meet with him. He publicly debates them, while accusing them of being "without manners, without courtesy," so that to meet one along the way is no better than to "meet a horse or a cow." In the end, Williams taunts Fox with a volume titled *George Fox digged out of his Burrowes.*

### George Fox: Prophet and Rebel

In 1650 George Fox (1624 – 1691) is sentenced by a judge to six months in prison for preaching a blasphemous message, claiming by his own testimony to be free from sin, perfectionism later reinforced by his Pendle Hill vision — a vision depicting "a people to be gathered to the Lord," freed from the power of sin in their lives. Fox gathers followers and founds a movement that becomes known as the Society of Friends (commonly called Quakers). His appearance sets him apart. Thomas Carlyle, a nineteenth-century Scottish historian, rates Fox alongside Luther and captures his essence in a suit of clothes:

The most remarkable incident in modern history perhaps is not the Diet of Worms. . . . The most remarkable incident is passed over carelessly by most historians and treated with some degree of ridicule by others — namely, George Fox's making for himself a suit of leather. No grander thing was ever done than when George Fox, stitching himself into a suit of leather, went forth determined to find truth for himself — and to do battle for it against all superstition and intolerance.

Although Fox has never risen to the height of Luther as a historical figure, he deserves attention for his prophetic role — a role that would become critical in the later developments of cultic and charismatic movements of the nineteenth and twentieth centuries.

The oldest of four children, Fox grew up near Leicester, England, the son of a prosperous weaver and devoted Anglican churchman. His testimony is very unlike that of John Bunyan and others who recalled living a sinful life until they were marvelously converted. Fox testified that he possessed a "gravity" and "spirit not usual in children" that caused him to be distressed when he witnessed levity in others. "When I came to eleven years of age," he later remembered, "I knew pureness and righteousness; for while a child I was taught how to walk to be kept pure." Indeed, he later claimed that throughout his youth, "I never wronged man or woman in all that time; for the Lord's power was with me and over me, to preserve me." His concern for religious matters as a youth paves the way for his becoming a lonely prophet as he moves through his twenties. In his journal he describes his solitary days and being set apart by God.

In the late 1640s the perfectionism that has been a key element in Fox's religion since early childhood comes to full flowering. Unlike John Wesley, who would later teach perfectionism (entire sanctification) but never claim it for himself, Fox is exhibit A. "Now I was come up in spirit through the flaming sword, into the paradise of God," he wrote. "I knew nothing but pureness, and innocency, and righteousness; being renewed into the image of God by Christ Jesus, to the state of Adam, which he was in before he fell." Indeed, he goes beyond the perfection of Adam and by his own testimony attains the perfection of Jesus: "I was immediately taken up in spirit to see into another

George Fox

or more steadfast state than Adam's innocency, even into a state in Christ Jesus that should never fall."

That he is accused of blasphemy is not surprising. In 1649 he is imprisoned in Nottingham, a confinement that would be followed by many more. He is also assaulted by rowdies while civil and religious leaders look the other way. Yet the persecution provides publicity for his message. People come out to hear what this controversial prophet has to say.

Fox's ministry begins to solidify in 1652, after he encounters God through a visionary experience on Pendle Hill, an event that marks the turning point of his life. Of this experience he writes: "As we travelled we came near a very great hill, called Pendle Hill, and I was moved of the Lord to go up to the top of it; which I did with difficulty, it was so very steep and high. When I was come to the top, I saw the sea bordering upon Lancashire. From the top of this hill the Lord let me see in what places he had a great people to be gathered." Through his outdoor preaching, he soon gains a following. Like John the Baptist and the Old Testament proph-

James Bird/www.flickr.com

Pendle Hill

ets, he calls people to repentance. He walks barefoot in his homemade leather breeches, raising his hands and shouting out God's curses on the cities and towns. Making his way through the crowded markets of Litchfield, he bellows, "Woe unto Litchfield, thou bloody city! Woe unto Litchfield!" Persecution and imprisonment inevitably follow.

Like the sixteenth-century Anabaptists, he urges his followers not to make use of "carnal weapons." Rather, they should use "spiritual weapons." Pacifism is the rule. "Let the waves [of persecution] break over your heads." There is a strong apocalyptic theme to his message. He believes that the world has entered the "New Age of the Spirit" (similar to what the Montanists had taught) and that he is ushering in the millennial age virtually by himself—as a perfected man in the image of Adam.

Fox emphasizes the uniqueness of his perfectionist beliefs. "Of all the sects in Christendom," he writes, "I found none that could bear to be told that any should come to Adam's perfection, into that image of God, that righteousness and holiness that Adam was in before he fell; to be clean and pure without sin, as he was." Indeed, he views it as his mission in life to bring people out of the carnal sects and into a "spirit-filled" life: "I was to bring them off from all the world's fellowships, and prayings, and singings, which stood in forms without power; that ... they might pray in the Holy Ghost, and sing in the Spirit, and with the grace that comes by Jesus."

Tongues-speaking was reported among the Quakers as well as a wide variety of religious excitement. Fox himself believes that he has the power to work miracles and discern spirits, and his followers claim similar charismatic gifts. Court testimony offers a glimpse of Quaker enthusiasm: "Men, women, and little children at their meetings are strangely wrought upon in their bod-

ies and brought to fall, foam at the mouth, roar and swell in their bellies." Richard Baxter gives a similar account. "At first they did use to fall into violent Tremblings and sometimes Vomitings in their meetings, and pretended to be violently acted by the spirit; but now that is ceased."

Fox was the charismatic prophet-founder of the movement—a movement that might have died out like other contemporary sectarian movements, but for a major difference: the conversion of an influential woman who would wield power in the movement for a half century.

## Margaret Fell Fox: Mother of the Friends

Margaret Fell (1614–1702) was a key figure in the Society of Friends and led the movement for more than a decade after her husband, George Fox, died. Her home at Swarthmoor Hall became administrative and spiritual center of the Quaker movement. Born into the landed gentry, she married an older man when she was yet in her teens. Thomas Fell, also of landed gentry, was a highly respected judge and member of Parliament. Riding the circuit kept him away for long periods of time, leaving the estate in the capable hands of Margaret. Long after his death, she reflected on their marriage: "We lived together twenty-six years, in which time we had nine children. He was a tender and loving husband to me, and a tender father to his children, and one that sought after God in the best way that was made known to him. I was about sixteen years younger than he."

Part of caring for her large household involved spiritual oversight, "being desirous to serve God, so that I might be accepted of Him." Indeed, she is a spiritual seeker who is always "inquiring after the way of the Lord" and travels "often to hear the best ministers that came into our parts." Of these ministers, she invites "the most serious godly men" to come to the estate to have "prayers and religious exercises in our family." She continues this practice for some two decades. Then, in 1652, "it pleased the Lord ... to send George Fox into our country, who declared to us the eternal truth, as it is in Jesus; and by the Word and power of the eternal God, turned many from darkness unto light, and from the power of Satan unto God."

Fox is still an itinerant preacher and evangelist with no organized following. She is so impressed with his message that she invites him to stay over at Swarthmoor Hall. The next morning he shows up at church and stands up to speak. As she later recollects, he offered his standard message: "You will say Christ saith this, and the apostles say this; but what canst thou say? Art thou a child of Light, and hast thou walked in the Light, and what thou speakest is it inwardly from God?" While others regard him an eccentric vagabond, she stands up to defend him and is profoundly affected by his words, as she later testifies: "This opened me so, that it cut me to the heart, and then I saw clearly we were all wrong. So I sat down in my pew again and cried bitterly: and I cried in my spirit to the Lord, 'We are all thieves; we have taken the Scripture in words, and know nothing of them in ourselves.'"

Before Thomas Fell returns from his circuit, Margaret and the children and servants have all been converted to the new religion. A short distance from his home he is met by concerned citizens, who warn him that his wife and family have been carried away in enthusiasm. Margaret later recalls the circumstances:

> When he came home, and found the most part of his family changed from our former principles and persuasions, which he left us in,

he was much surprised at our sudden change; for some envious people, our neighbors, went and met him, and informed him that we had entertained such men as had taken us off from going to church, which he was very much concerned at.... And so it so happened that ... some other Friends ... discoursed with him, and did persuade him to be still, and weigh things before be did anything hastily, and his spirit was somewhat calmed.... And then he was pretty moderate and quiet; and his dinner being ready, he went to it, and I went in and sat down by him. And while I was sitting, the power of the Lord seized upon me; and he was struck with amazement, and knew not what to think.... That night George Fox returned. After supper my husband was sitting in the parlor, and I asked him if George Fox might come in? And he said, yes. So George came in.... He spoke as excellently as ever I heard him, and opened Christ's and the apostles' practices.... And he opened the night of apostasy that had occurred since the apostles' days, and he exposed the priests and their practices in the apostasy. So well did he speak, that I thought if all in England had been there, they could not have denied the truth of those things.

In the following years the Fell home is opened for Friends meetings, and Margaret, with her husband's sanction, becomes a strong financial supporter of the movement. But as with most sectarian prophets, some of the followers aspire to be leaders themselves. Differences in both belief and practice create rifts. And even though Fox rails against Anglicans and Dissenters alike for their hierarchical structures and obsession with propriety, he himself wields dictatorial power and demands proper respect. When James Nayler, a leading Quaker preacher, refuses to properly bow before Fox, he is declared unfaithful. "There was now a wicked spirit," Fox warns, that has "risen amongst Friends."

Besides his claims of perfectionism, Fox is deemed a heretic for his disdain of the sacraments. The true sign of religion is inward, he argues, and there is no place for outward church rituals such as baptism or communion. Shocking as these "heresies" are to most people of the era, they are the very declarations that draw people to the new movement. Indeed, during the late 1650s, while Cromwell is in power, Fox imagines that the Friends will grow to dominate the religious landscape. Persecution, however, serves not only to keep the numbers down but also Fox's spirits. He easily falls into depression.

In the late 1650s Margaret also suffers depression. When her beloved husband dies, the estate is divided. She receives Swarthmoor Hall, and her son inherits the large tracts of land. She not only loses her dear companion but also the only real friend of the Friends in high places. With Cromwell's death and the restoration of King Charles II, persecution increases. Authorities ride into Swarthmoor, arrest Fox, and incarcerate him in a dungeon in Lancaster Castle, where he languishes in vile conditions for several months.

With the help of others, Fell secures his release, but then she is incarcerated herself—for refusing to take an oath of allegiance to the king. She is surely not trying to exacerbate the situation in order to become a martyr: "I love, own, and honor the King and desire his peace and welfare [and to] live a peaceable, a quiet and a godly life under his government, according to the Scriptures." But this only, she insists, "is my allegiance to the King. And as for the oath itself, Christ Jesus, the King of Kings, hath commanded me not to swear at all, neither by heaven, nor by earth, nor by any other Oath."

She is sentenced to six months in jail, only to be given a life sentence following her trial. Although she ends up serving less than five years, her time in jail is hardly wasted. While her religious inclinations focus inward, she has a very outward practical bent as expressed in a lengthy pamphlet written behind bars: *Women's Speaking Justified, Proved and Allowed of by the Scriptures, All Such as Speak by the Spirit and Power of the Lord Jesus And How Women Were the First That Preached the Tidings of the Resurrection of Jesus, and Were Sent by Christ's Own Command Before He Ascended to the Father, John 20.17.*

Swarthmoor Hall, where Margaret Fell lived and organized the Society of Friends

But if women's speaking can be justified by Scriptures, where does the opposition to women's speaking come from? From "the bottomless pit, and the spirit of darkness that hath spoken for these many hundred years together in this night of apostasy," she argues. In marriage, too, women enjoy equality. Did not God tell Abraham: "In all that Sarah hath said to thee, hearken to her voice"? Two years after the booklet appears, she would have an opportunity to practice equality in marriage. In the summer of 1669, eleven years after Judge Fell died, Fox testifies to a revelation: "I had seen from the Lord a considerable time before that I should take Margaret Fell to be my wife. And when I first mentioned it to her, she felt the answer of life from God thereunto." After consulting with the children, Fox and Fell are married later that autumn in Bristol before a company of Quakers. She is fifty-five, he, eleven years her junior.

There is no time for a honeymoon (a luxury that was hardly compatible with Quaker sensibilities anyway). On returning home to Swarthmoor, she is once again imprisoned for having broken the Conventicle Act, which forbad individuals to lead unauthorized religious meetings. Separated from the groom, she languishes in jail for most of a year. Soon after she is released, Fox sails for America. Shortly after his return, he is again imprisoned and not freed until 1675. Such separations characterize their marriage. They rarely live together for any extended period of time. When Fox dies in 1691, at the age of sixty-seven, the movement is still disorganized and scattered.

In the decade following her husband's death, Fell struggled with factions and individuals who sought to bring a legalistic "silly poor gospel" into the movement. Such views were in her mind *narrow* and threatened the very core of

## Quakers Abroad

One of the most well-known names among Quakers is William Penn (1644–1718), the founder of Pennsylvania. Born into wealth and converted at age twenty-two, he later acquires a vast tract of land in the New World where Quakers and others can enjoy religious freedom. He is remembered for his championing democracy, for his call for a union of the American colonies, and for his fair and honest treatment of Native Americans.

William Penn

Two years after Penn died, John Woolman (1720–1772) is born into a Quaker family in New Jersey. As a young man he earnestly seeks an opportunity to serve God. Then the opportunity comes: "My employer, having a negro woman, sold her, and desired me to write a bill of sale." Woolman obeys, but that incident sets him on a lifelong crusade to make abolitionism a key element of Quaker belief and practice. That Quakers were opposed to slavery from the beginning is a common misunderstanding. In fact, many of them were wealthy slaveholders. For the next three decades, Woolman travels on foot and on horseback to one Quaker home after another, convincing families of the sinfulness of slavery. He speaks at meetinghouse, writes essays, and sets the stage for Quakers as leading abolitionists and sponsors of the Underground Railroad, a system for helping fugitives find safety from slavery.

Quaker beliefs. Rules and regulations would quench the Spirit: "Let the Spirit of God ... lead us and guide us," she admonished. "Let us stand fast in the liberty wherewith Christ hath made us free." She continued to write and lead meetings in her home until her death at eighty-seven.

From the beginning of her involvement with the Friends, Fell had served as an effective apol-ogist for the movement. In 1660, she had written "Declaration," which laid out the Quaker position on pacifism, a position that has served the Society well in the centuries since. Her life and ministry, like that of her husband's, had a profound and long-lasting influence not only in her homeland but also in America and around the world.

## What if ...

What if Roger Williams had buckled under the Puritan regime and not been banished from the Bay Colony? Would he have founded Providence Plantation and befriended Indians and warded off the potential annihilation of Bay colonists? How did his demand for freedom of religion affect the future of American liberty?

What if Thomas Fell had not supported Margaret's ministry among Quakers? Would she have gone on to marry George Fox after Fell's death? Without her influence and organiza-tional skills would the Quakers be a mere foot-note in history like other seventeenth-century Civil War sects? Would the Quaker movement today be associated with pacifism?

What if John Woolman had not been convicted by God to make the abolition of slavery his life's work? Many of the nineteenth-century abolitionists were Quakers. Without the pro-found Quaker influence might abolitionism have been slowed and the freeing of slaves in America been delayed beyond the 1860s?

## Further Reading

Davis, J. C. *Fear, Myth and History: The Ranters and the Historians.* London: Cambridge University Press, 2002.

Fell, Margaret. *Undaunted Zeal: The Letters of Margaret Fell.* Edited by Elsa Glines. Richmond, Ind.: Friends United Press, 2003.

Fell, Margaret. *Women's Speaking Justified.* Introduction by David J. Latt. Berkeley: University of California Press, 1979.

Fox, George. *The Journal of George Fox.* Richmond, Ind.: Friends United Press, 2006.

Gaustad, Edwin S. *Roger Williams.* New York: Oxford University Press, 2005.

Hill, Christopher. *The World Turned Upside Down: Radical Ideas During the English Revolution.* New York: Penguin, 1991.

Knox, Ronald A. *Enthusiasm: A Chapter in the History of Religion.* South Bend, Ind.: University of Notre Dame, 1994.

LaPlante, Eve. *American Jezebel: The Uncommon Life of Anne Hutchinson.* New York: HarperOne, 2005.

Mack, Phyllis. *Visionary Women: Ecstatic Prophecy in Seventeenth-Century England.* Berkeley: University of California Press, 1995.

Purkiss, Diane. *The English Civil War: A People's History.* New York: HarperPerennial, 2007.

Williams, Selma. *Divine Rebel: The Life of Anne Marbury Hutchinson.* New York: Holt, Rinehart and Winston, 1981.

Woolman, John. *The Journal and Major Essays of John Woolman.* Edited by Phillips P. Moulton. Richmond, Ind.: Friends United Press, 1989.

# CHAPTER 18

# The Catholic Church

*Centuries of Struggle*

*We have a little farmhouse in northern Michigan where we go—MacBook in tow—to get away from phones, email, and the bustle of greater Grand Rapids. Located in the "town" of Isadore, we are the only residents except for Father Don, who lives across the road next to Holy Rosary Catholic Church. On the far side of the church is Holy Rosary cemetery.*

*Here in our town of three residents (two part-time), stands a living—and passing—memorial to the staying power of the Catholic Church worldwide. Whether the church came into being with the apostle Peter or centuries later with Pope Leo the Great, its long history of endurance and expansion is impressive—and absolutely fascinating. The Catholic Church is anything but static and steady, however. Its ups and downs, its cruelty and compassion, its profligacy and charity, offer stark contrasts.*

*Even the picturesque Holy Rosary Church, situated in the timeless rolling hills of Leelanau County, embodies the opposite extremes of its Mother Church. Traditions of community service and caregiving are everywhere. But hidden beneath the brick façade is a secret that lies in a nearby unmarked grave. Like many of the secrets of church history, this one is closely guarded, and even readers of the church's hundred-year history are left in the dark.*

*On August 23, 1907, Sister Mary Janina, a nun serving at the Isadore parish, went missing. Newspapers later reported that she was murdered by the priest's housekeeper, who was apparently upset by the close relationship between the nun and the priest. The housekeeper was tried and convicted in 1919, but that was not the end of the story. In the 1970s, Broadway and Hollywood presented their versions in* The Runner Stumbles, *and history faded into fable.*

*Last year author Mardi Link spent a long weekend at our little farmhouse (which doubles as Isadore Writers' Retreat), writing perhaps the definitive story of this incident. Published in 2009 by the University of Michigan Press,* Isadore's Secret: Sin, Murder, and Confession in Northern Michigan *is a well-researched and absolutely absorbing page-turner.*

History fades into fable; fact becomes clouded with doubt and controversy; the inscription molders from the tablet: the statue falls from the pedestal. Columns, arches, pyramids, what are they but heaps of sand; and their epitaphs, but characters written in the dust?
WASHINGTON IRVING

Ancient history marches toward the present, and columns and arches crumble into sand. We sometimes imagine that what remains are mostly museum artifacts. But the stories of the ancient church are also the stories of the eighteenth century and of the church of today. It is true that history fades into fable and great saints fall from their pedestals even as the inscriptions molder. But we recognize the voices as our own and those of our contemporaries, clouded as they are with doubt and controversy.

Church historians are sometimes tempted to emblazon the headlines with renewal, reformation, and revival. Whether inspired by monks or Puritans and Pilgrims, renewals are newsworthy. The same goes for the Reformation and later revivals, whether German Pietism or trans-Atlantic awakenings. The eccentric sectarians likewise grab headlines: from St. Francis to George Fox, their names are familiar. But alongside these movements and individuals, the established institutionalized church carries on, amid fragmentation and internal challenge, with its own colorful cast of characters, including Pope Innocent X and Olimpia, Blaise Pascal, Jeanne-Marie Guyon, Ann-Marie Javouhey, and John Henry Newman.

The Catholic Church emerged from the battering of the Protestant Reformation in some ways stronger than it was before. Overseas discoveries and colonization went hand in hand with mission outreach as religious orders expanded the church abroad. But at the same time, nationalistic impulses in Protestant and Catholic regimes ignited armed conflict, creating havoc in both countryside and city. Such rivalries were the staple of the Thirty Years War that raged in central Europe from 1618 to 1648. Simple summaries are inadequate, but the centuries-old House of Habsburgs, headed by two generations of Ferdinands, faced opposition from all sides. Maximilian I was an ally, while Frederick V rallied German troops in opposition. Calvinists, Lutherans, and Catholics were all prominent in the geographical and national upheaval that included Austria, Germany, France, Spain, Holland, Sweden, and Denmark. Borders shifted amid civil wars and feuding militias.

Throughout this period social status and mobility were swept by the winds of change. As

## PARADE OF HISTORY

The Catholic parade of pomp and splendor is continuous through the generations of church history. Whether in the Vatican or in local cathedrals, the processions of clerics is never-ending. But the vibrancy of the institution is another matter. In fact, the church veers seriously off course as it confronts Enlightenment thinking. The procession of philosophers from Descartes and Voltaire to Hume and Kant wreaks havoc on the supremacy of religious faith among both Protestants and Catholics. But rationalism is met by Quietism and other forms of renewal and revival. Madame Jean Guyon is one of many who journeys through the countryside and cities on evangelistic tours. She preaches in marketplaces and private homes, often with a parade of followers in her wake.

the merchant class gained prominence, concepts of freedom and individualism came to the fore, even as aristocratic power and church tradition was challenged. New Enlightenment ideals clashed with the old institutional hierarchies that were propping up both the monarchies and the church. Beneath the aristocracy simmered the bourgeoisie and the impoverished masses.

Despite the turmoil on every level of society, the Catholic Church continued to wield power as popes, cardinals, bishops, and lesser clerics came and went. The enormous wealth of the church in currency, jewels, art, and real estate combined to promote a prestige that was equaled only in its own pomp and ceremony. Notwithstanding the reform efforts of the Council of Trent, church offices were often bestowed on the basis of family or political connections. Few popes stood out as spiritual leaders or even as savvy corporate CEOs.

Because holding church office brought wealth and prestige to families, nepotism was all too common. Pope Urban VIII, who reigned for more than twenty years (1623–1644), named a brother and two nephews as cardinals and gave lesser positions to many other family members. His unrelated enemies, not surprisingly, were numerous. So fearful was he that he

retained magicians to ward off evil and astrologers to read his horoscope. Such activities were not perceived as threatening to the authority of the church even when practiced by lesser clerics or lay people. But sectarian movements were another matter. Urban, like most popes and Catholic clerics, did not tolerate individuals or groups that challenged papal authority or competed with the Vatican for loyalty. In 1633 he referred his one-time friend, the ailing Galilei Galileo (1564–1642), to the Inquisition, an action that led to Galileo's imprisonment and recantation. He also banned the writings of Cornelius Jansen (1585–1638), founder of a "Calvinistic" Catholic sectarian movement.

Urban's successor, Innocent X, shifted papal favoritism from France to Spain during his decade-long reign (1644–1655). His successor, Alexander VII (reigning for twelve years), is particularly remembered for his bitter conflicts with King Louis XIV of France. In fact, the situation became so strained that Louis marched French troops into Rome—a military venture that ended with a humiliating defeat for Pope Alexander, the terms of surrender spelled out in the Treaty of Pisa of 1664. Both, however, agreed on their condemnation of Jansenism.

## A ROYAL REVOCATION THAT BACKFIRES

Since the Huguenots of France were in large part artisans, craftsmen, and professional people, they were usually well-received in the countries to which they fled for refuge when religious discrimination or overt persecution caused [hundreds of thousands] to leave France [following the Revocation of the Edict of Nantes by Louis XIV in 1685]. Most of them went initially to Germany, the Netherlands, and England, although some found their way eventually to places as remote as South Africa. Considerable numbers of Huguenots migrated to British North America, especially to the Carolinas, Virginia, Pennsylvania, and New York. Their character and talents in the arts, sciences, and industry were such that they are generally felt to have been a substantial loss to the French society from which they had been forced to withdraw, and a corresponding gain to the communities and nations into which they settled.

National Huguenot Society

## THE CATHOLIC CHURCH ON THE DEFENSIVE

The Protestant Reformation had placed the Catholic Church on the defensive, and it would remain there until the middle of the twentieth century, fiercely combating the Enlightenment, the French Revolution, Italian nationalism, modern intellectual movements, and especially theological and biblical scholarship.... Paul V (1605–21) will always be remembered as the pope who [first] censured the astronomer Galileo — a censure removed almost four centuries later in the pontificate of John Paul II (1978–2005). Gregory XV (1621–23) decreed that papal elections should thereafter be conducted by secret ballot — a practice still in effect today. Urban VII (1623–44) consecrated the new St. Peter's Basilica in 1626.... Alexander VII (1655–67) permitted Jesuit missionaries in China to use Chinese rites in the Mass.... Clement XI (1700–21) reversed Alexander VII's approval of the use of Chinese rites — a disastrous decision that completely undercut the Catholic missionary effort in China. The memory of Clement XIV (1769–74), a Franciscan, is dishonored by his suppression of the Jesuits in 1773.... Pius VI (1775–99) denounced the French Revolution and died a prisoner of Napoleon Bonaparte.

Richard McBrien, *Lives of the Popes*

King Louis XIV symbolizes the seventeenth-century Age of Absolutism — especially in his declaration *"L'etat, C'est Moi"* (I am the state). As such, he had no inclination to buckle under the authority of a mere pope. Yet he was a staunch defender of Catholicism, expressed perhaps most visibly in his revocation of the Edict of Nantes in 1685. Instituted to protect Protestants, the Edict of Nantes (1598) had allowed Huguenots (French Protestant Calvinists) to live and worship in relative peace. With the revocation, however, there is a mass exodus of Christians from his domain. The Huguenots and Jansenists were not the only sectarian movements the popes sought to suppress, however. Gallicanism, a French national movement giving the monarch priority over the pope, gained momentum with the Declaration of the Clergy of France in 1682. In the eighteenth-century spirit of nationalism, other domains followed suit, much to the chagrin of the papacy.

But these were surely not the only battles the Church of Rome was confronting. The Age of Enlightenment took a major toll on the Christian faith as the eighteenth century produced philosophers who challenged the very foundations of Christian belief. Within a matter of generations the whole of Western society was infected. In the generations following the mid-seventeenth century, the philosophical foundations of the church were severely battered.

Before this time, faith and reason were generally seen as complementary. But then came Descartes, often labeled the father of philosophy. Spinoza likewise helped initiate the seventeenth-century era of rationalism through his attack on the validity of miracles. David Hume insisted that God's existence could not be proved by the intelligent design of the universe. Immanuel Kant viewed the existence of God as a reality only in human consciousness. And Friedrich Schleiermacher insisted that the Christian faith could not be supported by rational evidence. All of this took its toll on the underlying suppositions of natural theology expressly defined by Thomas Aquinas.

## Demonic Obsession and Witchcraft

Even as science and philosophy are making their way into the modern world, superstitions of every variety abound. In the generations following the Reformation the witchcraft frenzy leads to tens of thousands of executions. Nor are Catholics alone in their accusations and torture. Protestants are equally determined to rid the land of demonic menace. Between 1500 and 1660 an estimated fifty thousand witches are executed, four out of five of them women. Germany led in executions, with France coming in second, and England far behind with some one thousand sentenced to death.

As was true in Salem, Massachusetts, spectral evidence is frequently called forth in determining guilt. The charge that an individual (typically a woman) had made a pact with the devil and signed her name to worship him is often seen in court records. Women were accused of casting "spells for getting a husband, spells for the marriage, spells before the child is born, spells before the christening."

Were women actually practicing witchcraft and casting spells and making pacts with devils? There is evidence women were involved in superstitious rituals, but that they made pacts with the devil and renounced their Christian faith and desecrated the Mass is doubtful. Nor did they ride through the sky at night on broomsticks or ritually sacrifice babies. There was already a long history in medieval Catholicism of women allegedly committing atrocious acts spurred on by the devil. Thomas Aquinas joined the discussion by claiming "demons reap the sperm of men and spread it among women."

In 1484 Innocent VIII alleged that people—particularly in Germany—were making pacts with the devil, casting spells and causing stillborn babies and crop failure. He appointed two Dominican friars, Heinrich Kramer and Joseph Sprenger, to investigate and publish a full report—known as Malleus Maleficarum, "Hammer of Witches." Among other things,

### A GREAT COMPANY OF BEWITCHED PEOPLE

Perhaps no chapter in human history is more revolting than the chapter which records the wild belief in witchcraft and the merciless punishments meted out for it in Western Europe in the century just preceding the Protestant Reformation and the succeeding century. In the second half of that century, the Church and society were thrown into a panic over witchcraft, and Christendom seemed to be suddenly infested with a great company of bewitched people, who yielded themselves to the irresistible discipline of Satan.... No Reformer uttered a word against it.

Philip Schaff, *History of the Christian Church*

the report explains *"Why Superstition is chiefly found in Women* ... why a greater number of witches is found in the fragile feminine sex than among men."In sum, it all started with Eve.

Men like the Dominican friars, however, were certainly not responsible for inventing all the unusual accusations against women. Women incriminated themselves. In 1582, at the St. Osyth witch trials in Essex, England, Ursley Kempe testified that she assigned specific tasks to her familiar spirits:

> Bursting out with weeping and falling on her knees, she [Ursley] said, yes, she had the four imps her son had told of, and that two of them, Titty and Jack [a gray and a black cat] were "hees" whose office was to punish and kill unto death; and two, Tiffin [a white lamb] and Piggin [a black toad], were "shees," who punished with lameness and bodily harm only, and destroyed goods and cattle.

To be fair, such confessions were sometimes elicited through torture or promises of release from prison. Likewise, witches were often identified through a strip search for body blemishes that were evidence of the "devil's mark."

Earlier, in 1571, witchcraft hysteria broke out in France after Trois-Echelles, who served in the court of King Charles IX, testified that, besides himself, there were one hundred thousand other witches roving through the countryside. Rumors spawned panic, and magistrates sometimes locked up and executed suspects without a trial. In many cases children accused their parents of heinous crimes. By the late seventeenth century, at the very time the Salem witch hysteria was breaking out, witchcraft accusations in Europe were on the wane.

As early as 1615, the Inquisition denounced Galileo (1564–1642) for his support of the Copernican theory, proving the earth is not the center of the universe—a theory "false and contrary to Scripture." In 1632 he was found "vehemently suspect of heresy" by the Inquisition and given a life sentence of house arrest. But Galileo, the father of modern science, had begun a revolution that could not be undone by a pope or anyone else. Added to the problems caused by the new rationalism were outbreaks of witchcraft and magic that keep inquisitors busy.

The worldwide spread of the Catholic faith faces severe losses as the Chinese Rites Controversy rages among the religious orders, particularly between the more "liberal" Jesuits and the more "conservative" Dominicans. Pope Alexander VII had signed a decree favorable to the Jesuits in 1656 that permitted the widespread use of Chinese religious forms, including ancestor worship and the word *Tien* (heaven) for God. In the following century, however, the Jesuits are suppressed—put out of business in many regions of the world—by a papacy with French influence, and they are not reinstated until 1814. In the meantime, the French Revolution, beginning in 1789, would take a terrible toll on the already battered Catholic Church.

## THEOLOGY THROUGH THE AGES

During the years 100 to 600, most theologians were bishops; from 600 to 1500 in the West, they were monks; since 1500, they have been university professors. Gregory I, who died in 604, was a bishop who had been a monk; Martin Luther, who died in 1546, was a monk who became a university professor. Each of these life styles has left its mark on the job description of the theologian, but also on the way doctrine has continued to develop back and forth between believing, teaching, and confessing.

Jaroslav Pelikan, *The Christian Tradition*

### Pope Innocent X and Olimpia: Scandal in the Vatican

With the rise of national states and the spread of absolutism, popes were easily sidelined as monarchs began to reign supreme. The prestige of the papacy had declined during the long reign of nepotism under Urban VIII. His successor, a "dark-horse" compromise candidate, was hardly the man to revitalize the office. Indeed, in many respects, Giambattista Pamfili (1574 – 1655), who would become Innocent X, was a non-

Pope Innocent X

descript pope. He studied law and worked his way up the institutional ladder under three popes to the position of cardinal. In carrying out the guidelines of the Council of Trent and the Inquisition, he was faithful to a fault. As a pope, however, he was ineffective and inefficient.

Because he was perceived to favor France, Innocent X soon became embroiled in a widespread church dispute. French church militants were threatening to invade the Papal States. Later, when one of his bishops was murdered, the pope's henchmen mercilessly attacked those whom he suspected were responsible and created problems that would long haunt him. During his reign the Thirty Years War was winding down and was finally ended through the Peace of Westphalia in 1648. But late that year he issued a bull nullifying much of what had been agreed upon. In his "Zelo Domus Dei," he decreed that there would be no compromises on the part of the Roman Church.

Innocent was not a strong pope in his own right, and his eleven-year reign might have gone down in history as just one more in a gradual weakening of the papacy. In the eyes of many contemporaries he was considered weak but for one ace in the hand. He was propped up by a powerful woman behind the papal throne. Olimpia Maidalchini, his sister-in-law, possessed all the tenacity and qualifications to be a politically powerful pope herself, but for her gender. Born into a poor family, she was sent to a convent as a teenager, only to escape and marry her way into prestige. At twenty she became a rich widow, and at twenty-one she married a nobleman, age forty-nine and well connected. With her wealth and his noble blood, she relocated to Rome and was soon living in a mansion with a massive ballroom decorated by the most prestigious artists of the day.

But power, more than wealth, was her ambition. Her opportunity came when her brother-in-law was elevated to cardinal and later became Pope Innocent X. Indeed, she wielded so much control over the new pope that a cardinal commented, "We have just elected a female pope." Banners appeared outside churches proclaiming the reign of "Pope Olimpia I." Indeed, papal medals appeared showing Olimpia with the keys of St. Peter, crowned with the triple tiara and seated on the papal throne. The other side of the medal featured the pope spinning wool, wearing a bonnet over his curls.

She was denounced as a whore by one cardinal, and another bemoaned the "monstrous power of a woman in the Vatican." But most cardinals and lesser clerics paid her homage, one cardinal acknowledging her authority by hanging a large portrait of her in his outer lounge. When officials had business with the pope, they sought her authorization before assuming a decision was final. Publicly, Olimpia presented herself as the papal hostess, but her oversight of daily Vatican activities included far more than serving tea and pastries. Her authority was considerable, extending to the selection of cardinals, purchasing properties, and conducting diplomacy with foreign emissaries. All the while she took generous perks for herself from the papal treasury.

Rumors that she and the aged pope were lovers flourished, but her aspirations were far

### DONNA OLIMPIA WAS POPE

There has never before been heard of nor seen that the popes allowed themselves to be so absolutely governed by a woman. There was no more talk of the pope; all the discourse was of Donna Olimpia, many taking occasion to say, *That it were fit likewise to introduce the women to the administration of the Sacrament, since that Donna Olimpia was pope.*

A Contemporary Chronicler

beyond that of a sexual dalliance. Her lust was for power and prestige. The French ambassador reported to King Louis XIV that she was indeed a "great lady." Even her chief nemesis conceded that she had "intellect of great worth in economic government" and a great "capacity for the highest affairs." Yet there was widespread embarrassment that the church was being ruled by a woman. So unpopular was she that when the pope lay dying in 1655, she fled Rome, though not before filling her luggage with gold coins. At eighty-two, Innocent had long been failing. With her sudden flight, his corpse lay three days before he was reported dead.

Two years before he died in 1653, Innocent had issued a bull taking aim at the Jansenists, who were located primarily in France. His predecessor, Urban VIII, had also condemned the movement, a move based largely on a book written by Bishop Cornelius Jansen (1585–1638), who had drawn heavily on the theology of Augustine. According to Jesuit heresy hunters, the book was no more than warmed-over Calvinism, though Jansen had insisted his teachings were as Catholic as was St. Augustine himself. Like Calvin (and Augustine), he affirmed God's sovereignty and man's inability to come to God or perform good works apart from unmerited grace—grace bestowed only on the elect. His three-volume *Augustinus* (published posthumously in 1640), recounted the history—and heresy—of Pelagianism as a theology of works-based righteousness that denied original sin. The book also took aim at "modern" denials of Augustine's theology of God's sovereign grace. It became a seventeenth-century bestseller in France and the Low Countries, and ten professors at the Sorbonne endorsed it. However, in 1641 Urban VIII added it to the Index of Prohibited Books and issued a bull against it.

## Blaise Pascal: Mathematician and Philosopher

The most noted proponent of Jansenism was Blaise Pascal (1623–1662), mathematician and philosopher. The son of a scientist, Pascal was a precocious but sickly child. Introduced early to the best education of his day, he would be considered one of the most brilliant minds of his era. As young as eight he began in writing scientific papers, and in his teens he developed new concepts in geometry and invented a mathematical calculator. He later made great strides in the field of calculus and various fields of physics. But all the while he is struggling with doubt about God and his religious heritage. He lives at a time when new discoveries in astronomy point to the vastness of space. "The eternal science of these infinite spaces," he confesses, "terrifies

Blaise Pascal

me." Where is God, he wonders, in the midst of the vast universe?

His sister is a nun, and in 1655 he converts to Jansenism through her influence. Her abbess, Jacqueline-Marie-Angelique Arnauld (1591–1661), is one of the leading supporters of Jansenism in the seventeenth century. One of twenty children, she had entered the Cistercian convent at a young age and was appointed abbess before the age of twelve. Some three decades later she is introduced to the teachings of Cornelius Jansen, and for the remainder of her life she spreads his teachings. She wields theological influence over two Port-Royal convents and is also instrumental in bringing her brother, philosopher Antoine Arnauld, into the Jansenist camp.

Pascal's identification with the movement comes during a two-week retreat at the Port-Royal Convent, and in the following years he participates in other religious retreats there, even as he contemplates philosophical and psychological and scientific puzzles. Responding to questions in an era of increasing religious doubt, he makes his famous wager—known as Pascal's wager: "I should be much more afraid of being mistaken and then finding out that Christianity is true than of being mistaken in believing it to be true." Truly thoughtful people, he argues, should put their wager on the truth of Christianity. If it is false, what have they to lose? If it is true, they gain an eternal life of infinite happiness. Thus one could thoughtfully be a committed

Christian in the midst of seriously questioning the very existence of God.

Belief in God rises far above reason, as Pascal suggests in one of his most often-quoted aphorisms: "The heart has its reasons which reason knows nothing of." Just before he had gone to the Port-Royal Retreat, Pascal found this true in his own life. His discovery came through a profound mystical experience, which he recorded on paper and pinned inside his coat. It was found at the time of his death. Dated November 23, 1654, "from about half past ten in the evening until half past midnight," it was his "nuit de feu"—his night of fire.

### Fire

'God of Abraham, God of Isaac, God of
    Jacob,' not of philosophers and scholars.
Certainty, certainty, heartfelt, joy, peace.
God of Jesus Christ....
Joy, joy, joy, tears of joy.
Sweet and total renunciation....
Total submission to Jesus Christ and my
    director.
Everlasting joy in return for one day's effort
    on earth.
I will not forget thy word. Amen.

Although transformed by a mystical experience, he, like his contemporary René Descartes, rates rational thought as the crowning capability of humankind:

Man is but a reed, the most feeble thing in nature, but he is a thinking reed. The entire universe need not arm itself to crush him. A vapor, a drop of water suffices to kill him. But, if the universe were to crush him, man would still be more noble than that which killed him, because he knows that he dies and the advantage which the universe has over him, the universe knows nothing of this. All our dignity

then, consists in thought. By it we must elevate ourselves, and not by space and time which we cannot fill. Let us endeavor then, to think well; this is the principle of morality.

Thinking well is what Pascal is known for— despite serious health issues. Tormented by severe neurological problems most of his life, he is unfit for strenuous activities. But he excels in cognitive capabilities and not simply in complex mathematical and philosophical puzzles. His thoughts are captured by practical problems as well. For example, he engineers a plan for a mass transit system in Paris—large-capacity carriages transporting passengers on scheduled routes. At the same time, he is challenging Descartes on how we know things to be true. He insists that experiences and experiments are the starting point for the discovery of truth, not pure reason, though empiricism and reason go hand in hand for the scientist.

In some respects France of the seventeenth century was not big enough for two hardheaded, brilliant mathematician philosophers. "I cannot forgive Descartes," Pascal laments. "In all his philosophy he did his best to dispense with God. But he could not avoid making Him set the world in motion with a flip of His thumb; after that he had no more use for God." During Pascal's lifetime philosophy is being turned on its head by Descartes. As Pascal recognizes, Descartes' philosophy was more toxic to the faith than outright atheism would have been. To have a distant, mechanistic God was no better than having no God at all. God is not, Pascal insisted, "the god of philosophers."

Descartes' god of philosophy would reign over the Enlightenment, an era when the very truthfulness of religion was being questioned. Was there, in fact, a personal God who was concerned with human affairs, or was the biblical

God more myth than reality? The Renaissance had placed an emphasis on humanity—Renaissance humanism—while leaving the biblical concept of God essentially intact. But with the dawn of the Enlightenment, the traditional concept of God is challenged.

## René Descartes and Enlightenment Philosophers

Often referred to as the Father of modern philosophy, René Descartes (1596–1650) was a dutiful Catholic throughout his life. Ever conscious of the church dogma vigorously defended by the dreaded Inquisition, he nevertheless put forth a shocking proposition more radical than the ancient Greek philosophy from which he had so heavily drawn. Convinced that the rational mind was the only source of knowledge, he insisted that everything must be doubted—even one's very existence. He is considered the first in a series of genuinely secular philosophers. Philosophy, like his specialty of mathematics, must be autonomous—not subservient to religion. Indeed, religion and philosophy must not be mixed.

Born in La Haye, France, he grew up in modest wealth and studied at a prestigious Jesuit school. He then went on to Paris where, at the behest of his father, he graduated with a law degree. But settling down in a legal profession or continuing on in graduate studies was not suited to his temperament, as he later related: "I entirely abandoned the study of letters. Resolving to seek no knowledge other than that of which could be found in myself or else in the great book of the world, I spent the rest of my youth traveling, visiting courts and armies, mixing with people of diverse temperaments and ranks."

More than merely visiting armies, he serves as a military officer for both Dutch and German forces, though he is remembered more for his sloth than for any commanding presence. Leaving military life, he supports his traveling lifestyle with inherited money. While on his journeys he becomes captivated by mathematics and physics—particularly by questions related to gravity. In 1628 he settles in the Netherlands, where he establishes his reputation as a writer and university lecturer. A stylish dresser and life-long bachelor, he dotes over Francine, his daughter by a servant girl, and is devastated when she dies of a fever at age five.

The philosophical discovery for which he is most known comes in 1618, when he is in his early twenties serving with the Bavarian army. The scene is a cold winter day. He is contemplating epistemology—the science of knowing. *How can we know anything for sure?* The setting is most unusual. He is "in a stove"—perhaps a heated room or a large wood stove near which he huddles to keep warm. It is here that he suddenly recognizes the most basic foundation of knowledge: *Cogito ergo sum* (I think, therefore I am). That night he has dreams that serve as a symbolic confirmation of his mystical discovery. That thinking—or doubting—would prove one's existence would seem on the surface to have little to do with mathematics. But for Descartes the universe cannot be understood apart from the absoluteness of the hard science of mathematics. He allows no room for mere speculation and uncertainty. True knowledge requires absolute true and false answers.

Although he does not combine religion and philosophy as a single discipline as had Thomas Aquinas and others, he nevertheless takes a page from Anselm and seeks to prove God's existence through philosophy. For Anselm, God is that which nothing greater can be conceived. For Descartes, God's existence is proved by the same rationale that proves his own existence: *I think, therefore I am.* God likewise exists, he reasons, on the same foundation—essentially, *I think of the idea of God, and the cause of my thinking of God proves God exists.* But unlike Anselm, he is anything but a Christian apologist. In 1643 the University of Utrecht condemns his philosophy, and in 1663, more than a decade after his death, the pope includes his works in the Index of Prohibited Books.

If Descartes paved the way for the Enlightenment, Francois-Marie Voltaire (1694–1778) would stand as its most controversial representative. Like his predecessor, he acquired his razor-sharp thinking skills by way of a Jesuit education, but unlike Descartes he turned against his church heritage. His religious contempt wounded the church more severely than the guns of a mighty army could have. Yet for all the unbelief that flowed from his acerbic pen, he was no atheist. He was a deist. "I shall always be convinced," he wrote, "that a watch proves a watch-maker, and that a universe proves a God." But his God was not the personal God of the Bible, as he explained in his *Philosophical Dictionary*: "The Theist is firmly persuaded of the existence of a supreme Being as good as He is powerful.... The Theist does not know how God punishes, or how He favours and pardons, and is not rash enough to flatter himself that he knows how God acts, but that God acts and that He is just, this he knows."

Even more than Descartes or Voltaire, the brilliant Scottish thinker David Hume (1711–1776) stands out as a philosopher of skepticism. He maintained that no credible scholar could any longer honestly believe in the Bible. He challenged the cosmological argument for God, insisting that it is impossible for a cause (God) to be known only by its effect (the existence of the universe). He likewise argued that it is false to assume that the cause has any other

qualities than those related to causing the effect. Thus, one cannot identify the first cause as the Christian God or give this cause intelligence or moral attributes.

> *In general, the art of government consists of taking as much money as possible from one class of citizens to give to another.*
> Voltaire

"A miracle is a violation of the laws of nature," he argued, "and as a firm and unalterable experience has established these laws, the proof against a miracle from the very nature of the fact, is as entire as any argument from experience can possibly be imagined." In fact, all religions, he pointed out, depend upon miracles—and how, he demanded, can all religions be right? Yet he sometimes doubted his own methods so much that he experienced "melancholy and delirium," cured only by activities: "I dine, I play a game of backgammon, I converse, and am merry with my friends; and when, after three or four hours' amusement, I would return to these speculations, they appear so cold, and strained, and ridiculous, that I cannot find in my heart to enter into them any further."

Like his predecessors, Immanuel Kant (1724–1804) was unable to entirely rid himself of God. He was born into a poor Prussian family. His mother was a devout Christian whose faith had been profoundly influenced by the heritage of Jakob Spener, Auguste Hermann Francke, and other German Pietists. Through her influence he was immersed in evangelical religious values. But as he developed his speculative philosophy, he argued that no generation should be bound by the religious beliefs of earlier generations. He rejected biblical claims and attempts to prove the existence of God. But while he had no patience with the concept of a personal God who answers prayer and offers guidance, he nevertheless acknowledged that the universal human understanding of moral codes pointed to God. Jesus, for him, was a model worthy of recognition. He was convinced that because God is beyond our human comprehension, there is no value in attempting to prove his existence. But one might seek to know God not by looking for a deity but by starting with man and his quest for moral values.

These philosophers and many others had a profound effect on Christianity. Unlike the previous renewals and reformations and revivals that challenged the church to mend its ways, this movement aimed its arrows straight at God. The damage had only begun. Friedrich Nietzsche and others would carry on the fight.

## Madame Jeanne-Marie Guyon: Catholic Evangelist

Flourishing alongside philosophical speculation in every age are charismatic and mystical beliefs. On the opposite end of the spectrum from Descartes and his colleagues was Madame Guyon (1648–1717). Born into a wealthy family, she was a sickly child who spent her early life in a convent. Her desire was to become a nun, but her parents instead arranged a marriage when she was sixteen to a wealthy forty-year-old aristocrat whose mother treated her cruelly. The loss of her parents, a sister, and a son and daughter added to the anguish of her

Jeanne-Marie Guyon

twelve-year marriage. Widowhood at the age of twenty-eight comes as a relief.

All the while, however, she is finding solace in God through mystical experiences, convinced that suffering is drawing her closer to God. Influenced by a French Barnabite monk, Père Lacombe, she adopts a passive spirituality, one that opens the consciousness to deep meditation and comprehension of God. So consumed is she with spiritual discoveries that she leaves her two young children behind and begins an evangelistic tour. Her confessor, she insists, gives not only his blessing but also the command of the Lord: "My Father, I am a widow, who has little children four and six years of age. What else could God require of me but to rear them?" He responds: "I know nothing of it. You know whether God had made you recognize that he wished something of you. If it is so, there is nothing which should hinder you from doing his will. One must leave one's children to do it."

She journeys to Geneva where Father Lacombe has settled. But the local bishop orders them out of town. She later returns to France, where she publishes her mystical insights and is once again forced into exile by a local bishop. Her flight from persecution becomes an opportunity to evangelize. She preaches in marketplaces and private homes and is amazed at the spiritual hunger she finds. On entering the town of Thonon, she writes: "I have never in my life had so much consolation as in seeing in that little town so many good souls who vied with each

## Elizabeth Ann Bayley Seton

When Elizabeth Seton (1774–1821) converted to Catholicism in 1805, there was an uproar in her family. The daughter of a noted professor of anatomy and granddaughter of an Episcopal priest, she was devoted to her faith from childhood. Indeed, a battle began, with bishops on both sides fighting for her religious devotion. But on Ash Wednesday of 1805, she made her commitment official and never looked back. Despite a series of ministry failures, she attracted other women who joined with her in an informal religious community. In 1809 she took vows to enter a religious vocation. Property for a charitable complex in Maryland came through a donation as did other necessities. Eight women committed themselves to work with her, including her three daughters and a sister-in-law. Soon they had established an infirmary, a school, a chapel, and later an orphanage. Their own impoverished lifestyle — including a leaky roof and an infestation of fleas — replicated that of those who came for aid. In 1811, her ministry was recognized by the Vatican as an American order of the Sisters of Charity. By the time of her death in 1821, the order had expanded to a total of twenty communities. In 1975, she was canonized by Pope Paul VI.

other in giving themselves to God with their whole heart. There were young girls of twelve and thirteen years of age, who worked all day in silence in order to converse with God."

Her ministry reaches every social class and vocation, from an impoverished "laundress" to a prominent physician: "I entered into conversation with him on the subject of religion," she writes. "He acknowledged that he had known something of the power of religion, but that the religious life had been stifled by the multitude of his occupations.... The conversation was greatly blessed to him. And he became afterwards a decided Christian." Later on he "had occasion to bring to me some of his companions, and God took them all for himself." She preaches to those she encounters along the way and also seeks the rich and famous. In Paris she forms a group of "ladies of rank," including a countess and two duchesses. Nor does she assume clerics are off limits. Convents and monasteries become regular stops on her journeys. In fact, she is permitted to present her message at the monastery of the Grande Chartreuse, where no woman has before entered.

When she encounters a suicidal nun, she writes, "I endeavored to explain to her she must no longer rely upon observances, or trust to personal merits, but must trust in Christ and resign herself to Him alone." With further counsel, "she was so much changed that she became the admiration of the Religious community." Even if her words were true to the dogma reaffirmed by the Council of Trent, a female itinerant evangelist is not acceptable to the church hierarchy — particularly one considered mentally unstable. Indeed, she is regularly given to bizarre behavior. In an effort to gain holiness and comprehend the suffering of Christ, for example, she sucks bitter herbs, rolls in stinging nettles, puts stones in her shoes, and pulls out healthy teeth. She is convinced that in identifying with Christ she has actually ceased to exist and has become one with God.

Church authorities seek to silence her, but she is a Quietist who will not be quieted. Both she and Lacombe are imprisoned on orders of Louis XIV. Following her release, she is examined by theologians and signs a recantation. But she continues on with her ministry and is again imprisoned, this time in the Bastille. In 1703, after seven years of suffering, the last two years in solitary confinement, she is released. She lives the rest of her life with her son, writing poetry and following the injunction not to preach. "I found myself in happiness equal to that of the Blessed," she said of her suffering. "Nothing here below affected me; and neither at present do I see anything in heaven or in earth which can trouble me as regards myself."

## Anne-Marie Javouhey: Missionary to Africa and the World

Since medieval times large numbers of women have served alongside men in the Catholic Church, particularly in humanitarian ministries. Barred from the priesthood and the church hierarchy, they volunteered in droves to serve among those on the margins of society. Although many girls were sent to the convent by their parents, others felt called by God when they were very young. Anne-Marie Javouhey (1779–1851), the fifth of ten children born in the French countryside to prosperous pious farmers, grew up in an era of ferment which would erupt violently as the French Revolution, an uprising against both the state and the church.

Ten-year-old Anne Marie, like her family, was loyal to the church. As the

Anne-Marie Javouhey

Revolution ignited she feared that the church— her very Mother—might be destroyed by the waves of violence. Nuns and priests were persecuted. What could a child do? She found her niche in keeping watch as priests surreptitiously perform the Mass.

At nineteen she takes vows to become a nun, hoping to help undo some of the ravages of the Revolution. But she is restless until a vision awakens her one night. Before her is a nun with children from around the world pressing in from all sides. The nun calls to her: "These are the children God has given you. He wishes you to form a new congregation to take care of them. I am Teresa [of Avila]. I will be your protectress."

In the following years, she founds the Congregation of St. Joseph. Then in the 1820s, learning of an epidemic in Gambia, she journeys there with several nuns to serve the sick and dying. She establishes hospitals, schools, and agricultural colonies; within a few decades her blue-robed sisters are spread out over the world.

She supervises the work and is referred to by a sea captain as "my most seasoned sailor." Her mission outreach corresponds to the beginnings of the nineteenth-century Protestant modern missionary movement, predating the Women's Missionary Movement that began in the 1860s.

Like many of her male counterparts, she is an authoritarian leader who does not tolerate dissent. Her decisions are final: "God has made known to me what he wants me to do." Her superior, Bishop d'Hericourt, is not convinced, however. Her motherhouse is in his diocese, making him in his own mind the superior general. Before becoming a cleric, he

had been in the military, and he is not about to be bested by a woman. For nearly two decades a fierce tug-of-war would consume precious ministry time on both sides. Accused of demanding obedience from her nuns while disregarding obedience to him, she insists that the bishop is her superior only in personal matters—that he is not the superior over her religious order.

Despite her remarkable success—or because of it—the bishop's stance hardens as the years pass to the point of his excommunicating her, and she observes her nuns taking communion while she is forbidden to participate. Her aim, he charges, is to "extricate herself from Episcopal authority." Among her violations: she is appointing nuns without approval, and her business affairs are in "total disorder." She is carrying on like a bishop and a doctor of the church. He appeals to the archbishop, but she fights back: "I am not only the Superior General of the Congregation of St. Joseph of Cluny; I did not merely cooperate in the foundation of that Order; I am its sole and solitary foundress. I am its Mother General as God is its Father, since it is I who created and have developed it."

In the end, the archbishop comes down on her side. But it is a Pyrrhic victory. She is worn out by the long ordeal. Indeed, within a year both she and the bishop are dead, he before her. When she learns of his death, she writes to one of her nuns: "We almost met, he and I, on that very day, before the judgment seat of God. So he's gone in ahead of me, that good

Cardinal Newman

Bishop. Well, that is correct; that is how it ought to be."

## John Henry Newman: Catholic Convert and Apologist

As the Catholic Church marched into the modern era, controversy increased. Not only was it fighting philosophy and science and sectarian movements from within, but it was also clashing with Protestants in a battle for souls worldwide. By the mid-nineteenth century, the Protestant missionary movement was expanding, and Catholics, whose worldwide mission ventures were already centuries old, were not amused. Whether in Africa or Asia or the Pacific Islands, territorial battles raged. Catholics' eagerness to baptize infants and terminally ill individuals of all ages often led to horror stories that little ones (and others) were being poisoned, and Protestants did nothing to quell the rumors.

While Catholics faced competition from Protestants in world mission, they also competed for celebrity conversions from Protestantism to Catholicism. The much-publicized conversion story of Mother Seton was only equaled by the triumph of John Henry Newman (1801–1890), who departed the Church of England to become a Catholic. An Anglican priest and tutor at Oxford University, he was the founder of the Oxford movement that sought to stem the tide of low church liturgy and more closely conform to Catholic

## A HYMN FOR THE AGES

Lead, Kindly Light, amidst th' encircling
    gloom
Lead Thou me on!
The night is dark, and I am far from home —
Lead Thou me on!
Keep Thou my feet; I do not ask to see
The distant scene — one step enough for me.

John Henry Newman

liturgy and beliefs, including apostolic succession. In addition to sermons and books, he began writing "Tracts for the Times," defending high-church "ancient" liturgy.

Accused of being too cozy with the Catholics, he insists that he is not. "If there ever was a system which required reformation, it is that of Rome at this day," he argued, referring to the Catholic system as "Romanism or Popery." But as the years pass, he comes more in line with Rome than with the Church of England. In 1841 he publishes Tract Ninety, making the case that the Anglican Thirty-Nine Articles are compatible with Catholic doctrine. The tract creates an explosion among Anglicans, and he soon finds himself a cleric without a church.

He remains in limbo for a time even as the Oxford movement disintegrates. Then, in 1845, to the chagrin of his Anglican friends and colleagues, he formally joins the Catholic Church. The following year he is ordained a Catholic priest, helping to establish Catholic schools, publishing treatises, and serving in other clerical roles. In 1879 he is named a cardinal. His intent is not necessarily to pull others away from the Church of England into Catholicism. "You must be patient, you must wait for the eye of the soul to be formed in you," he writes to an inquiring friend. "Religious truth is reached, not by reasoning, but by an inward perception."

In both Catholic and Protestant circles Newman is today remembered as a deeply thoughtful writer in the field of spiritual formation, especially that which intersects with the rationalism and romanticism of his age. In *The Grammar of Assent* (1870), he makes a case for faith in the face of rational religion. Religious faith, he argues, is a legitimate outcome of cognitive activity. His chief opponents are British empiricists David Hume, John Locke, and John Stuart Mill. His *Apologia* challenging that philosophy also prefigures C. S. Lewis:

I understood ... that the exterior world, physical and historical, was but the manifestation to our senses of realities greater than itself. Nature was a parable, Scripture was an

## HAWAII SAINT

HONOLULU — The Congregation of the Causes of Saints at the Vatican has voted to canonize Father Damien of Molokai to sainthood.... Supporters of the sainthood effort are overjoyed that now the world will know what Hawaii has known for 100 years — that Father Damien of Molokai is a saint. He was born Joseph De Veuster in Tremeloo, Belgium, in 1840. De Veuster's older brother, Pamphile, was set to travel to the "Sandwich Islands," but was too sick to go. Instead, De Veuster traveled to Hawaii in his brother's place. The Roman Catholic priest arrived in Hawaii in 1864 and took the name Damien. He served the leprosy patients at the Molokai colony at Kalaupapa for 12 years before he succumbed to Hansen's disease at age 49.

*Honolulu News*, July 1, 2008

allegory; pagan literature, philosophy, and mythology, properly understood, were but a preparation for the Gospel. The Greek poets and sages were in a sense prophets.

Newman's writings have had a long shelf life. Thoughtful Christians in the generations since have looked to him for spiritual direction when facing intellectual struggles and doubt.

## What if ...

What if there had been a series of strong popes to confront kings like Louis XIV? What if the Catholic Church had held to an egalitarian position that would have allowed Olimpia, with her diplomatic and financial skills, to actually serve as pope? Like many strong papal predecessors, she had no inclination toward spiritual development, but she might have successfully protected the Vatican's interests against the power of seventeenth-century monarchs.

What if Pascal's "Christian" philosophy and science had prevailed in the Age of Rationalism and following? What if Descartes and other of the leading philosophers had followed his line of thinking?

What if Ann-Marie Javouhey had been allowed to expand her mission outreach with encouragement and support like that enjoyed by the Jesuits two centuries earlier? Would her band of missionaries have become a nineteenth-century Society of Jesus?

What if John Henry Newman had not converted to Catholicism? Might he have become a key ecumenical leader, bringing the Church of England and the Church of Rome closer together?

## Further Reading

Beik, William. *Louis XIV and Absolutism: A Brief Study with Documents.* New York: Macmillan, 2000.

Clarke, Desmond M. *Descartes: A Biography.* London: Cambridge University, 2006.

Collins, Roger. *Keepers of the Keys of Heaven: A History of the Papacy.* New York: Basic Books. 2009.

Dirvin, Joseph I. *The Soul of Elizabeth Seton.* San Francisco: Ignatius Press, 1990.

Guyer, Paul. *Knowledge, Reason, and Taste: Kant's Response to Hume.* Princeton, N.J.: Princeton University Press, 2008.

Herman, Eleanor. *Mistress of the Vatican: The True Story of Olimpia Maidalchini.* New York: William Morrow, 2008.

Link, Mardi. *Isadore's Secret: Sin, Murder, and Confession in Northern Michigan.* Ann Arbor: University of Michigan Press, 2009.

McPherson, Joyce. *A Piece of the Mountain: The Story of Blaise Pascal.* Lebanon, Tenn.: Greenleaf, 1995.

Pascal, Blaise. *Pensees and Other Writings.* Edited by Anthony Levi. New York: Oxford University Press, 2008.

Scarre, Geoffrey, and John Callow. *Witchcraft and Magic in Sixteenth- and Seventeenth-Century Europe*, 2nd ed. New York: Macmillan, 2001.

Strange, Roderick. *John Henry Newman: A Mind Alive.* London: Darton, Longman & Todd, 2008.

# CHAPTER 19

# Trans-Atlantic Awakenings

## *Revivals in England and America*

*Some years ago on a weekday afternoon I stood on a gravestone outside an Anglican Church in Epworth, England, and preached to an audience of one—my husband. The tomb in the cemetery alongside the church was that of Samuel Wesley, and the gravestone the very one on which his son John stood to preach when he was barred from preaching inside the church itself.*

*In that same town of Epworth is the Wesley manse, where Susanna held forth as the now-famous Mother of the Wesleys. As we toured her home, I imagined her—this feisty woman who stood up to her abusive husband—as my sister, brought together over the span of three centuries. But she and I are far removed from each other. Hers was a very different culture from mine.*

*I was reminded of that last night after returning home from seeing* Mama Mia!— *a lively filmed production of a Broadway musical with a southern European setting and lots of frivolity and dancing. Less than an hour later, my husband was back into his usual nighttime reading to me, in this case George Marsden's biography,* Jonathan Edwards. *The cultural milieu in that book could hardly have been more different from what we had just seen at the theatre.*

*Edwards, a dutiful son of the Puritans, was a minister in Northampton, Massachusetts, and was determined to stamp out any signs of silliness and mirth in the town. In* Mama Mia! *Meryl Streep and her middle-aged girlfriends are jumping on the bed and dancing down the stairs and laughing themselves sick. For my husband and me, the movie was a feel-good flick—an escape from all the bad network news of Baghdad and bank failures and floods and fires. For Edwards—or for Susanna Wesley—it would have been a shocking symbol of the evil times we live in when professing Christians are enjoying such entertainment.*

*History challenges us as we identify role models, but we should not fool ourselves in imagining that we could easily reach across the centuries and find cultural—or even religious—commonality. For Edwards and Whitefield and John Wesley and his mother, the "worldliness" of twentieth-first-century evangelicalism would be anathema.*

> We can learn from history how past generations thought and acted, how they responded to the demands of their time and how they solved their problems. We can learn by analogy, not by example, for our circumstances will always be different than theirs were. The main thing history can teach us is that human actions have consequences and that certain choices, once made, cannot be undone.
>
> GERDA LERNER, *WHY HISTORY MATTERS*

It is true that we learn more by analogy than by example when we look back over history—especially those of us who imagine that we would resonate with noted evangelicals of the past were they to be suddenly resurrected in the twenty-first century. Because our worldview is so much a part of us, we do not easily see it for what it is, and we sometimes imagine that our circumstances and our responses to circumstances would be similar to those who lived long ago. The main thing history offers us is the knowledge that actions have consequences that cannot be undone. For good and for ill, the actions of our evangelical forbearers had consequences that could not be undone.

Revival leaders of this era were a breed apart from those who would make headlines in the twentieth century. They were well educated and theologically astute, concerned more about correct doctrine than about making a quick convert. Among them are Susanna Wesley, John Wesley, George Whitefield, and Jonathan Edwards.

The eighteenth-century evangelical revivals in England and America were in many respects distinct and separate. Both, however, were the step-children of Puritanism, linked together through the person of George Whitefield and also through a long, rich heritage of Pietism that had its beginnings on the Continent. The historical roots of Pietism go back to seventeenth-century Germany where Philip Jakob Spener (1635–1705) called for a warm personal religious faith that would supercede the cold formalism of the Lutheran state church. His classic *Pia Desideria* (Pious Longings), published in 1675, laid out the prerequisites and principles for renewal and reform. His focus was on personal piety and the "new birth" that manifested itself in good works and social action. The movement spread through conventicles that offered opportunity for Bible study, prayer, and personal testimonies.

Spener's "dutiful son in the faith" was Auguste Hermann Francke (1663–1727). At Spener's encouragement, Francke became a pastor and professor at the University of Halle,

## PARADE OF HISTORY

As the tour of church history reaches the eighteenth century, popular revivalists leave behind settled congregations and march from town to town stirring sinners. Some, like Wesley and Edwards, slowly rise to the occasion. Others, like Whitefield, are natural-born actors who revel in an outdoor pulpit with nature's dramatic backdrop. Rumors that a Whitefield show is coming to town often spurs a frantic procession like one that occurred in Middletown, Connecticut, in 1740. Dusty roads were jammed with horses and buggies and runners on foot as though "fleeing for our lives," wrote a contemporary, "all the while fearing we should be too late to hear the sermon."

where he also established a community to aid ministers in spiritual development. His aim was to bring renewal to the church and stimulate evangelism at home and abroad. His motto was "a life changed, a church revived, a nation reformed, and a world evangelized." He was a preacher, scholar, and tireless humanitarian worker. Among his outreach endeavors were homes for widows, an orphanage, a hospital, a rescue mission, a school for poor children, and food and medicine for the needy.

The German Pietism of Spener and Francke spawned Lutheran mission outreach to India as well as a worldwide Moravian evangelistic movement founded by Nicolaus Ludwig von Zinzendorf (1700–1760), a Lutheran nobleman. Raised by his Pietist grandmother, Zinzendorf was educated under the guidance of Franke at the University of Halle, where he joined with other students in spiritual disciplines. Several years later, while visiting a museum, he saw the painting *Ecco Homo* by Domenico Feti, portraying Jesus crowned with thorns. The inscription read, "I have done this for you; what have you done for me?" The work of art had a profound impact on him. "I have loved Him for a long time," he said, "but I have never actually done anything for Him. From now on I will do whatever He leads me to do."

In the following years, Zinzendorf turned his grandmother's vast estate into a spiritual retreat and a refuge for Christians fleeing persecution. Named *Herrnhut* (meaning "the Lord's watch"), the center attracted many refugees who were descendants of the *Unitas Fratrum* (United Brethren), followers of John Hus. Lutheran Pietists and Anabaptists also moved to the community. In 1727, five years after the community was formed, there was a spiritual awakening that launched an around-the-clock "prayer watch" that lasted more than one hundred years.

The revival also set the stage for the worldwide Moravian mission venture. Prior to this time the land-locked Protestants—with the exception of certain German Pietists—had focused very little attention on overseas evangelistic outreach. But the Herrnhut revival changed that, and Zinzendorf offered his own theological foundation, believing that Christ's presence permeated the whole world through the Holy Spirit and that individuals were thus prepared to receive the gospel message. Missionaries were merely the agents who presented Jesus with no doctrinal defense of the faith. Zinzendorf argued that missionaries should not "be blinded by reason as if people had to ... first learn to believe in God, after that in Jesus." Nor should missionaries be concerned for their own physical well-being. They were to live on the same socioeconomic level as that of the people they served—including becoming slaves to bring the gospel to slaves, as Leonard Dober, who served on the island of St. Thomas, wrote in a letter:

> When the gracious count [Zinzendorf] came back from his trip to Denmark and told me about the slaves, it gripped me so that I could not get free of it. I vowed to myself that if one other brother would go with me, I would become a slave.... The word of the cross in its lowliness shows a special strength to souls. As for me, I thought: even if helpful to no one in it, I could still give witness through it of obedience to our Savior!... On the island there still are souls who cannot believe because they have not heard.

In the decades that followed, Moravian missionaries faced persecution, largely from other Christians, as they spread out over the world. But they also profoundly influenced other Christians by their unflagging faith. So it was

## EVERYDAY LIFE

## Midwifery and Childbirth

Teenage brides were not the norm in the seventeenth century. Susanna Wesley married at nineteen (her husband at twenty-six), but most brides were in their mid-twenties. The first baby typically was born within a year. If a woman did not conceive, the blame was placed on her; it was her failure to properly incubate her husband's seed.

Because childbirth was such a dangerous endeavor, women of means sought out the most competent midwife available. German midwives of the era were trained and paid by local municipalities. In other regions a form of licensing was available. But most midwives operated by reputation alone, often having been trained by a mother or grandmother. Training involved years of assisting the older experienced woman. Books, however, were available. The first such volume written by a woman appeared in the early seventeenth century. Written by Louise Bourgeois, a midwife for the French royalty, it became a bestseller and was soon translated into English and other languages.

London midwives of the seventeenth century were expected to obtain a license for which they paid substantial fees to Anglican officials. However, Quakers who gained a reputation as capable midwives did not seek church sanction because they refused to baptize the infant if it were stillborn and to carry out the tradition of bringing ribbons for the baby's adornment.

Although there were some male midwives, typically childbirth was attended by women only. Sometimes the bedchamber would be filled with female relatives and neighbors, all encouraging the woman in her often-arduous labor. In England most women gave birth lying in bed. In Holland a birthing chair was brought in by the midwife, a tradition that made its way to the New World. Massachusetts Judge Samuel Sewall notes in his diary that

### FOUR WEEKS OF LYING-IN

In the seventeenth century the new mother could expect a lying-in period of four weeks when she would be free from the demands of domestic and other responsibilities. If the family could not afford the expense of providing the necessary domestic help, the parish would often pay a poor parish woman to attend the new mother during her four-week recovery period. In some cases, the parish paid for the woman's delivery and four weeks' room and board at approved parish homes such as widow Bull's of St Olave Jewry or "nurse" James' and "nurse" Ray's of St Bride's. Midwives, however, avoided carrying out deliveries in their own homes lest they be accused of performing abortions.

Dorene Evenden, *The Midwives of Seventeenth-Century London*

a collapsible "birth stool" was used for the birthing mother. This "portable ladies' solace" featured a hole like that of a toilet seat, allowing the midwife to catch the baby from below.

There were many old wives' tales that offered counsel for difficult labor. Indeed, the tricks of the trade were endless. The mother-to-be needed strength, so the women filling the room busied themselves by bringing broth or mutton or toast and eggs. Wine was the beverage of choice, particularly for calming down an excitable new mother. Some midwives were accused of getting the birthing mother drunk in order to make their work easier. Another trick was "sneezing powder." Inserting a quill-full of such powder up a woman's nose caused her to sneeze and thus "dislodge" the baby in a difficult birth. Such an infant was called a "quilled baby."

when John Wesley encountered Moravians—men and women who demonstrated no fear of death—onboard ship. Of them he wrote: "In the midst of the psalm, wherewith their service began … the sea broke over, split the mainsail in pieces, covered the ship, and poured in between the decks, as if the great deep had already swallowed us up. A terrible screaming began among the English. The Germans looked up, and without intermission calmly sang on."

This encounter with the Moravians was one in a series of influences that would influence John Wesley in his becoming the most influential Christian leader of the eighteenth century. The outlook for renewal in the decades before the revival was bleak. According to a contemporary observer, the very continuation of Christianity was in jeopardy: "A new century was dawning, but it seemed as if in the spiritual sky of England the very light of Christianity was being turned by some strange and evil force into darkness." Yet it is a mistake to characterize the eighteenth century as an era devoid of religion. Loyalty to a particular perspective—be it Anglican, Puritan, Catholic, or sectarian—was alive and well.

An understanding of John Wesley is not complete without some knowledge of his mother—the person who offered the most formative spiritual influence in his life—including her reading to him and his siblings the stories of Moravian missionaries.

## Susanna Wesley: Mother of John and Charles

Susanna Wesley, the mother of John and Charles (and seventeen other children) is perhaps rightly regarded as the "mother" of Methodism—not because she was an active Methodist herself but because of her enormous influence over her two sons. Indeed, it was John's mother who had the most formative influence on his character and ministry. Though not strictly speaking a Puritan, hers was a Puritan mentality, especially as it related to family issues. Born in 1703 at the Epworth rectory in Lincolnshire, England, John was her fifteenth child.

Susanna is often viewed as the ultimate Christian mother, whose strict standards of child discipline have been more often praised than emulated. Her time-consuming commitment to her children was not a sacrifice most women were able or willing to make. "No one can, without renouncing the world, in the most literal sense, observe my method," she later wrote. "There are few, if any, that would entirely devote above twenty years of the prime of life in hopes to save the souls of their children, which they think may be saved without so much ado; for that was my principal intention, however unskillfully and unsuccessfully managed."

Despite her sacrifice and devotion, Susanna's method had mixed results at best. Her children, one after another, had problems in their relationships and struggled in failed marriages. Such problems were no doubt exacerbated by her own rocky marriage to an erratic and authoritarian minister. Samuel Wesley abandoned the family and his parish on one occasion when he took offense at her lack of wifely submission — her failure to say "amen" to his prayer for King William of Orange, whom Susanna regarded as a usurper of the throne. In his absence, Susanna

Susanna Wesley

conducted Sunday services that overflowed the parsonage. This time of worship began with her own children, and word quickly spread until the crowds exceeded two hundred. When her husband, who was away in London, vehemently objected, her response was matter-of-fact: "I cannot conceive why any should reflect upon you, because your wife endeavors to draw people to church, and to restrain them from profaning the Lord's day.... As to it looking peculiar, I grant it does. And so does almost any thing that is serious, or that may in any way advance the glory of God, or the salvation of souls."

That she was forced to defend her ministry illustrates the continuing constraints placed on any woman who sought ministry beyond the family circle. But her example influenced her son and set the stage for women's active involvement in Methodist ministry. John later referred to his mother as a "preacher of righteousness," a description that aptly fits many of the early Methodist women. Margaret Davidson, Sarah

## JACOB ARMINIUS

Born more than a century before John Wesley, Jacob Arminius (1559–1609) was a Dutch minister, theologian, and professor at the University of Leiden, who challenged Calvinistic beliefs, especially as they were filtered through Theodore Beza. Arminius emphasized God's foreknowledge in the work of election. "God decreed to save and damn certain particular persons," he wrote. "This decree has its foundation in the foreknowledge of God, by which he knew from all eternity those individuals who *would*, through his ... grace, believe, and, through his subsequent grace *would* persevere by which foreknowledge, he likewise knew those who *would not believe and persevere*." The most noted proponent of Arminianism was John Wesley.

Crosby, Sarah Mallet and others all preached in front of large crowds, though they were often admonished to step down from the pulpit, or to break their sermons into short exhortations with hymns interspersed, or to avoid speaking in a high, shrill voice. Many of these women grew up in poor working-class neighborhoods. Others, like Lady Selina, Countess of Huntingdon, easily mixed with royalty and the upper classes of society. She donated large sums for the training of Methodist ministers and became actively involved in theological issues and ministry placement, showing favor to those who supported George Whitefield's Calvinism as opposed to Wesley's Arminian stance. For decades the "Huntingdon Connection" was a power to be reckoned with.

## John Wesley: Founder of Methodism

By the time of his death, John Wesley (1703–1791) was recognized for his important contribution not only to the religious atmosphere of England but to the social and economic milieu as well. After he died, the *Gentleman's Magazine* eulogized him by underscoring his having done "infinite good to the lower classes of the people." For Wesley, social involvement was intrinsically tied to evangelistic outreach, and thus prison reform, employment assistance, poverty relief, and antislavery were a natural aspect of early Methodist ministry.

Both of Wesley's grandfathers were religious dissenters who had opposed the form and ritual of the Church of England. His parents, however, independently returned to the Anglican Church before they married. The most often-repeated tale of Wesley's childhood has been the story of the Epworth rectory fire and the miraculous rescue of the five-year-old John. The incident became legendary and was depicted in paintings, copies of which were hung in people's homes. Wesley's journal entry offers his own recollection.

This was a Thursday night, February 9, 1709, I believe between 11:00 and midnight, which completely destroyed the building. All were quickly evacuated except for me. As my rescue came none too soon, I have frequently thought of myself (to use those words of the prophets) as a "brand plucked from the burning." From that moment on, my mother seemed to take special pains to see that I was wholly committed to God.

In his early twenties, he began to seriously contemplate entering the ministry. In preparation, he radically changed his life style: "I began to alter the whole form of my conversation, and to set in earnest upon a new life. I set apart an hour or two a day for religious retirement.... I watched against all sin, whether in word or deed. I began to aim at, and pray for, inward holiness." But at Oxford he is shocked to find those preparing for holy orders living a frivolous and degraded lifestyle. Out of this worldly atmosphere is born the "Holy Club," an accountability group that includes his brother Charles and friend George Whitefield. Like similar small groups among German Pietists, they commit themselves to spiritual disciplines and good works.

When his aging father pleads with him to come home and serve as his successor at Epworth, Wesley declines: "The question is not whether I could do more good to others there or here; but whether I could do more good to myself; seeing wherever I can be most holy myself, there I can most promote holiness in others." His later decision to journey to Georgia to minister to the colonists and Indians is made on similar grounds. To his father he writes: "My chief motive, to which all the rest are subordinate, is the hope of saving my own soul.... But you will perhaps ask: 'Cannot you save your own soul in England as well as in Georgia?' I answer, No; neither can I hope to attain the same degree of holiness here which I may there."

Despite his good intentions, however, Wesley does not attain holiness during his mission to America. He had come to Georgia with high hopes of evangelizing the "poor heathens," but his hopes are soon dashed when he realizes they are not interested in the words of an Anglican priest. He finds the nearby Indians to be "implacable" and "unmerciful," and when he asks permission to make an expedition to a more distant tribe, Governor Oglethorpe insists that he work among the colonists in Savannah and the neighboring settlements. But his mission to the settlers fails as well. He appears to them to be self-righteous, aloof, and authoritarian. "I like nothing you do," complained a village magistrate. "All the people are of my mind, for we won't hear ourselves abused." Others express similar sentiments, and on one occasion Wesley is physically assaulted by an angry woman.

In the midst of these problems, he becomes embroiled in a personal matter. In 1737, a year after he arrives, he finds himself consumed by "an unholy desire" for Sophy Hopkey, the wealthy eighteen-year-old niece of a colonial official. In his estimation, her "soul appeared to be wholly made up of mildness, gentleness, longsuffering," He apparently makes a feeble marriage proposal but later vacillates, convinced that he is "not strong enough to bear the complicated temptations of a married state." In the meantime, Sophy agrees to marry another man. Wesley is dumbstruck. Then the couple elopes without the customary publishing of banns. When they return, Wesley denies her communion. She and her husband sue him on the grounds that he has

defamed her and denied her the Lord's Supper. Wesley defends himself but then decides to get out of town. "The hour has come for me to fly for my life, leaving this place; and as soon as evening prayers were over, about eight o'clock, the tide then serving, I shook off the dust of my feet, and left Georgia, after having preached the Gospel there ... not as I ought, but as I was able, one year and nearly nine months."

Wesley left Georgia an utter failure. On his voyage home he wrote, "I went to America to convert the Indians; but oh! who shall convert me!" An understandable rhetorical question asked in the midst of depression and self-doubt, it was also a timely question, considering what happens next. Back home in London, he is thirty-five, single, and not in a good mood. He would have rather stayed home from the church meeting that spring evening in 1738. "I went very unwillingly to a society in Aldersgate Street, where one was reading Luther's preface to the Romans," he later confessed. "About a quarter before nine, while he was describing the change God works in the heart through faith in Christ, I felt my heart strangely warmed. I felt I did trust in Christ alone, for salvation; and an assurance was given me, that He had taken away my sins, even *mine*, and saved *me* from the law of sin and death."

Exactly what this experience entailed has been the subject of much debate. Some historians and theologians characterize it as one of many turning points in Wesley's pilgrimage of faith. Others view it with far greater significance. His own family, except for Charles, is confused by his experience. His older brother Samuel writes: "What Jack means by his not being a Christian till last month I understand not.... I do not hold it at all unlikely, that a perpetual intenseness of thought, and want of sleep, may have disordered my brother."

Wesley's seeking after holiness is offset by struggles in his personal life. In November of 1738, only six months after the Aldersgate Street experience, he is despairing that his heart is "cold and senseless" with "no love or joy in the Holy Ghost." These ups and downs continue in the following years. Then, in 1749, more than ten years after his muddled affair with Sophy, he is again seriously contemplating marriage—this time to Grace Murray, a Methodist class leader. John Bennett, however, is also interested in Grace, and Charles Wesley—fearing his brother will be distracted from the ministry—meets privately with the couple and convinces them to marry before his brother John finds out. When John discover's his brother's duplicity, he is devastated. His relationship with Charles might have been permanently severed had it not been for the intervention of George Whitefield, weeping in great distress and pleading they not let this matter ruin the ministry. Charles, after all, holds a key role in the new movement as the writer of thousands of hymns that have great public appeal.

Just a year after this wrenching ordeal, Wesley is again contemplating marriage—this time without his brother's knowledge. He hastily marries widow Molly Vazeille before giving proper notice. But the marriage does not last. They live together "only occasionally," by his own account, for the next twenty years. After that Molly moves away to live with her daughter, "never to return." Wesley is indifferent: "I did not desert her; I did not send her away; I will never recall her."

In light of the strife he encounters on a personal level, Wesley's doctrinal focus on "entire sanctification" may seem unusual. He strongly objects to Whitefield's claim that a truly converted person is eternally secure. Such a position, Wesley believes, is a license to sin. He insists that justification is not a blanket forgiveness of sins: "If a justified person does not do good, as he has opportunity, he will lose the grace he has received, and," he adamantly insists, will perish eternally. A person who is justified is to "go on unto perfection." He is certain that believers can reach a state of sinless perfection—a conviction based in part on testimonies of those who claim to have attained it. "Nothing is sin," he argues, "but a voluntary transgression of a known law of God."

John Wesley

The doctrine of perfection—that Wesley made the "grand depositum" of the Wesleyan movement—is the most controversial of Wesley's beliefs. It created conflict throughout his ministry, and certain followers took the doctrine to an extreme. In fact, this controversy virtually tore the whole movement apart. Either it was neglected or it was carried too far, but rarely was it preached to his satisfaction. Perfection simply did not work on a practical level. Even after he had published *The Plain Account of Christian Perfection* (1766), he frequently confronted preachers who refused to preach the doctrine.

One of the questions frequently raised concerning Wesley and perfectionism has been

## METHODIST MARY FLETCHER

Early Methodism grew out of Wesley's tight organizational genius and discipline. The basic unit was the Society, consisting of a large group that gathered to listen to preaching and sing hymns. Societies were subdivided into small groups or classes. It was within this system that women found meaningful ministry. Mary Bosanquet Fletcher (1739–1815) actively served in the ministry from age eighteen until her death at seventy-six. Born into wealth, she used her inheritance to found an orphanage, where she served for two decades while preaching and leading societies on the side. At the age of forty-two she married John Fletcher (the most esteemed theologian in the movement), only to be widowed four years later. A powerful preacher, she sometimes spoke to crowds numbering in the thousands. Wesley did not approve of women preachers, but was convinced that "Methodism is an extraordinary dispensation" and thus did "not fall under the ordinary rules of discipline." To Mary Fletcher, whose ministry was often criticized, Wesley had written: "I think the strength of the cause rests there — on your having an extraordinary call."

whether he experienced entire sanctification himself. He never publicly claimed the experience, and in private correspondence he was vague at best. In 1763, he wrote to Charles, "I often cry out 'Give me back my former life!' Let me be again an Oxford Methodist! I am often in doubt whether it would not be best for me to resume all my Oxford rules, great and small. I did then walk closely with God and redeemed the time. But what have I been doing these thirty years?" Some years later he confesses, "I tell you flat I have not attained the character I draw."

On June 28, 1788, as he celebrated his eighty-fifth birthday, he reflected on how little he had suffered amid "the rush of numerous years!" He was remarkably alert, despite some short-term memory loss: "I find likewise some decay in my memory, with regard to names and things lately past; but not at all with regard to what I have read or heard twenty, forty, or sixty years ago ... nor do I feel any such thing as weariness, either in traveling or preaching. I am not conscious of any decay in writing sermons which I do as readily, and I believe as correctly, as ever." The day after his birthday is Sunday,

and he holds to his preaching schedule of three sermons at three different locations: "At eight I preached at Misterton, as usual; about one to a numerous congregation at Newby, near Haxey; and about four at my old stand in Epworth market place, to the great congregation." This is how he had carried out his ministry for almost a half century.

## George Whitefield: Trans-Atlantic Revivalist

The names Wesley and Whitefield are inseparably linked in the eighteenth-century English revival movement — in cooperation and later in conflict. Wesley is the organizer, Whitefield the flamboyant speaker and international traveler. But it is theology that separates them the most. Wesley's Arminian views of perfectionism and free will clash with Whitefield's Calvinism. "No living preacher ever possessed such a combination of excellences," writes Whitefield's contemporary biographer J. C. Ryle — excellences "of pure doctrine, simple and lucid style, boldness and directness, earnestness and fervor, descriptiveness and picture-drawing, pathos and feeling—united with a perfect voice, perfect delivery, and perfect command of words. Whitefield, I repeat, stands alone. No man, dead or alive, I believe, ever came alongside of him."

The son of prosperous innkeepers, George Whitefield (1714–1770) was the youngest of seven children (eleven years younger than Wesley). Two years after he was born, his father died, and his widowed mother was left to rear the children alone. It was an arduous task, and he was a difficult child, as he later recalls: "Lying, filthy talking, and foolish jesting I was much addicted to, even when very young. Sometimes I used to curse, if not swear. Stealing from my mother I thought no theft at all, and used to make no scruple of taking money out of her pocket before she was up." From his youth, he imitated ministers and dreamed of being in the pulpit himself. But play-acting was his foremost ambition: "I was very fond of reading plays, and have kept from school for days together to prepare myself for acting them. My master seeing how mine and my schoolfellows' vein ran, composed something of this kind for himself, and caused me to dress myself in girls' clothes, which I had often done, to act a part before the corporation."

At seventeen his life takes a different turn as he makes plans to enroll at Oxford. He is "delivered out of the snare of the Devil," he recalls, and "resolved to prepare ... for the holy sacrament." Entering academic life as a "servitor," the lowliest of students, he meets the Wesleys and becomes a member of the Holy

George Whitefield

Club. Ordained to the Anglican ministry at twenty-two, he is such a dynamic preacher that he reportedly "drove fifteen mad." (Anglicans and others often equated religious enthusiasm with madness.) He is the biggest show in town, bringing all his emotions to the pulpit. "I hardly ever knew him go through a sermon without weeping," writes an observer. "I could hardly bear such unreserved use of tears, and the scope he gave to his feelings, for sometimes he exceedingly wept, stamped loudly and passionately, and was frequently so overcome, that, for a few seconds, you would suspect he never could recover, and when he did, nature required some little time to compose himself."

Appearing to take great pleasure in his growing fame, he records an important breakthrough in 1737: "My name was first put into the public papers." No less satisfying is his reception in public: "I could no longer walk on foot as usual, but was constrained to go in a coach, from place to place, to avoid the hosannas of the multitude." His critics are many, but news—good or bad—only adds to his fame. Then, in 1738, he seems to turn his back on his celebrity to serve as a missionary in the remote colonial outpost of Georgia, following in the footsteps of John Wesley. Unlike Wesley (who had already left Georgia), Whitefield becomes the darling of the colonists. "I looked for persecution, but lo! I am received as an angel of God." He preaches, organizes schools, and supports economic endeavors. But his most illustrious efforts are in behalf of orphans. His vision to establish an orphanage will become a lifelong focus of his travel and preaching, always tied to charitable fund-raising. In September he sails back to England, vowing to return to his newfound friends.

On returning to England, Whitefield discovers that his star has risen, and with every fiery sermon against the established clerics, his popularity only increases. When barred from churches, he preaches outdoors — often using the elements to enhance his dramatic oratory. On one occasion, when a storm is approaching, he does not let the incident pass unnoticed: "And where will you be, my hearers, when your lives have passed away like that dark cloud?" His deep voice booms with no need of a megaphone. "Let not the wrath of God be awakened! Let not the fires of eternity be kindled against you! See there!" he exclaims, as lightening flashed across the sky, "it is a glance from the angry eye of Jehovah!" "Hark!" he cries out, as a crack of thunder roars over his words, "it was the voice of the Almighty as He passed by in His anger!"

The popularity of Whitefield as an open-air evangelist on both sides of the Atlantic is illustrated by the account of Nathan Cole. On October 23, 1740, a man on horseback gallops through the countryside spreading word that Whitefield will be preaching in the nearby town of Middletown, Connecticut. Cole's response is typical:

> I was in my field at work. I dropped my tool ... and ran home to my wife, telling her to make ready quickly to go on and hear Mr. Whitefield preach at Middletown, then ran to my horse with all my might, fearing that I should be too late. Having my horse, I with my wife soon mounted. ... We improved every moment to get along as if we were fleeing for our lives, all the while fearing we should be too late to hear the sermon, for we had twelve miles to ride.

As they approach Middletown, they realize they are not alone in their frenzied effort to hear the famous preacher:

> I saw before me a cloud of fog arising. I first thought it came from the great river, but as I came nearer the road I heard a noise of horses' feet coming down the road, and this cloud was a cloud of dust made by the horses' feet. ... When I came within about 20 rods of the road, I could see men and horses slipping along in the cloud like shadows, and as I drew nearer it seemed like a steady stream of horses and their riders, scarcely a horse more than his length behind another, all of a lather and foam with sweat, their breath rolling out of the nostrils every jump. Every horse seemed to go with all his might for the saving of souls. It made me tremble to see the sight.

Whitefield's sermon meets all of Cole's expectations and pricks his conscience: "I saw that my righteousness would not save me."

In the following years, Whitefield's popularity in America increases, and he regards the colonies his second home, making a total of thirteen trans-Atlantic voyages before he dies. He plays a key role in what becomes known as the Great Awakening and is credited with helping to unify colonies. His friendship with Ben Franklin is legendary, as Franklin acknowledged with his typical touch of humor.

> I happened soon afterwards to attend one of his sermons, in the course of which I perceived he intended to finish with a collection, and I silently resolved he should get nothing from me. I had in my pocket a handful of copper money, three or four silver dollars, and five in gold. As he proceeded I began to soften and

concluded to give the copper. Another stroke of his oratory made me ashamed of that and determined me to give the silver, and he finished so admirably that I emptied my pocket into the collection dish, gold and all.

Unlike Wesley, Whitefield does not leave behind a tightly organized following. He is a preacher far more than an organizer. But he does have a powerful patron in Selina, Countess of Huntingdon, who erects chapels with her ample finances. In addition, she purchases theatres and halls and other buildings and refurbishes them for Christians who desire evangelical preaching. She also establishes a college to train preachers for the chapels and to ride the circuit. Indeed, she divides England into six circuit districts and maps out the routes for her young preachers. She is also deeply involved in doctrinal affairs, particularly the Calvinist-Arminian controversy that separates Whitefield and the Wesleys. Although she is not a preacher herself (as were many other women in Wesley's Methodism), in her role as the chief administrator of the "connection" and as the arbiter of doctrinal disputes, she serves essentially as a bishop and wields extraordinary control over church-related matters.

> *When Whitefield came, it was like an appearance of Billy Graham, Garth Brooks, and Bill Clinton all rolled into one.*
> Nathan O. Hatch

Whitefield's spectacular oratory in an age before electronic recording has been lost to succeeding generations. But he did leave behind a physical presence that lived on for decades: his corpse. In fact, his decaying body became such an object of veneration that in 1775, five years after his death, a chaplain accompanied by military officers (including American traitor Benedict Arnold) went inside his tomb in Newburyport, Massachusetts, and removed some of his clothing for souvenirs.

When Methodist Jesse Lee and two fellow clerics entered his tomb in 1789, they were not disappointed. Lee left a record of their visit: "Removing the coffin lid, [we] beheld the awful ravages of 'the last enemy of man.' How quiet the repose, how changed the features." When another Methodist minister visited the tomb in the 1820s, he took Whitefield's skull into his hands and "examined it with great interest." By the 1830s, the viewings were becoming less

## A Not-So-Great "Great Awakening"

In the 1970s and 1980s, various historians have seen in it nothing less than the first unifying event of the colonial experience, the origins of the American evangelical tradition.... This emphasis on the "Great Awakening" may say more about subsequent times than about its own. The term was not contemporary, nor was it known to the historians of the revolutionary and early national periods.... Internal descriptive and analytical inconsistencies belie the event's importance and even its existence; it is difficult to date, for example, because revivals linked to it started in New England long before 1730 yet did not appear with force in Virginia until the 1760s.... It missed most colonies, and even in New England its long-term effects have been greatly exaggerated. On reflection, it might better be thought of as an interpretive fiction.

Jon Butler, *Awash in a Sea of Faith*

frequent and less interesting. A Freewill Baptist minister wrote of his visit in 1834: "The coffin was about one third full of black earth, out of which projected a few bones. The skull bone was detached from the rest, and was turned over."

## Jonathan Edwards: New England Preacher and Theologian

Whether the last of the Puritans or the first American intellectual of the modern age, Jonathan Edwards (1703–1758) is a controversial historical figure even as he was a controversial minister and theologian in his own era. Most often associated with the Great Awakening and revivals in his own church in Northampton, Massachusetts, he was also well known for his extensive writings on revivals. Decades before the awakenings in his own church, his grandfather, Solomon Stoddard (who served the same church for sixty years), had reaped five "harvests" between 1679 and 1718. The number of conversions exceeded that of any other parish in New England.

Edwards descended from a long line of Puritan preachers on both sides of the family and grew up in a pious home filled with women—ten sisters of nearly his height, prompting his father to joke about his sixty feet of daughters. From his earliest childhood he was home-schooled by his parents and older sisters. Deeply religious and studious, he kept detailed notebooks on scientific and philosophical and religious topics. At thirteen, he entered Yale, graduating four years later as valedictorian. After further independent study, he accepted a short-term pastoral position in New York City, followed by a position as tutor at Yale. His next career move was to Northampton to serve as an assistant minister under his renowned grandfather, Solomon Stoddard.

As a youth Edwards had struggled with the "horrible doctrine" of election that predestines some to eternal life and others to eternal damnation. But in his final year at Yale he comes to see the doctrine as "exceedingly pleasant, bright and sweet." Ever striving for holiness, he also records his spiritual progress in his journal, later published in his *Personal Narrative*:

> As I was walking there, and looking up on the sky and clouds, there came into my mind so sweet a sense of the glorious *majesty* and *grace* of God, that I know not how to express. [It was] an awful sweetness; a high, and great,

### SINNERS AND SPIDERS

The God that holds you over the pit of hell, much as one holds a spider, or some loathsome insect over the fire, abhors you, and is dreadfully provoked. His wrath towards you burns like fire; he looks upon you as worthy of nothing else but to be cast into the fire.... It is nothing but his hand that holds you from falling into the fire every moment.... And there is no other reason to be given, why you have not dropped into hell since you arose in the morning, but that God's hand has held you up. There is no other reason to be given why you have not gone to hell, since you have sat here in the house of God, provoking his pure eyes by your sinful wicked manner of attending his solemn worship. Yea, there is nothing else that is to be given as a reason why you do not this very moment drop down into hell.... You hang by a slender thread, with the flames of divine wrath.

Jonathan Edwards, "Sinners in the Hands of an Angry God"

and holy gentleness.... After this my sense of divine things gradually increased, and became more and more lively, and had more of that inward sweetness.... My longings after God and holiness, were much increased.

At twenty-four he marries seventeen-year-old Sarah Pierpont, who also comes from a distinguished Puritan line. He is smitten most by her spirituality: "God comes to her and fills her mind with exceeding sweet delight, and she hardly cares for anything, except to meditate on him.... She is of a wonderful sweetness, calmness and universal benevolence of mind; especially after this Great God has manifested himself to her mind." But they are in many ways polar opposites: she vivacious and optimistic; he awkward, studious, and stern. She immediately steps into the role of assistant pastor's wife in Northampton. But two years later, when Stoddard dies, they are on their own with a congregation that looks back with great fondness on the nearly sixty-year tenure of their beloved pastor.

Studying sometimes thirteen hours a day, Edwards is not popular among the townspeople who support him with their tax dollars whether they frequent church regularly or not. Yet ten years into his ministry, in this very church under his scholarly preaching, a revival suddenly breaks out. Within a year all of Northampton seems to have abandoned its "dullness in religion," and some three hundred souls are converted. Edwards documents the awakening in *A Faithful Narrative* (1737), which helps spread the revival to other areas through its dozens of printings. Conscious of critics, he seeks to stifle emotional outbursts. In less than a year the excitement in Northampton subsides, but it continues to spread as he travels to other churches.

The sermon for which he is best remembered, "Sinners in the Hand of an Angry God," was first delivered at Enfield, Connecticut, where it created a considerable stir. Although he read the sermon with composure, an observer reported: "There was such a breathing of distress and weeping, that the preacher was obliged to speak to the people and desire silence, that he might be heard." Edwards laments the criticism and scoffing, especially from the Boston elitists, most specifically his nemesis, the Reverend Charles Chauncey, who spurns enthusiasm. "Is it not a shame to New England that such a work should be much doubted of here?" Edwards asks his readers. "We have a rule near at hand, a sacred book that God himself has put into our

The American Colonies

## BUNDLING IN NEW ENGLAND

There was a curious New England custom in those days called Bundling, which was love-making under peculiar circumstances.... Boys and girls who bundled went to bed together, with their clothes on, and stayed until morning. Sometimes they got married afterward. And sometimes they didn't.... Hardly anybody thought it was wrong — except the Reverend Jonathan Edwards and his cultured associates.... But after Mr. Edwards' first "hell-fire and conniption-fit sermon," his colleagues took up the subject. And one of them wrote a poem with twenty-seven verses dedicated to "Ye Youth of Both Sexes," that ended like this:

Should you go on, the day will come
When Christ your judge will say,
"In bundles bind each of this kind,
And cast them all away.

"Down deep in hell there let them dwell,
And bundle on that bed.
There burn and roll without control
'Till all their lust are fed."

Eleanor Early, *A New England Sampler*

hands, with clear and infallible marks, sufficient to resolve us in things of this nature; which book I think we must reject ... if we reject such a work as has now been described."

As more revivals are reported throughout New England, ministers and theological professors begin to split into two warring camps. The followers of Edwards and others who support awakenings are referred to as "New Side" (or "New Lights"), and those opposed (including most of the teachers at Harvard and Yale), "Old Side" (or "Old Lights"). Opponents criticize Edwards for purposely stirring up emotion and causing unnecessary distress. In fact, during the height of a revival season, Edwards' uncle, Joseph Hawley, a highly respected merchant, takes his own life by slitting his throat. Hawley is depressed in part because he knows he can never be good enough for God. Edwards' preaching is not designed to spur suicides, but his sermons, if taken seriously, are frightening.

There is no expressing the hatefulness and how hateful you are rendered by it in the sight of God. The odiousness of this filth is beyond all account because 'tis infinitely odious; you have seen the filthiness of toads and serpents and filthy vermin and creatures that you have loathed and of putrefied flesh ... but there was but a finite deformity or odiousness in this.... 'Tis but a shadow. Your filthiness is not the filthiness of toads and serpents or poisonous vermin, but of devils which is a thousand times worse. 'Tis impossible to express or conceive or measure how Greatly God detests such defilement.

Edwards is strict and uncompromising, especially in matters of public morality. His campaign against taverns, for example, infuriates many who frequent the local saloon. He himself is too busy to socialize and seems uninterested in the mundane problems and concerns of his parishioners. In some situations he deals with issues in a seeming callous manner. In 1744 stories surface that certain young men in the church are making lewd remarks to young women and are secretly reading a midwives' manual and passing it on to friends. Shocked by the scandal, he conducts a hasty investigation and then publicly reads a list of those involved, without differentiating between the guilty and those who reported them, creating an uproar in the church and community.

There were other matters that created serious dissention in the church, most notably his opposition to the Half-Way Covenant, a ruling that allowed individuals who had not professed a conversion experience to become members of the church and to have their children baptized. He regards the policy detrimental to the church, even though grandfather Stoddard had helped formulate it. This issue, more than any other, causes turmoil during his long ministry in Northampton. Church attendance decreases, and between 1744 and 1748 no new applications are received for membership. In 1750 two

hundred church members sign a petition to have him removed from the pulpit. The matter is taken to the ministerial association, where he is judged by his peers. In a vote of eight to seven he is dismissed from his ministry of twenty-three years. He has no place to go, however, and the church finds no replacement, so he serves as a substitute in his own pulpit.

After some months in limbo, he receives a call to be a missionary to the Housatonic Indians in the frontier settlement of Stockbridge. Though hardly a promotion, it allows for solitude to pursue his writing. "Wife and children are well-pleased with our present situation," he writes after they have settled. "They like the place much better than they expected. Here, at present, we live in peace; which has of long time been an unusual thing with us. The Indians seem much pleased with my family, especially my wife." The situation soon deteriorates, however. Those who claim to be responsible for the mission school are some of his own cousins, who (having been influenced by Grandfather

## REVIVALISM IN THE MIDDLE COLONIES

American revivalism did not begin with Whitefield and Edwards, nor did it begin in New England. Of Theodore Frelinghuysen, Whitefield observed: "He is a worthy soldier of Jesus Christ and was the beginner of the great work which I trust the Lord is carrying on." A Dutch Reformed minister, Frelinghuysen sparks revivals in the Raritan Valley in New Jersey in the 1720s. Reformed Church authorities in Amsterdam are not surprisingly displeased by the reports of "enthusiasm."

Also serving in the Middle Colonies are Reverend William Tennent and his four minister sons. All "New Side" Presbyterians, they combine "enthusiasm" with great miracles. William, one of the sons, reportedly dies and is "laid out on a board" for three days, after which he is resurrected from the dead. Later, one night when he is sleeping, all his toes on one foot go missing with no explanation other than his having been attacked by the devil. John Tennent is known for his extraordinary weeping — so much so that "even some Strangers ... were much affected therewith; the *Tears* trickling down their Cheeks like *Hail*." Another son, Gilbert, with his father, founds the Log College to train evangelical ministers. In some respects the revivals of the Middle Colonies are more spectacular than the revivals of New England, and Edwards, among others, is suspicious of all the miraculous claims.

Stoddard), had opposed his ministry in Northampton. In the years that follow, many of the natives leave Stockbridge, angry with settlers they do not trust. Natives among the Mohawk and Iroquois, spurred by French traders, view all white settlers as their enemies. In Stockbridge, the Edwards family is terrified especially when they learn of nearby settlers who are set upon and killed — incidents that lead to the French and Indian War of the late 1750s.

Despite the threats from neighboring Indian tribes, the family stays put and Edwards continues to write and publish. In his *Thoughts on Revivals, Religious Affections*, and *A Faithful Narrative*, he seeks to defend biblically what others have panned as mere "enthusiasm." In his most substantial work, *Freedom of the Will* (1754), he makes a case against the Arminian belief that individuals can choose to follow or to disregard Christ. He holds that "the power

and grace, and operation of the Holy Spirit, in, or towards, the conversion of the sinner, is immediate (and not mediated by the concurring action of the will)." A person is free to do what he wills; he enjoys freedom of the will in the exercise of this liberty. But Edwards further insists, in what some might regard circular reasoning, that *will* is not its own cause but is determined by something outside and beyond itself, that being the Holy Spirit.

Edwards departs Stockbridge in 1758. The situation with the natives is dangerous, but more pressing is the need for a new president of the college in New Jersey (that would later become Princeton). The death of the young president, his son-in-law, Rev. Aaron Burr (father of a future vice president), leaves the school floundering, and Edwards is invited to fill the vacuum. Fearing the smallpox epidemic, he volunteers to be inoculated — a procedure still in its early and

## DAVID BRAINERD

The legacy of Jonathan Edwards is closely related to the Protestant missionary movement. That he himself served as a missionary was less significant than his writing *The Life of David Brainerd* — a book that influenced the cause of missions for generations. Expelled from Yale for an intemperate remark, David Brainerd (1718–1747) went on to serve as a missionary to Native Americans. While on leave, he visited the Edwards home and became engaged to daughter Jerusa, but he died before the wedding took place. His ministry to the natives had been hindered by his own inability to understand or speak the language and by his dark moods, as evident in his journal: "It seemed to me I should never have any success among the Indians. My soul was weary of my life; I longed for death, beyond measure." He blamed himself for his lack of success, but he also blamed the Indians. He found them "brutishly stupid and ignorant of divine things" and given to asking "frivolous and impertinent questions," such as why they would want to go to a white man's heaven when they had a perfectly suitable happy hunting ground of their own.

Brainerd reported revivals, but the emotional outpourings were often short-lived and superficial. How much of his preaching the natives understood — through a sometimes drunk interpreter — is difficult to assess. Edwards' biography, however, inspired others. John Wesley found a soul mate in the often-depressed young missionary and published an abbreviated version in 1768; and his most prominent ministers in America, Francis Asbury and Thomas Coke, were also profoundly challenged by the book, as were a long succession of missionaries, including Fredrick Schwartz, William Carey, Samuel Mills, Robert Morrison, David Livingstone, and Jim Elliot.

risky experimental stages. Five weeks after he arrives at Princeton, he dies.

One death follows another, bringing a sudden end to the Edwards story. Only weeks after her husband dies, Sarah receives word that her daughter Esther (wife of Burr) has also died of the smallpox vaccination. Amidst all this sorrow, she now has the responsibility of young orphaned grandchildren. The mother of eleven children, she is no longer young at fifty-one. The emotional strains and added burdens lead to her own death later that year.

## What if ...

What if Samuel Wesley had not walked out of the house when Susanna refused to say *Amen* to his prayer for the king? Son John, referred to as the child of his parents' reconciliation, was conceived shortly after his father returned home from an extended absence. What if young John had not survived the house fire to be a "brand from the burning"? How different would worldwide Christianity be today without John Wesley?

What if George Whitefield had become an actor instead of an evangelist? Was he a "flash in the pan" as an exciting preacher, or did his ministry have enduring effects? Without Wesley's organization, there would be no centuries-old movement that harks back to Whitefield.

What if Jonathan Edwards had been a more moderate pulpit preacher? Would he have the renown he has enjoyed if he had emphasized the sweetness of God's glory in his sermons more than the odious hatred God has for sinners?

## Further Reading

Ayling, Stanley. *John Wesley*. Nashville: Abingdon, 1979.

Bready, J. Wesley. *England Before and After Wesley*. London: Russell & Russell, 1971.

Brown, Earl Kent. *Women of Mr. Wesley's Methodism*. New York: Edwin Mellen, 1983.

Butler, Jon. *Awash in A Sea of Faith: Christianizing the American People*. Cambridge: Harvard University Press, 1990.

Byrd, James P. *Jonathan Edwards for Armchair Theologians*. Philadelphia: Westminster John Knox, 2008.

Dallimore, Arnold A. *George Whitefield: God's Anointed Servant in the Great Revival of the Eighteenth Century*. Wheaton: Crossway, 1990.

Dodds, Elisabeth D. *Marriage to a Difficult Man: The Uncommon Union of Jonathan and Sarah Edwards*. Hanson, Mass.: Audubon Press, 2005.

Edwards, Jonathan. *The Life and Diary of David Brainerd, Missionary to the Indians*. Goodyear, Ariz.: Diggory Press, 2006.

Edwards, Jonathan. *The Religious Affections*. Goodyear, Ariz.: Diggory Press, 2007.

Marsden, George. *Jonathan Edwards.* New Haven: Yale University Press, 2003.

Newton, John A. *Susanna Wesley and the Puritan Tradition in Methodism.* London: Epworth Press, 2003.

Thuesen, Peter J. *Predestination: The American Career of a Contentious Doctrine.* New York: Oxford University Press, 2009.

Tomkins, Stephen. *John Wesley: A Biography.* Grand Rapids: Eerdmans, 2003.

Wesley, John. *The Journal of John Wesley.* Kindle Edition. Signalman, 2008.

# CHAPTER 20

# An Age of Societies

## Nineteenth-Century Revival and Social Outreach

*When my son was an adolescent in the 1980s, we traveled to the Finger Lakes region of New York for a family reunion. On our way we stopped at various historical sites, among them Seneca Falls, the setting for the first Women's Rights convention and the hometown of Elizabeth Cady Stanton, a nineteenth-century feminist leader.*

*Further west we toured the childhood home of Joseph Smith. We walked into the woods where Smith reportedly received his first vision and went to Hill Cumorah where he later claimed to have dug up a gold bible that he subsequently "translated" into the Book of Mormon. It was in this region that Smith, at the same age as my son, roamed the hillsides digging for buried treasure and employing various kinds of magic, an activity almost any kid would relish.*

*Spiritualism was part of the popular magic and superstition of this region. Of particular interest were the famous Fox sisters, who conducted séances and entertained devotees from near and far. Besides feminism, magic, and spiritualism, the region was noted for revivals. In fact, it became known as the "Burned Over" district—burned over repeatedly with the fires of revival.*

*But revival fires burned far beyond the borders of New York. Indeed, for anyone following the revival road of history, Cane Ridge, Kentucky, beckons. Here campfires shot sparks into the night sky as revivalists planted terrors of hellfire into the hearts of weeping, sometimes barking, converts. We studied the map, watched for signs, and asked for directions, wondering how thousands of people could have found their way to this remote site two centuries ago.*

*The destination proved to be a disappointment. There was a tidy building, marking with photos and newsprint the site of this famous revival, but not a caretaker or tourist was in sight. We were relieved, however, to have missed the summertime Cane Ridge Day celebration, a specious effort to recreate an event forever lost in time. How easily we visualize such happenings with amusement and nostalgia, with little thought of how controversial and bizarre they were at the time and would be today.*

> Any good history begins in strangeness. The past should not be comfortable.
> The past should not be a familiar echo of the present,
> for if it is familiar why revisit it?
> The past should be so strange that you wonder how you
> and people you know and love could come from such a time.
> RICHARD WHITE, *REMEMBERING AHANAGRAN*

Good history truly does make the past uncomfortable. Good history makes us wonder how such past strangeness produced what seems to be the completely normal generation we live in. Past generations are not like us, and that is why we revisit them. In the cosmic scheme of things, the nineteenth century is recent history. Many families easily trace their genealogies back to this era. On the surface we have much in common with those who seem almost to resemble us in old photographs. Those with European ancestry know and understand the nineteenth-century Western mind—a mind brimming with curiosity and invention—and nineteenth-century books can be found in any of our bookshelves.

Like our nineteenth-century forebears, we live on this side of the Enlightenment, where religious belief is no longer taken for granted. And like them, we look to charismatic leaders to show us the way to God. These people are not distant ancestors, and yet there is a strangeness when we try to cross the divide and listen to their preachers and participate in their religious activities. In their temptations and travesties they look like us, but there is a chasm that separates us, as is evident in the lives and ministries of Richard Allen, Charles Finney, Phoebe Palmer, C. H. Spurgeon, and D. L. Moody.

Nineteenth-century religion is difficult to quantify or summarize—or even grasp. With every generation that passes since the Reformation (or since the time of Christ, for that matter), Christianity becomes more complicated and more variegated. In England and on the Continent the established churches wield power. They baptize and marry and bury, but they fail to stir passion among people in the pews.

Many circumstances and events factor into this dismal religious equation. The French Revolution had a profound influence on spiritual values, not only in France and in the Catholic Church, but in the entire western European psyche. So also with the American Revolution more than a decade earlier, though the effects were more provincial and less profound. It was a time when religious revivals and church membership were declining.

## PARADE OF HISTORY

The nineteenth-century procession of the faith assumes a multicultural and gender-inclusive hue. Indeed, in many instances people of color and women are leading the parade. A poignant example of this occurs when Richard Allen and his poor "colored" followers march right out the door of the Methodist church where they have been rudely treated. Though it was not intended at the time, this was the first step in the formation of the African Methodist Episcopal Church — a parade of believers that has grown to some two million strong.

Along with political revolution came revolutions in thinking, and not for philosophers only. Thomas Paine was no ivory-tower philosopher. His books and pamphlets, including *Common Sense*, *The Rights of Man*, and *The Age of Reason*, were written for ordinary thinkers. They challenged not only political perspectives but also religious faith.

Indeed, if one were to time-travel back to nineteenth-century established churches and denominations, one might conclude that religious passions were lying dormant. Matthew Arnold captures the spirit of the times in his poem "Dover Beach" (1851): "The Sea of Faith was once, too, at the full. . . . But now I only hear its melancholy, long, withdrawing roar." There were new ideas in the old churches, to be sure. Modern philosophy paved the way not only for atheism but for deism and Unitarianism as well. In fact, Unitarianism became downright respectable in England and later among New England Congregationalists such as Theodore Parker, Ralph Waldo Emerson, and others.

Nor was there a dearth of theologians or biblical scholars in the nineteenth century. Much of the writing, however, was academic and thus not easily accessible to laity. German theologian Friedrich Schleiermacher (1768–1834), referred to as the "father of modern theology," was a Reformed minister and professor who blended the Romantic spirit of the age with religious concepts. "God consciousness," he maintained, "is the feeling of absolute dependence upon God," and "true religion is sense and taste for the infinite." German "higher criticism" of the Bible was also aimed at other academics or educated ministers rather than people in the pews.

Outside the halls of academia, religion often drew its ardor from spirited revivalists and social activists who stirred emotions and drew crowds. These religious "enthusiasts" filled the vacuum created by "cold formalism" with apocalyptic visions. In Scandinavia, Hans Nielsen Hauge (1771–1824), amid Lutheran church "deadness," stirred up revival, traveling some seven thousand miles—often on skis. In America, the evangelical revivalism of the Second Great Awakening spurred evangelistic and humanitarian ministries at home and abroad. But many of the older denominations lost members.

Indeed, as church attendance dwindled, new sects and denominations and parachurch movements flourished. A spirit of democracy spurred ordinary individuals to imagine they could establish their own religion—a religion true to the spirit of the apostles of old. In America, with no state churches to support and with Puritanism on the wane, anyone could become a prophet and purveyor of new religions teachings. Joseph Smith (1805–1844) is an example. His visits by God the Father, Jesus, and angels grabbed the attention of both seekers and scoffers. When he translated his gold bible, he became even more popular. All that was needed to solidify the movement was his martyrdom in 1844.

The year of Smith's death was also the year of the Great Disappointment. Baptist lay preacher William Miller had been traveling and holding revivals during which he predicted the Lord's return. When October 22, 1844, came and went, he admitted his mistake, while others, including Ellen G. White, reinterpreted his prophecy. As the founder and prophetess of the Seventh-day Adventist Church, White insisted that Miller's date had been correct. The miscalculation related to the place: on that very date, Christ had not returned to earth as had been expected; rather, Christ moved from one apartment in heaven to another to begin his work of "investigative judgment."

Because Smith had a new bible and White offered new truths through her "spirit of prophecy," these sectarian movements were quickly deemed "cults." But the spirit of prophecy was also alive and well in many less-than-cultic movements. In England Edward Irving offered an apocalyptic gospel that included tongues-speaking, and Henry Drummond turned it into a denomination—the Catholic Apostolic Church. Included in his circle was John Nelson Darby, who formulated a complex system of dispensationalism (a belief that biblical history is divided into periods of God's unique activity) and founded the Plymouth Brethren movement.

Dispensational premillennial speculation spurred the Bible conference movement and its most heralded offshoot, the Niagara Conference. The interest in Christ's imminent return was not confined to sectarian movements, however. Premillennialist writings attracted widespread interest in more mainline circles.

Prophetic preaching and writing was largely a male domain. Indeed, men dominated society in virtually every arena. But Victor Hugo was not far off when he proclaimed, "The nineteenth century is the woman's century." Although women continued to be barred from most political and church offices, they were at the forefront of social activism, including the beginning of the women's rights movement. Some early feminists, like Elizabeth Cady Stanton (1815–1902), dismissed biblical orthodoxy as merely one aspect of male chauvinism. Others, like anti-slavery activist Sojourner Truth (1797–1883), found evangelical faith and feminism perfectly compatible.

Nineteenth-century democratic ideals had paved the way for a vast increase in the number of societies and reform movements, so that one historian has identified this period as the "age of societies." Reaching out to those marginalized by the Industrial Revolution was on the top of their agenda, and there were societies for every need that could be identified. Florence Nightingale took Victorian England by storm with her sacrificial service as a nurse in the Crimean War (1853–1856), inspiring others to follow in her footsteps. Antislavery movements, typically headed by men, captured the support of women, white and black alike. Quakers Sarah and Angelina Grimke, through education and publishing, were key figures in the abolitionist movement, as was runaway slave Harriet Tubman, a famous Underground Railroad conductor.

Temperance, more than any other issue apart from overseas missions, captured women's attention. The Woman's Christian Temperance

---

## AMERICA'S MOST HONORED REFORMER

In the Capitol in Washington, D.C., each state is represented by a statue of its most honored citizen. Of all the fifty states only Illinois, the Land of Lincoln, is represented by a woman.... At the time of her death in 1898, Frances Willard was the most famous woman in America. Flags flew at half-mast in New York, Chicago, and Washington, D.C. She died in New York, and her body was transported by rail to Chicago, pausing for services along the way like a presidential funeral train. In Chicago, 30,000 persons filed by her casket in one day. Ruth Bordin writes, "The nation mourned her with a grief, admiration, and respect it would have bestowed on a great national hero or martyred president. No woman before or since was so clearly on the day of her death this country's most honored woman."

Faith Martin, "Frances Willard: America's Forgotten Feminist"

Union (WCTU) was in the forefront of fighting poverty caused by high alcohol consumption. Frances Willard (1839–1898), a proper Victorian lady, devoted her life to preaching temperance, giving the WCTU a respectable reputation. On the other side of the ledger was the six-foot-tall Carry Nation, wielding her hatchet as she conducted her ministry of smashing saloons. Women were also in the forefront of social agencies like the Salvation Army and the Sunday school movement—an outreach focused on literacy for poor children with no access to public education. In London, Elizabeth Fry brought attention to the deplorable condition of incarcerated women and children through her celebrated prison ministry. In fact, when John Randolph, a Virginia planter and legislator went to London and visited Westminster Abbey, Parliament, and the Tower of London, he remarked that they "sink into utter insignificance in comparison to Elizabeth Fry." In Germany the deaconess movement enlisted an army of women to go into the slums to serve those living on the margins of society.

Often forgotten in histories of this era are people of color and the poor. They are not portrayed as movers and shakers. If they are visible at all, they are often objects of pity. But this vast *underclass* had a narrative in its own right—a narrative that included leading players in the drama of history.

## Richard Allen: Founder of the African Methodist Episcopal Church

One of the denominations that sprouted up in the decades following the American Revolution was the African Methodist Episcopal Church (AME). Had blacks been welcomed to worship alongside their white counterparts, the history of American religion might have been very different. The pervasive racism of slavery and segregation led to inevitable denominational splits both before and after the Civil War. The trend began when a former slave, Richard Allen (1760–1831) separated from the Methodist Church and founded the AME in 1816.

While recognizing the cruelty of slavery, Allen paid tribute to a particular slaveholder, Mr. Stokley of Delaware: "He was a very tender, humane man. My mother and father lived with him for many years." But such tenderness only went so far: "He was brought into difficulty, not being able to pay for us; and mother having several children after he had bought us, he sold my mother and three children." Such was the emotional torture of a slave family.

Converted at a Methodist revival meeting when he was seventeen, Allen taught himself to read and write and later earned his freedom. But freedom did not mean free time. He frequently worked two shifts a day, cutting wood, laying bricks, and driving wagons. Determined that long work days would not prevent him from following his call to preach, he found time to conduct revivals in the evenings—sponsored by both Methodists and Quakers. "In the year 1784 I left East Jersey, and laboured in Pennsylvania," he recalled. "Many souls were awakened, and cried aloud to the Lord to have mercy upon them.... Seldom did I ever experience such a time of mourning and lamentation among a people. There were but few coloured people in the neighbourhood—the most of my congregation was white."

Settling down in Philadelphia in 1786, he establishes a Methodist society of more than forty members and contemplates a building to house his growing congregation. But he soon faces strong opposition from white Methodist leaders, including one who "was much opposed to an African church, and used very degrading

## EVERYDAY LIFE

## The Christian Household

The nineteenth century was a time of budding feminism and of women's active role in society, but it was also an era of the "Cult of True Womanhood," both concepts supported by biblical texts. On the one hand, there was a rash of best-selling advice books telling ladies how to behave and how to rear their children. Paintings show delicate females fanning themselves to prevent fainting or taking to bed as lifelong invalids. Their bodies were constricted with tight corsets hidden under layers of petticoats. Manners and mores

were likewise restrictive Queen Victoria, who nearly sixty-four years

On the other hand, were far less concerned causes. Their mission them. In the streets and haggard mothers who to prostitution to feed their drunken factory- their off-hours in the Little children ventured to peddle trinkets and nies. This too was Victo- away from the myth of

Men were as involved anhood as were women

"A Christian House" illustration from Catherine Beecher and Harriet Beecher Stowe's *The American Woman's Home, or Principles of Domestic Science*

Harriet Beecher Stowe Center, Hartford, CT

in this era named for reigned in England for (1837–1901).

there were women who with corsets than with field was all around back alleys they found sometimes resorted their little ones while working husbands spent gin mills and saloons. into crime-ridden streets reclaimed trash for pen- rian life, though a world "True Womanhood."

in the cult of true wom- themselves, and preach-

ers spread the new religion from their pulpits. The nuclear family was becoming more isolated and independent from the surrounding community than it had been in earlier pre-industrial society. Middle-class homes (particularly in America) were compartmentalized with separate pantries and parlors and porches to accommodate sophisticated tastes. Designed for indoor living, the home extended into the surrounding gardens. The once-communal "women's work" of washing clothes, gardening, and tending the chickens was becoming the responsibility of a single household, jobs suitable for a servant and gardener. Gender roles were becoming fixed, with men in the workplace and women in the home. A woman found her place within a domestic system defined by advice books, sermons, songs, painting, crafts, architecture, and contemporary culture.

That the Victorian era was marked by sexual repression and prudishness is a claim often challenged by historians. There is more myth than reality in the common belief that proper ladies covered the legs of furniture because legs stir sexual passion. But as homes featuring a master bedroom became commonplace, intimacies carried on behind closed doors took on secretive, illicit implications not associated with a common family sleeping room of past eras. Proper behavior was defined by the niceties of True Womanhood. The Puritan father who was God's minister in the home was a relic of the past. The middle-class nineteenth-century father was away at work, and the housewife was in charge of family religious training, prayers, and devotion. As such, Victorian religion is characterized by its softer, more feminine touch. Children are no longer relegated to eternal damnation in hell when they become boisterous on the Sabbath. They are rather "little buds from heaven."

There were strict Sabbatarian households still around, to be sure. Indeed, John Ruskin told how his mother, on the Lord's Day, turned all the decorative paintings and wall hangings to face backward so as to preclude enjoyment and keep minds from worldly pleasures.

---

and insulting language to us, to try and prevent us from going on." Allen is informed that he and his congregation can attend St. George's Methodist Church. However, as a result of Allen's evangelism, attendance soon grows, and blacks spill over into sections reserved for whites. Amid prayer one Sunday morning, the "coloured people" are told to move. Insisting that they do not want to create a commotion, they remain on their knees—until one of the church trustees begins pushing and shoving and beckons to another trustee for help.

Richard Allen

"By this time prayer was over, and we all went out of the church in a body," Allen recalled, "and they were no more plagued with us in the church. This raised a great excitement and inquiry among the citizens, in so much that I believe they were ashamed of their conduct." The "coloured" contingent, poor as they were, had been paying their pledges for remodeling St. George's Church, "and just as the house was made comfortable, we were turned out from enjoying the comforts of worshiping therein." They initially rented a storeroom for their own worship but were threatened by trustees who wanted them back paying their pledges.

Throughout his personal narrative, Allen shows deference to Methodist leaders despite ill-treatment. Many local blacks want nothing to do with the Methodists, opting rather to associate with Anglicans. But Allen is opposed. "I was confident that there was no religious sect or denomination that would suit the capacity of the coloured people as well as the Methodist.... All other denominations preached so high-flown that we were not able to comprehend their doctrine." Others organize a church, however, and in 1793 they solicit him to be their minister, "for there was no colored preacher in Philadelphia but myself. I told them I could not accept of their offer, as I was a Methodist."

## HALLOWED GROUND IN PHILADELPHIA

If you go to Philadelphia today and stop at the corner of Sixth and Lombard streets, you stand on hallowed ground. Here one of early America's leading reformers built an internationally famous church, wrote pamphlets of protest that served as models for generations to come, and championed liberty and justice for all. "He was one of the most talented people of his generation," a distinguished scholar of the American Revolution has written; he was a true "Apostle of Freedom," an early biographer declared. His name was Richard Allen.

Richard Newman, *Freedom's Prophet*

Then, in 1794, Allen purchases an old blacksmith shop, has it moved to another lot, and hires a carpenter to remodel it. With his own money and that of his followers and sympathetic whites, he raises enough funds for his new Bethel Church. "I hope the name of Dr. Benjamin Rush and Mr. Robert Ralston [both Presbyterians] will never be forgotten among us," Allen gratefully wrote. "They were the two first gentlemen who espoused the cause of the oppressed and ... the first African church in America."

But problems with the Methodists are not over. Local leaders demand that the new property be turned over to the Conference. Allen balks. He is now free from their demeaning oversight, and he wants independence. One of the leaders agrees, offering to draw up incorporation papers. "We cheerfully submitted to his proposed plan," Allan recalled. But once again he had been double-crossed: "He drew the incorporation, but incorporated our church under the Conference, our property was then all consigned to the Conference for the present Bishops, Elders, and Ministers, &c., that belonged to the white Conference, and our property was gone."

Initially, Allen, "being ignorant of incorporations," does not even realize what has occurred, but some years later this dishonest man (identified by his initials as J.S.) is placed in charge of the Philadelphia Methodist churches. He demands the keys and books of the church and forbids holding any meetings except by orders from him. After protracted deliberations, the incorporation papers are finally changed, giving the Bethel congregation ownership of its property, but the mean-spirited conduct of the local Methodists continues. The new church, in order to be properly Methodist, has to be served periodically by licensed Methodist preachers — white lay preachers who are less qualified than Allen himself. For this service they demand six hundred dollars a year, far beyond what the tiny poverty-stricken congregation is able to pay. The amount is decreased to four hundred and finally two hundred. But when a lay minister is sent only five times for the year, Allen and his followers discontinue his services.

That African American Christians are demanding control of their own religious affairs is galling to some Methodist leaders. Finally, writes Allen, "an edict was passed ... that if any local preacher should serve us, he should be expelled," and "a circular letter [was published] in which we were disowned by the Methodists." But it is not enough to merely throw them out of the denomination. Preachers were also sent to force their way into their place of worship. "But having taken previous advice we had our preacher in the pulpit when he came, and the house was so fixed that he could not get but more than half way to the pulpit." Finally, the little congregation is faced with a lawsuit, which ultimately fails. "We bore much persecution from many of the Methodist connexion," Allen concluded, "but we have reason to be thankful to Almighty God, who was our deliverer."

The blacks in Philadelphia, however, were by no means alone. "About this time our colored friends in Baltimore were treated in a similar manner by the white preachers and Trustees, and many of them driven away," Allen wrote. "Many of the colored people in other places were in a situation nearly like those of Philadelphia and Baltimore, which induced us in April 1816 to call a general meeting, by way of Conference." Delegates come to Philadelphia from surrounding areas and determined to form a new denomination.

Resolved: That the people of Philadelphia, Baltimore, &c., should become one body, under the name of the African Methodist Episcopal Church. We deemed it expedient to have a form of discipline, whereby we may guide our people in the fear of God, in the unity of the Spirit, and in the bonds of peace, and preserve us from that spiritual despotism which we have so recently experienced — remembering that we are not to lord it over God's heritage, as greedy dogs that can never have enough. But with long-suffering, and bowels of compassion to bear each other's burthens, and so fulfil the Law of Christ, praying that our mutual striving together for the promulgation of the Gospel may be crowned with abundant success.

Not surprisingly, Allen is elected bishop of the new organization. In the following years he founds the Free African Society, a benevolent organization that helps newly freed slaves get on their feet. And for those still in the bonds of slavery, he oversees a station on the Underground Railroad for more than three decades. Amid his other activities he and his wife Sarah rear six children. The tiny church that he founded in a shed would grow to more than seven thousand by the end of the 1920s.

Despite his own ill treatment, Allen resists opening the door for full ministry to women. When Jerena Lee, one of his converts, tells him God is calling her to preach the gospel, he tells her that the AME has no place for women preachers. She nevertheless goes out on her own as an evangelist, as does Amanda Smith and other African American women.

## DELIVERED FROM THE SNARE OF THE DEVIL

My aunt was very religiously inclined naturally. She was much like my mother in spirit. So as we walked along, crossing the long bridge ... and were looking off in the water. Aunt said, "How wonderfully God has created everything, the sky, and the great waters." ... Then I let out with my biggest gun; I said, "How do you know there is a God?" and went on with just such an air as a poor, blind, ignorant infidel is capable of putting on. My aunt turned and looked at me with a look that went through me like an arrow; then stamping her foot, she said: "Don't you ever speak to me again. Anybody that had as good a Christian mother as you had, and was raised as you have been, to speak so to me. I don't want to talk to you." And God broke the snare. I felt it. I felt deliverance from that hour. How many times I have thanked God for my aunt's help. If she had argued with me I don't believe I should ever have got out of that snare of the devil.

Amanda Smith, *Autobiography*

## THE SECOND GREAT AWAKENING AND BEYOND

When one looks for evidence of religious awakenings in this period, one finds it everywhere: not only in the astonishing variety of religious sects, both imported and native, but also in literature, politics, educational institutions, popular culture, social reforms, dietary reforms, utopian experiments, child-rearing practices, and relationships between the sexes. In terms of duration, numbers of people involved, or any other measure, the Second Great Awakening dwarfed the First.... By the middle of the nineteenth century, an estimated one-third of the population affiliated with organized religion, twice the percentage of 1776, even though church membership was often deliberately demanding and difficult to achieve.... But the Second Great Awakening put religious practice in the United States on an upward trajectory that would continue through the twentieth century. The contrast with Europe, where religious faith declined in the same era, is striking.

Daniel Walker Howe, *What Hath God Wrought*

### Charles G. Finney: Evangelist of the Second Great Awakening

The best-known revivalist of the Second Great Awakening that swept America in the early decades of the nineteenth century was Charles G. Finney (1792–1875). In many respects, however, he was an unlikely candidate for this role. During his earliest years of ministry, he was insecure and ambivalent about his ability to preach. "Having had no regular training for the ministry," he confessed, "I did not expect or desire to labor in large towns or cities or minister to cultivated congregations. I intended to go into the new settlements and preach in schoolhouses and barns and groves as best I could."

Licensed and commissioned by the Western New York Female Missionary Society, Finney's initial term was for three months. In the village of Evans Mills, New York, he finds people hardened to the gospel. They attend his

Charles G. Finney

meetings, but there is no visible response except for their "ruinous rejection of the gospel of God's dear Son." Then one Sunday evening he throws out a challenge, asking all those who want to become Christians to stand and the rest to remain seated. The audience is stunned. "They looked at one another and at me, and all sat still, just as I expected." Then they begin walking out. He assumes his revival ministry is over, but amazingly, the building is packed at the next meeting and conversions follow.

His own conversion had been a highly charged emotional experience. As a young lawyer, he was alone in his office one evening when he suddenly met "the Lord Jesus Christ face to face." He fell down, confessing his sins and weeping "like a child." He arose to be about his business. "But as I turned and was about to take my seat by the fire, I received a mighty baptism of the Holy Spirit.... The Holy Spirit descended upon me in a manner that seemed to go through me, body and soul ... like a wave of electricity.... Indeed it seemed to come in waves of liquid love."

Like his own conversion, Finney's revival ministry is accompanied by high emotion. At one meeting people suddenly begin falling from their chairs and crying out to God: "If I had had a sword in my hand, I could not have cut them off as fast as they fell." His methods differ from those used in the First Great Awakening. The frontier spirit of individualism goes hand in hand with the Arminian concept of free will. While earlier preachers looked at revivals as miraculous acts of God, Finney emphasizes the human element, condemning the "notion that sinners should continue under conviction of sin until God should grant them repentance." In discussing the nature of revivals, he pointed to the necessity of "appropriate means," including familiarity with God in prayer, entering towns uninvited, expanded roles for women, and the use of the "anxious bench"—a place set aside (often in front of the auditorium) where those contemplating conversion could pray. "A revival is not a miracle," he insisted; "a revival is the work of man, nothing else!"

Like Edwards he is a postmillennialist, believing that revival will hasten the millennial age preceding the return of Christ. Indeed, he argues that if Christians had been evangelizing ten years earlier, "the millennium would have fully come in the U.S. before this day." But all is not lost. "If the church will do all her duty, the millennium may come in this country in three years."

After many years on the revival circuit, Finney settles down in New York City as the minister of Chatham Street Church. He is at home in this socially conscious "free" church (that welcomes poor people by not charging for pews). Nor is he alone among evangelicals in his concern for the poor. Orange Scott, a New England abolitionist preacher, severed ties with the Methodists over slavery, forming the Wesleyan Church. Then, in the mid-1830s, Lewis Tappan, with the support of Asa Mahan, established Oberlin College—soon to become a hotbed of abolitionist ferment. Tappan invites Finney to devote six months each year to Oberlin as a professor of theology. Here antislavery activism is mixed with Puritan covenant theology and Wesleyan perfectionism. Theodore Weld, another prominent abolitionist, joins the faculty, training students to become agents of the antislavery cause. Meanwhile, back in New York, Finney's congregation is expanding to become the new Broadway Tabernacle, a center for revival and reform.

> "By the law of the [Methodist] church through all these years, a single man's salary was $100 per year, and a married man's was $200. If, in the interim between sessions of the annual conference, a married man should lose his wife by death, immediately he was placed at the salary of a single man."
> Rev. James B. Finley (b. 1781)

As a postmillennialist, Professor Finney teaches that the means of bringing in the millennium is through holiness—by a baptism of the Holy Spirit, manifested in many outward forms. A godly Christian society, he insists, offers women opportunities to pray and speak publicly. And not just white women; black women are also enrolled at Oberlin. All the while, he rails against slavery: "How perfectly obvious is it, that slavery is from hell," he writes. "Such a barefaced, shameless, and palpable violation of the law of God.... And even religious teachers, gravely contending that the Bible sanctions this hell-begotten system? 'Oh shame where is thy blush?'"

In this Jacksonian era of land speculation, bank failures, and capitalist schemes, Finney berates merchants who charge exorbitant fees and

## John Jasper

Like Finney, John Jasper (1812–1901) lived into his eighties and conducted a wide and varied ministry that lasted more than five decades. Like Finney he was initially recognized only as a regional revivalist but later became nationally known. But unlike Finney, Jasper was black. Born a slave of slave parents, his father was a preacher and his mother, Nina, was a kindly overseer and medical assistant as well as a deeply pious Christian. On his twenty-seventh birthday in 1839, Jasper was soundly converted and began preaching the same day. His most famous sermon, "The Sun Do Move!" — preached some 250 times, to thousands of people — was taken from the story of Joshua. Challenging the biblical critics of the day, he insisted that the sun moves, assuming its rotation around the earth. People — black and white alike — sometimes traveled a day's journey just to hear the sermon:

> As a fact, Joshua was so drunk with the battle, so thirsty for the blood of the enemies of the Lord, and so wild with the victory that he told the sun to stand still til he could finish his job. What did the sun do? Did he glare down in fiery wrath and say, "What are you talking about my stopping for, Joshua. I ain't never started yet. Been here all the time, and it would smash up everything if I was to start?" Naw, he didn't say that. But what does the Bible say? That's what I ask to know. It says that it was at the voice of Joshua that it stopped. I don't say it stopped; it ain't for Jasper to say that, but the Bible, the book of God, says so. But I say this; nothing can stop til it has first started. So I know what I'm talking about. The sun was traveling along there through the sky when the order came. . . .

conduct their affairs on "principles of commercial justice rather than by Christ's commands." As to the land speculators, they must "give back their ill-gotten gains" or be condemned to the flames of hell. At his death, he leaves behind no denomination, but his legacy has profound social implications for American culture.

## Phoebe Palmer: Revivalist and Social Activist

Remembered as the mother of the Holiness Movement, Phoebe Palmer (1807–1874) was a teacher, evangelist, and writer who strongly promoted Wesley's doctrine of Christian perfection. She was also a leading social activist and an early feminist who maintained that women could minister equally alongside men. Born in New York City to devoted Methodists, she was immersed in the faith from infancy. Her father, a prosperous engineer, often recalled how he

had sneaked away as a child from his Anglican home in Yorkshire, England, to hear the aged John Wesley preach. "Ye must be born again" was the message that marked his conversion.

At nineteen, Phoebe married Walter Palmer, a homeopathic physician who shared her commitment to Methodism. In the following years she mourned the deaths of her little ones, convinced that God was taking them to teach her a lesson. "God takes our treasure to heaven, that our hearts may be there also," she penned in her diary. "The Lord has declared himself a jealous God. . . . After my loved ones were snatched away, I saw that I had concentrated my time and attentions far too exclusively, to the neglect of the religious activities demanded."

Religious activities become Phoebe's priority in the following decades, activities marked by her experience of entire sanctification. Such perfectionism was still an important theme in Methodism, though many ministers, finding it impossible to live out, had abandoned the doctrine. But several years into their marriage both Phoebe and Walter claim the experience of "perfect love." At the same time, Phoebe's sister, Sarah Lankford, is hosting Tuesday Meetings for the Promotion of Holiness. In attendance are both women and men, including prominent Methodist leaders. Phoebe joins Sarah, and so popular is her teaching that she receives invitations to speak at camp meetings and other venues. She leaves her surviving children behind with Walter and a maid, though he later joins her part time. "Never have we witnessed such triumphs of the cross as during the past summer and fall," she reports in 1857. "Not less than two thousand have been gathered into the fold.... Hundreds of believers have been sanctified wholly, and hundreds have received baptism of the Holy Ghost, beyond any former experienced."

Her ministry corresponds with the Prayer Revival of 1857–58 that begins inauspiciously when Jeremiah C. Lamphier, a lay minister serving at a declining Dutch Reformed church, posts fliers for a weekly noonday prayer meeting near New York City's financial district. With six in attendance at the first meeting, it spreads across the city and across the county, spurred in part by the events of October 14, 1857, when Wall Street was suddenly in the throes of a crushing financial panic.

In addition to her revival ministry, Palmer establishes the Five Points Mission in New York that offers housing, health care, and education to needy families. Often the brunt of criticism for pushing the boundaries of women's roles, she responds with *Promise of the Father* (1859), defending women in ministry. Earlier she had written:

> Last night I wrote, as the caption of an article I intend to write ... "has the spirit of prophecy fallen on woman?... The promise of the Father has either been fulfilled, or has not ... 'And it shall come to pass, after those days, that I will pour out my Spirit upon all flesh, and your sons and your daughters shall prophesy.'" And did one of that waiting company wait in vain?... Male and female were now one in Jesus Christ. The Spirit now descended alike on all. And they were *all* filled with the Holy Ghost, and began to speak as the Spirit gave utterance....

Palmer left behind no organized movement but her teachings paved the way for the later Holiness and Pentecostal movements. Her daughter, Phoebe Knapp, wrote many hymn tunes, including the familiar tune for Fanny Crosby's popular hymn, "Blessed Assurance."

---

## METHODIST CIRCUIT RIDERS

A Methodist preacher in those days, when he felt that God had called him to preach, instead of hunting up a college or Biblical institute, hunted up a hardy pony of a horse and some traveling apparatus and ... cried "Behold the Lamb of God, that taketh away the sin of the world." In this way he went through storms of wind, hail, snow, and rain; climbed hills and mountains, traversed valleys, plunged through swamps, swam swollen streams, lay out all night, wet, weary, and hungry, held his horse by the bridle all night, or tied him to a limb, slept with his saddle blanket for a bed, his saddle or saddle bags for his pillow, and his old big coat or blanket, if he had any, for a covering. Often he slept in dirty cabins, on earthen floors, before the fire.... His text was always ready, "Behold the Lamb of God."

Peter Cartwright, *Autobiography*

## GEORGE MÜLLER

Born in Germany the son of a government bureaucrat, George Müller (1805–1898) was a troubled teen, drunk the night his mother died, and imprisoned before he was sixteen. Prodded by his father, he enrolled at the University of Halle for religious studies aimed at a lucrative clerical career. At the invitation of a friend, he attended a prayer meeting and was soon after converted. In his twenties he moved to England and became the pastor of a small chapel. During that time he was struck by the words of Psalm 68, portraying God as the "father of the fatherless." With that challenge, he and his young wife rented a house in Bristol and soon had more than twenty orphans in their care. Within months they opened a second orphan home with thirty more children, and soon a third home was opened. In the following years, larger and bigger homes were acquired, some of them housing as many as three hundred children.

At seventy, Müller turned the work over to his son-in-law while he traveled around the world raising support and conducting missionary work. He became a celebrity as his miracle stories circulated. He told how one morning the children arose to the bell only to find their breakfast bowls empty. He had no more than said *amen* after his prayer of blessing, when there was a knock at the door. The local baker, with fresh bread, told how he had been awakened in the night thinking of hungry children. As the baker was leaving, another knock at the door brought the milkman. With a broken-down wagon, he was offering the milk to the orphans before it spoiled. Miracles multiplied as stories were repeated and funds came in.

### Charles Haddon Spurgeon: London's Boy Preacher

Known as the "Prince of Preachers," Charles Haddon Spurgeon (1834–1892) was London's most celebrated megachurch minister of his day. The son and grandson of independent Nonconformist ministers, his training began early with *Pilgrims Progress* and *Foxe's Book of Martyrs*. When his grandmother offered him a penny for each of Isaac Watts's hymns that he memorized, she soon reduced the pay "to a half-penny, then to a farthing, to keep from being quite ruined in the deal." When his grandfather offered him a shilling for every dozen rats he could kill around the house, he was torn: "I found rat-catching paid me better than learning hymns." Growing up in a Nonconformist household, he had a mediocre childhood education and studied Greek for only a short time; the first-rate classical education enjoyed by Anglicans was not available to him.

He was converted as a teenager in a tiny Primitive Methodist chapel. It was a cold winter night, and only eight people were present. On his way to a church social, he had stopped at the chapel, seeking shelter from a snowstorm. A "swarthy faced and grimy handed blacksmith" rose to speak. He read from Isaiah 45, "Look unto me, and be ye saved." His pointed and personalized commentary was simple: "Well, a man needn't go to college to learn to look. Anyone can look. You may be a fool and yet you can look. You will never find comfort in yourself. Look to Christ. Young man, you look very miserable. You always will be miserable if you don't obey the text; but if you obey now, this moment you may be saved."

"Free will carried many a soul to hell, but never a soul to heaven."

C. H. Spurgeon

Spurgeon's life was transformed. "I could dance all the way home," he remembered. "I understand what Bunyan meant when he declared that he wanted to tell the crows on the plowed land all about his conversion." Spurgeon preached to more than crows, and his reputation as a mesmerizing speaker quickly spread. At eighteen he was invited to be a pastoral candidate at the New Park Street Chapel, a large prestigious church whose parishioners were frustrated by the dry sermons of the other candidates. "The effect was amazing," wrote an observer. "After the service people too excited to leave the building gathered in groups talking about securing him for pastor." He was called, and so began his long and much-publicized career in ministry, bringing some twenty thousand into his church and prompting him to boast that "there was not a seat in the Tabernacle but someone had been saved in it."

In 1861, still in his twenties, his congregation moved to the new Metropolitan Tabernacle. Here his preaching ministry continued to thrive. He paced the platform as he took on the character of biblical figures, bringing Scripture stories to life. His illustrations featured pathetic tales of penitent prisoners and prostitutes and wayward children dying before their time. It was the best Sunday show in town, especially for evangelicals, whose Sabbath strictures limited their activities. But as his popularity soared, so did the sneers of his critics. Sometimes compared with the popular entertainer Tom Thumb, he was called a "pulpit buffoon" and worse. As an authoritarian strongman, he

Caricature of Charles Spurgeon from *Vanity Fair*, December 10, 1870

wielded power in the church and was referred to as a pope. Theological issues, however, created the most bitter controversies of his ministerial career. A staunch Calvinist, he condemned those who disagreed with him. "Arminian perversions," he railed, "are to sink back to their birthplace in the pit." Teaching that one could lose salvation was "the wickedest falsehood on earth."

> "A vigorous temper is not altogether an evil. Men who are easy as an old shoe are generally of little worth."
>
> C. H. Spurgeon

But the most publicized and drawn-out battle of his ministry involved the "Downgrade Controversy" within his own Baptist Union. He was convinced that many of his fellow ministers were becoming liberal on the issues of biblical infallibility, eternal reprobation, Christ's atonement, and other long-held orthodox doctrines. Those who are the targets of his accusations charge him with magnifying minor differences. Finger-pointing deteriorates into nasty allegations, Spurgeon claiming that some of his Baptist brethren do not preach enough gospel "to save a cat." Accusing him of arrogance and impudence, some of the students in his own preachers' college part company with him. In the end, the Baptist Union votes to censure him—after he has already resigned. The theological storm has negative consequences for the Baptists as well as for Spurgeon. His supporters

## SEX SCANDAL OF THE CENTURY

Long before Jim Bakker, Jimmy Swaggart, and Ted Haggard were making headlines, Henry Ward Beecher (1813–1887) captured the attention of the world in a lurid court case. Son of celebrated minister Lyman Beecher and brother of Harriet Beecher Stowe (author of *Uncle Tom's Cabin*), he was the most famous preacher in America of his day. As minister of the prestigious Plymouth Church in Brooklyn, he was middle-aged and at the peak of his career when the bubble burst. The woman (twenty-two years younger than he) was Elizabeth (Libby) Tilton, wife of a prominent church member. Libby sought Beecher's counsel for marital problems. Beecher was sympathetic, and for more than a year he counseled and kissed. Then Libby told her husband. In the spring of 1871, the story broke publicly. The case dragged out for several years, Beecher admitting kissing but denying adultery. After a six-month trial, he was acquitted of any wrongdoing. A church committee, alleged to be stacked in his favor, later exonerated him. All the while, the presses cranked out the scandal of the century.

lament that the uproar took a toll on his health, resulting in a premature death. In their eyes, he had become a martyr to orthodoxy.

Prior to this storm of controversy, he had offended "conservatives" in his midst—and around the world. Already having been criticized for drinking alcohol, he made matters worse when he went public with his smoking. In 1874 an American preacher was invited to join Spurgeon on the platform and make some remarks. Spurgeon's sermon had been on forsaking sin, and the visiting minister made application by challenging listeners to leave behind their besetting sins—including smoking. Instead of allowing the remarks to pass, Spurgeon had the last word: "Well, dear friends, you know that some men can do to the glory of God what to other men would be a sin. And ... I intend to smoke a good cigar to the glory of God before I go to bed tonight." The press had a heyday with the story, also reporting on his lavish lifestyle and his country estate "fit for a prince."

Spurgeon is a Victorian gentleman who hires servants and bestows jewels on his wife. And Susannah, for her part, is a most dutiful wife. Like too many Victorian women, she takes to her bed as an invalid. But from her boudoir, she is a powerhouse of publicity for her husband. She writes letters and raises large sums of money for the Sermon Fund and the Book Fund, supplying poor ministers with bound copies of her husband's writings. The books are a godsend, often more than doubling the minister's library holdings of the Bible, *Foxe's Book of Martyrs*, and *Pilgrim's Progress*. At the same time, Spurgeon's star rises as he becomes the most quoted source in Sunday sermons throughout England and far beyond.

Susannah is not the only family member actively involved in Spurgeon's ministry. His

Spurgeon preaching at Surrey Music Hall

brother James serves as assistant pastor of the Metropolitan Tabernacle, and, when he dies at fifty-seven, he is succeeded by his son Thomas.

## Dwight L. Moody: Father of Modern Campaign Evangelism

Dwight L. Moody (1837–1899), the most indomitable and influential evangelist of the nineteenth century, turned revivalism into big business. His boundless enthusiasm was contagious, and evangelical religion came of age under his ministry. His work became the benchmark for all revivalists who followed him. A pushy shoe salesman turned pushy evangelist, he refused to be limited by his lack of education and low social status, turning private religion into a public campaign. It is said that he once stopped a man on the street and asked, as was his custom, "Are you a Christian?" "It's none of your business," the offended pedestrian replied. "Yes, it is," insisted Moody. "Then you must be Mr. Moody," the man said.

Born in Northfield, Massachusetts, he had a difficult childhood. His alcoholic father died at forty-one when Moody was four. His mother was left deeply in debt and alone with nine children under the age of thirteen. Creditors quickly made their move. The farm was put into foreclosure. Furniture and anything else of value was divided like spoils. The older children were sent out to families, where they worked for their room and board. Even little Dwight was soon sent to live with a family, working for them more than attending school and barely learning to read. At seventeen he moved to Boston to work in his uncle's shoe store. Here, living under his uncle's rules, church attendance was required—a requirement that led to his conversion. Mr. Kimball, a Sunday school teacher, tells the story:

I started down to Holton's shoe store. When I was nearly there, I began to wonder whether I ought to go just then, during business hours. And I thought maybe my mission might embarrass the boy.... While I was pondering over it all, I passed the store without noticing it. Then when I found I had gone by the door, I determined to make a dash for it and have it over at once. I found Moody in the back.... I simply told him of Christ's love for him and the love Christ wanted in return. That was all there was. It seemed the young man was just ready for the light that then broke upon him, and there, in the back of the store in Boston, he gave himself and his life to Christ.

Despite his enthusiasm to follow Jesus, Moody was initially denied church membership, having failed the most simple Bible knowledge test. "I can truly say," Kimball recalled, "that I have seen few persons whose minds were spiritually darker than was his when he came into my Sunday school class." But what he lacked in book learning he made up for in street smarts and salesmanship. He moved to Chicago where

> "Everything I could get hold of in print that he ever said I read.... Oh, Lord, help me to preach and minister like Charles Spurgeon!"
> D. L. Moody

he excelled in sales and organized evangelistic outreach, shoddy as it was. "The first meeting I ever saw him at was in a little old shanty that had been abandoned by a saloon-keeper," wrote an observer. He was "standing up with a few tallow candles around him, holding a negro boy, and trying to read to him the story of the Prodigal Son and a great many words he could not

## FANNY CROSBY AND REVIVALISM

When one reflects on the phenomenal rise of the evangelical movement in the latter quarter of the nineteenth and the early years of the twentieth centuries, three spiritual stalwarts stand out as the most influential: Evangelist Dwight L. Moody, musician Ira D. Sankey, and hymn writer Fanny J. Crosby. In his later years, Sankey himself once remarked that the success of the Moody-Sankey evangelistic campaigns was due, more than any other human factor, to the use of Fanny Crosby's hymns.

In the period of 1870 to her death in 1915, it is estimated that Fanny Crosby wrote between 8,000 and 9,000 gospel hymn texts, more than any other known hymn writer.... These include such popular hymns still found in our hymnals as "Safe in the Arms of Jesus," "Blessed Assurance," "Pass Me Not, O Gentle Savior," "Jesus, Keep Me Near the Cross," ... "To God Be the Glory," and "Rescue the Perishing."

Kenneth W. Osbeck, *101 More Hymn Stories*

read out, and had to skip. I thought, *If the Lord can ever use such an instrument as that for His honor and glory, it will astonish me.*"

This work led to the founding of a Sunday school of some six hundred children and sixty volunteers. It was so noteworthy that on November 25, 1860, President-elect Abraham Lincoln visited and offered remarks to the class. How did Moody attract so many youth in his ministry outreach? As a salesman he used the tricks of the trade: passing out candy and offering free pony rides. Needing a permanent home for the growing class, he started a church in Chicago, the Illinois Street Church, its purpose to be a home for poor immigrant families. For several years he also headed up the Chicago YMCA.

The most momentous event of his early ministry is his meeting fifteen-year-old Emma Revell. Despite the striking difference in their social status, they marry four years later in 1862. Throughout their marriage she works beside him, manages the family, and anguishes over wayward sons. He regards her as a more effective teacher and one-on-one evangelist than he is. According to their son Paul, "Till the day of his death he never ceased to [be amazed at] the

miracle of having won the love of a woman he considered so completely his superior."

In 1871 Moody teamed up with gospel singer Ira D. Sankey. Later that year, Mrs. O'Leary's cow kicked over the lantern and all of Chicago was ablaze. Moody later remarked that he lost everything except his Bible and his reputation. It was a terrible circumstance, but it launched him out of one city and into the world. In the summer of 1873, he and Sankey set out for England. As a self-made American rags-to-religion hick, he quickly rises to superstar status. After preaching for two years in England, Scotland, and Ireland, he can point to revivals not only among miners

"If eloquence is measured by its effect upon an audience and not by its balanced sentences and cumulative periods, then there is eloquence of the highest order. In sheer persuasiveness, Mr. Moody has few equals, and, rugged as his preaching may seem to some, there is in it a pathos of a quality which few orators have ever reached, and appealing tenderness which not only wholly redeems it, but raises it not unseldom almost to sublimity."

Henry Drummond

and urban poor but also among the aristocrats and university elite. Students flock to his meetings. Among his converts are the "Cambridge Seven," some of them England's most celebrated cricket players, who will soon head overseas as missionaries with the China Inland Mission.

He returns to America in 1875 as an internationally famous revivalist. Every city wants him to hold a campaign. By trial and error he develops his methods: an ecumenically diverse invitation, house-to-house canvassing, funding from wealthy philanthropists, free newspaper publicity, rental of large buildings, trendy music, and volunteer counselors for an enquiry room.

Unlike modern-day evangelists, Moody did not invest heavily in print advertising. Reporters jostled each other in getting the lead story, his eccentricities and homespun personality serving them well. His self-deprecating style and his quotable quips perfectly suited the hungry press, eager to sell penny-papers; and his lack of education and proper etiquette, his poor grammar and pronunciation made him all the more endearing. Newspapers who ignored or belittled him did so to their financial peril.

Moody's uncle once quipped, "My nephew Dwight is crazy, crazy as a March hare." An unrelated observer offered a different slant: "There was the revivalist Moody, bearded and neckless, with his two hundred and eighty pounds of Adam's flesh, every ounce of which belonged to God." Still another reported that he was "a genuine kick-in-the-pants." H. L. Mencken, the wit and satirist of the day, was the source for much of the contemporary reflection on Moody. "When he started out, an evangelist had no more dignity and social position among us than a lightening-rod salesman," wrote Mencken. "When he finished, he was friendly with leading merchants, industrialists, and public figures of the day, including Cyrus McCormick and such august characters as John Wanamaker, Morris K. Jesup, and General O. O. Howard." Again, Mencken wrote:

> He wore a bristling beard, cultivated a paunch, and [had] the hearty innocent manner of a high-geared drummer in the pulpit; he was, indeed, always far more the business man than the theologian.... He discharged the obvious with all the explosive effort of an auctioneer. And, he knew how to weep, and how to make others weep. His pathetic stories— of drunkard's children, wives, sisters, aunts, grandmothers ... of atheist soldiers dying on the battlefield, of heroic missionaries garroted in the slums—were famous in their day, and kept the country damp [with tears].

## MOODY AND THE PRESS

It was Luther who remarked that the printing press was "God's highest act of grace" because the spread of his ideas help to make the Reformation possible. Moody certainly felt a similar solicitude. "I pray Heaven's richest blessing to rest upon the press in Chicago," he told them in a widely quoted benediction that was adapted for every occasion. "I hope they will continue to spread the Gospel of Christ as they have done during these meetings." He could pay them no higher compliment.... Moody and Chicago's mass media grew up together, knew each other, and needed one another. Moody needed to reach those at a distance through the pages of the press. Newsmen needed a good story. Together they crafted a civic spectacle of unprecedented proportions.

Bruce J. Evensen, *God's Man for the Gilded Age*

Moody, however, was more than a charismatic revivalist. The uneducated shoe salesman became an educator, establishing three schools in Northfield, Massachusetts, and Moody Bible Institute in Chicago—all founded in part to train more evangelists. When Moody died three days before Christmas in 1899, it was a time of mourning and homage. "Chicago at one time claimed this mighty preacher," a hometown newspaper eulogized. "But when he died the whole world claimed him." The *New York Tribune* offered a similar tribute: "The death of D. L. Moody is an almost irreparable loss to evangelical Christianity.

He was probably the greatest religious revivalist of the present century."

Moody lived and died in the nineteenth century, but his evangelistic legacy, as well as that of Finney, would profoundly influence virtually every twentieth-century evangelist, including Billy Graham. Moody Bible Institute in Chicago would likewise serve as a benchmark for the Bible institute/college movement that fueled worldwide evangelism for several decades following Moody's death. Twentieth-century evangelism was a direct descendant of its nineteenth-century forebears.

## What if ...

What if Richard Allen had backed down and submitted to Methodist leaders instead of leaving the church and organizing a black denomination with other disgruntled African Americans? Without the African Methodist Episcopal Church would blacks have fallen away from the Methodist Church altogether?

What if Charles Finney had given up after his early apparent failures as an evangelist? How did his ministry affect not only evangelical theological foundations but also abolition and women's rights?

What if a teenage boy heading for a church social had not stopped by a Methodist chapel on a stormy night? And what if the uneducated layman at that service had been too fearful to stand up and preach? Would C. H. Spurgeon have become the "prince of preachers," still read and admired today?

What if Edward Kimball had not turned around and gone back into Holton's shoe store to share the gospel with young Dwight L. Moody? How different might the evangelical world be today without his ministry more than a century ago?

## Further Reading

Bradley, Ian. *The Call to Seriousness: The Evangelical Impact on the Victorians*. New York: Macmillan, 1976.

Curtis, Richard K. *They Called Him Mr. Moody*. Grand Rapids: Eerdmans, 1962.

Dallimore, Arnold. *Forerunner of the Charismatic Movement: The Life of Edward Irving*. Chicago: Moody Press, 1983.

Evensen, Bruce J. *God's Man for the Gilded Age: D. L. Moody and the Rise of Modern Mass Evangelism.* New York: Oxford University, 2003.

Finney, Charles G. *Autobiography of Charles G. Finney: The Life of America's Great Evangelist.* Edited by Helen Wessel. Minneapolis: Bethany House, 2006.

Gundry, Stanley N. *Love Them In: The Life and Theology of D. L. Moody.* Grand Rapids: Baker, 1976.

Hambrick-Stowe, Charles E. *Charles G. Finney and the Spirit of American Evangelicalism.* Grand Rapids: Eerdmans, 1996.

Howe, Daniel Walker. *What God Hath Wrought: The Transformation of America, 1815-1848.* New York: Oxford University, 2007.

Knight, Mark, and Emma Mason. *Nineteenth-Century Religion and Literature: An Introduction.* New York: Oxford University, 2007.

Magnuson, Norris. *Salvation in the Slums: Evangelical Social Work 1865–1920.* Grand Rapids: Baker, 1977

Newman, Richard. *Freedom's Prophet: Bishop Richard Allen, the AME Church, and the Black Founding Fathers.* New York: New York University, 2008.

Polloch, John C. *Moody: A Biographical Portrait of the Pacesetter in Modern Mass Evangelism.* New York: Macmillan, 1963.

White, Charles Edward. *The Beauty of Holiness: Phoebe Palmer as Theologian, Revivalist, Feminist, and Humanitarian.* Grand Rapids: Zondervan, 1986.

# CHAPTER 21

# The Modern Missionary Movement

*Families in Cross-Cultural Ministry*

*As a child I imagined missionaries were super saints. As an adult I have come to realize they are beset with sins and flaws and failures like everyone else.*

*A 2010 cover story in* Christianity Today *exposes the dark side of missionary work. It tells of the horrific abuse of children at a West African school for missionary kids, Mamou Alliance Academy. Here things had gone very wrong for decades. How much Alliance leaders knew during this time and how much cover-up and foot-dragging occurred once they were informed is unclear. But with large numbers of victims coming forward, officials agreed to investigate, and an effort to come clean has been in process since the 1990s.*

*My own connection with the Academy is as indirect and distant as it is profound. In the late 1950s, when I was thirteen, I spent a week at Pigeon Lake Bible Camp in northern Wisconsin. Back in those days, mornings were devoted to preaching and Bible study, afternoons to recreation, and evenings to evangelistic meetings. The guest speaker for the week was a missionary from West Africa. At the end of his message on the last evening there was a double invitation—the usual one for salvation and then the clincher: all those who would commit themselves to be missionaries were to stand up.*

*I will never forget the tension of that night. The room was filled with teen campers sitting on benches, all anxious for the meeting to end and the campfire to begin. The missionary, however, was not about to let us escape so easily. Millions in Africa and elsewhere around the world were going to hell for want of someone to tell them of Jesus. How could any of us say no to God's call? As the pressure mounted, I remained seated, trembling and clutching the bench. To go to Africa for my whole life was terrifying. But if I didn't go, I'd be sending people to hell. I wavered as guilt engulfed me.*

*There is someone out there God is speaking to, the missionary intoned. If you don't say yes now, there may never be another chance. I stood. It was the hardest thing I had ever done. For the next decade I was haunted by this "call," determined to become a missionary. It never happened. Short-term, yes, but not a career missionary.*

*Over the decades I wondered about that missionary speaker, his name imprinted on my memory. Then sometime ago his name popped off the page as I read that he was among those who had molested little children at Mamou.*

World Christianity ... is the result of the great missionary expansion of the last two centuries. That expansion, whatever one's attitude to Christianity may be, is one of the most remarkable facts of human history. One of the oddities of current affairs ... is the way in which the event is so constantly ignored or undervalued.

LESSLIE NEWBIGIN

World Christianity has its origins with the apostle Paul and evangelists in the centuries following. Later Nestorianism spread as far east as China, and the age of Catholic missions corresponded with the age of discovery. Worldwide Protestant Christianity is the result of the great missionary expansion of the nineteenth century begun by William Carey and others. It is remarkable that this phenomenon is so constantly ignored in history texts, even *church* history texts. Today the Christian faith in the Southern Hemisphere is very different from that which was planted by missionaries in the nineteenth and twentieth centuries. But the origins of this rapidly expanding movement are, almost without exception, traced to those evangelical missionaries of generations past.

Nineteenth-century revival movements and social outreach were closely identified with overseas missions. The same individuals—whether Charles Spurgeon or D. L. Moody—were involved in evangelism and humanitarian outreach both at home and abroad. A missionary from Syria wrote to Susannah Spurgeon that the

"1500 copies of Sermons" that her fund had sent were "distributed to school children ... after they had been exhorted by their teachers to read them to their parents." Moody was a powerhouse behind the Student Volunteer Movement that originated at Cambridge University and spread throughout universities across America. Long before Spurgeon and Moody spurred overseas evangelism, however, pioneer missionaries like William Carey and David Livingstone were setting the stage for others to follow, including Hudson Taylor, Mary Slessor, Lottie Moon, Kanzo Uchimura, and Eliza Davis George.

Protestants had gotten off to a slow start in the overseas mission venture in part because their centers of strength were found largely in land-locked countries. The sea-faring nations of Spain, France, and Portugal were solidly Catholic, and missionary monks and friars accompanied explorers and merchants. Thus, as continents were colonized and countries were claimed by European powers, the natives in the New World were evangelized and baptized into Catholicism. In the eighteenth century, Dutch

## PARADE OF HISTORY

The Protestant parade to foreign lands was slow in getting underway, but by the late nineteenth century the sparse militias had turned into a vast army. Pearl Buck described the militant march to the mission field in colorful terms: "No weak or timid soul could sail the seas to foreign lands and defy death and danger unless he did carry religion as his banner." As this missionary parade advanced into unknown regions, religion — Christianity in capital letters — was the banner. In China, Pastor Hsi led the parade through towns and villages with his "gospel cart" emblazoned with "Holy Religion of Jesus" in Chinese characters.

Reformed, Danish Lutherans, and Moravians had ventured out in mission forays but on a much smaller scale. And even with the expansion of the British Empire, Anglicans and other Protestants were typically more concerned with trade and colonization than with missions.

Theological presuppositions frequently factored into the equation. The Protestant emphasis on the sovereignty of God and predestination caused some to wonder what part human effort played in salvation. Some argued that Jesus' commissioning of disciples to "go into all the world and preach the gospel" (the Great Commission) was fulfilled by the apostles, who, according to tradition, spread out as far as Spain, North Africa, and India. This commission, it was argued, was not given to succeeding generations.

Church historian Gustav Warneck (1834–1910) wrote that he missed "not only action, but even the idea of missions" in the lives of the Reformers, insisting that "fundamental theological views hindered them from giving their activity, even their thoughts, a missionary direction." Kenneth Scott Latourette (1884–1968), author of a multivolume history of missions, also saw a lack of missionary concern among the Reformers. In his survey of the history of Christian missions, Stephen Neill maintained that the Reformers showed little concern for "the progress of the preaching of the Gospel through the world." In recent years historians with Reformed leanings have challenged this account, though sometimes with less-than-convincing arguments.

Luther had argued in his commentary on Haggai that it was crucial for "the kingdom ... to be spread throughout the world to all nations," but he and his followers failed to put the missions mandate into practice. Calvin's record on overseas missions barely exceeds that

of Luther. The work for which he is best known, the *Institutes*, includes very little that could be considered mission theology. In his commentaries he gives a nod to missions because the text demands it. In reflecting on Isaiah 12:5, for example, he argues that it is the church's responsibility to ensure that the gospel is not "concealed in a corner" but is "everywhere proclaimed." Likewise, he asserts in a sermon that "it is not enough for us to have an eye to our own salvation, but the knowledge of God must shine generally throughout all the world."

In defense of Calvin, historians point to his sending out evangelists in Catholic regions to bring the Reformed message. He sent ministers — the Venerable Company of Pastors — from Geneva back to his homeland of France as well as to Italy, Germany, England, and Scotland. They traveled, often under cover of darkness, and planted churches in attics and barns and caves. In 1556 ministers M. Pierre Richier and M. Guillaume sailed to Brazil at the directive of Calvin to serve as chaplains to Huguenots who had settled there. But outreach to "the heathen" would be largely ignored for more than two centuries.

The history of modern missions is inescapably bound with the history of colonialism. As with Catholic missionary efforts in the preceding centuries, nineteenth-century Protestant missionary endeavors followed the flag. The expansion of the British Empire ("on which the sun never sets"), as well as colonization by the Dutch and other Western Europeans, occurred simultaneously with the expansion of Christian missions. Thus the modern missionary movement sends mixed messages — one that symbolizes the conqueror, and the other that symbolizes the cross. Historians have often emphasized the former, speaking of missions and imperialism and exploitation in one breath. But there is

## Letters from the Field

For nineteenth-century missionaries, letter writing was the only means of communication with family and supporters. But before the advent of airmail, letters from overseas often took months to reach their destination. Writing letters, however, was no mere pastime; it was a primary function in the vast enterprise of Christian missions. Letters served to raise funds and recruit more missionaries, but they were also very personal in nature.

Some letters carried the devastating news of death, often months after the fact. Others reveal shocking information, as when Andrew Fuller, head of the Baptist Mission Society, opened his mail in 1795. "Mrs. Carey has given us much trouble and vexation," wrote Dr. John Thomas. "She has taken it into her head that C[arey] is a great whoremonger, and her jealousy burns like fire unquenchable.... She has made some attempt on his life."

Letters, of course, went both ways. Letters and packages often crossed in the mail, as was the case for Narcissa and Marcus Whitman, missionaries to Native Americans in the Oregon Territory. In 1839, when their two-year-old Alice wandered away on a Sunday afternoon and drowned, news did not reach family back in New York for many months. A year after the tragedy, Narcissa opened a package from her mother, only to find little dresses and shoes for a toddler who would never wear them.

Ann Judson was America's premier missionary letter writer. Her letters were filled with the drama of missionary life in Burma, and each installment was widely printed in church magazines and newspapers. When her husband was imprisoned in a dungeon for more than a year, her newsy letters were devoured and financial support soared. A Baptist agent in New York reported the response of one young woman to Ann's most recent missive printed in the *New York Baptist Register:* "I heard a deep sigh from the young woman ... with her cheek bathed in tears, and handing me a quarter of a dollar (all the money she had) with trembling she said, 'Will you send that money to Burma?' ... and pointing to the letter, turned away to weep."

Lottie Moon, a Southern Baptist missionary to China, wrote letters—often laced with sarcasm—pleading for more recruits: "It is odd that a million Baptists of the South can furnish only three men for all China. Odd that with five hundred preachers in the state of Virginia, we must rely on a Presbyterian to fill a Baptist pulpit [here]. I wonder how these things look in heaven. They certainly look very queer in China."

After David Livingstone had sent his wife and children back to England while he himself remained in Africa, he expressed in writing what he could not say in person:

> My dearest Mary—How I miss you now, and the dear children. My heart yearns incessantly over you. How many thoughts of the past crowd into my mind. I feel as if I would treat you all more tenderly and lovingly than ever.... I never show my feelings; but I can say truly, my dearest, that I loved you when I married you, and the longer I lived with you, I loved you the better.

another side of modern missions that portrays sacrifice and self-denial and fierce opposition to colonial exploits.

Such a profile fits the majority of nineteenth- and early twentieth-century missionaries. When new recruits died within months of entering Africa ("the white man's graveyard"), more missionaries were sent to fill their places. Livingstone's words were typical: "It is a venture to take wife and children into a country where fever—African fever—prevails. But who that believes in Jesus would refuse to make a venture for such a Captain?" Ann Martin Hinderer expressed similar sentiments when she and her husband went to Africa in 1852 to serve as Anglican missionaries: "I had a strong desire to be a missionary.... When I see what is the need, I feel that if I had twenty lives I would gladly give them to be the means of a little good to these poor ... people."

That missionaries risked their lives to preach the gospel is not debated, but that they were on the leading edge of humanitarian outreach is often ignored. William Carey fought hard against cultural practices such as *suti* that presumed a wife would be burned on a funeral pyre at her husband's death. Mary Slessor battled against the practice of twin murder. David Livingstone waged war against slave traffic; Lottie Moon, against famine. Although some imagined that their work would be strictly evangelism, rare were the missionaries who were not deeply involved in health care and social causes.

In the early decades of modern missions, women served alongside their husbands, often in independent ministry, as was true of Ann Judson. Sending agencies viewed them merely as ministers' wives. But as single women clamored to be a part of this grand enterprise, the Women's Missionary Movement was born. Initiated in 1861, it spawned some forty "female agencies" in the next four decades, and by the turn of the century women—single and married—outnumbered men by nearly two to one in many areas. It became a vast network encompassing millions of women on the home front supporting thousands of women serving abroad. Fading away in the twentieth century, the movement was subsumed under denominational or independent mission board control. Men were in charge, and never again would women have such a prominent role in developing mission strategy and overseeing worldwide evangelism.

Four years after the first female agency was launched, Hudson Taylor founded the China Inland Mission. The first of dozens of "faith" mission agencies, its recruits, with no salaries, raised financial support "by faith." Taylor welcomed single women into the ranks and focused on *inland* tribal groups, as did later faith missions, including the Sudan Interior Mission, the Africa Inland Mission, New Tribes Mission, and the Regions Beyond Mission. Most of the missionaries were trained in the burgeoning Bible institutes of the early twentieth century.

In the late nineteenth century, spurred by the preaching of Moody, the Student Volunteer Movement was born. Capturing the hearts and minds of university students, this movement focused its mission outreach primarily on the educated elite of India and East Asia. Without Bible institute or seminary training, the missionaries became more liberal as time passed and the movement eventually died a natural death. Missionaries were by nature evangelistic and evangelical. Those with a liberal or modernist bent often opposed converting people to Christianity, so the era of modern missions is largely a story of evangelicals. Mission outreach is also a story of family life. Unlike their Catholic predecessors, Protestants took no vow of celibacy. Marriage and family created major cross-cultural stress that was virtually unknown among their peers in the homeland. One after another, missionary families were broken by death and dysfunction.

## William Carey: Shoemaker and Missionary Hero

Often labeled the father of modern missions, William Carey (1761–1834) influenced generations of Protestant missionaries by his self-sacrifice and his staying power among the "heathen" of Bengal for some forty years. He stands out as a judicious team leader of the misnamed "Serempore Trio" composed of himself, William Ward, and Joshua *and Hannah* Marshman—a team whose efficient division of labor served as a model for future mission enterprises.

William Carey

Born in Northamptonshire the son of a weaver, Carey became a shoemaker's apprentice and then opened his own shop. But poverty pursued him and his growing family. On the side he served as a licensed minister in a tiny Baptist church. Fascinated with seafaring discoveries—particularly the voyages of Captain Cook—he took to heart the message of Jesus to "go into all the world and preach the gospel." Joining with other Baptist ministers, he helped to organize the Baptist Missionary Society and volunteered to serve with Dr. John Thomas on the society's first mission venture.

In the following years he became a legend in his own time, serving some four decades in India without home leave. His dozens of translations, though raw and seriously flawed, would become a mark of his brilliance, and the fire that destroyed them would become a landmark tragedy in missions history. With his colleagues he developed schools and humanitarian programs. A recognized Sanskrit scholar, he was often involved in the "secular" work of translating Hindu writings—much to the chagrin of some of his supporters back home. The accomplishments of the Serampore mission (located in a Danish territory near Calcutta) were wide-ranging and noteworthy.

But for all his renown as a multifaceted missionary, Carey was far less successful in the arena of family life. Indeed, it was this aspect of his ministry that has most marred his image—and not just since the late twentieth century when family issues assumed a high priority. In Carey's own day there were those who questioned his seeming insensitivity to family concerns. He was nineteen when he married Dorothy ("Dolly"), who was then in her mid-twenties. As was true of many women of low social standing in that era, she was illiterate and signed her name with an "X" on the marriage register. It would be a mistake, however, to imagine that Dorothy had snared the town's most eligible bachelor. He was a "poor journeyman-shoemaker," and his own mother was appalled by their abject poverty when she visited them shortly after their marriage.

Despite their financial hardships, Dorothy supported his pastoral ministry to the point of being rebaptized as a Baptist—a noteworthy decision, considering her devout Puritan upbringing. But her support for his ministry had its limits. When he announced that he had volunteered to serve in India, she adamantly refused to join him. There is no evidence that he had previously shared his dreams with her or that he had sought to make her a partner in his passions for missions. Her opposition to serving overseas has been perceived by critics not only as a lack of wifely submission but also as an indication of spiritual weakness. But considering the immediacy of the departure, the permanency of the cross-cultural move, and the woeful lack of funding, it is not difficult to understand her frame of mind. Even if they were to survive the dangerous sea voyage, the disease-ridden tropical climate of India would be their home and perhaps their graves.

## A BROTHER'S LETTER

Mudnabatty, March 11, 1795

My Dear Sisters,
   Many changes have taken place with me since I left England.... Though I have abundant cause to complain of my leanness from day to day ... I am surrounded with favours, nay, they are poured in upon me; yet I find the rebellion of my heart against God to be so great as to neglect, nay, forget him, and live in that neglect day after day without feeling my soul smitten with compunction....
   With the natives I have very large concerns.... I have so much knowledge of the language as to be able to preach to them for about half an hour, so as to be understood, but am not able to vary my subjects much.... I hope in time I may have to rejoice over some who are truly converted to God.
   Poor Peter is removed from us by death. — I have had much better health here than in England....

I am,
Your affectionate brother,
W. Carey

In the spring of 1793 Carey abandoned his pregnant wife and two little children (taking his older son Felix with him) and boarded the *Oxford* on the Thames to begin his voyage to India. But the voyage ends almost as quickly as it begins. Accompanied by Dr. and Mrs. John Thomas and their daughter, Carey is devastated when officials turn them back, refusing to allow Thomas to leave the country until he has paid his debts. The delay, however, affords more opportunity for both men to pressure Dorothy (now having given birth to another child) to join them. She reluctantly agrees and sets sail with her husband and little ones. Storms at sea and appalling living conditions in India turn unhappiness into deep depression. Then the death of five-year-old Peter in 1794 pushes her over the edge. Not long after, she is described by an observer as being "wholly insane."

But such a description of Dorothy's condition is misleading. She suffers from delusions — particularly that her husband is having affairs with other women — yet she is not entirely out of touch with reality. Indeed, at times she is coherent and believable enough to convince others of the charges. Sometimes she follows her husband into the streets berating him; at times she is seen attacking him physically; at other times she talks and acts rationally. But as the years pass, her condition worsens to the point that Carey confines her in a locked room. He works on his translations, according to an observer, "while an insane wife, frequently wrought up to a state of most distressing excitement, [is] in the next room."

During these years their sons fend for themselves. Carey is consumed with his work and is lax in discipline. "The good man saw and lamented the evil," Hannah Marshman wrote, "but was too mild to apply an effectual remedy." She provides a motherly influence, and

## FORM OF AGREEMENT

Many mission ventures have fallen apart for lack of common purpose and honest supervision. Carey established a Form of Agreement that has valuable practical lessons for today. The expectations were clearly enumerated, and regular meetings offered times of accountability and venting grievances. Read three times yearly, it summed up the guiding principles:

1. To set an infinite value on men's souls.
2. To acquaint ourselves with the snares which hold the minds of the people.
3. To abstain from whatever deepens India's prejudice against the gospel.
4. To watch for every chance of doing the people good.
5. To preach "Christ crucified" as the grand means of conversions.
6. To esteem and treat Indians always as our equals.
7. To guard and build up "the hosts that may be gathered."
8. To cultivate their spiritual gifts, ever pressing upon them their missionary obligation, since Indians only can win India for Christ.
9. To labour unceasingly in biblical translation.
10. To be instant in the nurture of personal religion.
11. To give ourselves without reserve to the Cause, "not counting even the clothes we wear our own."

William Ward takes Felix under his wing. At sixteen the boy begins preaching to the native people, and six years later, in 1807, his father ordains and commissions him to serve as a missionary in Burma. Later that same year Carey made the following entry in his diary: "Tuesday, Dec. 8, 1807. This evening Mrs. Carey died of the fever under which she has languished some time. Her death was a very easy one; but there was no appearance of returning reason, nor any thing that could cast a dawn of hope or light on her state."

In May of 1808, just five months and a day after her death, Carey marries Charlotte Rumohr, a Danish woman not connected with the mission. She had moved to India for health reasons and had become a baptized believer through his ministry. Described as petite, elegant, well-educated, cultured, and wealthy, she is the same age as Carey—forty-six—at the time of their marriage. For Carey she is a dream come true. But their marriage so soon after the death of Dorothy creates no small scandal in the mission community. So agitated are some of the missionaries that they circulate a petition against it. Carey brushes them off, and he and Charlotte form an effective partnership, working together on translations and parenting the younger children. When she dies in 1821, after thirteen years of marriage, he writes: "We had as great a share of conjugal happiness as ever was enjoyed by mortals." Two years after her death, now sixty-two, he marries Grace Hughes, a widow seventeen years younger than he is.

To view Carey's home life only in terms of the nuclear family is missing the fundamental dynamics of his extended family relationships, however. After locating in the Danish settlement of Serampore in 1800, he formulated a pattern for communal family living whereby all members of the mission would share meals and devotional times and live out of a common treasury. The purpose was to bring family life and ministry together to enhance both. Earlier

Carey had written, "Our families should be considered nurseries for the Mission."

Carey ranks high as a team leader. He spoke well of his colleagues, focusing on their positive traits rather than their faults. The mission operated by a strict set of expectations. Wake-up call in the morning is 6 a.m. The Benedictine motto *Ora et labora* (pray and work) might well have been Carey's. He spends his early morning hours in meditation and prayer while at the same time tending his large garden, complete with flowers, vegetables, and fruit trees. (He was known in India and back home as a first-rate horticulturalist.) At 8 a.m. breakfast is served, followed by the day's work, when each of the missionaries conduct their own assignments—the Marshmans in various facets of educational ministry, William Ward working the printing press, and Carey primarily involved in transla-

tion work. The main meal of the day is taken in mid-afternoon, and all are then active in evangelistic outreach—both home visitation and street preaching, with Carey, Marshman, and Ward singing their own "Hindu" Christian ballads, printed and distributed to curious bystanders. Lyrics are contextualized for their hearers:

> In serving vain idols, why thus spend my
>    days,
> Since nought but destruction attends all my
>    ways?
> The Lord of the world did descend from on
>    high
> And was born in our nature all sin to
>    destroy
> Seeb, Doorga, and Kallee, could give me
>    no aid,

## The Judsons and Ko Tha Byu

Unlike the work of Carey, that of the Judsons in Burma continued through the generations and to this very day. Like Carey, Adoniram Judson had three wives: Ann, Sarah, and Emily. But the Judson women were equal partners in every sense of the word. Remembered as America's first missionaries, Ann and Adoniram sailed from Boston in 1812. Ann set forth her agenda soon after her arrival in Burma: "I desire no higher enjoyment in this life, than to be instrumental of leading some poor, ignorant females to the knowledge of the Saviour." During her husband's imprisonment on suspicion of being a spy, she defended him before government officials and wrote gripping letters to supporters back home. When she died in 1826, she left behind a grieving husband and a portfolio of biblical translation work. Adoniram would continue the work, though not without bouts of mental illness and religious doubt. "God, to me, is the Great Unknown," he confided. "I believe in him but I find him not."

In the following years, with the assistance of wives Sarah and later Emily, he built up the work in Burma and completed the translation of the Burmese Bible. Through his convert, Ko Tha Byu, thousands of the despised Karen people were converted to Christianity. Indeed, after a revival broke out, Ko complained that his house was broken down as a result of people pressing in to see him. A colleague wrote to Adoniram requesting assistance: "We are in distress and send to you for relief. For the last several days, our house and the house of Ko Tha Byu, ten cubits square, have been thronged.... Karens are thronging in from many places." In the generations since the Judsons served in Burma, Christian ministry has been largely conducted by native workers, many serving as missionaries beyond their regional borders.

No Debta nor Debbee, of off'rings were
    made,
No Brammhan, or Yogee....
I now lay all down at Christ Jesus' feet,
And trust, though a sinner, I mercy shall
    get.

In many respects, Carey was ahead of his
time in his appreciation for Indian culture and
his efforts to develop a well-rounded and comprehensive Christian ministry. He was both
confident and humble. But his leadership did
not transfer to the next generation of missionaries. The fault lay on both sides. As new candidates arrived — including his own nephew,
Eustace Carey — tempers flared and sides were
drawn when a new competing mission venture
was established. The newcomers accused the
old-timers of being authoritarian; the old-timers accused the newcomers of being selfish and
unwilling to submit to proper authority — an
all-too-common story in mission history. Carey
would live to see his work largely in shambles.
He would not live to see his reputation soar and
biographies multiply as he is turned into the
father of modern missions.

## David Livingstone: Africa Explorer

The most celebrated missionary of the nineteenth century — perhaps of all times — was
David Livingstone (1813–1873), who was barely
a missionary at all. He was the great explorer
to Africa who became the darling of Victorian
England when he returned from his excursions
and filled lecture halls with his gripping tales of
adventure. He had dreamed of being a missionary when he was a youth working fourteen-hour
days in the textile mills of Blantyre, Scotland.
Having heard reports of Karl F. A. Gutzlaff
smuggling gospel tracts and scripture portions

David Livingstone

into port cities of China, he vowed to carry on
with the work. However, the outbreak of the
Opium War frustrated his plans.

    Enter Robert Moffat. A great missionary
patriarch from Kuruman in Southern Africa,
Moffat is the featured speaker at an evening
church service. His appeal is gripping: "There
is a vast plain to the north where I have sometimes seen, in the morning sun, the smoke of
a thousand villages where no missionary has
ever been." Within months Livingstone is on
his way to Africa, only to discover Moffat's
vast exaggerations. The region is sparsely populated, prompting Livingstone to begin a series
of exploratory expeditions looking for natives
and new terrain, though always returning to
the Moffat mission compound at Kuruman
for rest and recovery, once after being mauled
nearly to death by a lion. During one of his visits he courts Mary Moffat, daughter of Robert
and Mary. Referring to this occasion, he later

recalled that he had "screwed up" enough "courage to put the question beneath one of the fruit trees," proposing marriage to this "sturdy" and "matter-of-fact lady."

If the bride imagined that marriage would mean stable mission work like that of her parents, she quickly learned otherwise. Livingstone is a traveling man, an explorer who cannot settle down in one place. In the following years, she is often left alone to care for their little ones. He bemoans her frequent pregnancies as comparable to the output of an "Irish manufactory," obviously ignoring his own culpability. After seven years of frequent separations and difficult living conditions, he accompanies Mary and the children to the coast and ships them back to England. In the months and years that follow, she is described as friendless, homeless, penniless, and drowning her sorrows in alcohol.

> I have been following a narrative [Livingstone's Missionary Travels and Researches in South Africa] of great dangers and trials, encountered in a good cause, by as honest and as courageous a man as ever lived.... The effect of it on me has been to lower my opinion of my own character in a most remarkable and most disastrous manner. I used to think I possessed the moral virtues of courage, patience, resolution and self-control.... I find that (these) turn out to be nothing ... my self-esteem oozed out of me.
>
> Charles Dickens, 1958

Meanwhile, Livingstone pushes deeper into the interior, seeking a trade route along the Zambezi River. He dreams of transforming southern Africa, guided by his mission philosophy, "Commerce and Christianity" (as opposed to Robert Moffat's philosophy, "the Bible and the Plough"). He is incensed by Portuguese and Arab traffic in human cargo and is convinced that his efforts will counteract such degradation. In the end, however, his exploration and map-making only serve to aid the slave trade. Nevertheless, when he returns to England in 1856 (nearly five years after parting from Mary and the children), he is greeted by cheering crowds. His heroic tales of trekking the wilds of dark Africa capture the collective imagination of his countrymen.

With the publication of his *Missionary Travels and Researches in South Africa*, he establishes his reputation as a heroic explorer—a reputation that lasts more than a century. But his return to Africa in 1858, now commissioned by the government (having resigned from the London Missionary Society), does not lead to a glorious finale. His health and personal relationships and grand strategies are strained to the breaking point. During his final fifteen years, he returns to England only once. Africa is now his home, and his closest companions are Africans who accept the cranky, toothless, bearded old man for who he is. His dream of finding the source of the Nile remains unfulfilled. He dies kneeling in prayer—a fitting legend for this legendary man. His closest African companions, Susi and Chuma, bury his heart in Africa and deliver his sun-dried, mummified body to the coast, where it is transported to England.

Dignitaries come in droves to pay their respects at the state funeral at Westminster Abbey. So also do his family, including children who hardly know him. For the seventy-eight-year-old Robert Moffat, it is a somber event. He walks slowly in front of the cortege bearing the casket of the man who decades earlier caught the vision of "a thousand villages, where no missionary had ever been."

## Hudson Taylor: Father of Faith Missions

The Opium War (1839–1842) that prevented Livingstone from going to China paved the way for Hudson Taylor and other missionaries to enter. The East India Company needed a market for its opium, and China was a perfect choice. The only problem was that Chinese emperors had adamantly opposed such trade. Smuggling opium into coastal cities was a major industry, and missionaries like Gutzlaff smuggled Scriptures in with the opium. But smuggling was not the solution. So the Royal Navy settled the issue, and China, in defeat, signed the Treaty of Nanking permitting opium—and missionaries—to legally enter five treaty ports.

J. Hudson Taylor (1832–1905), was born in Yorkshire, England, the son of Amelia and James Taylor, a pharmacist and Methodist lay preacher. Growing up in an atmosphere of Christian piety, he was captivated by China missions as a youth. After studying medicine and serving in urban mission work in London, he sailed for China in 1853, sponsored by the inept Chinese Evangelization Society. Depressed by his inability to learn the difficult language, he spent his early years in lonely, aimless wandering.

Hudson Taylor

Resigning from the mission did not improve his prospects. He was robbed of all his belongings and ridiculed when he decided to "go native," wearing Chinese dress, complete with dyed hair and a pigtail.

Taylor's fortunes take a turn for the better in 1857 when he meets Maria Dyer. He falls des-

> "China, China, China is now ringing in our ears in that special, peculiar, musical, forcible, unique way in which Mr. Taylor utters it."
> C. H. Spurgeon

perately in love but is bitterly opposed by a defiant, headstrong guardian, who vows her young charge will never marry this uneducated, unordained, uncouth stranger with no mission connections or credentials. But Taylor prevails, and in 1858 they are married. Two years later they return to England with their young daughter for a lengthy furlough (during which time four more children are born, one dying at birth). It is here in 1865 that Taylor is convinced that God is calling him to establish his own society, the China Inland Mission (CIM). Molded around Taylor's own personality and experiences, the CIM is to be an independent mission that appeals largely to England's massive laboring classes, both men and women. As such, Taylor avoids competition with other mission agencies. His previous experience with ineffective mission operations prompts him to establish headquarters in China, where he is personally in control (eventually, as a virtual dictator). Mission recruits, serving by faith alone, are offered no salary or set support.

The Taylors return to China with their four children and fifteen raw recruits, including seven single women. During the furlough, Taylor had publicized the work and had made many new friends and gained numerous supporters.

## PREPARATION FOR CHINA

After concluding my last service about ten o'clock that night, a poor man asked me to go and pray with his wife, saying that she was dying. I readily agreed, and on the way asked him why he had not sent for the priest, as his accent told me he was an Irishman. He has done so, he said, but the priest refused to come without a payment of eighteen pence, which the man did not possess as the family was starving.... Up a miserable flight of stairs into a wretched room the man led me, and oh, what a sight there presented itself! Four or five children stood about, their sunken cheeks and temples telling unmistakably the story of slow starvation, and lying on a pallet was a poor, exhausted mother, with a tiny infant thirty-six hours old moaning rather than crying at her side....

"You asked me to come and pray with your wife," I said to the man; "let us pray." And I knelt down. But no sooner had I opened my lips with, "Our Father who art in heaven," then conscience said within, "Dare you mock God? Dare you kneel down and call Him 'Father' with that half-crown in your pocket?" ... I put my hand into my pocket and slowly drawing out the half-crown, gave it to the man.... Not only was the poor woman's life saved, but my life as I fully realized had been saved too.

Hudson Taylor, *Hudson Taylor's Spiritual Secret*

The sea voyage to China allows time for the missionaries to stir up a revival among the ship's crew. But it also affords time for feuding among themselves. The "germs of ill feeling and division" were rife. "The feeling among us appears to have been worse than I could have formed any conception of," Taylor wrote. "One was jealous because another had too many new dresses, another because someone else had more attention. Some were wounded because of unkind controversial discussions, and so on." Taking each one aside, Taylor "privately and affectionately" staves off a near collapse of the infant China Inland Mission.

But the dissention is not over. When recruits realize that other English missionaries are ridiculing their native dress, some rebel. Harmony is temporarily restored in the summer of 1867 when eight-year old Gracie, whom her father idolized, becomes ill and dies. The mission comes together in grief, but greater crises are still to come. In 1868, the mission house in

Yangchow is attacked and set on fire by angry citizens. Maria and others barely escape with their lives.

Although Taylor had not expected British protection, some politicians in England charge that the attack is provocative and demand that the Royal Navy crush China once and for all. Though shots are never fired, the *Times* of London despairs that England's "political prestige" has been injured and blames it on "a company of missionaries assuming the title of the China Inland Mission." The adverse publicity is devastating. Support plummets, prospective recruits lose interest, and Taylor becomes so depressed that he nearly succumbs to "the awful temptation" of taking his own life.

Besides the Yangchow uproar, Taylor is undergoing a spiritual battle: "I hated myself; I hated my sin; and yet I gained no strength against it." The more he seeks spiritual wholeness, the less he finds: "Every day, almost every hour, the consciousness of failure and sin oppressed me." He is at the point of a mental collapse when a friend shares his spiritual secret in a letter: "To *let* my loving Savior work in me *His will. . . .* Abiding, not striving or struggling." Convinced he has discovered the secret, he testifies that "God has made me a new man." But the trials continue, most devastating a scandal involving him and two single women who are living in the family home. Rumors spread by a disgruntled missionary lead to an investigation. Both Jennie Faulding and Emily Blatchley deny intimacy beyond "good-night kisses." Jennie is transferred elsewhere in China, and Emily accompanies three of the Taylor children to England for their education. Only months later, Maria dies in childbirth.

Later that year Taylor sends word that he will be returning home for a visit. As a surrogate mother, Emily secretly hopes that he will also return home to marry her. But in the meantime, Taylor renews his close friendship with Jennie, now twenty-seven, and when he returns to England, they are engaged to be married. The news devastates Emily. "I feel sure from what I know of my own nature that I should, if I had had the chance, have been Mrs. [Taylor]," she writes in her diary. "And so it is in love and mercy my God cut off my flowing stream at which He perhaps saw I should drink too deeply. Such a sweet sweet stream, such a painful weaning! Therefore such a great blessing must await me for Jesus to bear to see me have so much pain." Taylor returns to China with Jennie, and the following year Emily dies—some say of a broken heart.

Jennie is a strong, independent woman, on one occasion returning to China alone to head up a humanitarian program while he stays in England recuperating from illness. But Taylor does not let sickness deter him. He is determined to reach all of China with the gospel: "Souls on every land are perishing for lack of knowledge; more than 1,000 every hour are passing away into death and darkness." His solution is to recruit one thousand evangelists, each of whom would reach two hundred and fifty people a day. Then the whole of China could be evangelized in less than four years. Although this fanciful dream is not fulfilled, his mission outreach exceeds that of other Protestant agencies. By 1895, after three decades, the CIM has more than six hundred missionaries serving throughout China.

More dark days are ahead of him and the CIM, however. In June of 1900 orders come from Peking to execute foreigners and exterminate Christianity. The greatest disaster in the history of Protestant missions follows. Nearly two hundred missionaries and their children are killed, many of them with the CIM. Ill in Switzerland, Taylor is shielded from the worst of the news. He returns one last time to China in 1904, where he dies a year after his arrival.

## Mary Slessor: White Mother of West Africa

Among those inspired by the life and death of David Livingstone was Mary Slessor (1848–1915), who ventured alone into Calabar, a remote area of present-day Nigeria. She was one of the thousands of women who flooded into foreign missions in the late nineteenth and early twentieth centuries. Scottish Presbyterians sponsored her even as they had sponsored her hero David Livingstone. Indeed, by the time she ventured into Africa in the mid–1870s, denominational mission boards were beginning to open the doors to women.

Like Livingstone, Mary Slessor had grown up in poverty and had worked long hours in textile mills as a child. Unlike the Presbyterian missionary wives serving in Calabar, she lacked sophistication, and in her leisure time she preferred climbing trees to attending afternoon tea parties. Her initial assignment was to teach in a school at Duketown, but dissatisfied with the social niceties and ample lifestyle of the other missionaries, she convinced the mission director to assign her to a post in the interior, where she adopted the African way of life. She ate native food and lived in a mud hut with her adopted African children—often children who were deemed demonic and rejected by their families.

In the following years she served as a teacher and medical specialist among the local people. On Sundays she traveled on a circuit deep into the jungle, preaching to any who would listen. But always restless, she was convinced that her calling was to preach in an even more remote area. In 1888, with the help of a local chief, she moved "up country" to the Okoyong district. "In the forenoon I was left alone with the mud and the rain and the general wretchedness," she wrote. "I looked helplessly on day after day at the rain pouring down on the boxes, bedding, and everything." There was no privacy. Packed tight in the tiny hut with a mud floor were two girls and three boys as well as the locals who "crowded in on every side"—not just men, women, and children, but also "goats, dogs, fowls, rats and cats all going and coming indiscriminately."

For more than a quarter century she would continue her multifaceted ministry in a region where no missionary had ever gone before. In 1892 she became the first British vice-consul to Okoyong, serving as a highly respected judge among the people. Twelve years later she moved on to an even more remote tribe, always considering her work as paving the way for other missionaries rather than church planting. She turned down a marriage proposal and was unable to work effectively with single women who joined her. Africa was her home, and Africans were her people. Today she continues to be remembered in Nigeria as the great Mother Slessor. Of her legacy, journalist Mary Kingsley wrote:

> This very wonderful lady has been eighteen years in Calabar; for the last six or seven living entirely alone, as far as white folks go, in a clearing in the forest near one of the principal villages of the Okoyong district, and ruling as a veritable white chief over the entire district. Her great abilities, both physical and intel-

---

### PICTURED ON A TEN-POUND NOTE

It is safe to conclude that aside from David Livingstone, no Protestant missionary has been more celebrated, more romanticized, more critiqued and mythologized than Mary Slessor, in print (over three dozen biographies and scholarly studies . . . ), in film, in music, and on stage. With a term of service that began in 1876, she was honored in the British Isles long before her death in 1915, while in the "field" her ministry was sought, even begged for, a privilege few missionaries have enjoyed the world over. In Scotland, her face adorns the ten-pound note, and in a Dundee museum her adventures are pictured in a stained glass window. In Nigeria, where she was trusted with the role of Vice Consul, a local judge for Pax Britannica, her name is everywhere—on a hospital, a chapel, a women's shelter, a school, a road. In 1956, Queen Elizabeth II placed a wreath on her grave.

Shirley Nelson, "Along Came Mary"

## OPIUM ADDICT TURNED MISSIONARY

Xi Sheng Mo (c. 1836–1896), known by China missionaries as Pastor Hsi, was a Confucian scholar and opium addict who became a Christian through the ministry of the China Inland Mission. "I tried to break it [opium] off by means of native medicine but could not," he later recalled. "At last I saw, in reading the New Testament, that there was a Holy Spirit who could help men. I prayed to God to give me His Holy Spirit. He did what man and medicine could not do; He enabled me to break off opium smoking." Xi opened a small drugstore selling cures for health problems, but soon addicts were coming. As the numbers grew, he opened an "opium refuge." As word of his success spread, more refuges were opened. To support the ministry he sold his property, and his wife sold her expensive wedding garments and jewels. In the following years some forty refuges were established. "On account of many onslaughts of Satan," he wrote, "my wife and I for the space of three years seldom put off our clothing to go to sleep in order that we might be the more ready to watch and pray." A recognized poet, he wrote hymns that were culturally appealing to his listeners. He and his wife traveled separately, each involved in refuge ministries, sometimes not seeing each other for months on end. His "gospel cart" was emblazoned with the Chinese characters reading "Holy Religion of Jesus."

lectual, have given her among the savage tribe a unique position, and won her, from white and black who know her, a profound esteem. Her knowledge of the native, his language, his ways of thought, his diseases, his difficulties, and all that is his, is extraordinary, and the amount of good she has done, no man can fully estimate. Okoyong, when she went there alone ... was given, as most of the surrounding districts still are, to killing at funerals, ordeal by poison, and perpetual internecine wars. Many of these evil customs she has stamped out.... Miss Slessor stands alone.

### Charlotte Digges "Lottie" Moon: Patron Saint of Southern Baptist Missions

Like Mary Slessor, Charlotte Digges "Lottie" Moon (1840–1912) found sponsorship through a denominational mission board, the Southern Baptist Convention. Born on a plantation in the American South, she sailed for China in 1873, only to find that opportunities for single women were severely limited. As a refined "Southern belle," she balked at her assignment. Feeling called to "go out among the millions" as an evangelist, she was instead stuck in a school of forty "unstudious" children. What a "folly" this was. "Can we wonder," she seethed, "at the mortal weariness and disgust, the sense of wasted powers and the conviction that her life is a failure, that comes over a woman when, instead of the ever broadening activities she had planned, she finds herself tied down to the petty work of teaching a few girls."

As a competent woman, she resented her second-class status. "What women want who come to China is free opportunity to do the largest possible work.... What women have a right to demand is perfect equality." Despite opposition, she moved to the outpost of Pingdu and launched an evangelistic campaign, initially targeting women. But soon men were showing interest as well. "Such eagerness to learn! Such spiritual desires!" she reported. "Something I had never seen before in China." The first baptisms in Pingdu had come in 1889, and during the next two decades that region became the most successful Baptist evangelistic center in China, largely due to her focus on training and ordaining national leaders. Despite loneliness and opposition from male directors, she was convinced of her calling. "Surely there can be no deeper joy," she wrote, "than that of saving souls."

Her enthusiasm and her appeals to Baptists back home not only brought missionaries to China but also raised much-needed funds. The first Christmas offering in 1888 brought in generous gifts. In the years that followed the offerings increased, but not enough to feed hungry people during a famine in 1911. Overwhelmed, she withdrew funds from her own bank account to buy food and gave hungry children every morsel in her pantry. When it was discovered that she had quit eating and that her health was rapidly failing, arrangements were made for her to return home. But she died aboard ship a week after her seventy-second birthday in 1912. Significantly, she died on Christmas Eve. In her memory the "Lottie Moon Christmas Offering," sponsored by Southern Baptist women, has continued for decades to bring millions of dollars annually for overseas missions.

Lottie Moon

The sacrifices made by Moon and other women missionaries were exceeded only by the sacrifice of native women evangelists. These were typically impoverished, illiterate women who traveled a circuit as Bible women because they carried the Bible in their heads through a vast store of memorized verses. In many cases their children were grown, but leaving aged parents behind was an enormous sacrifice, especially in cultures where honoring one's parents was a profound obligation. Without Bible women, missionary women would have been stymied not only in evangelistic and Bible-related activities but also in health and humanitarian ministries.

## Kanzo Uchimura: Leader of Japanese Independent Churches

As Lottie Moon was dying aboard ship at a port in Kobe, Japan, Kanzo Uchimura (1861–1930) was struggling to preach a gospel message that was culturally relevant. Born in Tokyo the son of a Confucian scholar, he enrolled at the Sapporo Agricultural College founded by William Smith Clark, an American educator. Through Clark's evangelistic zeal, the first class of students had been converted and had signed a covenant to evangelize succeeding classes of students. By the time Uchimura entered the school, Clark had returned home, but like his classmates Uchimura became part of the Sapporo Band. Though baptized by a Methodist missionary, he simply considered himself a Japanese Christian. However, when he planted a church with mission support and was later told that he must return the money if the church was not Methodist, he gave the money back and severed his ties with missionaries.

## MARY MCLEOD BETHUNE AND MISSIONS

One of seventeen children born into a family of sharecroppers in South Carolina, Mary McLeod Bethune (1875–1955) is remembered as a leading American educator. She might have been a missionary to Africa but for the endemic racism of the era. Having been financially supported by a Quaker woman, she graduated from Moody Bible Institute. But when she applied to mission agencies, she learned that there were no openings for black missionaries in Africa. The enforced segregation of travel and living arrangements would create too many problems. Denied mission service, she went on to establish a college (now Bethune-Cookman University) and hospital in Florida and helped to found the National Council of Negro Women.

This incident spurred him to form the non-church movement in Japan, much to the chagrin of Western missionaries. His response to them was in keeping with his cultural understandings. "Why blame me for upholding Japanese Christianity while every one of them upholds his or her own Christianity?" he demanded. "Is not Episcopalianism essentially an English Christianity?" Methodists, too, were culturally oriented, as were many other denominations: "Why, for instance, call a universal religion 'Cumberland Presbyterianism'? If it is not wrong to apply the name of a district in the state of Kentucky to Christianity, why is it wrong for me to apply the name of my country to the same?"

More than a minister and evangelist, Uchimura was a writer and scholar whose works kept his reputation alive long after his death. In addition to a twenty-two volume biblical commentary, he published *The Biblical Study*, a monthly journal. He was also a social critic who challenged Western—and particularly American—influence on Japanese Christianity and culture in general. He lamented that Christianity had been turned into a religion of numbers and money:

> Americans must *count religion* in order to see or show its value.... To them big churches are successful churches.... To win the greatest number of converts with the least expense is their constant endeavour. Statistics is their way of showing success or failure in their religion as in their commerce and politics. Numbers, numbers, oh, how they value numbers!... Mankind goes down to America to learn how to live the earthly life; but to live the heavenly life, they go to some other people.

### Eliza Davis George: African American Missionary to Liberia

Founder of the Eliza George Baptist Association, Eliza Davis (1879–1979) grew up in Texas in a large family, her parents having risen from slavery to share-cropping. She excelled in her studies and was permitted to enroll at Central Texas College with the dream of becoming a missionary to Africa. But African Americans were not welcomed in such roles by mission agencies. In her sense of calling, Davis envisioned Africans before the judgment seat of Christ crying out, "But no one ever told us you died for us!" When she sought support, however, she was informed that there were no openings for her in Africa. After she had appealed to the board of the Texas Baptist Convention, however, the trustees found her testimony and determination so convincing that she was accepted as a candidate and commissioned to Liberia. Arriving in 1914, she worked with another single woman in the interior, where they conducted evangelism and established the Bible Industrial Academy, enrolling dozens of boys.

Despite positive developments, Davis was ill-prepared to oversee a broad-based mission program, however. And news from home was not good. The Texas Baptist Convention had separated from the National Baptists, who were in charge of the work in Liberia, putting Eliza's ministry in limbo. Then comes word from the Convention that her work in Africa is being terminated. An ordained minister and his wife will take over her leadership of the Bible Industrial Academy and the newly planted churches.

Although her work is hardly a model of fiscal responsibility, the decision has all the signs of underlying racism and sexism. Feeling vulnerable and utterly alone, she makes a critical decision that will haunt her for years to come. She agrees to marry Thompson George, a native of British Guyana who is working in Liberia with a Portuguese company. Having previously shunned his advances, she now sees him to be the only solution to her problem. Turning her work over to others who know nothing of the people and her ministry is more than she can endure, so she marries a man she does not love. George joins her in the work, but his alcoholism and his desire for sexual intimacy create problems. Yet despite marital conflicts, they together conduct an effective ministry for many years.

In 1939 George dies, freeing Eliza from the bonds of a bad marriage. By 1943 she is supervising four substations in addition to the main mission complex, receiving a small stipend from the National Baptist Convention. Now approaching her sixty-fifth birthday, she again receives a directive from the Convention insisting that she return home and turn the work over to others. A letter informing her of this decision indicates concern for her health, but she knows otherwise. She records the facts in a terse sentence: "In 1945 the Foreign Mission Board of the National Baptist Convention of America saw fit to discontinue my services as a missionary."

From that point on, she worked "by faith," supported largely by "Eliza Davis George Clubs" in the United States. Her mission acquired thousands of acres of land, and by 1960 there were twenty-seven churches in the Eliza George Baptist Association. She actively served into her nineties and lived to age one hundred. She had become famous in Liberia, twice honored by Liberian presidents for her service to the country. She left behind mission stations and churches, but was virtually unknown in her homeland — one of thousands of missionaries whose names are all but forgotten.

Kenneth Scott Latourette, long-time professor of Religion at Yale, identified the modern missionary movement of the nineteenth century as the "Great Century" of missions: "Never before had Christianity been as widespread; never before had so many missionaries been sent; never before had so much money been given for missions; never before had humanitarian efforts been as diverse and widespread." Protestants were making up for their slow start in world missions, and this remarkable expansion continued to accelerate throughout the twentieth century.

## What if ...

What if William Carey had stayed home, honoring his wife's wishes? Might he, like A. B. Simpson a century later, have established a large mission society? Failing to convince his wife to serve with him in China, Simpson founded the Christian and Missionary Alliance that commissioned thousands of missionaries to foreign lands.

What if David Livingstone had waited and gone to China as he had planned? How might African Christianity be different today without his profound influence on Africa mission outreach?

What if the leaders of the Women's Missionary Movement had maintained their leadership roles as the agencies merged with denominational missions? Would mission agencies be different if they had a strong feminine influence?

How have Mary Slessor, Lottie Moon, and Eliza David George changed the course of missions?

## Further Reading

Anderson, Courtney. *To the Golden Shore: The Life of Adoniram Judson*. Grand Rapids: Zondervan, 1972.

Beck, James R. *Dorothy Carey: The Tragic and Untold Story of Mrs. William Carey*. Grand Rapids: Baker, 1992.

Brumberg, Joan Jacobs. *Mission for Life: The Story of the Family of Adoniram Judson*. New York: Free Press, 1980.

Buchan, James. *The Expendable Mary Slessor*. New York: Seabury Press, 1981.

Buxton, Meriel. *David Livingstone*. New York: St. Martin's Press, 2001.

Chung, Jun Ki. *Social Criticism of Uchimura Kanzo and Kim Kyo-Shin*. Seoul: University Bible Fellowship, 1988.

George, Timothy. *Faithful Witness: The Life and Mission of William Carey*. Birmingham: New Hope, 1991.

Hutchinson, William R. *Errand to the World: American Protestant Thought and Foreign Missions*. Chicago: University of Chicago Press, 1987.

Lutz, Lorry. *When God Says Go: The Story of Eliza Davis George*. Grand Rapids: Discovery House, 2002.

Pollock, J. C. *Hudson Taylor and Maria: Pioneers in China*. Grand Rapids: Zondervan, 1976.

Ransford, Oliver. *David Livingstone: The Dark Interior*. New York: St. Martin's, 1978.

Robert, Dana L. *American Women in Mission, 1792–1992*. Macon, Ga.: Mercer University Press, 1996.

Tucker, Ruth A. *From Jerusalem to Irian Jaya: A Biographical History of Christian Missions*. Grand Rapids: Zondervan, 2004.

# CHAPTER 22

# Fragmentation and Revival

## Salvation Army to Foursquare Gospel

*Growing up in the 1950s in a farming community in Northern Wisconsin, I was actively involved in a small Christian and Missionary Alliance Church. At the time I was unaware of the painful divisiveness that tore apart our denomination decades earlier over the issue of speaking in tongues. Pentecostal inroads into Alliance churches eventually led to a split and the beginnings of the Assemblies of God, today the much larger sister church.*

*When my little country church joined with other evangelical churches for occasional special functions, Pentecostals, still on our enemies list, were not welcome. Nor were Methodists, who were too liberal for our tastes. Wesleyan Methodists, however, were part of the mix, having broken from Methodists over "holiness" issues nearly a century earlier.*

*John Wesley was a hero of our faith as was Luther, though the local Lutherans were too worldly to participate in our functions, had they wanted to. As a young adult I was associated with breakaway fundamentalist movements, including the Bible Presbyterians and Bible churches affiliated with the IFCA (Independent Fundamentalist Churches of America).*

*I remember a business meeting at the Woodstock Bible Church where discussion centered on the possibility of an outsider coming in and speaking in tongues (though no one had ever done so before). It was decided that a deacon would escort the offending individual out of the church. Today such actions appear harsh, if not humorous. (Unlike early Catholics and Calvinists, however, we did not even contemplate burning an offender at the stake.)*

*The fragmentation of denominations that I encountered as a youth is a microcosm of the larger evangelical movement that stumbled and split its way through the course of the twentieth century.*

> The good historian is like the giant of the fairy tale. He knows that wherever
> he catches the scent of human flesh, there his quarry lies.
> MARC BLOCH, *THE HISTORIAN'S CRAFT*

As one studies the story of twentieth-century evangelicals, fundamentalists, and Pentecostals, one cannot help but catch the scent of human flesh, knowing that this is where the quarry lies. And there are giants far bigger in this fairy tale than the historian. Indeed, in this century of modern media any scent of celebrity is sniffed out, served up, and devoured by hungry spectators, allured by glamour and novelty. Whether attracted by "Halleluiah Lassies" and a street corner brass band or a sports-star-turned-revivalist, religious seekers are looking for more than the old-time religion of John Wesley or Jonathan Edwards.

But celebrity and novelty do not translate into a modernistic religion. Among these new Christian leaders there is no inclination to question, for example, the reliability of biblical texts or the validity of miracles and mystical experiences. And not all evangelicals, whether fundamentalist or Pentecostal, were enamored of flashy revival preachers. In fact, until the last decades of the twentieth century, most evangelicals were bringing up the rear in cultural innovation. They were conservative in every sense of the word. Among those who stood out and gained wide recognition are Evangeline Booth, Pandita Ramabai, William Seymour, Billy Sunday, Aimee Semple McPherson, and John Sung.

Twentieth-century evangelicalism is a strange mix of innovation and convention, of celebrity and banality, of fragmentation and unity. It divided and subdivided at a rate never seen before in history. With the onset of the Holiness Movement of the late nineteenth century, one group after another sought to out-distance the rest in claims of holiness and sometimes in bizarre teachings. Benjamin Irwin, of the Fire-Baptized Church forbade his male followers, for example, to wear neckties. Other restrictions separated his group from other tightly strung holiness churches. Irwin's following further fragmented in the spring of 1900, when it was learned that he was involved in "open and gross sin."

This acceleration of splintering had begun much earlier in the nineteenth century in Europe and particularly in America. The dynamic democracy of the young nation, combined with its westward movement and frontier spirit, only exacerbated the rapid proliferation of splinter groups and sectarian movements.

## PARADE OF HISTORY

The nineteenth-century parade of the faithful marched into inner-city degradation — into teaming tenements filled with impoverished peons displaced by the ravages of the Industrial Revolution. Trumpeting the gospel, Salvation Army bands offered good news for body and soul. "Booth led boldly with his big bass drum," proclaimed the opening lines of Vachel Lindsay's tribute. Decades later, baseball player Billy Sunday would be lured into the Pacific Garden Mission in Chicago through the ministry of the rescue mission's band. He was loitering in the street when the band marched by, playing hymns that stirred memories of his mother singing the same songs when he was a small child.

## FIRE-BAPTIZED RELIGION

Several developments between 1898 and 1900 prevented the Fire-Baptized movement from developing into the national church that it promised to become. One was the inclusion of additional doctrines that frightened even "radical" holiness people.... [Benjamin] Irwin began to teach that there were additional "baptisms of fire." These he named the baptisms of "dynamite," "Lyddite," and "Oxidite." By early 1900 the Fire-Baptized faithful were being taught not only a "third blessing" but also a fourth, a fifth, and even a sixth. This "chemical jargon" never took root within the movement and was later rejected. But for a time the movement was pervaded by the "pathetic pursuit of this religious rainbow's end."

Vinson Synan, *The Holiness-Pentecostal Movement*

Early nineteenth-century religious leaders like Ann Lee and her followers, known as Shakers, and John Humphrey Noyes, who founded the Oneida Community, sought to create utopian communal living—the former with celibacy as the hallmark; the latter featuring communal marriage.

Other Christians called for primitivism, the recreation of the lifestyle and practices of the New Testament believing community. This so-called Restoration Movement—the Christian Church (Disciples of Christ)—emerged under the leadership of Alexander Campbell and Barton W. Stone. Campbell pleaded for Christian unity founded on "the testimony of the Apostles" alone. He was distressed by dissention among Christians and by the proliferation of denominations but was unable to prevent his own movement from fragmenting, frequently over minor differences.

Also contributing to the fragmentation was the multiplication of societies. Under the umbrella of the Women's Missionary Movement, more than forty separate agencies arose. The first of these societies, founded by Sarah Doremus, was the Woman's Union Missionary Society. The term *union* was significant. She was seeking to bring women from different denominations together. But the societies proliferated,

each representing different denominations and theological and social perspectives. Likewise, the Sunday school movement quickly fragmented in its association with various denominations. Missionaries took the Christian faith, packaged in a multiplicity of denominational forms, around the world, where the church was further fragmented as new leaders and movements sprang up in "foreign" soil, often utterly bewildering to those they sought to convert. An amusing—and confusing—example developed when the Southern Baptists entered northern China and the Northern Baptists, southern China.

Revivalists like D. L. Moody and his successors easily crossed denominational lines. In fact, Moody was one of the leading lights for evangelical unity in the late nineteenth century, refusing to become entangled in controversial issues that were tearing other Christian groups apart. Those who supported his evangelistic campaigns hailed from a wide spectrum of denominations and social classes. Women also played important roles in his outreach. Indeed, women's roles were greatly expanded in virtually every new religious movement. But as religions became institutionalized, lay ministers and women were pushed aside in favor of status-conscious, ordained, career clerics. Women were particularly active in the Pentecostal movements that sprang up around the turn of the century, although two of the leading figures associated with one such movement, the Azusa Street Revival, were men: Charles Parham and William J. Seymour.

Women's active involvement in leadership roles, in the eyes of their critics, would lead to a more emotional and less intellectual form of faith. While this may have actually been true, there was certainly no emotion lacking in the fiery fundamentalism of Billy Sunday and other male evangelists who traveled the circuit. Sunday, and later Aimee Semple McPherson, sought to save souls while hammering against the twin evils of alcohol and evolution. The "Scopes Monkey Trial" in 1925 pitted William Jennings Bryan against Clarence Darrow in a climactic showdown between biblical creationism and the theory of evolution.

The "muscular Christianity" of Sunday and Bryan was worlds away from the boys-only club of Princeton Seminary and its cor-

responding Princeton theology that flourished between the American Civil War and World War I. Among its leading lights were Charles Hodge (1797–1878) and Benjamin Warfield (1858–1921). Both sought to hold the line against the liberalism in biblical and theological studies that was raging in Europe, particularly in Germany. Their Old School Presbyterianism represented Calvinist orthodoxy, holding to a high standard of scholarship in the context of a warm evangelical spirit.

But the Princeton theologians were surely not spared fights and fragmentation. Even Princeton (previously known for biblical orthodoxy) became the target of those who were more conservative. Theologians wrangled and churches split in the wake of J. Gresham Machen's blast against liberal theologians and ministers. A professor of New Testament at Princeton, Machen led what has been called a "conservative revolt" and left Princeton to form

## CARL McINTIRE: "P. T. BARNUM OF FUNDAMENTALISM"

For nearly three-quarters of a century, the irrepressible McIntire used Collingswood, New Jersey, as a launch pad for firing opinions on matters ranging from the Westminster Confession of Faith to the Communist Manifesto. At the height of his influence during the Cold War, McIntire's empire extended from Collingswood, the home of his Bible Presbyterian Church and Faith Christian School, to Elkins Park, Pennsylvania (Faith Theological Seminary), Cape May, New Jersey (Shelton College), and Pasadena, California (Highlands College).

He ran a conference center in Florida and had designs for a theme park there that would have celebrated America's military campaign in Vietnam. McIntire's radio program, 20th Century Reformation Hour, reached homes throughout North America, until his bombast and blatant violation of the fairness doctrine prompted the Federal Communications Commission to force him off the air....

McIntire was so prone to separatism that ... he separated from the very congregation he had formed 75 years earlier. His separatism recalled that of Roger Williams in the 17th century. A Puritan minister in Salem, Massachusetts, Williams parted ways with the Puritans in 1636, going away to Rhode Island, where in 1639 he formed the first congregation of Baptists in North America. Then he separated from them four years later. By the end of his life, Williams believed that only he and his wife were truly regenerate.

Randall Balmer, "Fundamentalist with a Flair"

## EVERYDAY LIFE

## Muscular Christianity

With the increase of women's public ministry, there was a corresponding backlash that only got louder at the turn of the twentieth century as well-known evangelists and church leaders like Evangeline Booth and Aimee Semple McPherson gained prominence. "Muscular Christianity" was a British reaction to the perceived feminine spirituality of the Victorian Age. D. L. Moody preached a masculine Christianity that appealed to Cambridge athletes.

Masculine organizations sprang up in Victorian times to challenge the spirituality of the day—spirituality that saw women as keepers of the home in charge of moral values, that is, keeping their husbands and children from falling into sin. Strong men were needed to reverse the domestication of religion and emphasize the "manliness of Christ." Overseas mission ventures, whether to "savages" or to ancient civilizations, also corresponded with manly Christianity.

Muscular Christianity was also a reaction to what was perceived to be women's dominance in the Sunday school movement and various other humanitarian endeavors. Male-oriented organizations included the Young Men's Christian Association (YMCA), Boy Scouts, and the Boys' Brigade. Building athletic, muscular bodies was an important theme in the Christian novels of the day by Charles Kingsley, Thomas Hughes, and others. Indeed, a focus on sports was seen as a way to bring men into the church—a "net" to catch young men and bring them to Christ. One female critic of the YMCA accused the organization of hiding religion in sports "like a pill in strawberry jam."

### MEN AND RELIGION FORWARD MOVEMENT

With speeches by Bishop David H. Greer, John D. Rockefeller Jr., James G. Cannon, and many of this country's most prominent clergymen and laymen, the Christian Conservation Congress of the Men and Religion Forward Movement held its final session yesterday at Carnegie Hall.... [D]uring the past two years [the movement] has held 7,062 meetings, with a total attendance of 1,500,000. It has led 7,580 men who were not church members to pledge themselves to personal allegiance to churches, and has inspired 26,000 men already church members to pledge themselves to active personal service.... "The National Committee of Ninety-seven has completed its labors, and now hands over the work of winning men to Christ's service to the local organizations in the 1,000 towns and the seventy-five large cities in which the movement has been organized," said Mr. Smith ... while preparing to return to his place in the International Y.M.C.A. office here which he has held for twenty-four years.

*The New York Times*, April 25, 1912

This macho Christianity was not just for weightlifters and jocks, however. The Prayer Revival (1857–1858) that began in New York City was also referred to as the "businessmen's revival." That fact was not lost on those who had railed against the emotionalism of typical revivals that called forth weeping and falling down in trance-like states.

The term "muscular Christianity" had been used as early as the 1860s and was becoming a recognized theme in both Christian and secular periodicals. The height of the movement was seen in one of the most pointed efforts to set forth a masculine spirituality. An interdenominational, lay-led organization, the Men and Religion Forward Movement was launched in 1911. It was a not-so-subtle effort to replace feminized religion with a manly faith that was integrated with capitalism and rugged individualism—a precursor to Promise Keepers. Efforts to take the movement to China, Japan, the Philippines, and South Africa fizzled.

---

Westminster Theological Seminary in 1929. Later difficulties with the Northern Presbyterian Church prompted him, along with others in 1936, to form the Orthodox Presbyterian Church. Splitting from him was the all-time king of splits, Carl McIntire, who founded the Bible Presbyterian denomination.

The more wide-ranging modernist-fundamentalist controversy pitted those emphasizing the social gospel against those stressing historic orthodoxy. It was an unfortunate dichotomy. Humanitarian outreach was certainly not confined to the "modernist" church. Robert Speer, long-time secretary for the Board of Presbyterian Foreign Missions, sought to walk the tightrope between the two sides, particularly regretting the unfortunate effect the fighting was having on mission outreach worldwide. He spoke for many evangelicals caught in the middle of the infighting. "I wish we could get up such a glow and fervor and onrush of evangelical and evangelistic conviction and action," he wrote to a missionary in China, "that we would be swept clear past issues like the present ones so that men who want to dispute over these things could stay behind and do so, while the rest of us could march ahead, more than making up by new conquests for all the defections and losses of those who stay behind."

The Salvation Army was determined to march ahead and remain above the fights and fragmentation. But even that movement was wracked by dissention.

## Evangeline Booth: Salvation Army General

From 1904 to 1934, Evangeline Booth (1865–1950) served as Commander of the Salvation Army in the United States. That role ended when she was promoted to General of the Army.

> Hardship, unbelief, suffering and poverty have not stopped our soldiery from rendering their service to God and man. The Salvation Army is a great empire, an empire without a frontier, made up of a tangle of races, tongues and colors such as never before in all history gathered together under one flag.
> Evangeline Booth

The Booth dynasty incorporated all the sons and daughters of William and Catherine Booth as high-ranking officers in this quasi-military movement, but Evangeline out-ranked them all in style and celebrity. Youth was not a deterrent to assuming key roles in the Salvation Army. In fact, when she was only fifteen she served as a sergeant in the dangerous streets of London. At twenty-one she was a corps officer and was known as the Army's most effective trouble-shooter, with her father's full support and confidence. Her three sisters would marry with their parents' blessings, but Evangeline was her father's favorite, and he was determined that no man would ever get between her and the singular demands of the Army.

Evangeline Booth

But if Evangeline was denied a wedding for herself, she conducted many wedding ceremonies for others during her long ministerial career. Indeed, a true daughter of her mother, she was a remarkable feminist of her day. Like other women evangelists before and after her, she would conduct revival meetings. But she would be the first to wield authority as a female executive of a vast Christian corporation—coming to power in America long before the "Roaring Twenties" and the Nineteenth Amendment (1920) that gave women the right to vote.

Before she headed the Salvation Army in America, Evangeline served for ten years as Commander in Canada. During that time she held revivals in the mining boomtowns of the Yukon—towns rife with every sin and vice imaginable. She entered the region with a flourish, setting up medical centers and soup kitchens. "Vain in her appearance" and speaking with grand gestures, she captured the attention of the miners, bringing some twenty-five thousand together for a revival meeting. Among them was Soapy Smith, the most notorious outlaw of the region. He reportedly promised her that he would mend his ways, but vigilantes found him first.

She was a show-stopper, whether in small groups or mass meetings. On one occasion she was lowered into a mineshaft in an ore bucket, singing "Nearer, My God, to Thee" to the astonished miners. After becoming the American General, she continued to make headlines. Her "lassies" were among

## SALVATION ARMY "HALLELUJAH LASSIES"

Handbills with this message were distributed in Philadelphia in 1879:

Blood and fire! The Salvation Army
Two Hallelujah females
will speak and sing for Jesus
in the old chair factory
at Sixth and Oxford Streets
Oct. 5th at 11 a.m. 3m. 8m.

All are invited to attend.

Attendance on the first night was only twelve, but within weeks, the factory building was filled to capacity. The "Hallelujah Lassies" played a key roll in the early outreach ministry of the Salvation Army, though they were often the object of ridicule and the target of assault by street rowdies.

the first at the scene of the San Francisco earthquake of 1906, and during World War I she sent them to the front lines to care for wounded soldiers, for which she was later honored by General Pershing. When she was appointed General of the Salvation Army in 1934, she was escorted by New York City Mayor Fiorello La Guardia in a ticker-tape parade.

The seventh of eight children born to William and Catherine Booth, founders of the Salvation Army, Evangeline exhibited the best qualities of both. From her father she inherited a natural predisposition to lead a large organization with troops marching in lockstep behind her, and from her mother, an ability to capture the rapt attention of an audience and a strong sense of egalitarian ideals. From both she inherited a profound empathy for the poor.

Evangeline's father, London pawnbroker William Booth (1829–1912), had been converted at a Methodist class meeting. Impressed by the "scientific" methods of Charles Finney, he vowed to be a different kind of evangelist. Instead of long sermons and conventional hymns, he attracted crowds with lively tunes that critics charged "belong to the devil." Following the musical performance he would give a short pitch for salvation and issue calls for decisions while collecting names and inviting those interested to meet him for further instruction. Though poorly educated, he went on to serve as a minister of a small church. In this capacity he met his future wife, Catherine.

Catherine Mumford (1829–1890) was raised largely by her mother; her father was a lay Methodist minister brought down by alcoholism. Home-schooled, she was an eager student who loved reading the Bible and reveled in theological and historical studies. In 1851 she met William Booth and married him after a three-year engagement—waiting to make sure

---

### "GENERAL WILLIAM BOOTH ENTERS HEAVEN"

Booth led boldly with his big bass
    drum —
(Are you washed in the blood of the
    Lamb?)
The Saints smiled gravely and they said:
    "He's come."
(Are you washed in the blood of the
    Lamb?)
Walking lepers followed, rank on rank,
Lurching bravoes from the ditches dank,
Drabs from the alleyways and drug
    fiends pale —
Minds still passion-ridden, soul-powers
    frail: —
Vermin-eaten saints with mouldy breath
Unwashed legions with the ways of
    Death —
(Are you washed in the blood of the
    Lamb?)...

Vachel Lindsay (1879–1931)

---

he was committed to an egalitarian marriage. Influenced by the ministry of Phoebe Palmer, she was convinced that God was calling her to preach. "Oh, that the ministers of religion would search the original record of God's word," she pleaded, "in order to discover ... whether God really intended woman to bury her gifts and talents, as she now does." Her ministry as a preacher began inauspiciously in her husband's congregation, but soon she was preaching regularly to a more sophisticated congregation on London's West End.

While Catherine was preaching in the West End of London, William raised support to operate a mission in East London in the midst of a filthy slum crowded with dilapidated tenement buildings and gin houses. There, in 1878, the

## BALLINGTON BOOTH

The Booth Children inherit their parents' domineering personalities, all resenting their father's authoritarian ways. Evangeline is the apple of his eye, but she locks horns with eldest son Bramwell; and second son Ballington locks horns with both Bramwell and his father — to the point of leaving the movement and starting his own similar organization, Volunteers of America, of which he becomes General.

The American secession was the most dramatic of the rebellions because Ballington, the proudest and the most impetuous of William Booth's children, reacted to Bramwell's instructions with a public show of defiance, which his brothers and sisters understood but deplored. Their discipline held.

Roy Hattersley, *Blood and Fire*

Salvation Army is born. In the ensuing years Catherine and William work side by side while raising their eight children and preaching regularly on Sundays. Her ministry paves the way for young women to serve with men on equal terms. From the beginning the movement had welcomed women into its ranks. But in 1875, when Evangeline is ten, Clause 14 of the Foundation Deed specifies that women can hold "any office" and are permitted "to speak and vote" at official Army meetings.

On William Booth's death in 1912, son Bramwell succeeds his father as General, and after him Edward Higgins, who serves for a five-year term. Evangeline's promotion to General is not without controversy. She is a powerful woman, having increased the size of the Army in America to far surpass that of England during her thirty-year tenure as Commander. Before her father died, the Army had begun spreading throughout the world due in part to her unstinting work in sending Americans abroad. Brother Bramwell, however, had sought to undermine her by dividing the American work into three regions, each with its own commander. But his plan backfired, weakening his hold over the movement. He had also insisted that he, not the High Council, had the right to appoint a successor. But the Council overruled his claim.

Evangeline's popularity in America and her recognition worldwide made her promotion to General a celebratory event. During her five-year term she traveled throughout the world and established new outposts in several countries, including the Philippines and Mexico. She enjoyed having a good time and was known for her athletic and musical skills. Whether galloping her favorite gelding or entertaining crowds on her harp, she was the star of the show. After her retirement as General in 1939, she lived in upstate New York for the final decade of her life. America had become her home.

### Pandita Ramabai: Founder of Mukti Mission

In the early twentieth century, as Evangeline Booth was assuming the role of American commander of the Salvation Army, a series of Pentecostal revivals broke out in southern Appalachia and around the world, none of them stirred up by well-known evangelists like Finney or Moody. One such "outpouring of the Spirit" occurred in the Welsh Revival of 1904, where it is estimated that some one hundred thousand were converted and experienced charismatic signs and miracles, with the expectation of the imminent return of Christ. The following year revival broke out at the Mukti Mission in India under the ministry of Pandita Ramabai. She had received word of the Welsh revival and was convinced that the same signs and wonders could occur at Mukti, where hundreds of young women and girls made their home. Frank Bartleman, an early Pentecostal leader, reflected on how world-wide revival was "rocked in the cradle of little Wales," after which it was "brought up" in India, and finally became "full grown" at Azusa Street.

Pandita Ramabai

Pandita Ramabai (1858 – 1922) was born into a high-caste Hindu Brahmin family. Her father was a Sanskrit scholar always in search of religious truth. Convinced that girls should have the same educational opportunities as boys, he taught her to have an open and questioning mind. She learned Sanskrit as a young child and memorized thousands of Hindu stories and sayings. Then suddenly her life is turned upside-down. Amid economic hard times her father lost his wealth, circumstances that spurred him to take his family on a religious pilgrimage. Later, after her parents fell ill and died, she continued to travel with her brother in the search for truth, ever grateful for her father's legacy and influence: "I am a child of a man who had to suffer a great deal on account of advocating Female Education," she wrote. "I consider it my duty, to the very end of my life, to maintain this cause and to advocate the proper position of women in this land."

Critical of her own culture's perspective on women, she points out that Hindu belief is varied and inconsistent—except on the topic of a woman's place. There is general agreement, she insists, "that women of high and low caste, as a class, [are] bad, very bad, worse than demons, as unholy as untruth" and that their only hope of being liberated from karma is "the worship of their husband"—the "woman's god." With the hope of reforming Hinduism, she travels, delivering lectures on women's education. She gains recognition and is soon celebrated as a scholarly and sophisticated Indian reformer.

Alone after the death of her brother, she marries a lawyer. But his lower-caste status creates a stir. Indeed, in the eyes of many Indians she has disgraced herself—a disgrace that is not mitigated by her husband's death. Now a widow, her options are severely limited, apart from her steadfast determination. Driven by her belief in gender equality, she establishes a women's society with the aim of promoting female education and banning child marriages. During this time she develops a friendship with Sister Geraldine, an Anglican nun who invites her to visit England. Encouraged by Geraldine, she studies the Bible, makes profession of faith, and is soon thereafter baptized.

But she is not a compliant convert. Indeed, she challenges the creeds of the Christian faith even as she had challenged the beliefs of Hinduism. "I am, it is true, a member of the Church of Christ," she writes to Geraldine, "but I am not bound to accept every word that falls down from the lips of priests or bishops." She reminds Geraldine of her former faith: "I have just with great efforts freed myself from the yoke of the

> ## BIOGRAPHIES INSPIRE THE FOUNDING OF THE MUKTI MISSION
>
> About twelve years ago, I read the inspiring books, [Hudson Taylor's] "The Story of the China Inland Mission," "The Lord's Dealings with George Muller," and the "Life of John G. Paton," founder of the New Hebrides Mission. I was greatly impressed with the experiences of these three great men.... I wondered after reading their lives, if it were not possible to trust the Lord in India as in other countries. I wished very much that there were some missions founded in this country that would be a testimony to the Lord's faithfulness to His people, and the truthfulness of what the Bible says, in a practical way.... Then the Lord said to me, "Why don't you begin to do this yourself, instead of wishing for others to do it?"
>
> Pandita Ramabai, "Telling Others"

Indian priestly tribe, so I am not at present willing to place myself under another similar yoke by accepting everything which comes from the priests as authorized command of the Most High." Geraldine reacts with dismay and expresses disappointment for her own role in Ramabai's conversion.

"I regret that I have been the cause of making you feel yourself wrong for the part you acted in my baptism," Ramabai responds. "I wish I knew that your Church required a person to be quite perfect in faith, doubting nothing in the Athanasian Creed, so that he had left nothing to be learnt and inquired into the Bible after his baptism."

Suspicious that the problem lies in Ramabai's refusal to make a complete separation from Hinduism, Sister Geraldine is convinced that her unwillingness to eat egg-based puddings indicates she is "clinging to caste prejudice which ought to have been thrown to the winds."

"You may, if you like, trace my pride in pies and puddings," Ramabai fires back, "I confess I am not free from all my caste prejudices, as you are pleased to call them." Then she turns the tables on Sister Geraldine: "How would an Englishwoman like being called proud and prejudiced if she were to go and live among the Hindus for a time but did not think it necessary

to alter her customs when they were not hurtful or necessary to her neighbors?" She is determined to go her own way despite the criticism of Geraldine and other Western Christians. Hindu culture is Indian culture, she argues, and she is unapologetically a Hindu Christian. She refuses to break ties with Hindus, maintaining friendships and professional relationships. She also continues to read from Hindu scriptures, making them available to the girls at the Mukti mission as well. Her independence creates controversy among both Christians and Hindus, but she is undeterred. She reflects on her struggles with no regrets: "I am having a right good time in the storm of public indignation that is raging over my head."

The Mukti Mission had been founded by Ramabai in 1889 as a place of refuge for young women, many of them widows who as little girls had been married to old men and then abandoned by their families. *Mukti* means 'liberation' in the Marathi tongue. Here the girls found love and liberation from a culture of rejection. Here they found not only a home but also health care, education, vocational training, and freedom to choose their own religious preference. Freedom was the operative philosophy. Ramabai was essentially a reformer who sought to emancipate Indian women from the tight restrictions that limited their options whether they were high or low caste.

She encouraged the girls to consider the tenets of Christianity, and many of them did so even before the outbreak of the "Pentecost" revival in 1905. Preceded by months of prayer, the "outpouring" resulted in thousands of conversions, often marked by weeping and tongues-speaking and miracles. The most spectacular miracle Ramabai reported was the provision of water during a drought so severe that the wells at the Mukti mission had gone dry. "Each of the two wells had all its contents used up every day," she recalled. "But there came a fresh supply in the morning to each well, and it lasted all day."

Many young women committed their lives to ministry, and in the ensuing years dozens of bands of female evangelists spread out through the region. A role model through her various ministries as a reformer, writer, poet, and Bible translator, Ramabai challenged the girls to find their own gifts and calling. She was recognized in India and England with prestigious awards both before and after her death, and she still stands today as a monument to freedom for women worldwide.

## William Seymour: Azusa Street Revivalist

The Azusa Street Revival of 1906 in Los Angeles is widely regarded as the key event that launched the twentieth-century Pentecostal and charismatic movements. In itself, however, it was just another in a series of revivals and "outpourings" that had begun in the late nineteenth century. What is profoundly different in the case of Azusa Street is publicity. Indeed, it could be argued that this is a revival spurred largely by religious journalism—most notably the widely distributed stories of journalist Frank Bartle-

man. His accounts of miracles and transformed lives distributed to religious magazines throughout the country and around the world prompted pilgrims to visit and seek the same experiences. Ministers among the crowds returned home with Pentecostal enthusiasm and ignited revivals in their own congregations. But Azusa Street remained the "mother" of all Pentecostal revivals, thanks to Bartleman.

A skillful journalist, Bartleman zeroes in on a key personality. The man of the hour is William Seymour (1870–1922), a little-known African American evangelist. That his ministry, despite his low-key style, could gain such a wide following prompts Bartleman to conclude that "the color line was washed away in the Blood." But others pounce on this "race mixing" perpetrated by the "dirty, collarless and uneducated" Seymour. From the *Los Angeles Times* comes the report that "colored people and a sprinkling of

### AGNES OZMAN AND TWENTIETH-CENTURY PENTECOSTALISM

On December 31, 1900, at a "watch-night" service at Bethel Bible School in Topeka, Kansas, student Agnes Ozman ushered in the twentieth-century Pentecostal movement. She was "the first person since biblical times to speak in tongues," according to one report. Actually, countless Christians had spoken in tongues through the centuries, but without the publicity. The report that she had spoken in Chinese with a halo surrounding her head was heralded in apocalyptic terms as the key to worldwide evangelism that would hasten the return of Christ. The founder of Bethel Bible School, Charles Fox Parham, was a leading proponent of glossolalia (tongues-speaking) and a one-time follower of Benjamin Irwin and his "fire-baptized" gospel.

## ALMA WHITE AND THE KKK

The first American woman to hold the office of bishop was Alma White (1862–1946), presiding over the denomination she founded in 1901, the Methodist Pentecostal Union Church in Denver, also known as the Pillar of Fire. White was a strong supporter of women's equality, while at the same time arguing for white supremacy and collaborating with the Ku Klux Klan in an effort to deny African Americans basic rights. She was also anti-Semitic and stirred up opposition to immigrants, particularly Catholics. But her support of the Klan more than anything else brought her notoriety — support that included cross burning and the publication of three books that she wrote: *The Ku Klux Klan in Prophecy* (1925), *Klansmen: Guardians of Liberty* (1926), and *Heroes of the Fiery Cross* (1928).

whites compose the congregation, and night is made hideous in the neighborhood by the howlings of the worshippers who spend hours swaying forth and back in a nerve-racking attitude of prayer and supplication."

Born in Louisiana to parents who had spent their early years in slavery, Seymour had moved to Indiana and later Ohio, where he abandons his Baptist background for holiness teachings of sanctification and divine healing. Employment as a railway porter and a restaurant waiter offers him opportunities to develop his interpersonal skills. From Ohio he moves in 1903 to Houston to study at Charles Fox Parham's Bible Training School. He is permitted to take courses, but only if he is properly segregated and listens from outside the classroom. Offended by such racism, he leaves, convinced that integration will hasten the return of Christ. But through Parham's influence, tongues-speaking becomes a key aspect of his ministry as a lay preacher in Houston.

From Houston he accepts a call from a church in Los Angeles, only to be released soon after his arrival because of his Pentecostal leanings. Without a pulpit, he sets up shop in a run-down, abandoned building on Azusa Street. What is perhaps most unusual about the revival that follows is the personality of the preacher. "Meek and plain-spoken and no ora-

tor," observes a contemporary, "he spoke the common language of the uneducated class. He might preach for three-quarters of an hour with no more emotionalism than that there post. He was no arm-waving thunderer by any stretch of the imagination." While others are responding with great emotion, Seymour is typically kneeling in prayer with his head under a pulpit fashioned from shoebox crates.

Women played a major role in the ministry of the Azusa Street Revival. Among them is Florence Crawford, who angrily separated from Seymour in 1909, taking the ministry's critical mailing list with her to Portland, Oregon, where she established her own Apostolic Faith Mission. Rumors spread that she was jealous of Jennie Evans Moore, who had become Seymour's wife in 1908. Moore frequently preached while Seymour was traveling, and after his death in 1922, she carried on the ministry for nearly a decade.

### Billy Sunday: Showman Evangelist

Among the successors of D. L. Moody, who had turned revival campaigns into big business, is Billy Sunday (1862–1935), who would turn preaching into a stage performance. Like Moody, Sunday was profoundly influenced by the poverty of his widowed mother who reluctantly relinquished him to an orphanage. Both evangelists appealed to the common man. But Sunday, more than any revivalist before him, preached a *manly* gospel — "muscular Christianity."

A lover of sports, Sunday rises through the ranks in baseball to play for eight years with the Chicago Whitestockings (now White Sox). He entertains the crowds with his lightening speed, running the bases in a record fourteen seconds. But stealing bases is his specialty, with ninety-four steals in one season. He also enjoys a good time — anything that involves drinking. One Sunday in 1886, while loitering on a street corner in Chi-

Billy Sunday

cago, a rescue mission band marches by, playing hymns his mother had sung to him when he was a child. He follows the band back to the Pacific Garden Mission, where he is converted.

Leaving baseball behind, he works with the YMCA and later joins evangelist J. Wilbur Chapman on the revival circuit. As the advance man, he learns the revival business from the ground up. When Chapman takes a settled ministry in Philadelphia in 1895, Sunday is asked to fill his schedule. His initial success spurs him to launch into full-time evangelism. In 1901 he hires a singer and directs revival organizers to erect wooden tabernacles for his meetings. By 1904 he has his own advance man as

well as an architect to design the tabernacles and supervise their inexpensive construction. Sawdust on the dirt floor minimizes dust, and thus the phrase "hitting the sawdust trail" emerges as a synonym for conversion. In 1909 he hires Homer Rodeheaver as songleader, a twosome that lasts for more than two decades.

Referring to himself as the "rube of rubes" because of his rural background, he gestures wildly, and every sermon becomes a dramatic show. He waves his arms and shakes his fists; he runs and jumps and gyrates, sometimes smashing chairs in a "rage against Satan." He mocks and chides everything from saloons to "dandy" preachers: "I want to preach the gospel so plainly that men can come from the factories and not have to bring a dictionary." But his plain speaking often draws criticism. "I don't believe your own bastard theory of evolution," he howls to his opponents. "I believe it's pure jackass nonsense."

Billy Sunday preaching

*Such skillful boob-bumpers as the Rev. Dr. Billy Sunday know what that culture is; they know what the crowd wants. Thus they convert the preaching of the alleged Word of God into a rough-and-tumble pursuit of definite sinners — saloon-keepers, prostitutes, Sabbath-breakers, believers in the Darwinian hypothesis, German exegetes, [bookies], poker-players, adulterers, cigarette-smokers, users of profanity. It is the chase that heats up the great mob of Methodists, not the Word.*

H. L. Mencken

Evolution is not his only enemy. He rails against the fashion of the Roaring Twenties. "It's a damnable insult some of the rigs a lot of fool women are wearing up and down our streets," he fumes. But his harshest attacks are against alcohol — its invention causing a "jubilee in hell." Indeed, his sermons are so effective that people are said to abandon alcohol in droves. After a campaign in Wilkes-Barre, Pennsylvania, bars reportedly close for lack of business.

Sunday also links his message to patriotism. In one sermon during World War I, he calls on God, in no uncertain terms, to damn the Germans. When the government announces registration for the draft, Sunday purchases $25,000 worth of liberty bonds. In another sermon he announces that if hell could be turned over, it would be stamped "Made in Germany." But by the 1930s, Sunday's influence is waning as cultural values change and other evangelists come to the fore.

## Aimee Semple McPherson: Founder of Foursquare Gospel

Coming to the revival stage on the heels of Sunday is Aimee Semple McPherson (1890–1944). A Canadian with Salvation Army and Methodist roots, she is converted to Pentecostalism through Robert Semple, soon to become

### MEL TROTTER

Like Billy Sunday, Mel Trotter was awakened spiritually through the ministry of the Pacific Garden Mission in Chicago. The son of an alcoholic, Trotter developed the same patterns as his father, losing one job after another. Blaming himself for the death of his small son, he vowed never to drink again. Two hours later he was stone cold drunk. Making his way to Chicago from his home in Iowa, he was converted through the ministry of Harry Monroe, director of the mission. He worked as an assistant for Monroe until a group of businessmen from Grand Rapids, Michigan, contacted him to start mission work there.

Beginning in 1900, Trotter's ministry blossomed. He organized a mission Sunday school, attracting hundreds of children, and soon he was presiding over the largest rescue mission in the country. His wife, Martha, joined in the work, reaching out to homeless women and prostitutes. But there were difficult times as well. During World War I, he had gone on the road to minister to troops. "After twenty months of work in the Army," he wrote, "I returned home to find everything gone that is dear to the heart." His wife had left him and later brought him to court "on the most horrible charge." News of the scandal quickly spread. "While I was thoroughly vindicated [in 1922] by the decree, I became a marked man literally around the world." He was soon back on the speaking circuit, however, conducting revivals and preaching at conferences through the 1930s.

## THE RISE OF WOMEN PREACHERS

So it is with women preachers. They do good, but how much harm they do! First, the rise of women preachers has meant the rise of multiplied sects of people with false doctrines of every kind.... [For example,] Mrs. Aimee Semple McPherson and the so-called "Foursquare Gospel," Pentecostalism and its vast majority of women preachers with the blight of sinless perfection doctrine, radical emotionalism, "speaking in tongues" and trances, its overemphasis on healing.... Women preachers have given the world an impression that Christians are emotionally unstable, that preaching is a racket.

John R. Rice, *Bobbed Hair, Bossy Wives, and Women Preachers*

her husband and a missionary to China. His death two years later in 1910 leaves her alone with a baby daughter. In 1912 she marries Harold McPherson and soon after gives birth to a boy. In the years following, while her marriage unravels, she travels as an evangelist across the United States and Canada with her mother, Minnie Kennedy.

Launching her coast-to-coast revival ministry in Los Angeles in 1919, she soon becomes a household name and an evangelical star. Clad in fashionable flowing white gowns and wearing makeup and jewelry, the glamorous "Sister Aimee" brings sex appeal to the stage. Adding props to the platform, she makes Billy Sunday's performances seem stale. On one occasion, she arrives on stage aboard a motorcycle and dressed as a traffic officer—one of her many dramatic openings. Unlike Sunday, she settles down in ministry. In 1922 she founds the Foursquare Gospel, and the following year she builds her own megachurch in Los Angeles. Angelus Temple has a seating capacity of more than five thousand and is a Southern California tourist attraction. In 1924 she goes on the air with her own radio station. Pentecostalism has come a long way in the less than two decades since the Azusa Street Revival.

The scandal of Pentecostalism in the first two decades of the century had been its "race-mixing" and the low social status of its adherents, both black and white. McPherson changes that, not only through outward appearances of success but also through her close connections to Hollywood and key local political leaders. Media consultants manage publicity as money pours in. But beneath the surface there is loneliness and depression.

Aimee Semple McPherson

The Angelus Temple, started by McPherson

The disappearance of Sister Aimee, reportedly while swimming at the beach on May 18, 1926, quickly captures the nation's attention. Teams in airplanes and watercraft search the waters along the coast, while thousands of her followers keep vigil on the shore. No trace of her can be found. Finally, after weeks of accusations and rumors, she appears from out of the desert near Douglas, Arizona. She tells reporters and law enforcement officers that she has been kidnapped, tortured, and held hostage in Mexico. Was she really the victim of shadowy criminals who inadvertently allowed her to escape by walking thirteen hours and made no attempt to recapture her? Her detractors argue

that she showed no signs of having undergone a month of torture, nor is there any other evidence to support the kidnapping claim apart from her own testimony. Theories and rumors abound—most specifically that she had spent the time with a married man, Kenneth Ormiston, her radio operations manager.

Charged with perjury by the Los Angeles district attorney, "Sister Aimee" weathers the storm, especially after the court case is dropped in 1927. In 1931 she marries again, only to divorce three years later. Public feuds with her mother also bring scandal, and when she dies in 1944, rumors surface that the overdose of barbiturates might not have been accidental. But through it all Sister Aimee is what might be described as the "Teflon evangelist." Scandal does not stick long enough to smear her success as a Pentecostal leader and as founder of the Church of the Foursquare Gospel that grows to more than two million in the decades after her death.

Some church leaders judged McPherson's ministry to be nothing more than a show and a sham. But the records show Angelus Temple as a haven for the poor and disadvantaged, especially during the Great Depression. Actor Anthony Quinn later spoke of the fear that immigrants had of coming forward requesting aid. "During the Depression," he related, "the one human being that never asked you what your nationality was, what you believed in and so forth, was Aimee Semple McPherson. All you had to do was pick up the phone and say, 'I'm hungry,' and within an hour there'd be a food basket there for you."

Aimee McPherson with her "gospel car."

## J. FRANK NORRIS: A TWO-GUN PARSON

During most of the first half of the twentieth century, John Franklyn Norris (1877–1952) was the minister of the Fort Worth, Texas, First Baptist Church, known as the "home of the cattle kings." The richest church in Texas, it had a sister church in Detroit and a total membership of some twenty-five thousand. When Norris's efforts to shut down a house of prostitution failed, he began advertising his Sunday evening sermons as forums for exposing the names of clients. Crowds overflowed the auditorium, and a tent was erected. The mayor ordered the tent removed, leading to a prolonged conflict between mayor and preacher and their supporters. In February of 1912, the church was burned to the ground, and a month later the Norris home was burned. The mayor was blamed, but Norris (rumored to have planned the arson in order to blame others) was the primary suspect though never charged. Another conflict erupted in 1925 when Norris sought to avert a land purchase by local Catholics. A city hall official came to Norris's office, and, according to Norris, threatened him. Norris pulled out his gun, fired four shots, and killed the man — muscular Christianity at work. He claimed self-defense, the jury agreed, and he was found "not guilty." Other Baptists were embarrassed by his behavior and parted company with him, but his radio audience grew as he increased his attacks against Catholics, communists, and organized labor. His influence impressed politicians, including Herbert Hoover, who invited him to his inauguration in 1929. Norris stands out as the premier "fighting fundamentalist" of the 1920s.

## John Sung: Asian Intellectual and Evangelist

In 1944, the same year that McPherson died in California, another church leader on the other side of the world died. One of the most extraordinary evangelists of the twentieth century, John Sung (1901–1944) has been all but forgotten in the Western world today. Born in Southeast China, he was the sixth child of an impoverished Chinese Methodist preacher. His mother, the wife in an arranged marriage, was a fervent Buddhist until she converted to Christianity the year before John was born.

Following in his father's footsteps, young Sung becomes recognized throughout the region as a celebrated boy preacher. He accompanies his father on preaching missions, and when his father is ill or engaged in other activities, he preaches his father's sermons that he has memorized. After completing secondary school in 1919 he is contacted by an American woman

offering to fund his education at Ohio Wesleyan University. A brilliant student, he graduates in 1923 with highest honors; he is elected to Phi Beta Kappa and awarded the gold medal and the cash prize for physics and chemistry. So remarkable are his academic achievements that newspapers around the country publish his story. The following year he completes a master's degree at Ohio State University, and in 1926 he is awarded a Ph.D. in chemistry.

Despite invitations to join faculties at various American universities, Sung is having second thoughts about pursuing an academic career. Unable to set aside the sense of calling to the ministry he felt years earlier, he takes the advice of a friend and enrolls at Union Theological Seminary. Here he is introduced to a liberal theology that is difficult to refute. Facing doubts and depression, he turns to the religion of his ancestors and begins to chant Buddhist scriptures. He also studies Taoism, hoping to find peace. But the more he searches, the more confused and distressed he becomes. "My soul wandered in a wilderness," he later confessed. "I could neither sleep nor eat. My faith was like a leaking, storm-driven ship without captain or compass. My heart was filled with the deepest unhappiness."

In the midst of his struggles he is invited to attend nightly meetings at New York City's Calvary Baptist Church, where the celebrated fundamentalist preacher John Roach Straton is minister. He had been told that the speaker would be Dr. Haldeman, a brilliant Bible scholar—a man whose message would address his doubts. Instead, the speaker is Uldine Utley, a fifteen-year-old evangelist whose simple message has no correlation with his intellectual struggles. But as he listens to her, he is reminded of his own childhood preaching. He returns the following nights to hear her preach, and as a result his life is transformed.

Back at the seminary he spends his nights praying and his days reciting Scripture and singing—and evangelizing Union seminary students. Convinced that he is mentally unstable, administrators admit him to a psychiatric hospital, where he is confined for more than six months against his will. During this time he reads through the Bible some forty times and shares his faith with other patients. Released in August of 1927 through the intervention of the Chinese Department of State, he returns to China to follow his call to ministry. Working under the auspices of the Bethel Mission, he is on a nonstop preach-ing circuit, traveling to more than thirty cities and speaking at nearly nine hundred meetings in a six-month period. Thousands join the Bethel Bands as full-time evangelists.

In 1934 Sung launches out on his own, and in the following years he travels throughout China, often speaking to crowds of thousands. He also travels to the Philippines, Formosa (Taiwan), Singapore, Malaysia, and Thailand, where thousands more are converted and enrolled in his locally organized Bible training centers. Here his ministry is multiplied as students spend half their days evangelizing neighboring communities.

Despite his success, many missionaries view him as a sensationalist performer and resent his criticism of them. Yet most concede that he has a connection with the Asian people that has eluded them, burdened as they are with their Western cultural baggage. In 1942, after fifteen years of exhausting ministry, health problems force his retirement at age forty. He dies two years later, leaving a ministry that lives on into the next generations.

This was an era of transformation. The revivalism featuring Salvation Army bands and a down-trodden Azusa Street Mission had come of age in the "Roaring Twenties" with theatrical performances and Hollywood connections. Wrapping itself in popular culture and patriotism, it positioned itself against the high-profile sins of the day. Conversion consisted of receiving Jesus and renouncing booze.

---

## What if ...

What if William Booth had gone through life as an obscure pawnbroker? What if Catherine Mumford had decided he was simply not the right one for her? What if Evangeline had not expanded the ministry in America and worldwide? What is the significance today of the Salvation Army?

What if Pandita Ramabai had not had the

opportunity to read biographies of great ministers and mission leaders? Would she have launched out on her own as a faith mission leader without the examples of others to follow?

What if the early decades of revivalism had been initiated by individuals like William Seymour rather than stars like Billy Sunday and Aimee Semple McPherson? How might evangelicalism look today if it had grown to maturity with a humble spirit?

## Further Reading

Blumhofer, Edith L. *Aimee Semple McPherson: Everybody's Sister.* Grand Rapids: Eerdmans, 1993.

Carpenter, Joel A. *Revive Us Again: Reawakening in American Fundamentalism.* New York: Oxford, 1997.

Douglas Carl Abrams. *Selling the Old-Time Religion: American Fundamentalists and Mass Culture, 1920 – 1940.* Athens: University of Georgia Press, 2001.

Dorsett, Lyle W. *Billy Sunday and the Redemption of Urban America.* Grand Rapids: Eerdmans, 1991.

Dyer, Helen S. *Pandita Ramabai: The Story of Her Life.* Whitefish, Mont.: Kessinger, 2004.

Frank, Douglas W. *Less Than Conquerors: How Evangelicals Entered the Twentieth Century.* Grand Rapids: Eerdmans, 1986.

Hankins, Barry. *God's Rascal: J. Frank Norris and the Beginnings of Southern Fundamentalism.* Lexington: University of Kentucky Press, 1996.

Hattersley, Roy. *Blood and Fire: William and Catherine Booth and Their Salvation Army.* New York: Doubleday, 2000.

Lyall, Leslie T. *John Sung: A Biography.* Singapore: Armour Publishing, 2004.

Marsden, George M. *Fundamentalism and American Culture.* New York: Oxford University Press, 2006.

Martin, Robert F. *Hero of the Heartland: Billy Sunday and the Transformation of America.* Bloomington: Indiana University Press, 2002.

Robeck, Cecil M. *The Azusa Street Mission and Revival.* Nashville: Thomas Nelson, 2006.

Sutton, Matthew Avery. *Aimee Semple McPherson and the Resurrection of Christian America.* Cambridge: Harvard University Press, 2009.

Synan, Vinson. *The Holiness-Pentecostal Tradition: Charismatic Movements in the Twentieth Century.* Grand Rapids: Eerdmans, 1997.

Trout, Margaret. *The General Was a Lady: The Story of Evangeline Booth.* Nashville: A. J. Holman, 1980.

# CHAPTER 23

# Theological Ferment

*Twentieth-Century Protestants and Catholics*

*Albert is not welcome in my church. He's there every Sunday, but to most people he is either invisible or ignored—or dismissed outright—by everyone except my husband and me, though we've never actually conversed with him. We give him a nod or perhaps an inconspicuous salute. He is a big man. Indeed, with the exception of Jesus, he is the largest full-bodied figure in the wall of stained glass that towers behind the pulpits and choir loft in the front of the sanctuary.*

*Albert Schweitzer, the great missionary medical doctor to Africa—and "heretic"—found his way into our church, not by invitation but by artistic license. The artist commissioned to create this spectacular set of images took the liberty of giving him a place alongside other recognizable "saints," including Martin Luther and John Calvin.*

*But Schweitzer, unlike the others, is considered less than orthodox. He challenged liberal interpretations of the gospel accounts of Jesus in his well-known book,* Quest for the Historical Jesus, *but was himself outside the realm of historic orthodoxy. So what was La Grave Avenue Christian Reformed Church to do? Could this big man be taken out of the glass? Yes and No. No, short of firing a cannon ball through the glass, he is there to stay. Yes, we can rid ourselves of him, as we have done, if we simply deny he is who he is. We can say the figures in the glass are generic representations of generic people and that one of them may appear to look like a generic Schweitzer.*

*Schweitzer's less-than-orthodox doctrine was balanced by his passion to follow Jesus in sacrificial service. It seems to me that he ought to get credit for that. How many Christians who are fully orthodox in church dogma, I ask, fail to follow Jesus as he commanded? "Take up your cross and follow me."*

Civilizations have arisen in other parts of the world. In ancient and modern times, wonderful ideas have been carried forward from one race to another.... But ... it has been always with the blast of war trumpets and the march of embattled cohorts. Each idea had to be soaked in a deluge of blood.

ANAND SINGH

The twentieth century was a time when wonderful ideas were carried forward from one race to another—but always, it seems, soaked in blood. It was a century of war. The national revolutions and civil wars that marked the mid-nineteenth century pale in comparison to the carnage of the world wars of the twentieth century and the accompanying holocausts that spanned the globe, beginning with that perpetrated on the Jews by the Nazis, followed by Joseph Stalin's bloodbath in Russia. And before the century was over, millions more would be slaughtered by the likes of Idi Amin in Uganda and Pol Pot in Cambodia as well as in civil wars from El Salvador to Rwanda and Sudan.

War, genocide, racism, tyranny, and terror in all its guises formed an incongruous backdrop for the unparalleled twentieth-century expansion of Christianity around the world. This was the century of evangelicals—earnest Christians populating chapels and churches and Bible institutes of every kind—from Plymouth Brethren and Baptist to Methodist and Presbyterian. Alongside of—and often in opposition to—

the evangelicals were liberals (and those accused of being liberal) of every stripe, both Protestant and Catholic. Social outreach was certainly not confined to the liberal camp, but many of the more progressive church leaders sought to infuse theology with social concern. Among those speaking out against totalitarianism and for the marginalized were Abraham Kuyper, Dietrich Bonhoeffer, Albert Schweitzer, Karl Barth, and Oscar Romero.

Severely bruised by the Enlightenment and by evolution and other scientific and technological revolutions, many European churches responded either by moving with the times and abandoning historic orthodoxy or by reacting to the liberalizing trends by tightening the reins. Protestant denominations, following the lead of their respective seminaries and schools of religion, were swayed by biblical criticism and a corresponding diminished authority of Scripture. Such moves, however, often resulted in church splits and the formation of new denominations that claimed to be the rightful heirs of the original founders.

## PARADE OF HISTORY

As Hitler reviews goose-stepping SS guards parading before the Reichstag in Berlin, the procession of church history moves onward. There are those who seek to rain on his parade, but far too many professing Christians cheer him on. They applaud during his boisterous birthday parade on April 18, 1939. "We celebrate in exultant joy the fiftieth birthday of our Fuhrer," reads a greeting from the German Protestant Church. "In him, God has given the German people a true man of wonders." Dietrich Bonhoeffer is in town that day, vowing to stand strong against the tyrant. His own parade will end at dawn on April 9, 1945, at the gallows.

## RELIGION IN DENMARK, CIRCA 1855

We have what one might call a complete inventory of churches, bells, organs, benches, alms-boxes, foot-warmers, tables, hearses, etc. But when Christianity does not exist, the existence of this inventory, so far from being ... an advantage, is far rather a peril, because it is so infinitely likely to give rise to a false impression and the false inference that when we have a complete Christian inventory we must of course have Christianity, too.

Søren Kierkegaard

Fearing similar liberalizing trends, the Catholic Church reacted by tightening its own reins. Pope Pius IX, who reigned for more than thirty years (1846–1878), stands above other nineteenth-century religious leaders in seeking to stem the tide of modernism. Initially a social liberal who cared about the concerns of those living under the oppressive regime of the Papal States, he quickly reversed his position in the face of revolution. Having earlier fled for his life, he later returned to the Vatican in 1849, his political power significantly weakened.

In this atmosphere, he directed his influence to strengthening the spiritual authority of the Church. Catholicism, he vowed, would not cave in to cultural trends. "Tradition—I am tradition!" was reportedly his dictum. With a heavy hand he brought Catholics in line with official church teaching, including the teaching on the Virgin Mary. Although Mary had long been revered in the church, he decreed in 1854 (with the support of bishops) that she was conceived without "any taint of sin"—the doctrine of the Immaculate Conception. Some years later he reaffirmed *Unam Sanctam*, specifying that for anyone outside the Roman Catholic Church there is no salvation. Fearing heretical teachings outside narrow church boundaries, he issued the *Syllabus of Errors*, which censured what he considered profane movements and ideas—from Bible societies and secular education to religious toleration and civil marriages.

For those who challenged his power, his response was straightforward—papal infallibility *ex cathedra* (by virtue of office). The first Vatican Council affirmed this doctrine in 1870. Thus, when the pope is speaking officially as head of the church on faith and morals, his word must be accepted as gospel truth. Opponents argued that such a decree elevated the pope above councils, thus making councils unnecessary. One year later, in 1871, dissenting bishops who claimed to be true heirs of apostolic succession formed the Old Catholic Church.

The same year that papal infallibility was defined, Friedrich Nietzsche (1844–1900) enlisted in the military and was on his way to fight against France. He watched with pride as the German cavalry passed through Frankfurt. "I felt for the first time that the strongest and highest Will to Life," he later wrote, is in a "Will to War, a Will to Power, a Will to Overpower."

Have you ever heard of the madman who on a bright morning lighted a lantern and ran to the market-place calling out ... "Where is God gone?... We have killed him,—you and I! We are all murderers!... Do we not hear the noise of the grave-diggers who are burying God?" ... At last he threw his lantern on the ground, so that it broke in pieces and was extinguished. "I come too early," he then said, "I am not yet at the right time."

Friedrich Nietzsche

Born into a family of Lutheran preachers, he had read the Bible with passion as a boy and was referred to as "the little minister." But in 1864, as a university student he, like many of his fellow students, abandoned the faith. In the years that followed, he became known as an evangelist of unbelief and the founding philosopher of the "death of God" movement. He was the poster child for religion gone awry.

When Nietzsche died in 1900, Paul Tillich (1886–1965), another son of a German minister was coming of age. Though sometimes wrongly associated with death-of-God theology, he identified his perspective as the "theology of doubt." Escaping Hitler's Germany in 1933, he became a professor of religion at Union Theological Seminary and later at Harvard, all the while pushing Luther's emphasis on justification by faith to its outer limits: "Not only he who is in sin but also he who is in doubt is justified through faith. There is faith in every serious doubt ... even if the only truth we can express is our lack of truth." Thus, according to Tillich, "there is no possible atheism." Although most Protestants were not comfortable with such a position, Tillich was widely viewed as America's leading theologian.

In the midst of this decades-long reign of liberalism, Karl Barth emerged with his theology or crisis, more commonly known as neo-orthodoxy. In his train were a host of young scholars also seeking to stem the tide of modernism. But many of them, including Rudolf Bultmann, went far beyond Barth. In his *New Testament and Mythology: The Problem of Demythologizing the New Testament Message*, Bultmann, taking form criticism to its logical end, challenged the historical value of the Gospels.

American theologians in the mid-twentieth century were among those who looked to Barth in their efforts to hold on to historic orthodox beliefs. Among them were the Niebuhr brothers,

Reinhold and Richard, both born in Missouri and both following their father into ministry. After seminary studies, Reinhold Niebuhr (1892–1971) took a call to a small mission church in Detroit. When he left more than a dozen years later, the largely working-class congregation had grown to nearly seven hundred. Though leaving the pastorate behind to become professor of practical theology at Union Theological Seminary, his concern remained with workers and the negative effects of industrialization.

Reinhold's younger brother, Helmut Richard Niebuhr (1894–1962), served in a church in St. Louis before going into a teaching career that culminated in a post at Yale. His specialty was Christian ethics, and he was best known for his seminal work, *Christ and Culture*, in which he sought to explain historically how Christianity has responded to various cultures: Christ against culture, Christ of culture, Christ above culture, Christ and culture in paradox, and Christ transforming culture.

As Christianity moved into the early decades of the twentieth century, the three branches of Christianity all confronted grave obstacles, and they responded in very different ways. As the Catholic Church turned inward and tightened restrictions on clerics and scholars and laypeople alike, mainline Protestant churches largely accommodated themselves to culture. For Orthodox Christians — especially Russian Orthodox — the enemy was a totalitarian communistic regime. More than one generation of children was schooled in an educational system that did not allow for God. In many respects the twentieth century, with its world wars, Nazism, communism, and liberal theologies was not a warm environment for Christianity. Yet even in the midst of all this, the church continued to play a significant and often positive role in society.

## Male Perspectives on Women in Ministry

Evangelical women in ministry found their role models in such dedicated pioneers as Phoebe Palmer and Catherine Booth as well as in the women serving with Jesus and Paul. Nor were they without male cheerleaders. "There is no prohibition in the Bible against women's public work," wrote Frederik Franson, founder of The Evangelical Alliance Mission, "and we face the circumstance that the devil, fortunately for him, has been able to exclude nearly two-thirds of the number of Christians from participation in the Lord's service through evangelization."

Presbyterian minister A. T. Pierson, also called for expanded roles for women in ministry. The argument was simple. More, not fewer, workers are needed in the vineyard of the Lord. The world will never be evangelized if women are excluded. Such an argument had been voiced in the early stages of sectarian movements throughout history. From Moravians and Quakers to Methodists and Pentecostals, women fought in the trenches alongside men and often rose through the ranks — but not in the status-conscious institutionalized churches.

Though it is often assumed that "liberals" support a more feminist agenda and "conservatives" do not, that was not true during much of the twentieth century. Mainline Protestant churches, like Roman Catholicism, were deeply entrenched in an institutionalized corporate system that encouraged competition and defense of one's turf. Opening the doors to women was seen as an unnecessary move that would only threaten male status and position.

Nor were women welcomed by liberal theologians of the twentieth century. Indeed, they are noticeably absent, except for behind-the-scenes involvement as in the case of Karl Barth and Charlotte von Kirschbaum, his often-unrecognized female researcher and co-author. Similar circumstances were present in the scholarship of Paul Tillich. Liberal and neo-orthodox theologies were part of a larger intellectual realm where women's voices were rarely heard. Even in the Social Gospel movement, women were less likely to hold prominent positions than in humanitarian outreach programs spawned by evangelicals. Largely

### KARL BARTH AND THE WOMEN'S ISSUE

Barth's views on women were traditional. He affirmed a distinction between men and women both "physiologically and biblically." Barth's concept of the "I-Thou" encounter is discernible here. Man has strength, woman has weakness, but she is not inferior. There is "super- and subordination." God has established an order, with man having headship over woman.

Ruth A. Tucker and Walter L. Liefeld, *Daughters of the Church*

intellectuals and lobbyists, the leading lights of the American Social Gospel movement were Richard Ely, Washington Gladden, and Walter Rauschenbusch.

Such a separation of the sexes and the assumption that women were not fit for intellectual and leadership positions was more of an old world European tradition than an American one. The received tradition was an assumption that women were basically inferior to men. In reflecting on the Samaritan woman in the gospel of John, Abraham Kuyper denigrates her despite her lively interaction with Jesus and her subsequent key role as an evangelist. He describes her not only as "positively uncouth" but also as "superficial, mundane, and gullible." Such language had a profound effect on the generations of Reformed Christians who followed him.

## Abraham Kuyper: Dutch Reformed Pastor and Prime Minister

Many nineteenth-century European Christians, like their eighteenth-century Pietist forebearers, felt as though they were being swept away in the torrent of liberalism. The confessions and catechisms of their youth were giving way to revolutionary ideas from the universities. Where would it end? Would their children and grandchildren be able to swim against the raging liberal theological current? Some succumbed to fear; others, like Pietje Balthus, took it upon themselves to do whatever they could to stem the tide. A pious young peasant woman, she confessed her simple faith to her scholarly minister. Through her testimony, the pastoral ministry of Abraham Kuyper (1837–1920) was transformed.

Kuyper, the son of a Dutch Reformed minister who had sought to straddle confessional

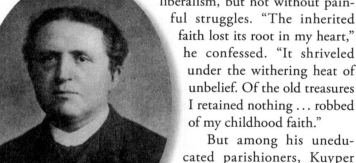

Abraham Kuyper

orthodoxy and modernism, had the advantage of the best education of his day, receiving his doctorate in theology in 1862. The following year he accepted a call to a small village church and married Johanna, with whom he would have eight children. Before entering the ministry he had gravitated toward liberalism, but not without painful struggles. "The inherited faith lost its root in my heart," he confessed. "It shriveled under the withering heat of unbelief. Of the old treasures I retained nothing ... robbed of my childhood faith."

But among his uneducated parishioners, Kuyper reclaimed his childhood faith, recognizing his own deficiencies: "I could not measure my impoverished Bible knowledge, the fruit of university study, with that of these plain people." As he met with them, his perspective slowly began to change: "What drew me most to them was that here the heart spoke—there was inner experience." He was

## RICHARD MOUW DISCOVERS KUYPER

I discovered Kuyper in the 1960s when I was struggling with fundamental tensions between my evangelical pietism and what I had come to see as the non-negotiable biblical mandate to work actively for justice and peace in the larger human community. Kuyper helped me, more than any other thinker, to see the profound connection between the atoning work of the loving Saviour who is my "only comfort in life and death" and that Saviour's kingly rule over all spheres of human interaction.

Richard Mouw, "MINE! Kuyper for A New Century"

torn: "I found myself ever at the fork of the way. Either must I take sharp position against them or go with them without conditions, putting myself under sovereign grace."

While visiting the Balthus home, he listened for two hours to Pietje's message of faith and hope. She was outspoken in the presence of her minister, warning him that unless he also believed through simple faith, he would have no hope for eternal life. He might have been offended by her audacious confrontation, but instead he returned time and again to her family home. Indeed, she became his teacher. So influential was she in his spiritual life that he kept her picture on his desk in the following years, ever reminding him of the commitment he had made.

Pietistic renewal had arisen earlier in the Dutch churches, but such movements had spread primarily among the lower classes and were either ignored or scorned by most religious scholars. With Kuyper behind the renewal, however, other scholarly ministers came on board. He published articles in journals, and in 1867 he accepted a call to Utrecht to minister in a church with thousands of members and several ministers. Three years later he moved on to Amsterdam to serve in an even larger church, the most prestigious congregation in the Netherlands.

Regarded by many as the most eloquent and engaging preacher in the Dutch language, Kuyper spured renewal with his biblical teach-ing. Soon a majority of the ministers and members in the Amsterdam congregation are in his camp. But those who are of a liberal persuasion mount strong opposition. As part of a state church, their views are protected. Nor are there only two sides; the state church includes several factions. Later in 1886 Kuyper and his followers split to form what in 1892 became the *Gereformeerde Kerken in Nederland* (Reformed Churches in the Netherlands).

Kuyper's interests extend far beyond biblical and theological studies and pastoral ministry. His worldview is summed up in his most oft-quoted aphorism: "There is not a square inch in the whole domain of our human existence over which Christ, who is Sovereign over *all*, does not cry: 'Mine!'" God's grace, he argues, is not active in matters of salvation only but in every area of life. This "common grace," associated with what is called Neo-Calvinism, is evident in all that is good, whether initiated by the followers of Christ or by others. This perspective was forcefully articulated and widely disseminated in 1898, when Kuyper visited North America to deliver the Stone Lectures at Princeton Theological Seminary. Opposition, however, was strong. Critics argued vehemently against common grace, insisting that God's *special* grace reigned — that Jesus died to save sinners, not sinners and the environment or sinners and political parties.

Kuyper, a renaissance man of his times, had left the pastoral ministry in 1874 to become a member of parliament. In the years that followed, he became a labor activist, a newspaper publisher, an educator (founder of the Free University, where he taught theology and literature), and then from 1901–1905, prime minister of the Netherlands. At the same time, he is a husband and the father of eight children. But the hectic schedule takes an emotional toll. On two occasions he succumbs to severe depression, his recovery aided by retreats to the Swiss Alps. He nevertheless continues to be politically active in his later years.

Kuyper died in 1920, before the rise of Hitler's Nationalism Socialism. During that era, the Kuyperian perspective on common grace — "grace that curbs the destructive power of sin" — was sorely tested by the horrors of Nazism — and not just on a grand scale. Indeed, his son, H. H. Kuyper, was a Nazi collaborator and his grandson Willem fought with the Waffen SS and died fighting on the eastern front. A granddaughter, however, risked her life to save Jews. Johtje Vos later recalled that she and her husband "did what any human being would have done." Their efforts were unplanned. "You started off storing a suitcase for a friend, and before you knew it, you were in over your head." By the end of the war they had hidden twenty-seven Jewish children. Nothing extraordinary. "When you see a person in need, you help them."

## Dietrich Bonhoeffer: Pastor and Protester Against Nazism

In the late summer of 1943, nineteen-year-old Maria von Wedemeyer received a letter from cell 92 of the military prison at Berlin-Tegel. Beginning "My *dearest* Maria," it continues with the mundane routine of confinement: "I've just had some hot gruel for supper." But it quickly becomes personal: "I'm sitting at the desk with my sleeves rolled up and my collar open, thinking longingly of you. I'd like to drive through the woods with you to the lakeside, go swimming and lie in some shady spot with you, listening to you for ages without saying a word." The letter ends on an optimistic note: "Goodbye for now, dear, good Maria. Wait a little while longer, and all will be well. I'm waiting with you. Ever Your Dietrich." She is his fiancée.

Having been arrested for his involvement in a conspiracy to assassinate Adolf Hitler, Dietrich Bonhoeffer (1906–1945) is sometimes presented as a saint who stoically endures prison and deprivation as a privilege of radical discipleship. But Bonhoeffer loves life, and when he writes about the cost of discipleship, he knows from experience what that cost entails. Born into a nominally Lutheran family, he is the son of a university professor. He enrolls at Tübingen University at seventeen and then goes on to Berlin University the following year to study theology. A brilliant scholar, he is invited to return to the university as a lecturer in systematic theology at age twenty-four.

But before he takes the position, he spends a year in America for further study. At Union Theological Seminary he is exasperated by the atmosphere: "Union students ... intoxicate themselves with liberal and humanistic expressions, laugh at the fundamentalists, and basically they are not even a match for them.... I never heard the Gospel of Jesus Christ ... of the cross, of sin and forgiveness, of death and life [while] in New York ... only an ethical and social idealism which pins its faith to progress."

Even churches fit that description, with the exception of a black church in Harlem that profoundly influenced his future ministry. He had become a friend of Frank Fisher, an African

American student. Together they attended the Abyssinian Baptist Church, taking turns teaching a boy's Sunday school class and working with the neighborhood boys' club. In this black church he finds a sense of community where joy and suffering mingle. Here he finds people who sing their suffering, and he takes their spirituals back to Germany.

Returning to Berlin, he assumes his prestigious assignment as a theology professor in the ivory tower of academia, but not as a stuffy intellectual. In a series of lectures on Christology—delivered the very year Hitler comes to power—he asks penetrating questions: "Who is Jesus in the world of 1933? Where is he to be found?" Jesus, he is convinced, would be identifying with "the persecuted Jew and the imprisoned dissenter in the church struggle." It might have been tempting for him to lie low and take the safe course during the turmoil of the 1930s, following other church leaders in their support of Hitler or at least not voicing opposition. Indeed, many of his fellow students and colleagues do just that. They remain silent when German Lutheran bishops declare: "We German Protestant Christians accept the saving of our nation by our leader Adolf Hitler as a gift from God's hand."

But Bonhoeffer is convinced that one cannot be a follower of Christ and a follower of Hitler at the same time. He abhors the ways of Hitler and the complicity of German Christians. Hermann Grüner, a Lutheran minister, speaks for many German people: "The time is fulfilled for the German people in Hitler. It is because of Hitler that Christ, God the helper and redeemer, has become effective among us. Therefore National Socialism is positive Christianity in action.... Hitler is the way of the Spirit and the will of God for the German people to enter the Church of Christ."

Bonhoeffer's own Lutheran Church finds its place in Nazism with little apparent twinge of conscience. In fact, the clergy conference in September of 1933 is dubbed the "Brown Synod" because many of the ministers wear the brown Nazi uniform and give the *Heil Hitler* salute. Bonhoeffer is distraught, particularly after anti-Jewish legislation becomes publicly associated with Nazism. He demands that the church stand against such laws and implores those who call themselves Christians to "jam the spokes of the wheel" of the state unless the laws are repealed. As time passes he is more and more uncomfortable in his teaching position at the University of

---

### A NEW KIND OF CHRISTIAN

Our church, which has been fighting in these years for its self-preservation, as though that were an end in itself, is incapable of taking the word of reconciliation and redemption to humankind and the world. Our earlier words are therefore bound to lose their force and cease, and our being Christians today will be limited to two things: prayer and righteous action among men. All Christian thinking, speaking, and organizing must be born anew out of this prayer and action.... It is not for us to prophesy the day (though the day will come) when men will once more be called so to utter the word of God that the world will be changed and renewed by it. It will be a new language, perhaps quite non-religious, but liberating and redeeming — as was Jesus' language; it will shock people and yet overcome them by its power; it will be the language of a new righteousness and truth, proclaiming God's peace with men and the coming of his kingdom.

Dietrich Bonhoeffer, *Letters and Papers from Prison*

## THE TEN BOOMS AND THE DUTCH UNDERGROUND

Recognized by Israel and by individual Jewish groups, the Ten Boom family has been repeatedly honored for saving some eight hundred Jews during the Holocaust. Devout Dutch Christians, the family sheltered those who sought refuge. When Nazi SS troops searched the home and arrested family members in 1944, four Jewish refugees and two members of the Dutch Underground escaped by hiding behind a fake bedroom wall. When the family patriarch, Casper ten Boom, was told by his captors that hiding Jews was a capital offence, he responded: "It would be an honor to give my life for God's ancient people." He died in prison shortly after he was captured. His daughters, Elizabeth and Corrie, were incarcerated at Ravensbrück concentration camp, where Elizabeth died and Corrie, due to a clerical error, was released in December 1944. She went on to write her bestseller *The Hiding Place* and to travel in a speaking ministry.

Berlin. Much of the university administration, faculty, and student body have joined the tidal wave of popular support for Hitler. In late 1933 he leaves his prestigious post and takes a pastorate in London, where he continues to speak against Hitler and to rally the ecumenical community outside Germany against Nazism.

Then, in 1935, he accepts an invitation to head an illegal seminary for the Confessing Church near the Baltic Sea. This is a daring move, but the school is closed by the Gestapo less than two years later. The Confessing Church initially stands against policies of the Third Reich, but it too loses nerve. Bonhoeffer, however, is determined to stand firm against evil—to follow Jesus as a disciple, a worldview of "costly grace" that his testimony laid bare in *The Cost of Discipleship* (1937):

> Such grace is costly ... because it costs a man his life, and it is grace because it gives a man the only true life. It is costly because it condemns sin, and grace because it justifies the sinner. Above all, it is costly because it cost God the life of his Son: 'ye were bought at a price,' and what has cost God much cannot be cheap for us.... God did not reckon his Son too dear a price to pay for our life, but delivered him up for us. Costly grace is the Incarnation of God.

In an effort to avoid military service and arrest by the Gestapo, he sails for America in 1939. By this time his opposition to Hitler and Nazism has taken a new turn. He has not only spoken against the regime but is secretly conspiring to overthrow it, having been part of a close inner circle that includes his brother-in-law, Admiral Wilhelm Canaris, and others. Shortly after his arrival, however, he realizes he is in the wrong place. "I have made a mistake in coming to America," he writes to Reinhold Niebuhr. "I will have no right to participate in the reconstruction of Christian life in Germany after the war if I do not share the trials of this time with my people."

Back in Germany he is prohibited from teaching, but he continues writing until his arrest on April 5, 1943. Prison is a terrible setback, but here he writes some of his most enduring works, including his prison letters. One of these letters, smuggled from prison, further clarifies his theme on discipleship:

> If we refuse to take up our cross and submit to suffering and rejection at the hands of men, we forfeit our fellowship with Christ and

have ceased to follow him. But if we lose our lives in his service and carry our cross, we shall find our lives again in the fellowship of the cross with Christ. The opposite of discipleship is to be ashamed of Christ and his cross and all the offense which the cross brings in its train.

Discipleship means allegiance to the suffering Christ, and it is therefore not at all surprising that Christians should be called upon to suffer.

He is later transferred to Buchenwald and from there to the death camp at Flossenbürg. On April 9, 1945 — just days before Flossenbürg is liberated by the allies — he is hanged.

## Albert Schweitzer: Missionary Medical Doctor and Theologian

Whether he was the greatest missionary of the twentieth century or a liberal theologian who wreaked havoc on the Gospels, Albert Schweitzer (1875 – 1965) was one of the most fascinating figures of the last hundred years. His sacrificial mission outreach and his challenge to Christian orthodoxy were both driven by his obsession with Jesus, spurred in part by his passion for the music of Johann Sebastian Bach and his keen interest in the writings of Emmanuel Kant. The son and grandson of ministers, Schweitzer grew up in Gunsbach in Alsace, on the border of France and Germany. His nationality was both French and German, and the church building where his father served was shared by both Protestants and Catholics, who held separate services. Indeed, he grew up with a spirit of toleration that remained with him for the rest of his life. Philosophical and religious ideas permeated his world, but his passion was music. Both sides of the family were known not only in the academic world but also in the world of Bach and organ playing.

By his mid-twenties, Schweitzer was an ordained Lutheran minister, recognized for his scholarly work on Bach as well as on Kant and Jesus. He was also a highly acclaimed organist. But his obsession is his calling to follow Jesus. Having made a vow that at age thirty he would pursue a humanitarian ministry, he shocked family and friends when he submitted his name to a Paris mission society in 1905. Although there are serious questions about his doctrinal views, he is accepted to serve as a medical doctor on the Ogooue River at Lambaréné (in present-day Gabon). Only then does he begin his medical studies.

In 1906, his landmark controversial book, *The Quest for the Historical Jesus*, appears. Here, as in prior works of biblical scholarship, he emphasizes the eschatological nature of Jesus' mission — arguing that Jesus went to his death fully expecting to bring to fruition the kingdom of God and not merely a spiritualized kingdom. Jesus, Schweitzer argues, failed to accomplish his mission but gave his very life to serve others, that alone making him worthy of devotion and discipleship.

While in medical training, Schweitzer continues his theological studies and organ concerts. In fact, the concerts are part of his fund-raising activities — his quest to equip a hospital in Africa. In 1912, having published more studies on Bach and Jesus as well as on the apostle Paul, he marries his longtime friend and confidant, Helene Bresslau, daughter of a Jewish historian. The following spring they sail for Port Gentil on the coast of French Equatorial Africa and then make a two-week journey upriver by raft. They set up their medical center in a shed and begin work. Word quickly spreads, and thousands of sickly and injured Africans make their way to Lambaréné as workers begin construction of a hospital.

If the Schweitzers had imagined they would be able to settle into a routine medical ministry, they were rudely shaken by the onset of World War I. Lambaréné is not spared. The Schweitzers and the staff are placed under house arrest, initially not even permitted to continue treating patients. In this French colony, German missionaries are apparently considered a risk, even though Schweitzer considers himself more French than German. Realizing that closing the medical work is not accomplishing their purpose, however, the troops soon relent. But in 1917 the Schweitzers are taken to France and incarcerated with other prisoners, despite outrage from Schweitzer's French relatives and friends.

When they are finally freed near the end of the war, both are in ill health and Helene is pregnant with their first and only child. For the next several years they remain in Europe seeking to regain their health. Added to the physical problems are the postwar economic realities of the devastated Alsace and surrounding regions. Coping with anxiety and depression, Schweitzer repairs organs to make ends meet, imagining that his years as a scholar, musician, and missionary are over. But an invitation to present lectures in Sweden revives his optimism. Following his lecture series, he is invited to present fund-raising organ concerts in some of the most prestigious churches in Europe.

In 1924, after some seven years of absence, he returns to his mission hospital, finding it in serious disrepair. Because of health issues Helene remains in Europe with their young daughter, but others—including doctors and nurses—volunteer to serve with him. In the years that follow, he periodically returns to Europe for family and fund raising, but his home is Lambaréné. During the late 1930s, with Hitler's rise to power, Helene, with daughter Rhena, moved to New York and from there made fund-raising tours that helped keep the work financially sound. During World War II, and again prior to her death in 1957, she joined her husband in Africa.

Schweitzer's greatest work, in his own estimation, was not his philosophical writings but his missionary work. "We must all die, but when I can save a life from days of torture—that is what I feel as my great and ever new privilege," he writes. "The greatest reward I know is when a patient takes my hand after awakening from an operation and says: 'I feel no pain.'" His work in Africa is largely an act of atonement. Outraged with the conduct of European colonial regimes, he writes:

> Who can describe the injustice and cruelties that in the course of centuries they [the Africans] have suffered at the hands of Europeans?... If a record could be compiled of all that has happened between the white and the coloured races, it would make a book containing numbers of pages which the reader would have to turn over unread because their contents would be too horrible.

Schweitzer traces such ethical deficiencies and accompanying ideas of racial superiority to Enlightenment philosophers as well as to the more recent popularity of Fredrick Nietzsche, who regards pity as weakness and celebrates the superman. Nietzsche and the missionary doctor are diametric opposites in both preaching and practice. As a man of his times, however, Schweitzer himself is criticized by some for treating Africans as less than equals. His own sacrifice trumps such censure, however, and in 1952 he is awarded the Nobel Peace Prize.

For Schweitzer life is serious, but his light-hearted self-deprecation is evident in personal encounters as well as in his writing. An example is found in his children's book, *The Story of My Pelican*. The little pelican gives an account of being brought to the hospital with its two brothers and gives more than a nod to the kindly doctor. But there is also a reference to the doctor's impatience when he was first preparing a cage in which to house the new guests: "He busied himself all afternoon under the house, crawling about and making no attempt to hide the bad temper these extraordinary activities put him in. I never had any experience of man and I found it very strange that such a good man could grumble such a lot."

> He comes to us as One unknown, without a name, as of old by the lakeside, He came to those who knew Him not. He speaks to us the same word: "Follow thou me!" and set us to the tasks which He has to fulfill for our time. He commands. And to those who obey Him, whether they be wise or simple, He will reveal Himself in the toils, the conflicts, the sufferings which they shall pass through in His fellowship, and, as an ineffable mystery, they shall learn in their own experience Who He is.
>
> Albert Schweitzer

Despite his own claims to be merely a man, the story of his saintliness persisted. Even his detractors — both colleagues and theological critics — could not quell the myth of the missionary. In some ways he was the epitome of Nietzsche's superman: "Dr. Schweitzer still performs as many as eight hundred operations a year," wrote an observer. "Halfway through his eighties, he has been known to go seventy-two hours without sleep when one of his patients has been in danger. He has kept up his writing — twenty-four major works of philosophy, religion, ethics, and a survey of world problems are to his

credit. An organ given him by those who loved him also claims his attention." Upon his death at the mission hospital in 1965, Schweitzer was buried alongside the remains of his wife, Helene.

## Karl Barth: Leading Theologian of the Twentieth Century

In 1911, when Schweitzer, in his thirties, was making his final preparations to serve as a missionary doctor in Africa, another minister, also engaged to be married, was settling into his first parish in the Swiss industrial town of Safenwil. The parsonage in the small village was in disrepair, hardly a showpiece for his fiancée, Nelly Hoffmann, yet Karl Barth (1886 – 1968) was convinced that this was where God wanted him.

Here in this economically depressed and seemingly God-forsaken place, Barth got his start in pastoral ministry, though he was surely not unfamiliar with the task. Born in Basel, Switzerland, he was, like Schweitzer, the son and grandson of ministers. Family connections, however, had not paved the way for a prestigious parish. "I am not speaking to you of God because I am a pastor," he tells his listeners in his inaugural sermon. "I am a pastor because I *must* speak to you of God." But despite his sense of mission, the people are stone-faced — if they attend church at all. "I always seemed to be beating my head against a brick wall," he later confessed, concluding that "going to church is contrary to the nature of the people."

Part of his difficulty lies in the fact that the congregation is deeply divided: the affluent factory owners and managers expect religion to sustain their lifestyle and ideals of progress, while the poor seek consolation and assistance. "I was sorry for everything that my congregation had to put up with," he later wrote. "I am tormented by the memory of how greatly ... in the end I *failed*

Karl Barth

as a pastor of Safenwil." But amid his failure he is convinced that he has grown in his understanding of pastoral ministry: "It was there that I first began at least to become aware of the full scope of the task of a Reformed preacher, teacher and pastor." Despite pressure from the most prosperous in his congregation, Barth stands alongside the poor. Realizing how impoverished most of the people are due to long hours, ill health, and low wages, he organizes a Workers' Association: "I regard socialist demands as an important part of the application of the gospel."

It is during his early ministry that he begins to recognize the weakness of the liberal theology that has long been in vogue in European universities. Of what relevance are such teachings to his parishioners or to the wider militaristic European culture that is deeply embroiled in an arms race? He digs into Scripture for answers, focusing heavily on Paul's letter to the Romans. Here he is confronted with the sovereignty of God—not a domesticated god of the liberals, but an awesome "divine incognito" beyond the comprehension of human beings. The only hope of knowing God is through Jesus Christ and the *power* of his resurrection.

Barth's commentary on Romans appears in 1919, and the following year he begins teaching at the University of Göttingen in the field of Reformed theology. Considering his later celebrity as a theologian, his confession to a friend about his "dreadful theological ignorance" combined with a "quite miserable memory" is surprising. But with the help of student assistants and colleagues, he presses on in his challenge to liberal theology.

Although the first edition of his commentary on Romans gets off to a slow start, the timing

---

PASTORAL REFLECTIONS ON "UNION WITH CHRIST"

That Christ links Himself with the Christian settles the fact that the latter, too, does not go alone. To do justice to Christ as his Counterpart he is not directed to believe in Him and to obey and confess Him on his own initiative or resources. He is certainly summoned to believe, obey and confess. And both as a whole and in detail this will always be the venture of a free decision and leap. It will always be a venture in which no man can wait for or rely on others, as though they could represent him or make the leap for him. Even in the community and therefore with other Christians, he can believe, obey and confess only in his own person and on his own responsibility. But does this mean on his own initiative and resources? No, for the act of the Christian is not to be described as a leap into the dark or a kind of adventure. . . . The Christian undertakes these things as through the Spirit he is called to do so by the risen One in whom he believes and whom he obeys and confesses.

Karl Barth, *Church Dogmatics*, Vol. IV, Part 3.2.

## Exactly When Was Barth Saved?

In 1962 when Barth was visiting the United States on a lecture tour, he was challenged by a questioner about his salvation and whether he could point to the moment he was saved. Nonplussed, he responded: "It happened one afternoon in A.D. 34 when Jesus died on the cross."

is right. Liberal theology is bankrupt. Students, ministers, and laity alike are seeking something more substantial for their spiritual diet. He insists on the absolute primacy of Christ—that Christ is the very *Word* of God and therefore is the foundation of theology. The Bible is foundational for all of his studies, particularly in pointing to Christ, but it is only secondarily the word of God. No book—not even the Bible—can challenge the primacy of Christ. The publication of his first volume of *Church Dogmatics* in 1932 further solidifies his place as a leading biblical scholar and theologian, though never without heated exchanges with both liberals and conservatives.

Challenging any form of religion aligned with national interest, Barth insists that Christians must look to the cross of Christ in seeking to live out their lives in a perilous world. And indeed, world affairs *are* very perilous as Hitler is coming to power. From his first teaching position in Göttingen, he has moved on to the universities in Münster and Bonn; but in 1935, after refusing to take an oath to Hitler, he returns to Switzerland to teach in Basel. He had been part of the founding of the Confessing Church, but it failed to rally the majority of German Christians against the *Führer*.

Barth's theological teaching and writing are more contextualized and practical than systematic. Indeed, *Church Dogmatics* grows out

of his lectures and the questions students raise. He challenges not only theological liberalism but also the Reformed teaching of Calvin. He argues that any theoretical dogma that seeks to balance election with reprobation would trump the very sacrifice of Christ on the cross. Yet his own "dialectical theology" balances grace with judgment as well as other biblical paradoxes.

Throughout his career, Barth accuses liberal colleagues of allowing philosophical constructs to usurp the message of Christ. But he is likewise critical of those who argue for the inerrancy of Scripture, thus putting the written word above Christ. The supreme role of Scripture in his mind is that of revealing Christ. Neither philosophical nor theological constructs, nor the text of Scripture itself, he insists, must ever be presumed to be one and the same with God's revealed wisdom.

After the first volume of *Church Dogmatics* appeared, many more volumes followed—a work in progress still being revised at the time of his death in 1968. How could one man accomplish so much? Barth acknowledged colleagues' input in his writings, and one name rose above all others as a behind-the-scenes collaborator in his academic life. Beginning in the 1920s, before the first volume of *Church Dogmatics* was published, he began working closely with Charlotte

## Casting Agency's Professor

Barth looked like a casting agency's idea of a German professor, with his shock of wavy gray hair, high forehead and cheekbones, craggy eyebrows. His owlish eyes peered occasionally over his horn-rimmed glasses, which often sat at the tip of his nose. He was known for his geniality, modesty, patience and sympathy, and above all a pixyish sense of humor.

Thomas Oden, *The Promise of Barth*

Charlotte von Kirschbaum

her presence in the Barth household created tension in the marriage and with the children.

In 1962 Barth was featured on the cover of *Time* magazine, and in the years after his death he was regarded as the greatest theologian of the twentieth century — perhaps even since Aquinas, as Pope Pius XII suggested. He was heralded as the father of neo-orthodoxy, a term he himself rejected.

In many ways Barth's work represents a finale to the German — or European — supremacy in theological studies (though Rudolf Bultmann and others would carry on with this most German pursuit). But by the 1970s theologians outside Europe were coming to the fore, including ones hailing from Africa, Asia, and Latin America.

von Kirschbaum, who served as far more than a secretary and editor. In fact, so dependent is he on her that in 1929 she moves into his home so that she can be awakened during the night when he needs her assistance. She reads widely in theological fields (learning additional languages in order to keep up), attends lectures, and keeps copious notes. Whether their relationship went beyond theological pursuits has been debated over the decades. But it is true that they traveled together, sometimes sharing the same room, and

> *As I look back upon my course, I seem to myself as one who, ascending the dark staircase of a church tower and trying to steady himself, reached for the banister, but got hold of the bell rope instead. To his horror he had then to listen to what the great bell had sounded over him and not over him alone.*
>
> Karl Barth

## Dorothy Day

A writer, social activist, and spiritual sage, Dorothy Day (1897–1980) was the most well-known American Catholic social activist in the twentieth century. She was born in Brooklyn, but her family soon moved to San Francisco, where her father was on the road to success as a journalist. The earthquake of 1907, however, overturned their lives. Having lost both home and income, the family moved to Chicago, where they lived in a rundown tenement building. Her mother was so ill that she could barely function at times. After her father found work as a sport's editor, the family fortunes improved considerably, but Day would never forget the shame and struggle of poverty. Setting up shop in New York City, she went on to become a lightening rod on social issues. As co-founder of *The Catholic Worker*, a newspaper published by the Catholic Worker Movement, she was accused by Catholics and capitalists alike of being a communist sympathizer. Her writing combined with her various humanitarian outreach endeavors profoundly influenced succeeding generations of Catholics.

## Oscar A. Romero: Latin American Martyr for the Poor

Three years after he was named archbishop of San Salvador in 1977, Oscar A. Romero (1917–1980) was gunned down while he was officiating at Mass. His name is often linked with liberation theology, and rightly so, but his path to that way of thinking was based on circumstances as much as on theological scrutiny. One of seven children, he was born into a poor family in a village near the border of Honduras. He attended a local school and then became a carpenter's apprentice. But he was determined to enter the priesthood. At thirteen he began the twenty-year process, completing his studies in Rome, where he was ordained in 1942. His plan to pursue doctoral studies was thwarted, however, when he was called to El Salvador to serve in the Diocese of San Miguel.

Oscar A. Romero

Except for his flair for radio ministry, Romero did not stand out among his fellow priests. "Strong-willed and seemingly born to lead," a colleague wrote, "yet he submitted unquestioningly to a structure that encourages conformity." A loyal church bureaucrat, he was a staunch supporter of the Catholic hierarchy and a social and theological conservative. Yet he demonstrated deep concern for the poor. While serving as bishop of Santiago de Maria, he traveled on horseback to outlying villages. Here he encounters dire poverty and often digs into his own pocket to provide medicine and food.

He recognizes, however, that such acts of charity will never solve the underlying societal problems. "The world of the poor teaches us that liberation will arrive only when the poor are not simply on the receiving end of handouts from the government or from

---

### POPE JOHN XXIII

One of thirteen children born into a poor Italian peasant family, Angelo Giuseppe Roncalli (1881–1963) was seventy-seven and relatively obscure when he was crowned Pope John XXIII. When "the cardinals of the Holy Roman Church chose me," he wrote, "everyone was convinced that I would be a provisional and transitional pope. Yet here I am, already on the eve of the fourth year of my pontificate, with an immense program of work in front of me to be carried out before the eyes of the whole world, which is watching and waiting." The event that caused the eyes of the world to watch and wait was Vatican II. With his unmistakable imprint, the Council purposed to seek how best to engage the modern world as well as other religions and Christian bodies outside the Catholic Church. In his opening address, he piqued the interest of Protestants: "The Catholic Church, raising the torch of religious truth by means of this Ecumenical Council desires to show herself to be the loving mother of all, benign, patient, full of mercy and goodness toward the brethren who are separated from her." But the most far-reaching change was the option to say Mass in the vernacular rather than in Latin only. It was, in the words of an American archbishop, "a vote against old ideas." At eighty-one, two years before the Council is concluded, Pope John dies of stomach cancer.

churches," he writes, "but when they themselves are the masters and protagonists of their own struggle for liberation." His thinking is slowly evolving as he listens to his priests and as he acknowledges the growing chasm between the wealthy and the impoverished. In a 1976 pastoral letter, he writes of the destitution of workers, particularly those on the vast coffee plantations:

> It saddens and concerns us to see the selfishness with which means and dispositions are found to nullify the just wage of the harvesters. How we would wish that the joy of this rain of rubies and all the harvests of the earth would not be darkened by the tragic sentence of the Bible: "Behold, the day wage of laborers that cut your fields defrauded by you is crying out, and the cries of the reapers have reached the ears of the Lord" [James 5:4].

Yet Romero is wary of social activism, including that of his superior, Archbishop Luis Chavez. His sympathies are with government law and order—government controlled by what was known as the "fourteen families." Power and wealth were in the hands of these aristocrats, and those who fought for change were labeled Marxists and imprisoned. His appointment to the office of archbishop of San Salvador is a disappointment to many priests, who had hoped for someone more attuned to the needs of the poor. But government officials are pleased—though not for long. Only weeks after Romero's consecration, Rutilio Grande, a friend and Jesuit priest is gunned down, along with two other social activists.

Rutilio had been involved in establishing Christian base communities (CEBs), considered by officials to be camps for radicalizing the poor. He had refused to be intimidated and fearlessly preached a provocative sermon after government officials had expelled a Colombian priest: "Very soon the Bible and the Gospels will not be allowed to cross the border," he warned. "All that will reach us will be the covers, since all the pages are subversive.... So that if Jesus crosses the border ... they will not allow him to

The porch (west entrance) to Westminster Abbey with statues of 20th-century martyrs. From left to right: Maximilian Kolbe of Poland, Manche Masemola of South Africa, Janani Luwum of Uganda, Elizabeth Fyodorovna of Russia, Martin Luther King Jr, of the United States, and Oscar A. Romero of San Salvador

enter." In the eyes of officials he was a trouble-maker. In the eyes of Romero, a friend.

With Rutilio's death, Romero's worldview comes full circle. It is a defining moment. "When I looked at Rutilio lying there dead, I thought 'if they have killed him for doing what he did, then I too have to walk the same path.'" Now in his radio programs he is unwavering in demanding justice for the poor. He calls on Catholics to come to the cathedral for a national Mass where justice for the poor becomes a rallying cry, much to the chagrin of government officials and most of the country's bishops, who remain loyal to the ruling party.

In 1979, when the Revolutionary Government Junta takes control, violence escalates. Times are desperate. Visiting Rome, Romero pleads with Pope John Paul II to intervene — anything to stop the bloodshed. He likewise sends a message to President Jimmy Carter imploring him to suspend American military assistance to the new government, but without success. He fears the worst and desperately appeals to military leaders: "We are your people. The peasants you kill are your own brothers and sisters.... In the name of God, in the name of our tormented people whose cries rise up to heaven, I beseech you, I beg you, I command you, stop the repression." The day after this message is sent, he is assassinated. He is not marching in the streets but is simply saying Mass at the Carmelite Sisters' medical complex where he resides. The bullet strikes his heart, and he is dead at the altar.

The prophetic words of his homily minutes earlier saw no immediate fulfillment: "Those who surrender to the service of the poor through

## LIBERATION THEOLOGY

From the beginning, the theology of liberation posited that the first act is involvement in the liberation process, and that theology comes afterward, as a second act. The theological moment is one of critical reflection from within, and upon, concrete historical praxis, in confrontation with the world of the Lord as lived and accepted in faith.

Gustavo Gutierrez,
*The Power of the Poor in History*

love of Christ will live like the grain of wheat that dies.... The harvest comes because of the grain that dies." As tens of thousands crowded around the cathedral to mourn, gunfire broke out. What followed was all-out civil war that lasted a dozen years and cost tens of thousands of lives, with countless thousands fleeing the country.

Though not canonized as a saint, Romero is the patron saint of the poor in El Salvador — and in all of Latin America. His words ring in their ears: "The church would betray its own love for God and its fidelity to the gospel if it stopped being ... a defender of the rights of the poor."

The systemic evil manifested in twentieth-century totalitarian regimes severed the sheep from the goats as no other circumstance in history had done. Some too easily hid behind the pretext of patriotism and the depraved decrees of dictators. Not so Dietrick Bonhoeffer, Oscar Romero, the ten Booms, and countless others. For them, Jesus' words, "Come, follow me," meant literally taking up the cross.

## What if ...

What if Pietje Balthus had been too intimidated to challenge her highly educated minister on spiritual matters? Would Abraham Kuyper have gone on to become known as a liberal theologian? How would contemporary Christianity be different without his profound influence?

What if young, unmarried Maria Anna Schickelgruber had gotten an abortion in 1836 and never given birth to Alois, the father of Adolf Hitler? How would world history and church history be different today had Hitler not been born?

What if Albert Schweitzer had taken an easier route to fame as an organist and theologian and not given his life to serve in Africa? Would he be remembered today? Would he be encased in stained glass alongside Luther and Calvin?

What if Angelo Roncalli had not been elected pope? How would the Roman Catholic Church look today without his influence and without Vatican II?

## Further Reading

Brabazon, James. *Albert Schweitzer: A Biography.* Syracuse: N.Y.: Syracuse University, 2000.

Brockman, James R. *Romero: A Life.* Maryknoll, N.Y.: Orbis, 2005.

Forest, Jim. *Love Is the Measure: A Biography of Dorothy Day.* Maryknoll, N.Y.: Orbis, 1994.

Franke, John R. *Barth for Armchair Theologians.* Philadelphia: Westminster John Knox, 2006.

Grenz, Stanley J., and Roger E. Olson. *20th-Century Theology: God and the World in a Transitional Age.* Downers Grove, Ill.: InterVarsity, 1997.

Haynes, Stephen R. *The Bonhoeffer Phenomenon: Portraits of A Protestant Saint.* Minneapolis: Fortress Press, 2004.

John XXIII. *Journal of a Soul: The Autobiography of Pope John XXIII.* New York: Image, 1999.

McGoldrick, James E. *God's Renaissance Man: The Life and Work of Abraham Kuyper.* London: Evangelical Press, 2000.

Romero, Oscar A. *The Violence of Love.* Trans. by James R. Brockman. Maryknoll, N.Y.: Orbis, 2004.

Schweitzer, Albert. *Out of My Life and Thought: An Autobiography.* Trans. by Antje Bultmann Lemke. Baltimore: Johns Hopkins University Press, 2009.

Selinger, Suzanne. *Charlotte von Kirschbaum and Karl Barth: A Study in Biography and the History of Theology.* University Park: Pennsylvania State University, 1998.

Ten Boom, Corrie. *The Hiding Place.* 1971. Reprint: Peabody, Mass: Hendrickson, 2009.

# CHAPTER 24

# Worldwide Christian Outreach

## *The Twentieth Century and Beyond*

*Sunday school at Maranatha Baptist Church. The setting, Plains, Georgia. The lesson, Queen Esther. The teacher, former President Jimmy Carter. This church was one of the many churches I visited while researching my book* Left Behind in a Megachurch World. *Some were tiny chapels, others the size of stadiums.*

*I also visited churches beyond the shores of North America in travels that took me to England and Scotland and several countries on the Continent. Whether in Italy, the Netherlands, or Russia, as so many others have said, the once-vibrant Christian faith is in serious decline.*

*In some areas of the world Christianity has barely gained a foothold after generations of mission work. My time in Singapore, Malaysia, and Japan confirmed that very fact, though I found some Methodist churches in Singapore that were flourishing. In Africa the exploding faith is still passionate, though sometimes, in the words of my Kenyan students, a mile wide and an inch deep.*

*I found the faith most fervent in Korea. Hosted by friend and former student Chung Ki Jun, a professor at a Korean Presbyterian seminary, I preached and he interpreted. Most Korean churches are offshoots of American denominations: Methodist, Presbyterian, Assemblies of God. This visit, however, was sponsored by University Bible Fellowship, an authentic Korean Christian movement that has expanded worldwide.*

*My last speaking venue was at Bethesda Christian University, founded by David Yonggi Cho, pastor of Yoido Full Gospel Church, the largest church in the world. Here, in a country where Christianity did not even gain a foothold until the end of the nineteenth century, the faith is vibrant, churches are expanding, and missionaries are carrying the gospel around the globe.*

*What would the great apostle Paul have thought had he known his message would one day virtually die out in the cities and towns along the dusty roads of his missionary journeys while finding root in distant unknown lands? From Plains to Seoul, his message of "victory through our Lord Jesus Christ" rings out, though ever balanced by "take heed, lest you fall."*

*History, like a vast river, propels logs, vegetation, rafts, and debris;*
*it is full of live and dead things, some destined for resurrection;*
*it mingles many waters and holds in solution*
*invisible substances stolen from distant soils.*
JACQUES BARZUN, *CLIO AND THE DOCTORS*

The history of Christianity is not always the river glorious of God's perfect peace, in the words of a familiar hymn. This river of faith is full of debris, live and dead, invisible substances stolen from distant soils. From its source in Palestine two thousand years ago, it mingles many waters from distant lands, some destined for resurrection.

Twentieth-century Christianity is far more diverse than was the faith in the first century and in the generations since. The New Testament writings open themselves to different interpretations, and in the ensuing centuries these differences in doctrine and practice have multiplied. Today the differences are so vast that some might wonder if certain variations even belong to the same religion. But despite the differences in doctrine and practice that have arisen across centuries and cultures, core beliefs hold Christians together. Commonalities are greater than differences as is seen in the lives and ministries of C. S. Lewis, Martin Luther King Jr., Mother Teresa, Desmond Tutu, and Billy Graham.

World Christianity of the past half century — Catholic and Protestant — is largely the product of mission and evangelism, often performed at great sacrifice to the most remote corners of the earth. Before quinine was available as a cure for malaria in the early twentieth century, a majority of missionaries died soon after arriving in Africa. Disease continued to be an obstacle throughout the twentieth century, as was opposition from native peoples, totalitarian governments, and terrorism. Yet the faith took root, perpetuated by indigenous evangelists who gave the gospel cultural context.

The big business of revivalism (following the era of Sunday and McPherson) was carried on by Billy Graham and others in the middle years of the twentieth century. Among them was Oral Roberts, the leading Pentecostal of his day, who conducted large campaigns and later branched into radio and television. Known for his healing ministry, Roberts founded a university and a medical center, both of which were later plagued by widely publicized financial losses and corrupt management. His contemporaries included Rex

## PARADE OF HISTORY

As church history marches into the twenty-first century, we find Billy Graham on the final night of his final crusade, March 12, 2006, leading a parade of sixteen thousand followers from the vast New Orleans Arena to Bourbon Street to claim the infamous French Quarter for Christ. Riding a motor scooter, Graham serves as grand marshal, as Christians lift their voices singing "When the Saints Go Marching In." What a fitting climax to one man's career and to a two-thousand-year parade of history! Problem is, the story is an Internet hoax. It is a reminder that even sacred history includes lies and urban legends.

Humbard, A. A. Allen, and Billy James Hargis, the latter brought down by a shocking series of sordid affairs involving male and female students at his own school.

In the closing decades of the twentieth century, with the rise of television evangelism, scandal continued to plague the industry as both Jim Bakker and Jimmy Swaggart were caught in extramarital affairs. Financial improprieties also brought disgrace. But televangelism did not spell the end of the traveling revivalist. Argentinean Luis Palau took his campaigns worldwide, following in the preaching tradition of Billy Graham. At the same time, German-born Reinhard Bonnke conducted campaigns in Africa and around the world featuring healing miracles. The most spectacular was in 2001, when he reportedly raised Nigerian Pastor Daniel Ekechukwu from the dead.

With severely limited funding, mission agencies were less vulnerable to the scandals that plagued televangelists. Their flaws and failings related more specifically to the area of strategy. Task-oriented North Americans often came with a ready-made agenda and were frustrated when local Christians did not rise to the occasion. Americans in particular offered grand schemes. Japan could be evangelized, Charles and Lettie Cowman promised, by turning their mission house into a military headquarters, utilizing military maps to plot out neighborhoods, and distributing mountains of literature—all to execute their "Every Creature Crusade."

Some mission agencies were highly specialized. William Cameron Townsend founded Wycliffe Bible Translators to make Scripture available in every language. Donald McGavern presented the Homogeneous Unit Principle (HUP) as the way to bring the gospel to individual people groups. Ralph Winter, founder of the US Center for World Mission, turned the mission focus to "Unreached Peoples." Among these unreached were Muslims, a vast population that became a major target of mission outreach, with much wrangling over the most effective method of approach. Intertwined with the wide-ranging mission strategies were the *third wave* (following the *first wave* of Pentecostalism and the *second*

## RETIRED BISHOP REDIRECTS MISSION OUTREACH

After serving for thirty-five years in India, Anglican Bishop Lesslie Newbigin retired in Birmingham, England, only to realize he had returned to a mission field more irreligious than the one he had left. Evangelism was "much harder than anything I met in India," he wrote. "There is a cold contempt for the Gospel which is harder to face than opposition." He quickly became convinced that the "pagan" West "is the greatest intellectual and practical task facing the Church." His retirement years became the most influential of his life as he engaged in evangelism and in writing — particularly *Foolishness to the Greeks: The Gospel in Western Culture*. Birmingham became his mission field. "As I visited the Asian homes in the district, most of them Sikhs or Hindus," he later recalled, "I found a welcome which was often denied on the doorsteps of the natives" — referring to his own countrymen. In his last addresses before a conference of the World Council of Churches, he challenged the notion that "the sins of the old missionaries" are only redressed by giving of ourselves and making no exclusive claims for Jesus. "I am an old missionary, and I have committed most of those sins," he confessed, but it would be wrong to respond by saying, "I will refrain from talking about Jesus and will instead offer my own life as a witness that will enable people to believe."

*wave* of the charismatic movement), so labeled by C. Peter Wagner, and its accompanying spiritual warfare (namely, warfare against demonic powers of darkness that purportedly hindered the receptivity of the gospel).

In the midst of these developments a trend emerged, emphasizing not missionaries per se, but the "missional church." Spurred by the writings and teachings of Anglican Bishop Lesslie Newbigin, scholars and practitioners insisted that mission outreach was most effectively conducted through the local church. Another Anglican cleric who profoundly influenced the worldwide church was John Stott (author of dozens of books, including *Basic Christianity* and *The Cross of Christ*), who became deeply involved in furthering theological training of non-Western Christians. John Perkins focused on community development in Jackson, Mississippi, establishing Voice of Calvary Ministries, a multifocused program that has been the inspiration for dozens of other urban ministries

Years before Newbigin began redirecting his energies to evangelizing the West, parachurch organizations, many of them originating in North America, were evangelizing universities and expanding around the world. InterVarsity Christian Fellowship, Young Life, and Campus Crusade for Christ all sought to evangelize youth and commission them as lay evangelists in the campus and workplace. While Bill Bright expanded Campus Crusade worldwide from his American base, Francis and Edith Schaeffer sought to reach the youth culture from L'Abri, their mountain compound in Switzerland. Their outreach was focused particularly on disillusioned university students who often found atheism more tenable than Christianity.

Idolized as a pop theologian, Schaeffer, a fundamentalist Presbyterian, influenced a generation of Christian leaders, as did Harold Ock-

enga and Carl F. H. Henry, both theologians and founding editors of *Christianity Today*. Starting out as a big city soap-box preacher, Henry soon found his calling in the more subdued environments of teaching, editing, and writing. Ockenga introduced "neo-evangelicalism," much to the chagrin of Carl McIntire and other fundamentalists.

J. I. Packer, a leading North American theologian, had a profound influence on Christians beyond his own Anglican circles. A Canadian of British birth, he was a professor at Regent College for many years and the author of dozens of books, including his seminal work, *Knowing God*. From Germany, through the teaching and writing of Jürgen Moltmann came theology of hope, an effort to combine an ecumenical, evangelical, and liberation spirit under the banner of an all-inclusive biblical theology. Also focused on a biblical theology approach was the British New Testament scholar Bishop N. T. Wright.

From Africa came a wide variety of biblical and theological perspectives, including that of Kwame Bediako from Ghana, who drew on the church fathers in his contextualization of African theology. Also contributing important theological insights were scholars from Korea, where Minjung theology (an Asian liberation theology) found root. From Canada came the controversial "open theism," presented in introductory form by Clark Pinnock in *The Openness of God* and later fleshed out by American theologian John Sanders and others. A more liberal version of this theology, process theology, had been introduced earlier in the century by Alfred North Whitehead. This theology essentially argued that God is a verb rather than a noun; God is ever in process even as the universe is in process. At the same time, liberal theology was flourishing under Emerson Fosdick and William Sloane Coffin, both ministers at New

## EVERYDAY LIFE

## Christianity Online

Google the word *Christianity* and you might get 89 million results (or only 74 million, depending on the date). Christianity online is big business. Every denomination and most churches have sites, as do mission organizations, magazines, and Christian schools. Angels are featured prominently (132 million results), compared to demons (only 55 million). Apologetics—defending the faith and arguing with atheists—is a major online ministry. Atheism, both for and against, is also a huge online category.

One of the largest sites featuring a wide range of religious resources is belief.net. Billed as a site that offers "Inspiration, Spirituality, Faith, and Religion," it promotes not only Christianity but also a daily horoscope. Blogs are a prominent aspect of this site, including Michele McGinty's "Reformed Chicks Blabbing" and Scot McKnight's "Jesus Creed." On the opposite spectrum of belief.net is "ExChristian.net" (including ExChristian.net/Facebook) and similar sites that tell the stories of people who have walked away from the faith.

People long dead also have their sites. "Into the Wardrobe" is a C. S. Lewis site hosted by Lewis's stepson, Douglas Graham. The C. S. Lewis Foundation hosts another major site, as does the C. S. Lewis Institute. "Mother Teresa of Calcutta Center" is her official site, but there is also an official site for her "Cause of Canonization." The Vatican site invites the browser to enter in one of eight languages. John Calvin pops up primarily in English and has no apparent official site, but his name is referenced in millions of sites and his *Institutes of the Christian Religion* is online, free for the taking. Church history sites abound, including ones like "Medieval Sourcebook" that offer original documents that can be cut and pasted and emailed in a matter of moments to the research historian's hundred closest friends.

"Emergent Village" features Brian McLaren podcasts and other resources for those interested in the Emergent Church. "CBE International" is the official website for Christians for

### THE HOLY OBSERVER

"The Holy Observer" bills itself as being "God's #1 Source for Christian News." Among its mix of clever and lame humor is a full-color advertisement sponsored by "Joel Osteen's Blessed Whitestrips." He is pictured with his usual toothy smile and a subscript: "If your soul is white as snow, why shouldn't your teeth be?"

A May 2009 lead article is titled, "How big is your PRAYER FOOTPRINT?" with short subtitles and text:

> Church Leaders Urge Christians to Reduce Their Prayer Footprints:
> Experts warn of a looming shortage of "supernatural resources"

Biblical Equality, offering a wide variety of materials. "The Council on Biblical Manhood and Womanhood" offers a similar range of materials from the opposite perspective.

Jews for Jesus, founded by Moishe Rosen, hosts a flashy interactive site filled with resources and ministry opportunities, while their opponents host a multiplicity of sites challenging their activities and beliefs. Clicking the Jews for Jesus tab "Get Saved" takes the Internet surfer through a series of four steps, each with Bible verses and questions, ending with the "sinner's prayer." That step leaves another click that asks for contact information.

"Pulpit Jokes" and "Church Bulletin Bloopers" and sermon humor sites abound, as do Christian cartoon sites such as "ReverendFun" and "The Back Pew." "The Jolly Blogger" is a personal site hosted by David Wayne that offers not only humor but also poignant accounts of struggling with cancer and other issues. He is a Presbyterian minister whose online bio reads: "I'm a Christian, husband, father, pastor and all around goof who believes that God is at His best when man is at his worst." Greg Albrecht is one of many online preachers. His website church, complete with a hymnbook and an opportunity to partake of communion, is "Christianity Without Religion," appealing to those with no other church home.

Christianity online reaches far beyond the blogosphere, as was evident in March 2011 with the publicity surrounding mega-church minister Rob Bell's book *Love Wins: A Book about Heaven, Hell, and the Fate of Every Person Who Ever Lived.* He is a universalist, critics screamed, launching him onto morning news programs on television and the pages of the *New York Times* and *USA Today* and the cover of *Time* magazine.

York's prestigious Riverside Church. From the same pulpit, Norman Vincent Peale gained wide acclaim through his book *The Power of Positive Thinking,* even as the influence of liberalism was on the decline.

The issues of homosexuality and feminist theology led to church splits in mainline denominations in America and around the world. Speaking out forcefully for traditional values was Anglican Archbishop Peter Akinola of Nigeria, who insisted that an acceptance of the gay and lesbian lifestyle and same-sex unions was not consistent with Christian teachings. Decades earlier such lifestyle issues were brought into the political arena by Jerry Falwell's Moral Majority and other networks of the religious right, including James Dobson's Focus on the Family. But the most influential religious figure in this era, holding the line against liberalism in all of its forms, was John Paul II, who reigned as pope for more than twenty-six years (1978–2005).

In the meantime, from the Americas to Africa to Asia, megachurches mushroomed and celebrity ministers built networks and wrote books. Rick Warren's *Purpose-Driven* series became a worldwide industry. In Korea, Assemblies of God preacher David Yonggi Cho built the world's largest church based on the concept of cell groups.

One of the most striking and least publicized religious developments of the late twentieth century was the transformation of the Worldwide Church of God. Founded by Herbert W.

## A TRANSFORMING MOMENT IN THE HISTORY OF CHRISTIANITY

We are currently living through one of the transforming moments in the history of religion worldwide. Over the past five centuries or so, the story of Christianity has been inextricably bound up with that of Europe and European-derived civilizations overseas, above all in North America. Until recently, the overwhelming majority of Christians have lived in White nations.... Over the past century, however, the center of gravity in the Christian world has shifted inexorably southward, to Africa, Asia, and Latin America.... This global perspective should make us think carefully before asserting "what Christians believe" or "how the church is changing." ... The era of Western Christianity has passed within our lifetimes, and the day of Southern Christianity is dawning.

Philip Jenkins, *The Next Christendom*

Armstrong in the 1930s, the movement drew from a wide range of unorthodox teachings and was tightly controlled by its authoritarian leader. On his death in 1986, under the direction of Joseph Tkach, the movement began assessing its beliefs and in the following years moved fully into evangelical orthodoxy. Never before in church history had a cultic movement turned so completely around and become part of the wider community of Christians.

### C. S. Lewis: Fiction Writer and Apologist

His books have been translated into dozens of languages and have sold more than 100 million copies. Hollywood versions of *The Chronicles of Narnia* (beginning in 2005) grossed more than a billion dollars worldwide. Yet, C. S. Lewis (1898 – 1963), despite his autobiographical books and articles, remains elusive. By his dress and appearance and associations he was hardly "cool" and might even have been described as an "old fogey," but today he steps out of his writings as the freshest and most fashionable of his contemporaries. Yet he remains a mystery. Formative events in his childhood offer insights. One episode perhaps rises above all others. He is ten years old. Lying in bed unable to sleep, he hears footsteps in the hall, and then the creaking of his bedroom door. Shivering in the darkness, he waits for the words he has so dreaded. The silhouette framed in the doorway is his father. There is no way to soften the news. His mother is dead. He knew it was coming; her cancer has been worsening. But nothing can ease the awful aching.

Life had been carefree for him growing up in Belfast, Northern Ireland, in the first decade of the twentieth century. He lived on the outskirts of town with his parents and his older brother Warren, and every day the boys were out in the fields and woodlands looking for new adventures. Young "Jack" and "Warrie" went to church on Sundays with their parents and were taught to say their prayers every night. During his mother's illness, his faith was actually strengthened. He prayed fervently for her recovery, and he believed God would heal her. If there was a God who answers prayers, why wouldn't God heal his mother? These questions haunted him in the years that followed while he was away at prep school. Sometimes he found himself doubting whether there was any point in praying at all. Yet during this time he began to listen in church and read the Bible. The fear of hell so gripped him that sometimes he prayed passionately on his knees long into the night, pleading for God to hear him.

This struggle to find God begins to fade during his teenage years when he transfers to a different prep school, however. Here the house matron reaches out to him as a surrogate mother and fills a missing void in his life. Her fascination with spiritualism soon becomes his own. Intrigued by the occult world of spirits and the supernatural, he gradually comes to regard Christianity as no more than a legend.

His life changes drastically in 1917, three years after England is swept into World War I. He enlists in the army and is soon on the front line in France confronting daily the horrors of combat. He loses two of his closest buddies and is sent home wounded. "My memories of the last war haunted my dreams for years," he later wrote. "I think death would be much better than to live through another war." For Jack Lewis there were no easy answers. Where was God in this carnage?

Following the Great War he enrolls at Oxford and then moves on to a teaching career. Influenced by George MacDonald, G. K. Chesterton, J. R. R. Tolkien, and others, he is drawn into Christian ways of thinking through their imaginative writings. Of MacDonald's *Phantastes*, he writes: "What it did to me was to convert, even to baptize ... my imagination." He begins to sense that God is hunting him down and closing in on him. Finally, while a teaching fellow at Magdalen College, Oxford, he realizes he can no longer escape:

> You must picture me alone in that room in Magdalen, night after night, feeling, whenever my mind lifted even for a second from my work, the steady, unrelenting approach of Him whom I so earnestly desired not to meet. That which I greatly feared had at last come upon me. In the Trinity Term of 1929 I gave in, and

admitted that God was God, and knelt and prayed: perhaps, that night, the most dejected and reluctant convert in all England.

In the years that follow he becomes a strong defender of the faith, writing and speaking widely. This apologetics period of his life, however, ends on a negative note. In 1948, British Catholic philosopher Elizabeth Anscombe delivers a devastating critique of his book *Miracles* to the Oxford Socratic Club. With logic and razor-sharp wit, she demonstrates that his proof for the supernatural is wanting. Lewis defends his position, but the consensus is that he has been defeated. His own reaction is one of bitter disappointment and depression. In the following years he turns to Christian mythology.

Magdalen College, Oxford

## A Doubting Apologist

*A Grief Observed* reveals many things about Lewis but none more important than that he was ultimately undone by the problem of contrary evidence.... The later Lewis had felt the full impact of religious doubt, and although he could not abandon his faith, neither could he claim a greater certainty than he had attained. His perplexities remained, and he acknowledged them with a degree of intellectual integrity that is as remarkable as it is rare. The Lewis of the '60s is no longer the Apostle to the Skeptics, acutely surveying the present state of the evidence, but the Reminder to the Forgetful, humbly searching for just enough light to face the day that lies ahead. Yet this is the Lewis of greatest personal stature, the Lewis who survives the collapse of his own arguments, and the Lewis who remains worthy of our highest and unqualified respect.

John Beversluis, "Beyond the Double Bolted Door"

*The Lion, the Witch and the Wardrobe* (1950), the first and best-known volume of the *Chronicles of Narnia*, had its origins in Lewis's teen years, when he imagined "a Faun carrying an umbrella and parcels in a snowy wood." Decades later he retrieves the image from his memory and begins toying with a story. Then "Aslan came bounding into it" — Aslan, who "pulled the whole story together." As he allows the story and the characters to develop, he presents in narrative form a theology of incarnation, atonement, and resurrection.

> *"God whispers to us in our pleasures, speaks to us in our conscience, but shouts in our pains: It is His megaphone to rouse a deaf world."*
>
> C. S. Lewis

In 1956, in his late fifties, Lewis marries Joy Davidson, an American with whom he had corresponded. It is a marriage made in heaven — but for its brevity. After her death in 1960, he relives the unanswered prayer of a ten-year-old boy. He feels utterly abandoned. "Meanwhile, where is God?" he demands, in *A Grief Observed*. "Go to him when your need is desperate, when

all other help is vain, and what do you find? A door slammed in your face, and a sound of bolting and double bolting on the inside. After that, silence." In the midst of such silence some turn away from God. Lewis does not. Rather, he confronts God in his anger. "All that stuff about the cosmic sadist was not so much the expression of thought as of hatred. I was getting from it the only pleasure a man in anguish can get: the pleasure of hitting back."

Although Lewis moved beyond his bitter grief, during the last years of his life he expressed less certainty than he had in earlier years. Yet he left behind a body of work that offered a sense of security that had eluded him.

## Martin Luther King Jr.: Preacher and Civil Rights Activist

Perhaps as much as any other figure in recent times, Martin Luther King Jr. (1929 – 1968) illustrates the influence of church history on a life and ministry. When he was five years old, he traveled to Germany with his father. Inspired by the life and legacy of Martin Luther, Mike King changed his own name and that of his son. If a mere monk could transform the course of history, so also could a black preacher and his son from Atlanta. In the following years that name would inspire and prod the young boy. Indeed, living up to the legend of Luther was daunting for a black youth in the American South.

King's father was not an obvious Reformation tourist. The son of an often-drunk sharecropper, Mike King grew up barely literate on the bottom rung of rural black society. Though ridiculed by classmates, themselves impoverished, for having manure on his shoes and smelling no better than a barnyard mule, Mike King had dreams. Making his way to Atlanta, he edged his way into the lowest level of church work and set his mind to marrying the preacher's daughter, Alberta Williams, the most eligible young lady at Ebenezer Baptist Church. Marrying her set the stage for Mike to succeed his father-in-law in 1931. With some four hundred in attendance, the church struggled amid a sea of poverty. But King was determined to turn things around. Before the decade was over attendance was in the thousands as the authoritarian young preacher developed ingenious fund-raising tactics and wielded tight control of the congregation.

One of three children, Martin Luther King Jr. grew up under the rousing "talk-back" preaching of his father. At seven he stepped forward to get saved and join the church. He later admitted that he "joined the church not out of any dynamic conviction, but out of a childhood desire to keep up with my sister." Approaching his teen years, he began to challenge his Sunday school teachers. Simply accepting the given wisdom "was contrary to the very nature of my being," he remembered. "I had always been the questioning and precocious type." Despite his doubts he was part of the church community, and simply walking away from faith was not an option. Then, in his mid-teens he sensed his own calling: "My call to the ministry was not a

miraculous or supernatural something, on the contrary it was an inner urge calling me to serve humanity." Skipping two grades in high school, he entered Morehouse College at fifteen. Not until three years later did he deliver his first sermon. However, it was devoid of the flare and showmanship of his father, who sang out the words in rhythmic waves. In fact, young Martin deplored such preaching, opting rather to present a more serious and intellectually stimulating discourse.

From Morehouse, King (now ordained) enrolled at Crozer Theological Seminary and later Boston University, where he was awarded a doctorate in 1955. In the meantime he marries Coretta Scott and becomes the minister at Dexter Avenue Baptist Church in Atlanta. In the ensuing years the routine of family life with four young children is mixed with pulpit ministry and social activism. His involvement with the NAACP (National Association for the

Martin Luther King Jr.

> *I have a dream that my four little children will one day live in a nation where they will not be judged by the color of their skin but by the content of their character.*
>
> *I have a dream today....*
>
> *This will be the day when all of God's children will be able to sing with new meaning "My country 'tis of thee, sweet land of liberty, of thee I sing. Land where my father's died, land of the Pilgrim's pride, from every mountainside, let freedom ring!"*
>
> *Let freedom ring.... Let freedom ring.*
>
> Martin Luther King Jr.

Advancement of Colored People) and his service with the Alabama Council on Human Relations paves the way for a leading role in the Montgomery Bus Boycott and directing the Southern Christian Leadership Conference. He knows well, however, that such leadership offers few rewards and many perils—perils that often put families at risk.

His most persistent philosophical theme is nonviolence—a worldview that solidifies in his mind while visiting the Gandhi family in 1959. "Since being in India," he writes, "I am more convinced than ever before that the method of nonviolent resistance is the most potent weapon available to oppressed people in their struggle for justice and human dignity. In a real sense, Mahatma Gandhi embodied in his life certain universal principles that are inherent in the moral structure of the universe, and these principles are as inescapable as the law of gravitation."

His followers are becoming weary of the rhetoric when beaten back by clubs and tear gas. But King keeps the volunteers in line with sit-ins throughout the South staged by black students and their white allies. However, this peaceful protest is met with violence, particularly

as "freedom riders" board busses and demand accommodations at hotels. Amid the backlash, King is jailed. The night following his release, he is alone in his kitchen thinking back on his wedding night spent in a friend's funeral home because accommodations for blacks were not available. Conscious of his wife and little girl sleeping close by, he senses God's presence:

> And I sat at that table thinking about that little girl and thinking about the fact that she could be taken away from me any minute. And I started thinking about a dedicated, devoted and loyal wife, who was over there asleep.... And I got to the point that I couldn't take it anymore. I was weak.... I had to know God for myself. And I bowed down over that cup of coffee. I will never forget it.... I said, "Lord, I'm down here trying to do what's right. I think I'm right. I think the cause that we represent is right. But Lord, I must confess that I'm weak now. I'm faltering. I'm losing my courage." ... And it seemed at that moment that I could hear an inner voice saying to me, "Martin Luther, stand up for righteousness. Stand up for justice. Stand up for truth. And lo I will be with you, even until the end of the world."

Spurred by a new sense of calling, he vows to fill jails to overflowing with nonviolent agitators "to create a situation so crisis-packed that it will inevitably open the door to negotiation." With that goal in mind, Birmingham becomes the focus. As had been true elsewhere, peaceful marches and boycotts are met with vicious attacks. Yet his grand strategy of nonviolent protest paves the way for the demise of the segregationist Jim Crow laws. The 1963 March on Washington is the setting for his "Let Freedom Ring" speech to more than a quarter-million people both black and white. *I have a dream* becomes embedded in American consciousness. But the protest for which King is best remembered occurs in Selma. Indeed, President Lyndon Johnson declares that Selma will be remembered in American history along with Lexington and Concord and Appomattox.

Just before Selma, King travels to Norway to receive the Nobel Peace Prize and to the White House to talk with President Lyndon Johnson. "I left the mountaintop of Oslo and the mountaintop of the White House," he later recalled, "and two weeks later went on down to the valley of Selma." The issue brought to the fore in Selma is voting rights for blacks, and King vows that his work will not be complete until blacks have equality at the ballot box. Once again he meets with fierce resistance and is jailed. He misses the next march from Selma to Montgomery: "I had been away for two straight Sundays and therefore felt that I owed it ... to my parishioners to be on hand for the Sunday service ... to administer the Lord's Supper and baptism."

When what was supposed to be a peaceful march turns into "Bloody Sunday," he is filled with remorse: "I shall never forget my agony of conscience for not being there when I heard of the dastardly acts perpetrated against nonviolent demonstrators that Sunday." When the march eventually takes place, some inside the movement accuse King of being too weak. His speech at the end of the march on the steps of the Alabama state capitol offers conciliatory words — too conciliatory, critics say — in the midst of hate and violence: "Our aim must never be to defeat or humiliate the white man," he reminds the crowd, "but to win his friendship and understanding. We must come to see that the end we seek is a society at peace with itself, a society that can live with its conscience. And that will be a day not of the white man, not of the black man. That will be the day of man as man."

In the three short years that follow, King continues to march and organize and to preach at Ebenezer Baptist Church. Early in 1968 he leads the Poor People's Campaign to Washington D.C. In late March, he travels to Memphis to offer his support to black sanitary workers who are on strike, demanding equal pay with whites. In a speech on April 3, he reflects on a death threat that had delayed his flight to Memphis:

## REFLECTIONS ON RACISM AND MARTIN LUTHER KING JR.

The Ku Klux Klan had an almost mystical hold on our imaginations.... I remember a Fourth of July rally held at a fairgrounds [where] ... hooded Klansmen ... began beating [black men] with fists and axe handles.... Although nearly four decades have passed, I can still hear the crowd's throaty rebel yells, the victims' pleas, and the crunch of the Klansmen's bare fists against the flesh.... These memories of racism from my youth all came flooding back as I read biographies of Martin Luther King Jr.... He faced death threats from segregationists as well as the FBI. A bomb went off in his home. Black churches were burning every week in the south.... I better understand now the pressures that King faced his entire adult life, pressures that surely contributed to his failures.... I certainly once dismissed him. Yet now I can hardly read a page from King's life, or a paragraph from his speeches, without sensing the centrality of his Christian conviction. I own a collection of his sermon tapes, and every time I listen to them I am swept up in the sheer power of his gospel-based message, delivered with an eloquence that has never been matched.

Philip Yancey, *Soul Survivor*

I don't know what will happen now. We've got some difficult days ahead. But it doesn't matter with me now. Because I've been to the mountaintop.... I just want to do God's will. And He's allowed me to go up to the mountain. And I've looked over. And I've seen the promised land. I may not get there with you. But I want you to know tonight, that we, as a people, will get to the Promised Land. And I'm happy tonight.... Mine eyes have seen the glory of the coming of the Lord.

The following day King was killed by an assassin's bullet. His last words were to the musician who was scheduled to play at an evening event: "Ben, make sure you play 'Take My Hand, Precious Lord,' in the meeting tonight. Play it real pretty." His legacy, as perceived by many evangelicals, is often more negative than positive. They point to plagiarism, marital unfaithfulness, and liberal theology. But a dismissal of him fails to recognize the incredible role he played in serving as a Moses to his people. "I am many things to many

Mother Teresa

people," he wrote in 1965, three years before his death, "but ... I am fundamentally a clergyman, a Baptist preacher. This is my being and my heritage, for I am also the son of a Baptist preacher, the grandson of a Baptist preacher, and the great-grandson of a Baptist preacher."

## Mother Teresa: Missionary Servant from Calcutta

The youngest of three children, Agnes Gonxha Bojaxhiu (1910–1997) was born into a prosperous family in Albania. When she was nine, however, her father died and left the family in dire straits. Her mother carried on with humanitarian outreach in the community—selfless service that does not go unnoticed by her youngest daughter. Assured of her mother's blessing, she makes plans to become a missionary in India.

After training as a novice, Agnes takes vows in 1931 to become a Loreto sister (named Teresa) and is assigned to teach geography at St. Mary's and later to serve as headmistress at that school. But she is not satis-

---

### ATHEISTIC AUTHOR OF *GOD IS NOT GREAT* SLAMS MOTHER TERESA

One of the curses of India, as of other poor countries, is the quack medicine man, who fleeces the sufferer by promises of miraculous healing. Sunday [October 20, 2003, when Pope John Paul II beatified Mother Teresa] was a great day for these parasites.... More than that, we witnessed the elevation and consecration of extreme dogmatism, blinkered faith, and the cult of a mediocre human personality. Many more people are poor and sick because of the life of Mother Teresa.... She was a fanatic, a fundamentalist, and a fraud.

Christopher Hitchens, "Mommie Dearest: The Pope Beatifies Mother Teresa"

## MOTHER TERESA, PATRON, NO PLASTER SAINT

I am surprised at the flurry of discussion and concern about this aspect of Mother Teresa's inner life, because spiritual teachers have long taught about the dark night of the soul. St John of the Cross spoke eloquently about this phenomenon.... Mother Teresa wonderfully was no plaster cast saint. She has helped to affirm many who are passing through this period of desolation and dryness when God seems so remote.

Desmond Tutu, "On Faith"

fied educating the daughters of India's elite. She sees the desperately poor in the streets of Calcutta and envisions them as her mission field. She insists, however, that her calling has not come from the poor but rather from God: "This is how it happened. I was traveling to Darjeeling by train [for her annual retreat], when I heard the voice of God.... The message was clear. I must leave the convent to help the poor by living among them. This was a command, something to be done, something definite. I knew where I had to be. But I did not know how to get there."

With students from the Loreto school working alongside her, Teresa applied to Rome for permission to form a new congregation—and to India for citizenship. Wearing saris, not habits, she and her followers made themselves part of the culture. The Missionaries of Charity, which she founded in 1950, was not a convent separated from the world of vice and degradation. "Our Sisters must go out on the street," she insisted. "They must take the tram like our people, or walk to where they are going. That is why we must not start institutions and stay inside. We must not stay behind walls and have our people come to us."

In the 1960s, after the Missionaries of Charity had experienced significant growth, Teresa departed from her adopted homeland for the first time in more than three decades to establish mission outposts around the world.

Although she avoided publicity, publicity found her. In 1971 Malcolm Muggeridge published *Something Beautiful for God.* Because of that book and other flattering media exposure, more young women committed their lives to the work. Money poured in, and lay ministries were organized. The little woman in the Indian sari and tattered sweater became a saint long before the Vatican could conduct an investigation. In 1979 she was awarded the Nobel Peace Prize.

When asked how she identified herself, Teresa responded: "By blood and origin, I am all Albanian. My citizenship is Indian. I am a Catholic nun. As to my calling, I belong to the whole world. As to my heart, I belong entirely to Jesus." Yet she struggled throughout her life with doubts: "Jesus has a very special love for you," she wrote to a cleric. "[But] as for me, the silence and the emptiness is so great, that I look and do not see—Listen and do not hear—the tongue moves [in prayer] but does not speak."

### Desmond Tutu: Bishop and Warrior Against Apartheid

Recipient of the Nobel Peace Prize (1984) as well as the Albert Schweitzer Prize for Humanitarianism and the Gandhi Peace Prize, Desmond Tutu (1931- ) is recognized far beyond the borders of his homeland of South Africa. He survived childhood sickness and demeaning racial segregation to become the first black Anglican archbishop of Cape Town and one of the foremost Christian leaders of his time.

One of three children, he was born in Klerksdorp, Transvaal. His father was a teacher who struggled with alcohol, while his mother kept the family together with her menial labor. He moved with his family to Johannesburg when he was twelve, at that time dreaming of becoming a medical doctor. Unable to afford the education, he enrolled in a teacher training school and then taught at a black high school. However, he left that profession in protest when the government passed legislation downgrading education for all blacks.

From the field of education, he turned to theological studies and was ordained an Anglican priest in 1960. Two years later he was awarded funding for further theological training at King's College, London. Joining him there were his wife, Leah, and their two children. After returning to Africa, he served as a chaplain and taught theology. In 1972 he returned to London to serve as a director for the World Council of Churches. Throughout his career he was an outspoken social critic. "Why do the expatriates live in so much better homes, segregated by a green belt from the village where the national staff live? Because the mission boards pay the rents for missionaries and the nationals can't afford the rents. Well, damn the mission boards."

It is in the realm of theological studies, however, that Tutu finds himself to be most out of touch with the Western worldview. He insists that

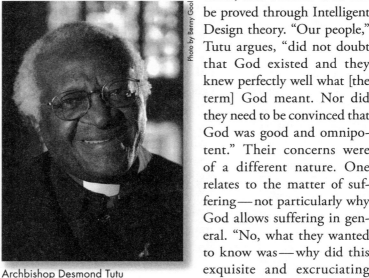

Archbishop Desmond Tutu

there is no one theology that can be universally applied to all cultures. The very questions theology seeks to answer are culturally biased. Western theologians, he points out, deal with matters of *who* or *what* is God, whether God actually exists, and whether God can be proved through Intelligent Design theory. "Our people," Tutu argues, "did not doubt that God existed and they knew perfectly well what [the term] God meant. Nor did they need to be convinced that God was good and omnipotent." Their concerns were of a different nature. One relates to the matter of suffering—not particularly why God allows suffering in general. "No, what they wanted to know was—why did this exquisite and excruciating suffering seem to isolate and concentrate so particularly on them?" Africans, he insists, must not claim to have a superior or universal theology but rather one that is relevant to their own circumstances:

> Black theology is an engaged not an academic, detached theology. It is a gut level theology, relating to the real concerns, the life and death issues of the black man.... It is a clarion call for man to align himself with the God who is the God of the Exodus, God the liberator, who leads his people, all his people, out of all kinds of bondage—political, economic, cultural, the bondage of sin and disease, into the glorious liberty of the sons of God.
>
> Black theology is not so naïve as to think that white oppression is the only bondage from which blacks need to be liberated. Sin and evil are as dehumanizing as white racism....

In his work with the World Council of Churches, Tutu travels to many African countries and forms networks with both political and religious leaders. This sets the stage for his role in fighting against apartheid when he returns to South Africa three years later in 1975 to serve as dean (senior minister) of the largely white St. Mary's Cathedral in Johannesburg. The following year he is named bishop of Lesotho (a small country surrounded by South Africa). Leaving Johannesburg is a painful decision made more difficult in the weeks that follow by the Soweto Uprising. Students protesting the effects of apartheid — their progressively worsening educational system — take to the streets. Police crush the uprising with tear gas, dogs, and firearms. Before it is over, hundreds of youth are dead. Tutu is outraged by the lack of concern in his own white congregation.

From his position as bishop of Lesotho, he presses hard for changes, warning of even greater violence. In 1978, when P. W. Botha becomes prime minister, Tutu challenges him from his new post as general secretary of the South African Council of Churches. From that key position he calls for economic sanctions against the government of his own country. It is a call for nations and corporations to take their investments out of South Africa. While President Reagan is calling for "friendly persuasion," Tutu insists that nothing short of a radical economic shunning will force the white government to give equal rights to blacks. In the decade that follows he is on a roller coaster of highs and lows. On the one hand he is terrorized by death threats to his family and tortured by the fear that boycotts will only bring more suffering to poor blacks. On the other hand he is awarded the Nobel Peace Prize and elected archbishop of Cape Town.

In the end, the anti-apartheid forces win. The most stunning signal comes in 1990, when political prisoner Nelson Mandela is freed after nearly twenty-seven years in prison. Four years later Mandela is the duly elected president of South Africa. But Tutu's hardest work is just beginning. As chair of the Truth and Reconciliation Commission, it is his duty to investigate more than three decades of accusations and crimes and to bring about reconciliation. Forgiveness is required — a concept that at one time seemed impossible on a national level. It is nothing short of "crazy," as Tutu admits, but it is the only way to move ahead. Whether demanding an end to apartheid or calling for reconciliation, he looks to one book more than any other

## AN AFRICAN PERSPECTIVE FROM A YALE PROFESSOR

We cannot afford to be churlish about the missionary roots of Christian renewal in Africa. We should recognize today's immense vernacular gains as springing out of the translation ferment of the previous missionary era and the anticolonial sentiment it nursed.... Africans came to their sense of cultural and national self-awareness through the grammars, dictionaries, and the vernacular literacy of Christian missions. The missionary contribution of outsiders to the modern reawakening of Africa has few parallels, and should stand as a monument to the scaling down of cross-cultural barriers. We should give praise and honor to God that he raised in the Western church servants of his cause in Africa and elsewhere. The dry bones of many of these missionaries, rising from their unmarked graves, gave voices to our ancestors.

Lamin Sanneh, "Africa"

as his guide. "Why should you need Marxist ideology," he asks on one occasion. "The Bible is dynamite.... Nothing could be more radical."

> "I don't preach a social gospel; I preach the Gospel, period. The gospel of our Lord Jesus Christ is concerned for the whole person. When people were hungry, Jesus didn't say, "Now is that political or social?" He said, "I feed you." Because the good news to a hungry person is bread."
>
> Desmond Tutu

Looking back over his career, Tutu reflected on the struggle against apartheid: "Many of us had moments when we doubted that apartheid would be defeated, certainly in our lifetime." How then did he maintain his optimism? "When you look at something like Good Friday, and saw God dead on the cross, nothing could have been more hopeless than Good Friday. And then Easter happens, and whammo! Death is done to death, and Jesus breaks the shackles of death and devastation, of darkness, of evil. And from that moment on, you see, all of us are constrained to be prisoners of hope."

### Billy Graham: Evangelist to the World

The pious, unsophisticated Christian faith that dotted the rural landscape with clapboard churches in mid-twentieth-century America had all but vanished as the century came to a close. As hymnbooks and Wednesday-night prayer meetings gave way to worship teams and PowerPoint, the "old-time religion" was all but gone.

This was the faith that nourished William Franklin (Billy) Graham (1918- ) as he was growing up, a faith passed down from his parents. His mother remembered how she made sure she had her Bible with her on their honeymoon: "I just wouldn't have felt like a clean person without my Bible with me." Before they went to bed on their wedding night, his parents knelt together to dedicate "our marriage and our family to the Lord." Billy grew up immersed in a simple and strict piety. "We had Bible reading and prayer right after supper, even before I cleaned up the kitchen," his mother recalled. "We all got down on our knees and prayed, yes we did, sometimes from twenty to thirty minutes. That was the main event of the day in our house." Sundays were devoted to Sunday school, morning and evening church services, devotional reading, and sitting around the radio listening to Charles Fuller's *Old-Fashioned Revival Hour*. Recreation was strictly forbidden.

After graduating from high school, Graham enrolled at Bob Jones University. But after struggling with all the rules and regulations, he soon transferred to Florida Bible Institute, aiming for a career in ministry. Following the completion of his degree, he enrolled at Wheaton College, graduating in 1943 and soon after marrying fellow student Ruth Bell, a missionary kid from China. "I saw her walking down the road towards me and I couldn't help but stare at her as she walked," he later recalled. "She looked at me and our eyes met and I felt that she was definitely the woman I wanted to marry." In the following years, he conducted a radio ministry, served as the president of Northwestern College in Minneapolis, and co-founded Youth for Christ, working alongside Charles "Chuck" Templeton, who would also become a well-known evangelist—until he abandoned his faith as he later related in his memoir, *Farewell to God*.

Graham went on to conduct his Los Angeles campaign that would launch his evangelistic ministry in America and around the world.

## FOLLOWING IN THE FOOTSTEPS OF BILLY SUNDAY

That old time religion has gone as modern as an atomic bomb in the thunderous revival meetings that Rev. Billy Graham conducts nightly in a giant tent.... Nothing detracts from the traditional fury and power of an old-fashioned gospel gathering. That's what his listeners, many of whom remember with pleasure the late Billy Sunday, want. And that's what they get.

Richard Reynolds, *Los Angeles Daily News*, September 30, 1949

But not before he settled the matter of his own doubts that continued to haunt him. Indeed, just prior to his first campaign, "everything came to a climax." Alone on a moonlit night at a retreat center in the San Bernardino Mountains, he knelt down, as he later testified, and prayed a prayer that would set the stage for his future ministry. Gripping a Bible, he poured out his heart: "Father, I am going to accept this as Thy Word — by *faith*. I'm going to allow faith to go beyond my intellectual questions and doubts, and I will believe this to be Your inspired Word."

The retreat center where Graham made his commitment is Forest Home Christian Conference Center, founded by Henrietta Mears who served as the director of Christian education at Hollywood First Presbyterian Church. Knowing Graham's struggles, she had invited him to come at a time when he could be alone. He later

Billy Graham

wrote: "I doubt if any other woman outside my wife and mother has had such a marked influence on my life. She is certainly one of the greatest Christians I have ever known."

Like D. L. Moody generations earlier, Graham is aided considerably by print media.

The California newspaper magnate William Randolph Hearst sends a telegram to his editors: "Puff Graham." Puff they do, and rival news outlets quickly join in. As was true with Moody's ministry, the stories of his revivals sell papers. The favorable press reports put Graham in the spotlight. Thousands make their way to the Big Top, and the Los Angeles campaign is extended an additional five weeks. By the 1950s he is a celebrity. His picture is on the cover of *Time* magazine. In the following years he holds campaigns at one spacious venue after another, primarily in large cities from New York and London to Moscow and Beijing. Thousands sing in the choir, and tens of thousands fill the auditoriums.

One of the most unexpected developments in Graham's ministry was his evangelistic tours to communist bloc countries and the Soviet Union at a time when such ministry was rare, particularly by one who spoke so adamantly against communism. Such cozying up with communists was controversial, as was his involvement in American politics, particularly when he publicly supported Richard Nixon over John F. Kennedy in 1960. He later vowed to stay

## HAROLD OCKENGA AND BILLY GRAHAM

The Rev. Harold John Ockenga, pastor of the influential Par Street Church at the edge of the Boston Common, brought Graham to Boston and did as much as anyone to give Graham's mission its larger shape. Ockenga and Graham both heralded the revival of 1950 as the greatest in New England since the Great Awakening. While Graham could well assume the role of Whitefield, the revival had no towering theologian to assume the role of Jonathan Edwards. . . . Yet Ockenga, a scholarly pastor who had earned a Ph.D. under J. Gresham Machen at Princeton and Westminster seminaries, did more than anyone else to launch a neo-evangelical movement that balanced revivalism with intellectual rigor.

George M. Marsden, "Minding a Malleable Movement"

out of politics, and his five decades of ministry were relatively free from controversy, except for opposition from fundamentalists.

In the early 1960s Graham took a stand against segregation. Indeed, on one occasion his temper flared when he spotted ropes designed to separate whites from blacks in his crusade, and he tore them down in protest. During his 1957 crusade in New York City, he invited Martin Luther King Jr. to join him at the pulpit, and he maintained a warm relationship with him in the years that followed. Throughout his ministry he made a conscious choice to avoid the religious right and in fact is accused by some of "cozying up to liberals." When invited by Jerry Falwell in 1979 to be part of the newly formed Moral Majority, he declined: "Evangelists cannot be closely identified with any particular party or person. We have to stand in the middle in order to preach to all people, right and left. I haven't been faithful to my own advice in the past. I will be in the future."

As Graham was reaching out to church leaders beyond the bounds of his own Southern Baptist denomination, he was also reaching out geographically. He conducted crusades on every continent and sponsored two major world congresses on evangelism, the first in Berlin (1966) and the second in Lausanne (1974), the latter hosting some twenty-four hundred delegates from one hundred and fifty countries. He also sponsored training conferences for thousands of itinerant evangelists (including women) from developing countries. A twentieth-century evangelist, he continued on into the twenty-first century — his last Crusade in New York in 2005 — and lived to see all of his children following him in evangelistic ministry.

Late twentieth-century Christianity is far too encompassing to even begin to summarize. It draws from all nations and all denominations — more than two billion people who today identify themselves as Christians. Its worldwise influence and its celebrity adherents made it a force to be reckoned with. But outside the portals of power exists the essence of the faith — ordinary people simply seeking to follow Jesus, the man from Galilee.

## GRAHAM'S PRODIGAL SONS

As Franklin grew older, I'd get calls from the police. . . . There's quite a gap in age between Franklin and my fifth child, Ned. He was a loving child, but he also went through a period where he was involved with drugs. Looking back on it, it seems like just a few weeks ago. But it dragged on for years.

Ruth Bell Graham, Prodigals —
And Those Who Love Them

## What if ...

What if Elizabeth Anscombe had not attacked C. S. Lewis on matters of miracles and the supernatural, thus pushing him away from apologetics into Christian fantasy? How would contemporary Christianity be different without the *Chronicles of Narnia*?

What if Mother Teresa had continued teaching geography to elite Indian girls? Would the world be poorer without her ministry, or are more people poor and sick, as Christopher Hitchens has claimed, because of her ministry?

What if Daddy King had not changed his name and that of his son and vowed to change the world even as Martin Luther did? What if Desmond Tutu had been funded for medical training? What if Billy Graham had starred in baseball instead of preaching? How would the world be different today?

## Further Reading

Aikman, David. *Billy Graham: His Life and Influence.* Nashville: Thomas Nelson, 2007.

Allen, John. *Desmond Tutu: Rabble-Rouser for Peace.* Chicago: Lawrence Hill Books, 2008.

Balmer, Randall. *Mine Eyes Have Seen the Glory: A Journey into the Evangelical Subculture in America.* New York: Oxford University Press, 2006.

Bormley, Beatrice. *C. S. Lewis: The Man Behind Narnia.* Grand Rapids: Eerdmans, 2005.

Graham, Billy. *Just As I Am: The Autobiography of Billy Graham.* New York: HarperOne, 2007.

Jenkins, Philip. *The Next Christendom: The Coming of Global Christianity.* New York: Oxford University Press, 2007.

Lewis, C. S. *Surprised by Joy: The Shape of My Early Life.* New York: Houghton, Mifflin, Harcourt, 1995.

Lischer, Richard. *The Preacher King: Martin Luther King Jr. and the Word that Moved America.* New York: Oxford University, 1997.

Loveland, Anne C., and Otis B. Wheeler. *From Meetinghouse to Megachurch: A Material and Cultural History.* St. Louis: University of Missouri Press, 2003.

Marsden, George. *Reforming Fundamentalism: Fuller Seminary and the New Evangelicalism.* Grand Rapids: Eerdmans, 1995.

Peters, Thomas C. *Simply C. S. Lewis: A Beginner's Guide to the Life and Words of C. S. Lewis.* Wheaton, Ill.: Crossway Books, 1997.

Rosell, Garth M. *The Surprising Work of God: Harold John Ockenga, Billy Graham, and the Rebirth of Evangelicalism.* Grand Rapids: Baker, 2008.

Teresa, Mother. *Mother Teresa: Come Be My Light — The Private Writings of the Saint of Calcutta.* Edited by Brian Kolodiejchuk. New York: Doubleday, 2007.

Turner, John G. *Bill Bright and Campus Crusade for Christ: The Renewal of Evangelicalism in Postwar America.* Chapel Hill: University of North Carolina Press, 2008.

Wainwright, Geoffrey. *Lesslie Newbigin: A Theological Life.* New York: Oxford University Press, 2000.

# Epilogue

Where will the parade of the Christian faith lead in future generations? Monumental changes have occurred since believers were first called Christians in Antioch—even in the five hundred years since Luther nailed his Ninety-five Theses to the church door. In my own lifetime I have seen significant changes. No longer are denominational differences underscored. And the old debates about Calvinism and Arminianism are easily shrugged off by a generation that does not really care. When I think of the future, I wonder if Jayber Crow might represent the direction the faith is headed:

> I kept on as janitor of the church.... I still walk up on Fridays to clean, as I have always done, and on Sunday mornings I go up to ring the bell and sit through the service. I don't attend altogether for religious reasons.... I am not sectarian or evangelical. I don't want to argue with anybody about religion. I wouldn't want to argue about it even if I thought it was arguable, or even if I could win. I'm a literal reader of the Scriptures.... I am, maybe, the ultimate Protestant, the man at the end of the Protestant road, for as I have read the Gospels over the years, the belief has grown in me that Christ did not come to found an organized religion but came instead to found an unorganized one.

Jayber, a small-town Kentucky barber, is the creation of Wendell Berry in his novel *Jayber Crow*. He represents a mindset that will undoubtedly grow in coming generations. But organized churches will surely not cease to be. So how will the final chapters of church history be formulated in the twenty-second century and beyond? Might North America be as Europe is today—a massive museum of a once-vibrant Christian faith? Will the Catholic Church be headed by a female pope? Might Christianity be expanding most rapidly in Iran and Iraq—and North Korea?

Will the Sunday morning sermon be a relic of the past? Instead of going to church, might Christians be downloading to a gold ear stud all the spiritual songs and sermons and Scripture they could ever want?

Might the earth be in ruins in the wake of a nuclear catastrophe? A day of utter doom and gloom. People crawling out of caves and picking through rubble. The marks of civilization wiped out—but for a tattered old textbook, *Parade of Faith*.

Whatever uncertainties the future holds, Christians of all generations and cultures look forward with hope, knowing the grandest of all parades—that vast multitude from every tribe and tongue and nation—will one day end in New Jerusalem *when the saints go marching in*.

*O Lord, I want to be in that number.*

# Index

## Share Your Thoughts

**With the Author:** Your comments will be forwarded to
the author when you send them to *zauthor@zondervan.com.*

**With Zondervan:** Submit your review of this book
by writing to *zreview@zondervan.com.*

## Free Online Resources at
# www.zondervan.com

**Zondervan AuthorTracker:** Be notified whenever your favorite
authors publish new books, go on tour, or post an update
about what's happening in their lives at www.zondervan.com/
authortracker.

**Daily Bible Verses and Devotions:** Enrich your life with daily
Bible verses or devotions that help you start every morning
focused on God. Visit www.zondervan.com/newsletters.

**Free Email Publications:** Sign up for newsletters on Christian
living, academic resources, church ministry, fiction, children's
resources, and more. Visit www.zondervan.com/newsletters.

**Zondervan Bible Search:** Find and compare Bible passages in
a variety of translations at www.zondervanbiblesearch.com.

**Other Benefits:** Register yourself to receive online benefits
like coupons and special offers, or to participate in research.